PRECARIOUS EMPLOYMENT

Precarious Employment

Understanding Labour Market Insecurity in Canada

EDITED BY LEAH F. VOSKO

McGill-Queen's University Press
Montreal & Kingston · London · Ithaca

© McGill-Queen's University Press 2006
ISBN 0-7735–2961-6 (cloth)
ISBN 0-7735–2962-4 (paper)

Legal deposit first quarter 2006
Bibliothèque nationale du Québec

Printed in Canada on acid-free paper that is 100% ancient forest free
(100% post-consumer recycled), processed chlorine free.

This book has been published with the help of a grant from the Canadian
Federation for the Humanities and Social Sciences, through the Aid to
Scholarly Publications Programme, using funds provided by the Social
Sciences and Humanities Research Council of Canada.

McGill-Queen's University Press acknowledges the support of the Canada
Council for the Arts for our publishing program. We also acknowledge
the financial support of the Government of Canada through the Book
Publishing Industry Development Program (BPIDP) for our publishing
activities.

Library and Archives Canada Cataloguing in Publication

Precarious employment: understanding labour market insecurity
   in Canada / edited by Leah F. Vosko.

   Includes bibliographical references and index.
   ISBN 0-7735-2961-6 (bnd)
   ISBN 0-7735-2962-4 (pbk)

      1. Industrial hygiene – Canada. 2. Labor laws and legislation –
   Canada. 3. Labor unions – Canada. 4. Labor market – Canada.
   I. Vosko, Leah F.

   HD8106.5.P74 2006   331.12'5'0971   C2005-905267-8

This book was typeset by Interscript in 10/12 Sabon.

In memory of
KAREN HADLEY
scholar, activist, and friend

Contents

Preface

This book emerged out of a Community-University Research Alliance on Contingent Work, a five-year project funded by the Social Sciences and Humanities Research Council of Canada and based at York University. This collaborative project involved a network of researchers from universities, national non-governmental organizations, an agency of the government, and several local community groups in Ontario and Quebec. The alliance was built on a community-university partnership between Toronto Organizing for Fair Employment (now the Workers' Action Centre of Toronto); Parkdale Community Legal Services Clinic; the Occupational Health Clinics for Ontario Workers; the Ontario Federation of Labour; the Institute for Work and Health; the Canadian Council on Social Development; the Housing, Family, and Social Statistics Division of Statistics Canada; George Brown College; McMaster University; York University; and Université du Québec à Montréal.

The goal of the project was to examine the growth of precarious employment in order to foster new social, statistical, legal, political, and economic understandings of this phenomenon – understandings grounded in workers' experiences of their work and directed at improving their quality and conditions of work and health. The research agenda of the alliance was divided into two phases, beginning with a southern Ontario component and followed by a Quebec comparison. It encompassed four interlocking streams of research: on the shape, size, and location of precarious employment; on labour laws, regulations, and policies concerned with precarious employment; on work organization and health; and on improving working conditions. From the outset, the work of this alliance was interdisciplinary in its approach, and participants were committed to action-oriented research. Each stream of research was designed to explore the intersections of race, class, gender, and other social relations in shaping the legal and social regulation of precarious employment and to take workers' experiences as its point of departure in defining research questions, devising methodological tools, and disseminating findings.

This book represents one avenue for reporting on the findings of this community-university research alliance as well as for reflecting upon and recording its multiple approaches to research and action. Chapter 1 advances a theoretical and methodological framework for studying precarious employment, offers a conceptual and technical description to the phenomenon, and describes the interdisciplinary and multi-method approach orienting the alliance and framing the contents of the volume. The four parts structuring the body of the volume mirror, yet build links across, the streams of research organizing the alliance. The volume's remaining sixteen original chapters are a mixture of meta-level investigations into the phenomenon of precarious employment and its wide-ranging manifestations, drawing on statistical, legal, and sociological research methods; case studies of workers' experiences crossing the public and private sectors; regulatory developments and challenges in various jurisdictions in Canada and internationally; and thought-experiments bridging theory, history, and contemporary challenges to consider prospects for social change.

The Community-University Research Alliance was a collaborative project, and this book grew out of the extensive contributions and creativity of all its members. This effort included authors who contributed chapters – true to our research protocol, where authorship is alphabetical, it reflects equal contribution. The larger effort also included academic researchers and community activists who participated in the alliance in other ways, as well as a group of graduate students, research colleagues, and workers who were committed to its activities and its broader success. The richness of the collaboration is a testament to all these individuals and to the organizations that contributed resources to the broader endeavour.

It takes a great deal of energy to nourish a collaborative research project of the size and magnitude of the Community-University Research Alliance on Contingent Work. As academic director, I extend my appreciation to its community director, Alice de Wolff; the graduate and undergraduate students who participated in the project; the community and university researchers involved in the alliance; as well as the many supporters within and beyond the community organizations and universities involved. The alliance owes a great debt to the Social Sciences and Humanities Research Council of Canada for funding the five-year research project; to the School of Social Sciences and the Office of the Dean, Atkinson Faculty of Liberal and Professional Studies, York University, as well as the Office of the Vice-President Research, York University, for their in-kind and direct financial support; and to Statistics Canada and all the universities, research institutes, and community organizations participating in the research for their in-kind support. I am also very appreciative of the outstanding work of the staff at McGill-Queen's University Press (special thanks to Philip Cercone, Joan McGilvray, and Brenda Prince) and the press's broader commitment to publishing interdisciplinary scholarship on labour issues. And, on behalf of all the contributors, I extend my sincere thanks to the two anonymous reviewers for their incisive comments on all aspects of this volume.

Many individuals contributed to the production of this book. However, several deserve special mention here. Lynn Spink worked with me in putting together the glossary. To ensure that the research findings of the alliance reached all of our desired audiences, she also prepared clear-language materials to accompany this book and for other forums. I am grateful to Lynn for lending her tremendous skill to these tasks and for her larger commitment to every aspect of the alliance. Rochelle Goldberg provided superb support in coordinating events and activities of the alliance that contributed ultimately to this book. Rosemary Shipton gave editorial guidance in preparing the manuscript for publication. Krista Scott-Dixon was of enormous help in formatting the figures. And the following individuals provided excellent research assistance to the volume's contributors: Isabelle Aubé, James Beaton, Simon Enoch, Cindy Gangaram, Joel Harden, Beth Jackson, Krista Johnston, Jacqueline Krikorian, Tariq Khan, Erika Khandor, Kate Laxer, Annick Legault, Rob Maxwell, Maude Randoin, Lina Samuel, Kayla Scott, and Christina Toutounis.

On a more personal note, I extend my sincere thanks to colleagues inside and outside the alliance who have seen me through the past five years with the challenges and pleasures of this project. I also want to acknowledge and thank my family: Gerald, Phyllis, Judith, David, Morry, Rachel, Philip, Nella, Edith, Anthony, Charles, Alexandra, Bram, Matthew, Simon, Sara, and Andrew consistently support my work and bring joy to my life.

This volume is dedicated to Karen Hadley, fondly remembered for her outstanding scholarly contribution, her activism, and her friendship.

Leah F. Vosko
September 2005

PRECARIOUS EMPLOYMENT

Precarious Employment: Towards an Improved Understanding of Labour Market Insecurity

LEAH F. VOSKO

Precarious employment is a defining feature of the Canadian labour market, yet it is poorly understood and the consequences are far-reaching. They include our inability to apprehend the nature and scope of labour market insecurity, misdiagnoses of work-related sources of ill-health, the growing misfit between labour law and policy and workers in need of protection, and legal and institutional obstacles inhibiting vulnerable members of society from expressing their voices collectively. If we are to understand and limit precarious employment, we must engage in a dialogue involving theory (how we understand our social world), methodology (how knowledge is produced), empirical realities (what we see), and the goal of social change (what we want) – a dialogue that is simultaneously conceptual and technical.

This chapter initiates the conversation between theory, method, evidence, and practice that is the focus of this book. It conceptualizes precarious employment, probes its dynamics in Canada, and identifies avenues for fostering understanding in the service of positive social change by way of several linked arguments set out in the three major sections that follow.

Precarious employment encompasses forms of work involving limited social benefits and statutory entitlements, job insecurity, low wages, and high risks of ill-health. It is shaped by employment status (i.e., self-employment or wage work), form of employment (i.e., temporary or permanent, part-time or full-time), and dimensions of labour market insecurity as well as social context (such as occupation, industry, and geography), and social location (the interaction between social relations, such as gender[1] and "race,"[2] and political and economic conditions).[3] The first section of the chapter advances this argument by setting the historical backdrop and elaborating on the conception of precarious employment framing this volume as well as the book's guiding methodological approach, with attention to the research on employment restructuring in which it is situated.

The dynamics of precarious employment reflect continuity through change. Certain precarious forms of employment are spreading while others persist, especially among historically disadvantaged groups. Precarious employment is racialized and gendered in familiar as well as new ways, due partly to continuities in how resources beyond the wage are distributed by the state via the household and partly to continuities in divisions of unpaid work. The second section of this chapter develops these claims by exploring the nature, size, and scope of precarious employment in early 21st-century Canada.

Understanding precarious employment requires thinking outside the labour force – or the sphere of jobs – and re-examining assumptions that are often taken for granted, such as how we define "choice," "control," and "constraint." It entails embracing different entry points, and identifying a range of practical solutions attentive to workers' experiences. The third, and final, section of this chapter advances these contentions by charting the main areas of investigation in the book, as set out in its four parts, and locating individual chapters within them.

PRECARIOUS EMPLOYMENT

Precarious employment is not a new phenomenon. Rather, it takes expression in different ways in different periods and different places. It is shaped by historical circumstances, conceptual and theoretical understandings, social norms, and concrete developments in the labour market.

Since precarious employment is multi-dimensional, conceptualizing it involves working at different levels of analysis, from the individual and the job level to the occupational and industrial levels, and considering various axes of social differentiation and inequality. Fully comprehending it requires an interdisciplinary approach, informed by multi-method analysis, exploring household dynamics, institutional processes, social and legal norms, and workers' expression of their agency. After a brief historical sketch, this section sets out the conceptual framework for the book and its guiding methodological approach.

Historical Context:
Precarious Employment from the Late 19th to the Late 20th Century

There is a large body of literature documenting the manifestations of precarious employment from the late 19th to the late-20th centuries both in

Canada and in North America more broadly. Many interventions focus on particular labour market niches or employment forms (Arat-Koc 1997; Bakan and Stasiulis 1997a; Calliste 1993; Johnson and Johnson 1982; Satzewich 1991), some consider workers' strategies of resistance (Heron 1996), and others address the theme of precarious employment by considering the relationship between industrial organization and immigration policy of a given period (Avery 1979, 1995).

In Canada in the late 19th and early 20th centuries, precarious employment was the norm, especially among immigrant workers. Between 1880 and 1920, labour needs in key areas of economic expansion led the government to alter its immigration policy, which had long focused on attracting permanent settlers to contribute to the expansion of the British settler colony (Arat-Koc 1997; Avery 1995). Canada's nation-building objectives remained Eurocentric and gendered well into the 20th century. Yet employers' demands for male workers in agriculture, industry, construction, and other forms of work critical to building railways and physical infrastructure in urban areas, and settlers' demands for female domestic workers, prompted various policy changes, such as policies facilitating the recruitment of workers through employment agents or labour brokers in Canada and abroad to fill labour needs. Moreover, despite the unscrupulous practices of employment agents, there was limited resistence to the growth of these entities, due mainly to the xenophobic views held by segments of the population, including some segments of organized labour, threatened by a more open immigration policy (Das Gupta, this volume; see also Anderson 1991; Avery 1979; Heron 1996).

Employment through intermediaries, across a wide range of sectors, was a key manifestation of precarious employment in the early 20th century, one that takes expression in new and continuous ways to date (Vosko 2000). Another occupation-specific manifestation was live-in domestic work, which involved the recruitment of women from abroad (Arat-Koc 1997). These practices, too, continue to prevail (Bakan and Stasiulis 1997b; Langevan and Belleau 2000). Yet another manifestation was seasonal agriculture work, a mainstay of the Canadian economy around the turn of the 20th century, and a domain of employment where workers still have limited access to social and labour protections such as occupational health and safety (Tucker, this volume; see also Satzewich 1991).

Many forms of industrial work also exhibited qualities of precariousness before the emergence of large oligopolistic multi-plant firms in North America (Doeringer and Piore 1971; Morse 1998, 32). The contract labour system prevailed in the factory before the triumph of bureaucratic mass production in the early 20th century. This system varied, depending on the nature of the industry, the degree of unionization, and the management's competitive strategy; for example, the garment industry was plagued by sweating, due to its labour-intensive processes and limited requirements for capital investment (Frager 1992).

Some skilled male craft workers also confronted high degrees of insecurity through to the early 1940s; workers in the transportation industry (first driving wagons and hacks and then trucks) and early taxi-drivers were often compelled to be owner-vendors or owner-operators because of the mobile nature of their trade. This employment status exacerbated the high occupational health and safety risks they confronted as well as the lack of stability in their employment relationships.

These examples highlight the array of precarious employment from the turn of the 20th century to World War II. Their diversity is striking. They traversed work arrangements and varied by occupational and industrial context, and this heterogeneity continued and expanded through to mid-century. Then Canada entered an age of rapid accumulation, economic expansion, and productivity growth in which a sizeable group of workers successfully secured associational rights and collective bargaining gained legitimacy. Still, many workers lacked these rights in this oft-labelled "golden age"– trade union membership was extremely uneven after World War II, benefiting mainly male workers in the resource, mass-production, and transportation industries, who joined their skilled craft brothers in the ranks of organized labour (Heron 1989, 92), and excluding many workers in the public sector and the secondary segments of the private sector (Jamieson 1968, 348–49; Ursel 1992, 250; see also Fudge and Vosko 2001a). Yet this period was marked indelibly by the entente between employers and workers, brokered by the state, cultivating the rise of a normative model of employment – the standard employment relationship – whose material referent facilitated the reproduction of a sizeable segment of the working population well into the 1970s.

In this era, the standard employment relationship came to be identified with a full-time continuous employment relationship where the worker has one employer, works on the employer's premises under his or her direct supervision, normally in a unionized sector, and has access to social benefits and entitlements that complete the social wage (Butchtemann and Quack 1990, 315; Mückenberger 1989, 267). The standard employment relationship was associated, first, with male workers in blue-collar and, subsequently, white-collar occupations, and it was organized around a particular employment status (i.e., employee status), a particular form of employment (i.e., full-time permanent wage work), and a particular set of work arrangements (i.e., work at a worksite specified by the employer and under his or her direct supervision). It was designed to cushion workers from unemployment, to "incorporate a degree of durability and regularity in employment relationships," and to enable workers to reproduce themselves and their families via a social wage or a bundle of social benefits and entitlements beyond earnings that shapes the overall standard of living of workers and their households (Rodgers 1989, 1; see also Picchio 1998).

Although it is characterized by a series of identifiable features, varying only slightly by time and context, the standard employment relationship has always amounted to more than the sum of its parts. Growing up in the post–World War II period, it initially constituted an ideal type around which the state, under pressure from workers and employers in large firms concerned with making productivity gains, organized labour and social policies. It was built as a normative model, existing independently of individuals and encompassing prescriptive and descriptive elements. For example, from the outset, the social wage model integral to the standard employment relationship took as its guiding assumption that statutory benefits and entitlements, as well as employer-sponsored extended benefits, are best distributed to workers and their dependants via a single earner; through such assumptions, the standard employment relationship shaped not only labour-force patterns but familial obligations (Fudge and Cossman 2002, 8) and household forms as well (McKeen 2004; Porter 2003).

Significantly, legislated collective bargaining and policies such as unemployment insurance, workers' compensation, and public pensions were constructed, grew up around, and perpetuated the standard employment relationship from its inception. During and immediately following World War II, when workers' militancy was strong and both employers and the state took the threat of revolt seriously, this normative model of employment gave a systematic character to the emerging labour policy platform (Langille 2002) and its exclusions (Fudge, Tucker, and Vosko 2003b). It also shaped, and was shaped by, a particular gender contract or normative and material basis around which sex/gender divisions of paid and unpaid labour operate in a given society (Rubery 1998, 23; see also Fudge and Vosko 2001b). This gender contract assumed a "male breadwinner," normally a wage-earner, pursuing employment in the public sphere and in receipt of a family wage, and a "female caregiver" confined to the private sphere, subject to protective measures, and primarily gaining access to the social wage through her spouse. Together, the standard employment relationship and the male-breadwinner/female-caregiver contract contributed to curtailing job insecurity, improving wages, and augmenting control over the labour process for a group of (largely white) male industrial workers, and then white-collar workers. Organized around these norms, postwar labour law, legislation, and policy fostered the ascendance of the Keynesian Welfare State, whose elements are well documented.[4]

The central pillar of the labour policy framework evolving with the Keynesian Welfare State is noteworthy: Order-in-Council PC 1003 (1944) attempted to limit precarious employment among an unprecedented (though limited) group of workers. The most important piece of labour legislation in this period, its key elements consisted of union certification by membership cards and majority vote, exclusive bargaining agent status defined by bargaining units, protection against unfair practices, and enforceable obligations on employers to bargain in good faith (O'Grady 1991; see also Fudge and Vosko 2001a). It installed a range of features that came to characterize the standard employment relationship, including industrial unionism and worksite-based collective bargaining, and it encouraged the provision of fringe benefits, such as pensions, holiday pay, regular hours, sick pay, and disability insurance, via collective agreements (Fudge and Vosko 2001a, 275).

PC 1003 was accompanied by a range of other pillars critical to the postwar labour policy platform, such as the provision of unemployment insurance. Unemployment insurance policy of the period played a critical part in inaugurating other lasting features of the standard employment relationship tied to the social wage; the earliest *Unemployment Insurance Act* (1940) was designed to protect mainly male workers in jobs in industry and commerce from the ills of unemployment.

Casting and upholding the normative model of (white) male employment also involved securing the flipside of the standard employment relationship. By their nature, norms, and the material realities they aim to reflect, foster exclusions. The ideal of the standard employment relationship cultivated a conception of the "normal job" pivoting around full-time, full-year work with a single employer at a single worksite, and it tied a host of benefits and entitlements to this model. Thus early exclusions related to employment status, forms of employment, and work arrangements deviating from the standard employment relationship became linked to precarious employment. The notion of "flipside" (Vosko 2000) has a double meaning: it connotes forms of employment and work arrangements differing from the standard employment relationship and their much more limited bundle of statutory benefits and entitlements; and it attempts to capture the always tenuous (and historically contingent) character of the standard employment relationship as well as the connection between policies, such as those related to temporary and permanent migration, employer practices, and constructs (including the gender contract), cultivating this norm and persistent gendered and racialized inequalities. Early unemployment insurance policy, for example, upheld the flipside of the standard employment relationship by way of its exclusions. Not only did it treat men and women differently, dividing women into wife/mother and female worker (Pierson 1990), but it excluded a host of gendered and racialized occupations, such as teaching, nursing, and domestic work, and cemented the male-breadwinner/female-caregiver norm by denying wage-earning women their individual entitlement to benefits if they were married (Porter 1993). The regulations flowing from it contributed, at once, to constructing the standard employment relationship as a male norm, which, paradoxically, meant modifying its qualifying requirements where necessary, as in industries such as fisheries where coverage was extended to self-employed fishermen [sic] on the premise that they were employees of the merchants and plant owners who bought their fish,[5] and cementing deviations from this norm (Clement 1988; Neis 1993). Such modifications reveal both the malleable character of the standard employment relationship and the way it can readily be manipulated to cultivate labour market segmentation along gendered lines. In this era, even though the average fisherman did not engage in a prototypical standard employment relationship, the federal government extended unemployment insurance coverage to him and other groups of seasonal male workers. Women, especially married women and/or women presumed to be dependent on a male wage, had, in contrast, to prove their entitlement to unemployment insurance by demonstrating a commitment to waged work through engaging in a form of employment that resembled a narrower prototype (Vosko 1996).

In the last quarter of the 20th century, the stretch of the standard employment relationship became more limited as its terms eroded; so, too, did the male-breadwinner/female-caregiver model, although their normative power persists and no equivalents have yet replaced either the dominant employment norm or its associated gender contract. Cracks are now evident across labour and social policies conforming to this norm, from unemployment insurance (Porter 2003), social assistance policy (Bashevkin 2002; Vosko 2002), and training (Cameron 1995; Stephen 2000) to pensions (Townson 1997) and employment standards (Fudge 2001).

Because initial cracks in the standard employment relationship and early attempts to fill them[6] were linked to the expansion of deviations from the standard employment relationship, and because its flipside was interpreted narrowly, precarious employment in Canada came to be associated, as early as the mid-1970s, with part-time and temporary wage work, solo self-employment (where the worker has no employees), and multiple job holding.

Subtle variations on this theme were also apparent in other industrialized countries in this period. In some contexts, including at the supranational level in Europe, there was growing attention to the relationship between the growth of "atypical work" and social exclusion (Silver 1994). In others, such as in the United Kingdom, where early analysts adopted the appellation "flexible work" (Atkinson 1986, 1988), scholars who wished to reflect the balance of power between workers and employers more accurately posed the pivotal question "Whose flexibility?" to warn of heightening "casualization" (Huws, Hurstfield, and Holtmaat 1989; Pollert 1989).[7] In still others, such as in the United States, concerns about the rise of "contingent work" mounted (Polivka and Nardone 1989). Each distinct angle on this issue – as well as the terms chosen to capture insecurity in labour markets – reflected the manifestations of deviation from the standard employment relationship in the different contexts (Vosko 2004b). For example, in the United States, the moniker "contingent work" gained prominence to reflect the prevalence of conditional and transitory employment relationships, owing to the high level of employment uncertainty characterizing not only wage work that is technically temporary but also solo self-employment and even so-called permanent employment because of the limited protections against unfair dismissal (Hyde 1998; Summers 2000). The debates surrounding employment restructuring in industrialized contexts in the post-1970 period, especially the large body of research critical of attempts to cast employment trends in a value-neutral or evenhanded fashion, inspire many of the chapters collected in this volume.[8]

Returning to the Canadian context, three government reports, dating to the mid-1970s, spelled out the association between the spread of precarious employment and the cracks in the standard employment relationship, both as a norm and in numeric terms. *People and Jobs* (1976) made this tacit link by tying the changing demographic profile of the labour force – specifically, rising participation rates among married women with children and among young people – to the challenges and transitions faced by these "new" workers, and mounting pressures on the state from employers who viewed a diversity of employment forms and work arrangements as the key to "flexibility" or moderating fluctuations in the demand for labour.

The now commonplace association between precarious employment and forms of employment and work arrangements differing from the norm of the standard employment relationship crystallized in Canada in the early 1990s. The second government report, *Good Jobs, Bad Jobs: Employment in the Service Economy* (1990), articulated the decline of the prototypical full-time, full-year job and embraced the following dualism in describing employment change: "Employment is becoming increasingly polarized into two categories – good jobs and bad jobs ... the growth of non-standard employment forms is leading to the emergence of a related dichotomy in the labour force: workers with well-paid, relatively stable jobs and with extensive legal protections; and workers in employment that is often more tenuous, usually less well-compensated, and nearly always less protected." Seven years later the third report, *Collective Reflection on a Changing Workforce* (1997), written by a tripartite advisory group to the federal minister of labour, offered a more finely grained analysis of the same set of developments. It concluded that "only a minority of workers in Canada today hold ... 'good jobs' – full-time, full-year jobs that pay at or above the average industrial wage," while observing that "increased precariousness and insecurity" and "increasing intensity of work" characterize many so-called good jobs (76). *Collective Reflection* devoted greater emphasis to poor-quality jobs. Its conception of the flipside of the standard employment relationship was more nuanced than that in *Good Jobs, Bad Jobs*. It implicitly recognized fault lines in the full-time, full-year job, observing that "most so-called 'core' workers are working longer and longer hours in more stressful jobs" (76). But this report still cast developments in a relatively neutral (Fudge 1997, 5) and dualistic fashion, even more neutral than in the United States. There analysts sharpened their early focus on the notion of "contingent work," although they continued to debate its precise definition (Barker and Christensen 1998; Polivka 1996). Less recognized, even in policy discussions of the late 1990s, was the declining quality of forms of employment closely resembling the standard employment relationship.

Both *Good Jobs, Bad Jobs* and *Collective Reflection* drew a close connection between the growth of "non-standard work," a catchall term covering forms of employment and work arrangements deviating from the prototypical standard employment relationship, and labour market insecurity (Krahn 1989, 1995). Perhaps this association should be predictable, given the centrality of the standard employment relationship to the post-war labour policy platform and the Keynesian Welfare State in Canada. Yet, despite the significance of this norm in shaping policy design and employment practices to the present, there are fundamental problems with the standard/non-standard employment distinction, problems that take sharp expression in attempts to understand labour market insecurity and to conceptualize and measure precarious employment. The rigidity of the distinction neglects dimensions of precarious employment. It obscures central differences between the prototypical standard employment relationship and non-standard work, and especially among the employment forms and work arrangements comprising the non-standard catchall, and it fails to capture the deterioration of full-time permanent employment – the closest proxy for the standard employment relationship.

Conceptual Framework:
Precarious Employment in the Early 21st Century

In the early 21st century, precarious employment encompasses forms of work characterized by limited social benefits and statutory entitlements, job insecurity, low wages, and high risks of ill-health. This conception is rooted in an understanding of the diverse manifestations of precarious employment over time and in the history of the standard employment relationship and its flipside. It departs from the framework advanced in influential Canadian policy studies of the late 20th century in its attempt to interrogate, deepen, and rethink what have come to be normalized descriptive concepts – terms such as "standard," "non-standard," and "contingent." In so doing, this conception builds on a long tradition of research on employment restructuring dating to the mid-1970s and extending beyond Canada, including both quantitative and qualitative studies (studies rooted in action research and ethnographic approaches as well as more conventional sociological analyses) and, in many instances, studies informed by feminist, anti-racist, and worker-centred approaches.[9] It is process-oriented, preoccupied with social relations and workers' experience, interested in multiple dimensions and in continua rather than dichotomies, and attentive to social context and to social location. It is thus sensitive to gender relations, specifically the ways in which sexual difference forms the basis for exclusions and inclusions and constitutes inequalities in power, authority, rights, and privileges. And it is concerned with the processes of racialization, racism,[10] and resistance to racism.

This understanding of precarious employment brings together legal, economic, political, psychosocial, sociological, and statistical insights. These distinct perspectives allow for the analysis of precarious employment at multiple levels – from the level of employment status and form of employment to the levels of the individual and the job, and from the level of occupation to the levels of industry and geography.

Legal definitions are central to any conception of precarious employment. They relate to whether workers confront insecurity because of whom a given law or policy is designed to cover, the parameters around which it is framed, and how it is applied. They are critical to revealing how and in what ways law and policy on the books shape, mirror, or contrast law and policy in practice (Armstrong, Cornish, and Millar 2003). In legal terms, employment status and form of employment are particularly important. The need to categorize and define workers by employment status and form of employment is central in law. The law uses employment status to determine the personal scope of labour protection and social benefits – whether or not a worker is an employee under a given law or policy is a central question (Fudge, Tucker, and Vosko 2002). Yet, under some laws and policies, hours of work (e.g., employment insurance) and continuity of service (e.g., employment standards) also come into play.

Still, laws on the book and laws and policies in practice rarely operate in isolation. For example, workers deemed to be independent contractors under a given law or policy, and counted as self-employed in dominant statistical measures, may perceive their client as an entity accountable on similar terms to an employer. They may nevertheless come together with other workers and use pressure tactics outside the law, such as public campaigns, to advocate for change in employer practices (Cranford and Ladd 2003). How laws are interpreted by judges and other types of adjudicators and how laws are applied are also affected by economic considerations, including the costs and benefits of extending or limiting protection, and who will bear these costs.

Commonplace understandings of key pairs of terms denoting employment status and form of employment – pairs such as wage work versus self-employment, permanent versus temporary, full-time versus part-time – also convey different meanings at different times and in different contexts. Yet these pairs, and their individual definitions, are influenced by the structure of society and by broad social understandings – the central preoccupation of sociologists (Mills 1959; Porter 1987). Sociological analysis is, by its very nature, attentive to individuals, jobs, and especially their interrelationship. Sociological methods, ranging from qualitative analyses so central to grasping the complexities of workers' experiences to quantitative analyses critical to mapping developments across labour markets, contribute to textured understandings of precarious employment.

Statistical definitions and analyses offer yet another angle to approach precarious employment. They enable researchers to paint a portrait of the phenomenon in Canada sensitive to the social locations of gender, "race," immigration status, age, (dis)ability, and region, as well as to changes at the firm, industry, and occupational levels. And they encourage scholars to address a range of questions unanswerable through case law or interview-based analysis: Are the same workers in precarious employment year after year? How long are typical spells of precarious employment? What role does precarious employment play in labour market entry, exit, and re-entry and in the retirement process? How do events such as marriage, divorce, the birth of children, and injury or disablement affect employment relationships?

Statistical analyses provide unique means of breaking down the labour force, but they are limited in their capacity to improve the state of knowledge on work-related health outcomes. They do not capture stressors and strains associated with the direct experience or mounting threat of precarious employment, the effects of employment uncertainty, piecing together a living from multiple sources, or cycling in and out of employment. In contrast, psychosocial approaches that mix "objective" indicators, such as weekly hours of work, and "subjective" indicators, such as workers' experience of work intensity, offer openings for considering how peoples' employment situations and broader working environment relate to physical health and well-being (Cooper 2002; Johnson 1991).

Political understandings, too, are integral to this conception of precarious employment. Terms such as "non-standard" often reflect an attempt to neutralize social problems. They are thus inadequate in explaining the dynamics, level, or form of precarious employment or how it relates to a given institution of interest, such as trade unions. Engaged social science scholarship strives to be transparent in the assumptions and guiding principles that shape its theories and methods. The chosen term "precarious employment" reflects these aims. It reflects the understanding that job insecurity and uncertainty, ill-health, limited social benefits and statutory entitlements, and a lack of certainty in continuing employment relationships have their effects.

Bringing together such diverse perspectives and insights presents challenges because of the distinct analytical lenses they employ and because of dissimilarities in terminology. But the challenges posed by an interdisciplinary approach to conceptualizing precarious employment are also its central strengths. They compel us to ask questions of the taken-for-granted and to move beyond commonsensical understandings.

Methodological Approach: Understanding Precarious Employment

The conception of precarious employment orienting this book reflects the attempt to engage in a conceptual dialogue with data, be they statistics, law on the books, case law, qualitative interviews, or survey results. Rather than proceeding inductively, the methodological approach unifying it takes a basic knowledge of precarious employment as its starting point and employs multiple theories and methods to understand it.

The notions of "lumping" and "slicing" are integral to this approach (Armstrong 2004). Lumping offers a means of examining what is common among people. Slicing, in contrast, is central in using data, theory, and concepts to create multiple and complex pictures of people in different places. Armstrong (2004) argues that it is important to lump because certain things are universal: for example, "every society we know about has defined some work as men's and some as women's" (2). The practice of lumping enables social scientists to make this work visible. At the same time, it is also important to slice (Glucksman 2000), a practice consistent with the work of scholars concerned principally with intersections (Brenner 2000; Das Gupta 2002; Gabriel 1999; Glenn 1992). Slicing is perfectly compatible with lumping, but it allows for the recognition of difference and the possibility of developing several angles into the same set of issues, circumstances, and evidence.

The "lumping/slicing" coupling is instructive in studying precarious employment. Feminist scholarship has long demonstrated that sex/gender divisions of labour pervade households, the labour force, and their interrelation (Armstrong and Armstrong 1994; Barrett 1988; Luxton 1980; Luxton and Corman 2001). In turn, a complementary body of anti-racist scholarship highlights the powerful social construct "race," processes of racialization, and their intertwinement with racism, to demonstrate the centrality of racialized divisions within these spheres (Cranford, Grant, and James 2000; Dua and Robertson 1999; Gabriel 1999; Galabuzzi 2004; Miles 1987). Long-established axes of social differentiation shaping labour market dynamics in Canada include age, (dis)ability, and spatially related distinctions, and they are often tied in with the situation of vulnerable populations such as women, youth, Aboriginal people, and people of colour (Juteau 2003).

A methodological approach aimed at developing a meaningful conception of precarious employment must begin with social constructs such as race and gender, yet it must also remain open to their shifting character. Given the axes of social differentiation shaping workers' experiences, understanding precarious employment also calls for slicing various types of data in different ways. It requires embracing a range of entry points or paths of investigation and, hence, multiple methods.

Multiple avenues of inquiry are essential to furthering knowledge in the service of fostering social change – a further goal of this book. The pursuit of change involves, first, envisaging and then advancing a broad notion of security that encompasses dimensions such as control over the labour process, a decent income, and adequate social and regulatory protection. Consistent with the slicing/lumping coupling, this notion takes the household and the labour force as sites of social relations often characterized by continuity yet open to challenge and change.

Adopting a suitable approach to the study of a complex and persistent social problem like precarious employment is also challenging from a technical point of view. The conception of precarious employment framing this book calls for analyses addressing forms of employment in relation to dimensions of precarious employment. This conception draws inspiration from European approaches to studying precarious employment, particularly those first advanced by Rodgers (1989) and his colleagues (see Bettio and Villa 1989; Butchtemann and Quack 1990; Mückenberger, 1989; Rubery 1989), as well as approaches to understanding labour market insecurity developed more recently by Standing (1992). (For formative studies critiquing notions of labour flexibility, see also Huws, Hurstfield and Holtmaat 1989; Jenson 1989; MacDonald 1991; Pollert 1989; Walby 1989).

In Europe and North America, precarious employment is structured by employment status and by form of employment, yet focusing solely on status and forms of employment as a means of exploring employment change is overly rigid, as it fails to probe relationships integral to this phenomenon. To remedy this problem, bringing together studies of developments across Europe in the post-1970 period, Rodgers (1989, 3–5) identifies several dimensions central to establishing whether a job is precarious. The first dimension is the degree of certainty of continuing employment. The second is control over the labour process linked to the presence or absence of a trade union and, hence, control over working conditions, wages, and work intensity. The third is the degree of regulatory protection, or whether the worker has access to an equivalent level of regulatory protections through union representation or the law. The fourth is income level, indicating that a given job may be secure in that it is stable and long-term, but precarious in that the wage is insufficient to maintain the worker and any dependants.

This broader matrix opens space for multiple research methods, ranging from statistical and legal methods to survey research elevating psychosocial issues. It allows for cross- and interdisciplinary exchange. Yet the dimensions identified by Rodgers and his counterparts, while useful, are somewhat narrow. They assume the situation of a wage worker, even though precarious employment traverses forms of self-employment and wage work. Dimensions also often operate at different scales, and they are location and context sensitive. Indicators of a dimension such as uncertainty, or shift or on-call work, take on particular meanings in industries in the public and private sectors.

Qualitative analyses and case studies exploring workers' experiences reveal the importance of taking a multifaceted approach in elaborating dimensions of precarious employment at a macro level and analyzing their play in practice. For example, while union coverage is a good indicator of control over the labour process, it also guards certain groups of workers against other dimensions of precarious employment, such as low income or degree of regulatory protection (Akyeampong 2001). Case studies of groups of hotel workers, and analyses of racism and activism around anti-racism in the labour movement and their effects on precarious employment, give texture to this claim. In adding depth to the dimensions of precarious employment, it is also necessary to reflect jurisdictional differences – or variation across different legal regimes and provinces. The situation of particular groups of workers (e.g., agricultural workers in Ontario) excluded from key social protections such as occupational health and safety is a case in point. Similarly, constraints on access to justice for workers with atypical contracts in different places make a dialogue between data and concepts necessary.

Extending the insights of European scholars on the importance of considering the form of employment in relation to dimensions of precariousness involves developing indicators of precarious employment and cultivating explanatory insights through statistical and legal methods, policy analysis, ethnography, and survey research. A methodological approach to conceptualization and measurement via statistics involves devising statistical indicators of wages and the social wage that complement knowledge of laws, legislation, and policy emerging from survey research informed by critical (dis)ability theory – by, for example, allowing for more complex analyses of occupational context, introducing more expansive notions of regulatory protection to reflect ethnographic research findings, and embracing understandings of (dis)ability as a social construct. Considering developments in specific industries, such as the health-care industry, and among specific subgroups of workers, such as ancillary workers in contrast to those in the private sector, also yields new methods for understanding the relationship between precarious employment and privatization (Armstrong and Laxer, this volume). Case studies exploring key subsectors of the eroding public sector and in privately delivered but (often) public services also extend new understandings and causal insights into precarious employment (in this volume, see Borowy; and de Wolff).

Insights into the micro- and meso-level factors shaping precarious employment are especially instructive if the sites of social reproduction remain in view. Social reproduction refers, on the one hand, "to training and the development of skills and the continued well being of the worker for the labour process and, on the other hand, the general standard of living,[11] education and health sustained in society" (Clarke 2000, 137). And it is intimately intertwined with the social relations of gender and race. Institutions connected to social reproduction, including the state, the education system, immigration, the public sector, the family,[12] firms, and trade unions, share an interest in reproducing the working population. Social reproduction thus occurs at various levels (Muszynski 1996; Picchio 1992). Still, even though labour is a central factor in the production process (Sengenberger 2002), it is normally produced and maintained in households, performed mainly by women, and managed by the state through labour and social policies, from family policies to immigration and migration policies and programs (Fudge and Vosko 2003, 185).

Dominant approaches to understanding precarious employment tend to separate work performed in the labour force from social reproduction, with scant attention to the latter (Krahn 1995; Lowe, Schellenberg, and Davidman 1999). Yet feminist scholarship in the social sciences, economics, and law teaches us that the labour market encompasses not only the production of goods and services for sale but the social processes and labour that go into the daily and intergenerational maintenance of the working population (Picchio 1992; Seccombe1992) and, by extension, that social reproduction is integral to the dynamics of precarious employment (Armstrong and Armstrong 1994; Bernstein, Lippel, and Lamarche 2001; Fudge 1997; Jenson 1996; MacDonald 1997). It illustrates that government policies and employer practices, in their interaction with social norms and gender ideologies, often come together to confine women, especially women of colour, to jobs in the market, such as nursing and service occupations, that reflect the racialized sex/gender division of domestic labour (Das Gupta 2002; Glenn 1992).

Explorations that take racialized sex/gender divisions of labour in households and the labour force into account are highly valuable in comparing regulatory models in countries cast as exemplars in mitigating precarious employment, as are interventions that refuse to take "choice" or "uncertainty" uncritically. Joining theoretical insights into the relationship between production and social reproduction with research methods capable of capturing complexity makes possible a fuller response to the countless studies observing a correlation between precarious employment and people presumed to have access to subsistence outside the wage relationship (see, for example, Luxton and Corman 2001; Peck 1996). It opens space for a richer explanatory response to the observation that, where a state "relies on the provision of services to households on an informal basis as essential supplements to goods and services purchases from the formal economy, the demand for precarious labour is likely to be high" (Rubery 1989, 67).

Understanding precarious employment involves building a methodological approach considering form of employment and dimensions of labour market insecurity that is sensitive to social location and context as well as the dynamics of social reproduction and open to multiple entry points. This approach makes it possible to develop a sketch of precarious employment in early 21st-century Canada. The ensuing profile brings statistical data together with legal and policy analysis and with survey and qualitative research to set the context for the chapters to follow.

PATTERNS OF CONTINUITY AND CHANGE:
PROFILING PRECARIOUS EMPLOYMENT IN CANADA

Precarious employment in contemporary Canada reflects continuity through change. These dynamics are evident in forms of employment exhibiting dimensions of precariousness, and they relate to both occupational and industrial context. They are apparent also in racialized and gendered patterns shaped by divisions of unpaid work and relations of distribution at the level of the household and the state, or "sequences of linked actions through which people share the necessities of survival" (Acker 1988, 478), and the social norms they engender.

A Statistical Portrait:
Forms of Employment Exhibiting Dimensions of Precariousness

Forms of employment characterized by multiple dimensions of precarious employment are spreading. These trends come into view by breaking from the standard/non-standard dichotomy and embracing an approach to statistical conceptualization and measurement that captures the deterioration of forms of employment resembling the standard employment relationship and the heterogeneity inherent in the catchall "non-standard work."

This book employs a new approach to profiling precarious employment in Canada that considers form of employment in relation to dimensions of precarious employment in an attempt to respond to longstanding criticisms of crude aggregations of disparate forms of non-standard employment (see, for example, Casey and Creigh 1988; Fudge 1997; Huws, Hurstfield, and Holt-maat 1989). Emerging out of early collaborative research conducted through the Community University Research Alliance on Contingent Work (Vosko, Zukewich, and Cranford 2003),[13] this approach involves breaking down total employment into a typology of mutually exclusive forms. This represents a necessary first step in exploring precarious employment statistically that is now possible using national and supranational survey instruments, such as the European Foundation's New Ways to Work Survey, the European Household Panel Survey, and the Current Population Survey in the United States as well as the Labour Force Survey in Canada, but that analysts in Canada and elsewhere are just beginning to take up. Depicting this typology visually, figure 1.1 differentiates employees from the self-employed to reflect the diversity in the forms of employment falling within the catchall "non-standard." It then divides the self-employed into those without employees (solo self-employed) and those with employees (employers). In parallel, it separates employees who are temporary from those who are permanent. Finally, it splits each subgroup of employees and self-employed people by full-time and part-time status.

This typology is the methodological and technical backdrop to Part One of this volume, *Mapping Precarious Employment in Canada: New Statistical Insights*, as is the ensuing statistical profile, whose framework reflects and expands upon research examining the shape, size, and location of precarious employment conducted by Alliance members (see especially, Vosko, Zukewich, and Cranford 2003; in this volume, see also Armstrong and Laxer; Anderson, Beaton, and Armstrong; Cranford and Vosko; and Vosko and Zukewich). Applying a critique of the standard/non-standard dichotomy to the Canadian case, along with the insights of European scholars concerned with precarious employment, it links dimensions of precariousness to forms of employment by capturing the degree of certainty of continuing employment, control over the labour process, and degree of regulatory of protection. Its first order of distinction between employees and the self-employed is central to workers' capacity to exercise control over the labour process and their degree of regulatory protection. Few self-employed people have access to collective representation through a union, limiting conventional modes of control, and most labour and social protections pivot around the norm of the standard employment relationship. In its second layer, the typology addresses the degree of certainty of continuing wage work by grouping employees by job permanency and by distinguishing between the solo self-employed and employers, since the former are more vulnerable to uncertainty (Fudge, Tucker, and Vosko 2002; Hughes 1999). By separating each form of employment by part-time and full-time categories, the third and final layer also addresses social and regulatory protection, since eligibility for certain social benefits, such as employment insurance, is based on hours worked.[14]

Figure 1.1
Mutually exclusive typology of total employment, 2003

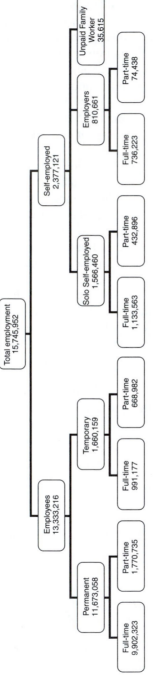

Source: Labour Force Survey Public Use Microdata Files Custom Tabulation, 2003

Employees with full-time permanent jobs still constitute the majority of the employed population in Canada, highlighting the continuing significance of the standard employment relationship. Yet full-time permanent jobs became less common over the 1990s and early 2000s, dropping from 67 per cent in 1989 to 64 per cent in 1994 and 63 per cent in 2003 (table 1.1). It should therefore not be surprising that policy studies of the late 1990s drew attention to the growth of forms of employment and work arrangements deviating from this norm.

But forms of employment differing from the standard employment relationship are not mutually exclusive: for example, temporary employees often work part time, as do many solo self-employed. Nor are they necessarily precarious on multiple dimensions. In Canada, prevalent approaches to conceptualization and measurement based on the notion of non-standard are inadequate because they group all forms of employment and work arrangements differing from the full-time permanent job into a single category. They therefore cannot reveal the forces driving the deterioration of those forms of employment resembling the standard employment relationship or the changes in forms of employment. An examination of mutually exclusive forms of employment, in contrast, illustrates that solo self-employment and full-time temporary wage work grew most sharply over the 1990s. Self-employment grew until 1998, reaching one of the highest levels in the OECD (Lin, Yates, and Picot 1999). Furthermore, its decline after 1998 was due primarily to the decreasing prevalence of self-employed employers, the least precarious type of self-employment; the share of self-employed employers declined from 7 per cent in 1989 to 5 per cent in 2003 (table 1.1). In contrast, solo self-employment grew from 7 per cent to 10 per cent in the same period (table 1.1). The share of employed people with temporary jobs rose steadily throughout the 1990s; this growth was fuelled by full-time temporary jobs, which rose from 4 per cent in 1989 to 6 per cent in 2003 (table 1.1). Racialized gendered patterns are apparent in this form of employment, which is characterized by several key dimensions of precarious employment.

Policy studies such as *Collective Reflection* observe that the overall share of employed people in non-standard work stabilized at high levels in the late 1990s, although this narrative is thin on description. In contrast, breaking down this catchall shows that the relatively more precarious forms of wage work and self-employment became more widespread in the 1990s – temporary full-time jobs and solo self-employment. This finding makes better sense of the growing reports of insecurity among the workers whose experiences are documented across this book.

The movement away from full-time permanent jobs since the mid-1970s has affected women and men differently. Increases in full-time temporary wage work and solo self-employment are observable for both sexes, but while the absolute decline in full-time permanent jobs was slightly greater

Table 1.1
Typology of Mutually Exclusive Employment Caterogies by Sex, Selected Years

Category	1989	1994	1997	1998	1999	2000	2001	2002	2003
				thousands					
Total employed*	12,669	13,035	13,775	14,140	14,531	14,910	15,077	15,412	15,746
Men	7,060	7,193	7,508	7,661	7,866	8,049	8,110	8,262	8,407
Women	5,609	5,841	6,266	6,479	6,665	6,860	6,967	7,150	7,339
				per cent of total employment					
Employees									
Full-time permanent	67	64	62	62	62	63	63	63	63
Men	71	67	65	65	65	66	66	66	66
Women	63	61	58	58	58	59	60	59	59
Full-time temporary	4	5	6	6	6	6	6	7	6
Men	4	5	6	6	6	7	7	7	7
Women	3	4	5	6	6	6	6	6	6
Part-time permanent	11	12	12	11	11	11	11	11	11
Men	5	6	6	5	5	5	5	5	5
Women	19	19	19	18	18	17	17	17	18
Part-time temporary	3	3	4	4	4	4	4	4	4
Men	2	2	3	3	3	3	3	3	3
Women	4	3	5	5	5	6	6	6	6
Self-employed									
Employer	7	6	6	6	6	6	5	5	5
Men	10	8	8	8	8	8	7	7	7
Women	4	3	3	3	3	3	3	3	3
Solo self-employed	7	10	11	11	11	10	10	10	10
Men	8	10	12	12	12	12	11	11	12
Women	6	9	9	9	9	9	8	8	8

Sources: General Social Survey, 1989 and 1994; Labour Force Survey, 1997–2003
*Totals for 1997 to 2003 include unpaid family workers.

Table 1.2
Part-time Employment Rates, Selected Years

Year	Total	Employees			Self-employed		
		Total	Permanent	Temporary	Total*	Employer	Own-account
Both sexes							
2003	19	18	15	40	22	9	28
2002	19	18	15	41	22	9	28
1997	19	19	16	39	21	8	29
1994	19	19	15	34	21	8	29
1989	17	16	14	43	19	7	27
Men							
2003	11	10	8	31	12	5	17
2002	11	10	7	31	13	5	18
1997	11	10	8	29	12	4	17
1994	11	11	8	28	12	4	18
1989	9	9	6	32	10	4	16
Women							
2003	28	26	23	49	38	20	44
2002	28	26	23	50	38	21	44
1997	29	28	· 25	49	39	20	46
1994	29	28	24	42	39	20	45
1989	27	26	23	54	39	18	46

Sources: Labour Force Survey; General Social Survey (figures in italics)
*Includes unpaid family workers for 1997, 2002, and 2003.

for men between 1989 and 2003, they were considerably more likely than women to be in this form of employment in 2003 (66 per cent versus 59 per cent) (table 1.1). The share of men who were solo self-employed increased between 1989 and 2003, while the share of men who were employers declined. More men are engaging in self-employment, but most male self-employment continues to be full time and hence less precarious along the dimension of income, unlike female self-employment.

Numerous studies document women's disproportionate participation in part-time work in Canada (see, for example, Armstrong and Armstrong 1994; Duffy and Pupo 1994). This overrepresentation is true of both employees and the self-employed, a fact receiving far less emphasis. In 2003, 44 per cent of solo self-employed women worked part time, compared with just 17 per cent of their male counterparts (table 1.2). The work of female part-time employees also became more precarious as the share with temporary jobs grew between 1989 and 2003 (table 1.1).

Young people aged 15–24 are also considerably more likely to be in precarious forms of employment than middle-aged people, prompting analysts to question whether precarious employment decreases over the lifecycle or whether the sizeable proportion of young people in the most precarious forms signals rising insecurity for the future work force (Cheal 2003). Among young people the likelihood of temporary wage work grew between 1989 and 2003, while the percentage with full-time permanent jobs declined (table 1.3).[15]

The majority of workers in precarious forms of employment that are growing in number are women (figure 1.2). In 2003, women accounted for over six in ten of those with part-time temporary jobs and part-time solo self-employment and nearly three-quarters of part-time permanent employees (figure 1.2). Men, in contrast, accounted for the majority of those engaged in full-time employment, whether in temporary or permanent jobs, as solo self-employed or self-employed employers. When the category of temporary employment is broken down into seasonal, agency, and casual work, gendered patterns also emerge (figure 1.3). Women make up the majority of temporary employees classified as "casual," a group that mainly works part time (figure 1.3). In contrast, men dominate in seasonal forms of temporary wage work, most of which are full time, and also in core segments that are highly racialized, such as seasonal agricultural work, many of which are underprotected (Tucker, this volume).

Age and sex interact in shaping precarious employment (figure 1.4). Mid-aged men still dominate in full-time permanent jobs and full-time employer self-employment, situations that are relatively secure, and very few men aged 25–54 are engaged in any form of part-time employment (figure 1.4). Yet many men aged 15–24 are in forms of employment that deviate from the standard employment relationship. The salient gender difference here is that women of all ages fill these forms, alongside mainly young men. Among men and women aged 15–24, 22 per cent and 33 per cent, respectively, were part-time permanent employees in 2003. However, 14 per cent of women and only 2 per cent of men aged 25–54 were part-time permanent employees (figure 1.4).

The distribution of forms of employment across industries is also gendered. In general, men with full-time forms of employment are more likely than women to be in the goods-producing sector. For example, in 2003, 45 per cent of men with full-time permanent jobs worked in goods-producing industries, compared with just 19 per cent of women, and the figures were similar for both forms of full-time self-employment (table 1.4). When parallel occupational contexts are examined in ensuing chapters, it becomes clear that these gendered patterns are also racialized (Cranford and Vosko, this volume).

Table 1.3
Typology of Mutually Exclusive Employment Forms by Sex and Age, Selected Years

	15 and over		15 to 24		25 to 54		55 and over	
	Men	Women	Men	Women	Men	Women	Men	Women
Total				000				
1989	7,060	5,609	1,151	1,091	5,041	3,986	869	532
2002*	8,262	7,150	1,209	1,158	5,993	5,279	1,060	713
2003*	8,406	7,338	1,220	1,187	6,038	5,337	1,148	814
			% of total employment					
Employees								
Full-time permanent								
1989	71	63	58	53	76	66	57	57
2002	66	59	45	35	73	66	53	51
2003	66	59	45	36	73	66	53	51
Full-time temporary								
1989	4	3	6	5†	3†	3	5	F
2002	7	6	14	11	6	5	5	4
2003	7	6	14	10	6	5	4	3
Part-time permanent								
1989	5	19	21	30	1†	16	F	22
2002	5	17	22	32	2	14	5	19
2003	5	16	22	33	2	14	4	19
Part-time temporary								
1989	2	4	7†	7†	F	3	F	F
2002	3	6	14	18	1	4	2	5
2003	3	6	14	17	F	3	2	5
Self-employed								
Employer								
1989	10	4	F	F	11	4	18	6†
2002	7	3	F	F	7	3	13	6
2003	7	3	F	F	7	3	14	6
Solo Self-employed								
1989	8	6	5†	F	8	7	14	10†
2002	11	8	3	4	11	8	22	15
2003	11	8	3	4	11	8	22	14

Sources: General Social Survey, 1989; Labour Force Survey, 2002 and 2003

F sample size too small to provide reliable estimates.

*Include unpaid family workers.

† Use with caution.

Figure 1.2
Women's share of forms of employment by full- and part-time status, 2003

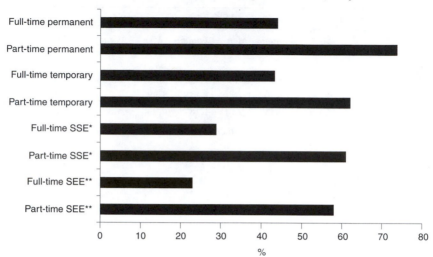

*Solo self-employed   **Self-employed employer
Source: Labour Force Survey, Public Use Microdata Files, Custom Tabulation, 2003

Figure 1.3
Types of temporary work

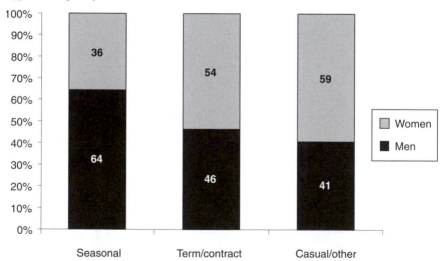

Source: Labour Force Survey, Public Use Microdata Files, Custom Tabulation, 2003

Figure 1.4
Forms of employment by age and sex

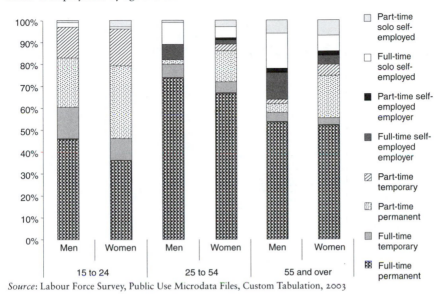

Source: Labour Force Survey, Public Use Microdata Files, Custom Tabulation, 2003

Social services, a category that includes the health-care industry and covers core segments of public sector employment in the federal and provincial jurisdictions, is the most common industry of employment for women with any form of paid work. It is also an important domain of employment for women from racialized groups (Das Gupta 2002). This concentration is not surprising given the gendered (female) character of care work in households and the labour force. Yet women's participation in this industry is correlated with women's precarious jobs. In 2003, 17 per cent of women with part-time temporary jobs, 22 per cent of those with part-time permanent jobs, 18 per cent of those with full-time temporary jobs, and just 19 per cent of women with full-time permanent jobs worked in health care and social assistance.

Part-time employees of both sexes are highly concentrated in the services sector. In addition to the concentration of female part-time employees in the social services, large shares of both sexes with part-time jobs are also employed in retail trade and other consumer services industries.

The business services industry is the most common industry of employment for self-employed people. It hosts the largest shares of women and men who are solo self-employed (on either a full- or part-time basis), as well as part-time self-employed employers. This fact appears to reflect a dual process of economic restructuring and changes at the level of form of employment, a process that amounts to the de facto reclassification of

Table 1.4
Form of Employment by Select Industries and Sex, 2003

Category	Goods Producing			Service Producing			Total
		Construction	Manufacturing		Retail Trade	Health Care/ Soc Assist	
Employees							
Full-time permanent	Men	40	8	26	60	9	3	100
	Women	43	1	13	57	11	19	100
Full-time temporary	Men	9	20	12	91	6	3	100
	Women	11	1	9	89	6	18	100
Part-time permanent	Men	16	2	5	84	29	5	100
	Women	15	1	3	85	25	22	100
Part-time temporary	Men	4	4	4	96	22	4	100
	Women	5	1	3	95	21	17	100
Self-employed							
Full-time SEE*	Men	33	16	8	67	11	7	100
	Women	17	5	6	83	19	11	100
Full-time solo†	Men	37	18	2	63	5	2	100
	Women	11	2	2	89	8	24	100
Part-time SEE*	Men	24	12	4	76	6	13	100
	Women	27	9	6	73	14	7	100
Part-time solo†	Men	23	13	2	77	7	3	100
	Women	8	2	1	92	8	12	100

Source: Labour Force Survey, Public Use Microdata Files, Custom Tabulation, 2003.
*Self-employed employer.
† Solo self-employed.

workers from a variety of industries who have shifted status from employees to solo self-employed (Purcell 2000).[16] The largest concentration of full-time male self-employed employers is also in this industry.

Breaking down total employment illustrates that solo self-employment and full-time temporary work grew in the late 20th and early 21st centuries. Employees with full-time permanent jobs still remain the majority, but this form of employment is becoming less common even though the standard employment relationship is still the norm at a policy level.

Women and men are differentially affected by continuities and changes in precarious employment – the fact that a considerably higher percentage of men than women held full-time permanent jobs in 2003 shows the difference that prevails. Women continue to dominate in part-time forms of wage work and self-employment, and men's participation in full-time solo self-employment has become more significant. Moreover, age and gender come together to reveal the persistence of gendered inequalities in the most precarious forms of employment – women of all ages, in contrast to mainly young men, are disproportionately represented in forms of employment that are neither full-time nor permanent. Accenting racialized gender differentiation, (white) male domains of employment remain the key contexts in which the standard employment relationship holds sway – the goods-producing sector and occupations unique to primary industries are cases in point, although many such industries are suffering from economic restructuring, evident in rising levels of company uncertainty (Cohen 1994).

This portrait reveals the importance of examining continuities in unequal gender relations and underexplored social relations, such as (dis)ability, as well as changes tied to racialized inequalities – all central concerns in this book. It also calls for probing dimensions of precarious employment more deeply and for examining how various forms of social differentiation shape workers' experiences.

Dimensions of Precarious Employment Enlarged

A portrait of forms and dimensions of precarious employment attentive to the social relations of gender and "race," as well as occupational and industrial context, is integral to understanding developments in the Canadian labour market. The movement to mutually exclusive measures fosters a relational analysis concerned with continua rather than dichotomies and the exploration of multiple dimensions. Yet statistical insights gain greater precision and meaning in dialogue with analyses of laws, legislation, and policies, original survey research, and qualitative case studies. Adding texture to the statistical portrait, such analyses reveal how and in what ways precarious employment is taking shape in Canada, especially on what dimensions and along which axes of differentiation.

Certainty On the dimensions of the degree of certainty of continuing employment and regulatory protection, several troubling tendencies are evident. Social benefits and entitlements continue to be tied to the eroding norm of the standard employment relationship. Consequently, labour and social protections are accessible to fewer and fewer workers, from occupational health and safety protections, to employment standards and collective bargaining rights, to employment insurance and the Canada/Quebec Pension Plan (this volume, see Bernstein; Tucker; and Lippel). Continuity through change is evident in the misfit between labour laws and social policies and the realities of the labour market. Where they apply, many labour and social protections also remain primarily job-specific or benefit mostly those with full-time full-year jobs.

These tendencies call for an expansive conception of the degree of certainty of continuing employment. This dimension is often still tied to a given job, but the need to consider multiplying actors involved in employment relationships is growing, from employers and workers to employment agencies and client firms. Degree of certainty of continuing employment is tied principally to form of employment and the contractual relations surrounding wage work, but the rise in solo self-employment (both full-time and part-time) and temporary wage work, together with the growing number of actors involved in employment relationships, makes it necessary for this dimension to address certainty (and uncertainty) beyond the single job. Research into employment-related sources of stress and ill-health substantiate this claim. It highlights the importance of considering both "job-strain" (a concept coined by Karasek in 1979), and "employment-strain" (strains tied to employment relationships), a notion advanced in this book.

Regulatory Effectiveness Another dimension of precarious employment relates to the legal regime governing work relations. In part, this dimension requires consideration of the scope of coverage, because some workers may be denied protection entirely. But an overly narrow understanding of regulatory protection tied to laws on the books must be displaced by a broader conception of regulatory effectiveness addressing the growing plurality of labour market locations and their intersection with diverse social locations. Degree of regulatory effectiveness can relate to legal coverage, awareness of coverage, legal design, policies on application and enforcement, employer avoidance, and disparities of power and inequalities between groups of workers – by design or omission (Bernstein, Lippel, Tucker, and Vosko, this volume). This interpretive shift is critical to understanding the varied situations of workers in need of protection – from temporary wage workers unable to access the basic occupational health and safety protections to which they are entitled (Lippel, this volume), to solo self-employed persons able to access extended medical and dental benefits only through a spouse (Vosko and Zukewich, this volume), to workers cycling in and out of precarious forms of employment and in and out of the labour force, lacking sufficient attachments to secure social benefits and statutory entitlements (this volume, Cranford, Das Gupta, and Vosko; Schenk). It makes room for addressing issues of access to the labour force and various segments within it, by way of employment supports such as counselling, training, and job-search advice (de Wolff, this volume). A broader approach to this dimension is particularly important for employees compelled to shift to solo self-employment due to privatization and contracting out and losing access to key labour and social protections (Borowy, this volume), while gaining other (often gendered) dependencies, such as the reliance on a spouse as a source of benefits, in the process. It is also critical to understanding fully what exclusion from legal coverage means, in practice, for specific groups.

In broadening conventional notions of the degree of regulatory protection, case studies of other jurisdictions offer a range of new insights. Yet being attentive to geographic or national context is important. For example, social democratic countries like Denmark take innovative approaches to regulating precarious employment, but they have done little to redress gendered divisions in the labour force, where women are largely excluded from high-level jobs in the private sector (even by comparison to liberal countries like Canada) and overrepresented in sectors emerging from the socialization of some care-giving responsibilities that were borne formerly by households (Jackson, this volume; see also ILO 2003a).

Control With respect to control over the labour process, workers in precarious employment are confronted with uneven access to traditional means of exerting their power, such as through unions. In response, many are testing out new modes of control rooted in community and community-union alliances. The most important indicator of control over the labour process has historically been union status. However, several chapters in this book illustrate that social fractures are developing around access to justice through unions not only because of legal hurdles but also because of challenges at the level of union structure and organizing practices (Cranford, Das Gupta, and Vosko, this volume; Schenk, this volume; see also Yates 2002). These social fractures are especially evident by race, gender, immigration status, and age (this volume, Anderson, Beaton, and Laxer; Cranford and Vosko; Das Gupta). They call for deepening our understanding of control along similar lines to the degree of regulatory protection, since workers' capacity to exercise control relates to disparities in power and in treatment. Control over the labour process is often expressed by way of union status, through formal grievance procedures or strikes, which remains a key indicator of this dimension. Yet "new" modes of control, some drawing on age-old models of trade unionism, are emerging through community organizing and hybrid community-union structures.

The Income Package With regard to income level, research indicates that this key dimension of precarious employment is best understood through a complex of lenses (or a composite set of indicators) that allow for comparative analysis of hourly wages, annual income, government transfers, or social wage protections, as well as through normative discussions. Regarding hourly wages, there is evidence of a gendered continuum of precarious wage work and a racialized gendering of jobs (Cranford and Vosko, this volume). A parallel gendered continuum also exists among the self-employed. A disproportionate share of full-time solo self-employed women earn below $20,000 per year (Vosko and Zukewich, this volume). Yet what constitutes a precarious income is still contested at a policy level. So, too, are the causal factors and broader social dynamics that lie at the root of precarious income and other core dimensions, including the degree of regulatory protection and control over the labour process.

This book demonstrates that relations of distribution fostered by the state, in its provision of the social wage, and replicated in households via the distribution of resources attached to wages and the social wage, contribute to the new and continuous ways in which precarious employment is racialized and gendered. Consistent with ethnographic studies in both industrialized and industrializing countries (Fernandez-Kelly 1983; Fernandez-Kelly and Garcia 1989), it illustrates further that unequal divisions of unpaid work also shape continuities in precarious forms of employment and in their gender. Even though they contribute to exposing gendered precariousness, indicators of precarious employment considering the labour force alone are insufficient. They provide only limited insight into the significant share of precarious employment among those social groups presumed to have access to forms of subsistence beyond the wage and its roots. When components of men's and women's "total work" (Picchio 1998, 207–8), a term used to capture all work (paid and unpaid) taking place in an economy, are compared, sharp differences in the types of work performed by women and men emerge. For example, women and men in two-parent households with children under 16 in Canada in 1998 performed, respectively, 4.9 and 3.3 hours of unpaid work daily and 5.5 and 6.9 hours of paid work daily (Statistics Canada 1998).

Even though the employment rates of women with children have risen dramatically in the last 30 years, women's share of unpaid work has remained constant, standing at about two-thirds of total unpaid work since the 1960s (Statistics Canada 2000; Statistics Canada 1995).[17] Sharp differences in men's and women's unpaid child-care and housework persist. The largest percentage of men employed 30 hours or more per week with children under 6 report doing 5–14 hours of child-care per week. In contrast, the largest percentage of women report doing 30–59 hours of child-care per week. Men are also doing less housework than women. The largest percent of men employed 30 hours or more per week with children under 6 report doing 5–14 hours of housework per week. The largest percentage of women, in contrast, report doing 15–29 hours of housework per week. Shares of housework and child-care only equalize between employed men and women who are also lone parents, although women are the majority of lone parents.

Moreover, men's versus women's main reasons for engaging in part-time work highlight a set of gendered tradeoffs: many men trade off part-time work for education, but few trade off part-time work for caregiving. Many women also trade off part-time work to attend school, yet an equivalent percentage cite caregiving responsibilities as their central reason for working part time.[18] Women are also nearly eight times more likely than men to opt to be self-employed due to caregiving responsibilities – 13.2 per cent of women versus 1.7 per cent of men cite "balancing work and family" as their main reason for becoming self-employed (Delage 2002). This set of tradeoffs contributes to the betterment of men's labour market position and the entrenchment of precariousness among many women.

The relationship between unpaid work, relations of distribution, and gendered precariousness also makes it necessary to consider the rise of "precarious households" – another important theme considered in various chapters of the book – whether they are composed of two or more income-earners (cycling in and out of precarious employment) struggling to sustain a decent standard of living for their members or a single parent with children. This development, too, is inseparable from prescriptive assumptions about gender roles and racialized inequalities. What constitutes precariousness on the dimensions of the income package or regulatory effectiveness depends on the unit of analysis chosen (e.g., the individual or the household).

TOWARDS UNDERSTANDING AND LIMITING PRECARIOUS EMPLOYMENT

Understanding precarious employment requires an analysis of developments inside and outside the labour force and a re-examination of the way we conceive of choice, control, and constraint. Limiting it requires identifying the conceptual bases for positive social change and a range of parallel practical solutions.

The chapters in the body of this volume take up this dual challenge, pursuing four overarching avenues of investigation. Every chapter is guided by a common conception of precarious employment, yet the four parts into which the book is divided represent different entry points into understanding this social problem. Part One, "Mapping Precarious Employment in Canada: New Statistical Insights," draws on data from Statistics Canada to explore the contours of precarious employment in early 21st-century Canada and examines several of its central facets in depth.[19] The analysis is extended in Part Two, "Precarious Health at Work and Precarious Work in an Unhealthy Public Sector," by drawing on original survey data, legal analysis, and case studies to explore the health effects of precarious employment. Part Three, "Regulating Precarious Employment: Institutions, Law, and Policy," devotes attention to the way that workers in precarious employment, from a range of social locations and social contexts, are affected by gaps and changes in labour and social policy. Finally, Part Four, "Unions, Unionisms, and Precarious Employment," explores the obstacles that the precariously employed confront in organizing to improve their conditions of work and health, and considers several innovative organizing efforts. Each of the four parts of the volume begins with a contribution providing an overview of the vocabulary, concepts, and approaches organizing the chapters to follow. Readers may wish to refer to these contributions to assist them in navigating a given section or, alternatively, they may prefer to turn immediately to the case studies.

Part One develops a textured statistical portrait of precarious employment in Canada. Chapter 2, "Conceptualizing Precarious Employment: Mapping Wage Work Across Social Location and Occupational Context," by Cynthia J. Cranford and Leah F. Vosko, advances a new methodological approach to understanding precarious wage work, taking the statistical portrait of precarious employment described previously as its point of departure and setting the stage for the mapping methodology employed in several subsequent chapters. This approach considers how race and gender, as they intersect with occupation, shape and, in turn, are shaped by precarious employment. Its main empirical finding is that a "racialized gendering of jobs" characterizes the contemporary Canadian labour market. Following this effort, chapter 3 applies a complementary approach to the self-employed. "Precarious by Choice? Gender and Self-Employment," by Leah F. Vosko and Nancy Zukewich, layers forms of self-employment by select dimensions of precarious employment and finds a gendered continuum of precarious self-employment. The chapter also illustrates that many dimensions of precarious employment characterize key forms of self-employment, such as part-time and full-time solo self-employment. The conclusion of these authors supports challenges to contemporary definitions of "entrepreneurship" (Fudge, Tucker, and Vosko 2002; Hughes 1999; Mirchandani 1999), yet the adoption of a gender lens allows them to interrogate and challenge the notion of "choice" underpinning prevailing understandings of main reasons for self-employment.

These two overview chapters are followed by an in-depth examination of a significant social location as well as an industrial context that is essential to the public/private divide. Chapter 4, by Emile Tompa, Heather Scott, Scott

Trevithick, and Sudipa Bhattacharyya, shifts to a different level to explore precarious employment among workers with disabilities, examining how and in what ways certain forms of employment and dimensions of precarious employment exacerbate insecurity for groups that are already disadvantaged. In "Precarious Employment and People with Disabilities," these authors explore the contemporary employment-related experiences of people with disabilities with reference to the rise of precarious employment since the mid-1970s. Reflecting the volume's central concern with social reproduction and relations of distribution, this chapter offers an analysis of labour market trends; it considers how the movement in and out of employment among people with disabilities relates to their experience of precariousness. The authors pay considerable attention to remedial legislation, such as federal and provincial pay and employment equity legislation, designed to facilitate access to employment and how, and in what ways, it influences (or fails to influence) conditions of work.

Finally, chapter 5, by Pat Armstrong and Kate Laxer, applies the mapping approach to an important industrial context and a central domain of women's employment. In "Precarious Work, Privatization, and the Health-Care Industry: The Case of Ancillary Workers," these authors paint a portrait of precarious employment in the increasingly privatized Canadian health-care industry. In the face of dramatic restructuring in this industry, they reveal that a growing number of women health-care workers, especially those performing what is deemed to be "ancillary work," are subject to conditions of work that make not only ancillary health-care workers but patients too at greater risk of ill-health.

By highlighting the public health costs of precarious employment, the last chapter of Part One offers a bridge to Part Two, whose goal is to consider the health implications of precarious employment, especially among workers delivering increasingly privatized public services, as they relate to policy design as well as state, employer, and union practice. This segment of the volume includes chapters linking precarious employment, work organization, and health to develop the notion of "employment strain" through the use of survey data, by examining the impact of contracting-out on state workers and by exploring the relationship between precarious employment and declining access to once public employment supports. It is oriented by an approach to health that emphasizes social determinants and is grounded in an understanding of precarious employment focusing on the connections between households and the labour force.

The lead chapter in this segment, "The Hidden Costs of Precarious Employment: Health and the Employment Relationship," illustrates that the conventional notion of "job strain" – understood to result from the interaction between workload and control at work – does not reflect the situation of workers in precarious employment. Wayne Lewchuk, Alice de Wolff, Andrew King, and Michael Polanyi argue that this construct must give way to the notion of "employment strain," which captures the unique aspects of control in contexts where workers are constantly searching for work. The concept employment strain emerged from spirited exchanges across the Community University Research Alliance on Contingent Work and it frames contributions in Part Two in particular. In their research, these authors began with the objective of probing the health impacts of precarious employment with reference to Karasek's job demand-control model. But, in encountering the research findings of other groups, they discovered that although Karasek demonstrates the importance of control over the labour process at the level of the workplace, the study of precarious employment necessitates a break from his model – the Karasek model assumes a standard employment relationship but the phenomenon under study is neither place-specific nor characterized by a singular employment relationship or work arrangement. Understanding precarious employment, work organization, and health thus calls for examining how workers piece together a living and considering the relationship among households, the state, and firms (both production and social reproduction). For these authors, making this shift meant constructing a research tool that challenged the norm of the (white) male industrial implicit in the job demand-control model. The result is an innovative survey with questions probing how workers train and prepare themselves for work as well as their strategies for retaining work and for survival among and across different work contexts – adding texture to the notion of employment strain. Chapter 6 reports on the findings of this survey research.

Chapters 7 and 8, in contrast, explore the employment practices and policies of an unhealthy public sector and their role in shaping the dynamics of precarious employment and thereby employment strain. Chapter 7, by Jan Borowy, focuses on the state as an employer; it is concerned with precarious employment among state employees (and former employees) involved in the delivery of public services, their deteriorating conditions of employment, and the impact of this decline on public safety. In "Essential but Precarious: Changing Employment Relationships and Resistance in the Ontario Public Service," Borowy examines the situations of three groups of state workers – court workers, workers in Ontario's Trillium Drug Program, and meat inspectors – whose work is critical to maintaining public health and welfare, yet who confront multiple dimensions of precarious employment. Following a similar thematic thread, yet placing greater emphasis on workers using public services, chapter 8 probes the relationship between the privatization of a key state-run institution – the public employment service – and the social and state regulation of precarious employment in Toronto. In "Privatizing Public Employment Assistance and Precarious Employment in Toronto," Alice de Wolff considers the effects of contracting-out of public employment services for employment placement workers, on the one hand, and, on the other, the workers seeking employment whom they serve. In so doing, she reveals a range of important connections, from linkages at the policy level between changing immigration policy and the provision of employment supports at the provincial level, to connections, by way of a common attachment to precarious employment, between community workers, working largely in serial fixed-term temporary contracts contingent on public funding, and their clients.

With changes in the normative model of employment and the spread of precarious employment, more and more workers experience gaps in protection. There is a disjuncture between labour law and policy and the realities of the contemporary labour market. Part Three addresses developments in Canadian labour laws, regulations, and policies pertinent to the spread of precarious employment. Chapter 9, by Stephanie Bernstein, Katherine Lippel, Eric Tucker, and Leah F. Vosko, initiates this endeavour with an intervention paralleling the effort to conceptualize precarious employment statistically in chapters 2 and 3 and to develop the concept of employment strain in chapter 6. "Precarious Employment and the Law's Flaws: Identifying Regulatory Failure and Securing Effective Protection for Workers" moves beyond the dimension of regulatory protection to reflect a more holistic understanding of regulatory effectiveness aimed at remedying failures in not only legal design and coverage but misinformation among workers and poor enforcement mechanisms. This chapter is concerned with identifying the many symptoms associated with the inadequacy of workers' protection that the study of precarious employment makes visible. After outlining some of the definitions, concepts, and tendencies essential to an understanding of regulatory effectiveness and failure, contributors probe key themes central to regulatory failure in the context of precarious employment, including disparity of treatment between workers in precarious employment and workers with greater security, gaps in legal coverage, the interaction between labour market position and social location, and the lack of compliance and enforcement. To frame the chapters that follow, they also identify the interdisciplinary and methodological challenges to securing regulatory effectiveness.

The chapters included in Part Three respond to the call for improving regulatory effectiveness, though in different ways, focusing primarily on Ontario and Quebec. Chapter 10, by Stephanie Bernstein, addresses Quebec's approach to reforming its *Labour Standards Act*. "Mitigating Precarious Employment in Quebec: The Role of Minimum Employment Standards Legislation" examines developments in Quebec in the early 2000s, with attention to efforts by the government to evaluate the situation of "atypical workers" (e.g., Bernier, Jobin, and Vallée 2003) in an attempt to mitigate precarious employment in this jurisdiction. The next two chapters shift focus to examine precarious employment and occupational health and safety regulation. Chapter 11, by Katherine Lippel, offers an analysis of existing legislation, case law, and legal literature on the application of occupational health and safety and on workers' compensation legislation in Quebec. The central argument of "Precarious Employment and Occupational Health and Safety Regulation in Quebec" is that meta-analyses are critical to specifying the health effects of precarious employment – indeed, they inform workers' compensation research – but there are very few tools available to examine regulatory effectiveness from a legal perspective. In order to improve the occupational health and safety of workers in precarious employment in Quebec, Lippel argues that it is crucial for legal researchers to join with researchers determining health effects. Chapter 12, by Eric Tucker, also focuses on occupational health and safety regulation, but in Ontario. In "Will the Vicious Circle of Precariousness Be Unbroken? The Exclusion of Ontario Farm Workers from the *Occupational Health and Safety Act*," Tucker critically examines the rationale offered to justify the exclusion of agricultural workers from occupational health and safety legislation which lasted until 2005. His chapter is a case study of marginalized workers denied the benefit of labour law protections. Part Three ends with an intervention by Andrew Jackson, "Regulating Precarious Labour Markets: What Can We Learn from New European Models?" Offering a segue into the discussion of alternatives, chapter 13 explores how more widespread collective bargaining, minimum wages, and minimum standards, modelled on efforts to regulate precarious employment in Nordic countries like Denmark, could have a favourable impact on the ways in which labour markets operate at the micro-level.

Part Four concludes the volume by considering avenues for improving workers' quality and conditions of work and health, with attention to workers' historical and contemporary struggles. Chapter 14, "The Union Dimension: Mitigating Precarious Employment?" by John Anderson, James Beaton, and Kate Laxer, examines the degree to which unionization, a key indicator of control over the labour process identified in several chapters in Part One, limits precarious employment among workers. It also explores how, and in what ways, union coverage mitigates precarious employment for workers in distinct social locations and thereby provides a backdrop for the chapters that follow. In so doing, these authors weave together statistical data and an analysis of union policy and practice. Although unionization mitigates precariousness for some workers, it contends that inequalities based on race still prevail. Chapter 15 examines union responses to precarious employment. In this instance, Tania Das Gupta's focus is "Racism/Anti-Racism, Precarious Employment, and Unions," as she is concerned with the way the mainstream labour movement has historically treated non-white workers in precarious employment and the role of history in shaping contemporary practices. Das Gupta's chapter offers a qualitative analysis of the perceptions and experiences of labour activists of colour and of alternative advocacy strategies for building more inclusive resistance movements. Chapter 16, by Chris Schenk, is also concerned with the experience of workers of colour. However, his chapter offers a case study of workers in a large Toronto-based hotel and their campaign, first, to attain just working conditions, and then to retain them in the face of the SARS crisis. "Union Renewal and Precarious Employment: A Case Study of Hotel Workers" considers the question of resistance by examining how a union locale in a sector confronting precarious employment successfully transformed its politics and, hence, challenged conventional notions of labour militancy. Yet, even though it won important terms and conditions designed to mitigate precarious employment in its collective agreement, crisis in the hotel industry with the onset of SARS allowed precarious employment to resurface.

The final chapter in Part Four, "Thinking Through Community Unionism," offers a case study based on multi-year ethnography of the efforts of a group of workers organizing with Toronto Organizing for Fair Employment (TOFFE), now the Workers' Action Centre of Toronto, an active community partner in the Community University Research Alliance on Contingent Work. Chapter 17, by Cynthia J. Cranford, Tania Das Gupta, Deena Ladd, and Leah F. Vosko, attempts to conceptualize community unionism by locating the efforts of TOFFE in relation to two intersecting continua – a continuum of location that includes constituency, site, and issue-based organizing, and a continuum of process, defined by hierarchical organizations at one pole and participatory organizations at the other pole. According to these authors, community unionism is located at the intersection of these two axes. It is a highly participatory process of organizing among workers around a variety of social locations, including a diversity of issues, sites, and constituencies, while maintaining a central interest on labour concerns – and it is critical to limiting precarious employment in Canada.

The conclusion, "What Is to Be Done? Harnessing Knowledge to Mitigate Precarious Employment," synthesizes the central findings of the volume. It explores the implications of precarious employment for workers, households, and communities as well as its larger public costs and identifies several avenues for improving knowledge in an attempt to better workers' conditions of work and quality of health.

PART ONE

Mapping Precarious Employment
in Canada:
New Statistical Insights

2

Conceptualizing Precarious Employment: Mapping Wage Work across Social Location and Occupational Context

CYNTHIA J. CRANFORD AND LEAH F. VOSKO

The dominant measures of precarious employment are out of sync with the realities of the Canadian labour market. Accepted measures focus narrowly on the form of employment and on work arrangements, yet precarious employment is a multi-dimensional phenomenon shaped by race and gender as well as by occupation.

There is growing scholarly attention to the spread of non-standard forms of employment, such as work through a temporary agency and solo self-employment, and work arrangements, including shift work, on-call work, and telework (Bourhis and Wills 2001; Duffy and Pupo 1994; Gurstein 2001; Hughes 1999; Johnson 2002; Zeytinoglu and Mutsehi 1999). Marking a departure from previous research, more studies pay attention to the quality of different forms of employment and work arrangements (Lowe, Schellenberg, and Davidman 1999). Still, scholarship remains limited by the conceptual focus of the dominant statistical measures and their normative power.

How is precarious employment best conceptualized and measured? This chapter contributes to conceptualizing precarious employment by offering a new methodological approach. This approach centres on the relationship between the form of employment and other dimensions of precarious employment – income level and the social wage, regulatory protection, and control and contingency – with attention to the social locations of gender and "race"[1] and to occupational contexts.

Form of employment continues to shape precarious employment, yet the relationship between employment forms and additional dimensions of precarious employment varies by social location and by social context. Precarious employment is highly gendered, and gender relations intersect with race-ethnicity and other social locations to shape different groups' experiences of precarious employment. Occupation is another layer influencing precarious employment. Some occupations are characterized by low earnings, limited access to the social wage, and a lack of regulatory protection and control, regardless of form of employment, and key forms of employment are polarized by occupation.

The chapter uses the analytic concept of the "feminization of employment norms" to highlight the multi-dimensional character of precarious employment. The feminization of employment norms denotes the erosion of the standard employment relationship and the spread of forms of employment exhibiting qualities of precarious employment associated with women, immigrants, people of colour, and other marginalized groups.

The ensuing discussion unfolds in four sections. The first section sets out the theoretical framework; it joins scholarship on changing employment relationships and intersecting inequalities of race, ethnicity, and gender through the notion of the feminization of employment norms. The second section advances the methodological approach, conceptualizing precarious employment along multiple dimensions and introducing new statistical indicators. The third section applies this methodology to four forms of wage work[2] – full-time permanent, full-time temporary, part-time permanent, and part-time temporary – across select social locations and occupational contexts. Finally, the fourth section concludes the chapter with a discussion of how these findings illustrate a key facet of the feminization of employment norms – the gendering of jobs.

PRECARIOUS EMPLOYMENT
AND THE FEMINIZATION OF EMPLOYMENT NORMS

From "Non-standard Work" to Precarious Employment

A direct and linear relationship between form of employment and other dimensions of precarious employment is too often assumed. In the post-World War II period, labour and employment legislation supported a standard employment relationship, primarily for white men, which linked decent wages, benefits, working conditions, and job security to the full-time permanent job. Despite the continued numerical and normative importance of the standard employment relationship, the standard is eroding, with broader labour market and political restructuring, resulting in increasing insecurity for all workers. Within this context, important differences between the temporary and part-time forms of employment, usually lumped together in the category non-standard work, have emerged.

The category of non-standard work is used to group together a broad range of employment forms and work arrangements (Carre, Ferber, Golden, and Herzenberg 2000; Economic Council of Canada 1990; Krahn 1991). The categories comprising this catchall are part-time employment; temporary employment, including employees with term or contract, seasonal, casual, and all other forms of wage work with a pre-determined end date; solo self-employment (i.e., self-employed persons with no paid employees); and multiple job holding. These categories are unified by their deviation from the standard employment relationship. Yet the broad grouping "non-standard" is limited in its capacity to capture precarious employment because of the diversity in the categories "standard" and "non-standard." Some distinctions within a given category, such as solo self-employment, which may be part-time or full-time, are not reflected in the dominant framework, since "non-standard work" is not a mutually exclusive measure. Other differences, such as income differentials among full-time permanent employees, are also overlooked, since considering forms of employment and work arrangements alone neglects the mix of dimensions characterizing precarious employment.

Rather than focusing exclusively on forms of employment and work arrangements, a growing body of literature highlights the importance of considering their relationship to dimensions of precarious employment. For instance, part-time temporary employees are more precarious than part-time permanent employees in terms of the dimensions of control over the labour process, degree of regulatory protection, and income level. Similarly, the solo part-time self-employed are more precarious than full-time self-employed employers on the dimensions of control, social and regulatory protection, and income level (Vosko and Zukewich, this volume). This approach allows for an analysis of continuity and change in the form and content of employment relationships. It yields a more complete portrait of precarious employment that maintains an emphasis on employment status (i.e., self-employment or wage work) and form (part-time/full-time or temporary/permanent) at the same time as it expands the dimensions of precarious employment under consideration.

This effort to conceptualize precarious employment also opens space for examining how precarious employment varies by social locations, such as gender, race, immigrant status, and age, and by social contexts, such as occupation and industry. Both erosion of the norm and inequalities within forms of non-standard employment are shaped by industrial/occupational context. Some occupations are particularly vulnerable to economic restructuring, such as those in primary industry and manufacturing (Bakker 1996a; Cohen 1994; Luxton and Corman 2001), while others are characterized by decentralized and fragmented work organization, ranging from trades and transport to service sector occupations (Madar 2000; Smith 1997). Economic restructuring may mean that full-time permanent wage work in some industrial or occupational contexts is more precarious than part-time permanent wage work in others. Industrial and occupational trends in turn contextualize intersecting relations of gender and race. Because of enduring racism and nativism, women of colour and immigrant women are particularly disadvantaged by shifts to a polarized service sector and the downgrading of manufacturing (Das Gupta 2002; Gabriel 1999; Glenn 1992; James, Grant, and Cranford 2000). Thus, an understanding of precarious employment also requires attention to social location.

The Feminization of Employment Norms: Elevating Social Location and Occupational Context

Feminization is typically associated with either women's mass entry into the labour force or simply with the changing gender composition of jobs. In contrast, the feminization of employment norms (Vosko 2003) encompasses four facets of racialized and gendered labour market trends: high levels of formal labour force participation among women; continuing industrial and occupational segregation; income and occupational polarization both between women and men and among the sexes by social locations such as race, ethnicity, and immigrant status; and the gendering of jobs to resemble more precarious work associated with women and other marginalized groups assumed to have access to alternative sources of subsistence beyond the wage. Armstrong (1996) refers to a similar process tied to economic restructuring as "harmonizing down."

An approach informed by the analytic concept of the feminization of employment norms takes as its starting point that understanding precarious employment requires attention to social location, particularly to gender as it intersects with race and age, given continuous sex/gender inequalities in the labour force. Each of the facets is linked to men's and women's differential responsibilities for social reproduction and to the unequal relations of distribution in households. An expanded space for analysing the relationship between race, gender, and other axes of inequality and precarious employment is necessary, given that changing employment relationships are accompanied by enduring racialized gender inequalities both inside and outside the labour force (Brenner 2000; Cranford 1998; Gabriel 1999; Spalter-Roth and Hartmann 1998).

In conceptualising precarious employment, with attention to social location and occupational context, this chapter focuses on one facet of feminization – the gendering of jobs. The gendering of jobs is inextricably connected to social reproduction. Women, particularly women from racialized groups, are often confined to jobs in the market that reflect the sex/gender division of domestic labour, such as child-care, nursing, and service occupations (Armstrong and Armstrong 2001; Das Gupta 2002; Glenn

1992; Luxton 1980; Vosko 2003). In turn, these jobs are precarious along multiple dimensions. They typically pay low wages, offer few benefits, have limited regulatory protection, allow for little control over the labour process, and are often of short duration. These precarious conditions, in turn, are often justified with reference to women's perceived access to male wages and social benefits. The expansion of gendered jobs to more segments of the labour force reflects the erosion of the standard employment relationship in normative and numeric terms.

The ensuing empirical analysis is framed by the notion of the gendering of jobs. It explores the relationship between precarious employment and the social locations of race and gender as they intersect within occupational contexts. The concern here is less with identifying occupations characterized by high levels of precarious employment than with placing social context on a par with social location in the new methodological approach.

METHODOLOGICAL APPROACH

Mapping Precarious Wage Work

The methodological point of departure in this chapter is a mutually exclusive typology of total employment. For a description of this typology, see the introduction to this volume. The focus here is on the four forms of wage work – full-time permanent, part-time permanent, full-time temporary, and part-time temporary.[3]

Elsewhere, we layer the four forms of wage work with three indicators of precarious employment and examine how this relationship is gendered.[4] Using this approach, the main empirical finding is that the Canadian labour market is characterized by a continuum of precarious wage work, where full-time permanent employees are the least precarious, followed, in order, by full-time temporary employees, part-time permanent employees, and part-time temporary employees. Sex differences along this continuum reveal gendered inequalities between full-time permanent employees. Sex differences also highlight multiple gendered dimensions of precarious employment among part-time and temporary employees and two facets of the feminization of employment norms – the gendering of jobs and income polarization between men and women. The central methodological finding is that conflating non-standard forms of employment and precarious employment masks nuances central to understanding labour market insecurity.

The notion of a continuum of precarious employment has several merits. It moves beyond the standard/non-standard employment dichotomy while acknowledging the significance of the standard employment relationship as a normative model of employment shaping the legal and social regulation of wage work and self-employment. The continuum also offers a range of possibilities for elevating social location: for example, applying a gender lens to the continuum reveals that women's concentration in certain forms of employment reflects continuities in gender inequalities; even though more men than in the past, especially young men, are in precarious forms of employment, women are concentrated in the most precarious forms of employment. Examining gender inequalities within forms of employment also allows for a detailed investigation of the full-time permanent category – that is, an exploration of continuities in gendered inequalities in this form of wage work. At the same time, it permits an exploration of how gender inequalities are being reconstituted through the gendering of jobs. Finally, considering indicators of precarious employment across the forms of wage work along the continuum highlights inequalities among men and among women. For example, part-time young men have lower incomes and lower levels of regulatory protection and control than other men. Still, a range of questions remains: How are inequalities between women and men, and among women and men, racialized? Do these inequalities vary along other indicators of precarious employment? How do they vary by occupational context?

These questions, and the concern to replace unitary with multi-dimensional indicators, lend themselves to the metaphor of a map (or a multi-dimensional continuum). It is nevertheless important to be cognizant of relativism. Precarious employment is still structured by form of employment. Moreover, as the concept of the feminization of employment norms reminds us, gender differentiation inside and outside the labour force remain. This analysis reveals how the process of feminization is also highly racialized.

Dimensions of Precarious Wage Work

Precarious employment includes job, person, household, and community levels of analysis.[5] This discussion considers one piece of this larger puzzle: the characteristics of individual employees in their main job. A focus on the main job has both merits and drawbacks. Because more and more individuals hold multiple jobs, and because people reproduce themselves in households, a focus on a main job does not capture fully the ways in which people piece together a living. However, addressing the person level or household level of analysis is impossible without first understanding how precariousness is manifest at the level of an individual's main job.

This analysis focuses on four dimensions of precarious wage work: earnings, social wage, regulatory protection, and control and contingency.[6] Each dimension has several indicators of precarious employment. The indicators are defined as the proportion of employees (in a particular form of wage work, social location, or occupation) who fall into the category conceptualized as "precarious." Each dimension also operates at different scales. For example, roughly 70 per cent of all employees lack dental benefits, demanding a wide scale, while only 15 per cent of all employees have hourly earnings at or below the minimum wage, calling for a more concentrated or finely grained scale. Modifying the scales for different dimensions reflects, visually, that earning below the minimum wage is as strong an indicator of precarious employment as not having dental benefits, if not a stronger one.

Income is, arguably, the most important dimension of precarious employment. Earnings are an important component of income and the focus of this individual-level analysis of a person's main job.[7] This analysis considers four indicators of earnings. First, it includes a measure of an extremely precarious wage – namely, those earning the minimum wage or less. However, many employees who earn more than the minimum wage are also in poverty. Second, an intermediate measure includes all those who earn less than $10 an hour, one consistent with the poverty line defined by the Low Income Cut Off for an individual in a large city working 35 hours a week, year round. It is also used in community unions' campaigns for fair wages (Cranford, Das Gupta, and Vosko, this volume). However, many individuals do not work 35 hours a week or on a permanent basis. The analysis therefore includes a third measure of precarious wages: the median industrial wage. The median wage, standing at $14.13 an hour, is also the measure of a precarious wage preferred by many trade unionists (Anderson, Beaton, and Laxer, this volume). Finally, the analysis includes a measure of precarious yearly earnings those who earn less than $20,000 a year, in order to include a measure that comes closer to the earnings of individuals with temporary and part-time work.

Earnings represent but one dimension of precarious employment. The social wage is another important part of the wage package; it is the bundle of elements beyond earnings, and it significantly shapes the standard of living of individuals and households as well as the relations of distribution within households (Picchio 1998). Employer-sponsored benefits are a component of the social wage with a significant bearing on precarious employment. This analysis selects four indicators of a precarious social wage: the lack of extended health coverage, dental coverage, a pension plan, and life/disability insurance.

Together, regulatory protection and control represent an important dimension of precarious employment related to unions, law, and policy. This pair of dimensions shapes working conditions, yet the two concepts operate at different levels of analysis. "Control" is used here to denote workers' ability to influence the labour process. In contrast, "regulatory protection" has a broader impact on a worker's standard of living, whether through legislation or through a collective agreement (Forrest 1995; Fudge 1991; Rodgers 1989). Despite these differences, measuring regulatory protection and control with available statistics is best achieved through proxies that measure both dimensions at once. In other words, it is difficult to separate regulatory protection and control using the available data. Union coverage is the first indicator of regulatory protection and control. It is a suitable indicator because unionized workers have a higher degree of protection written into collective agreements (Rodgers 1989; White 1993). It is also a good measure of control over the labour process because unionized workers have grievance procedures as well as job-based solidarities that allow them to influence the level and speed of their work (White 1993). Firm size less than twenty is a good indicator of the degree of regulatory protection among employees, since some labour laws do not apply in these firms, and those that do are often ill-enforced or difficult to use (Fudge 1993; O'Grady 1991). For example, small firms are not required to abide by equal pay and employment equity legislation (Armstrong and Armstrong 2001, 28).[8]

Measures of contingency generally focus on conditional, transitory, and temporary employment contracts (Polivka and Nardone 1989; Polivka 1996). Within a context of declining job tenure, that of less than one year is a suitable measure of conditional employment relationships. With this measure, it is particularly important to control for age, because all young workers have lower tenure. This analysis also measures contingency through two additional indicators, since the notion of contingency as temporary employment contracts is overly narrow. Not all short-term employment relationships are inherently precarious, such as highly paid consultants who increase their earnings each time they move. Being in and out of work is a more precise measure of precarious employment, since regulatory protections and employer-provided benefits are highly correlated with a continuous relationship with an employer – the linchpin of the standard employment relationship (Fudge and Vosko 2001a). Finally, the analysis includes a measure related to broader processes of economic restructuring labelled "company uncertainty," which measures job separation due to layoff or business slowdown or to the fact that the company has moved or is going out of business.

These indicators are summarized in table 2.1, which also defines proxies for the social locations of gender and race and for the social context of occupation/industry. The analysis uses the 10 categories of occupational/industrial groupings in order to ensure sample sizes that are large enough for each of the indicators. The data used in this analysis are from the Survey of Labour and Income Dynamics (SLID), 2000, cross-sectional files. The data used here are also for Canada as a whole, for reasons of sample size.[9] The empirical analysis focuses on the prime-aged population (persons aged 25–54) for two reasons tied to the feminization of employment norms. First, young people, especially young men, tend to move out of the forms of wage work exhibiting multiple dimensions of precarious employment as they move through the life cycle (Drolet 2001; Lochhead and Scott 1997; Townson 1997). Second, the analysis is concerned to elevate the relationship among aspects of social reproduction, gender, and precarious employment – specifically, sex/gender divisions of unpaid work and how they shape the racialized gender of precarious employment (in this volume, see Armstrong and Laxer; and Vosko and Zukewich). It is logical, therefore, to draw attention to age groups where children are most likely to be present.

This methodological approach is depicted in figure 2.1 and taken up by Armstrong and Laxer (this volume) and by Anderson, Beaton, and Laxer (this volume).

PRECARIOUS WAGE WORK IN CANADA

Dimensions of Precarious Wage Work in Canada

The standard/non-standard distinction still structures insecurity in important ways. Full-time permanent wage work is the least precarious on several dimensions, specifically earnings, social wage, regulatory protection, and control (figure 2.2). At the same time, the patterns do not lend themselves to the notion of a strict standard/non-standard dichotomy.

A comparison of temporary and part-time forms of wage work confirms that there are important inequalities, along several dimensions, among those grouped together in the non-standard category. With respect to income, full-time temporary employees are less likely than part-time permanent employees to earn the minimum wage. In turn, part-time permanent employees are less likely than part-time temporary workers to have this extremely precarious wage (figure 2.2 income). These results reflect the continuum of precarious wage work identified in our previous research and are consistent with the finding of a continuum of precarious self-employment presented in chapter 3. However, the notion of a continuum is complicated in that differences between forms are greater along some dimensions than others. For example, full-time permanent employees are much more likely to have low tenure and to move in and out of work than are those in the part-time permanent form. At the same time, differences between the two part-time forms are less along the dimensions of regulatory protection and control (figure 2.2).

The erosion of the standard employment relationship along key dimensions also breaks with the notion of a continuum. High proportions of workers across all forms lack the regulatory protection and control of a union. Nearly 70 per cent of full-time permanent employees are not covered by a union, even though they are more likely to be covered than the other three forms of wage work. Given the importance of union status to shaping precarious employment (Anderson, Beaton, and Laxer, this volume), the significant proportion of full-time permanent employees who are not unionized is important to recognize. Full-time permanent employees are

Table 2.1
Variables of Employment

Forms of Employment

Forms of Wage Work
Full-time permanent employees
Full-time temporary employees
Part-time permanent employees
Part-time temporary employees

Indicators of Precariousness

Earnings
Less than minimum wage
Poverty wage (less than $10.00/hr)
Median industrial wage (less than $14.13/hr)
Poverty earnings (less than $20,000/year)
Social Wage
No extended medical benefits
No dental benefits
No pension plan
No disability/life insurance
Regulatory Protection and Control
Not covered by a union contract
Firm size less than 20
Contingency
Less than 12 months job tenure
In and out of work*
Company uncertainty[†]

Social Locations

Visible minority women (women of colour)
Visible minority men (men of colour)
Not-a-visible minority women (white women)
Not-a-visible minority men (white men)

Occupational Context (Occupation/Industry)

Management occupations (A011-A392)
Business, finance, and administrative occupations (B011-B576)
Natural and applied sciences and related occupations (C011-C175)
Health occupations (D011-D313)
Occupations in social science, education, government service, and religion (E011-E216)
Occupations in art, culture, recreation, and sport (F011-F154)
Sales and service occupations (G011-G983)
Trades, transport and equipment operators, and related occupations (H011-H832)
Occupations unique to primary industry (I011-I216)
Occupations unique to processing, manufacturing, and utilities (J011-J319)

---

*Those who have work part of the year but are also unemployed or out of the labour force part of the year.
[†] Job separation due to layoff/business slowdown, or to company having moved or being out of business.

Figure 2.1
Indicators of precarious wage work

also the most likely to experience company uncertainty – an important dimension of contingency. These results highlight the importance of examining differences within the forms of wage work in relation to social location and occupational context.

Precarious Occupational Contexts

Examining dimensions of precarious wage work across occupational contexts illustrates further the conceptual problems with the standard/non-standard dichotomy. This distinction is still relevant. Yet inequality between occupations remains within the most precarious form of wage work at the same time as the erosion of the norm is in evidence.

The relevance of the standard/non-standard distinction is clear in comparing full-time permanent and part-time temporary wage work. Employees in all occupations are less precarious if they are full-time permanent than if they are part-time temporary, along all dimensions (figure 2.3). This trend is particularly significant for occupations in sales and service, health, social science, education, government service, and religion, which have relatively high proportions of part-time temporary employees. In contrast, few part-time temporary employees are in occupations unique to trades, processing, primary industry, transport and equipment, or manufacturing and utilities (figure 2.4).

Figure 2.2
Indicators of precarious wage work by form of employment, Canada, 2000 (ages 25–54):
Income, social wage, regulatory protection and control, contingency

Figure 2.2a
Income

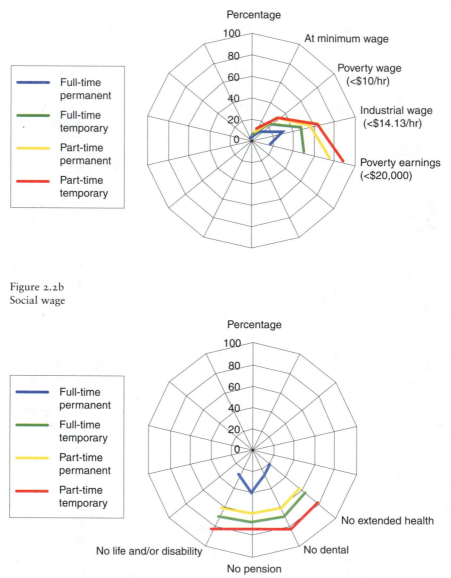

Figure 2.2b
Social wage

Figure 2.2c
Regulatory protection and control

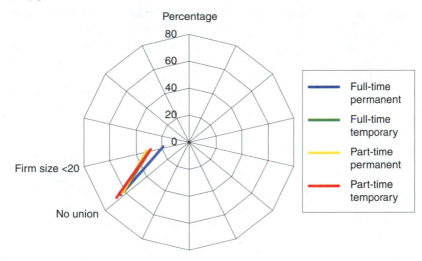

Figure 2.2d
Contingency

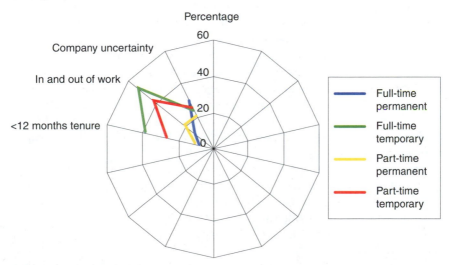

An examination of part-time temporary wage work illustrates inequality between occupations despite form of employment. Along all dimensions, sales and service occupations are more precarious than health, social science, education, government service, and religion occupations.

Differences in union coverage between public and private service sector occupations are particularly notable: approximately 60 per cent of part-time temporary employees in occupations in health, social science, education, government service, and religion are covered by a union, compared to just over 20 per cent in sale and service occupations. There are also significant differences along the social wage – in pension coverage in particular. Part-time temporary sales and service workers are also more contingent than their public sector counterparts along all indicators,[10] but the rates of sales and service employees who are in and out of work are notably high (figure 2.3). These findings of stark inequalities between private sector and public sector service occupations reinforce the analysis of Armstrong and Laxer (this volume) on the link between privatization and precarious employment.

An examination of the full-time permanent category reveals that these jobs are not always "good jobs." Employees in some occupations are highly precarious along multiple dimensions, even if they have full-time permanent jobs (figure 2.3); and significant proportions of employees, across all occupations, are still employed in full-time permanent jobs (figure 2.4).

The dimension of earnings highlights the limits of equating full-time permanent wage work with a "standard" or "good job" devoid of occupational context. Even when sales and service employees have full-time permanent wage work, 30 per cent earn a poverty wage and an even a greater proportion earn less than the average industrial wage. In addition, many full-time permanent employees in occupations unique to primary industry and processing, manufacturing, and utilities earn below the average industrial wage (figure 2.3). These results are particularly notable because 82 per cent of employees in occupations unique to processing, manufacturing, and utilities are full-time permanent (figure 2.4).

Along the dimension of regulatory protection and control, low rates of union coverage illustrate downward harmonization. In all occupations except health and those in social science, education, government service, and religion, few full-time permanent employees are covered by a union contract. Occupations unique to primary industry stand out in terms of the proportion employed in small firms (figure 2.3). These employees are the prototypical industrial workers who, through labour militancy, laid claim to the standard employment relationship previously common primarily among professional men. Since the standard employment relationship is premised on large workplaces, it is not surprising that, today, high percentages of these workers are without a union and earning below the median industrial wage.

Along the dimension of contingency, significant numbers of full-time permanent employees in processing, manufacturing, and utilities occupations

Figure 2.3
Indicators of precarious wage work by form of employment and occupation,
Canada, 2000 (ages 25–54)

Figure 2.3a
Full-time permanent

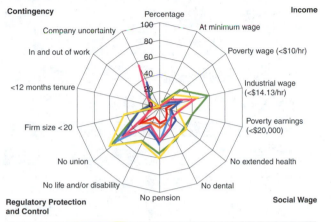

Figure 2.3b
Part-time temporary

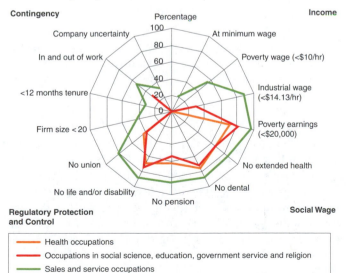

Figure 2.4
Forms of wage work by occupation

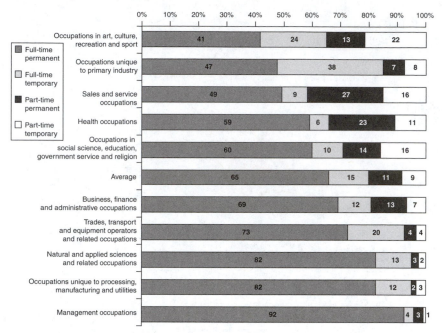

are enduring company uncertainty. Trades, transport, and equipment operators are a distant second along this important indicator of economic restructuring (figure 2.3).

Precarious Form of Wage Work and the Gendering of Jobs

Understanding the nature and experience of precarious employment requires attention to social location as well as occupational context. Precarious employment is highly gendered, as evidenced in the enduring unequal positions of women and men in the labour force (see, for example, Armstrong and Armstrong 1994; Duffy and Pupo 1994; Luxton and Corman 2001). Gendered disparities in paid work are, in turn, shaped by unequal relations of distribution and unpaid work in households. These continuities and changes in gender relations reflect the gendering of jobs. Gender is not a unitary category; rather, gender relations are shaped by other social locations such as race, ethnicity, immigrant status, age, disability, and others, making it essential to examine intersecting axes of inequality (Collins 1990; Cranford 1998; Morris 1993; Stasiulis 1999; Zavella 1997). Processes of racialization, in particular, are a key aspect of the gendering of jobs.[11]

The form of employment is highly gendered. Women, as an undifferentiated group, are more concentrated in the most precarious forms of employment than are men, as an undifferentiated group. Women are more likely than men to have part-time permanent wage work across all age groups. In all the age groups except the youngest, women are also considerably more likely to be employed in part-time temporary wage work. In contrast, men are more likely than women to have full-time permanent wage work across all age groups. Men aged 15–24 are also more likely to have full-time temporary wage work, compared to women (Vosko, Zukewich, and Cranford 2003). There are also gender differences among people with disabilities. Women with disabilities are more concentrated in part-time permanent and part-time temporary forms of employment than are men with disabilities.[12]

People of colour are also differentiated by gender across form. Women of colour are less likely to have full-time permanent jobs than their male counterparts and more likely to hold part-time permanent jobs (figure 2.5). Race intersects with immigrant status as well as gender to shape workers' labour market position. Among immigrants of colour, women are more likely to be part-time permanent employees than are men.[13]

Changing employment relations are also gendered in more complex ways. The concept of the gendering of jobs points to ways in which some men are experiencing more precarious situations alongside many women. Men of colour are slightly more likely than white men to be in the more precarious part-time temporary and part-time permanent forms of employment (figure 2.5). Racialized men are experiencing downward pressure alongside many women, both white women and women of colour. As racialized men converge with most women at the bottom, the greatest difference by form becomes that between women of colour and white men. These findings point to the need to examine more closely the ways that social locations of gender and race intersect.

The gendering of jobs is occurring through the concentration of some men (i.e., young and racialized) in precarious forms of wage work alongside many women across social locations. However, an analysis focused primarily on form of employment does not illuminate well the degree or manner in which the feminization of employment norms may result in heightened inequalities among women along social locations of race. Women of colour, as an undifferentiated group, are more likely to be in full-time permanent wage work than white women. They are also less likely to be in part-time permanent forms than white women, although the differences are small in the most precarious part-time temporary form. This finding may emanate from the considerable diversity within the category of "visible minority." For example, Black and South Asian women are more likely to be in full-time temporary wage work than non-visible minority women, whereas Chinese women are more likely than other ethnicities to be in part-time temporary wage work (Cranford, Vosko, and Zukewich 2003b, figure

Figure 2.5
Form of wage work by sex and visible minority status, Canada 2000

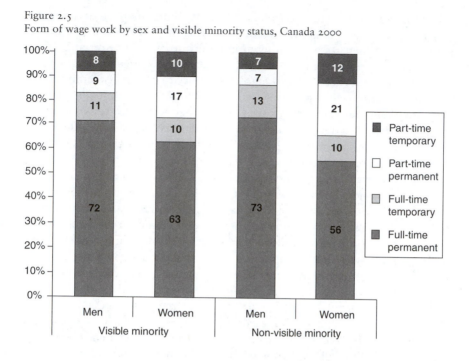

4). At the same time, the form of employment may not be the most important in-dicator of precarious employment for some. Immigrant women of colour are more likely to work full-time and longer hours than white women, but they still earn less (Boyd 1992, 295).[14] These complexities highlight the utility of a meth-odological approach that maps multiple dimensions of precarious employment.

The Racialized Gendering of Jobs: Social Location in View

There is a strong relationship between racialized-gendered social locations and dimensions of precarious employment, regardless of form. White men are less precarious than white women, consistently across all dimensions, just as they are less precarious than both women and men of colour. The differences between white men and the other three groups are the largest along the dimensions of income and social wage (figure 2.6).

The degrees of difference between the other three groups vary more by dimension. For example, both groups of women have high proportions with poverty earnings (figure 2.6). Thus, elevating social location supports the casting of precarious employment as multi-dimensional.

The erosion of the standard employment relationship is racialized. In terms of regulatory protection and control, this pattern is clear with regard to union status. Men and women of colour are less likely to be covered by a union contract than white women and men. Along the dimension of contingency, women and men of colour are also more likely to experience company uncertainty compared to white women and men. Moreover, the degree of difference among men is greater than it is among women along most indicators. For example, men of colour are much more precarious than white men along the dimension of income. These findings point to the need to conceptualize the erosion of the standard employment relations as both racialized and gendered.

RACIALIZED GENDERING OF JOBS IN CONTEXT

This analysis reveals clearly that the complex set of trends driving labour market insecurity is best understood as a racialized gendering of jobs. This conceptualization places intersecting social locations of both gender and race and industrial/occupational contexts on a par with the form of employment. In doing so, it allows for a fuller understanding of precarious employment in the contemporary Canadian labour market – one that requires a new methodological approach.

Too many discussions of labour market insecurity still rest on a simple standard/non-standard dichotomy undifferentiated by social location or social context. Many empirical studies proxy "good jobs" with "full-time permanent jobs" and lump everyone else into a "non-standard" category that is to represent "bad jobs." In contrast, scholars have long argued that the industrial/occupational context structures labour market insecurity, bad pay, and poor working conditions (Edwards, Reich, and Gordon 1975), yet many of these analyses also posited a dichotomous "primary/secondary" labour market undifferentiated by gender. Feminist scholarship points to the way social location, particularly gender, structures precarious employment, since the standard employment relationship is a male norm that has historically relegated women and other marginalized groups to more precarious forms of employment (Fudge and Vosko 2001a). Because of its institutionalisation in law, legislation, and policy, the standard/non-standard distinction still shapes an individual's level of precariousness. Yet as precarious forms of employment spread, the "standard" is eroding, resulting in increasing insecurity for all workers across employment contracts. In addition, recent theorizing of intersectionality (Collins 1990; Cranford 1998; Stasiulis 1999; Zavella 1997) helps to explain how these processes are simultaneously racialized.

This broad conceptualisation of precarious employment has required a new methodological approach that allows for a deeper theorization of location and context. The first step in breaking with the standard/non-standard dichotomy was to deconstruct "non-standard" employment into a mutually exclusive typology as described in chapter 1. Recent scholarship focused on

Figure 2.6
Indicators of precarious wage work by sex and visible minority status,
Canada, 2000 (ages 25–54)

Figure 2.6a
Income

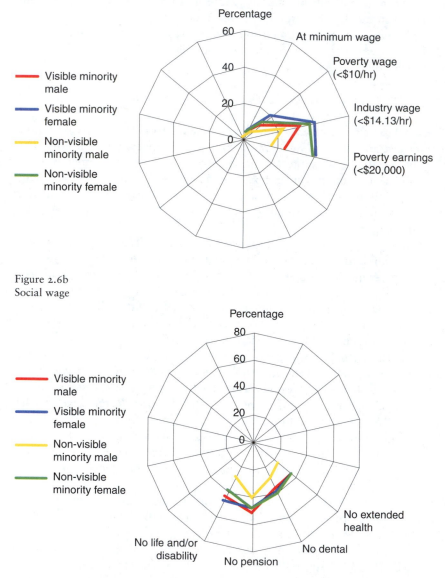

Figure 2.6b
Social wage

Figure 2.6c
Regulatory protection

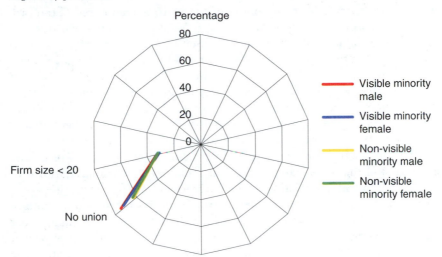

Percentage

80
60
40
20
0

Firm size < 20

No union

Visible minority
male

Visible minority
female

Non-visible
minority male

Non-visible
minority female

Figure 2.6d
Contingency

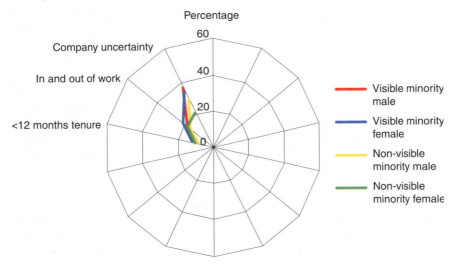

Percentage

60

Company uncertainty

40

In and out of work

20

<12 months tenure

0

Visible minority
male

Visible minority
female

Non-visible
minority male

Non-visible
minority female

the relationship between employment status and form, on the one hand, and other indicators of precariousness, on the other, and it found that distinctions by form are more akin to a continuum than to a dichotomy (Cranford, Vosko, and Zukewich 2003a; Fudge 1997; Vosko and Zukewich, this volume). The metaphor of a continuum is useful for maintaining a necessary tension between the continuing impact of the standard/non-standard distinction and the more complex changes. However, these same studies also find gender inequalities both between and within statuses and forms of employment, thereby complicating the notion of a uni-dimensional continuum. There is a pressing need for both a conceptual framework and a methodological approach that captures this complexity. This chapter contributes to advancing this approach by placing the intersecting social locations of gender and race and the industrial/occupational social contexts alongside form of wage work and additional indicators of precarious employment.

The notion of a racialized gendering of jobs brings together four components essential to understanding precarious employment – the employment relationship/contract, additional dimensions of precarious employment (such as income), occupational/industrial context, and social location. The concept of the "gendering of jobs" was coined originally to denote the downgrading of jobs to resemble work associated with women and other marginalized groups assumed to have access to alternative sources of subsistence beyond the wage. Historically, the work done by women of all races, as well as by both men and women of colour, has been poorly remunerated and characterized by poor working conditions; and it was most common in temporary, seasonal, and part-time employment contracts and in the competitive and service sectors. By considering gender as a social relation, rather than as a fixed identity or characteristic, this concept also incorporates the more recent dynamics of the spread of precarious forms of employment beyond the competitive and service sector, beyond temporary and part-time employment contracts, and beyond women. By these means, this relational concept opens space for examining how other inequalities intersect with gender to perpetuate precarious employment.

Deepening this concept, the preceding empirical analysis examined intersecting social locations of gender and race and industrial/occupational contexts in order to elevate the ways in which the gendering of jobs is racialized. The importance of social location and occupational context becomes clear when multiple indicators of precarious employment are included. This chapter mapped four forms of wage work along additional dimensions of income, social wage, regulatory protection, and control and contingency. Measuring multiple dimensions of precarious employment, in turn, highlighted a racialized gendering of jobs. The empirical results illustrate how form of employment still structures precariousness and the erosion of the norm, resulting in a gendering of jobs in distinctively racialized ways.

Mapping wage work along additional dimensions of precarious employment reveals how the standard/non-standard distinction still structures insecurity and how this structuring is highly gendered. Full-time permanent employees are the least precarious wage workers along all indicators but one. Women are more likely to have the form of wage work that is the most precarious along the majority of dimensions – part-time temporary – and they are least likely to have full-time permanent wage work, the most secure form. This gendered pattern holds across other social locations, including age, disability, race, and immigrant status. Clearly, it is still important to conceptualize precarious employment as a process of *gendering*. At the same time, the standard/non-standard distinction obscures important differences within a given form of wage work, as well as between temporary and part-time employees – differences that reflect how gendering processes are *racialized* as well as the broader shifts in occupational/industrial structure.

A contextual examination of precarious employment shows that this phenomenon is best understood as a racialized gendering of *jobs* – that is, a process shaped by occupational context. Even full-time permanent jobs are gendered if they are located in private sales and services or in primary industry. In these sectors, many full-time permanent employees earn a very precarious wage and have few benefits. Erosion of the norm of the standard employment relationship is in evidence. Many categories of private sector employees have very low unionization rates – a dimension historically alleviating insecurity among the working class, particularly for white men. Erosion is also evident in the high rates of company uncertainty among full-time permanent employees in processing, manufacturing, and utilities occupations and among trades, transport, and equipment operators. This erosion of the standard is linked to the spread of the more precarious forms of employment. Form matters the most for the public sector occupations. There are above-average proportions of part-time temporary employees in the public sector, and these workers are worse off than their full-time permanent counterparts along all dimensions. At the same time, the dual effect of holding a part-time temporary job and having that job located in private sales and services results in extensive levels of precariousness that are, along some dimensions, off the map. These trends illustrate the need to understand both which workers are in the more precarious (part-time and temporary) forms, and which workers are full-time permanent employees and precarious.

An analysis that elevates social location reveals a *racialized* gendering of jobs. The erosion of the standard employment relationship is racialized. It is men and women of colour who are least likely to be covered by a union and the most likely to labour in companies that experience business slowdown, move, or go out of business. Women of colour are the most likely to be in and out of work and to have less than a year on the job – two important indicators of contingency. Differences between women along lines of race are less stark along the dimension of income and the social wage. Contrary to the popular assumption that "men," as an undifferentiated group, are faring badly with economic changes, white men have the highest income, social wage, and regulatory protection and control; white men are also the least likely to be contingent, except along the lone, but significant, indicator of company uncertainty, where they are more precarious than white women but less so than women and men of colour. The racialized gendering of jobs apparent in mapping precarious employment underscores continuities in unequal gender relations as well as changes tied to racialized inequalities and to broader processes of economic restructuring.

CONCLUSION

The relationship between form of employment, other dimensions of precarious employment, social location, and occupational context underscores the importance of altering normative measures of insecurity to better reflect the 21st-century labour market. New and continuous patterns are evident in the racialized gendering of jobs. A narrow emphasis on employment forms and work arrangements fails to disclose these linkages and limits the possibilities for understanding the dynamics of precarious employment. In contrast, mapping multiple dimensions of precarious wage work offers promise not only in understanding the nature of precarious employment but also in devising statistical measures that support efforts to mitigate its spread. An understanding of who is in precarious wage work, and in which contexts, points to areas for further research, including studies of whether people mitigate their precariousness through multiple jobs and/or household economies.

3

Precarious by Choice?
Gender and Self-employment

LEAH F. VOSKO AND NANCY ZUKEWICH

The contemporary Canadian labour force is characterized by an expansion of self-employment. Consistent with the spread of forms of wage work differing from the standard employment relationship (Cranford and Vosko, this volume), self-employment grew faster than wage work for most of the 1990s, accounting for nearly three-quarters of job growth between 1990 and 1997 (Lin, Yates, and Picot 1999).[1]

The form and gender of self-employment are also changing. In the 1980s, most of the increase in self-employment came from self-employed employers, or those who hire paid help. In the 1990s, growth came from the solo self-employed, or people who work on their own (Hughes 1999; Lin, Yates, and Picot 1999; Statistics Canada 1997; Vosko, Zukewich, and Cranford 2003). An influx of women into self-employment accompanied the trend towards more solo self-employment. Although men are still more likely than women to be self-employed, self-employment grew faster for women than for men in the 1990s at the same time as it became more heterogeneous, as certain forms exhibited more dimensions of precarious employment.

Yet despite these trends, dominant approaches to analyzing the dynamics of self-employment still rest on a narrow normative model – the male entrepreneur choosing risk, autonomy, and independence over stability and direct supervision. They pay scant attention to the quality of self-employment and they neglect to subject trends to a gender analysis. The dual tendency to take the choice of self-employment at face value and to construct it in gender-neutral terms obscures the differential and textured reasons informing men's and women's participation in self-employment. It perpetuates the assumption that among people who "choose" self-employment, the experience and gender of precariousness is a private matter rather than a public concern.

This chapter explores the ways in which self-employment can be precarious, considers how gender relations shape precarious self-employment, and interrogates the notion of choice underpinning dominant approaches to understanding and analyzing self-employment. The first section looks inside the category of self-employment, examining conventional definitions of self-employment and how they are gendered. It highlights the heterogeneous character of self-employment, discloses the male entrepreneurial norm implicit in statistical definitions that inform public policy, and initiates a critique of the notion of choice intrinsic to theories of self-employment applying "entrepreneurial pull" and "recession push" frameworks. The second section identifies dimensions of precarious self-employment and statistical indicators of these dimensions sensitive to gender relations.[2] The third section explores dimensions of precarious self-employment and the construction of "choice" through the lens of gender, using data from Canada's Labour Force Survey and Survey of Self-employment. These data reveal a continuum of forms of self-employment which is polarized by gender. They illustrate, further, that a gender-neutral approach to choice obscures how sex/gender divisions of unpaid caregiving and dependencies produced by the gendered form of the social wage shape precarious self-employment.

LOOKING INSIDE "SELF-EMPLOYMENT"

Conventional approaches to defining self-employment treat the self-employed as a unified group, distinct from employees. Yet self-employment is not a homogeneous category. Generally, the self-employed are set apart by their mode of remuneration – they receive profits, in contrast to employees, who earn wages (Fudge, Tucker, and Vosko 2002). But some self-employed people resemble employees in that they derive a significant proportion of their income from a small number of clients, use clients' equipment and office space, and do not have employees (Delage 2002; OECD 2000b). There are different ways to approach the measurement of self-employment. Some people counted as self-employed by the Labour Force Survey are classified as wage workers by the Census of Population (e.g., babysitters, cleaners for private households, and newspaper carriers). Incorporated self-employed people are also counted as wage workers in certain types of income analysis using census data (Statistics Canada 2002).

The employment situations covered by the different definitions of self-employment also vary, related, in part, to the gendered assumptions on which they rest. One dominant statistical approach to conceptualizing self-employment – worker's main job as measured by the Labour Force Survey – includes a diverse group of workers, ranging from the self-employed who hire paid help to the solo self-employed to unpaid family workers[3] (Statistics

Canada 2003b). The first group is composed mainly of men, and the last mainly of women. Based on this conceptualization, both change and continuity are apparent in the gender of self-employment: the share of self-employed women and men who were full-time employers declined during the 1990s, while full-time solo self-employment grew. Men also experienced modest increases in part-time forms of self-employment. Continuity in gendered patterns of self-employment is revealed through the representation of women and men across different forms of self-employment. At the end of the 1990s, women accounted for over six in ten of those with part-time self-employment, while men accounted for the majority of those engaged in full-time self-employment, whether solo or employers (Vosko, Zukewich, and Cranford 2003). The persistent concentration of women in part-time self-employment suggests that gendered continuities remain alongside the movement of more men into solo and part-time forms of self-employment.

Despite evidence of the heterogeneous and gendered nature of self-employment, many approaches to analyzing it perpetuate an implicit normative model – the self-employed profit-maximizing male business owner who owns his own tools and exhibits qualities of control over the production process that distinguish him from the typical wage worker (Eardley and Corden 1996, 13). This normative model equates self-employment with entrepreneurship (Fudge, Tucker, and Vosko 2003a and 2003b; Hughes 2003b, 5) and reflects theories based on men's lives (Mirchandani 1999, 225).

A male model of self-employment shapes, fundamentally, the theories of "entrepreneurial pull" and "recession push" into self-employment.[4] These theories posit that people are either pushed or pulled into self-employment: push factors are described as "involuntary," and pull factors are described as "voluntary." The framework they employ suggests that the latter group of workers chooses self-employment freely; it "assumes entrepreneurs as individuals with particular abilities and argues that self-knowledge of these particular abilities motivates them to engage in risk-taking entrepreneurial pursuits" (Lin, Yates, and Picot 1999, 6). In contrast, the group cast as involuntary is assumed to enter self-employment as a "job of last resort" because of labour market hardship – that is, a lack of suitable wage work (Lin, Yates, and Picot 1999). Statistically, "push" and "pull" factors are conceived of as dichotomous, and they are measured by a series of subjective questions related to reasons for engaging in self-employment. People who state they became self-employed owing to lack of suitable wage work are said to have been "pushed" into self-employment, while others are said to have been "pulled."[5]

Push/pull theories are inadequate, given their neglect of gender relations and their failure to scrutinize the entrepreneurial norm underpinning dominant understandings of "choice." Under this framework, reasons for being pulled into self-employment encompass "entrepreneurial values" (such as independence, being one's own boss, decision-making latitude, and creative challenges) as well as other reasons such as more money, lower taxes, taking over the family business, "nature of the job," and "time-related reasons" (flexible hours, balancing work and family life, and working from home). On the "pull" side, there is also a tendency to oppose two clusters of factors – "entrepreneurial values" and "time-related reasons." A study by Human Resource Development Canada finds that both women and men are most likely to cite "entrepreneurial values" as the main reason for self-employment. At the same time, it emphasizes that nearly a quarter of women cite "flexible hours" or "balancing work and family" as their main reason for becoming self-employed, while few men mention "time-related reasons" (Delage 2002). In contrasting these two main reasons as a means of exploring differences between women and men in self-employment, this approach "create[s] these differences ... by 'seeing' certain and not all differences as significant" (Mirchandani 1999, 229) and by failing to see women's domestic responsibilities as a structural concern that fits uneasily on the "pull" side of the dichotomy. This comparison also neglects the ways in which entrepreneurial values themselves are situated within gendered processes. Explanations for the differences observed between women and men rest on an acceptance of particular sex roles (Connell 1987, 50–2). This sex-role approach fails to consider why individuals maintain stereotypical views of female and male behaviour and, in so doing, neglects power dynamics shaping claims to individual choice (Mirchandani 1999, 226).

Qualitative research by Hughes (2003b) highlights the importance of considering the "interrelation of different factors" (440) shaping the decision to pursue or remain in self-employment, illustrating that a narrow focus on main reason for self-employment dichotomizes individual choices, when choice is rarely clear cut. Conceiving of choice as shaped by an interrelation of factors may reveal "forced choice"; some so-called pull factors, such as independence, decision-making, and flexible hours may, in fact, reflect the push "posed by eroding working conditions and job quality, as well as work-family considerations" (450). For example, wage work may be unsuitable because of a lack of adequate child-care, flexible hours, or the absence of workplace policies that take into account the responsibilities of workers outside of the labour force (Duxbury and Higgins 2001). Push factors may be defined too narrowly, contributing to an overemphasis on pull factors which masks dimensions of precarious self-employment and how gender relations shape "choice."

CONCEPTUALIZING PRECARIOUS SELF-EMPLOYMENT

Precarious employment is a useful concept in examining changing employment relationships linked to the decline of the standard employment relationship and related concerns over underemployment, income insecurity, and social exclusion. This concept highlights the limits of approaches to understanding employment change that focus solely on "forms" of employment, and it casts greater attention on social relations such as gender and "race." Yet, while there is a growing body of literature on precarious employment among wage workers, few studies inquire into how self-employment can be precarious or into the relationships between gender, forms of self-employment, and dimensions of precariousness among the self-employed.

Forms of Self-employment

Elsewhere, we develop a mutually exclusive typology of total employment to add texture to overlapping and overly broad conceptions of employment forms (see chapter 1, figure 1.1, this volume). This typology first breaks down total employment into wage work and self-employment; then separates wage workers by temporary and permanent status, and the self-employed by employers and the solo self-employed as well as unpaid family workers; and, finally, divides every group except unpaid family workers into full-time and part-time work.[6] Its aims are to reveal which forms of employment have been driving the rise of non-standard work – to take apart this catchall category – and to highlight the diversity in both wage work and self-employment.

This typology is instructive in advancing understandings of precarious self-employment because it improves on conventional measures of non-standard work that cast the full-time self-employed entrepreneur as the baseline of analysis. Indeed, the only group of self-employed people excluded from the conventional definition of non-standard work (Krahn 1991 and 1995) is full-time self-employed employers, a group populated mainly by men and resembling ideal typical entrepreneurs most closely. Looking at people's main jobs, this inquiry considers the following forms of self-employment: full-time employer self-employment, full-time solo self-employment, part-time employer self-employment, and part-time solo self-employment (see table 3.1).

Dimensions of Precarious Self-employment

Four dimensions related to the quality of jobs are critical to establishing whether a job is precarious (Rodgers 1989, 3–5). The first dimension is the degree of certainty of continuing work; here, time horizons and risk of job loss are emphasized. The second dimension is control over the labour process, linked to control over working conditions, wages, and pace of work. The third dimension is the degree of regulatory protection – whether the worker has access to an equivalent level of regulatory protections, normally through union representation or the law. The fourth dimension is income adequacy – a given job may be secure in the sense that there is little risk of job loss but precarious if earnings are insufficient for the worker to maintain a decent standard of living (Picchio 1998).

Table 3.1
Distribution of Types of Self-employment by Sex, Canada, 1989 and 2000

	Total		Women		Men	
Category	1989	2000	1989	2000	1989	2000
Self-employed	100%	100%	100%	100%	100%	100%
Full-time employer	43%	32%	27%	23%	50%	38%
Full-time solo	40%	48%	36%	45%	41%	51%
Part-time employer	3%	3%	6%	5%	2%	2%
Part-time solo	14%	17%	31%	31%	8%	10%

Sources: Statistics Canada, Labour Force Survey, 2000

Several of these dimensions assume the situation of a wage worker. Yet even if a self-employed person is dependent on the sale of his or her labour power, few self-employed people are permitted to form or join recognized trade unions in Canada (Cranford, Fudge, Tucker, and Vosko 2005). In addition, the statutory benefits and entitlements that make up the social wage available to wage workers (e.g., collective bargaining, basic employment standards, Employment Insurance) are not available to most self-employed people (Fudge, Tucker, and Vosko 2002), and they must either purchase or acquire through some other means the extended benefits normally provided to wage workers by their employers. Furthermore, although income is a concept that applies equally to employees and the self-employed, it is measured differently for employees and the self-employed in most statistical vehicles.

It is nevertheless possible to conceptualize dimensions of precarious employment for the self-employed. The following modified dimensions of precarious employment are suitable to the self-employed: regulatory protection and social benefits; job certainty; control over one's employment situation; and income adequacy (see figure 3.1).[7] Incorporation status, access to extended benefits, and membership in a professional association are good indicators of regulatory protection and social benefits among the self-employed. Incorporation status minimizes personal financial risk for the self-employed and allows them to draw a salary from the business. Extended health and dental coverage, as well as disability insurance, are examples of elements of the social wage as applicable to self-employment. Professional, occupational, or trade associations represent the interests of self-employed people and they may help regulate the practices of self-employment in a given industry or sector; they may also offer group rates on various forms of insurance coverage, training or information about training, and networking opportunities.

In the absence of an employment contract, it is impossible to analyze statistically whether a person is engaged in self-employment on a temporary

Figure 3.1
Dimensions of precarious self-employment

Dimension	Proxy			
regulatory protection and social benefits	incorporation status	association membership	has at least one extended benefit	source of benefits*
job certainty	job tenure	dislike uncertainty		
control	main reason for self-employment*	favoured job aspects of self-employment*		
income adequacy	annual income	dislike income fluctuations	retirement planning	personal financial difficulties

*Proxies for gender relations.

or a permanent basis, as is possible for wage workers. The length of time a person has been in the same employment situation (job tenure) is a good proxy for job certainty among the self-employed. Feelings of insecurity, uncertainty, and risk also provide a more subjective measure of job certainty. Annual income from self-employment represents a measure of income adequacy: low and high income (annual income under $20,000 and over $60,000) are the two poles explored here. Previous research into income indicates sharp polarization between the unincorporated solo self-employed and incorporated employers, and it highlights the gendered character of this phenomenon (Fudge, Tucker, and Vosko 2002). Data on the retirement savings and self-employed workers' perceptions of income fluctuations and personal financial difficulties add texture to this analysis. Finally, since autonomy and control over the labour process are hallmarks of the ideal typical model of self-employment, multiple reasons for self-employment are indicators of control over one's employment situation, yet they do not replicate the notion of control, as resistance, epitomized by union status.

Gender and Dimensions of Precarious Self-employment

Scholarship examining wage work illustrates that gender is inextricably linked to precarious employment.[8] Considered historically in Canada, the post-World War II gender order (Connell 1987) was shaped by the standard employment relationship, based on what some characterize as a "patriarchal model" (Eichler 1997) and others conceive as a "family wage" model (Fraser 1997). This model was designed to provide a wage sufficient for a *man* to support a wife and children. After World War II, it became the statistical reality for many (primarily white) men wage workers, while many women, as well as immigrants and workers of colour, were relegated to forms of wage work, such as part-time permanent and temporary work, characterized by dimensions of precarious employment (see Arat-Koc 1997; Duffy and Pupo 1994). In this period, the standard employment relationship became the reference point for labour law and policy. And it remains so to the present despite the growth of certain deviations, including self-employment and unprecedented levels of labour force participation among women (Krahn 1991, 1995; Vosko, Zukewich, and Cranford 2003).

A narrow normative model of male self-employment also grew up in this period. Owing largely to the significance of agriculture to the economy, unpaid family work has always existed in Canada, as has solo self-employment, especially in sectors such as construction and industries such as book publishing, where workers have, in a few instances, been able to join or form recognized trade unions. Yet employer self-employment has been a significant phenomenon until recently. Standing at between 40 per cent and 45 per cent of self-employment through the 1980s, the size of employer self-employment alongside the pre-eminence of a male breadwinner model, built around an ideal of independence, has shaped the narrow equation between self-employment and "entrepreneurship" (Fudge, Tucker, and Vosko 2002).

Linked to the continued normative pre-eminence of the standard employment relationship and the male entrepreneurial norm, changing employment relations are accompanied by enduring racialized gender inequalities inside and outside the labour force (Das Gupta, this volume; see also Armstrong 1996; Bakker 1996b). The contemporary period is marked by continuing industrial and occupational segregation and by income and occupational polarization. Such polarization is apparent both between women and men and between the sexes along various social locations and the "gendering of jobs" to resemble more insecure work associated with women and other marginalized groups assumed to have access to sources of subsistence beyond the wage. Each of these trends is shaped by women's continuing and disproportionate role in unpaid caregiving (Vosko 2002; Zukewich 2003). This situation continues, in part, owing to limited government supports for and privatization in health care, elder care, and child-care in the face of the growth of dual breadwinning. For example, persisting occupational segregation between men and women reflects the gendered organization of unpaid caregiving: women are often confined to jobs in the labour force that reflect tasks associated with domestic labour, such as ancillary work in the health sector (Armstrong and Laxer, this volume).

The persistence of gendered relations of distribution, or "sequences of linked actions through which people share the necessities of survival" that perpetuate adult women's dependency on men, also shapes these trends (Acker 1988, 478). The distribution of the social wage remains gendered because of the persistence of two assumptions: first, that the male wage is a breadwinner wage and, hence, the appropriate locus for distributing the social wage to related members of a given household; and, second, that the male earner, be he self-employed or a wage worker, should determine the allocation of the household income (Armstrong and Armstrong 1994; Fraser and Gordon, 1994; Kessler-Harris 1982). The first assumption is particularly crucial here: fixing the male wage as the breadwinner wage, even in the face of dual earning in households, contributes to women's dependency on men for extended benefits such as dental, health, and prescription drug coverage, as well as retirement savings. It also assumes permanency in relationships between men and women, such as marriage, where it does not necessarily exist; for example, the common decision for women to take on part-time work to reduce job and caregiving conflict contributes at mid-life cycle to high proportions of lone-parent mothers and elderly women with incomes below the low-income cut-off. The household, moreover, is an inappropriate unit of analysis, especially if gender inequalities within it are not considered; it is inappropriate to assume, for example, that resources are shared or distributed equally in households and that this type of sharing is continuous across the life cycle.

Given that the self-employed lack access to the full range of benefits and entitlements of wage workers, unequal sex/gender relations of unpaid caregiving and the source and distribution of the social wage are critical to understanding the gender of precarious self-employment. They are also central to analyzing how "choice" is constructed in push/pull theories of self-employment. These relations are best explored by focusing on how women's and men's positions in the four forms of self-employment are mediated by sex/gender divisions of unpaid caregiving and relations of distribution, considered here as the gendered form of social benefit entitlement.

The ensuing empirical analysis selects the source of extended medical benefits as an indicator of the gendered form of the social wage and explores sex/gender divisions of unpaid caregiving via an analysis of the reasons that men and women take up self-employment. "Spouse or partner as source of benefit plan" is a good indicator of gendered access to benefits for two reasons. It highlights men's greater access to extended benefits via their employment, given their continued predominance in both the standard employment relationship and employer self-employment, even though both these forms are becoming less common. It also signals women's dependence on men for access to non-wage benefits. Several "time-related reasons" for engaging in self-employment are used as proxies for unequal sex/gender divisions of unpaid caregiving. These include "flexible hours," "work-family balance," and "working from home." These so-called voluntary reasons for self-employment are shaped by gender, since the time stress associated with juggling paid work and unpaid caregiving is a factor in the employment "choices" made by women with children.[9]

GENDER AND PRECARIOUS SELF-EMPLOYMENT

Considering the four forms of self-employment in relation to additional dimensions of precarious employment and gender relations, inside and outside the labour force, reveals a continuum of precarious self-employment that is polarized by gender. This division is due, partly, to how it is shaped by unequal sex/gender divisions of unpaid caregiving and to dependencies produced by the gendered form of the social wage.

Gendered Polarization and the Continuum of Precarious Self-employment

According to some measures, employers are less precarious than the solo self-employed. Both part- and full-time forms of employer self-employment are similar and less precarious than solo self-employment with respect to incorporation (regulatory dimension), long job tenure (job certainty dimension), and RRSP ownership (income adequacy dimension). These measures illustrate the greater stability associated with employer self-employment, the model resembling entrepreneurship most fully, regardless of full- or part-time status.[10] This finding is in contrast to trends observed for wage work, where full-time status, a central feature of the standard employment relationship, mitigates precariousness to a greater extent than other characteristics such as job permanency (Cranford, Vosko, and Zukewich 2003b).

Yet the interface between employer/solo self-employment and full-time status still shapes the dynamics of precarious self-employment. Contemporary self-employment is characterized by a continuum of increasing insecurity, moving from full-time employers to the full-time solo self-employed to part-time employers to the part-time solo self-employed. Along all indicators, full-time self-employed employers are least precarious, while along the majority of indicators, part-time solo workers are the most precarious. Regarding access to regulatory protection and social benefits, the part-time solo self-employed are less likely than those in all other forms of self-employment to be incorporated, to belong to an association, or to have extended benefits. They are also the group most likely to have short job tenure and least likely to have adequate incomes, as measured by the proportion with an annual income under $20,000 and the rate of RRSP ownership. Still, on some measures – dislike of the uncertainty, insecurity, risk and lack of stability inherent in their job (job certainty), dislike of income fluctuations (income adequacy), and entering self-employment because of a lack of suitable wage work (control) – the full- and part-time solo self-employed exhibit similarities, and both groups are more precarious than the full-time employers (see tables 3.2–3.5).

At a fundamental level, patterns of polarization along the continuum are gendered through the concentration of women and men in certain forms of self-employment. Women were three times as likely as men to be part-time

Table 3.2
Dimensions of Precarious Employment: Job Certainty, Canada, 2000

	Job Tenure* <2 Years	Job Tenure* 10 Years +	Dislike Uncertainty/ Insecurity/Risk/ Lack of Stability
Type of Self-employment			
	per cent		
Full-time employer	11	51	26
Women	14	42	25
Men	10	54	26
Full-time solo	22	37	36
Women	27	27	31
Men	20	42	39
Part-time employer	13	51	–
Women	14	44	–
Men	10	63	–
Part-time solo	30	29	37
Women	33	25	37
Men	27	36	38

Source: Statistics Canada,* Labour Force Survey, 2000; and Survey of Self-employment, 2000
– Indicates sample size too small to yield estimate.

solo self-employed (31% versus 10%) in 2000 and were less likely to be full-time employers (23% versus 38%) or full-time solo workers (42% versus 51%) (see table 3.1). Women also account for a larger share of the self-employed population as one moves towards the more precarious end of the continuum; just one-quarter of full-time self-employed employers were women, compared with three in ten full-time solo self-employed and six in ten part-time solo self-employed. Women make up the majority of those employed in the most precarious form of self-employment – part-time solo self-employment (see figure 3.2 and table 3.6).

Comparing the situation of women and men within forms of self-employment highlights other ways in which this continuum is gendered. First, evidence of gendered polarization exists across all forms of self-employment on basic measures of income adequacy and job certainty; women – even those in full-time forms of self-employment – were more likely than men to have an annual income of less than $20,000 and were less likely to have long

Table 3.3
Dimensions of Precarious Self-employment: Control, Canada, 2000

	Main Reason for Self-Employment				
Type of Self-employment	Could Not Find Suitable Paid Employment	Time-Related Reasons*	Because of Entrepreuneurial Values†	Other	Total
	per cent				
Full-time employer	15	6	52	27	100
Women	18	10 E	48	23	100
Men	14	4 E	53	28	100
Full-time solo	25	13	38	23	100
Women	23	27	26	23	100
Men	26	7	43	22	100
Part-time employer	–	–	–	–	100
Women	–	–	–	–	100
Men	–	–	–	–	100
Part-time solo	27	27	27	20	100
Women	25	38	17 E	20 E	100
Men	29 E	–	42	19 E	100

Source: Statistics Canada, Survey of Self-employment, 2000
– indicates sample size too small to yield estimate.
*Includes balance of work and family, flexible hours and work from home.
† Includes independence, freedom, own boss; control, responsibility, decision making; and challenge, creativity, success, satisfaction.
E High sampling variability (coefficient of variation between 16.6% and 33.3%). Use with caution.

job tenure. Yet there is also evidence of the gendering of jobs whereby some differences observed at the least precarious end of the continuum (full-time employer self-employment) disappear at the more insecure end (part-time solo self-employed). For example, women full-time employers were less likely than men to have at least one extended benefit (57% versus 69%), while among part-time solo workers, access was less common but similar for both sexes (48%). Mirroring findings for full-time permanent wage work, even full-time employer self-employment is not as "good" for women as it is for men (Cranford and Vosko, this volume).

Table 3.4
Dimensions of Precarious Self-employment: Regulatory Protection
and Social Wage, Canada, 2000

Type of Self-employment	Incorporated Business*	Association Member	Has Extended Health	Has Extended Dental	Has Disability Insurance	Has All Three Benefits	Has at Least One Extended Benefit†
			per cent				
Full-time employer	64	58	48	37	51	25	66
Women	60	52	43	32	39	18	57
Men	65	59	50	39	55	27	69
Full-time solo	22	36	39	33	33	13	57
Women	15	38	43	35	26	12	55
Men	25	35	37	32	36	13	57
Part-time employer	58	35 E	–	–	–	–	–
Women	60	–	–	–	–	–	–
Men	56	–	–	–	–	–	–
Part-time solo	12	31	39	35	17	8 E	48
Women	10	31	40	35	17 E	8 E	48
Men	13	31	38	34	18 E	–	48

Source: Statistics Canada,* Labour Force Survey, 2000; and Survey of Self-employment, 2000
† Has at least one of dental, health, or disability insurance.
– Indicates sample size too small to yield estimate.
E High sampling variability (coefficient of variation between 16.6% and 33.3%). Use with caution.

The dimension of control underscores important contradictions obscured by an approach to categorizing reasons for self-employment as "voluntary" or "involuntary" which neglects gender. Similar shares of women and men across all forms reported that their main reason for being self-employed was

Table 3.5
Dimensions of Precarious Self-employment:
Income Adequacy, Canada, 2000

Type of Self-employment	Income <$20,000	Income $60,000+	Dislike Fluctuations in Income/Cash Flow Problems	Experienced Personal Financial Difficulties as Result of Self-employment	Type of Retirement Preparation					
					RRSPs	Other Savings for Retirement	Pension from Paid Job	Equity Home/Cottage/Business	Land/Rental Property	Other Assets
				per cent						
Full-time employer	10	32	16	35	82	51	15	89	35	18
Women	19	23	16 E	35	77	43	15 E	85	29	11 E
Men	8	35	17	35	84	54	15	90	38	20
Full-time solo	25	10	26	42	62	40	13	72	22	12
Women	37	8 E	24	36	61	41	12	67	16	8 E
Men	20	11	27	45	62	40	14	74	25	14
Part-time employer	–	–	–	40 E	77	–	26 E	93	29 E	–
Women	–	–	–	–	78	–	–	93	–	–
Men	–	–	–	–	–	–	–	–	–	–
Part-time solo	48	–	28	36	56	37	19	69	19	9 E
Women	55	–	25	28	61	42	15 E	67	19 E	10 E
Men	39	–	31	48	49	30	25 E	71	20 E	–

Source: Statistics Canada, Survey of Self-employment, 2000
– Indicates sample size too small to yield estimate.
E High sampling variability (coefficient of variation between 16.6% and 33.3%). Use with caution.

Figure 3.2
Women's share of self-employment by type, Canada, 1989 and 2000

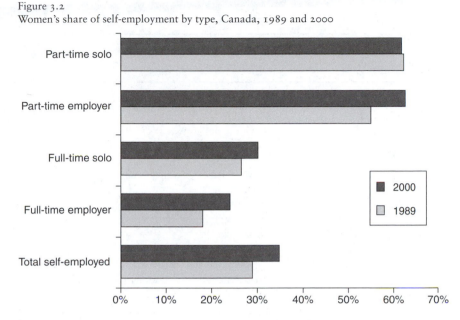

a lack of suitable wage work. This finding suggests that women and men were equally likely to have been "pushed" involuntarily into self-employment. However, analysis of the main reasons making up the "choice" or "voluntary" category reveals a difference between the sexes. Across every form, the main reason most commonly cited by men is "entrepreneurial values." The same is true of women within the masculine full-time forms of self-employment. Yet women in all forms of self-employment are more likely than men to cite "time-related reasons" for their "choice." Furthermore, as one moves towards the most precarious end of the continuum, the share of women citing entrepreneurial values declines and time-related reasons rises. For part-time solo women, the category of "time-related reasons" is the most commonly cited main reason for "choosing" self-employment. A more nuanced understanding of the gender of precarious self-employment thus requires closer scrutiny of the notion of "choice" (see tables 3.3 and 3.7).

Precarious by "Choice"?
Inequalities Shaping the Gender of Self-employment

Unequal divisions of unpaid caregiving and dependencies fostered by the means of distributing extended benefits are central to the gender of precarious self-employment – and understanding them is critical to unravelling the common yet perplexing assumption that certain groups of self-employed women are precarious by choice. A logical first step in this direction is to consider the demographic characteristics of self-employed people and to interrogate fully

Table 3.6
Women's Share of Self-employment by Type, Canada, 1989 and 2000

	1989	2000
Form of Employment		
	per cent	
Total self-employed	29	35
Full-time employer	18	24
Full-time solo	27	30
Part-time employer	55	63
Part-time solo	62	62

Source: Labour Force Survey, 2000

the reasons for self-employment, especially part-time self-employment. This, then, opens space for the analysis of gendered dependencies produced by the "choice" of self-employment among many women.

The characteristics of self-employed people highlight the role of sex/gender divisions of unpaid caregiving and the gendered form of the social wage in shaping the gender of precarious self-employment. Women who most closely resemble the ideal typical male entrepreneurial model, full-time self-employed employers, are less likely than their male counterparts to be partnered and to have a child under the age of 16 at home.[11] However, women in part-time forms of self-employment are more likely than men in these forms to be aged 25 to 54[12] and to live with a partner. They are also twice as likely to have at least one child under the age of 16 at home (see table 3.1).

Reasons for part-time work reflect these demographic differences and employed women's disproportionate responsibility for unpaid caregiving (Statistics Canada 2000). Among women part-timers aged 25 to 54, 37 per cent of solo workers and 49 per cent of employers report working part time owing to child-care or personal/family responsibilities, compared with a marginal share of their male counterparts. At the two ends of the life course, when the dual responsibility of child-care and employment is less pronounced, reasons for part-time self-employment are similar for women and men. Seven in ten part-time solo workers aged 15 to 24 were at school, while a similar share of those aged 55 and over cited personal preference.

Yet people citing any of these reasons for part-time work are considered to have voluntarily "chosen" part-time work (Marshall 2001). Only those who stated that they could not find full-time work are considered to be engaged in part-time self-employment involuntarily. Men in part-time self-employment were far more likely to note they could not find full-time work as their main reason. As a result, part-time work is cast as a matter of personal choice

Table 3.7
Types of Self-employment by Demographic Characteristics, Canada, 2000

Type of Self-employment	Age			Marital Status			Age of Youngest Child		
	15–24	25–54	55+	Married/ Common-Law	Separated/divorced/ widowed	Single Never Married	< years	6–15 years	no child < 16
				per cent					
Full-time employer	1	80	19	86	6	8	16	25	59
Women	1	85	14	81	–	10	14	22	64
Men	1	79	20	88	–	–	17	26	57
Full-time solo	4	78	19	76	9	15	15	20	65
Women	5	81	14	77	11	12	15	22	63
Men	3	76	21	76	8	17	15	19	66
Part-time employer	2	64	34	89	–	–	16	20	64
Women	–	75	23	93	–	–	21	23	56
Men	–	45	52	–	–	–	7	14	78
Part-time solo	13	60	26	69	8	23	15	17	69
Women	12	68	19	71	–	20	18	21	61
Men	14	48	38	65	–	28	8	10	82

Source: Statistics Canada, Labour Force Survey, 2000
– Indicates sample size too small to yield estimate.

rather than a public issue shaped by sex/gender divisions of unpaid caregiving, including that done by women citing child-care or personal/family responsibilities (see table 3.8).

The frameworks of entrepreneurial pull and recession push for analyzing self-employment associate a wide variety of reasons for self-employment with "choice." Time-related factors, such as flexible hours, balancing work and family, and work from home, are constructed as "pulls" into self-employment of the same order as entrepreneurial values such as independence, decision-making latitude, and creativity (Delage 2002). Analyzing motivations for self-employment beyond the "main" reason gives greater texture to women's and men's experience of self-employment. Considering the interrelation of factors in a gender-sensitive way is key to understanding whether it is strictly a matter of personal choice that some people, predominantly women, are concentrated in the most precarious forms of self-employment.

The three aspects of self-employment preferred by the greatest share of women and men full-time employers, people conventional analyses describe as having been "pulled" into this form of work, are "entrepreneurial values" (independence, freedom, being one's own boss – 68%), control (responsibility, decision-making – 38%), and challenge (creativity, success, satisfaction – 37%). Independence is also the aspect most commonly cited by the full-time solo self-employed, although the figure is lower for the women in this group (48%) than for the men (69%). However, flexible hours, a component of "time-related reasons," becomes the second favourite aspect for this group, reflecting a shift away from the ideal typical entrepreneurial norm represented by employer self-employment. The same trend is observed for men at the most precarious end of the continuum – part-time solo – but, for women, flexible hours (64%) replaces independence (43%) as the best-liked aspect of self-employment. Furthermore, the two other components of time-related reasons – "balancing work and family" and "work from home" – are cited by large shares of women in both forms of solo work, but by relatively few men (see table 3.9).

For many women, self-employment leads to highly gendered patterns of dependency. Many are accessing benefits through men, reflecting the persistence of the male wage as the locus for delivering social entitlements and benefits despite women's high rates of labour force participation. When source of extended health and dental benefits among those with these benefits is examined, a pattern of gendered dependency is evident. In moving from full-time employer to part-time solo self-employment, women's access to both sets of benefits through a spouse increases, as does the difference between men's and women's reliance on a spouse or partner as the source of extended benefits (see table 3.10).[14] In relation to women in full-time employer self-employment, women in part-time solo self-employment are doubly disadvantaged and economically dependent: not only are they precarious along multiple dimensions but they are twice as likely as women full-time employers to depend on a

Table 3.8
Main Reason for Part-time Employment by Sex and Age, Canada, 2000

Type of Self-employment	Caring for Children	Personal/Family Responsibilities	Going to School	Personal Preference	Couldn't Find Full-time Work	Other	Total
			per cent				
Part-time employer							
15+							
Women	27	12	–	44	10	4	100
Men	–	–	–	63	20	8	100
15–24							
Women	–	–	–	–	–	–	100
Men	–	–	–	–	–	–	100
25–54							
Women	35	14	–	35	12	–	100
Men	–	–	–	51	27	–	100
55+							
Women	–	–	–	76	–	–	100
Men	–	–	–	75	13	–	100
Part-time solo							
15+							
Women	19	8	10	40	18	4	100
Men	1	3	12	42	35	7	100
15–24							
Women	–	–	71	10	14	–	100
Men	–	–	72	–	19	–	100
25–54							
Women	27	10	2	35	22	4	100
Men	3	4	4	30	52	8	100
55+							
Women	–	6	–	77	11	6	100
Men	–	–	–	71	19	7	100

Source: Statistics Canada, Labour Force Survey, 2000
– Indicates sample size too small to yield estimate.

Table 3.9
Job Aspects Favoured by People "Pulled"* into Self-employment, Canada, 2000

Type of Self-employment	Flexible Hours	Balance Work/Family	Work from Home	Independence, Freedom, Own Boss	Control, Responsibility, Decision	Challenge, Creativity, Success, Satisfaction	More Money, Unlimited Income	Lower Taxes, Deductions	Less Stress
				per cent					
Full-time employer	23	9	5 E	68	38	37	16	–	–
Women	26	12 E	–	65	34	43	–	–	–
Men	22	8	–	69	39	35	19	–	–
Full-time solo	34	13	12	62	28	23	13	5	5
Women	36	23	26	48	22	24	11 E	–	6 E
Men	34	8	6 E	69	31	22	15	5 E	5 E
Part-time employer	–	–	–	–	–	–	–	–	–
Women	–	–	–	–	–	–	–	–	–
Men	–	–	–	–	–	–	–	–	–
Part-time solo	59	26	21	51	13 E	16 E	–	–	–
Women	64	35	26 E	43	–	–	–	–	–
Men	51	–	–	64	–	–	–	–	–

Source: Statistics Canada, Survey of Self-employment, 2000

* Respondents who reported they did not become self-employed because of a lack of suitable paid employment.

– Indicates sample size too small to yield estimate.

E High sampling variability (coefficient of variation between 16.6% and 33.3%). Use with caution.

spouse or partner for access to benefits. Given the large shares of women who "choose" self-employment for time-related reasons, this discrepancy suggests that many are trading off a high degree of precariousness and dependency in return for the ability to better manage the multiple time demands of the double day. This finding echoes Hughes's (2003b) qualitative research, which shows that self-employed women find great intrinsic value in their work (e.g., satisfaction and control over working conditions) but low extrinsic value (e.g., income and retirement planning).

Given that the majority of part-time solo women "choose" self-employment not because of entrepreneurial values but for time-related reasons, and given that many work part-time to accommodate child-care and family responsibilities, the gendered continuum of precarious self-employment underscores the resilience of the male entrepreneurial model at a normative and empirical level and, most notably, gendered dependencies of old. This model, like the male norm of the standard employment relationship, takes for granted that having the time to work only part time owing to unpaid caregiving responsibilities and having access to benefits through a spouse are not only acceptable but matters of private concern, ignoring the gender relations constraining choice and the very public dependencies they generate.

Women's dependency on men, shaped by unequal divisions of unpaid caregiving and the gendered form of the social wage, is intimately related to the gender of precarious self-employment. The situation of women in full-time employer self-employment, women who conform more closely to the male entrepreneurial norm, is shaped least directly by gender divisions of unpaid care work/responsibility and gendered relations of distribution, while the situation of their counterparts in part-time solo self-employment is shaped considerably by these factors. This finding is not to diminish the employment-unpaid caregiving dilemma confronted by women employers. Rather, these findings all illustrate that, on the one hand, "there are deep institutionalized forms of inequality between women and men," yet, on the other, "there are very significant transformations [among women] which need to be understood rather than denied" (Walby 2000, 166). There are significant differences between women in the degree to which their lives are affected by the changes and continuities characterizing new employment norms. In the case of self-employment, "change" means that women in full-time employer self-employment have higher incomes and access to social benefits and regulatory protection and, thereby, greater resources in confronting the employment-unpaid caregiving dilemma. It should not be surprising, however, that women employers are less likely than men to be partnered or to have children under the age of 16. Yet "new" employment norms also prompt age-old responses to this dilemma among women in part-time solo self-employment. Polarization among women is gaining increasing recognition, but, with the exception of research into occupational polarization among women by race (Das Gupta 1996; James, Grant, and Cranford 2000), this trend

Table 3.10
Source of Extended Health and Dental Benefits, Canada, 2000

Type of Self-employment	Source of Extended Health Benefits			Source of Extended Dental Benefits		
	Spouse or Partner	Purchased Own Plan	Other*	Spouse or Partner	Purchased Own Plan	Other*
	Per cent of self-employed with access to benefit					
Full-time employer	24	62	14	29	57	14
Women	39	51	–	49	48	–
Men	20	65	15	24	60	16
Full-time solo	57	33	11	66	24	10
Women	70	21	–	77	14 E	–
Men	49	39	12 E	60	29	11 E
Part-time employer	–	–	–	–	–	–
Women	–	–	–	–	–	–
Men	–	–	–	–	–	–
Part-time solo	75	–	16 E	78	–	–
Women	86	–	–	92	–	–
Men	57	–	–	58 E	–	–

Source: Statistics Canada, Survey of Self-employment, 2000
* Includes through a franchisor and through an employer at a paid job.
– Indicates sample size too small to yield estimate.
E High sampling variability (coefficient of variation between 16.6% and 33.3%). Use with caution.

is poorly understood because it is rarely examined empirically, let alone with attention to the role of unpaid caregiving and relations of distribution in households in shaping polarization (Walby 2000).

CONCLUSION

Dominant approaches to understanding and analyzing self-employment still rest on a narrow normative model of self-employment – the male business owner who owns his own tools and exhibits control over the production process. This norm fosters an association between self-employment and entrepreneurship, correlating this employment status with the values of risk, autonomy, and independence. It also masks dimensions of precarious self-employment and the gender relations at their root.

The polarized continuum of precarious self-employment illustrates clearly that full-time employers – fully three-quarters of whom are men – are the least precarious among the self-employed. This group resembles the normative model of self-employment most closely and, thus, remains the reference point in most statistical approaches and public policies. Yet the entrepreneurial norm and its associated characteristics (i.e., operating an incorporated business, membership in an association, a high income level, long hours, access to benefits, and long job tenure) run counter to the experience of many women (and some men) in part-time solo self-employment and mystify sources of gendered difference among the self-employed, both between women and men as well as among women.

Full-time self-employed employers are least likely to have entered into self-employment owing to lack of suitable wage work. The dual tendency to take the choice of self-employment at face value and to construct it in gender-neutral terms obscures the differential and textured reasons informing men's and women's participation in self-employment. It perpetuates the assumption that, among people who choose self-employment, the experience and gender of precariousness is a private matter. Yet unequal divisions of unpaid caregiving and the dependencies they engender – most notably, self-employed women's dependency on male partners for benefits – shape the gendered continuum of precarious self-employment.

This inquiry challenges the characterization of "entrepreneurial values" and "time-related reasons" for self-employment as "pull" factors by considering both new and continuous dependencies and shifting dynamics of unpaid caregiving and their interaction with dimensions of precarious self-employment. The highly gendered character of the most precarious form of self-employment is shaped by constraint (e.g., the limits on working hours posed by "family responsibilities") rather than by the pursuit of entrepreneurial values. Part-time self-employment may reduce job/family tension in the mid-life cycle, but it contributes to low retirement incomes among women and to the high proportion of female lone parents and elderly women living with incomes below the low income cut-offs (Marshall 2000; Statistics Canada 2000). Considerable consequences flow from this constrained choice – gendered inequalities and dependencies across the life cycle being chief among them.

4

Precarious Employment
and People with Disabilities

EMILE TOMPA, HEATHER SCOTT,
SCOTT TREVITHICK, AND SUDIPA BHATTACHARYYA

Over the past two decades important changes have occurred in the policy, legislative, and programmatic context in which vulnerable groups – such as women, people of colour, Aboriginal people, and people with disabilities – participate in the Canadian labour market. Concurrent with these developments, economic restructuring tied to globalization, growing competition associated with international trade, and technological innovation have contributed to fundamental changes in the organization of the labour market and the structure of employment relationships. In this context, what have been the labour market experiences of vulnerable populations – specifically, people with disabilities, including those confronting intersecting inequalities related to "race"[1] and gender? How, and in what ways, do people with disabilities experience precariousness in the labour market?

This chapter investigates the historical and contemporary work-related experiences of people with disabilities in the Canadian labour market, with reference to the rise of precarious employment. It is framed by two concurrent phenomena: legislative and programmatic initiatives aimed at increasing labour force participation among people with disabilities; and structural changes in the labour market tied to the spread of forms of employment and work arrangements exhibiting dimensions of precarious employment. Since the 1980s, there has been growing evidence of a relationship between the rise of forms of employment and work arrangements differing from the full-time permanent job and the spread of precarious employment, a phenomenon evident not only in these forms and arrangements but in the erosion of the standard employment relationship itself. Simultaneously, employment and pay equity policies have evolved unevenly across Canada. The spread of precarious employment, coupled with an uneven regional trend towards dilution of equity commitments, could mean that vulnerable populations face greater barriers today to labour force participation and within the labour force than they did a decade or more ago. Alternatively, equity legislation and programmatic initiatives could act as a brace against precarious employment among those in the labour force, protecting people with disabilities from the adverse consequences of structural changes in the labour market. A third possibility is some combination of the two trends.

The chapter proceeds in five sections. The first section discusses changes in the structure of the labour market, with attention to the growth of forms of employment and arrangements differing from the full-time permanent job over the past three decades. The close of this section relates these developments to people with disabilities, provoking a number of questions that guide the empirical investigation. The second and third sections canvass several theoretical approaches to disability and consider how they relate to the policy and legislative frameworks designed to help disadvantaged groups access the labour market. The fourth section then reviews empirical work, drawing on some Canadian and some US data on the labour market experiences, earnings, and socio-demographic characteristics of people with disabilities, and briefly reviews the limited literature on people with disabilities and precarious employment. The final section identifies data sources, outlines the methodology, and presents the results of the empirical investigation conducted here. The chapter closes with a discussion of the empirical findings and their implications for further research and policy-making.

ECONOMIC RESTRUCTURING AND THE GROWTH OF PRECARIOUS EMPLOYMENT

In the 1970s new forces began to erode employment norms that had originated in the postwar period. The high productivity growth of the 1950s and 1960s that contributed to dramatic improvements in living standards began to decline.[2] This macroeconomic slowdown was a major cause of the stagnation of real wage rates over the 1980s and 1990s, leading firms to seek new ways to cut costs and innovate in order to improve performance and remain competitive.[3] The expansion of international trade in conjunction with technological advancements extended market boundaries and intensified competition. The liberalization of trade and finance contributed to significant growth in the trade of goods and services and in financial flows across international borders (Longworth 1998). Concurrently, technological change, especially changes affecting the telecommunications and transportation sectors, has facilitated the mobility of physical and financial capital, as well as that of goods and services.

As a result of these changes, employment relationships are becoming more variable and complex. The standard employment relationship is a declining norm in Canada (Krahn 1995; Lavis 1998; Lipsett and Reesor 1997; Vosko 1997). Today, firms hire workers under a range of atypical contracts and rely increasingly on temporary and part-time workers as well as solo self-employed workers in an effort to cut costs and increase flexibility (see, this volume, Cranford and Vosko; Vosko and Zukewich; see also Barker and Christensen 1998). In some cases, entire functions within organizations are being outsourced. Many types of atypical employment contracts, such as fixed-term or temporary contracts, allow firms to alter the size of their workforces in response to market shifts. From the perspective of the firm, a system of ad hoc employment may facilitate adjustments to demand and, at the same time, avoid responsibility for benefits and fixed labour costs during slumps in demand. Workers in precarious employment are also less able to leverage desirable terms and conditions of employment owing to their frequent exclusion from worker-advocacy mechanisms such as trade unions (see, this volume, Anderson, Beaton, and Laxer; Borowy; Cranford, Das Gupta, and Vosko; see also Cappelli et al. 1997). For workers, forms of employment and work arrangements that differ from the full-time permanent job can be harmful or beneficial. On the positive side, they can offer worker-centred flexibility that makes it easier for individuals to manage competing demands on their time, including furthering their education and fulfilling family responsibilities. Some individuals may opt, for example, for solo self-employment for reasons of scheduling flexibility, but that may simply be due to the fact that it is difficult to find a full-time permanent job with the flexibility required to accommodate family and other commitments. Indeed, some authors in this volume question the notion of "choice" in the context of limited employment options, particularly for women with young children (Vosko and Zukewich, this volume). On the negative side, temporary and part-time employees are often poorly paid, lack benefits that complete the social wage, receive little employer-sponsored training, and have irregular schedules and/or inadequate hours (Armstrong and Laxer, this volume). In other words, they confront multiple dimensions of precarious employment.

Precarious employment is not spread equally across socio-demographic groups in society (Cranford and Vosko, this volume). Rather, vulnerable groups such as women, people of colour, and Aboriginal people bear a disproportionate share of the burden as firms resort to "new" forms of employment and work arrangements. Thus, trends towards individualized insecurity may exacerbate longstanding race, class, gender, and disability-based inequalities.

One set of questions grows from recognizing the danger that the drive for "flexibility" among firms will fall on vulnerable populations. What have the labour market experiences of people with disabilities been relative to those without disabilities? Specifically, how do the rates of employment and unemployment, and labour force participation and non-participation, compare between people with disabilities and the non-disabled populations? Additionally, how do these rates compare for people with disabilities among women and men and among people of colour and white people? Are people with disabilities who are women and people of colour more likely to find themselves in forms of employment and work arrangements differing from the full-time permanent job? In which of these forms and arrangements are they most highly represented? Is their presence in them voluntary or involuntary? To what extent do their labour market experiences, particularly their participation in certain employment forms and work arrangements, shape the character of precariousness? Have these experiences changed over time?

A second set of questions relates to the business cycle – the sequencing of periods of prosperity and downturn – and to federal and provincial government policies aimed at fostering labour force attachment among people with disabilities: What influence does the business cycle have on people with disabilities relative to their non-disabled counterparts? What effect, if any, have government policy and legislation had on the experiences of people with disabilities? Have these policies affected subsections of the disabled population equally?

THEORIZING DISABILITY

The extensive theoretical literature on disablement has important implications for disability policy. This literature is largely centred on two conceptual frameworks: those of Nagi and those of the World Health Organization (WHO). Nagi (1965) offers one of the first comprehensive conceptualizations of disablement. In his framework, disablement is a series of four interrelated concepts that describe the impact of a health condition on a person's body, activities, and involvement in society (Nagi 1965; Nagi 1991). These four concepts are pathology, impairment, functional limitation, and disability. Pathology refers to an "interruption of or interference with normal bodily processes," such as a disease or physical trauma to the body (Nagi 1991, 313). An impairment is a loss or lack of functionality in a part of the body resulting from an active or arrested pathology, such as fingers missing from the right hand. Functional limitation describes a limitation at the level of the body as a whole, such as the inability to hold objects in the right hand. Finally, a disability is "an inability or limitation in performing socially defined roles and tasks expected of an individual within a sociocultural and physical environment" (Nagi 1991, 315).

The WHO developed a conceptual framework for disablement comparable to, but independent of, the Nagi model (WHO 1980; WHO 2001). This framework also describes the consequences of disease as four interrelated concepts: disease, impairment, disability, and handicap.[4] The WHO model is similar to Nagi's. The disease (health condition) dimension is comparable to Nagi's pathology; the term "impairment" (body) is used in both models for the second concept; the disability (activities) dimension mirrors the notion of functional limitations; and handicap (participation) reflects disability. In both frameworks, disability is not taken as a characteristic of an individual but, rather, as a relational phenomenon that arises from the interaction of an individual and her or his personal characteristics with a particular social environment. A critical factor is the degree to which the physical and social environments create barriers to involvement for an individual with an impairment or functional limitation. Essentially, disability can be described as an inappropriate fit between the person and the environment (Pope and Tarlov 1991). Two avenues of resolution are possible when there is an inappropriate fit: one is to make the environment more accommodating, and the other is to enhance the abilities of the person. In many cases, where people suffer from health conditions, environmental modification is a more realistic alternative. To this end, at the level of public policy, efforts have focused on reducing the barriers to fuller participation of people with health conditions, impairments, and functional limitations through legislative reforms that prohibit discrimination and require accommodation.

THE POLICY AND LEGISLATIVE CONTEXT

People with physical or mental impairments have a long history of labour market disadvantage. Historically, dominant understandings and legislative frameworks defined disability as individually specific, locating its source in an individual's lack of "normal" physical or mental capacity. The burden arising from being unable to function in a normal fashion was placed on the individual (Bakan and Kobayashi 2000). However, more recent conceptualizations, such as those of Nagi and the WHO, situate disability at the point of interaction between the individual and her or his surroundings, locating the cause of the disability as much in the social environment as in the individual's mental and physical health conditions, impairments, and abilities. The evolution of Canadian public policy towards people with disabilities reflects this shift in understanding, but only in part.

Disability policy follows a similar trajectory in Canada and the United States. The traditional approach, which began to be challenged in the 1970s and 1980s, viewed disability as a medical deficiency at the level of the person, and it cast a person with a disability as requiring special assistance to function in a normal environment. The question became: What special devices and services does the individual need to fully participate, and what are the costs and benefits to society if the government purchases these assistive devices and services on behalf of the individual? In response to the efforts of disability advocates from the 1960s onwards, a new paradigm has at least partially supplanted the traditional one (Cook and Burke 2002, 542). This paradigm takes as its starting point the premise that people with disabilities have an inherent civil right to participate in society and that the primary obstacles to their doing so are the unwarranted discrimination of employers and their failure to make accommodations. The question broadened to become: What physical, psychological, or other barriers limit the participation of people with disabilities in society, and how can they best be removed (Cook and Burke 2002)?

In Canada, extending the notion of civil rights into the realm of disability has meant extending the guarantee of equal opportunity by eliminating discriminatory or unintentionally exclusionary practices that affect people with disabilities. One of the early pieces of legislation in this arena was the *Canada Human Rights Act* of 1978. The Act requires that people receive the same rate of pay for work of equal value, regardless of race, sex, religion, disability status, and other factors. The Act also forbids discrimination on the basis of sexual, racial, or cultural characteristics, including religion. It does not take into consideration whether members of disadvantaged groups are represented in proportions equal to their availability in the labour force. Rather, the Act is complaints-based; it operates on a case-by-case basis. The onus is on the individual to call upon the law when necessary.

The centrepiece of disability legislation in Canada is the federal *Employment Equity Act*, first implemented in 1987 and amended in 1996. The Act designates four historically disadvantaged groups: Aboriginal peoples, women, visible minorities, and people with disabilities. Unlike the *Canadian Human Rights Act*, it does not function through complaints. Rather, the *Employment Equity Act* assumes that, in the absence of discrimination, members of designated groups will be present in the private and public sectors in numbers proportionate to their availability in the labour force. In theory, the Act comes into play when these groups are not so represented, but whereas the *Canadian Human Rights Act* applies to both the public and the private sectors, the *Employment Equity Act* applies only to the federal government and to a limited number of organizations with sizeable contracts with the federal government and employing a large number of people.[5] The 1987 *Employment Equity Act* required federally regulated employers to submit a report on the number, occupations, and salary range of members of designated groups in their employ. However, it contained no mechanism for obligating employers with disproportionately low numbers of employees from the designated groups to increase their hiring of these groups. The 1996 amendments to the *Employment Equity Act* broadened the scope of the legislation to include all federal employers, including the civil service[6], the Armed Forces, the Royal Canadian Mounted Police, and the Canadian Security and Intelligence Service. It also created mechanisms for enforcement. Employers covered by the Act became subject to regular compliance audits by the Canadian Human Rights Commission. An Employment Equity Tribunal with the power to give directives similar to that of a federal court was also created.

In spite of their different structures, both the *Canadian Human Rights Act* and the *Employment Equity Act* conceptualize equity in broad, non-technical terms. Equity is understood as equality of opportunity rather than strict equality of treatment. This interpretation obliges employers to make special provisions to accommodate disadvantaged groups even if it entails minor expense, inconvenience, and disruption (Hucker 1997). In the realm of pay equity, the definition of equality has been broadened from *equal pay for equal work* to *equal pay for work of equal value* (Antecol and Kuhn 1999; Chicha 1999).[7]

In contrast to Canada, state and federal governments in the United States have introduced legislation for people with disabilities which applies to both the public and the private sectors. Such legislation often borrows the logic, enforcement structure, and, in some cases, the vocabulary of the original federal civil rights acts prohibiting discrimination on the basis of race, ethnicity, and sex (Mudrick 1997). For example, in many states the category of disability was simply added to other grounds on which employers cannot discriminate. At the federal level, new pieces of legislation were added to the existing *Civil Rights Act* of 1964 – the *Rehabilitation Act* of 1973,[8] the *Americans with Disabilities Act* of 1990, and the *Ticket to Work and Work Incentives Improvement Act* of 1999.

The *Americans with Disabilities Act* extended anti-discrimination to the private sector and combined the social environmental and civil rights models of disability. The Act closely resembles traditional civil rights laws in that it does not require employers to hire people with disabilities. Rather, it prohibits consideration of a person's characteristics beyond her or his ability to do the job in question (Mudrick 1997). It breaks with civil rights principles and with person-centred models of disability in requiring "reasonable accommodation." Additionally, the Act functions much like the *Canadian Human Rights Act* in prohibiting discrimination and requiring complaints, without considering whether people with disabilities are proportionately represented.

Canadian and US policy-makers and legislators also attempt to expand labour force participation among people with disabilities through a series of accessibility programs. In Canada, federal tax incentives like the Medical Expense Tax Credit are designed to improve the income security of people who require health-care aids. The Canada Study Grant for Students with Permanent Disabilities from Human Resources and Development Canada works to encourage post-secondary education through special subsidies. Other skill-enhancing initiatives include the Employability Assistance for People with Disabilities program, which helps fund provincial and non-governmental organizations' programs including employment counselling, pre-employment and skills development training, assistive devices, and wage subsidies. Other programs target difficulties with work scheduling and transportation and with finding suitable types of work. For example, the Canada Pension Plan Vocational Rehabilitation initiative offers a return-to-work program including vocational assessment, planning, skills development, and job search assistance (Government of Canada 2002).

The US *Ticket to Work and Work Incentives Improvement Act* is comparable to Canadian accessibility programs. The Act expands federal rehabilitation and vocational training opportunities for people with disabilities, while the Work Incentives Program allows people with disabilities to work while continuing to receive disability benefits and Medicare or Medicaid payments. These two programs provide incentives for the labor force participation among people with disabilities. Many state governments have similar programs (Blanck et al. 2000).

Provincial and municipal governments in Canada have adopted their own forms of anti-discrimination legislation. Each one aims to eliminate specific or systemic discrimination in the labour market, although they vary in scope according to the peculiarities and shifting tides of regional mandates. At the time of their introduction, the equity laws of Ontario and Quebec were the most extensive, pertaining to both public and private sector employers. However, Ontario's *Employment Equity Act* of 1994 was repealed shortly after the Mike Harris government took office in 1995 (Agocs 2002). Legislation in some of the other provinces has also undergone dilution due to the ascension of conservative political agendas constructed around economic deregulation and privatization. In all, there continues to be considerable variation across provincial jurisdictions (Bakan and Kobayashi 2000).

THE LABOUR MARKET EXPERIENCES
OF PEOPLE WITH DISABILITIES

A modestly sized body of literature in the United States and Canada has examined the labour market experiences of people with disabilities. Several studies have demonstrated that people with disabilities suffer considerable disadvantages relative to those without disabilities. A recent Canadian example is a study by Crawford (1998), which uses longitudinal data from 1993–94 from the Survey of Labour and Income Dynamics. Crawford finds that people with disabilities experience more unemployment, underemployment, or non-continuous employment, lower income levels, and higher poverty levels than the non-disabled population. In 1993 and 1994, 60 per cent of people without disabilities were continuously employed in the year. In sharp contrast, only 22 per cent of people with disabilities were continuously employed in 1993, declining to 19 per cent in 1994.

There is also significant variability in the employment experiences of people with disabilities. Additional layers of vulnerability can magnify the impact disability has on employment. Women with disabilities have a lower rate of employment than men (Crawford 1998). In 1993, 35 per cent of women with disabilities were employed all year in Canada, whereas this was true for 53 per cent of men;[9] furthermore, women with disabilities aged 36–69 were less likely to be employed (either continuously or part of the year) than those aged 16–36. Other studies show that people of colour with disabilities are seriously disadvantaged compared to whites with disabilities (Blanck et al. 2000).

Oi (as cited in Blanck et al. 2000) describes four dimensions critical to defining disability in relation to labour force participation: severity, age at onset of disability, anticipated duration of disability, and the effect of a disability on expected lifespan. Supporting Oi's emphasis on these dimensions, empirical studies show that the degree of labour market disadvantage increases with the severity and number of impairments (Baldwin and Johnson 2000; Fawcett 1996; Hum and Simpson 1996; Jongbloed 1990). Other research finds that the type of disability relates to the level of precariousness. For instance, Fawcett (1996) found that people with mental impairments are particularly disadvantaged relative to those with sensory impairments (e.g., hearing and vision impairments). The unemployment rate for the former was 21 per cent in 1991, whereas it was only 10 per cent for the latter. The latter was only 0.6 per cent higher than the unemployment rate of people without disabilities. People with congenital disabilities experience greater difficulty finding employment than people injured at work. In 1991, 16.8 per cent of those with disabilities caused by disease or illness were unemployed, compared to 11.9 per cent of those with disabilities arising from work-related accidents or illnesses (Fawcett 1996).

Educational attainment is strongly correlated with income; it is also a factor that distinguishes people with disabilities from the non-disabled population. Crawford (1998) suggests that people with disabilities tend to have lower education levels than the non-disabled. Higher education is associated with a higher probability of employment for people both with and without disabilities, although it has greater bearing on this probability for people without disabilities, with the exception of people with very high levels of education (Crawford 1998).

People with disabilities tend to have lower income than people without disabilities, particularly if they are female, people of colour, or Aboriginal (Barnartt and Altman 1997, as cited in Bunch and Crawford 1998). Crawford (1998) finds that the average annual salaries of Canadians reporting disabilities in

1993 and 1994 dropped from $4,585 to $4,258.[10] The lower earnings of people with disabilities are due to a combination of fewer hours worked and lower hourly wage rates. Of these two factors, fewer hours worked appears to be more important. Hum and Simpson (1996) substantiate this supposition. According to the 1989 Canadian Labour Force Activity Survey, the annual earnings of people with disabilities were 37 per cent less than people without disabilities, although the difference in average annual earnings was only 7 per cent. Government transfers offer alternative sources of income for people with disabilities. However, they are frequently insufficient to prevent poverty. Between 1993 and 1994, rates of poverty among people with disabilities in Canada were approximately three times those for the non-disabled – between 23.5 per cent and 27 per cent, compared to between 8.6 and 10.4 per cent for the non-disabled population (Crawford 1998). Higher rates of poverty among people with disabilities are due both to lower rates of employment and to lower hourly earnings (Kruse 1998).

Few studies investigate the labour market experiences of people with disabilities with reference to the form of employment or work arrangements or precarious employment more broadly. Indeed, our survey of several periodical indexes produced only three studies, each of which is based in the United States. Appropriately, both Blanck et al. (2000) and Schur (2002) comment on the relative dearth of studies on the participation of people with disabilities in forms of employment and work arrangements differing from full-time permanent jobs.

Using data from the 1997 U.S. Survey of Income and Program Participation and the U.S. Current Population Survey for the period 1991–2000, Schur (2002) finds that people with disabilities are more likely to be in some forms of employment than people without disabilities. Specifically, 44 per cent of workers with disabilities are in part-time or temporary employment, in contrast to only 22 per cent of workers without disabilities. The probabilities are more similar for independent contracting – 10.7 per cent and 6.6 per cent, respectively.

Evidence suggests that many people with disabilities are not engaged in these forms of employment voluntarily and would prefer full-time permanent jobs. More than half of temporary wage workers with disabilities stated this preference, as well as one-third of part-time workers; by contrast, only one-sixth of the self-employed had such a preference (Schur 2002).[11] Similar evidence is provided by a Harris poll from 1998, which found that 48 per cent of part-time wage workers with disabilities would have preferred full-time permanent work (Harris 1998). Furthermore, in each of these forms of employment, people with disabilities are significantly more likely than people without disabilities to desire the full-time permanent alternative to their current employment situation, including those in self-employment (Schur 2002).

On the matter of wages and benefits, workers with disabilities in these forms of employment fare poorly compared to people with disabilities in standard work and the non-disabled in both full-time permanent and other forms of employment. Not only do people with disabilities in part-time and temporary employment earn less per hour than people with and without disabilities in full-time permanent work but they also earn less than their non-disabled counterparts (Schur 2002). Workers without disabilities in full-time permanent work earn 14.1 per cent more per hour than workers with disabilities in temporary work (both full and part time), 21.9 per cent more than workers with disabilities in self-employment (both solo and employer self-employment), and 21.6 per cent more than workers with disabilities in part-time employment. As Cranford and Vosko (this volume) argue, another important dimension of precarious employment tied to the social wage is access to extended benefits. Surprisingly, workers with disabilities in both full-time permanent and other forms of employment are less likely to have benefits than their non-disabled counterparts. A critical concern in the US context is that workers with disabilities are not only less likely to have employer-sponsored health insurance in each form of employment but also less likely to have personal health insurance (Schur 2002).

A final issue critical to the dimension of income level is rates of exposure to poverty among people with and without disabilities in forms of employment differing from full-time permanent jobs. In this group, people with disabilities in every form of employment are more likely to be in poverty compared to those without disabilities (Schur 2002). Almost 20 per cent of workers with disabilities in these forms live in poverty, whereas only 10 per cent of the non-disabled do. There is also a higher probability of poverty for workers with disabilities in full-time permanent jobs, but it is only 2 per cent higher than their non-disabled counterparts. As one would expect, the highest rates of poverty for people with disabilities are among the unemployed.

For some labour force participants, part-time and temporary employment may represent a stepping stone to full-time permanent work. The extent to which this possibility is the case among workers with disabilities is similar to those without disabilities (Schur 2002). Blanck (1998) finds that out of 10 people working for a temporary agency at some point during the year, six had moved to permanent jobs by the following year. However, Schur (2002) finds that in all employment forms, those with disabilities are more likely to exit the labour force the following year than their non-disabled counterparts.

Widespread recognition of the disadvantages and overt forms of discrimination faced by people with disabilities has led to the passage of remedial legislation at the federal, provincial/state, and municipal levels in both Canada and the United States. A handful of studies and reports, both qualitative and quantitative, have evaluated the effectiveness of this legislation.

Some completed under the federal Employment Equity Act in Canada suggest that vulnerable populations face the fallout associated with a coincidence of waning equity practices and changing employment relationships (Christofides and Swidensky 1994). These reports find significant wage gaps between able-bodied non-minority men and disadvantaged groups, and also that hiring and promotion practices still favour the former, especially with respect to positions of power.

Several studies have investigated the effectiveness of Canada's 1986 Employment Equity Act and the Employment Equity plans it requires employers to implement. In general, the studies find that these policies affect people with disabilities differently, depending on social location. Leck and Saunders (1992) examine hiring trends for whites, Aboriginal people, people of colour, and women with disabilities, using the Employment Equity Employer reports submitted in accordance with the Employment Equity Act and telephone interviews with employers who were subject to it. Their findings indicate that all vulnerable groups have benefited from the Act, but they have not benefited equally. The Act has led to the hiring of white women into traditionally male-dominated occupations, such as supervisory and manual labour positions. By contrast, for Aboriginal women and women with disabilities, the Employment Equity Act has had its greatest impact in the traditionally female-dominated areas such as clerical work.

Research by Leck and Lalancete (1995) on whites, people of colour, Aboriginals, and women with disabilities finds similar variation in outcomes arising from the implementation of the Employment Equity Act. The authors examine the effectiveness of the Act at different salary levels in increments of $5,000. They find that, relative to those for white men, hiring rates increased for all four vulnerable groups in the earnings category of less than $35,000. However, in higher income categories, particularly $50,000 or more, gaps in hiring rates widened between white men and vulnerable groups of women. White women without disabilities were the only ones to achieve gains relative to white men in the $35,000 to $45,000 salary range. Earnings gaps also widened between the men and women in specific groups – people of colour, Aboriginals, and people with disabilities. Hence, wage gaps widened between minority men and women, and they did so even more rapidly between minority women and white men.

THE LABOUR MARKET EXPERIENCES
OF PEOPLE WITH DISABILITIES IN CANADA

What are the contemporary and historical labour market experiences of people with disabilities in Canada, and how have these experiences changed with policy shifts and labour market developments over the last decade? Through cross-sectional time-series analyses, this section addresses this question by way of an overview of the labour force participation and earnings experiences of people with disabilities in relation to other vulnerable groups. It is concerned principally with the contemporary labour force participation and earnings experiences of people with disabilities, with evaluating how they fare in the labour market in relation to people of colour and women, and in following how the layering of vulnerabilities can affect these experiences.

Data Sources

Data are drawn from two Canadian surveys, the Survey of Labour and Income Dynamics (SLID) and its predecessor, the Labour Market Activity Survey. Begun in 1986, the Labour Market Activity Survey provides annual information on patterns of labour force participation, as well as information on the characteristics of jobs held by Canadians. The survey sample is nationally representative and consists of 40,000 households.[12] In 1993 the Labour Market Activity Survey was replaced by the Survey of Labour and Income Dynamics, a similar, though more in-depth, study of labour force activity and income experiences. The Survey of Labour and Income Dynamics is a panel study of 15,000 households, focusing on how changes in work and family composition influence levels of economic well-being. Though both the Labour Market Activity Survey and the Survey of Labour and Income Dynamics were designed primarily as panel studies, each contains a cross-sectional component providing a representative overview of the experiences of Canadians. This cross-sectional component allows us to sketch trends in the labour market experiences of people in different social locations for the period 1989 through 2001.[13] Both the Labour Market Activity Survey and the Survey of Labour and Income Dynamics collect information on disability in general, as well as whether a person experiences specific limitations associated with employment. Information on visible minority status is also available. Because this chapter is concerned with patterns of employment among Canadians for whom employment is a primary activity, the analysis is restricted to individuals who are of working age (i.e., aged 17 to 64), excluding full-time students.

The indicators used in the analysis focus on patterns of labour force participation, work arrangements, and forms of employment. Since precarious employment is a multi-dimensional construct that reflects more than forms of employment and work arrangements (see Vosko, this volume; see also Rodgers 1989), the analysis considers two dimensions of precarious employment and develops appropriate indicators for each dimension: the degree of certainty of continuing employment and the income level. Although the methodological approach outlined in chapter 1 offers a suitable framework for examining the employment experiences of people with disabilities, this chapter does not employ this methodology for two reasons: first, the number of respondents with disabilities in the Survey of Labour and Income Dynamics is small, precluding further disaggregation of the sample into the layered categories that this methodology requires. Second, the mapping methodology, as Alliance on Contingent Employment researchers have developed it thus far, relies on a cross-sectional approach to the analysis that examines labour market experiences at a single point in time. It is not yet ready to be adapted to examine the *temporal evolution* of the labour market experiences of people with disabilities in conjunction with legislation and policy changes and labour market restructuring – a major objective of this chapter.

Table 4.1 lists and defines measures of labour force participation included in the analysis and defines the forms of employment and work arrangements under study. These forms and arrangements are limited by the nature of the data collected by the Labour Market Activity Survey and the Survey of Labour and Income Dynamics. Specifically, while the catchall term "non-standard" consists of forms and arrangements that are not mutually exclusive, it is the closest proxy for forms of employment and work arrangements differing from the full-time permanent job in these surveys. Furthermore, neither survey measures job permanence, making it impossible to determine which workers with full-time full-year work are permanent.[14] Consequently, while recognizing the validity of critiques of the concepts "standard" and "non-standard" and the dichotomy itself (Vosko, this volume), the analysis employs the catchall "non-standard work" because it is the only option available.

In the ensuing discussion, non-standard work comprises four employment situations: part-time hours,[15] job tenure of six months or less, solo self-employment, and multiple job-holding. Standard work, in contrast, describes work that does not meet any of these criteria – work that better approximates the postwar normative model of employment. Consistent with other chapters in Part One, in classifying work experiences this analysis focuses on characteristics pertaining to the respondent's main job, defined as the job with the most hours worked in a particular reference year, or, where this information is unavailable or unclear, the job with the longest tenure.

Identifying People with Disabilities

Questions used in population health surveys to determine disability status partly reflect recent conceptualizations of the disablement process. These questions generally take the following form: "Because of a long-term physical or mental condition or health problem, are you limited in the kind or amount of activity you can do at home, at school, at work, in other activities such as transportation to or from work or school or leisure time activities?"

Table 4.1
Measures of Labour Market Participation and Types of Work Arrangements

Measure	Definition
LABOUR FORCE PARTICIPATION VARIABLES	
Employed part-year	Employed at least one week during the year
Employed majority of the year	Employed at least 27 weeks of the year
Employed all year	Employed 52 weeks of the year
Unemployed part-year	Unemployed at least one week during the year
Unemployed majority of the year	Unemployed at least 27 weeks of the year
Unemployed all year	Unemployed 52 weeks of the year
In the labour force all year	Labour force participants – those employed or unemployed for the duration of the year
Out of the labour force all year	No labour force activity during the year
Individual income	Total individual income, all sources, for the year
Household income	Total household income, all sources, for the year
Low Income Cut-Off (LICO)	Statistics Canada measure of low income, adjusted for family size and composition
Low Income Measure (LIM)	Statistics Canada measure of low income, adjusted for family size and urban/rural classification
Labour force earnings – non-standard work	Total labour force earnings where the person is identified as in non-standard work form or arrangement
Labour force earnings – standard work	Total labour force earnings where the main job is identified as a standard work arrangement
FORMS OF EMPLOYMENT AND WORK ARRANGEMENTS	
Part-time employment	Person works no more than 30 hours each week (covers self-employment and wage work, permanent and temporary)
Involuntary part-time employment	Person works in part-time employment but would prefer full-time work (covers self-employment and wage work, permanent and temporary)
Solo self-employment	Self-employed without paid help
Short-tenure employment	Work with tenure of six months or less
Multiple job holding	Holding more than one job concurrently (wage work or self-employment)
Non-standard work	Refers to any form of employment or work arrangement differing from the full-time permanent job
Standard work	Work that does not fall into any category of non-standard work and is full time

Often, separate questions are used to inquire into different categories of role function, and sometimes categories are clustered together under one question (e.g., work and school, transportation, or leisure).

The foregoing question identifies people with disabilities in the Labour Market Activity Survey in 1989 and 1990 and the Survey of Labour and Income Dynamics from 1993 to 1999. The focus is on long-term disabilities and, therefore, individuals with transitory or intermittent conditions may not be identified as disabled. The question focuses on activities rather than role functions and does not inquire about the degree to which the environment accommodates limitations in basic functional capabilities. Consequently, people with similar functional capabilities may respond differently because of the different expectations and the different environments in which they perform these roles. Essentially, disability status across respondents is not measured by the same standards.

The above question is supplemented in the Survey of Labour and Income Dynamics with a catchall question: "Do you have any long-term disabilities or handicaps?" The Labour Market Activity Survey does not ask this question but uses several other ways of measuring limitations in the activities of daily life. Recent modifications to the roster of disability status questions from 1999 onward in the Survey of Labour and Income Dynamics have broadened the scope to focus equally on long- and short-term disabilities. In addition, the catchall question has been replaced with the following question: "Do you have any difficulty, hearing, seeing, communicating, walking, climbing stairs, bending, learning or doing any similar activities?" These modifications have broadened the definition of disability and, consequently, more people in the Survey of Labour and Income Dynamics sample are identified as disabled from 1999 onward. The new set of questions still focuses on activities rather than role function and does not probe the environmental context in which the activities occur.

Given the differences in the questions used to identify people with disabilities, the proportion of the population identified with disabilities varies with each survey. In the Labour Market Activity Survey, 13–14 per cent of the population have disabilities; in the Survey of Labour and Income Dynamics from 1993 to 1998, 10–12 per cent have disabilities, and from 1999 to 2001, 17–18 per cent. When comparing data on people with and without disabilities across years, it is important to keep these differences in mind. Another measurement issue also warrants mention: the Survey of Labour and Income Dynamics is a panel survey, with six-year overlapping panels. The first panel began in 1993, the second in 1996, and the third in 1999. Cross-sectional information from the Survey of Labour and Income Dynamics is drawn from observations taken from the overlapping panels. With the introduction of the second panel in 1996, the sample increased substantially. The increase in the sample inevitably requires a reweighting of observations. Statistically, this reweighting should not have an impact on the proportion of the population identified with disabilities, yet a small increase is found in this proportion (approximately 2 per cent) in the Survey of Labour and Income Dynamics in 1996 through 1998. Since there was no change in the questions used to identify people with disabilities in these years of the survey, this increase is likely a statistical artifact.

Trends in Labour Market Experiences of People with and without Disabilities

Two clusters of the working-age population are considered here: all individuals aged 17 to 64, and individuals in this age bracket who are in the labour force. Consistent with the methodological approach of this volume, these populations are then sliced by disability status, and further by gender and visible minority status,[16] to assess the impact of the layering of vulnerabilities. The analysis focuses on the labour force participation rates of people in different social locations and the relative precariousness experienced by those in the labour force. In assessing the experience of precarious employment among these groups, the degree of certainty of continuing employment and income level are of central concern. In particular, they relate to forms of employment and work arrangements.

The Working-Age Population

The proportion of people with disabilities employed at some point during the year is much smaller than for people without disabilities (43–63 per cent compared to 84–88 per cent) (figure 4.1). Fewer still are in the labour force all year and/or employed all year (43–58 per cent for the former, and 29–49 per cent for the latter). These trends remain relatively stable over time. Differences in participation rates also appear within the disabled population along the lines of gender and visible minority status. Women with disabilities are less likely to be employed at some point during the year than men with disabilities (36–57 per cent range over the observation period compared to 48–71 per cent range) (figure 4.2). They are also less likely to be employed all year or in the labour force all year (figure 4.3). In contrast, visible minorities with disabilities experience the same low levels of employment as non-visible minorities with disabilities, and the proportion in the labour force all year and/or employed all year is also similar between these groups. Anti-discrimination policies may have played a role in protecting visible minorities with disabilities, in that they are not incrementally disadvantaged relative to non-visible minorities with disabilities. The small differences suggest that visible minority women with disabilities are as engaged in the labour force as non-visible minority women with disabilities, though there are no data to substantiate this hypothesis.

Figure 4.1
Proportion of people with and without disabilities employed at least one week
during the year, 1989–2001

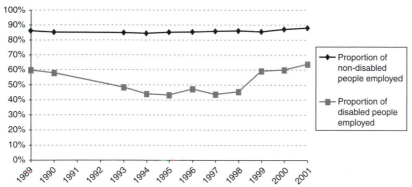

Figure 4.2
Proportion of women and men with and without disabilities employed at least
one week during the year, 1989–2001

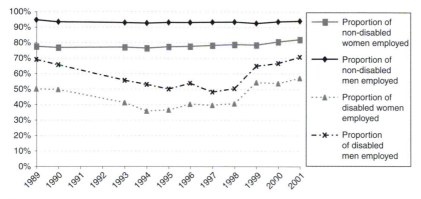

Figure 4.3
Proportion of women and men with disabilities employed all year
or in the labour force all year, 1989–2001

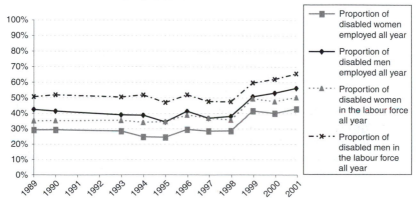

The business cycle influences the employment opportunities and labour force participation rates of people with disabilities more substantially than people without disabilities. That is true for both women and men with disabilities and visible minorities and non-visible minorities with disabilities. The impact of the business cycle is apparent in the substantial decrease in the proportion of working-aged people with disabilities employed at some point in the year in the mid-1990s recession. It is also apparent in the proportion that is out of the labour force all year. In contrast, the proportion of people without disabilities employed at some point during the year does not change significantly over the business cycle, nor does the proportion of this group that is out of the labour force all year. Once again, women with disabilities are considerably more affected by the fluctuations in the business cycle than are men with disabilities, based on these labour force attachment variables. By contrast, little difference is apparent between visible and non-visible minorities with disabilities. There is some evidence to suggest that anti-discriminatory policies have provided some support for at least those individuals who remain in the labour force. Specifically, the unemployment rates (unemployed at some point during the year) and the long-term unemployment rate (unemployed all year) are similar for all people with disabilities and the non-disabled.

Given the average looser labour force attachment of people with disabilities, it is not surprising they have average annual incomes of approximately $10,000 less than their non-disabled counterparts (an average difference of $10,200 over the nine-year period from 1993 to 2001). At the level of the household, incomes are lower by approximately $17,000 (an average difference of $16,900 over the same nine-year period), suggesting that the family members of people with disabilities also bring in less income than those of people without disabilities. This trend indicates that people with disabilities may, in many instances, be doubly disadvantaged, given their more precarious attachment to the labour force and the more meagre resources potentially available to them through the household. Once again, women with disabilities confront low incomes more than men with disabilities. In fact, men with disabilities are comparable to women without disabilities in terms of annual income levels. The household incomes of women with disabilities are comparable to those of men with disabilities, suggesting that their own high level of income insecurity may be offset at the household level while perpetuating other dependencies (Vosko and Zukewich, this volume). As with the labour force attachment variables, there are no apparent differences between visible minorities and non-visible minorities with disabilities at the level of individual income. At the level of household income, there are some differences. Somewhat unexpectedly, the household income of visible minorities with disabilities is, in fact, higher than their non-visible minority counterparts.

Data on the proportion below the Low Income Cut-Off (LICO), below the Low Income Measure (LIM), and receiving social assistance provide compelling evidence of the income-based precariousness of people with disabilities. Given their lower levels of labour force attachment and income levels, people with disabilities are more likely to have household incomes that fall below the Low Income Measure and the Low Income Cut-Off. They are also more likely to be receiving social assistance. These proportions are higher through the 1990s – approximately one in four, or more for the time period 1993 to 1998, compared to fewer than one in ten for the non-disabled population. Women with disabilities receive social assistance more than men with disabilities, whereas a similar distinction between visible minorities and non-visible minorities is not evident.

Labour Force Participants

We now turn to the subsample of the working-age population who are labour force participants. This group includes individuals who are working or searching for work at some point during the year.

Labour force participants with disabilities experience greater discontinuities in employment than their non-disabled counterparts. They are less likely to be employed all year (60–70 per cent versus 70–80 per cent), for the majority of the year (70–85 per cent versus 90 per cent), or at some point during the year (figure 4.4). Women with disabilities and visible minorities with disabilities are even less likely to be employed all year or the majority of the year than their disabled counterparts (i.e., men with disabilities and non-visible minorities with disabilities).[17] On the flip side, labour force participants with disabilities are more likely to be unemployed for the majority of the year or at some point during the year. Also, the unemployment and employment rates for this group appear, once again, to be affected more strongly by the business cycle. Furthermore, our trend analysis shows that this is so even more for women with disabilities and for visible minorities with disabilities. These groups experienced a larger drop in employment rates in the early to mid-1990s than other disabled groups.

In terms of individual and household incomes, people with disabilities are worse off than their non-disabled counterparts, but differences are smaller than those observed for the entire working-age population. The average difference in individual incomes is approximately $6,000 (average difference of $6,164 over nine years from 1993 to 2001), and in household income approximately $10,000 (average difference of $10,062 over nine years). Despite having higher average incomes than people with disabilities generally, labour force participants with disabilities are still more likely to be below the Low Income Measure and the Low Income Cut-Off , and more likely to be receiving social assistance than their non-disabled counterparts (figure 4.5). Income inadequacy is clearly a concern for many of these people.

Given that the forms of employment and work arrangements differing from the full-time permanent job are, on average, more precarious along the dimensions of income level, degree of regulatory protection, and control over the labour process than the employment norm (Vosko, this volume), the prevalence of these situations among people with disabilities is central to understanding the dynamics of precarious employment among this group. Non-standard work tends to be less secure than standard work in terms of hourly wages and benefits associated with the social wage, such as pensions (public and private), and employer-sponsored benefits, such as sick pay, dental coverage, and extended health care. The trend analysis shows that labour force participants with disabilities are consistently less likely to be in so-called standard work than non-disabled participants (figure 4.6). Once again, women with disabilities are more likely than men with disabilities to work in non-standard work and, therefore, they are potentially more vulnerable to various dimensions of precarious employment. In fact, even women without disabilities are quite vulnerable in this area. Men with disabilities are also more likely to hold standard work than women without disabilities. In contrast, no differences are apparent between visible minorities and non-visible minorities with disabilities.

The prevalence of the different forms of employment and work arrangements investigated remains similar over time for people with disabilities and for the non-disabled group, with the exception of part-time work. The prevalence of part-time work among people with a disability ranges from 11–14 per cent of labour force participants versus 15–21 per cent for those without a disability. Considering these trends by gender, part-time work is more common among women with disabilities than for men with disabilities. In fact, it is quite low for men with and without disabilities compared to women, with and without disabilities (figure 4.7). Here again, gender appears to be a critical factor. Furthermore, the prevalence of involuntary part-time work among people with disabilities is equal to that of those without disabilities who work no more than 30 hours a week. This would suggest that a greater proportion of people with disabilities choose part-time work, while recognizing the constraints that may surround this choice. For example, we might question the notion of "voluntary" in this case, since it may well be that these individuals opt for part-time work because the accommodation required to make full-time work (be it wage work or self-employment) possible is simply not available to them.

Data on satisfaction/dissatisfaction with the number of hours of work provides further insight into the perceived adequacy of hours of work for people with disabilities. As we might expect, this trend appears to have a cyclical pattern to it.[18] The proportion of all individuals satisfied with the number of hours of work is reasonably high in the peak years of the business cycle (approximately 72–79 per cent in 1989 and 1990, and 73–78 per cent in 2000 and 2001 for men and women with disabilities), though quite low in the

Figure 4.4
Proportion of people with and without disabilities employed all year
or employed a majority of the year, 1989–2001

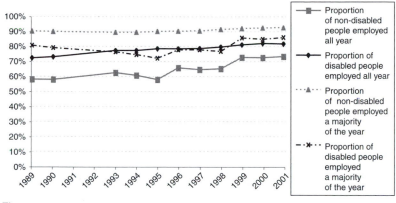

Figure 4.5
Proportion of people with and without disabilities who are economically vulnerable, 1989–2001

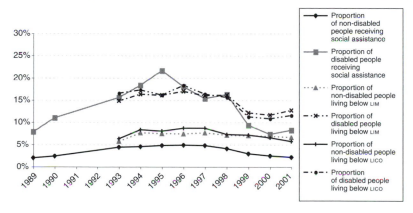

Figure 4.6
Proportion of people with and without disabilities in standard and non-standard work
arrangements, 1989–2001

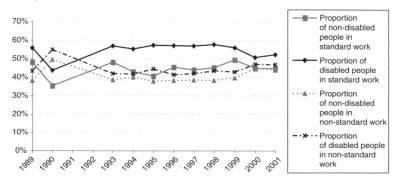

Figure 4.7
Proportion of women and men with and without disabilities
in part-time employment, 1989–2001

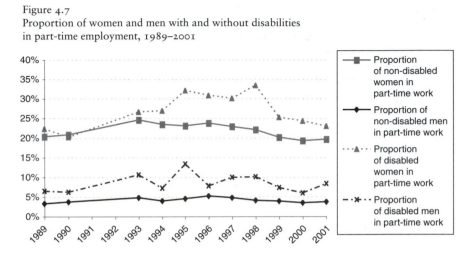

downturn of the cycle (approximately 55–61 per cent in the 1993–5 time period). A much smaller proportion of people with disabilities desire to work more hours. The range is from 14–27 per cent over the time period under analysis. Trends in the satisfaction/dissatisfaction with the number of hours of work are similar for women and men with disabilities, even though the prevalence of part-time work is higher for the former. The trends are also similar for visible minorities and non-visible minorities with disabilities.[19]

The average annual earnings of people with disabilities in standard and non-standard work are consistently lower than those for people without disabilities in the same types of arrangements (figure 4.8). That is true for every form of employment and work arrangement captured in table 4.1. Coupled with the information on low-income thresholds, it is reasonable to speculate that people with disabilities make up a substantial portion of this country's working poor.[20] Moreover, consistent with previous findings regarding the salience of gender, women with disabilities fare worse than men with disabilities in terms of average annual earnings across employment form. Men with disabilities also do better than women without disabilities. In contrast, there is little distinction between the annual earnings of visible minorities with disabilities and those of non-visible minorities with disabilities across forms of employment.

Lastly, it is important to review the prevalence of public sector employment among people with disabilities, since many of the employment equity programs discussed earlier are applicable primarily in this sector. Unexpectedly, the proportion of people with disabilities employed in the public sector is similar to the number of people without disabilities. However, the data show that a consistently greater proportion of women than men with disabilities are public sector employees, suggesting an emphasis on the employment

Figure 4.8
Average labour-market earnings of people with and without disabilities in standard
and non-standard work, 1989–2001

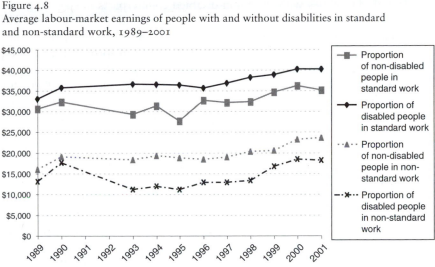

of people in social locations characterized by multiple disadvantages. Unfortunately, owing to small sample size, data was not available on public sector employment of visible minorities.

<h2 style="text-align:center">CONCLUSION</h2>

This chapter has begun to paint a picture of the more precarious labour market experiences of people with disabilities compared to those without disabilities. In the future, an enriched understanding of these experiences may be gained by drawing on studies that collect information from people with disabilities, such as the Health and Activity Limitation Survey (HALS). However, because the HALS is not conducted annually and because it lacks a comparison group (i.e., information on non-disabled people), researchers concerned to adopt a relational approach to understanding precarious employment must continue to rely on data sources like the Survey of Labour and Income Dynamics to set these phenomena in context. Our findings show that people with disabilities are more loosely attached to the labour force than people without disabilities. They are more likely to leave the labour force during downturns in the business cycle, and more likely to be unemployed if they remain. Their low levels of individual and household income shape their experience of precariousness. Finally, they are more likely to fall below Statistics Canada's low-income thresholds, and considerably more likely to require social assistance than people without disabilities.

Labour force participants with disabilities have lower average annual earnings than non-disabled participants. Even if the average annual earnings of people with disabilities with their non-disabled counterparts in specific forms of employment, from part-time work (temporary and permanent or self-employment or wage work) to full-time wage work (temporary and permanent), are compared, the former have lower earnings across all forms. Furthermore, they are more likely to be engaged in non-standard work and, in particular, part-time work. Though the levels of satisfaction with part-time employment for people with disabilities are similar to those of the non-disabled, it may be that people with disabilities assume that appropriate accommodation in full-time work (wage work or self-employment) is not feasible.

Lastly, though many policy initiatives are geared towards public sector employers, the proportion of labour force participants with disabilities employed in this sector is similar to the proportion of non-disabled participants. A higher proportion of women with disabilities than men with disabilities work in this sector, although, as noted, the aggregate of these two groups totals a public sector employment rate similar to that of the people without disabilities. Notably, there are some indications of improvements in public sector employment rates for women with disabilities, advances that, in the early-to-mid-1990s, were lower than those of women without disabilities.

One of the chief objectives of this chapter was to evaluate the impact, if any, of policy developments over the last 10 to 15 years on the labour market experiences of people with disabilities. Based on the trends observed, there is little indication that people with disabilities are catching up to their non-disabled counterparts. People in some social locations, within the disabled population, fare relatively better than people in others. Men with disabilities, both visible minority men and non-visible minority men, appear to be the least disadvantaged of this group. In fact, men with disabilities fare better than women without disabilities on many of the dimensions investigated. Whether this finding can be attributed to the protection provided by legislation is unclear. What is evident is that women with disabilities certainly experience greater disadvantage as labour force participants. Gender is thus a critical factor not addressed adequately in disability policy. In the face of the rise of precarious employment, policy developments have not demonstrably improved the labour market experiences of people with disabilities. At best, they may have kept the dramatic churnings of the labour market at bay.

Precarious Work, Privatization, and the Health-Care Industry: The Case of Ancillary Workers

PAT ARMSTRONG AND KATE LAXER

Health care is women's work. Wherever it is done, whether paid or unpaid, women provide the overwhelming majority of care. Women comfort, feed, bathe, toilet, keep records for, clean for, shop for, do laundry for, manage, and supervise those needing care, often combining these tasks with more clinical interventions. Forms of this work have traditionally been performed by women in the home, although a significant proportion of what is currently done in health care has not historically been provided in the household. Women have struggled hard to have the work of care recognized as both valuable and skilled, wherever it is provided. Nevertheless, much of the work and many of the skills remain invisible in terms of the acquired nature of the capacities and the contribution to health. They remain invisible in part because women are primarily responsible for social reproduction wherever it is done and because there is a great deal of overlap among the kinds of reproductive work women do in the private and the public realms.

Florence Nightingale struggled to emphasize the importance of the environment in health care and demanded that the skilled nature of nursing work be recognized. At the time, nurses were often the sole daily providers of paid care. As a result, they did everything, including in their work the full range of women's traditional care along with newly emerging clinical tasks. Since Nightingale's time, nursing has become more narrowly defined as others take over some of the work formerly included in nurses' responsibilities. Nevertheless, Nightingale's legacy is evident in the recognition of the skilled nature of nursing work and its contribution to care.

However, the struggle for recognition of both skills and contribution to health continues for those who have taken on the tasks previously done mainly by nurses and traditionally by women. The issue is highlighted in the recent Royal Commission on Health Care. *Building on Values: The Future of Health Care in Canada* (Romanow Report) draws a line between the jobs defined as direct and those defined as ancillary. It not only separates ancillary services from direct health-care services, implying that they have different connections to health care, but also suggests that, while there is little evidence to support privatizing direct services, ancillary services could be safely delivered by for-profit concerns.

This chapter considers some of the potential consequences of such privatization both for women's work and for health care. Like the other authors in this volume, we use a feminist political economy approach to bring an interdisciplinary lens to bear on these developments. In stressing the context of health care for understanding this work, we challenge the notion that there is a category called ancillary work that is generalizable across industries. We ground this challenge in both the determinants of health literature and the feminist literature on skills and social reproduction. The link between women's paid and unpaid work in social reproduction help explain why this work is so undervalued and so easily defined out of health care. We challenge as well the move to privatize the work defined as ancillary, seeking to show how such privatization simultaneously puts many women into a more precarious employment relationship and into more unpaid work at home. At the same time, we seek to fill some of the evidence gap on contracting out ancillary services. Specifically, we look at work in and outside care, mapping the extent to which work is precarious for ancillary workers in both the public and the private sectors. Our assumption is that greater precariousness means greater risks for both workers and recipients of care.

DEFINING ANCILLARY WORK

What work is ancillary work in health care? The Romanow Report, while not offering a specific definition of ancillary services, describes them as services "such as food preparation, cleaning and maintenance." Clerical workers and laundry workers would also seem to fit in with this understanding of ancillary, given that these workers, too, do not provide "direct" care. Because our primary interest is in jobs defined as women's work, our focus is on the female-dominated food services and cleaning, child-care and home-support workers and on secretaries and clerical occupations. Maintenance work is both male-dominated and more difficult to separate out as a category, and it is not included here as part of the analysis. In order to assess this definition, it is necessary to look at the specific nature of health-care work and the role ancillary services play.

A host of literature demonstrates that health is determined by a range of factors (see, for example, Evans, Barer and Marmor 1994). Social, physical, and psychological environments have, as various provincial reports (Deber, Mhatre, and Baker 1994) make clear, a significant impact on health. Secure employment and secure income are also critical, as are conditions within workplaces and the degree of control people have over their work (Karasek 1979; Karasek and Thorell 1990). In addition, biology, gender, and culture are recognized by Health Canada as determinants of health. However, much of the literature and policy in health care treats these factors as independent variables that are not relevant to the study of health care itself or to the health of workers who provide care. Indeed, health care is listed as a separate variable.

Yet we know that social, physical, and psychological environments are even more critical for those who are ill, frail, or suffer from chronic conditions that make them particularly vulnerable. The importance of these determinants is intensified within the health-care workplace, reflecting the specific nature of health-care work. Health care is about vulnerable individuals whose body parts cannot easily be separated out of their environments. Moreover, the environments for care are much more likely than other environments to constitute risks that are hazardous to those requiring care. In other words, health-care workplaces can be particularly dangerous and require special attention to the determinants of health.

Health-care laundry that has not been appropriately handled can become life threatening for patients (Orr et al. 2002). It can be equally dangerous to those doing the work, with hepatitis A or B providing only one example (Borg and Portelli 1999; Wa 1995). Similarly, food plays a critical role in care. The National Health Service in the United Kingdom describes health-care food as "a token of exchange between hospital and patient, and it matters tremendously how it is made available to patients, how it is prepared and how it is served" (NHSE states 2003a). While these aspects of food matter to us all, they have a particular importance in health care. Food not eaten, the wrong food eaten, or food eaten at the wrong time in the wrong way can be especially dangerous to the ill, frail, or disabled. So can food that is not correctly prepared. The environments for care are part of care, and they can be as critical to health as clinical interventions. Indeed, they can influence whether such interventions succeed or fail. That is, in part, why there is a term for illnesses that result from being treated in the system: *Iatrogenesis* refers to illness or death caused by health care.

Health care is an interactive process, and this factor, too, makes it a specific kind of workplace. Those needing care have an influence on both the structuring and the impact of care on a continual basis. The interaction is not restricted to direct providers and patients, however. Patients talk to those cleaning around their beds, and they often influence that cleaning in the process. Cleaning staff "play an important role in handing people blankets and out-of-reach items, opening drink containers, getting personal items, notifying a nurse of problems and conversing with patients" (Cohen 2001, 8). Feeding is an even more obvious example of interaction, one that depends on the relationship between provider and patients as well as on the quality of the food. Nor is the interaction restricted to that among patients and providers. Health care requires interaction among those who provide care, because care itself must be integrated through the complementary skills of a range of providers. Health care necessarily involves a team that includes those who do surgery and those who make sure the surgery is clean; those who determine whether patients eat and those that help them eat; those who determine what records should be kept and those who keep them.

Team members are interdependent in ways which mean that distinctions between ancillary and direct care are blurred. All those who work in health care require health-specific knowledge, and most describe themselves as health-care providers, whatever their job in care. The British House of Commons Health Select Committee (1999) warned: "The often spurious division of staff into clinical or non-clinical groups can create an institutional apartheid which might be detrimental to staff morale and to patients" (quoted in Sachdev 2001, 33).

Perhaps, most obviously, health care is about life and death, about healthy possibilities and dangerous consequences. The risks of poor quality are high, and the importance of skilled work is greater than in other sectors. It also means that the health of the workers can have an impact on those needing care. Workers without extended health benefits come to work sick, jeopardizing patient health. Temporary workers often lack familiarity with patients or workplaces, creating possibilities for critical errors. Lack of security in jobs or income can mean less commitment, less training, and more strain, all of which can lead to poor quality that creates risks to care recipients' health. Lack of control can mean that workers cannot use their skills to respond to the variability in work demands and to crises that are regular aspects of work in care.

IS CARE WORK GENERALIZABLE?

Together, these characteristics of care work differentiate it significantly from other employment sectors. The competitors that the Romanow Report suggests can take over this health-care work are, for the most part, those who service hotels. Indeed, food, laundry, cleaning, and maintenance services in health care are increasingly described as hotel services. The new industrial classification system at Statistics Canada even moves these services out of the health industry when they are privatized and into industrial categories that assume, for example, that all cleaning work is the same. Yet there are important reasons not to equate health and hotel work, reasons that reflect the specific nature of health care outlined above.

First, the demands are different in these different kinds of workplaces. Although the research on ancillary workers in either sector is limited, there are clear indications that the jobs in the two sectors cannot be equated. Health-care cleaning staff, for example, must work around complicated, delicate equipment and living patients, while hotel cleaners work in empty rooms. Laundry workers in health care must carefully separate laundry, and the process involves considerable risks and, often, protective clothing. Laundry from isolation wards has to be washed in manually loaded machines and specially treated (Cohen 2001,12). Records must be meticulously kept in ways that require considerable specialized knowledge about health issues. Food preparation, too, requires such knowledge, with special care taken to ensure that foods meet the specific dietary needs of the ill, frail, and disabled.

Second, the hazards are different in both kinds of work. The risks of infection are greater and distinct in health care. The chemicals handled are dangerous and varied. Indeed, health-care cleaners have three times the injury rate of other cleaners (Workers' Compensation Board, quoted in Cohen 2001, 9). Working around patients means exposure not only to disease but also to violence. Ill or drugged patients can lash out at the providers within reach. And those within reach are often the ancillary workers. Equally important, equipment not properly maintained could mean that a life is not saved as well as the creation of a health hazard for workers.

Third, the consequences of mistakes or poor quality are significantly greater and different in health care. Quality is important in both kinds of workplaces, and workers in either place may face job loss if the work is not safely done. However, a poorly prepared meal in the hospital could mean the difference between recovery and continued illness. The wrong meal delivered to the wrong patient could have even more serious consequences. Invisible germs in hospitals can mean contagion and death for patients with weak immune systems. The wrong data recorded could cause life-threatening mistakes.

Finally, hotel services work to different standards, and there is little evidence that quality is immediately evident to the customer, as the Romanow Report suggests. The work organization designed for profit in hotel services can result in standards of cleanliness that not only are low but may be dangerous to the health of even healthy customers. Research in the United States revealed a host of dangerous bacteria in hotel rooms. The invisible bacteria were found by microbiologists and were evident even in the most expensive, and seemingly clean, hotels (Gerba et al. in Cohen 2001, 11). Applying such methods of work organization through contracted services could well mean inadequate or even risky quality in health care. Taiwan provides one example. The Center for Disease Control there has argued

that the outsourcing of nursing aides, cleaners, and laundry workers contributed to the transmission of Severe Acute Respiratory Syndrome (SARS)
in that country. According to the director of the center, "nursing aides, who
did not have proper disease-prevention outfits, roamed freely in the hospitals and contracted the disease." Because they were not direct employees,
the hospitals could not "efficiently manage these workers" (Chen 2003).
The Taipei Foreign Workers' Consulting Center reported that, in one hospital, seven foreign nursing aides had contracted SARS, and three of them
died (Chen 2003). It is certain that the deterioration of quality would not
be immediately obvious, as the Romanow Report suggests. The issue is not
whether hotel employees are good at or committed to their work. Rather, it
is that the standards set for them, the way work is organized, and the requirements of the workplace are quite different from those in care.

In short, the Romanow Report does not produce evidence to support the
claim that quality is "relatively easy to judge" or that "competitors in the
same business" could provide appropriate ancillary services. Nor does it
consider the consequences of contracting out some services essential to care
while retaining others as part of a public or at least semi-public system.
And there is no discussion at all of this ancillary work as women's work,
even though gender clearly plays an important role in the understanding of
the nature of the jobs.

GENDER, SKILL, AND SOCIAL REPRODUCTION

More than 80 per cent of those employed in health care are women. Women
are also the overwhelming majority of those doing the cooking, cleaning,
laundry, and care work in the home. The kinds of skills and conditions of
women's ancillary work frequently involve those associated with the home,
where it is often assumed they know how to do the work because they are
women. This link between women's social reproductive work in the home,
where it is unpaid, and their social reproductive work in the labour force
has consequences for the visibility of the skills, effort, and responsibilities
involved in the work. The segregation of the work in the market helps make
possible the continuing invisibility and undervaluing of this women's work.

Research over the last two decades has shown that women's job characteristics are invisible in part because so many women do the work. As a result, skills, responsibilities, and effort are often considered to be simply a
natural part of being female, and working conditions are thought to be un-
objectionable to those doing the work. Evaluators often do not see skills
but, rather, see "qualities intrinsic to being a woman. Because of this, the
job evaluators were confusing the content and responsibilities of a paid job
with stereotypic notions about the characteristics of the job holder. We
find this happening with fine motor co-ordination, rapid finger dexterity

skills, and with the noisy and public working conditions associated with female blue collar and clerical work" (Shepela and Viviano 1984, 56).

Women's skills and responsibilities are also invisible because many of them are learned outside the formal education system, do not result in different credentials, and are often learned from other women on the job. For example, clerical workers frequently teach each other how to use computers and photocopiers. Cleaners teach each other how to use and fix the new equipment and chemicals that are introduced on a regular basis. They teach each other how to work with patients, sharing their knowledge about personal relations as well as about cleaning techniques. Neither worker ends up with a piece of paper saying she can do the work, even though she is required to have these skills (Treiman and Hartmann 1981, 49). The nature of the job tends to mean that women's service work disappears as soon as it is done, leaving the skills and tasks invisible. Moreover, such work often involves overlapping skills used in tasks that are frequently performed simultaneously. When so many tasks are done at the same time, it is difficult to see any particular task or to see the skill involved in juggling the tasks.

In addition, women's work is more likely to involve team work, cooperation, and coordination with other workers than it is to reflect a place in the hierarchy. The importance of a job is more visible if it is higher up on the formal organizational charts and done by few people. Those higher up in a hierarchy not only are more visible but have greater value attached to the work. It is assumed that they require more skill and have more responsibility if they tell others what to do than do those who must cooperate with others to get a job done. It is men and those with credentials who disproportionately fill the top jobs in the hierarchy. It is also men who have the power to define the work that others do.

Job descriptions for women's work are often based on formal rules and organizational charts that misrepresent or at least understate what women actually do – and are required to do – on a daily basis. Many simply fail to capture much of what women do on the job. The job descriptions for clerical workers often do not indicate that they do a great deal of management work, handle stressful phone calls, lift heavy boxes of supplies, or operate a wide variety of equipment (Statham, Miller, and O'Mauksch 1988). Yet male managers' job descriptions frequently emphasize their need for communication skills and their responsibility for both money and people. An Oregon study found that different "pictures of male and female work were implicit in different language used to describe the jobs, both in the written job composites and in the group discussions," and male jobs were described in much greater detail than were women's jobs (Acker 1989, 92).

These differences in the visibility and value of male and female jobs in care are not mere accidents of history or simply the fault of ideas about women's skills. They also reflect unequal power relations. Even though they form the overwhelming majority of providers, women have had to struggle hard against male medical dominance in health care and against assumptions made about their work. Women have enjoyed some success in having their value recognized in care. Nurses have managed to carve out a scope of practice and improve their conditions of work, demonstrating their contribution to clinical care. Ancillary workers too have made gains in protecting their jobs and conditions. Indeed, their very success may be a factor in the move to distinguish between direct and indirect care and to allow the contracting out of the latter as a means of reducing costs and increasing employer control.

PRIVATIZATION OF ANCILLARY WORK

When women clean, cook, or do laundry and clerical work in the private sector, the work is low paid and often precarious in other ways as well. The "hotel services" sector is characterized by low pay and job insecurity. Service and clerical work constitute two of the four low-wage occupational categories, and women account for two-thirds of low-wage earners (Maxwell 2002b). Employees in food and accommodation services are among those with the lowest job quality, and the quality is often low as well for those in part-time, temporary, and irregular shift employment (Hughes, Lowe, Schellenberg 2003, 22). Work in the public sector can be precarious for women doing such work (McMullen and Schellenberg 2003), but when the services are contracted out in the private sector, the degree of precariousness is likely to increase.

Research in other countries suggests that contracting out services makes work more precarious. Case studies in the United Kingdom and Northern Ireland "found that exposure to tendering led to the, often dramatic, erosion of terms and conditions of employment ... Estimates state that some 40 per cent of the NHS ancillary jobs were lost" (Sachdev 2001, 5). Moreover, the impact on women is more extensive, resulting in a widening of the gender gap. According to the Equal Opportunities Commission of Northern Ireland (1996), most work contracted out was female-dominated. The rate of female job loss was more than double that of men. While both women and men experienced wage reductions, the proportionate reduction was larger for women. Some benefits disappeared, along with some entitlements. Employers with the contracts were less likely than public sector employers to have policies that are critical for women, such as strategies to prevent sexual harassment.

Little research has been done on contracting out in Canada. The Romanow Report seems to be making its recommendations in the absence of sufficient evidence to support the move. The Canadian Union of Public Employees reports on a number of investigations by consulting firms. They indicate that laundry, food, and cleaning contracts have all resulted in few costs savings and poor working conditions. More important, contracting out may not improve quality of care and may even undermine it (Cohen 2001). In more than one case, contracting out has been reversed in favour of old forms of direct employment in the public sector. Manitoba homecare provides one example (Shapiro 1997).

Contracting out has an impact not only on those working in the firms with the contracts but also on those who remain in the public sector. In order to maintain their position, the public sector that remains is increasingly pressured to act like the contractors. The British research shows how the same practices applied by the for-profit firms were introduced in the public sector. Manual staff, which includes cleaners and caterers among others, "in particular, has borne the brunt of the changes that have been made in working methods, pay and conditions" (Walsh and Davis 1993, 163).

Not surprisingly, the contracting out strategy seems to have had an impact on the environment for care. This contracting out began more than a decade ago. Although it was supposed to improve quality while reducing costs, a "national listening exercise" by the current government indicated "the need for basic care to be reviewed." One response has been the introduction of ward housekeepers whose job it is to make "sure wards are clean, patients are fed properly and that the surroundings are well maintained and welcoming" (NHS estates 2003b). Another has been the introduction of strategies to assess and improve food and cleaning services in care. Both have been required by the failure of strategies that introduced for-profit methods in ancillary services.

METHODS AND DATA

The central social location is sex/gender and the context is the health care and social assistance industry. We map precarious wage work based on an approach initiated by Vosko, Zukewich, and Cranford (2003). This means examining a mutually exclusive typology of employment forms across several dimensions of precariousness and by several social contexts and social locations. Employment forms are broken down into four categories: full-time permanent or temporary, and part-time permanent or temporary. The key social contexts in our study include industry, occupation, and sector.

Our indicators of precarious wage work are grouped into four categories: income, social wage, regulatory protection and control, and contingency. In each category we use those indicators developed and described by Cranford and Vosko (this volume). However, given the nature of the work in the health-care and social assistance industry, we add the indicator of "poor schedule" within the category of regulatory protection and control. Poor schedule refers to night, rotating, on-call, or split-shift work. We use Statistics Canada's definition for our analysis of public and private sector employees. Here, the public sector includes all those employed by the federal, provincial, and municipal governments, along with those working in Crown corporations, liquor control boards, and other government institutions such as schools, universities, hospitals, and public libraries. The private sector includes all other employees. Self-employed persons are excluded from our sample.

Our distinction between direct and ancillary occupations within the health industry is based on the Romanow Report, which vaguely defines direct occupations as "services providing medical, diagnostic and surgical care" and ancillary occupations as "food preparation, cleaning and maintenance." Using the North American Industrial Classification System (NAICS), we have classified professional,[1] nursing, technical, social work, and clinical assisting occupations within direct occupations; and food services, cleaning, sales, protective services, clerical, child-care, and home-support occupations within ancillary occupations. We believe we are making a conservative estimate of those occupations that might face the consequences of the commission's proposals because some occupations we have classified as direct might be regarded as ancillary, though they were not specified within the report.

The NAICS presents an important challenge for profiling ancillary occupations in the health industry. When ancillary services are contracted out, they are usually classified under an industry other than health. For example, contracted food services are likely to fall within the accommodation and food services industry rather than health care and social assistance. Although workers in these contracted out services may continue to work at a worksite providing health care, their employer may no longer be the health-care establishment but some other establishment in another industry.[2] In order to work around this challenge, we compare ancillary occupations in the health industry with the same occupations grouped in all other industries. The occupations grouped in other industries serve as our proxy for ancillary occupations that have been contracted out, even though we lack confirmation of whether workers in these occupations are working at health-care sites. This shortcoming of the research results presented here, as well as how the data are categorized by Statistics Canada more generally, warrants further review but goes beyond the scope of this chapter.

Our data are derived from the results of custom tabulations from the 2000 Statistics Canada Survey of Labour and Income Dynamics (SLID). In using this survey, we made tradeoffs in terms of sample size and the availability of certain variables for analysis. The SLID provides excellent detail for our indicators of precarious wage work. Ideally, we would have preferred to look at employment form by indicators of precarious wage work throughout our analysis, following the method developed by Cranford and Vosko (this volume). However, sample sizes are often too small to provide reliable estimates for workers in the health-care industry when these workers are examined in terms of the mutually exclusive typology of employment forms *and* the indicators of precariousness. Consequently, our results and analysis are based on a method that separates out employment form from the indicators of precariousness.

GENDER, PRIVATIZATION, AND PRECARIOUS WORK IN ANCILLARY WORK

There are many different types of jobs in health care, ranging from professional occupations such as physicians to ancillary or support service occupations such as clerical, food service, cleaning, and maintenance. Women dominate in nearly all occupations in health care. Overall, they represent over 80 per cent of workers in the industry. However, there are important variations in the proportions of men and women in different occupations. Women form the overwhelming majority of workers in nursing, clerical, and home-support occupations, while men form above average proportions of workers in professional, managerial, maintenance, food service, and cleaning occupations. Important differences in levels of precariousness relate to the gendered segregation in health care. For example, physicians may encounter high levels of precariousness in terms of work arrangements. However, workers in other occupations such as clerical and home-support services are also precarious along dimensions of income, job security, and benefits. In all occupations, women are disproportionately precarious, although their concentrations in certain occupations contribute to their overall precariousness in the industry.

We begin with a general overview of precariousness in the health-care and social assistance industry. In this analysis we use the combined category of health and social services because their boundaries are unclear and work often overlaps. For example, some provinces administer homecare under social services, while others do so under health ministries. We will use the term health-care industry to refer to this Statistics Canada category in order to make the text more readable. After the overview of the industry, we turn to our comparison of sector and occupation within the industry. We conclude with a comparison of ancillary occupations in health care and the same occupations in other industries.

Figure 5.1 compares the precariousness experienced by men and women within the health-care industry with that experienced by men and women in other industries. Along many of the indicators, both men and women appear less precarious than their counterparts in other industries. However, there are a few instances in which these health and social services workers are more precarious. While women in these industries do better in comparison to women employed elsewhere, they do less well in comparison to men in other industries. For example, a majority of women have dental and extended health coverage, but considerably more men in the health-care industry have such coverage. Both men and women in health care are more likely to have a

Figure 5.1
Indicators of precarious wage work by industry and by sex, Canada, 2000

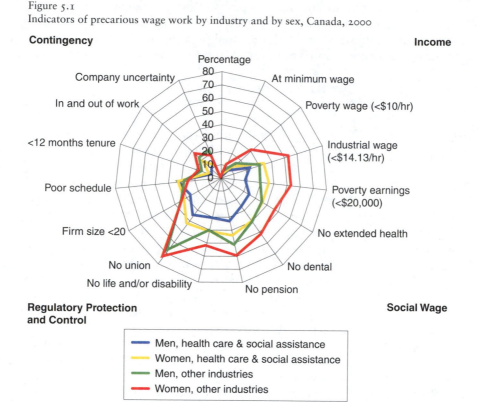

Contingency   **Income**

Regulatory Protection and Control   **Social Wage**

— Men, health care & social assistance
— Women, health care & social assistance
— Men, other industries
— Women, other industries

poor schedule than men and women in other industries, pointing in part to the nature of work in the health-care industry. The need for shift work accounts for some, but not all, of this difference.

The measure of union coverage indicates an even larger gap, this one in favour of health-care workers. Both women and men employed in health care are much more likely to be unionized than those in other industries. For men in health care, this higher rate of unionization correlates with a greater likelihood of extended health, dental, pension, and life and/or disability benefit coverage. The same cannot be said for women in health care and social assistance. While women in health care do have more benefits than women in other industries and their rates of unionization are much higher than for either men or women in other industries, their social wage coverage is quite close to that of men in other industries. These results suggest that the health-care industry is, in general, a less precarious industry to work in for men than for women. However, both men and women in other industries tend to experience higher levels of precariousness overall. In other words, working in this industry is better for both women and men.

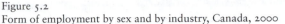

Figure 5.2
Form of employment by sex and by industry, Canada, 2000

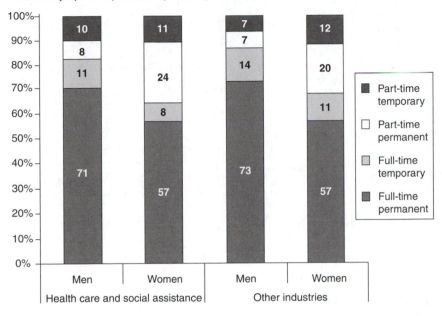

What this figure does not show, and what we aim to uncover in the following set of results, is the substantial variability in experiences of precariousness within the health sector, particularly when we layer on form of employment and social contexts such as sector (private/public) and occupation (direct/ancillary). To uncover this variability, we begin with layering the mutually exclusive typology of form of employment.

In comparing men and women in health care with those in other industries (figure 5.2), we find that women in health care are more likely to work in part-time permanent employment (24%) than their female counterparts in other industries (20%). Women in both health care and social assistance and other industries are nearly equally distributed in part-time temporary (11–12%). Men in health care are also more concentrated in part-time forms than men in other industries. Looking only at health-care employees, we find less full-time permanent employment among women (57%) than among men (71%) within this industry. How then, we ask, do these forms in health care and social assistance compare along dimensions of precariousness?

Full-time permanent employees within the health-care industry are less precarious than employees in other forms along almost all the indicators (figure 5.3). Part-time permanent, full-time temporary, and part-time temporary employees are more precarious along several dimensions compared with their full-time permanent counterparts.

Figure 5.3
Indicators of precarious wage work by form of employment within health care and social assistance, Canada, 2000

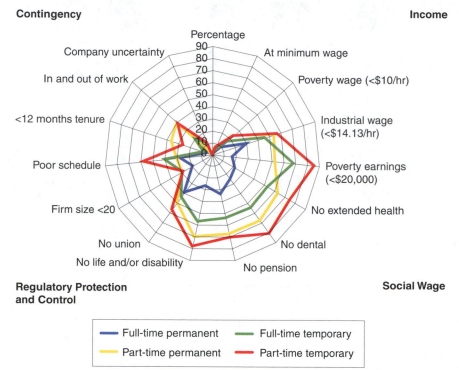

Contingency   **Income**

Regulatory Protection   **Social Wage**
and Control

— Full-time permanent   — Full-time temporary
— Part-time permanent   — Part-time temporary

Not surprisingly, the most precarious employees in the health-care industry are full- and part-time temporary employees, with part-time temporary employees being exceptionally precarious along several dimensions. Specifically, employees in these more precarious forms are less likely to receive extended health, dental, pension, and life and/or disability benefits than full-time permanent employees. For example, while only 22 per cent of full-time permanent employees do not have extended health coverage, 64 per cent of full-time temporary, 53 per cent of part-time permanent, and 75 per cent of part-time temporary employees lack this coverage. Similar results are observed for dental coverage. Only 25 per cent of full-time permanent employees do not have dental coverage, while 68 per cent of full-time temporary, 55 per cent of part-time permanent, and 81 per cent of part-time temporary lack dental coverage. Employees in these more precarious forms are also less likely to be covered by a collective agreement and more likely to work in small workplaces, have job tenure of less than one year, and have a poor schedule than their full-time permanent counterparts. A shift to temporary employment leads to precariousness on all measures, not only those pertaining to job security.

Approximately 50 per cent of workers in the health-care industry work in the public sector. With ongoing privatization in the industry, however, more of these workers are moving to the private sector. Women in the private sector are more likely to work in part-time permanent employment than women in the public sector, at 27 per cent and 21 per cent, respectively. Moreover, women in the private sector are less likely to have full-time permanent employment than men in the private sector and both women and men in the public sector. Specifically, only 53 per cent of women health-care and social assistance employees in the private sector have full-time employment, as compared to 67 per cent of men in the private sector, 61 per cent of women in the public sector, and 73 per cent of men in the public sector. We find that male health-care and social assistance employees working in the public sector are the most sheltered from working in the forms that are associated with greater precariousness. However, women in the public sector are less sheltered from working in the precarious forms and have greater concentrations in these forms than men in the private sector. In comparing all groups, those most likely to work in the forms associated with greater precariousness are women in the private sector (figure 5.4).

In comparing men and women health-care employees in the public sector with men and women in the private sector along dimensions of precariousness, we find that both men and women in the public sector are significantly less likely to experience precariousness along almost all indicators. The only instances in which public sector workers are more likely to be precarious than private sector workers are in the cases of poor schedule and moving in and out of work. For example, 38 per cent of women health-care workers in the public sector have poor schedules, compared with 27 per cent of women in the private sector.

The most dramatic differences in levels of precariousness are observed along dimensions of social wage and regulatory protection and control. Health-care workers in the private sector are significantly more likely to lack access to social wage benefits such as dental, extended health, pension, and life and/or disability coverage. In particular, women in the private sector are the most precarious along these social wage dimensions. For example, 51 per cent of women in the private sector lack extended health coverage, compared to 37 per cent of men in the private sector, 20 per cent of women in the public sector, and 18 per cent of men in the public sector. Pension coverage is especially polarized between the private and the public sectors. Among workers in the private sector, 67 per cent of women and 55 per cent of men lack pension coverage, while only 20 per cent of women and 21 per cent of men in the public sector lack this coverage. A similar pattern is observed with union coverage, where unionization rates are approximately twice as high in the public sector. The least precarious workers along this dimension are women health-care and social assistance workers

Figure 5.4
Indicators of precarious wage work by sector and by sex within health care and social
assistance, Canada, 2000

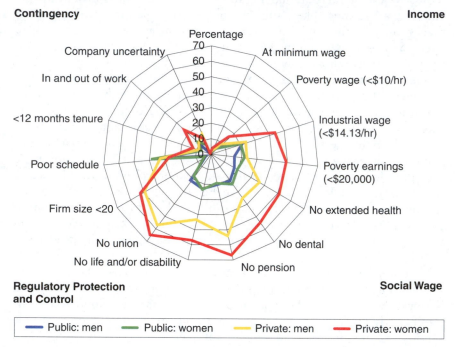

in the public sector, where 82 per cent are unionized. Men in the public sector are only slightly less unionized, at 79 per cent. The rate for men in the
private sector with union coverage is 43 per cent. The most precarious are
women in the private sector, where only 34 per cent are unionized.

With regard to income indicators, women in the private sector are especially precarious – and far more likely to be precarious than their male counterparts. For example, approximately 24 per cent of men in the private sector
earn at or below the industrial wage and have earnings below the poverty
cutoff, while among women in the private sector, 44 per cent earn below the
industrial wage and 49 per cent have earnings below the poverty cut-off.

Results described above indicate that men and women in the public sector
have very similar patterns in terms of precariousness along nearly all dimensions. Meanwhile, men and women in the private sector show greater dissimi-
larity along several dimensions, especially those pertaining to income, social
wage, and regulatory protection and control. In each of these cases, women in
the private sector are significantly more likely to be precarious than their male
counterparts. Critically, these findings suggest that the public sector helps to
mitigate precariousness for women and reduces sex/gender inequality.

After considering sector, we now layer in occupation. In particular, we aim to look closely at the ancillary occupations that the Romanow Report suggests are suitable for privatization. Knowing that public sector workers experience significantly less precariousness than private sector workers in the health-care industry, we aim to uncover both the current state of precariousness among ancillary workers and the likely state post privatization.

Direct occupations account for approximately 65 per cent of all occupations in health care, and ancillary occupations account for 35 per cent. Women dominate in both direct and ancillary occupations, but they form a larger proportion of the employees in ancillary than in direct. In particular, women represent 82 per cent of employees in direct occupations in health care and 88 per cent of employees in ancillary occupations. Where women form the smallest proportion relative to men is in professional occupations, at 55 per cent women and 45 per cent men. Not surprisingly, women account for very large proportions of workers among nursing (direct occupation) and among secretaries and clerical, child-care, and home-support occupations (ancillary occupations). In each of these examples, women account for more than 90 per cent of workers. If ancillary occupations are privatized, the impact on women workers will be disproportionate owing to their significant shares in these occupations.

We turn now to an exploration of how precariousness among ancillary workers compares with that experienced by direct workers within health care. Ancillary workers are less likely to have full-time permanent employment than direct workers. Among ancillary workers, 54 per cent have full-time permanent employment. In contrast, 60 per cent of direct workers work in full-time permanent employment. Ancillary workers are more likely to work in full-time temporary and part-time permanent employment than their counterparts in direct occupations. Among ancillary workers, 10 per cent are employed in full-time temporary jobs, compared to only 7 per cent of workers in direct occupations. At the same time, 25 per cent of ancillary workers work in part-time permanent positions, compared to 22 per cent of direct workers. There are no differences in the rates of participation in part-time temporary, where the average is approximately 11–12 per cent for all groups of workers. In general, these findings indicate that workers in direct occupations in health care are less likely concentrated in the precarious forms.

When we compare men and women in ancillary and in direct occupations in health care, we find that workers in direct occupations are less precarious along several dimensions than workers in ancillary occupations (figure 5.5). Moreover, there are important differences between men and women in each type of occupation. For instance, women in direct occupations are more precarious than men in direct occupations along several dimensions. Women in ancillary occupations are the most precarious among all groups of workers for all indicators except those pertaining to work arrangements.

Figure 5.5
Indicators of precarious wage work by direct and ancillary occupations and by sex, within health care and social assistance, Canada, 2000

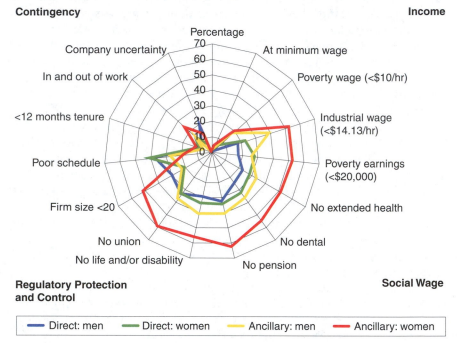

With regard to income, there is a significant difference in the level of precariousness experienced by women in direct occupations as compared to women in ancillary occupations. For example, 53 per cent of women in ancillary occupations have earnings below the poverty cut-off, compared to only 29 per cent of women in direct occupations. Similar disparities exist between workers in direct occupations and workers in ancillary occupations in terms of social wage and regulatory protection and control. For example, among women ancillary workers, 52 per cent do not have extended health coverage, 55 per cent do not have dental coverage, 63 per cent do not have pension coverage, and 60 per cent do not have union coverage. The least precarious workers are men in direct occupations, among whom only 24 per cent lack extended health coverage, 25 per cent lack dental coverage, 33 per cent lack pension coverage, and 34 per cent lack coverage by a collective agreement. In each of these cases, the rate of precariousness among female ancillary workers is approximately double that for male direct workers.

In general, there is slightly less difference between men and women in direct occupations than there is for men and women in ancillary occupations. This distinction suggests that direct occupations help to alleviate precariousness for

Figure 5.6
Indicators of precarious wage work by type of ancillary occupation within health care and
social assistance, women only, Canada, 2000

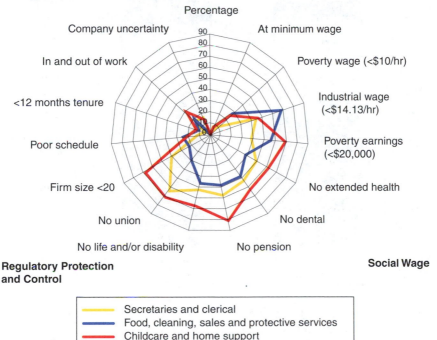

women and to reduce sex/gender inequality. These results parallel to some degree our results for sector, although the public sector diminishes sex/gender inequality to a greater extent than do direct occupations versus ancillary
occupations.

We see from the discussion above that there are significant differences
along dimensions of precariousness between direct and ancillary occupations in the health-care and social assistance industry. We now consider differences within ancillary occupations.

In comparing women in our three groupings of ancillary occupations (figure 5.6), we find that the two occupations in which women form the largest
proportion of workers – secretaries and clerical and child-care and home-
support occupations – are significantly more precarious along several dimensions than food, cleaning, sales, and protective services, where men form a
larger than average proportion. The latter group of workers has very high
levels of unionization within the health-care industry. Relative to the two

Figure 5.7
Form of employment by food services and cleaning occupations and by industry,
Canada, 2000

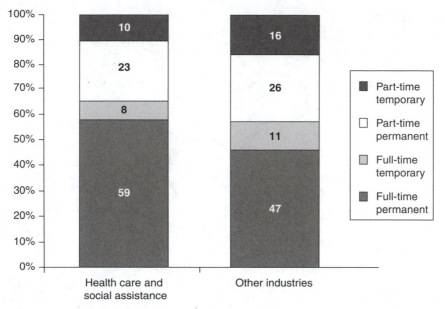

other ancillary groups, the group composed of food, cleaning, sales, and protective services fares quite well along dimensions of social wage.

From the above results, we still lack a clear portrait of the food services
and cleaning occupations that have been contracted out or otherwise privatized. As already stated, when these services are contracted out, it is im-
probable that they will continue to be classified within health care. Instead,
these workers are likely be classified within the accommodation and food
services industry or another industry within NAICS. Hence, in order to get a
sense of the precariousness experienced by these services post privatization,
we compare ancillary occupations within health care with the occupational
groupings of the same name in other industries.

Figure 5.7 exhibits one example of a comparison of ancillary occupations
within health care and social assistance with the same occupational groupings in other industries. This figure shows form of employment for food services and cleaning workers within health care and within other industries.
Keeping in mind that ancillary occupations grouped within "other industries" serve as our proxy for ancillary occupations that have been contracted
out and/or privatized, we find that food and cleaning services workers within
health care are more likely, on average, to have full-time permanent employment than their counterparts in other industries (59% versus 47%). Food

Figure 5.8
Indicators of precarious wage work by industry and by sex, ancillary occupations only,
Canada, 2000

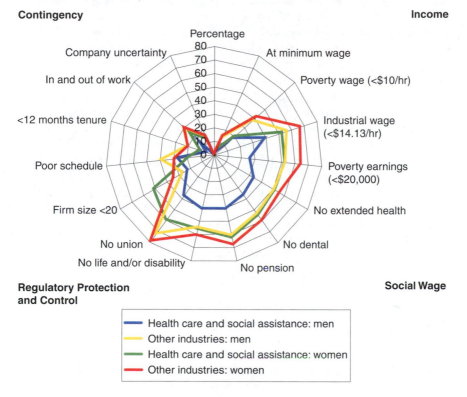

and cleaning services in other industries are more likely to be concentrated in the precarious forms such as full-time temporary, part-time permanent, and part-time temporary. Among food and cleaning services workers in other industries, 11 per cent work in full-time temporary employment, compared with only 8 per cent in health care and social assistance. Among these workers in other industries, 26 per cent work in part-time permanent jobs and 16 per cent work in part-time temporary jobs, compared with 23 per cent of health-care and social assistance workers in part-time permanent and 10 per cent in part-time temporary.

A comparison of grouped ancillary occupations within health care and within other industries reveals that men and women in ancillary occupations in health care are less precarious along several dimensions than their counterparts in other industries (figure 5.8). Workers in ancillary occupations in other industries show exceptionally high levels of precariousness along dimensions of income, social wage, regulatory protection, and control. In particular, these workers in other industries have a very high likelihood of earning the minimum wage, with 13 per cent of men and 15 per cent of women experiencing precariousness along this indicator. This figure is compared with negligible rates for men and 4 per cent of women within the health-care industry.

With regard to social wage dimensions, 56 per cent of women and 51 per cent of men in other industries lack extended health coverage, compared to the 52 per cent of women and 34 per cent of men in health care who lack such coverage. A similar pattern is observed for dental coverage, pension coverage, and union coverage. Interestingly, women ancillary workers in health care are far more likely to work in small firms than are men in health care and both men and women in other industries. Over all industries generally, women are the most likely to work in small workplaces, with men in health care being the least likely to work in small workplaces. This result suggests that whatever precariousness is associated with small workplaces may be offset when these workplaces are located in the health-care industries, since women ancillary workers in this industry fare better along several dimensions than women in other industries.

In general, figure 5.8 indicates where we might anticipate seeing both male and female ancillary workers face increased precariousness after privatization. In using the same groupings of occupations in other industries as our proxy for ancillary services that have been contracted out, we see higher levels of overall precariousness both along dimensions of precariousness and within form of employment.

FINDINGS: PRECARIOUSNESS AMONG ANCILLARY WORKERS BEFORE AND AFTER PRIVATIZATION

Beginning with the health-care industry as a whole, we find that workers in health care tend to be less precarious along most dimensions than workers in other industries. However, workers in health care tend to be more precarious along dimensions of work arrangements, in part because some of the work at least requires shifts. Delving within the health-care industry, we find substantial variability in terms of precariousness within the industry. We also find that sector and occupation are central social contexts that correlate to this variability. Employment in the public sector helps to mitigate precariousness for women and to reduce sex/gender inequality compared to the private sector.

Similar results are observed in comparing direct occupations with ancillary occupations, with the former having a comparable effect on sex/gender inequality. Overall, ancillary occupations within health care are associated with some of the highest levels of precariousness on several dimensions, even before contracting out. Gender is central here, as more women are concentrated in ancillary occupations, although women dominate in both direct and ancillary occupations. Looking specifically at ancillary occupations, we find the highest levels of precariousness in the occupations in which women form the highest proportions – among secretaries and clerical occupations and in child-care and home-support occupations.

The most dramatic results in terms of levels of precariousness are observed in our comparison of ancillary workers in health care with workers in the same occupations in other industries. We find that workers in these occupations in other industries are the most precarious along several dimensions and, in general, are significantly more precarious than ancillary workers in health care. These results suggest what we might anticipate for ancillary workers in health care in terms of precariousness after privatization.

Several methodological limitations arose from our examination of precariousness among ancillary workers in health care whose jobs have been contracted out. In particular, owing to the NAICS classification scheme for workers, we were unable to compare ancillary workers who have been contracted out directly with those in the public sector. We also encountered problems with small sample sizes. Hence, we restructured our analysis in order to work our way towards a portrait of how ancillary workers in health care fare in terms of precariousness once they are contracted out, but it remains a limited portrayal nonetheless.

CONCLUSION

The distinction drawn between ancillary and direct services in the Romanow Report differentiates the connection each has to health care and underestimates both the skilled nature of ancillary work and the potential negative consequences of contracting out these services. Women dominate in both ancillary and direct occupations. It is therefore women who will be the most negatively affected by privatization. Meanwhile, much of women's skilled work in health care remains invisible. No mention is made in the Romanow Report of women's role in ancillary services, even though gender is critical in understanding the nature of this work. Our research indicates that ancillary work in health care is distinct from what is considered comparable work in other industries. Comparisons between the two minimize the unique characteristics and outcomes of this work within health care. The risks of poor quality in health care are high, speaking to the importance of skill and to the potential negative implications for both workers' and patients' health if health-care work becomes increasingly precarious.

In our mapping of the mutually exclusive typology of employment forms across several dimensions of precariousness, we find substantial variability in the prevalence of precariousness within the health-care industry. Important differences are observed in relation to sex, occupation, and sector. Public sector and direct employees in health care are found to be less precarious than private sector and ancillary employees. Moreover, there is less sex/gender inequality among public sector and direct employees than among private sector and ancillary employees. In general, our findings suggest that women will be disproportionately affected by the privatization of ancillary jobs. This mapping approach deepens our understanding of the gendered nature of precariousness among health-care workers, the relationship of precariousness to occupation and sector, and some of the potential consequences of privatization for ancillary jobs.

PART TWO

Precarious Health at Work and Precarious Work in an Unhealthy Public Sector

The Hidden Costs of Precarious Employment: Health and the Employment Relationship

WAYNE LEWCHUK, ALICE DE WOLFF,
ANDREW KING, AND MICHAEL POLANYI

This chapter contributes to an understanding of the nature of precarious employment and its broader social implications, with an emphasis on its impact on health. It reports findings of a survey exploring connections between the employment relationship, the organization of work, and workers' health. A number of studies have shown the high risks of ill health associated with precarious employment. This chapter develops a new concept – "employment strain" – to examine how precarious employment relationships affect workers' health.

EMPLOYMENT RELATIONSHIPS AND HEALTH

The point of departure in this chapter is the Karasek Job Demand-Control model and the concept of "job strain" (Karasek 1979; Karasek and Theorell 1990). This approach to wage work and health examines risks associated with the organization of work, focusing attention at the level of the workplace. According to Karasek, workers are exposed to "job strain" when their jobs are characterized by high demands and low levels of control over how work is performed. Numerous studies find that "job strain" leads to exhaustion, depression, lower job satisfaction, and, ultimately, to stress-related illness, including cardiovascular disease. Karasek and Theorell (1990, 6) find that the incidence of heart disease is most prevalent among workers in low control–high-workload occupations. An analysis of British mortality data attributes an occupation-based social gradient in the incidence of heart disease among men to differences in work organization and levels of control (Marmot 2000). Another series of studies finds that chronic exposure to "job strain" increases blood pressure (Laflamme et al. 1998; Landsbergis et al. 1994; Schnall et al. 1992; Schnall et al. 1998). In their review of the literature, Belkic et al. (2000) conclude that "job strain" increases the incidence of heart disease.

"Job strain" captures mainly those dimensions of the control-demand-support trilogy that are associated with production processes: tasks tied directly to the production of goods and services. The Job Demand-Control model does not consider seriously links between health and the employment relationship itself – how people acquire work, how they keep work, and how they negotiate the terms and conditions of work. A fuller appreciation of the health effects of the employment relationship will lead to a deeper understanding of the links between work organization and health outcomes and the occupation-based social health gradient.[1]

This chapter is not alone in pointing to limitations of the "job strain" framework and the need to develop a relational analysis, one considering the social relations surrounding employment relationships themselves (de Jonge et al. 1999 and 2000; National Institute for Occupational Safety and Health 2002; Scott 2004; Sparks and Cooper 1999; Wall et al. 1995 and 1996). Cooper argues that "the psychological contract between employer and worker in terms of 'reasonably permanent employment for work well done [is] truly being undermined by the spread of outsourcing and the rise of a flexible workforce" (Cooper 2002, 355). He calls for models that incorporate the shift towards atypical employment contracts – common among workers in precarious employment – or a "short-term contract culture." However, his suggestion that the rise of this "contract culture" may actually give workers more control of their working life requires empirical scrutiny.

Karasek developed his analysis in the early 1970s in a world where, at least for most white men, the standard employment relationship was the norm (Vosko, this volume). The notion of "job strain" assumes a standard employment relationship and, at the same time, fails to take into account the range of possible strains associated with the employment relationship itself. Cooper's analysis of the "short-term contract culture" uses a limited notion of control, focusing narrowly on control over a production process. This focus enables him to suggest that atypical employment contracts may have positive health effects on workers because many may find it easier to refuse less desirable work assignments, or because, in the case of the self-employed and those working at home, they are freer to organize how they work in the absence of direct supervision. (For a related discussion of "control" as a dimension of precarious employment, see Cranford and Vosko, this volume.)

However, to suggest that workers in general have more control in this new "contract culture" is to misunderstand the nature of many forms of employment exhibiting dimensions of precariousness. This suggestion, moreover, underestimates the gains workers won in struggles to establish the bundle of elements that make up the standard employment relationship as a norm – specifically, the types of control that it extends to workers. Conditions at the beginning of the 20th century were so harsh that unions organized for more stable employment and "living wages." These struggles led to enforceable legal collective agreements and social protections that defined social entitlements and rights to continuing employment, decent working conditions, seniority, retirement support, and a process for renegotiating terms and conditions – key aspects of control tied to the standard employment relationship. Strong unions, especially in large workplaces, and a broad public understanding that stability created a platform for high-productivity workplaces, a robust economy, and healthy families and communities led employers and governments to retain the standard employment relationship as a norm until the early 1980s. Until the last two decades of the 20th century, economic and social policies pivoted on and upheld the standard employment relationship (Fudge and Vosko 2001a and 2001b).

Workers in precarious employment normally hold atypical employment contracts and lack a full range of social protections and entitlements. Labour victories around the "living wage" were constructed around the norm of a nuclear family with a male wage earner and a female caregiver who was not expected to participate in the paid labour market. Gains were enjoyed mainly by full-time permanent employees. Workers moving between jobs were not seen as part of the real labour force. These assumptions contributed to a system where most workers in precarious employment lack rights codified into a legally enforceable contract, have fewer rights in the system of labour market regulations, and have weaker protections under existing health and safety laws.

Since the mid-1980s, more mid-career men in the industrial sector, as well as women of all ages, recent immigrants, and youth, have become precarious workers (this volume, Bernstein; Cranford and Vosko; Vosko and Zukewich). This growth is a predictable outcome of employment strategies and policies of both private sector employers and governments seeking flexibility and new ways of controlling costs (Herzenberg, Alice, and Wial 1998). Together, business and governments have restructured employment so that increasing numbers of workers are "free agents" in a weakly regulated labour market. They have created a climate where employers have permission to break the implicit and explicit agreements associated with standard employment relationships, just as they have created new levels of uncertainty for workers who must continually search for work and renegotiate the terms and conditions of employment. Further, through exclusions from social and labour protections, governments and employers are downloading many of the costs associated with production, and the costs of social reproduction (medical benefits, family-related leaves, pensions, unemployment insurance, etc.) on workers (see, for example, Armstrong and Laxer, this volume).

Understanding the health effects of precarious employment requires a re-focus on the employment relationship. All employment relationships create health risks. Yet studies that take the standard employment relationship as the norm have not made these risks visible. Simply by showing up to work, workers in standard employment relationships have a degree of control over whether they will be employed the next day and the terms and conditions of their future employment. If their workplace is unionized, they may have some control over which job they do, based on seniority rights, as well as the right to participate in setting wage and benefit levels and even a say in how work is organized. The absence of many of these rights among workers in precarious employment suggests a possible contributor to work and health outcomes, one that is fundamentally different from the production process-based pathway outlined by Karasek.

Health and Safety in Precarious Employment

A sizeable body of literature suggests that many, but not all, workers in precarious employment are at risk of higher work-related injury or illness (Benavides and Benach 2000; Cameron 2001; Quinlan and Mayhew 1999). This literature highlights the need for an analysis that takes into account a range of factors across many forms of employment characterized by dimensions of precarious employment.

Quinlan (1999) identifies increased risks of injury and illness in related labour market contexts: outsourcing/self-employment and home/tele-work; labour shedding and growth of small business; and temporary and part-time labour. He proposes that higher risks are associated with three causal factors: economic and reward factors (competition, long hours, piecework, etc.); disorganization (ambiguity of rules, splintering occupational health and safety management systems, etc.); and increased likelihood that laws do not apply to these employment relationships.

In 2001, Quinlan, Mayhew, and Bohle reviewed 93 health and safety studies. Seventy-six of these studies established connections between precarious employment and poor health. Workers in outsourced/home-based work, downsized firms, small businesses, and temporary employment experience negative health and safety outcomes. In European studies, Dauba-Letourneux and Thebaud-Mony (2002) find that precarious employment results in more ergonomic risks, heavier workloads, and greater exposure to toxic substances, while Goudswaard and Andries (2002) find no greater exposure to noise, vibrations, and temperature hazards.

The European Foundation for the Improvement of Living and Working Conditions (EFILWC) conducted three waves of surveys in 1991, 1996, and 2000 with approximately 1,500 workers in each of the 15 member states of the European Union. This research found that specific dimensions of precarious employment are associated with poor health outcomes (Benach, Gimeno, and Benavides 2002; Dauba-Letourneux and Thebaud-Mony 2002; Goudswaard and Andries 2002). For example, workers in non-permanent work (i.e., lacking certainty of ongoing work) report lower levels of job satisfaction than permanent workers (Benach, Gimeno, and Benavides 2002). The self-employed report more back pain, muscular pain, and fatigue than those in wage work. Workers on full-time fixed-term contracts report high levels of back pain and fatigue, and small employers (those employing fewer that 15 workers) report high levels of fatigue and stress. Interestingly, non-permanent workers, in general, report *lower* levels of stress and *less* absenteeism than permanent workers do. EFIWLC's studies suggest that workers in forms of employment exhibiting dimensions of precariousness experience marginally more unhealthy working conditions, higher levels of job insecurity, lower levels of control over their working conditions and work arrangements, and poorer-quality social interactions than their full-time permanent counterparts.

Two sets of observations are particularly interesting here. Goudswaard and Andries (2002) and Parker et al. (2002) argue that less control, but also fewer demands, are characteristic of some forms of precarious employment compared to full-time permanent wage work. Quinlan, Mayhew, and Bohle 2001 suggest that considering dimensions of precariousness in an expanded job control concept may help account for findings that economic and reward factors, disorganization, and failure of the regulatory system are not equally relevant to all groups of workers in precarious employment.

EMPLOYMENT STRAIN:
MODELLING THE IMPACT OF PRECARIOUS
EMPLOYMENT ON HEALTH

The production process and the employment relationship affect the health of all workers. The health impact of the production process includes job strain and exposures to typical health risks at work, including exposure to toxic substances and biomechanical risks. This chapter argues that measures of the health impact of the employment relationship should be added to the broader analysis, and that they should include the extent of uncertainty over access to work and its terms and conditions, high wage variance, effort related to balancing multiple jobs, and effort searching for and maintaining work.[2] It uses the concept "employment strain" in developing a relational analysis of the health impacts of precarious employment. There are four components of employment strain: employment relationship uncertainty (control), employment relationship workload, employment relationship support, and household insecurity. While these measures are related to the components of Karasek's "job strain," they are not substitutes for them.

Employment Relationship Uncertainty

Employment relationship uncertainty is the control dimension of employment strain. It is related to control over access to work, where work is performed, the work schedule, and the degree of influence over setting the terms and conditions of work. It has three components: employment uncertainty, earnings uncertainty, and scheduling uncertainty. High levels of uncertainty indicate low levels of control.

Employment uncertainty measures the level of control over future employment and, hence, the extent to which employment is regularly renegotiated. The following indicators make up this construct: perceived uncertainty about whether current employers will offer more work, average contract length, and the extent to which discrimination and favouritism are factors in getting future work. *Earnings uncertainty* measures the level of control over future earnings. It emerges from the following questions: whether the worker can predict future earnings, the existence of written pay records, whether unemployment insurance and state pension contributions are deducted from earnings, whether workers are paid when they are sick, whether they are paid on time, and whether they have disability insurance and pension entitlements. *Scheduling uncertainty* measures the control workers have over when and where they will work. It is constructed from three questions: the length of advance notice of work schedules, hours to be worked, and work location.

Employment Relationship Workload

Employment relationship workload is the effort dimension of employment strain: it measures the effort required to find work, to balance the demands associated with multiple places of work and multiple employers, and to keep work. Workers in precarious employment are likely to have to travel to multiple places of work, to adapt to new co-workers and supervisors on a regular basis, and to face continual evaluation of their attitude and performance as a condition of being offered more work. They may also be more vulnerable to harassment and discrimination at work as a result of the temporary nature of their relationship with employers and co-workers. Employment relationship workload has three components: effort expended in finding work, in balancing the demands of multiple employers, and in keeping work.

Effort expended finding work measures the time spent looking for work. *Effort expended balancing the demands of multiple employers* measures the workload related to having more than one employer or workplace. This construct combines questions measuring the number of employers, supervisors, and work locations; unpaid time spent travelling between jobs; frequency of working with new sets of co-workers and in unfamiliar locations; and conflicts arising from having multiple employers or work locations. *Effort expended keeping work* measures the energy expended in keeping work when the employment relationship is temporary. The influence of evaluations of attitude and performance on the offer of more work and on the kinds of work assigned, the experiences of harassment and discrimination, as well as the frequency of being asked to do things unrelated to work are all part of this indicator.

Employment Relationship Support

Employment relationship support includes many of the same factors as the ISO-strain (social isolated and high strain occupations) version of support (Johnson 1991). For workers in precarious employment, the degree of uncertainty of continuing work may affect levels of support. Employment relationship support relates to the availability of help with a job, assistance if a worker is stressed, the presence of a union, and, if so, whether it provides sufficient support.

Household Insecurity

Precarious employment is often characterized by low wages and high variability in income levels over time. For workers in such positions, it may be difficult to satisfy not only their basic needs but also those of dependent household members. To capture how precarious employment shapes households, the construct *household insecurity* considers workers' individual and household earnings, household benefit coverage (drug, medical, dental, eye, life), and the presence of children 18 or younger in the household. Low levels of household insecurity may buffer a worker from the low control levels and high workload associated with the particular employment relationship; however, as Vosko and Zukewich (this volume) illustrate, this buffer may simultaneously foster gendered dependencies. Yet where household benefit coverage is low, workers unsure of their ability to provide basic economic needs may find it more difficult to deal with work-related health risks.

EMPLOYMENT STRAIN AMONG FOUR GROUPS OF WORKERS IN PRECARIOUS FORMS OF EMPLOYMENT

The analysis that follows is based on a survey of 404 workers conducted in 2002–3. Ninety per cent of these workers were engaged in precarious forms of employment, defined as fixed-term contracts, part-time wage work, and solo self-employment (for illustrations of the continua of precarious employment evident among wage workers and the self-employed, respectively, see Cranford and Vosko, this volume; Vosko and Zukewich, this volume). Workers responded to a fixed response self-administered survey designed to measure the components of employment strain described above, other work organization characteristics, and health outcomes. Questions on employment strain were developed for this project. Questions on job strain and health outcomes were taken from an existing survey used by members of the research team investigating the impact of work organization on health among full-time permanent workers employed in the manufacturing sector. These questions, and others identical to those in the National Health Population Survey, allow for future comparisons.[3]

One of the difficulties with this research was finding a sample of workers in precarious employment. It took researchers two years to construct this sample, drawing on contacts developed through community and worker-based agencies in Toronto. The resulting sample is not large, but it is sufficient to tell us an important story about working conditions and to suggest that the question of employment strain needs to be further explored in more extensive studies. It is also not random: it is a purposive sample made up of workers from three well-defined sectors, including homecare workers, university workers, community workers, and a diverse group of workers drawn from a variety of sectors, many of whom find work through a variety of channels such as temporary agencies, public employment agencies, and personal contacts. Within these sectors, the sample is representative of urban precariousness as a whole.[4] Response rates varied significantly across the different sectors, reflecting the different distribution strategies. The response rate was near 100 per cent in the homecare sector, 60 per cent in the diverse sector, just over 13 per cent in the community workers sector, and 7.4 per cent in the university sector. The overall response rate was 18.8 per cent.

The outreach strategy drew in a group of full-time permanent workers from three of the four sectors (university, community, diverse). This sample of workers is taken as a point of comparison in the analysis. A limitation of this strategy is that the comparison group has a different sectoral composition than the rest of the sample; the university sector is overweighted, and the other three categories are underweighted. The analysis nevertheless uses the full-time permanent category as a benchmark in measuring employment strain, since the level of employment strain experienced by full-time permanent workers is unlikely to be affected by sector. Using the full-time results as a benchmark for traditional workplace risks is riskier, since physical risks and job strain are likely to vary considerably by sector. Relative measures for these risks are set out below, but they should be interpreted with caution. The resulting sample is described in table 6.1.

Table 6.1
Survey Respondents (n = 404)

Respondents	HC	U	C	DIV	FT
Total number	131	94	23	107	49
average age	49.3	35.4	35.2	35.6	40.0
% age under 25	0.8	26.6	34.8	11.3	8.3
% female	94.6	75.5	87.0	50.9	71.4
% white	81.1	80.7	60.9	47.2	73.5
% lived in Canada less than 10 years	3.9	10.6	13.0	28.3	14.3
% highest education level some university or degree	7.7	79.8	26.1	47.6	32.7
% full time students	1.6	27.8	22.8	7.7	0.0

HC Homecare; U University; C Community; DIV Diverse; FT Full-time

Characteristics of the Sectors

The homecare workers surveyed belong to two unions. The majority worked for one non-profit employer. Most worked in the suburbs and rural areas surrounding Toronto in situations where they were assigned clients on a weekly or daily basis, many of whom were disabled or seniors. About one-quarter of the workers were on call full time and had preferential access to future work. The remainder worked part time. On-call full-time workers were excluded from the full-time category, as they were not guaranteed future work hours or pay.[5] The actual hours of work, for both full-time and part-time homecare workers, were scheduled with minimal advance notice. Most had been in part-time or full-time precarious work for over five years. This was the oldest group, with an average age of 49.3 years. Most were female, white, and had lived in Canada longer than 10 years. Of all four groups, they had the lowest level of education, with less than 10 per cent having some university courses completed or a degree.

The university workers in our sample were urban project support workers engaged in faculty research projects and short-term administrative assignments. Four of every five worked in a contract position, and the others worked part time. Although this group was approached through two unions, only half were unionized in every place they worked. About one-quarter had been in precarious work longer than five years. An equal number had been in this type of employment for less than one year. This group was younger than the homecare workers, with an average age of 35.4 years, and over a quarter being younger than 25 years. Three-quarters were female. Over 80 per cent were white and had lived in Canada longer than 10 years.

They had the highest level of education: most had some university courses completed or a degree. About one-quarter were full-time students.

Most of the community workers worked on contract, and about one-third worked part time. All of them worked in Toronto. Most were recent graduates of a college program, and this background was reflected in their employment situations. Over half had been in precarious employment for less than a year, and very few were unionized. This was the youngest group, with an average age of 35.2 years. One-third of the group was under the age of 25. Almost all were women. They were more racially diverse than the first two groups: almost 40 per cent were non-white. However, most had lived in Canada longer than 10 years. Their education level reflected their recent graduation from college, as only one-quarter had some university courses or a degree, and about one-quarter were full-time students.

The diverse group may be particularly representative of precarious workers in Toronto in general. They included day labourers, temporary agency workers, hospitality sector workers, high-tech workers, health workers, and others. Most worked on contracts, while one-quarter worked part time, and a few were self-employed. About one in 10 had full-time precarious employment: continuing positions without a commitment to hours of work. They were generally new to precarious employment: over half had been in precarious jobs less than a year. Few were unionized. They were about the same age as the university and community workers in our sample, with an average age of 35.6 years. But they were the most diverse group: half were female, less than half were white, and almost one-third had lived in Canada less than 10 years. They were also highly educated, with almost half having some university courses or a degree.

Full-time permanent workers in this sample came mainly from the university sector. Community workers made up one-quarter, and the diverse group just under one-fifth. These workers had both full-time hours and indefinite employment contracts. They were slightly older, with an average age of 40 years. Most were women, almost three-quarters were white, all worked in an urban centre and most had lived in Canada more than 10 years.

EMPLOYMENT STRAIN, JOB STRAIN, AND PHYSICAL RISKS

This section examines work organization characteristics that can result in employment strain, job strain, and exposure to physical risks. Its starting hypothesis is that workers in precarious employment are likely to be exposed to high levels of employment strain, but the levels of job strain and physical risks will be mixed, relative to those of full-time permanent workers.

Employment Strain

Table 6.2 provides a comparison of workers in precarious employment and in full-time permanent wage work. This comparison helps to define the level of employment strain and how it varies across sectors. In the process, it makes it possible to understand in greater detail the relationship between precarious employment and health. The four components of employment strain emanate from clusters of survey questions described above. Indices are calculated by summing the unweighted scores of questions making up each component. The aggregate *employment relationship uncertainty* and the *employment relationship workload* indices are calculated by summing all of the questions that make up the components of these indices.

Columns 1–4 report the results for the four groups of workers in precarious employment relative to the results reported by full-time permanent workers. A relative index of 100 indicates that those in precarious employment reported the same level of uncertainty, workload, support, or household insecurity as full-time permanent workers. Relative indices greater than 100 represent levels of uncertainty, control, support, or household insecurity greater than those reported by full-time permanent workers. Column 5 reports the actual index score out of 100 for the full-time permanent workers. Higher numbers represent higher levels of uncertainty, workload, support, and household insecurity.

With few exceptions, each of the four groups of workers in precarious employment has higher levels of employment relationship uncertainty, workload, and household insecurity than full-time permanent workers. The diverse group of respondents has higher employment relationship uncertainty, workload, and household insecurity, and lower support than the other groups in the survey. These findings confirm that employment strain is more of an issue for workers in forms of employment exhibiting dimensions of precarious employment than for those in full-time permanent employment. At the same time, table 6.2 illustrates how the characteristics of employment strain vary across the four groups of workers in precarious situations.

Workers in the "Diverse" Category
Have the Highest Uncertainty and Workload

Workers in the "diverse group" were highly uncertain about whether they could count on future employment. The level of overall employment relationship uncertainty was over three times higher than that for full-time permanent workers: almost half worked on contracts that were less than six months, or thought their employer would not offer them more work, and over half reported that discrimination and favouritism affected offers of future work.

Table 6.2

Employment Strain Indices for Precarious Workers Relative to Those Reported by Full-time Workers (Columns 1–4: FT = 100)

	HC	U	C	DIV	Actual FT Score Out of 100
Employment Strain Indices	1	2	3	4	5
Employment relationship uncertainty	305.6	215.4	313.6	368.9	14.3
Employment uncertainty index	123.8	172.0	267.1	298.8	16.4
Earnings uncertainty index	264.4	217.2	269.6	325.2	18.8
Scheduling uncertainty index	516.7	102.0	318.2	420.9	10.0
Employment relationship workload index	150.8	72.5	138.1	163.2	23.6
Effort getting work subindex	318.3	245.5	986.4	1659.1	2.2
Effort associated with multiple workplaces subindex	188.2	112.3	189.1	186.2	19.5
Effort keeping work subindex	119.2	50.3	106.7	139.3	31.2
Employment relationship support	119.5	123.5	105.6	58.5	36.0
Household insecurity index	179.9	161.0	229.3	228.8	25.9

HC Homecare; U University; C Community; DIV Diverse group; FT Full-time permanent
Notes: Columns 1–4: Reported results relative to full-time category scores. A relative index of 100 indicates precarious groups reported the same level of uncertainty, workload, support, or household insecurity as full-time workers. Relative indices greater than 100 represent higher uncertainty, effort, support, or household insecurity. Column 5: Actual index score out of 100 for the full-time workers. Higher numbers represent higher levels of uncertainty, workload, support, and household insecurity.

Their level of earnings uncertainty was over three times higher than full-time permanent workers: most could not plan on the same income level six months in advance; and over one in 10 were not paid on time half the time or more. A high proportion could not count on income support if they were unable to work: three-quarters lost pay when they were sick; just under half did not contribute to employment insurance or the state pension plan; very few were not covered by disability insurance, either their own or a spouse/partner's; and less than one-fifth were covered by an employer-sponsored pension plan, either their own or a spouse/partner's.

Members of this group had limited control over their work schedules: half did not know their work schedule more than a week in advance more than half the time. Employment relationship effort levels were also relatively high. More were expending effort looking for work than in the other sectors: over one-third had looked for work at least half the days in the previous month. The effort associated with multiple employers was similar to that of community workers and homecare workers: over half had more than one supervisor; 60 per cent worked with different co-workers half the time or more; and just under one-fifth reported conflicting demands by employers half the time or more – the highest of any group. They also reported extremely high levels of effort keeping work. Among the five groups, this one had the highest proportion of workers who were requested to perform tasks unrelated to their jobs (41.9%), the highest proportion of workers reporting that attitude evaluation affected the kind of work they were assigned (36.7%), and the highest proportion who encountered discrimination at work (62.6%).

Uncertainties related to maintaining a household were also high for this group, and they had the least access to support. Only one in five earned more than $25,000 per year; two-thirds lived in households whose total income was less than $35,000 per year, which in Toronto is close to the low-income cut-off; and 80 per cent had no benefit coverage of their own or from a family member. The majority of workers in this group belonged to households that provided limited additional income or benefits to supplement their own meagre earnings and benefit coverage. This group enjoyed significantly lower support at work: fewer than one in 10 expected assistance with problems from a union, and only one-quarter could expect support for stress at work.

Homecare Workers Have Earnings and Schedule Insecurity

Uncertainties common among homecare workers relate to earnings and scheduling. Employment uncertainty was slightly higher than that of full-time permanent workers – at the level of the employment contract, these workers were considered permanent employees, but they were not guaranteed hours of work or consistent pay. This variability is reflected in their earnings uncertainty, which was almost three times higher than full-time permanent workers: over 8 per cent could not plan on the same income level six months in advance. Very few received income when they were unable to work: almost all lost pay when they were sick; just over one-quarter had disability insurance through a spouse/partner; and less than one-fifth had pension coverage through a spouse/partner.

Homecare workers had high levels of scheduling uncertainty. Just over half knew their work schedule most of the time at least one week in advance, and under one-half knew how many hours they were to work at least a day in advance. The median number of work locations in the previous month was 12. They had the highest level of unpaid travel: over half travelled two or more hours each day without pay. They reported high effort levels related to keeping their work, in part because almost half the members of this group reported that the hours they were assigned were affected by daily performance evaluation and/or daily attitude assessments.

This group included the highest proportion of workers earning under $25,000 per year. They were an older group of women who had, apparently, more household support than community workers and the diverse group: half lived in households with an income over $35,000 per year, and just over half had benefit coverage – the highest rate of any group. Employment relationship support was relatively high for this group: most were members of unions everywhere they worked, and over half could call on the union for help with problems. However, they scored the lowest on the two other components of the employment relationship support index. Less than one-fifth could call on help to get their job done or could rely on help at work dealing with work-related stress.

Community Workers: Looking Inside the "Short-Term Contract Culture"

Most of our sample of community workers had graduated from college in the previous three years. They illustrate the consistently high levels of employment strain involved in moving into an occupation (i.e., community service work) where many entry-level positions involve fixed-term contracts (see also de Wolff, this volume). Community workers are not quite as precarious as the diverse group, but they were dealing with far more uncertainty than the university or full-time workers.

The community workers reported the highest levels of favouritism and discrimination in getting work, a factor that contributed to their high employment uncertainty index. One-quarter said their current employer was not likely to offer more work. Their earnings uncertainty was high: 60.9 per cent said they could not count on their income six months from now, and many could not count on continued income if they were not able to work. For example, more than one in five did not contribute to employment insurance or state pension plans, making it unlikely that they would be eligible for employment insurance benefits; around 80 per cent lost pay when they were sick, had no disability insurance, and had no employer pension.

Their scheduling was slightly more stable than that of the homecare and the diverse groups, but just over one-third often did not know their work schedule more than a week in advance or the hours they would work a day in advance. Their employment relationship workload was high because over half had multiple jobs, and almost 70 per cent reported working with different groups of co-workers half the time or more – higher levels than for any other group. These workers' employment relationship workload was moderated somewhat by familiar work locations: none reported regularly working in an unfamiliar location. They did, however, spend considerable time travelling: almost half spent two or more unpaid hours travelling to work. Over a third reported that daily performance and attitude evaluations affected the number of hours they worked and the type of work they were assigned.

More workers in this group lived in households with an income under $35,000 per year (81.0%) than in any other group. Employment relationship support was about the same as that reported by full-time permanent workers.

University Workers Have Uncertain Earnings
but Low Employment Relationship Workload

Most university workers thought their employer would offer them more work, even though four out of five were in contract positions. Their earnings were uncertain: just over half reported that they could not plan on the same level of earnings in six months. They were twice as likely to lose pay when sick compared to full-time workers, although that level was much lower than for other groups of workers in precarious forms of employment. Most had no disability insurance or employer pension.

This group spent less effort managing their employment relationship than full-time workers. They had more notice of their schedules and hours than any other group. Fewer were looking for work, and even though one-quarter had more than one employer, they reported little conflict associated with multiple employers or work locations. Of all the groups, strikingly low proportions of university workers felt that evaluations affected the hours or type of work they were asked to do, and they reported the lowest levels of harassment and discrimination.

About three times as many earned less than $25,000 than in the full-time group. However, they lived with less household insecurity than other precarious groups: almost 60 per cent were in households whose income was over $35,000, and just under half had some access to benefits. They reported the highest level of employment relationship support of any sector, mainly as a result of high levels of being able to call on help to do their job if needed and having help available at work to deal with stress.

JOB STRAIN

Table 6.3 shows the survey results of indicators of "job strain" – control at work, physical and cognitive workload, management relations, and employment relationship support. Columns 1–4 report results relative to full-time permanent workers, and column 5 reports the actual score for full-time permanent workers.

The first observation is that the relative index values for workers in all four groups in precarious employment differ less dramatically from the values of full-time workers than was the case for the indicators of employment strain in table 6.2. In table 6.2, four-fifths of the employment relationship uncertainty indices were at least twice as high as those reported by workers in full-time permanent wage work, and a number were three times higher. Over half of the sub-indices on workload were at least 50 per cent higher than those reported by full-time permanent workers. In table 6.3, no relative index differed from that of the full-time permanent group by 50 per cent. Workers in precarious employment generally reported less control

Table 6.3
Job Strain Indices for Precarious Workers Relative to Those Reported by Full-time Workers
(Columns 1–4: FT = 100)

Job Strain Indices	HC	U	C	DIV	Actual FT Score Out of 100
	1	2	3	4	5
Control at work index	66.7	100.8	95.2	82.1	76.7
Workload, physical index	142.1	65.6	53.6	129.1	30.2
Workload, cognitive index	102.4	79.3	79.2	111.4	41.1
Management relations index	81.4	124.1	122.7	68.8	66.0
Support	88.6	100.1	95.2	68.5	65.1

HC Homecare; U University; C Community; DIV Diverse; FT Full-time
Notes: Columns 1–4: Reported results relative to full-time category scores. A relative index of 100 indicates precarious groups reported the same level of control, workload, support, or management relations as full-time workers. Relative indices greater than 100 represent higher control, effort and support, and better management relations. Column 5: Actual index score out of 100 for the full-time workers. Higher numbers represent higher levels of control, workload, support, or better management relations.

than full-time permanent workers, with homecare workers reporting about one-third less control and the diverse group about one-fifth less. There was little difference between the control scores of full-time permanent workers and the other two groups of workers in precarious forms of employment (university and community).

Relative scores on the workload index present an even more diverse picture. Homecare workers scored almost 50 per cent higher than full-time permanent workers on the physical index but about the same on the cognitive index. The diverse group scored about 30 per cent higher on the physical index and just 10 per cent higher on the cognitive index. University workers and community workers reported lower physical and cognitive workloads compared to full-time workers. The results in table 6.3 suggest that workers in the homecare sector and the diverse sector might be exposed to marginally higher levels of job strain (conventionally defined), relative to full-time permanent workers. For diverse workers, the low levels of support may further increase the health effects of job strain.

PHYSICAL RISKS

Table 6.4 reports on the level of exposure to physical risks. Again scores relative to full-time permanent workers provide a mixed picture. Both the diverse group and homecare workers reported significantly higher exposure to all physical risks. The university workers reported conditions closer to those of the full-time permanent workers, while the community workers reported significantly lower physical risks. Overall, physical risks

Table 6.4
Frequency of Physical Risks for Precarious Workers Relative to Those Reported
by Full-time Workers (Columns 1–4: FT = 100)

Physical Risks	HC	U	C	DIV	FT Score (%)
Worked in awkward positions half or more of each day	313.2	76.7	26.3	194.0	16.7
Worked standing half or more of each day	569.8	117.4	45.3	330.2	8.6
Discomfort due to air quality, noise, and/ or temperature in previous month half the days or more	270.5	153.0	29.5	205.3	13.2
Hours worked last month	82.8	68.4	73.3	64.7	150.8 (#)

HC Homecare; U University; C Community; DIV Diverse; FT Full-time

Notes: Columns 1–4: Reported results relative to full-time scores. A relative index of 100 indicates that precarious groups reported the same risk frequency as full-time workers. Relative indices greater than 100 represent higher risk frequency. Column 5: Actual index score out of 100 for the full-time workers. Higher numbers represent higher risk frequency.

for workers in precarious forms of employment may be reduced by fewer hours, compared with those for full-time permanent workers.

HEALTH OUTCOMES AND THE EMPLOYMENT RELATIONSHIP

Does the nature of the employment relationship affect health outcomes? How does the construct *employment strain* challenge and build upon the conventional notion of job strain? Does employment strain reflect the distinct decision-making latitude and health issues facing workers in precarious employment? Given the small size of the sample and the complex relationship between work organization characteristics, personal characteristics, and health outcomes, only tentative conclusions are possible. However, studying the nature of the employment relationship itself deepens an understanding of how work affects health outcomes.

Table 6.5 reports relative health outcomes comparing workers in precarious employment and those in full-time permanent wage work. The diverse group consistently reported poorer health than full-time workers. It is worth remembering that, relative to full-time permanent workers, the diverse group is marginally younger (about four years on average) and better educated. Both of these factors should lead to better health outcomes. Homecare workers had similar self-reported health outcomes and pain severity, but much higher levels of pain frequency compared to full-time permanent workers. Community workers reported poorer health, but less frequent and severe pain. University workers reported better health outcomes on all three measures.

Table 6.5
Health Outcomes for Precarious Workers Relative to Those Reported by Full-time Workers
(Columns 1–4: FT = 100)

Health Outcomes	HC 1	U 2	C 3	DIV 4	FT Score (%) 5
Self-reported health less than very good	104.8	61.5	167.3	136.5	10.4
Work in pain half the time or more	247.7	59.6	79.8	192.7	10.9
Work with severe pain anywhere	84.1	38.2	51.2	134.7	17.0

HC Homecare; U University; C Community; DIV Diverse; FT Full-time
Notes: Columns 1–4: Reported results relative to full-time scores. A relative index of 100 indicates that precarious groups reported the same health outcome as full-time workers. Relative indices greater than 100 represent poorer health outcomes. Column 5: Actual index score out of 100 for the full-time workers. Higher numbers represent poorer health outcomes.

These findings on overall health outcomes are broadly consistent with the hypothesis that employment strain, so common among workers in precarious forms of employment, negatively affects health outcomes. The diverse group reported work organization characteristics suggestive of higher levels of employment strain and marginally higher levels of job strain. They also reported relatively poor health, high pain frequency, and high pain severity. Community workers were also exposed to high levels of employment strain and reported poor health but low incidence of pain. University workers were the least exposed to employment strain and reported the best health outcomes of any group in the study. Homecare workers reported high frequency of working in pain, a result that may reflect their high reported levels of physical risks.

Table 6.6 reports findings on questions related to stress levels at work. The diverse group consistently reported results which indicate that work is much more stressful for them than for full-time workers. The other groups of workers in precarious employment reported either similar or lower levels of stress factors compared to full-time permanent workers.

Finally, it is possible to estimate the health effect of the employment relationship on two different health outcomes: whether a person worked in pain at least half of the previous month, and whether self-reported health was very good or excellent. To make such an estimate requires knowing, first, if an employment relationship characteristic affects health outcomes and, second, the degree to which this characteristic varies by type of employment relationship. The analysis is limited to a comparison of the health effects of those in our diverse group and those in full-time permanent employment.

The logistic models estimated in table 6.7 had one of the health outcomes as the dependent variable, and age, sex, and an index value of an employment relationship characteristic as independent variables. Entering the individual

Table 6.6

Exposure to Stressors of Precarious Workers Relative to Those Reported by Full-time Workers (Columns 1–4: FT = 100)

Stressors	HC 1	U 2	C 3	DIV 4	FT Score (%) 5
Tense at work half the days or more	67.3	95.5	71.0	177.1	24.5
Tense outside of work half the days or more	90.2	96.2	98.5	142.3	26.5
Distaste going to work half the time or more	69.8	86.9	18.0	170.6	24.5
Frustrated with their jobs half the days or more	103.7	82.4	88.6	167.3	24.5
Exhausted after their shift most days	106.9	53.1	74.3	123.3	24.5

HC Homecare; U University; C Community; DIV Diverse; FT Full-time permanent

Notes: Columns 1–4: Reported results relative to full-time category scores. A relative index of 100 indicates precarious groups reported the same exposure to stressors as full-time workers. Relative indices greater than 100 represent higher exposure to stressors. Column 5: Actual index score out of 100 for the full-time workers. Higher numbers represent higher exposure to stressors.

index scores of an employment relationship characteristic into the model would provide only a point estimate of how that characteristic affects health outcomes. Dividing the individual index numbers by the difference in the mean index of the diverse group and the full-time group generates an estimate of both the effect of the characteristic on health outcomes and the total magnitude of the effect related to being in the diverse group relative to the full-time group. For example, the mean score on employment relationship uncertainty index was 14.3 for full-time permanent workers and 52.8 for the diverse group. Dividing the individual index scores by 38.5 and using these numbers in the estimation model provides an estimate of how a change of 38.5 points in the employment relationship uncertainty index affects the probability of reporting a health outcome. Results are presented in table 6.7.[6] They compare the relative probability of reporting a health outcome for two individuals whose score on the particular employment relationship index differed by an amount equivalent to the mean difference in that index between the diverse group and the full-time permanent group. For example, the figure 2.18 for employment relationship uncertainty and working in pain can be roughly interpreted as workers in precarious employment relationships having 2.18 times the risk of reporting pain relative to those working in full-time permanent wage work.[7]

A number of results are worth remarking on. First, poor health outcomes correlate with employment relationship uncertainty, employment relationship workload, employment relationship support, and household insecurity. As

Table 6.7
Impact of Precarious Employment Relationship on Health Outcomes
(Statistical significance of estimates in brackets)

Precarious Employment Indices	Estimate of the odds-ratio showing how precarious employment affects the probability of working in pain at least half the time relative to full-time workers	Estimate of the odds-ratio showing how precarious employment affects the probability of reporting excellent or very good health relative to full-time workers
Employment relationship uncertainty	2.18 (**)	0.59 (**)
Employment uncertainty	1.69 (**)	0.74 (**)
Earnings uncertainty	1.36	0.68 (*)
Scheduling uncertainty	1.21	0.80 (**)
Employment relationship workload	1.30 (**)	0.80 (**)
Effort getting work	1.03	0.85
Effort multiple jobs	1.14	1.00
Effort keeping work	1.15 (**)	0.86 (**)
Employment relationship support	0.81 (**)	1.38 (***)
Household insecurity	1.35	0.71 (**)
Control at work	0.74 (***)	1.20 (**)
Physical workload at work	1.17 (***)	0.91 (**)
Physical risks at work	1.39 (***)	0.89 (**)
Stressors at work	1.41 (***)	0.86 (***)

Significance of estimates: *.10, **.05, ***<.001

employment relationship uncertainty and employment relationship workload increase, the probability of working in pain rises and the probability of reporting excellent or very good health falls. Increases in household insecurity and decreases in employment relationship support have a similar effect. All but one of these relationships is statistically significant at the 5 per cent level or better. Second, the effect of employment relationship uncertainty appears to be quantitatively larger than the other measures of the employment relationship. Third, the traditional health risks reported in the last four lines of table 6.7 are statistically significant. However, their effect on the health of workers in precarious employment is less than employment relationship uncertainty. That is a result of the large differences between workers in precarious employment and full-time permanent workers on measures of the employment relationship. The differences were generally smaller with the measures of traditional work organization characteristics. These findings are consistent with the initial hypothesis that the explanation of the different health outcomes of workers in precarious employment relative to those in standard employment relationships requires researchers to look beyond the workplace itself and to the nature of the employment relationship.

CONCLUSION

This chapter developed a new construct, *employment strain*, to account for health outcomes among workers in precarious forms of employment. The survey results provide detailed descriptions of the uncertainties, workloads, and support levels related to the employment relationships of five clusters of workers. The new employment strain indices assist in identifying where homecare workers, university workers, community workers, a diverse group of workers, and full-time permanent workers are most and least precarious. The most salient finding is the high level of precariousness of the diverse group of workers relative to full-time permanent workers. They reported high levels of uncertainty in their employment relationship and high effort levels in finding and keeping employment. The results for the other three groups (homecare, university, community) were not as strong, but it was still the case that, on most measures, they reported more uncertainty and greater effort to sustain employment than the comparison group of full-time permanent workers.

The findings were more diverse respecting job strain and physical risks. On the work organization characteristics that lead to job strain, differences between full-time permanent workers and those in precarious employment were less pronounced. The homecare and diverse group reported less control and heavier workloads, but differences were much smaller than in the case of work organization characteristics that could lead to employment strain. Homecare workers and the diverse group reported significantly higher physical risks.

There is a rough correlation between health outcomes and work organization characteristics. The diverse group reported the worst health outcomes of any group, despite being younger and more educated than the full-time workers. The pattern for the other three groups was less pronounced relative to full-time permanent workers. The health effects of the employment relationship were confirmed in the final section of the chapter, which demonstrated that increases in employment relationship uncertainty, employment relationship workload, and household insecurity and decreases in employment relationship support are associated with poorer health outcomes.

Further work needs to be done to isolate the particular employment relationship variables that influence health outcomes, the interactions between these variables, and the interaction between employment strain and job strain. To this end, future research will involve focus groups and oral interviews, to gain a deeper understanding of how employment strain affects health outcomes, and more extensive survey work to increase the sample size to permit further analysis. There is, nevertheless, growing evidence of the health costs associated with the spread of the precarious employment relationship, costs that require greater public attention and scholarly scrutiny.

Essential but Precarious: Changing Employment Relationships and Resistance in the Ontario Public Service

JAN BOROWY

The Conservative Party was elected as the government in Ontario in June 1995 on a platform called the "Common Sense Revolution." A popularization of neo-liberal ideology, the recipe for this revolution included reforming the operation of the provincial government so that it would "do better for less."

An early target for the Common Sense Revolution was the provincial Ministry of the Environment. Early in 1996 the Tory government announced the privatization of its water analysis laboratories and the layoff of one-third of the enforcement officers and clerical workers in that ministry. By the summer of 1996 the Ontario Public Service Employees' Union (OPSEU) published a report detailing the impact of these cutbacks. It warned, "due to the cutback of 1,000 Ministry of Environment protection workers, amounting to one third of the Ministry, Ontario's environment faces a grave crisis" (OPSEU 1996). OPSEU pointed out further that the ministry had been underfunded for years and that "there is nothing left to cut."

In May 2000 the people of Walkerton experienced the tragic consequences of the cutbacks to Ministry of Environment enforcement staff and the privatization of water analysis. Water contaminated with E. coli 107 bacteria killed seven people and made more than 2,400 ill. Justice O'Connor concluded, in his report from the public inquiry into those events, that government cutbacks and the lack of new regulations for water testing were responsible for the events in Walkerton (O'Connor 2002). The government denied O'Connor's conclusions. When the ministry did move to implement O'Connor's recommendations for increased staff, initially it placed all the new environmental enforcement officers in short, fixed-term contracts.

In March 2002 Ontario's 45,000 Crown employees found themselves in the midst of a 54-day strike to hold back major concessions to their collective agreement. A court clerk, legislated to be an essential worker for the purposes of labour disputes, spoke to a rally in front of the downtown Toronto courthouse. She asked the crowd, "If I am so essential to this system, then why am I only on contract, get so few hours of work, and am paid so low?" Court workers are predominantly women and, in larger metropolitan areas, women of colour. During a strike they are deemed to be providing an "essential service" – a statutorily defined term that requires them to continue to work to ensure the administration of justice. Court workers perform a wide range of clerical duties and are often expected to assist judges with personal services. In the five years before the strike, court clerks' income had declined and the number who were on fixed-term contracts had increased dramatically. During the 2002 OPSEU strike, the court workers joined the strike from the inside, refusing to perform what they viewed to be non-essential duties and, some days, walking off the job entirely.

These two stories illustrate the attack by the 1990s neo-liberal government in Ontario on the standard employment relationship within its own workforce, the impact these changes have on the public, and the resistance by workers and their union. Many case studies document the Ontario Conservative government's dismantling of welfare state functions, including cuts to social assistance and the introduction of "Workfare," the cancellation of social housing programs, the withdrawal of employment equity legislation, the cuts to the public education system, and the deregulation of basic employment standards, as well as the privatization of different government services (Armstrong and Laxer, this volume; Bakker 1996b; de Wolff, this volume; Walkom 1997; see also Bashevkin 2002; Burke, Mooers, and Shields 2000). Yet fewer analyses document the story of front-line public service employees – specifically, how the emergence of the neo-liberal state led to a shift towards precarious employment among government employees themselves (see Broad 2000; Fudge 2002, 122; Morgan et al. 2000; Public Service Alliance of Canada 1993; Shields and Evans 1999).

Between 1995 and 2002 the Ontario state-as-employer pursued its goals of "flexibility" in three different ways: through internal restructuring; through changes to the legislative regime; and in its bargaining strategy with the Ontario Public Service Employees' Union. Relying on the tenets of "new public management" – the ideological foundation of neo-liberalism in the public sector – Ontario government workplaces underwent a profound restructuring between 1995 and 2002. The Common Sense Revolution entailed the typical components of an austere neo-lialism by shrinking the size of the public service, cutting spending, cutting taxes, cultivating public-private partnerships, and removing so-called labour market rigidities and legal regulations protecting workers (Albo 1994; Leys 2001; Pollert 1988; Whitfield 2001). As a result, the downsizing, privatization, and marketization, as well as the erosion of the standard employment relationship, have fundamentally reshaped the Ontario public sector.

This chapter presents three case studies to illustrate the growth of precarious employment in the Ontario public service (OPS), along with the consequences for public services and for the workers who deliver them. The three groups examined are meat inspectors, court workers, and clerical workers. The case studies rely on interviews with front-line workers in the Ontario public service conducted by the author.[1]

To better understand the restructuring in the Ontario public service, the chapter begins by locating these case studies within the typology of total employment described in chapter 1, "Precarious Employment: Towards an Improved Understanding of Labour Market Insecurity" (Vosko, this volume). Collectively, these case studies illuminate the variety of forms of employment and work arrangements that shape precarious employment in the Ontario public service. This typology, along with the mapping methodology advanced in chapter 2, "Conceptualizing Precarious Employment: Mapping Wage Work across Social Location and Occupational Context" (Cranford and Vosko, this volume), enables us to better understand how regulatory protection, control over the labour process via unionization, income level, hours of work, and access to a social wage all have an impact on workers within the public service. The typology opens space for more detailed analysis of several of the diverse manifestations of precarious employment in the OPS – specifically, part-time permanent wage work, short-term fixed contracts, solo self-employment (known as fee-for-service employment in the public service), and employment through temporary agencies. At the same time, this chapter illustrates that workers in the public sector are not passively accepting poor working conditions and low pay. Rather, each case study reveals the creative ways workers organize through their union to slow down or overturn the shift to more precarious employment.

WORK REORGANIZATION
AND PRECARIOUS EMPLOYMENT IN ONTARIO
GOVERNMENT WORKPLACES

As the Keynesian Welfare State and women's labour force participation expanded in Canada in the 1960s and 1970s, the public sector became a site for "good jobs," especially for women and workers of colour. Jobs within the state are categorized as part of the primary labour market. They are normally unionized jobs, with relatively high wages compared to the private sector, which offer primarily full-time permanent positions conforming closely to the prototypical standard employment relationship (Luxton and Reiter 1997; White 1993). Yet, beginning in the mid-1990s in the provincial public service in Ontario, the simple dichotomy of "good" jobs in the public sector and "bad" jobs in the private sector became increasingly misleading.

Historically, the province-as-employer has deployed a variety of practices, often through the legislative framework, to limit the rights of workers in the public service. It has codified these limits in the Public Service Act (PSA) and, later, the Crown Employee Collective Bargaining Act (CECBA). Public servants were prohibited from forming unions in Ontario before the mid-1970s and did not have access to the same rights as their predominantly male counterparts in the private sector. The Ontario public service won the right to unionize and, in 1974, formed the Ontario Public Service Employees' Union (OPSEU). Initially, the scope of collective bargaining was limited to specific areas, and it excluded areas and issues such as technological change, training, pensions, and management rights found typically in private-sector contracts. Public service workers were barred from political participation and excluded from whistleblowing. The union-recognition clause in the collective agreement was legislated by the employer. Workers in fixed-term contract positions and temporary contract positions, and those working through GO-Temp (the internal temporary-help agency of the provincial public service), were prohibited from unionizing. OPSEU won the fight to have these workers join the bargaining unit, under a new category of "unclassified workers," only in 1980, and workers working through GO-Temp were not recognized as union members until 1994 (Panitch and Schwartz 1993; Roberts 1994).

The state-as-employer used its legislative power to create flexibility in its workforce by controlling the right to appoint workers to the Crown. Ontario's direct employees are "appointed to the public service" through the *Public Service Act*, which delineates their job status as either a permanent full-time classified position or as an "unclassified" contract position. Crown employees are legislated by the *Crown Employees Collective Bargaining Act* (CECBA) into the union. If workers are not appointed to the Crown, and remain mere "employees of the Crown," they are excluded from the Act and from union representation. Moreover, as direct employees of the government, the workers are excluded from all major provisions of employment standards as well as the *Ontario Labour Relations Act*. These exclusions from provincial labour statutes profoundly affect workers' capacity to resist.

The provincial employees were further limited by their exclusion from the right to strike. The CECBA prohibited employees of the Crown from striking until 1994. Although workers in the OPS have the right to strike, this legislation still prohibits thousands of employees from withdrawing their labour. Their positions are deemed to be essential – necessary to prevent "danger to life, health or safety" or "disruption of the courts or legislative drafting."[2] The effect of this essential services regime is to limit the bargaining power of provincial public sector workers.

By 1995 the new provincial government demonstrated its willingness to make whatever policy and legislative amendments it deemed necessary to facilitate restructuring (Leeb 2002, 70). The first action removed legislative barriers to privatization, and divestments identified so-called market rigidities. The state-as-employer legislated away successor rights – workers' rights to have union protection follow them if their work is contracted out. Private sector workers did not face a comparable legislative onslaught. Downsizing and privatization became prominent. Many segments of the public service were eliminated completely, and many workers were laid off. Thousands of Crown employees were divested, as their work was transferred to other levels of government, to independent agencies, or to non-profit, broader public service agencies. Some segments were contracted out to private companies, including temporary-help agencies. Most ministries within the Ontario provincial government saw their workforces cut by at least one-third, and some, such as the Ministry of Environment, by 48 per cent. Between July 1994 and July 2002, the number of direct government employees shrunk by over 23,000. A climate of profound insecurity pervaded every public sector workplace across the province (OPSEU, OPS Populations Employee Lists, 1994–2002).

This downsizing altered significantly the occupational and gender composition of the public service. In 2003 women represented 60 per cent of the OPSEU bargaining unit, an increase from 55 per cent in 1994. The restructuring reinforced the traditional occupational segmentation of office and clerical work. In a gendered harmonizing down of the public service, jobs performed primarily by male workers providing a technical service, for example, were reduced by 60 per cent. The impact of downsizing and privatization in the OPS was threefold: specialized or technical jobs were contracted out; the proportion of the OPS that is female and in clerical occupations increased; and, all too often, these female clerical workers were not seen as providing direct public "services."

GENDER AND PRECARIOUS EMPLOYMENT IN THE OPS

Between 1995 and 2002 the Conservative government used whatever openings it could find in the collective agreement, in combination with new legislation, to create a far more precarious workforce. Full-time permanent wage work grew less common as job insecurity and underemployment rose. The standard employment relationship was under attack not only from the increased insecurity brought by downsizing and privatization or by the new legislative regime but as the norm for the OPS. Changes to the OPS bargaining unit shaped the manifestations of precarious employment in this era.

There are five defined employment situations in the OPS: full-time permanent classified jobs and regular part-time classified jobs form the core of the public service and have the most extensive set of benefits and entitlements under the collective agreement. However, three other employment situations are quite common: unclassified short-term fixed contracts, temporary agency and fee-for-service jobs, and "term classified" positions created in 2001. Each situation varies in its hours of work, degree of continuity or permanency, access to union protection, income level, and social wage benefits.

Rights to job security, benefits, and regulatory protection via the collective agreement are attached to full-time permanent classified positions. Regular part-time classified positions have the same level of job security and the same degree of regulatory protection, but only pro-rated benefits. Unclassified contract positions are in the bargaining unit and are covered by parts of the collective agreement, but they lack the same level of job security and access to benefits as full-time permanent classified positions. Unclassified workers receive a percentage in lieu of benefits and have the option of purchasing an extended pension plan. Hours of work range from 14 to 40 per week in these positions. The majority of unclassified contract workers are hired on short fixed-term contracts, generally for terms of six months to one year. The collective agreement provides for the conversion of these positions to full-time permanent positions after a specified period. The proportion of unclassified contract workers in the OPS bargaining unit increased from 15 per cent in 1994 to 26 per cent in 2001, or a 73 per cent increase in seven years. During the summer months, when students and seasonal workers were hired, the number of unclassified members increased to 34 per cent of the overall bargaining unit.

One of the most significant shifts between 1995 and 2002 was the increase in the proportion of part-time unclassified contract workers. These workers have very limited hours. In 1994 one in 10 unclassified contract workers were part time. By 2001 this number had more than doubled, so that fully 23 per cent of the unclassified contract workers were working part-time hours. In contrast, the proportion of classified regular part-time workers remained the same, standing at 3 per cent of the bargaining unit. The government used the unclassified contract part-time workers to implement a low-wage strategy rather than increase the number of classified or regular part-time permanent workers with access to more benefits.

The drive for greater flexibility did not stop with the increased resort to full-time or part-time unclassified workers. In 2001 the government legislated a new category of employee – "term classifieds" – a contract position with three-year terms. The state-as-employer has extra tools in its labour relations kit, as it has the power to legislate changes to its own employment relationships.

The Tory government openly articulated its objectives for these changes to the *Public Service Act*. David Tsubouchi, chair of Management Board Secretariat, stated, when defending the legislation at Queen's Park: "We live in a world that is faster, more dynamic, and which demands more flexibility than ever before. The policies and practices of today's government must meet those challenges or we will all get left behind. To do this, we must modernize the contextual framework in which we operate."[3] Not content with shorter-term unclassified positions, the government claimed that it needed to create positions for longer periods, primarily in the field of information technology.

OPSEU members protested. One of the central issues in the 2001–2 round of bargaining (and the 54-day strike) between OPSEU and the government was control over the conditions under which workers would be hired in these new "term-classified" positions. Workers fought to ensure that members in the term-classified positions would have access to the same wages and many of the same working conditions as full-time workers in the bargaining unit, and that they would not further undercut the standard employment relationship. A cap was bargained to limit the number of term-classified workers. Despite a strike, however, the increase in contract workers within the bargaining unit has only been slowed.

The final tier of workers working for the provincial government is made up of temporary workers. Between 1995 and 2002, temporary agency workers and fee-for-service workers were hired in increasing numbers, and their working conditions became more precarious. Historically, GO-Temp, the provincially run temporary employment agency, employed over 1,300 workers every week and, in 1994, OPSEU won recognition of these employees as members of the bargaining unit (Ontario Labour Relations Board 1998). In its efforts to deregulate, the Conservative government privatized GO-Temp in 1997. OPSEU launched claims of bad-faith bargaining, but was unable to halt the elimination of GO-Temp. As a result, a number of different private temporary agencies, many of them large transnational entities, now compete to provide workers to the provincial government.

Ontario's public accounts reveal an increased resort to temporary workers in the public service. In 1996–97 alone, the provincial government paid $30 million to temporary-help agencies. By 2001–2, expenditures increased to $60 million (Ontario Government, *Public Accounts*, 1997 and 2002). Two of the largest classifications of agency staff are in clerical positions and in institutional health-care groups, such as nurses. In the case of nurses, the resort to temporary agency workers is the product of an acute labour shortage. In office and clerical positions, it is both a low-wage strategy and a privatization strategy.

At the same time, fee-for-service consultants became increasingly common across a wide variety of ministries beginning in the mid-1990s. The dramatic increase in the use of fee-for-service workers or solo self-employed workers was documented in the November 2002 Provincial Auditor's report (Ontario Provincial Auditor 2002). However, the Auditor General focused primarily on so-named consultants in the areas of information technology and management consulting, rather than conducting a review of all fee-for-service work in the Ontario public service. Expenditures jumped from $271 million in 1998 to $662 million in 2001–2. The Ontario Provincial Auditor General reported (2002) that "hundreds of consultants were engaged at per diem rates that were on average two or three times higher than the salaries of Ministry employees performing similar duties. For instance, at the Ministry of Public Safety and Security, over half of the IT workforce was made up of consultants. In addition, more than 40 of these consultants were former Ministry employees who had left the Ministry in 2001 and returned within a few days at per diem rates that were more than double their salaries as employees."

Unfortunately, the Auditor General did not consider it to be within his purview to comment on either the employment status of the consultants or the actual number of consultants hired. However, evidence suggests that most of these former employees have joined the ranks of the solo self-employed. The use of solo self-employed workers is primarily political. It allows the government to claim that there are fewer employees on the payroll, even though it may pay two or three times more to have the same work performed.

Overall, the rise of forms of employment and work arrangements highly correlated with precarious employment has had a profound impact on the situation of provincial government employees. Approximately 63 per cent of frontline workers remain in standard employment relationships. The number of workers in unclassified short-term contracts rose by 73 per cent over a six-year period. In many worksites, temporary agency and fee-for-service or solo self-employed workers work side by side with full-time permanent staff performing the same work. The result is increased insecurity and increasing pressure to accept a downward harmonization in income levels and working conditions for all workers (Armstrong 1996).

Indeed, recent changes in the OPS have contributed to an erosion of the standard employment relationship. Three case studies, in particular, attest to this claim and show, specifically, how the rise of precarious employment in the OPS is gendered. These examples make the link between downsizing, privatization, and the rise of precarious employment. The first example explores developments in the Ministry of Agriculture and Food; the second considers restructuring within the Ministry of the Attorney General; and the third examines changes in the Ministry of Health Trillium Drug Program.

MEAT INSPECTORS

The Ministry of Agriculture and Food (OMAF) has historically been an advocate for Ontario's farming community inside the Ontario government. In

1998–99 the ministry refined its direction. It advanced a business plan with a new vision to "promote value-added agriculture, [and to] support increased exports and an improved agriculture and food trade balance" (OMAF Business Plan 1998). The ministry emphasized that the role of government was to assist Ontario's food system to expand within the global supply of food imports and exports.

During the 1996 OPSEU strike, provincial abattoirs had been forced to close because the meat inspectors were on strike. The meat inspection unit of OMAF was one of the first to be targeted for restructuring by the Conservative government.

In 1997 the Ministry of Agriculture, Food and Rural Affairs laid off all but seven of the 150 full-time permanent meat inspectors working in the provincial abattoirs. They were replaced with, or more often became, supposedly independent, fee-for-service workers working for the OMAF. The government argued that this change would not put food safety at risk because food-borne illnesses related to meat were minimal and largely a product of the lack of proper cooking. By implication, risks would henceforth be carried by individuals in their own homes. With the shift to fee-for-service inspectors and the associated rise of solo self-employment among meat inspectors, two distinct socioeconomic clusters of meat inspectors emerged (OPSEU 2003b). One group was made up primarily of older men, with considerable experience in the federal government's meat-inspection program. The second group was composed of workers entering the occupation for the first time; they were younger and they included more women (although not the majority) and more workers of colour. These workers were engaged by OMAF to conduct the inspections and were initially paid $20 per hour. At the time, this hourly wage represented a $3 per hour increase over the wage of the former meat inspectors. The fee-for-service contract meat inspectors received no employment benefits, however, and were required to cover all their own business expenses. Many worked only part-time hours.

Seven years later, the meat inspectors were still receiving $20 per hour, and they still had to cover the costs of running a business, including all travel and communication expenses. They had not benefited from wage increases negotiated for unionized Crown employees. Their hours of work varied from fewer than 20 to 50 hours per week. Their schedules and assigned work sites were tightly controlled by the ministry's area supervisors. Moreover, meat inspectors reported that if they raised questions or concerns perceived to be threatening, their hours were cut back. Newly hired inspectors received little training to learn their duties.

In 2000 meat inspectors began to challenge their status and their wages. That year, the Ministry of Labour ruled that they were employees. Revenue Canada agreed that the inspectors should be considered as employees for purposes of Employment Insurance and the Canada Pension Plan. The inspectors, however, were "employees of the Crown" and, as a result of the legislated "flexibility" within the *Public Service Act*, they remained excluded from all the substantive sections of the *Employment Standards Act* and were barred from organizing under the *Ontario Labour Relations Act* (OPSEU 2003a, Interview 1). Meat inspectors were prevented from joining a union by legislation. Even when they were successfully deemed as employees, they had little job security, they lacked control over the labour process, and they had virtually no regulatory protection.

The meat inspection program in Ontario of the 1990s and early 2000s was built on profound employment insecurity. With little regulatory protection, the state-as-employer resorted to using workers' hours of work as the means to ensure they did not challenge the Ministry of Agriculture. Because hours of work determined income, the turnover rate among meat inspectors was, predictably, over 32 per cent annually from 1995 to 2002 (Ontario Farm Council 2003).

Precarious employment in meat inspection contributed directly to a precarious food-safety system in the province. Working on contract meant that, once an inspector closed an abattoir because it failed to reach the provincial standards, the inspector would not get paid for the remaining hours of the day because there would be no meat to inspect as it went through the process. The system was designed so that inspectors faced an impossible alternative: the choice between minimum hours for them and protecting public safety.

The state-as-employer used precarious employment as a strategy not only to downsize and deregulate but to advance privatization (see also Armstrong and Laxer, this volume). Meat inspectors were treated as entrepreneurs, each individually responsible for carrying the costs of the food-safety program (see also Vosko and Zukewich, this volume). The state-as-employer consciously used solo self-employment and particular work arrangements to undermine the collective bargaining strength of the meat inspectors – and of the OPS front-line workers as a whole. It transferred the costs of the food-safety system onto the backs of workers. In these circumstances, it became increasingly unlikely that an abattoir would be closed, thereby threatening public safety.

COURT CLERKS IN THE MINISTRY OF THE ATTORNEY GENERAL

The provincial government justified the re-engineering of the Ontario Ministry of Agriculture and Food on the basis of bolstering Ontario's food production and sales in an increasingly competitive global market. A different set of motivations framed the actions of the Ministry of the Attorney General – the ministry responsible for running the court system. In the result, this ministry welcomed the private sector into running the court system in the province and reorganized work so as to undermine the standard employment relationship.

Between 1995 and 2002 the Ministry of the Attorney General identified its "core businesses" and promised in its administrative plans to provide "fair, co-ordinated, timely and accessible courts." The 1998–99 business plan illustrates the marketization of public services – a central feature of creeping privatization. This plan included several new performance measures: a reduction in the case backlog; an increase in the number of clients served from 20,000 to 23,000 in one year; and a reduction in the telephone waiting time for justice-related matters to an average of 15 minutes or less (Ontario Ministry of Attorney General, June 1998). In this example, commercialization entailed the expansion of precarious employment within the court system and an increase in private sector access to commercial contracts in the justice system.

Court workers assist judges in the courtroom and ensure the proper functioning of the courts. Historically, the courts have used a larger proportion of unclassified contract staff than other ministries – mainly women in clerical positions. In 2002, wages for unclassified workers were the same rate as for full-time classified staff. Clerical workers' wages ranged from $16 to $19 per hour, and they received pay in lieu of benefits (OPSEU Collective Agreement 2001–4). They could opt to pay into the pension themselves, but otherwise no such plan was available. The collective agreement provided unclassified workers with access to full-time classified positions after a specified number of hours. However, workers had no control over scheduling. Only by filing and winning a grievance, court workers eventually gained two hours of guaranteed payment if they were called into work, but the court did not function.

Both court managers and judges exercise control over the labour process of the clerical staff. Within the courtroom, the judge has complete control over timing and hours. A court may operate for less than one hour to more than 50 hours a week, depending on the cases and the evidence. In the past, this varied schedule worked well for some women, providing an opportunity for genuine flexibility in scheduling when raising their children. Some workers even described "an earlier paternalistic approach" when they got all the hours they needed and could also get time off to raise their family. Recalling her experience of the past, one worker noted: "At the time, I thought I had a perfect job. Now that has changed. They are just bullies" (OPSEU 2003a, Interview 3).

Two significant changes are worthy of note in this case: between 1995 and 2002, more part-time unclassified contract workers were hired, and the ministry reduced the number of hours a person could work (OPSEU 2003a, Interview 4). Depending on the size and location of the courthouse, workers reported an increased number of unclassified staff in this period. Some courts were run by 50 to 75 per cent unclassified part-time contract staff. When a job opening occurred, it was increasingly posted as a part-time unclassified contract position rather than a regular part-time position. Workers identified a lack of control over hours, a lack of access to full-time classified work, and a lack of seniority as the foremost challenges facing them in their workplaces. As one court worker noted, "before the Tories, people in my position would work 40 to 50 hours a week sometimes. With the Tories coming to power I effectively got a 40–50% pay cut" (OPSEU 2003a, Interview 5). Several workers commented that they felt like second-class citizens, with no supports, and that they were "effectively the working poor, which is very unusual considering the job we do" (OPSEU 2003a, Interview 5).

The connection between limited hours and income level affects court workers' ability to resist. These workers contend with favouritism in the allocation of hours of work. If a worker challenges a manager, the worker's hours are often cut back. They may work as few as 10 hours a week, but with a heavier workload and at a faster pace than in the past. Many court workers work for years without the certainty of a full-time, full-year permanent job. While court workers contend that the presence of a union limits the threat of dismissal, they are careful about when they vocalize their concerns. The state-as-employer uses access to hours of work as a controlling mechanism to undercut workers' access to greater control over the labour process through unionization.

While the Ministry of the Attorney General expanded precarious employment in the court system, it also introduced fee-for-service contracts in a new information technology project – the Integrated Justice Project. The project represented the largest private-public partnership in the OPS and involved EDS Canada Inc. – the Canadian-based arm of EDS International, one of the world's largest information technology transnational corporations (*Canadian Lawyer* 2002). Private sector involvement did not stop with EDS. A complex of subcontracted firms, primarily based in the United States, was established under EDS to create software applications and to supply the outside service provider. Initially budgeted at $180 million, project costs reached approximately $359 million by March 2001 (Ontario Provincial Auditor General 2002). The auditor general reported that the staff working on the project negotiated premium pay rates for themselves, about three times the rate paid to employees performing similar work in other ministries. One group of employees was ordered to quit their jobs, only to be rehired on a fee-for-service basis through a subcontracting firm used in the Integrated Justice Project. Workers in this group were then paid twice their hourly wage in exchange for relinquishing social benefits. These employees thought they had no other choice if they wanted a job (OPSEU 2003a, Interview 1).

This growth in precarious employment within the Ministry of the Attorney General is also gendered. While the clerical workers in the courts have less job security and lower income, they remain Crown employees and members of the bargaining unit. The technical staff working with information technology, largely men, are now solo self-employed with higher incomes, although they are no longer public service employees protected by a union. These examples demonstrate that the justice system, like the food-safety system, is increasingly staffed by workers in precarious employment. As the ministry introduced new programs to the justice system, it eroded the standard employment relationship. There is little evidence that any of the changes actually improved the system or provided the public with better access to justice. In the case of the Integrated Justice Project, information technology was developed as a new "market" and then split off into discrete units for private business to capture. The state directly supported the expansion of the use of transnational corporations in the delivery of public service.

CLERICAL WORKERS IN THE MINISTRY OF HEALTH TRILLIUM DRUG PROGRAM

The Ministry of Health Trillium Drug Program demonstrates clearly how the state-as-employer is contributing to precarious employment within the OPS. This program was introduced in early 1995 to provide financial assistance to individuals who could not afford the rising costs of drugs they required. In this instance, the government sought cost savings within the program from the pay packets of the clerical workers.

The staff of the Trillium Drug Program is 90 per cent temporary agency workers and 10 per cent unclassified contract workers and a few permanent classified workers. These positions are all clerical in nature and are performed primarily by women. In 1997 the Ministry of Health's temporary agency budget was 0.68 per cent of total expenditure on salaries and wages. By 2002 it had increased to 4 per cent of the overall ministry budget in this area – a 341 per cent increase.[4] The majority of the temporary agencies are large transnational corporations providing staffing services around the globe. In 1998 the provincial government explored the possibility of privatizing all mail and telephone operations in the entire OPS. That year, the Trillium Drug Program operations were also considered, but, rather than contract out the program to a private company completely, all new hiring went to temporary agency workers, not full-time permanent classified or unclassified contract staff.

The biggest problems identified by temporary help workers are a lack of job security, low pay, and a lack of benefits (OSPEU 2003a, Interview 6). In 2003 temporary agency workers were paid between $9.00 and $12.50 per hour, far less than the $16 to $19 per hour paid to classified or unclassified clerical workers. Workers reported that they asked for a wage increase every three months or so and bartered with the agency. Most of the time they received an increase, and they felt secure because "they had a pretty good relationship with the agency" (OPSEU 2003a, Interview 7). However, individuals have to seek this kind of increase on their own, and agency workers receive no benefits and no pension. As one former agency worker stated: "You live from pay cheque to pay cheque; you don't worry about anything else. You don't even ask them for vacation pay. You work for the money, that's all. You don't think about RRSP or retirement or anything" (OPSEU 2003a, Interview 6).

A lack of job security is another major concern identified by temporary agency workers. The contract with the Trillium Drug Program is open and on-going, based on the shifting needs of the program. Agency workers reported that they felt confident they would have work for a long time because clients used the phone often – "they depended upon us" – and the program was "under-staffed" (OPSEU 2003a, Interview 7). Still, as one woman explained, "there is no opportunity for advancement in the OPS." While many workers felt they had some security of hours of work so long as the program remained busy, their work was not secure. Many were angry that the government kept them in temporary positions; as one said, "They make the laws and then they break them" (OSPEU 2003a, Interview 7). Finally, when asked to consider why the government uses temporary workers, one agency worker replied, "It simply is to save a lot of money, mainly on many benefits" (OPSEU 2003a, Interview 6). The local union leaders also explained that the use of temporary agency workers has a critical impact on all workers: "It wasn't a question of money. They have money when they want it. Think about the fee-for-service consultants – they have the money. It's an ideological thing. It has an impact not only on the temps for not having any rights, but it has an impact on the unclassified and classified too. It generally depresses union activity and workers' expectations" (OPSEU 2003a, Interview 2). To this union leader, the erosion of the standard employment relationship in the OPS threatens all government workers.

The resort to temporary agency workers in the Trillium Drug Program is yet another illustration of erosion of the standard employment relationship in the OPS. It represents a strategy to avoid unionization and collective bargaining, deny workers a decent wage and benefits, and turn public money over to the private sector. This program is a discrete unit ready for privatization. When one form of privatization did not occur – the contracting out of the unit to a private company – managers simply turned to another type of "privatization" strategy, one premised on precarious employment.

WORKERS' RESISTANCE

Despite the pace and intensity of change between 1995 and 2002 and the multiplicity of strategies used by the Conservative government to implement its policies, workers and their union challenged the direction and the impact of restructuring in the OPS. While the government continued in its drive to undermine the standard employment relationship, workers fought back. They resisted precarious employment in the OPS in many ways, including broad-based public campaigns drawing attention to the importance of public services, the reorganization of privatized workers, direct challenges through grievances, and two major strikes. In 1996 and again in 2002, OPSEU members in the OPS bargaining unit went on strike against the new public management agenda and its effects.

In the 1996 strike, more than 65,000 workers were off the job for 37 days. The employer had tabled an opening offer below the basic provincial employment standards, and it rolled back more than 20 years of collective bargaining gains. Successor rights had been stripped away by legislation – rights that had to be bargained back. The state-as-employer sought complete and unregulated use of unclassified positions and a reduction in these employees' rights to access to full-time classified positions (Rapaport 1999). In 2002 the OPS struck for 54 days. In each round of bargaining since 1995, the state-as-employer has attempted to introduce flexible pay systems, such as pay for performance. In each round of bargaining, workers successfully opposed both measures.

In the 2002 round of bargaining and the subsequent strike, the employer's strategy on precarious employment was addressed more directly. Again, the employer came to the table looking for concessions to the rights of unclassified workers, as well as no rights for term-classified workers. The union's response was twofold: to gain access for unclassified contract workers to permanent employment, and to improve the wages and working conditions of these workers. At the conclusion of the strike, the union won improvements for contract workers – specifically, seniority for some contract workers, increased pay in lieu of benefits, and faster access to permanent jobs. The new contract included clear terms and conditions of employment for the new category of term-classified worker, including strict limits on the number of term-classified positions. Workers in these term contracts have access to the same wages as permanent workers, increased benefits, access to permanent jobs, and new seniority rights. As well, the employer agreed to work with the union on new options for part-time contract workers for conversion into regular part-time jobs. The union strategy has been to fight concessions and to seek new rights for contract workers, including their access to permanent full-time work (OPSEU *Table Talk* 2002). Women workers were clear that the 2002 strike was about preserving the integrity of good jobs for women and slowing, or stopping if possible, the exploitation of increased numbers of workers in precarious employment relationships.

OPSEU undertook an on-going grievance strategy and campaign to "chase" bargaining unit work that the employer attempted to make more precarious. The limits and possibilities of this strategy are surfacing through grievance arbitration awards. In 1999 and 2002 members were encouraged to file grievances relating to the "integrity of the bargaining unit," to try to bring contract work back within the coverage of the collective agreement. In 2002 a number of grievances were won in which work done by temporary agency and fee-for-service workers was returned to the bargaining unit.

Workers within the OPS are not victims of the rise of precarious employment but agents who are trying to resist, both individually and collectively (Barndt 2002). As the employer used a variety of strategies to expand the variety of the precarious employment, workers responded. One strategy focused on workers' key demand to gain access to permanent work. Another strategy involved calling for improved wages and working conditions among workers in precarious employment. Both contract workers and temporary agency workers are seeing improvements in their wages, working conditions, and union status. The erosion of the standard employment relationship has, at a minimum, been slowed. Women workers, in particular, have contested privatization and precarious employment. This resistance often goes unacknowledged and needs to be recorded.

GENDER, PRECARIOUS EMPLOYMENT, AND POWER

A number of key insights emerge from these three case studies. First, the Ontario provincial government is an active catalyst in the rise of a variety of precarious employment. A decade ago, proponents of new public management – the "new" approach to managing government workplaces – claimed that the way to resolve the crisis of the debt and deficits in the public sector was to rely on strategies from the private sector. Downsizing, privatization, commodification, and marketization are part of the neo-liberal strategy. The reliance on new public management had a profound impact on the organization of work within government workplaces, and it was considered critical to the emergence of a more "flexible" workforce.

Second, it is often argued that privatization is deeply political (Leys 2001). The emergence of precarious employment relationships is equally as political (Stanford 1996). These precarious relationships seek to fundamentally alter the power relations between the state-as-employer and the frontline workers and their union, and to ensure that the state-as-employer has even greater power.

Third, the changes brought about by the Ontario Conservative government are not monolithic. Power relations are contested, challenged, and resisted over time and space. Between 1995 and 2002 there were three sets of negotiations between the provincial government and the OPS bargaining unit of OPSEU. Two culminated in lengthy strikes – among the largest in

Canadian labour history. The core issues of each strike related to ways to stop or slow down the expansion of precarious employment. Through resistance, workers have had an impact on the shape and effectiveness of the flexibility strategies of the state-as-employer and, in a limited way, on the formation of the neo-liberal state in Ontario.

The undermining of the standard employment relationship within the Ontario Public Service is a complex and contradictory process. It provides an opportunity to reflect on gendered precariousness (Vosko 2002) in Ontario's labour market. The way the provincial government restructured its workforce had the effect of increasing the proportion of women workers, and the primarily women workers of the OPS, in the office administration job classification. Despite women's predominance in the OPS, traditionally female-dominated occupational categories such as clerical work continue to have lower wages compared to many of the male-dominated administrative positions. New public management has built upon, reinforced, and extended the existing sex/gender division of labour in the OPS. Women's power has not increased.

The strategies used by the state-as-employer are a clear example of a gendered harmonizing down (Armstrong 1996) and an increased precariousness. This trend has happened not only through downsizing and marketization of services but with the erosion of the standard employment relationship (see also Lewchuk et al., this volume). Downsizing and cutbacks hit the male-dominated operational-maintenance and technical positions the hardest. When sections of OPS work were restructured into discrete units ripe for privatization, such as Information Technology units, they did not transform into private companies with permanent jobs. Instead, the work went to fee-for-service workers – to solo self-employed people.

We might assume that solo self-employment represents a higher status than various forms of wage work, but the picture is much more complex. Solo self-employed people work on a fee-for-service basis and may be paid a higher hourly rate than Crown employees doing the same work, but they lack benefits, statutory protection, job security, and bargaining power. Furthermore, in the case of the meat inspectors, pay rates, while initially higher than those of the former employees of the OPS, remained stagnant for seven years. Scheduling of hours of work was used as a control mechanism and, as a result, the inspectors' income was unstable, and workers were expected to cover the costs of the province's food-safety system. These workers turned initially to the limited statutory protections, where they were found to be employees. Ultimately they turned to the union for creative strategies, and organized a public campaign to improve their wages and working conditions and to gain union status. Their struggle paid off, when, in November 2003, OPSEU won a grievance, under the notion of bargaining unit integrity, bringing meat inspectors back into the unit.

The shift to this form of employment has a clear impact on union strength. In the case of the meat inspectors, these workers had played an important role and provided bargaining power when their services were withdrawn during the 1996 strike. By placing their positions outside the bargaining unit, the state-as-employer aimed to reduce the bargaining power of the individuals and of the union as a whole.

Meat inspectors' status of solo self-employed is inseparable from gender. Why was meat inspection, formerly a domain of male employees, transformed into solo self-employment? Are these forms perceived to be of higher status or a domain of entrepreneurship? In truth, meat inspectors did not resemble entrepreneurs on any level. They lost, rather than gained, control over their work and income when they shifted from being employees to self-employed workers.

Different strategies were used in the female-dominated clerical category. In the courts, the state-as-employer turned to more unclassified short-term contract staff and more part-timers, especially in the unclassified category. These workers retained their union status, but their employer's use of hours of work as a mechanism of control undermined their ability to control their work environment. In the Ministry of Health, clerical work was privatized. Clerical workers hired through agencies received lower wages but, on a weekly basis, had a slightly higher take-home pay than the regular court workers because the agency staff had full-time hours of work. These temporary workers had no job security, no union, and little statutory protection.

The growth of precarious employment in the OPS has a profound impact on all front-line workers. Greater job insecurity, downward pressures on workers' wages and benefits, and decreased union coverage result in diminished power for the provincial public service workforce. This decrease, however, does not mean that workers are not resisting. As we have shown, they are resisting – and they are making a difference.

CONCLUSION

This analysis is but a starting point for assessing the major changes in public sector workplaces and in new public management strategies in the context of globalization and privatization. Central to the neo-liberal restructuring is the growth of gendered precarious employment relationships. All too often the analysis of the neo-liberal state ignores the view of the front-line workers and disregards the nature of the employment relationships with the state. This chapter attempts to provide a worker-centred perspective on the downsizing, privatization, and marketization of the public sector.

As the three case studies demonstrate, Ontario's front-line public sector workers confronted a multiplicity of strategies, from 1995 to 2002, designed to change the organization of work and to reduce their collective power. These changes are not gender neutral. Any analysis of the neo-liberal state is not complete without an assessment of the gender impact of these strategies: underlying the new public management, there is a specific gender bias. New public management, as the OPS case demonstrates, is built on and extends the existing sex/gender division of labour. Women's clerical work has grown as a proportion of the OPS, and this work is even more invisible and undervalued as service work with clients. There has been a gendered harmonizing down in the employment relationships in the OPS. Moreover, the gendered makeup of the increasingly precarious workers needs to be acknowledged; men tend to dominate fee-for-service, solo self-employed positions, and women tend to dominate either part-time contract positions or temporary agency positions.

Finally, we cannot overlook the resistance strategies used by the workers, some individual and some collectively, to fight back against the erosion of the standard employment relationship. This resistance demonstrates that global changes that are often thought to be too large and too powerful are indeed being challenged by workers. Resistance in the workplace does matter. Public sector workers have had an impact on the policies of the neo-liberal state. As long as the workers are resisting these changes, as they have done through these seven years, the neo-liberal state's new public management strategy of "doing less with more," of running public services "just like a business," will be slowed down and changed.

Privatizing Public Employment Assistance and Precarious Employment in Toronto

ALICE DE WOLFF

This chapter examines federal and provincial government policy changes in the provision of employment assistance. It focuses particularly on the privatization of federally funded employment services and its effect on non-profit agencies that provide employment assistance programs, on workers, and on precarious employment.

In the late 1980s and early 1990s the federal government adopted components of a neo-liberal approach to labour market competitiveness, with the primary goal of reducing spending and transferring greater labour market responsibilities to the provinces (Griffin Cohen 2003, 4, 8). Through the *Employment Insurance Act* of 1996, the federal government dramatically reformed its primary labour market policy mechanism – the unemployment insurance program. In the same period it backed away from a tripartite (employers, unions, and government) industrial development approach to labour market planning, most notably by closing the Canadian Labour Force Development Board. Other policies facilitated the labour market retention of the baby boom generation by cancelling pre-retirement programs and mandatory retirement in certain contexts, and by a general failure to tailor immigration policy to labour market cycles.

The 1996 employment insurance (EI) legislation set the framework for transferred responsibility for labour market training from the federal government to those provinces that were prepared to enter into a labour market partnerships. Over the same period, several provinces, most notably Ontario, have deregulated the labour market by lowering employment standards. And several provinces have undercut lower-wage markets by transforming social welfare programs to workfare programs (Klassen and Schneider 2002). Amid all these changes, employment counselling and assistance continue to be funded by both the federal and the provincial governments. Programs at both levels are shaped by a mixture of uncoordinated deregulation and by restraint in social spending. Community-based and college employment counselling and training have been severely cut back and replaced by a private training industry. New systemic barriers to women and other marginalized workers have emerged (Critoph 2003; Lior and Wismer 2003; McBride 1998; Stephen 2000). In Ontario, employment assistance programs are currently delivered almost exclusively by non-profit agencies, which have experienced dramatic changes in the past ten years. Ironically, the community workers who provide the counselling are themselves largely contract workers, so they, in turn, share many of the same dimensions of precarious employment as the clients they serve.

This chapter finds that even though the professional practices of employment counsellors are egalitarian in principle – that is, professionals in this field want their services to be available to anyone who wants to make changes in their employment situation, regardless of whether they are underemployed or unemployed – in practice, funding conditions restrict access to these services. The restrictions are reinforced by the barriers built into employment insurance and social assistance. This chapter highlights the consequences for workers in temporary and contract employment, older women and men, young people, aboriginal people, and recent immigrants, as well as their difficulties in accessing the core services of individual counselling and financial assistance. It concludes that collective action by both community-based agencies and workers in precarious employment is required to challenge the outcomes of the privatization of employment assistance and to work towards creating a just system that better meets workers' needs.

The project on which this chapter is based was designed in collaboration with Toronto Organizing for Fair Employment (TOFFE), a community-based workers' organization committed to improving wages and working conditions. This chapter is oriented by TOFFE's concern with conditions affecting immigrant workers and workers of colour in precarious employment. The community activists and researchers involved understand precarious employment to mean jobs that are not full-time permanent and that have few benefits, limited legal regulatory protection, short tenure, and low wages, jobs where workers are often underemployed. This chapter draws on 15 interviews conducted with non-profit program directors and managers of Toronto agencies where employment counselling is a core activity. These interviews were conducted in 2002 and 2003.

EMPLOYMENT COUNSELLING AND PRECARIOUS EMPLOYMENT

Many people who have attended job counselling sessions since the mid-1990s have heard this message: "There is no such thing as a permanent job" and "Get used to it, adjust, shape yourselves to the new economy."[1] Deena Ladd, the coordinator of TOFFE, often tells the story of her own experience at a mandatory employment counselling session when she was looking for work in 1998. "We were told that we had to get used to it, and that embracing the future meant looking at temporary jobs and contracts." Because a worker in a government-supported employment assessment centre delivered the message and because the message is, by no means, uncommon, the incident raises a number of questions about governments' role in the growth of precarious employment. The "get used to it" message is often delivered with urgency, particularly to young people and immigrants. Does this message influence the changing nature of employment in the Canadian labour force and the social location of workers that find themselves in precarious employment? How and to what extent does it reflect government policy?

The "get used to it" message describes the reality for a distressingly large number of workers in Canada, but not for the majority who still hold full-time permanent jobs. The proportion of full-time permanent jobs in Canada dropped from 67 per cent to 63 per cent between 1998 and 2002. This is a significant change that has affected 4 per cent of the workforce. In the same period the proportion of full-time temporary jobs increased from 4 per cent to 7 per cent; and workers who are solo self-employed increased from 7 per cent to 10 per cent (Vosko, Zukewich, and Cranford 2003; Vosko and Zukewich, this volume). In Toronto many recent immigrants are particularly likely to find themselves in these types of jobs. Most non-permanent jobs are not good jobs – most are low paid, have almost no benefits, and very few employment protections. Solo self-employment in particular is often promoted as an alternative to other forms of low-waged work, but it is not a high-income alternative for most people. In 1999 solo self-employed women earned an average of $13,032, compared to the average of $26,015 earned by employed women. Solo self-employed men earned $19,769, compared to the average of $40,183 earned by male employees (Fudge, Tucker, and Vosko 2002).

All the agency managers and program directors interviewed are familiar with and concerned about precarious employment and the quality of the jobs their clients are able to find. Most report that their agencies handle this reality by making certain that their clients are informed about conditions they are likely to find in the labour market. None of them feel that their agencies promote precarious employment, although many recognize that they are intermediaries in a labour market that does not provide a sufficient number of decent employment opportunities. As one agency manager explained: "In newcomer job search workshops we talk about advantages and disadvantages of temp work, contracting, home working, self-employment because we have to talk about labour market trends in Canada, so they aren't shocked, or take it personally when this is the only kind of work they are offered. We are not forcing them into it."

Young People and Recent Immigrants

Many young people and recent immigrants, particularly women, find that it takes them longer to break into full-time permanent jobs in Toronto than it took their predecessors before the mid-1990s. A large proportion of those in temporary work of various forms, ranging from seasonal, casual, and fixed employment to work provided through a temporary help agency, are under the age of 25. Only 10 per cent of Canadians who were full-time permanently employed were aged 15–24 in 2002, while 55 per cent of part-time temporary workers were in that age group (Vosko, Cranford, and Zukewich 2003). It may appear that a temporary job is a great way to enter the labour force, but increasing numbers of workers find that it is a dead end rather than a path to more satisfying employment. As one agency manager put it: "The longer you are in contingent work, the less likely you will get a permanent job."

Toronto has a labour market polarized and segmented by "race" and gender (Cranford, Das Gupta, and Vosko, this volume). The city's economy relies on an underemployed immigrant labour force to fill low-waged precarious jobs (Ornstein 2000; Statistics Canada 2003c). In the mid-1990s people of colour, especially from Africa, the Caribbean, South Asia, East and Southeast Asia, Arab and West Asia, and Latin America, experienced special difficulty in finding permanent stable employment, and many held precarious jobs with low incomes. Women in these groups earned lower incomes than men, from work that was neither full time nor full year. Men with the lowest incomes from work that was not full time or full year were from East and Southeast Asia and Latin America (Ornstein 2000). Those who immigrated between 1991 and 1996 arrived during a recession and found it more difficult than earlier groups to get work in the years immediately following their arrival. In this period, even those immigrants selected for their skills and labour market suitability did not do better economically, in the long run, than their family class counterparts (Wanner 2003). The "recovery" of the late 1990s still left 16.5 per cent fewer recent immigrants in employment than their Canadian counterparts in 2001. This gap is more dramatic for women than for men. In 2001, 8.8 per cent fewer recently arrived immigrant men were employed compared to Canadian-born men, down from 11.5 per cent in 1991. For recently arrived women, the gap in the employment rate was 22.9 per cent that year, a gap double the rate in 1991 (Statistics Canada 2003c). One manager described the experience of many of her clients this way: "Highly skilled individuals spend the first number of years trying to get licensed in their profession. Their wives, however, take any work that they can get and their professional experience goes by the wayside. To get 'Canadian experience' they work for temp agencies and get into temp work. Men tend to be the primary professional, so these have become women's issues."

Canada's immigration policy of favouring highly skilled workers does not make it easier for recent immigrants to find work. Even though the selection process appears geared to trends in the Canadian labour force, many highly educated individuals arrive in Canada only to find that there are no jobs in their field or that, without Canadian experience, they are not qualified for a job in their field, or that their credentials will not be recognized without further training in Canada.

Precarious Employment in Toronto

The growth of precarious employment is a predictable outcome of both government and employer strategies and policies. Employers in all sectors are scaling back the number of full-time permanent workers and increasing their reliance on temporary help agencies and subcontracting. At the same time, federal and provincial governments (except Quebec; see Bernstein, this volume) are weakening basic employment standards and reducing workers' access to EI and health and safety benefits (Lippel, this volume). Consequently, as Lewchuck, de Wolff, King, and Polanyi argue in this volume, growing numbers of workers are "'free agents' in a weakly regulated labour market."

Managers and directors of non-profit agencies are aware of the role of privatization and just-in-time production and flexible human resource management strategies in labour market deregulation. As one noted: "The jobs employers offer at job fairs are generally not good. They may get a lot of hires, but clients don't stay and the jobs may be part time, contract. There isn't good matching." Another manager links this observation to restructuring at the firm level: "Fewer companies are running their own recruitment, and are now using temporary agencies – the only way to get into 'pink-collar,' lower-end white-collar jobs is through a temp agency. I'm astounded at the number of companies that don't hire. Banks, for instance, show up at job fairs but hire only through an agency. Huge sectors of the labour market are being closed to unskilled youth." A third manager observed that "information technology (IT) and administrative workers are all hired through temporary agencies. Very few computer programming jobs are permanent."

GOVERNMENT EMPLOYMENT ASSISTANCE POLICIES

Employment assistance programs at both the federal and the provincial levels are increasingly linked to social assistance measures, with the primary program objective of moving people into employment. Many programs are not oriented to genuine labour adjustment – that is, they do not aim to identify labour market gaps, train people to fill these gaps, or promote better jobs.

Federal Policy: The Reprivatization of Employment Assistance

In 1996 the federal government privatized employment services through Bill C-111, *The Employment Insurance Act*. Services formerly handled by government-run centres, including employment assessment, employment counselling, job-finding assistance, and resource provision, were transferred to third parties, which, to date, are primarily non-profit organizations. One program manager addressed some of the transition difficulties: the government has "put unstable, under-funded not-for-profit agencies in the position of managing government policies – polices which made large numbers of people ineligible for assistance. They have to mediate a labour market that is increasingly casual."

This move signals a new chapter in a long history of the regulation of employment services in Canada. In the late 1800s and early 1900s, immigrant workers and labour organizations forced public debate about the abuses of private employment agencies that acted as employment brokers, mostly for new immigrants. In 1918 the federal government began to regulate private agencies and instituted a system of joint federal-provincial employment offices (Vosko 2000). For decades, this system was used as a policy tool for connecting Canadian-born and immigrant workers with jobs and for assisting industrial sectors through periods of employment growth and recession. The National Employment Service and the Unemployment Insurance program were established in 1940. The insurance fund provided consistent resources for federal employment counselling and training programs that remained a centerpiece of the public service until the deficit reduction policies of the early 1990s and the introduction of EI legislation of 1996.

The EI *Act* restructured the delivery systems dramatically. The Act was a core component of large federal government spending cuts and promised "savings" to the EI fund of $2 billion a year by 2001 (Torjman 2000). It introduced new measures for EI claimants that included wage subsidies, earnings supplements, self-employment assistance, job-creation partnerships, and lower levels of employment benefits. It reduced EI claims by limiting access to benefits for most workers who contribute to EI and by changing premiums and benefit levels. The legislation increased the qualifying period by between 180 and 300 hours in a 12-month period (Torjman 2000). Qualifying hours were raised for new entrants to the workforce – immigrants and young workers were raised significantly to a minimum of 910 hours in a 12-month period. As a consequence, the proportion of unemployed workers who were eligible for EI benefits dramatically dropped, from 83 per cent in 1993 to 38 per cent in 2001 (CLC 2003; Stephen 2000). The Act introduced individual voucher payments for training and created a niche for mostly private, short-term, labour market training. It also laid the groundwork for negotiating different models of responsibility for employment training with most provinces. Ontario is the only province that did not take this responsibility from the federal government, as of 2003.

At the same time, the Act privatized the delivery of employment assessment and counselling. In Toronto, only 7 of 20 federal government offices operated by Human Resources Development Canada (HRDC) remained open.[2] The new delivery system expanded to include 11 non-profit assessment centres, and over 30 non-profit employment resource centres. Before 1996, workers receiving unemployment insurance met with counsellors employed by the federal government. Now non-profit, community-based organizations handle employment assessment and counselling programs. Public service unions, anticipating a loss of unionized jobs (and, indeed, careers) and the removal of system-wide standards for delivering employment advice and benefits, opposed this change (National Union of Public and General Employees 1998). As the legislation emerged, unions made prototype agreements with sympathetic non-profit organizations, proposing that agencies should either reject federal funding for assessment or counselling or, if agencies accepted funding, they should insist that a union member be seconded from the public service to perform the work. Their efforts raised some awareness of the coming changes, but they did not halt the passage of the legislation or alter the pace of change.

In Toronto, the seven Canada Employment Centres have computerized job boards, electronic kiosks for filing EI claims, and information officers who direct people through the system. EI claimants and some social assistance recipients are referred to one of the 14 contracted-out assessment centres, where they attend individual and group employment counselling sessions and are required to complete return-to-work plans. Individual claimants can then be referred to one of the employment resource centres for job search assistance, occupation or language (English or French) assessment, counselling, workshops, and self-employment programs. Some specialized programs still exist for those claimants who need special assistance – specifically, women, youth, and recent immigrants.

The core services of this privatized infrastructure are designed to assist the reduced number of EI claimants. No equivalent strategy exists for people ineligible for EI. As one manager observed, "There is no incentive in the system to serve people who are not on EI." Workers who are not eligible for EI are entitled to use self-access components of the infrastructure but are ineligible for individual counselling in most programs and for training and wage subsidies.

Privatization of employment assistance has not been a smooth process. It mirrors the process of privatization in health care, and its effects on ancillary workers, as described by Armstrong and Laxer in this volume. In the absence of a labour market agreement between Ontario and the federal governments, HRDC managers based in each region have made the decisions about regional priorities and how the new network of programs will work. This regional autonomy has generated considerable unevenness in the system, introduced more complex internal decision-making procedures and funding criteria, and new levels of uncertainty for non-profit agencies.

In Toronto the guidelines for receiving funding are often unclear and uneven, and regional budgets have, at different times, been over-allocated and frozen. Since 2000, HRDC has been criticized very publicly for its mismanagement of grants. In response, rather than reversing the trend towards contracting out public employment services, the department developed an elaborate financial accountability process for all funds distributed as contracts or grants. The accountability mechanisms became tighter still in 2004, with the open bidding for services developed by non-profit agencies, deeper budget scrutiny, process audits, and twice-a-year financial audits.

Citizenship and Immigration Programs: No Employment Strategy

Many immigrants have been selected to come to Canada because of their training, education, and job experience. Yet there are very few mechanisms to assist newcomers in matching their experience with available jobs. Citizenship and Immigration Canada (CIC) funds short-term language training and some job-search workshops for immigrants who are seeking employment. It does not support employment counselling or training, but rather relies on the privately delivered, EI-funded employment assistance infrastructure to provide these services for newcomers. Recent immigrants are not offered substantial assistance with retraining, upgrading, or finding employment on their arrival, because, to qualify for these services, recipients must be eligible for EI. Language Instruction for Newcomers to Canada (LINC) programs are still offered by a range of non-profit organizations, although this funding has been cut back over the past decade.

Most agencies that support recent immigrants rely on CIC funding, which may include short job-search workshops and language instruction. Settlement programs that expand beyond CIC policies to provide employment counselling do so with HRDC and other funding. Several of the managers interviewed reported that the CIC-funded job-search workshops were far too short, and they criticized CIC for not creating the conditions for effective settlement experiences because of this lack of employment-related support. As one manager put it, CIC policy assumes "that somehow people can settle without being gainfully employed ... If the future of Canada is in immigration, then Canada has to create the conditions to come and settle, rather than immigrants coming and creating their own conditions for settlement." As it stands, immigrants make up a substantial part of the client base of most agencies in the HRDC system, although the majority of these agencies are not able to offer the specialized services needed by immigrants. In particular, new program supports are needed for the highly trained people currently selected by Canada's immigration policy. Some agencies are developing approaches that provide more profession-specific language programs and orientation sessions. Workers trained outside Canada also need support to gain entry into professional associations, many of which have rigid membership requirements. As long as professional bodies in Canada have their own systems of certification, immigrants without Canadian credentials will need effective advocates.

Workfare: The "Shortest Route to Employment"

The provincial government's clearest policy on employment training and counselling is embodied in the Ontario Works (OW) program. Ontario Works is a workfare program that replaced social assistance in 1996. The policy message it sends is that all adults in the province, including single parents and many of those with disabilities, should be in the labour force, not on social assistance. Programs "focus on supporting participants to participate actively in determining and taking steps that represent the shortest route to employment for the individual participant" (Ontario Government 2001).

Ontario Works relies on a privatized delivery system that overlaps with, but is distinct from, the HRDC system. Non-profit, community-based agencies and private companies are encouraged to provide training and employment experience. Income assistance is administered by government offices, but non-profit groups are funded to offer employment-related support, including assistance with job plans, job search, and basic education as well as job-specific training, literacy training, employment placement, wage subsidies, and supports for self-employment. Several programs are tailored to youth. A significant component of OW provides wage subsidies to employers for short-term job placements, and many agencies are involved in "job development" – finding employers who will hire and train participants in a subsidized position for a limited period of six months. One manager described a kind of responsibility "football" that is played between the levels of government as it relates to the six-month OW wage subsidies and EI. He noted the "tacit understanding that, after six months of employment, clients will be eligible for EI, and that if they become unemployed at that point they can be transferred to the federal system."

ORGANIZATIONAL EFFECTS OF PRIVATIZATION

As workers are facing the harsh realities of EI change and the accompanying employment counselling system, so are organizations. Non-profit agencies that act as HRDC-funded assessment centres include school boards, colleges, and large organizations like Goodwill, the YWCA, and settlement organizations. Agencies that have become employment resource centres include many that previously offered community-based training, as well as neighbourhood service centres and settlement agencies. New agencies have been created to provide programs for workers from specific neighbourhoods, occupations, or targeted groups. Some agencies are funded only by government programs, while others find charitable funding that makes it possible for them to broaden their programs. In either case, the overall impact of government policy changes and downloading on non-profit organizations is substantial.

Transforming Training into Employment Counselling

Many of the non-profit organizations making up the complex and increasingly privatized system have transformed their core services from skills and transition training to employment counselling, in a pragmatic response to funding requirements. With Bill C-111, the federal government withdrew from job training, leaving little support for community college and community-based training. Consequently, a new for-profit private training industry has emerged. The effects of this change include an explosion of training options, increased fees, and narrowly defined skills-based training, which have been well documented by Stephen (2000) and the Toronto Training Board (Viswanathan 2000). As one manager explained: "There used to be a program specifically for women who were re-entering the workforce. It was a six-month training program that really gave them a chance to get back into the workforce – skills training, a real opportunity to plan, and connections with employers. It worked for new immigrants as well. But it's gone."

EI training benefits have been paid by individual vouchers since the EI *Act* of 1996. This system is proving difficult to manage. The Toronto HRDC region has been unable to forecast its voucher budget with any accuracy, initiating cycles where training in the region is first over-allocated, then frozen, and then over-allocated once again. This fluctuation has put agency counsellors in situations where workers come to them, having done everything possible to be eligible for training – they have completed action plans, researched their options, and found space in an available training program – and counsellors have to inform them that no funding is available through EI.

In 2003, the type of training that counsellors were permitted to recommend narrowed: EI recipients can no longer use training funds to make significant changes in their occupation. Funds must be used to enhance individuals' existing employment opportunities and to get people back to work with the least time and expenditure possible. No matter how close they are to being qualified for an occupation of their choice (even in occupations where there are shortages, such as nursing), they receive support, if they are employed in another occupation, only to stay in that occupation. Workers trained outside Canada who are eligible for EI, but are not working in their chosen profession, experience this measure as particularly frustrating.

Measures of Success: Employment Goals

Professional and sympathetic counselling practice is about wanting the best for clients and, at the same time, helping them to assess the possibilities honestly. All the managers and project officers interviewed wanted their clients to find good jobs, and most stressed that they do not compel people to take the first job that comes along. As one of them said: "If employers tell us that they can't guarantee a job for longer than three months, the majority of our clients won't take it. We may wish that they take it because it will get them some experience, will modify their resume, but we don't force people ... They will just come back to us in three months."

However, HRDC contracts require that programs attract a certain number of clients, and that they match clients with programs or jobs. The most stringent requirements apply to agencies that are operating assessment centres. With privatization, decisions about the renewal of funding are tightly linked to formal assessments of how well agencies meet their targets.

Both the federal and the provincial governments have stated that their goal for HRDC and OW programs is to use the available funds to get people into work in the shortest time, while using the least resources. HRDC includes non-employment program goals in its formal evaluations – goals such as connecting clients to networks, increasing clients' self-confidence, and increasing job interview and job-search skills. But agency managers recognize that meeting these goals does not bring the same probability of future funding as getting people into employment.

HRDC expects assessment centres and employment resource centres to report that between 65 per cent and 80 per cent of their clients found work or participated in training during the contract period. Assessment centres are expected to see 80 per cent of their clients in work within three months of completing individual action plans. Agencies working with immigrants have the same targets or timelines; they have no capacity to reflect the particular difficulties facing this client group. These targets have not changed since 1996, but the opportunities for training have become much more restricted. Reaching the targets is not only more difficult because of reduced access to training but also, as one manager remarked, "it is difficult in this labour market." Agencies do not meet these targets easily.

This system encourages agencies to choose clients most likely to be successful in their programs, so their success rates stay high. "Cherry picking" successful clients may reduce access to counselling for those workers who need it the most. It takes a conscious effort on the part of everyone in an agency to resist this tendency. One project manager described the policy developed by her agency in these words: "Some people take the view that you have to pick the most employable clients to counsel. We've never taken that position. What we might do is counsel somebody and not count them in our total if we know that they are going to take longer."

One agency has a merit-pay system that reflects an effort to mix the requirement to find employment with other program goals. This system makes it possible for counsellors to increase their pay by a maximum of 10 per cent each year. It is weighted to take into account the complexity of clients' needs, how long clients stay employed, and the number of apprenticeship placements. Although this agency's effort to accommodate complex program goals is interesting, the fact that it has adopted merit pay for its staff reflects a significant change from the non-profit service culture to a for-profit culture.

A New Client Group

Most agencies now have a new core client group: EI claimants. Meanwhile, agencies struggle to find funds for programs available for non-claimants. Before privatization, government workers handled EI claims, and non-profit agencies offered a range of training and counselling programs for people who were not EI claimants. The constraints of the EI fund mean that counsellors in most programs are frustrated because they can offer EI claimants little support to help them make substantial changes in their employment. At the same time, they have little to offer their former non-EI claimants beyond self-service resource centres and job-finding clubs. As one project manager put it: "A year ago HRDC took 'people who are under-employed' out of our contract. Consequently, that program no longer serves people who want to be pro-active, people who are not using their skills, or who want to develop new ones."

In the late 1990s the Toronto HRDC region increased restrictions about eligibility for services. A number of agencies challenged these restrictions, arguing that the spirit of Bill C-111 was to use the EI fund to assist all unemployed and under-employed people in Canada. Several agency managers reported taking their challenge to the national HRDC director, but there has been no change at the regional level.

Among the managers we interviewed, three had seen significant restrictions in their core program after 1996. One program lost its ability to serve workers in the Live-In Caregiver Program. Another no longer serves under-employed workers: its manager said, "We can't serve anyone who is working more than 30 hours a week, including temp agency workers." Yet another is permitted to provide programs only during the day, effectively excluding most people who work part time.

The only EI-funded program that provides significant training, mentoring, and financial assistance is the Self-Employment Assistance Program. It provides support for developing business plans, training, a year's training allowance, plus whatever start-up profits are earned during the year. It is over-subscribed, with three times as many people applying, according to estimates, as are accepted.

In this context, it is not surprising that counsellors cannot find the way to encourage their clients to see a bright employment future. The only substantial change-oriented program in the HRDC system involves self-employment, a route to employment creation that leads to exclusion from a host of statutory entitlements, social and labour protections, and employer-provided benefits (Vosko and Zukewich, this volume).

Expanded Funding: Reliance on Charitable Status

To serve people who are unemployed but ineligible for EI, and to provide a range of services broader than those funded by HRDC, agencies are expanding their bases of funding. Most now rely on charitable status to provide them access to United Way and other foundation funding. Non-profit agencies in the arts, health, community sports, and the like were all compelled to adopt this strategy in the late 1990s as government funding shifted away from core grants (Scott 2003). Now, considerable senior administrative time and attention is paid to securing highly competitive funding and to maintaining relationships with a range of funders.

Charitable status is not available to organizations that offer services restricted to a specific group of people, including women and recent immigrants. A number of agencies have had to change their fundamental nature in order to expand their funding base.

A central concern about charitable status is that it limits the amount of advocacy in which an organization can engage. One manager who has experienced the loss and reinstatement of an agency's charitable status says that it is now very measured about how vocal it will be about concerns that may be interpreted as "political." Charitable status makes it more difficult for agencies to be the advocates for vulnerable and unemployed workers

Administering Public Funds: HRDC

Changing HRDC funding criteria and program priorities make the survival of agencies, and the survival of jobs within them, a constant preoccupation. According to some managers, the demand to survive prevents them from spending the time needed to challenge the new policy framework: "Our agencies are unstable, and we spend too much time trying to save jobs or the agency itself."

Managers fully recognize that they are managing public funds and that they need to be accountable. Many feel, however, that the system is too onerous. As one noted: "We are over-audited." All workers who receive EI benefits are "tracked" through the system. Assessment centre agencies must use Contact 4, a computerized government-operated system which records the times when counsellors have seen each client, the nature of the "intervention," and the places where the client was referred. Contact 4 is not compatible with other databases, so it creates more work for counsellors and administrators.

A number of increasingly punitive measures ensure that agencies follow HRDC rules to the letter. In 2002 HRDC installed an in-house computerized accounting system that will not release monthly payments to agencies until it has current Contact 4 information, other program statistics, the previous month's expense statement, and cash-flow projections. Agency managers must have a tight administrative system in order to maintain their funding. Furthermore, because employment is a measure of success, agencies must create a system for staying in touch with and tracking clients over the course of one year at least – by any measure, a labour-intensive exercise.

Administering Public Funds: CIC

In 2001 CIC introduced a standardized program accountability system, the Contribution Accountability Framework (CAF), and a computerized Immigration Contribution Accountability Measurement System (iCAMS), which is similar in its purpose to HRDC's Contact 4. These systems are intended to create comparable programs and administrative practices in LINC and other programs across the country. iCAMS records not only program and financial indicators but also certain types of personal information about program participants.

Several agencies report that both the provincial and the federal governments request that they enter security-related information about clients who are landed immigrants into iCAMS and that they keep copies of their clients' Immigration Record of Landing Cards. Agency workers who handle the iCAMS data are required to go through security checks by CIC. As one manager said, "We are all opposed to monitoring, but it's in our contracts." The iCAMS system has been introduced in a wide number of agencies, with 35,000 clients entered in the system as of July 2003 (CIC 2003).

Wage Subsidy Programs:
Limited Monitoring and Employment Standards Violations

EI and OW include wage subsidy programs, where employers are given a subsidy in return for providing participants with both training and work experience. The duration of subsidies is usually six months. Agency job developers connect employers and worker-participants. Funders attempt to ensure that these subsidized jobs become permanent, but most agencies do not have the resources for follow-up and monitoring. Some of these positions offer useful training, but the kinds of jobs created by wage subsidies are rarely long term and permanent.

Most agencies have little capacity for follow-up, even though there can be problems with wage subsidy placements. One agency manager dealt with potential problems in advance by requiring "employers to have workers' compensation, make employer contributions like EI, and [ensure] that the position must not intentionally be short term." Others also recognized that workers are quite vulnerable: "If the employer violates employment standards and the worker raises the issue, even if the worker has been amazing it is unlikely that s/he will get their all-important reference."

Counsellors at one agency, the Workers Information Centre, report a worrying number of complaints from workers in wage subsidy jobs. Incidents include situations where employers have harassed the worker, paid the worker only the subsidy (below minimum wage), not paid for overtime hours, not paid for holidays, laid off the worker before the end of the contract for no apparent reason, or not provided the worker with the training promised in the contract. Many of these workers had approached their placement agencies to help them sort out these types of problems but had received little support.

Who Can Expect a Good Job? Not Many Employment Counsellors

Many counsellors and support staff in non-profit employment agencies themselves work on contract. Employment assistance agencies do not receive multi-year or core funding. Government funding contracts are renewed each year, as are most charitable grants, and agency managers are increasingly reluctant to hire permanent staff. Many workers remain in contract jobs for years, without a standard employment relationship or benefits. This uncertainty creates constant insecurity and stress.[3] As one manager said, "All new positions in this agency are contracts."

HRDC and other funders limit the amount of money they are prepared to pay an employment counsellor or administrative support person, and they regularly indicate that they are not prepared to fund benefits beyond a basic wage. As one manager said: "Agencies I have worked with pay their staff only what funders will allow for staff costs. This means that funders are setting our human resource policy as well as other program directions." Those agencies wanting to be principled employers must therefore seek funds from multiple sources.

Another manager described her frustrations with the unions that organize workers in non-profit employment assistance agencies. Her experience is that, for every monetary raise the unions have won, she and other managers have had to create more contingent contracts. She is frustrated that there is no forum to have a discussion between non-profit agencies and unions about government funding levels and the working conditions of employment counsellors in non-profit agencies. She has attempted to engage the current chair of Toronto's United Way in discussions about this issue, hoping that the chair's union background would make her sympathetic to the issues and that she would instigate talks between agencies and the unions.

Impact on Workers: Agency Workers

The counsellor who encouraged Ms Ladd to get used to a future of temporary work may well have been a contract worker herself. She may not have been able to see how she would ever get a permanent job doing this work, and her message may have been an effort to convey her own coping strategies. She may have thought she had to deliver this message to meet the requirements of her job. Or she may have perceived that she needed to encourage people to get into employment quickly to contribute to her agency's quota of employed clients.

Her job likely made her more sensitive to the barriers and insecurities in the labour market rather than to employment success stories. She was probably familiar with the limited programs available for people who want to change their situation, even for the "elite" group of people who are eligible for EI. She likely knew about the relative "luxury" of the Self-Employment Assistance Program, for instance, and she may have felt that this option was the most viable in an otherwise limited array of opportunities. If this situation frustrated her, or if she could see systematic program failures, she was not likely in a position where she could easily do something constructive about it. The insecurity of contract work can keep program staff from making critical observations in public.

Impact on Workers Looking for Jobs

Workers' experiences with employment assistance programs are arguably the real test of current employment policies. Significant groups of workers are excluded from employment assistance: many workers who are already in precarious employment find that they are not eligible for EI or for most of the programs supported by HRDC. The process whereby workers find out what they are eligible for now involves much more effort, potential confusion, and frustration. Workers used to be able to visit one location for assessments, training recommendations, job-search support, and the like. As these services have spread across a changing network of different agencies and locations, it takes considerable communications ability, effort, and time for most people to find the services that are the best for them. Workers are usually surprised and disturbed when they discover that the EI system is not intended to support any dreams and aspirations they might have to find a better job than their last one. Workers do not necessarily let go of their dreams, but the system is meant to get them into work, not into work they want.

When workers find a program, there is often not enough support. Programs and counsellors who are themselves insecure are often not able to provide the consistent support needed by workers. If workers are encouraged to consider temporary or contract jobs, they are rarely given the information they need about their rights as workers in these types of jobs. Newcomers particularly need this information so they know what to expect from the moment they begin working in Canada. And some of those workers who are in wage-subsidy jobs find that their employers are not willing to train them, that they will not get a longer-term position, and, sometimes, that the employer is violating their rights as workers. When there are problems with employers, professional associations, or government policy, workers need advocates. Charitable status, counsellors' contract status, and the unpredictability of regional HRDC-funding criteria make it less likely that there will be individuals or agencies in the system that will advocate for workers.

THE SYSTEMIC ENCOURAGEMENT OF PRECARIOUS WORK

Federal employment and immigration policies and provincial workfare policies are partly responsible for the difficulty that workers experience in breaking out of precarious employment. This study found several program effects that make it difficult for workers to move into more satisfying permanent employment.

The subcontracting relationship with government draws non-profit agencies into a policy framework that fails to support their professional practices and the role they have played well for many years – to provide employment counselling and transition training for a wide range of people seeking work, most of whom were not EI claimants. The resulting infrastructure is based on a policy that excludes those who are not eligible for EI – the majority of people without adequate work in Canada. In particular, it excludes workers on short-term contracts and temporary workers, many of whom are recent immigrants and women. It also excludes young people and newcomers who have no experience in the Canadian labour market.

Lack of access to EI-funded employment counselling and training support is a significant systemic barrier for newcomers and temporary and contract workers who want to get into more formal employment. Government policy goals of getting people into employment via the shortest route, and the need to demonstrate "savings" to the EI fund, are in tension with most agencies' goals of assisting people to find good jobs.

The unpredictability of the subcontracting relationship with government keeps agencies themselves unstable, forcing them to pay very close attention to the needs of government. The conditions of funding, the annual renewals, and minimal contributions to salaries keep many jobs in the sector unstable and precarious. In addition, the lack of resources and strong agreements for monitoring wage-subsidy programs makes it more likely that jobs found through these programs will not last longer than the subsidy, and that workers in these jobs will be vulnerable to employment standards violations.

CHANGING THE SITUATION

The privatization that began in 1996 has required constant restructuring, though it has not yet presented much opportunity for collective reflection on the overall direction of the changes. The employment assistance network must take stock of recent developments and exercise more control over its future. Because agencies are the core of the delivery infrastructure, they are in a new position of power to conceptualize and work for new policy and programs.

Non-profit agencies could act collectively to make a number of policy and program changes. It would be necessary, first, to define the special contributions that can be made by non-profit agencies, and then to come to a different balance between government and non-profit delivery, so that the particular strengths of the non-profit sector can be used most effectively. The overall policy change that would make the most significant difference would be to secure coordinated government funding from EI, CIC, or general revenue for employment assistance for all workers who are under-employed, unemployed, or newcomers. That development would require a radically reformed EI program that included shorter qualifying periods.

A CIC labour market strategy for immigrants that is closely coordinated with HRDC strategies, but not restricted by EI eligibility, could make a tremendous difference to the experience of newcomers. Further, transparent licensing processes are needed in all professions, and immediate effort needs to be directed towards establishing fair equivalencies for international credentials.

In the shorter term, several changes could minimize employment standard violations. Contractual agreements among governments, agencies, wage-subsidy employers, and workers that explicitly prohibit employment standards violations could easily be introduced. Information about violations should be made public and shared among wage-subsidy programs. Information about precarious employment should be made more public and shared among employment services programs.

Several measures could make employment in the sector less precarious. The most obvious is multi-year government and foundation funding, and levels of funding that support staff benefits and permanent positions. This direction could be developed into sector-wide agreements on wages and benefits that are negotiated between agency managers, unions, governments, and foundations. Finally, lifting the limitations on advocacy that are placed on registered charities would make it more possible for employment services programs to act as advocates for unemployed workers.

PART THREE

Regulating Precarious Employment: Institutions, Law, and Policy

9

Precarious Employment and the Law's Flaws: Identifying Regulatory Failure and Securing Effective Protection for Workers

STEPHANIE BERNSTEIN, KATHERINE LIPPEL, ERIC TUCKER, AND LEAH F. VOSKO

A new immigrant who speaks no English or French sews clothing at home for a company that subcontracts with other companies that contract with a large retail chain. Not only is she being paid less than the minimum wage, but, because of the cramped conditions in her home, she works in an area that is dimly lit and poorly ventilated. She finds that she frequently has severe headaches that prevent her from working or properly caring for her infant daughter.

A young man who dropped out of high school finally found a part-time job in a non-unionized factory after months of being unemployed. There were obvious uncorrected hazards, but no health and safety inspections had been conducted in two years and the joint health and safety committee existed on paper but had not met in recent memory. This worker suffered a severe laceration that required him to be off work for six weeks, but he encountered difficulty with the calculation of his earnings basis for workers' compensation. His employer claimed he was not cooperating in a return-to-work program and fired him, so his compensation was terminated. The young man does not know where to turn for assistance.

A middle-aged woman recently lost her unionized job. She applied for work at several locations, but they seemed to be hiring only younger workers. When she confronted one employer, he denied that age was a factor in their decision-making. Finally, a company that delivered newspapers offered her work but made her sign a contract that clearly stated she was an independent contractor and not an employee. A union organizer contacted her, but she didn't think she had the right to join. Eventually an application for certification was filed with the labour board and a vote was held, but the employer is claiming that the carriers are not employees. A decision is pending.

Each of these stories involves workers with diverse characteristics encountering different work-related problems, but they all have two things in common. First, all the workers can be described as being in precarious employment relations. They do not fit into a model of relatively recent origin, the "standard employment relationship," or a full-time continuous employment relationship where a worker has one employer, works on the employer's premises under direct supervision, and has access to social benefits and other entitlements that complete the social wage. Second, all these workers are encountering difficulty in accessing the protections that labour, employment, and social security law currently offer to workers in standard employment relationships. Although these stories are composites, they describe a reality that has recently attracted the attention of numerous scholars who are concluding that the dominant framework for regulating employment is increasingly incapable of taking into account the realities of precarious employment (Bernier et al. 2001; De Munck 1999; Fudge and Vosko 2001; Muckenberger 1989; Rodgers 1989; Supiot 1999).

Despite the evolving nature of labour law, regulatory protection generated by the state at the national and subnational levels still pivots on the standard employment relationship, at a time when the prevalence of this relationship is declining. Of course, the extent to which a legal regime is based on the standard employment relationship can vary from one law to the next, depending on its objective and logic, as well as on its place in the historical spectrum of the development and evolution of labour and social protection legislation (Deakin 2002a; Fudge, Tucker, and Vosko 2002), but, nevertheless, the norm is almost always central. This misfit not only deprives workers in precarious employment of the regulatory protection they need but also cultivates the institutionalization or crystallization of unequal power relations in the labour market, both between workers and employers and between different groups of workers, such as those between men and women (Cranford and Vosko, this volume; Fudge and Vosko 2001; Rubery 1999). Finding remedies for the inadequacies of the existing model of labour and social security law is one of the main challenges facing policy-makers, not only in Canada but elsewhere too (Bellace and Rood 1997; Bernier, Vallée, and Jobin 2003; ILO 2000b; Standing, 1999; Vosko 2004).

The study of precarious employment brings to the fore many manifestations of the inadequacy of workers' protection, and this chapter identifies some of the regulatory issues surrounding it. The first section outlines some of the definitions, concepts, and tendencies essential to an understanding of regulatory effectiveness and failure. In the second section, the specificity of regulatory failure in the context of precarious employment is explored through an examination of four related themes: disparity of treatment between workers in precarious employment and workers with greater security; gaps in legal coverage; the interaction between labour market position and social location; and the lack of compliance and enforcement. Regulatory protection does not operate in a vacuum; thus, inquiry into the challenges posed by the rise of precarious employment calls for a multi-method approach. In identifying paths for future research, the third section canvasses some of the interdisciplinary and methodological challenges to improving regulatory protection.

REGULATING EMPLOYMENT: DEFINITIONS, CONCEPTS, AND TENDENCIES

The Concept of Regulation

The term "regulation" encompasses a broad range of norms or rules designed to shape behaviour and outcomes. A fairly narrow conception of regulation is the "promulgation of a set of rules, accompanied by some mechanism, typically a public agency, for monitoring and promoting compliance with these rules" (Baldwin, Scott, and Hood 1998, 3). This chapter addresses regulation in this narrow sense, its focus being state regulation of work relationships. Historically, labour and employment law has pursued a variety of objectives, including the imposition of discipline on recalcitrant workers (Hay and Craven 2004). However, precisely because workers resist working conditions that they perceive to be unfair, and because rule in liberal democratic countries requires the consent of the governed, the legal regulation of work has also included a protective dimension. It is the effectiveness of this normative dimension of the legal regulation of work that is the principal concern in this chapter. The analysis is premised on the idea that regulatory protection should guarantee decent working conditions, an adequate standard of living, and protection for the exercise of freedom of association to all workers – including, of course, those in precarious employment.

In evaluating the existence and adequacy of regulatory protection of workers, two separate issues must be examined. First, it is necessary to determine the nature of the regulatory framework and degree to which it espouses the normative objective of regulatory protection. If legislation does not aim to provide protection to workers, or to certain categories of workers, we can speak of regulatory failure in the broadest of senses (Quinlan, Mayhew, and Bohle 2001a, b). However, regulation may fail to protect workers, or some workers, not by explicit design but for various other reasons (lack of enforcement, access to justice issues, sloppy legislative language, employer resistance, etc.), which make it ineffective (Weil 1997). The only way to determine whether legislation that aims to protect all workers actually attains this objective is to measure regulatory effectiveness. From the workers' point of view, whether the legislation intends to exclude them from protection or whether other obstacles prevent adequate

application of the legislation is an academic question. Yet, from a methodological and law reform perspective, it is necessary to make these analytical
distinctions in order to identify the source of the failure to protect and, in
turn, to design the appropriate remedy.

Regulatory regimes are not monolithic but consist of many sub-regimes divided by jurisdiction and subject. Canadian provinces normally have jurisdiction over labour and social protection regulation. The federal jurisdiction is
narrow and applies to a short list of undertakings employing about 10 per
cent of the Canadian workforce. It also includes a limited number of social
protection schemes, such as Employment Insurance and the Canada Pension
Plan, the public contribution-based pension scheme outside Quebec. Regulation governing the labour force therefore varies from one province to the
next, depending on its particular circumstances. As a result, an analysis of
regulatory regimes must be strongly linked to geographic location and the
particular social context that led to the adoption of the regulatory instrument
and that shapes the state's willingness to ensure enforcement and remain
committed to the long-term survival of the scheme – all in a world that is increasingly promoting deregulation (Lippel and Caron 2004).

Protective Legislation

Protective legislation aims to redress a variety of injustices, including discrimination, the denial of compensation for work injuries, and unfair labour practices committed against workers seeking collective representation. These
issues are addressed in many different statutes, using a variety of administrative and legal tools to achieve their objectives, and further increasing the complexity of the protective regime. Moreover, for each particular protective
objective, different interests may become involved, resulting in diverse outcomes. For example, the primary aim of minimum employment standards legislation is to ensure adequate working conditions and income levels to
employees, often compensating for the absence of a collective agreement
(Bernstein, this volume; see also Fudge 1991; Malles 1976), but employers
will mobilize to ensure that their interest in keeping down labour costs and
controlling the organization of work is impaired as little as possible. As a result, the level and scope of protection will vary, depending on the balance of
power. The tradeoff between the worker's right to a minimum of protection
and the employer's freedom of contract and right to control and direct work is
limited to the context of a subordinated employment relationship. It is not intended to apply to self-employed workers,[1] who, in theory at least, enjoy adequate bargaining power and are free to organize their work as they see fit.

In contrast, workers' compensation schemes are designed to provide health
care, income replacement, and rehabilitation to workers injured on the job.
These schemes are funded by insurance premiums paid by employers, although

a substantial portion of these costs is shifted onto workers in the form of lower wages (Chelius and Burton 1994). This transfer, in addition to the fact that workers' compensation serves to reduce health-care and social support costs that would otherwise fall on state-financed programs (Lippel 1986), helps to explain why workers' compensation schemes are sometimes broader in their scope. Anti-discrimination legislation embodies the principle of equality in the workforce as well as in the provision of service to the public. Because the law is designed to apply beyond the workplace and because equality rights are constitutionally protected, it is more difficult for employers to claim that their interest in organizing work as they see fit should extend to discriminating against contractors. The application of human rights protections, therefore, does not normally require a dependent employment relationship; both employees and self-employed workers are covered (Fudge, Tucker, and Vosko 2002).

Substantive and Procedural Standards

To understand the regulatory context, it is important to distinguish between substantive standards and procedural (or process-oriented) standards (Freedland 1995). Work-related legislation and policy is both substantive and procedural in nature, the balance varying from one area to the next. Substantive standards generally contain a right or an obligation to proceed or not to proceed in a particular fashion. The determination of a fixed minimum wage is a clear example of a substantive standard, as is the establishment of a quantified exposure limit to a hazardous substance. Procedural standards set up a legal framework for substantive standard-setting, decision-making, and enforcement and can vary greatly depending on whether authority is vested exclusively in the state, shared between the state and the labour market parties, or delegated entirely to the labour market parties. The most obvious example is collective bargaining law, which creates a procedural framework within which trade unions and employers negotiate the terms and conditions of employment (Davidov 2002; De Munck 2000; Engblom 2001; see also Jackson, this volume). Other examples include the creation of mechanisms for tripartite dialogue, firm-based bipartite health and safety committees, or consultative bodies on issues such as gender equity (Smismans 2003; see also Davidov 2002, who discusses regulations designed to address economic unfairness and democratic process). Many protective schemes rely on a mixture of substantive and procedural standards. For example, in occupational health and safety, quantified exposure limits often coexist with procedural standards such as mandatory joint health and safety committees or occupational health and safety management systems (Frick et al. 2000; Gunningham and Johnstone 1999; Walters 2002).

In recent years there has been a shift towards greater use of procedural standards as an alternative to substantive standards. In part, this shift is driven by increasing resistance from employers to the command and control approach, based on substantive rules, which has stymied new regulatory initiatives. For example, recent experience with the regulation of ergonomic hazards demonstrates that procedural standards are sometimes the only ones that are allowed to survive in an anti-regulatory climate (Lippel and Caron 2004). Arup (1995, 37) comments that "the attack on the norm can ... be read as part of a general loss of faith in substantive regulation by law" – a decline that, according to some, undermines the law's legitimacy and leads to regulatory failure. Still, many commentators argue that the move away from state-generated substantive standards towards procedural standards that vest more authority in the workplace parties to "solve their mutual problems" is a positive step (Levine 1997, 475; also see Kaufman 1997; Ogus 2000). Although there is nothing intrinsic to precarious employment that favours a procedural approach, this type of standard may be becoming more prevalent as a response to the erosion of the standard employment relationship; certainly, international standard setting points in this direction (Vosko 2004). Ideally, under this approach, the state and its regulatory machinery determine normally binding rules surrounding the process, rules that, ideally, are founded on a series of legally entrenched principles such as human rights, including freedom of association and freedom from discrimination – two relevant dimensions of labour market regulation oriented towards social justice (Engblom 2001, 217–19).

However, many are concerned that the shift away from substantive to procedural standards may result in an erosion of worker protection, especially in a world where the imbalance of power between workers and employers is growing. For example, greater reliance on procedural standards in occupational health and safety is often premised on the view that the interests of workers and employers in this area are largely congruent and that the state, as promised, will use its coercive powers to deal with the "bad apples," but there is little empirical evidence to support these premises. As a result, the adoption of these models may relieve pressure on the state to intervene more forcefully to protect workers who lack the tools and capabilities to protect themselves in a more deregulated environment (Nichols and Tucker 2000). Moreover, in contrast to those who see procedural standards as being an appropriate response to precarious employment, others argue that because these workers have weak bargaining power and are underrepresented in participatory structures, they are particularly at risk when these strategies are adopted (Aronsson 1999).

Enforceability of Standards

Equally central is the question of enforceability of standards, since they can be binding or voluntary. Binding standards can be created publicly though legislation and regulations, as well as privately through collective agreements or individual contracts that can be enforced by arbitration or legal action in the courts. Voluntary standards, falling under a category coined by jurists as "soft" law, can also be created by the state, through private agreement, or by a combination of the two. Voluntary standards can result from binding procedural standards, since administrative bodies can be legally obligated to create a process or develop guidelines where certain objectives are set but no mechanism exists to enforce them (Mockle 2002). For example, the Ontario *Occupational Health and Safety Act* makes provision for state-approved codes of conduct, but the failure to abide by such a code does not constitute a breach of the statute.[2] Private bodies, such as the International Standards Organization (ISO), also generate standards that are privately enforced through a certification process, but no one is obliged to comply. Another example pertains to industry- or sector-based codes of practice, such as that found in the Canadian temporary employment agency industry (ACSESS 2003). In none of these cases is there worker input. Whether generated by the state or by private parties, compliance with soft law depends on the ongoing willingness of parties, particularly employers in this case. The effectiveness of such an approach can be severely hindered when the parties have conflicting interests (Hepple 2002; see also Kirton and Trebilcock 2004).

Both hard and soft regulation can be effective in protecting workers in at least two ways. First, many standards are legally binding and enforceable; they can change harmful employer behaviour through compulsion, whether it be through the issuance of an enforceable order, the withdrawal of a licence, or the levying of a fine or imposition of a jail sentence. Second, whether binding or not, public and private standards can influence attitudes and social norms, which in turn may influence how people and organizations behave (e.g., the prohibition on sexual harassment and the duty to accommodate workers with disabilities). Moreover, standard setting is not a static process but a dynamic, iterative one, in which standards shape social norms, which in turn shape standards. For example, the operative meaning of "reasonableness" standards, which are common in law, changes as social attitudes shift over time. Similarly, campaigns to change social attitudes about appropriate workplace behaviour (e.g., workplace harassment), may, more generally, lead to changes in the law or its interpretation (see Bernstein, this volume).

Standards also benefit from varying degrees of legitimacy and acceptance. For example, where standards are viewed as being irrelevant because they do not adequately translate into real situations or take into account emerging realities, compliance is likely to be low, regardless of whether they are legally enforceable. Social norms, or practices within workplaces or the labour market, may then predominate even though they contravene requirements set out in the law. An example is the often illegal practice of compensating overtime in the form of time off instead of additional remuneration; workers often prefer time off and tacitly or explicitly agree to such employer practices (Thoemmes 1999). The law can remain stagnant on such issues or may be modified to take into account these non-legal norms.[3] In other cases, norms are contested, and workers may need to challenge employer claims that some existing or proposed regulation unnecessarily interferes with their ability to organize work efficiently.

Regulatory Scope

Regulation can be of general application (e.g., general provisions of a labour code) or it can target specific sectors of activity, groups or categories of workers, or even regions. This variability raises the question of whether it is preferable, in some circumstances, to tailor standards to particular sectors with respect to occupation (e.g., the special legal regimes for artists,[4] decrees extending particular working conditions to a sector such as building maintenance or security services,[5] etc.) or employment status (e.g., framework laws enabling self-employed workers to organize and bargain collectively; see Bernier, Vallée, and Jobin 2003, 516ff;[6] Cranford, Fudge, Tucker, and Vosko 2005). The advantage of standards of general application is that their content relies less on bargaining power than is the case with sector-based standards (Sen 2000). Universal standards apply to all workers in a given jurisdiction, even to those who were absent from the legislative process. Sector-based standards heavily depend on target workers' capacity to put the need for these standards on the legislative agenda and to engage in negotiations with their providers of work. It should be borne in mind that certain groups of workers nevertheless remain excluded from otherwise universal standards (Benjamin 2002; Fudge, Tucker, and Vosko 2003a, b).

Labour Market Position and Social Location

Labour market position and social location are also intimately intertwined with regulatory effectiveness and, in turn, regulatory failure. A worker's labour market position emanates, in part, from occupation, work arrangements (i.e., multiple job-holding), and form of employment (i.e., different categories of wage work or self-employment, such as temporary wage work or solo self-employment). Social location, in contrast, refers to how social relations and political and economic conditions interact to shape peoples' actions and experiences. It refers to groups of people affected differentially by social relations of inequality such as gender, "race," ethnicity, immigrant status, disability, class, and age, as well as their intersections. Together, labour market position and social location affect workers' participation in the design, content, and extent of implementation of regulation (Schenk, this volume). The racialized and gendered dynamics of precarious forms of employment, such as temporary wage work and the phenomenon of low income among women engaged in solo self-employment, are cases in point (Cranford and Vosko, this volume; Vosko and Zukewich, this volume; see also Hughes 2003b).

What Is the Question?

In the scholarly literature, as well as among policy makers, sharp tensions exist over the extent, as well as the appropriate vehicles and processes, of labour market regulation (Jackson, this volume). It is important to emphasize, however, that the choice is not between regulation and deregulation, since, as Macdonald (1985) has shown, the decision to leave matters to be determined by market forces is a political one, made by the state, for which a legal foundation is required. The appropriate question, therefore, is not whether we should regulate but how and to what end? Proponents of reducing the scope of direct state regulation of the labour market frequently claim that regulation limits employment growth and labour market adaptation (see, for example, OECD 1994; for a detailed analysis, see also Card and Krueger 1995). Regular targets of this claim are fixed minimum wages and social protections. Others argue that the negative effects of protective legislation are greatly overstated and that the normative imperative of protecting workers against exploitative conditions by providing a modicum of income and job security, and thereby limiting precarious employment, is worth the small tradeoffs involved. Because we share the latter view, the central question here is whether and how existing regulation fails to protect workers in precarious employment and whether and how law can be adapted to provide better protection to these workers. A starting premise is that it is necessary to look beyond the legal boundaries of the employment norm and its associated regulatory framework, which is providing protection to a diminishing number of workers and offering little or no security to workers in the labour market whose relationship to their providers of work is increasingly ill-defined (Ichino 1998; Supiot 1999a).

REGULATORY EFFECTIVENESS AND REGULATORY FAILURE: ISSUES FACING WORKERS IN PRECARIOUS EMPLOYMENT

Form of Employment and Intentional and Inadvertent Failures

Laws based on the norm of the standard employment relationship fail to reflect the reality of the labour market, and this breakdown necessarily has an impact on regulatory protection (Lippel, this volume). There is an intimate relationship between the form of employment and the disparity in legal treatment between workers. This disparity of treatment may be intentional or inadvertent. The explicit exclusion of solo self-employed workers or home workers from all or from parts of legislation is an example of how this disparity of treatment can be by design. The hours-system around which Employment Insurance is organized, which extends coverage to all part-time wage workers while making it impossible for many to qualify, is an example of how disparity of treatment may arise by mistake (Vosko 2003). Another example of inadvertent failure to protect is illustrated by the drafting of the employers' obligations to protect the health of workers in Quebec. The "general duty clause" in the law lists several obligations, some with regard to workers employed by the employer, others with regard to "establishments under the employer's authority." The former apply to home-based workers while the latter do not, yet there seems to be no legislative rationale to vary the level of protection of home-based workers from one subparagraph to the next (Bernstein, Lippel, and Lamarche 2001).

In other instances, certain forms of employment are neither excluded specifically nor inadvertently denied protection by a flaw in the scheme's design; rather, there is simply no legislation applicable to their situation. Examples include the general lack of regulation of temporary employment agencies (Bernstein, this volume; Vosko 2000) and, in some cases, home work (Bernstein, Lippel, and Lamarche 2001). In Canada, people working via temporary employment agencies and doing essentially the same work as those hired directly by the client firm have no regulatory protection to ensure that they will be treated equally or even equitably. Home workers often have to pay work-related costs, such as electricity and materials, that on-site employees do not, and these expenses, in practice, reduce their wages. By not regulating certain employment situations, employer practices go unchecked and become institutionalized. Although at one time this lack might have been characterized as inadvertent, now that the problems of workers in precarious employment have been identified, it is perhaps more appropriate to characterize the failure of the state to protect as intentional.

Disparities in Treatment and Discrimination

Recognition that the existing legal framework, based on the standard employment relationship, is prompting growing disparities among different forms of employment has led to some regulatory solutions. They include equality of treatment provisions for part-time workers, measures that are being introduced with varying degrees of success (Bernstein, this volume). Still, it is difficult to design legislation sensitive to precarious employment in its multiple dimensions, rather than the standard/non-standard employment dichotomy that has shaped labour law and policy in Canada since before World War II. Although regulatory frameworks may respond to some dimensions of precarious employment, such as part-time wage work, they compensate less well for other dimensions, including low income and a lack of control over the labour process. They are also less able to consider directly some of the other dimensions of precarious employment such as social location: legislative exclusion of agricultural workers, particularly migrant workers who come to Canada on temporary visas, is an example of disparity of treatment based on citizenship, ethnicity, and race (Tucker, this volume).

In legal terms, disparity of treatment may translate into illegal discrimination against certain groups on the basis of particular characteristics such as sex, race, and disability. It is therefore important to identify the potential discriminatory or exclusionary effects of existing standards for workers in precarious employment. Discrimination can be direct (or explicit), although it is relatively rare for Canadian legislation to target particular groups on the basis of personal characteristics such as sex or race.[7] The law is usually, at least formally, oblivious to such distinctions. Yet indirect and systemic discrimination still remains prevalent in many areas of the labour market. A precarious employment situation can be both a source and a consequence of discrimination; that is true for the hotel workers, largely immigrants, working in the "back of the house" in Schenk's case study of workers struggling against precarious employment in Toronto (chapter 16, this volume), for agricultural workers (Tucker, this volume), and for ancillary workers in health care (Armstrong and Laxer, this volume). Being in a precarious employment situation can be considered a consequence of gender discrimination, since women have historically had less access to regular well-remunerated work because of stereotypes, cultural mores, and their reproductive and care-giving roles in society (Fudge and Vosko 2003). Women and people from racialized groups, for example, more often find themselves in certain types of precarious employment, and this can lead to multiple forms of exclusion (Das Gupta, this volume; Vosko and Zukewich, this volume). Like precarious employment, discrimination is multi-dimensional. Intersectional analyses give credence to such claims: the experience of a woman with a disability will not be the same as that of a woman who is not disabled or as that of a man who is disabled (Carbado and Gulati 2001; Crenshaw 1989).[8] The prohibition on discrimination is also transversal, or cross-cutting, in nature. All rights, such as freedom of association and the right to fair and reasonable working conditions, should be exercised without discrimination on the basis of a series of enumerated or analogous grounds (sex, race, national origin, etc.).

In theory, the experience of precarious employment could also be considered an illegal ground of discrimination, since it fosters exclusion and is tied to other grounds that are prohibited in some jurisdictions, such as "social condition" (Paquet 2005). At the same time, legal recognition of precarious employment situations as a ground of discrimination is in itself complex, since employment can be precarious by degree and differentially associated with other prohibited grounds. Anti-discrimination legislation in Canada does not explicitly recognize professional or occupational status as grounds of discrimination. There are some limited exceptions; specifically, in the 2001 *Dunmore* case,[9] dissenting Supreme Court justice L'Heureux-Dubé opened the door to a limited recognition of occupational status as an analogous ground of discrimination under the equality provisions of the *Canadian Charter of Rights and Freedoms*. This case dealt with the legislative exclusion of agricultural workers from the Ontario *Labour Relations Act*,[10] providing for organizing and collective bargaining rights. Justice L'Heureux-Dubé recalled that the Supreme Court has, on several occasions, confirmed that work is an essential part of a person's life and identity. Without deciding that "occupational status" will always constitute an analogous ground of discrimination, she nevertheless determined that the occupational status of agricultural workers, proven to be particularly vulnerable, is an analogous ground (pars. 165ff). In 1999 the Quebec Human Rights Tribunal, in the *Sinatra* case,[11] found that a person's precarious employment situation (freelance journalist) was included under "social condition" in the list of prohibited grounds of discrimination at section 10 of the Quebec *Charter of Human Rights and Freedoms*. This isolated decision recognized that a person's precarious employment situation could have a discriminatory effect, in this case outside of work, since the plaintiff was refused rental housing on the basis of his employment status.

Legal Coverage

The exclusion of certain categories of workers from regulatory protection creates an incentive for employers to move workers into those categories, thereby reducing regulatory effectiveness. The exclusion of self-employed workers from a whole series of regimes is one of the most obvious examples of this phenomenon. In other cases, legislative exclusions arise from the use of antiquated classifications, resulting in unanticipated and arbitrary differences in coverage. For example, several statutes exclude "outworkers," an archaic term that no longer has a clear referent. The wording of these provisions has the presumably unintentional effect of excluding from workers' compensation home-based workers doing industrial-type work, such as garment workers, but not tele-workers, a group arguably less vulnerable to work-related health problems than garment workers (Bernstein, Lippel, and Lamarche 2001).

The problem with interpreting language points to a deeper issue. Even modern legal terms, such as self-employment, are in danger of becoming incoherent as the sociological reality of the distinction between employees and the self-employed is being eroded. Decision-makers find it difficult to determine the scope of the employment relationship, with the result that a worker can be an employee for some purposes but not for others. For example, newspaper carriers for the *Winnipeg Free Press* were held by the labour relations board to be employees under collective bargaining law, but the tax court determined that they were not employees for the purpose of Employment Insurance and the Canadian Pension Plan (Cranford, Fudge, Tucker, and Vosko 2005). Under these circumstances, many workers are likely to be confused about their status and, hence, their legal rights. When workers are convinced they have no rights, even if they do, the best protective legislation will fail in its objectives (Mayhew and Quinlan 2002). Similarly, if ambiguity prevents the timely application of protective legislation, the right to protection may become moot. When an injured trucker working for a temporary employment agency does not know who must pay for the ambulance needed to take him home from the scene of an accident 400 kilometres away, he will not have access to the ambulance service, even if, in hindsight, it is possible to identify the responsible employer (Lippel, this volume).

Labour Market Position and Social Location

The maxim "the law is blind" overlooks how legal regulation "sees" labour market position and social location and how it responds to these dimensions of precarious employment. Labour market position and social location have an impact on workers' awareness of existing regulation, on their access to information on the various and complex regulatory regimes, and on the relationships between them. They also affect workers' ability to benefit from the legal rights they enjoy. For example, an unemployed worker who does not read or write either of Canada's official languages is less likely to be aware of her entitlement to Employment Insurance benefits or to successfully navigate the claims' process. Language may not be the only problem. Access to workers' compensation, for instance, often depends on medical evidence that will be provided by a medical expert for a fee, sometimes costing several thousand dollars, well beyond the means of most workers. In other instances, employers will contest claims, and workers will not have access to the economic means and resources to respond. The problem this adversarial reaction poses for workers was illustrated when McDonald's Restaurants successfully contested a decision of the workers' compensation appeals tribunal that had interpreted the governing Act in a way that was favourable to part-time employees and consistent with the text and the spirit of the Quebec workers' compensation legislation. The decision was overturned in Superior Court,[12] but only the employer was represented (Lippel 2004).

There are many other ways in which disparity of power, dependent on labour market position and social location, promotes regulatory failure. As actors in the legislative and policy-making process, workers in precarious employment have difficulty being represented and heard. The exclusion of agricultural and domestic workers and caregivers from much protective leg-islation is a clear example of this phenomenon (Tucker, this volume; Bern-stein, this volume). Union representation can also make a crucial difference in the ability of workers to benefit from protective regulation. Unionized workplaces, for example, are more likely to receive health and safety in-spections, and unionized workers exercise the right to refuse dangerous work far more frequently than non-unionized workers (Tucker 1995; Weil 1991). This difference highlights the need to develop alternative forms of representation, such as community unionism, so that the voices of workers in precarious employment can be heard and their rights enforced.

Compliance and Enforcement

The effectiveness of particular laws is dependent on the degree of compliance with them, not just their adequacy on the books (Collins 2000; Hepple 2002; Weil 1997). Compliance is, in part, related to the degree of adaptation of reg-ulation to the realities of the labour market. Workers and employers will often have very different ideas about those realities, however. The more that regula-tion challenges employers' freedom to organize their workforce as they see fit, the more resistance there is likely to be. In these circumstances, compliance will depend heavily on the capacity of the employees to influence employer be-haviour and on employers' expectations with regard to government enforce-ment. Precariously employed workers rarely enjoy sufficient power resources to overcome their employers' resistance to regulatory requirements – specifi-cally, access to union coverage (Anderson, Beaton, and Laxer, this volume) – leaving them particularly dependent on state enforcement to check unlawful employer behaviour. Unfortunately, the state often fails them as well.

Historically, governments have both limited the resources devoted to en-forcement and adopted enforcement strategies that are conducive to regulatory failure (Tucker 1990). This situation continues today. In British Columbia, for example, workers have to demonstrate to the authority responsible for enforc-ing the *Employment Standards Act*[13] that they have attempted to resolve the problem with their employer before they can file a complaint using a "Self-Help Kit," or their complaint will not be considered.[14] There are, however, sig-nificant variations between jurisdictions and regulatory schemes. For example, in Quebec the government agency responsible for enforcing the *Labour Stan-dards Act*[15] has recently adopted a more proactive approach to enforcement, including increased recourse to onsite inspections (Bernstein, this volume).

The dimensions of precarious employment experienced by many workers complicate enforcement for a variety reasons. One is spatial; precariously employed workers are often widely dispersed and located in "private" spaces. Ensuring safe and healthy working conditions for home workers or people working in other people's homes is a prime example of this problem.

It would be costly to inspect every home where paid work is performed, and inspectors resist entering private dwellings, or face legal impediments from doing so. A second problem is that the lines of responsibility are often blurred. To return to the home worker, for example, the employer may claim that he is not responsible for conditions there since he exercises no control over that workspace. The ever-present question "Who is the boss?" also routinely interferes with safe and healthy working conditions for temp workers (Vosko 2000, chap. 5). Specific provisions and enforcement strategies for such categories of workers are needed to promote regulatory protection (Bernstein, Lippel, and Lamarche 2001). A third problem is that power imbalances influence the degree of compliance and enforcement, as well as the allocation of enforcement resources (see, for example, the TOFFE campaign to enforce existing regulations governing vacation pay described in chapter 17, this volume).

Not only are workers in precarious employment less likely to know their rights but their lack of job security puts them at risk of being fired for exercising their rights, notwithstanding statutory prohibitions against this kind of employer retaliation. As noted earlier, unionized workplaces are more likely than non-union workplaces to be inspected. As well, an awareness of the potential length of legal proceedings may discourage workers whose time horizons in a job are short from registering claims, such as claims for back wages under minimum standards legislation (Cranford, Das Gupta, and Vosko, this volume). Another area where this problem manifests itself concerns the right of injured workers to return to work after an accident. The process is supposed to be self-managed, but precariously employed workers are less able to influence the self-management process. For example, workers in small workplaces do not have the support of unions to offset imbalances of power that shape the return to work process and its outcomes for injured workers (Eakin, Clarke, and MacEachen 2002). A final problem is that legal remedies are not necessarily designed to take into account the situations resulting from certain forms of employment. Temporary agency workers, for instance, may, according to the law, have the right to reinstatement if they are dismissed because they have claimed a right from their employer. Reinstatement may, however, be illusory, since, on the one hand, it is difficult to compel a client firm to take back an agency worker, and, on the other, an agency can claim that it has no other assignment to offer the worker.

INTERDISCIPLINARY CHALLENGES

"Labour law is inherently an interdisciplinary field in that its major questions, arising from its function and purpose, cannot be answered without input and analysis from more than one discipline or area of study" (Gahan and Mitchell 1995, 88).

Given the complex determinants of regulatory success and failure, no single discipline can provide all the analytic tools needed for its investigation. This is not to say, however, that the insights of any particular discipline should be ignored. Traditional legal scholarship, for example, can be used to develop an inventory of existing legislation, regulations, contracts, and voluntary guidelines. As well, it can improve understandings of how the law has been interpreted and applied by competent decision-makers such as tribunal members and judges. But knowing of the existence of standards and understanding case law and legal doctrine tell only part of the story. For example, in some instances the absence of case law with respect to a particular category of workers may be particularly significant for an understanding of regulatory failure. Why are these workers not filing complaints, or, if they are, why are their complaints not being adjudicated? The reasons behind this phenomenon must be explored, but traditional legal methodology is not well suited for such inquiries.

The field of socio-legal studies developed in response to these limitations, and its methods have been used to provide additional insights into precarious employment. For example, scholars in this tradition have gleaned, from the stories recounted in legal cases, insights into the factual conditions of precarious employment. As well, by aggregating the results of cases, scholars can identify systemic problems, such as discrimination (Lippel 2002). In other instances, sources beyond legislation and case law need to be examined to pinpoint the reasons for regulatory failure.

Statistical data is frequently used in policy design, implementation, and assessment, but, as with all methods, it must be used with care and in a way that is sensitive to the complex realities of the phenomenon it is attempting to comprehend. This sensitivity is not always present. For example, definitions used by statisticians to determine employee status do not necessarily correspond to the criteria used by courts: the statistical definition is based on a self-assessment, while tribunals and courts determine employee status based on the application of a legal test to the facts that they find (Delage 2002, 12; Fudge, Tucker, and Vosko 2002). Another example is a recent survey of self-employment in Canada, in which workers were asked if they provided their own tools and materials and whether they had more or less control over the labour process since they had become self-employed. While these questions could be used as a proxy, to determine whether individuals are self-employed legally or sociologically, the survey was designed on the presumption that the persons they were surveying were self-employed from the outset (Delage 2002). Statistical practices and definitions may distort reality in other ways. When questions about work are restricted to the main job of a multiple job holder, the cumulative risks to the health of the worker from all jobs will become invisible. So, too, may the fact that some "part-time" workers may be working more than 40 hours a week in paid employment. Not only do regulations fail these workers, who have no right to overtime because they work for multiple employers, but the tools designed to inform policy-makers fail even to disclose the existence of a problem that needs to be addressed.

Administrative data are another important source of information regarding regulatory protection; however, the under-reporting, or non-reporting, of claims or incidences of non-compliance can distort them. Workers' compensation is a prime example of this phenomenon. Workers in precarious employment may not report dangerous working conditions or make claims for accidents and occupational illnesses (Mayhew and Quinlan 1999a). This silence, in turn, affects the available data on occupational health and safety and on workers' compensation claims, distorting the portrait in a way that can lead to a false sense of security, since a reduction in accident statistics is inaccurately equated with improved prevention mechanisms. In other cases, data is not collected if the workers are excluded from the legislation. Solo self-employed workers excluded from workers' compensation legislation may, therefore, have similar work accidents and suffer from occupational illnesses that regulation could address, but, since their incidence does not appear in the data, they remain invisible.

The meaningful evaluation of regulatory effectiveness and failure requires surveys of workers in different forms of employment and in different sectors (Lewchuk, de Wolff, King, and Polanyi, this volume). To be effective, such surveys should include information on labour market position as well as social location, providing for more nuanced and multi-dimensional analyses, and be combined with a detailed and critical examination of existing regulation. This process, once again, involves dislodging the employment norm. Since regulatory frameworks do not take into account the multiple dimensions of precarious employment, the question remains how to translate these results into public policy ensuring genuine regulatory protection. This discussion highlights the need for careful and well-informed interdisciplinary research when investigating regulatory success and failure in regard to precarious employment. The use of research teams, involving both legal scholars and social scientists, is one of the ways to maximize the benefit of interdisciplinary investigations.

CONCLUSION

The goal of regulatory protection provides an important normative foundation for much of labour, employment, and social security law, but its realization has always required an ongoing struggle by working people. Achieving this objective for workers in precarious employment is particularly challenging because the risk of regulatory failure is high. As this chapter has demonstrated, workers in precarious employment encounter difficulties in making their voices heard in the political arena, often resulting in their exclusion from protective legislation, either by design or by virtue of their invisibility. Moreover, because modern labour, employment, and social security law was built on the platform of the standard employment relationship, its structure and design is often ill-suited to meet the needs of the increasing number of workers who no longer fit this norm, even though they may be covered by the law. Finally, securing compliance with laws that interfere with employer freedoms is always difficult, but the problem becomes even thornier when workers in precarious employment are in need of protection.

In order to begin to address this regulatory deficit, we need to better understand its causes and effects. Interdisciplinary research is necessary to avoid the pitfalls of seeing the world through a single lens that fails to capture the complexity of the phenomenon under investigation. More research alone is not a solution to the problem of regulatory failure, however. There still remains the challenge of developing policies that could provide workers with the protection they deserve. Comparative research can sometimes be helpful in identifying "best practices," but, in looking at what works, it is vital that the underlying social conditions on which a given practice is based be understood. This understanding is particularly important when considering practices that have been used in jurisdictions where the balance of power between workers and employers is more even than it is in contemporary Canada (Jackson, this volume; Tucker 1992). Finally, even if there are laws and policies that address the conditions of workers in precarious employment, there remains the even more daunting task of developing strategies to ensure their implementation. This challenge poses a series of other questions. What are the prospects for organizing precariously employed workers and what organizational forms would meet their needs? What is the role of the labour movement, and can collective bargaining make a positive contribution? Is there scope to pursue the goal of protection through constitutional litigation and, if so, can legal victories be translated into effective law? What positive role, if any, can international norms and institutions play in promoting regulatory protection for workers in precarious employment in Canada? How do you build the political will essential to the promotion and implementation of effective regulatory protection?

Clearly, there are no easy answers to any of these questions. Our ambitions here have been more modest: to make the problems of precariously employed workers more visible; to develop an analytical framework that can be used to develop a better understanding of the issue of regulatory failure; and to promote debate on the way forward.

10

Mitigating Precarious Employment in Quebec: The Role of Minimum Employment Standards Legislation

STEPHANIE BERNSTEIN

The call for the withdrawal of the state, for reasons of competitiveness and flexibility, from the regulation of employment raises serious questions about the means that are available to mitigate precarious employment – an expanding feature of many workers' experience. The need to assess the functions and the foundations of labour law, including the state's role in legal regulation, is always present (Conaghan 2003), yet the more immediate objective of finding ways to curb and lessen the dimensions of precarious employment must also be addressed. On the one hand, there is growing interest in a modernized contractual approach to regulating employment relations, as a partial response to the inability of labour law to cope with changes in workplace practices and employment forms, as well as the needs of workers traditionally marginalized by labour law – particularly women (Collins 2001; Stone 2001). On the other hand, the role of state regulation, in the form of universal minimum employment standards, and the need to establish a clear set of rules governing the workplace must be recognized, given precarious workers' limited individual and collective bargaining power. In each case this limitation, whether individual or collective, is both a consequence and a feature of precariousness. There are compelling reasons to strengthen minimum employment standards legislation, not least of which is its importance as a threshold for collective bargaining (Fudge 1991). At the same time, the role of minimum standards legislation in legitimizing precarious employment and the capacity of these laws to be truly universal, rather than, often inadvertently, to create new exclusions that increase dimensions of precarious employment for some categories of workers, must also be borne in mind.

The evolution of minimum employment standards legislation in Quebec in mitigating precarious employment provides some insight into the advantages and limitations of this form of legal regulation. The Quebec *Labour Standards Act (LSA)*[1] underwent an important reform process in 2002. The minister of labour had announced early in his mandate that the government's goal was to modernize Quebec's labour legislation and to adapt it to new realities both in the workplace and in the labour market, including the inadequate protection of non-standard workers (Ministère du Travail 2001a). By 2002 the issue of non-standard employment had been on the legislative agenda for close to 15 years, even though the tenor of legislative reforms had been uneven. Historically, the Quebec government has approached the regulation of non-standard employment in a piecemeal fashion, because of the influence of competing interests and a lack of political will to curb employer practices geared towards so-called flexibility. In most cases, "flexibility" can be understood as a code word for the spread of precarious employment.

The latest review of the *LSA*, initiated in the last year of the Parti Québécois's mandate, resulted in the adoption of Bill 143, the *Act to Amend the Act Respecting Labour Standards and Other Legislative Provisions*, which came into force in May 2003.[2] Despite the Quebec government's stated objective of bringing the legislation into line with the new realities of the labour market, the reform represents, in several respects, yet another missed opportunity to curb or lessen the effects of precarious employment. In the last 15 years, the government has introduced timid modifications to the *LSA*, selectively taking account of new realities in the labour market. This chapter retraces the path of legislative change in Quebec with respect to minimum employment standards and evaluates the success of the *LSA* in mitigating precarious employment relations. The first section provides a brief legislative chronology of minimum employment standard-setting in Quebec. The second section explores some of the regulatory issues surrounding precarious employment in relation to the evolution of the *LSA*. Three of the most pressing issues in Quebec, and elsewhere, are the determination of employee status and the scope of the employment relationship, a preliminary question to legislative coverage in a context where solo self-employment has risen significantly in the last 20 years (Vosko and Zukewich, this volume); the uncurbed recourse to temporary employment agencies, resulting in regulatory avoidance and inequitable working conditions; and, more generally, the increased disparity of treatment between workers in standard and non-standard forms of employment (this volume, Lippel; Tucker). The third section concludes the chapter by discussing whether the gap between employment standards and the realities of the labour market with respect to precarious employment is narrowing in Quebec.

KEEPING PACE WITH NEW REALITIES?
A LEGISLATIVE CHRONOLOGY

In 1979 the Quebec *Minimum Wage Act*[3] became the LSA. It introduced a more comprehensive, integrated, and universal approach to minimum employment standards by advancing norms not contemplated under the previous law, such as maternity leave and protection against dismissal or other reprisals. This leave brought the legislation into line with the maternity benefits provisions of the 1971 *Unemployment Insurance Act* and marked the introduction of a series of measures, over the next decades, to reconcile work and family life. The foundation of the 1979 law was the standard employment relationship; it did not contain specific provisions to counter precarious employment, though, indirectly, it did, through the new protection against unjust dismissal, including the right to reinstatement, after five years of service for the same employer.[4] One important change, however, was its broadening of the definition of the term "employee" for the purposes of the LSA. Despite a more universal approach, the law prioritized the protection of minimum wage earners. This preoccupation with protecting very low wage workers has remained a constant. Ten years later, amendments reinforced the law as a cornerstone of labour legislation, both for unionized and for non-unionized workers.

The important legislative review of 1990 had several objectives – notably, reinforcing the universal coverage of the law, reconciling work and family life, and expanding protection against unjust dismissal (Quebec 1990a, 5248ff). Partial and total exclusions from the law were reduced, especially for domestic and agricultural workers, who now gained somewhat broader coverage (Tucker, this volume). The number of years of service required for workers to be protected against unjust dismissal, with the right to reinstatement, was reduced from five to three, a measure that provided many workers with greater job security. One of the most debated measures concerned the new protection against wage disparity for part-time workers (Quebec 1990b, CAS-3067ff), signalling, for the first time, a legislative recognition that the standard employment relationship was insufficient as a model for protection.

Over a decade later, the imperatives of a changing labour market and certain failings in the existing legislation led to another relatively in-depth review of the LSA. In its initial discussion document, the government proposed four guiding principles for the 2002 reform: 1) broadening the scope of the law to eliminate most of the remaining partial and total exclusions; 2) further reconciling work and family responsibilities; 3) inducing greater compliance with the law and adapting its application to new forms of work organization and remuneration; and 4) ensuring the payment of a statutory minimum wage (Ministère du Travail 2002). (See table 10.1.)

Table 10.1
Changes to the *Labour Standards Act*

Issue	Minimum Wage Act (1940)	Labour Standards Act (1979)	Labour Standards Act (1990)	Labour Standards Act (2002)
Defining and determining employee status	1) Definition of the term "employee": "'employee' means any person, workman, functionary, clerk, or employee whatever entitled to a wage for work done for an employer."	1) Definition of the term "employee": "'employee' means a person who works for an employer and who is entitled to a wage; this word also includes a worker who is a party to a contract, under which he or she (i) undertakes to perform specified work for a person within the scope and in accordance with the methods and means determined by that person; (ii) undertakes to furnish, for the carrying out of the contract, the material, equipment, raw materials or merchandise chosen by that person and to use them in the manner indicated by him or her; and (iii) keeps, as remuneration, the amount remaining to him or her from the sum he has received in conformity with the contract, after deducting the expenses entailed in the performance of that contract" (s. 1(10)).	1) Unchanged	1) Unchanged 2) Determination of employee status: "An employee is entitled to retain the status of employee where the changes made by the employer to the mode of operation of the enterprise do not change that status into that of a contractor without employee status. Where the employee is in disagreement with the employer regarding the consequences of the changes on the status of the employee, the employee may file a complaint in writing ... with the Commission des normes du travail" (s. 86.1).

Table 10.1
Changes to the *Labour Standards Act* (*Continued*)

Issue	Minimum Wage Act (1940)	Labour Standards Act (1979)	Labour Standards Act (1990)	Labour Standards Act (2002)
Regulation of temporary employment agencies	No provisions (*Employment Bureaus Act* in force as of 1964)	No provisions (*Employment Bureaus Act* repealed in 1982)	No provisions	No provisions
Mitigation of disparity of treatment between workers	No provisions	No provisions	1) Partial equal rate for part-time workers: "No employer may remunerate an employee at a lower rate of wage than that granted to other employees performing the same tasks in the same establishment for the sole reason that the employee usually works less hours each week. [This] does not apply to an employee remunerated at a rate of pay which is more than twice the rate of the minimum wage (s. 41.1). "No employer may reduce the annual leave of an employee ..., or change the way in which the indemnity pertaining to it is computed, in comparison with	1) No change 2) No change 3) Calculation of indemnity for legal holidays (pro-rata basis): "For each statutory general holiday, the employer must pay the employee an indemnity equal to 1/20 of the wages earned during the four complete weeks of pay preceding the week of the holiday, excluding overtime." (There is a different method of calculation for employees remunerated in whole or in part on a commission basis) (s. 62).

Table 10.1
Changes to the *Labour Standards Act* (*Continued*)

Issue	Minimum Wage Act (1940)	Labour Standards Act (1979)	Labour Standards Act (1990)	Labour Standards Act (2002)
			what is granted to other employees performing the same tasks in the same establishment, for the sole reason that the employee usually works less hours each week" (s. 74.1). 2) Disparity of treatment on the basis of the date of hiring: "No agreement or decree may, with respect to a matter covered by a labour standard ..., operate to apply to the employee, solely on the basis of the employee's hiring date, a condition of employment less advantageous than that which is applicable to other employees performing the same tasks in the same establishment."(Certain restrictions and exceptions apply) (adopted in 1999: s. 87.1ff).	

Under this reform, broadening the scope of the law meant that partial exclusions relating to certain agricultural workers were to be repealed. No mention was made of dispensing with the oft-debated total exclusion of many caregivers in private homes in the discussion document. However, at the end of the legislative process, provisions were adopted to include them under the purview of the legislation as of June 2004.[5] The proposals to adapt the application of the law to new forms of work organization and remuneration included some restrictions on working time and a limited right to refuse overtime; an increase in job security, by reducing from three to two the minimum number of years of service required to be protected against unjust dismissal; pro-rata compensation for legal holidays; and an improved right of return to work following a leave of absence related to family obligations or illness. In the name of reconciling work and family obligations, the discussion document proposed amendments regarding parental leave and leave to look after a sick or injured relative, amendments that were adopted with some modifications. The principle of reinforcing the right to the general minimum wage entailed clarifying who is a tip earner (tip earners receive a lower minimum wage in Quebec) and certain restrictions on employer demands for payment for uniforms, tools, and materials. Another issue not contemplated in the initial discussion document, but introduced in Bill 143, was psychological harassment in the workplace. The relationship between precarious employment and harassment had been documented by, among others, an interministerial committee two years earlier (Ministère du Travail 2001b). The proposed provisions were eventually adopted after several amendments, most notably concerning changes to the definition of what constitutes psychological harassment.[6] The law now obliges employers to take reasonable measures to prevent and stop psychological harassment in the workplace, and, by creating a recourse for victims of harassment, this law leads to a wide range of remedies.

The scope of the legislation has, without question, expanded over the years, tending towards universal coverage and the inclusion of an increasing number of standards on a wide variety of issues related to work. Contrary to some other Canadian provinces, such as Ontario (Fudge 2001), there are no exemptions for firm size and very few for sector of activity or type of employment. Moreover, while the trend in some jurisdictions may be to eliminate the threshold of minimum employment standards in the presence of a collective agreement, Quebec has gone in the opposite direction. This expansion of the regulatory sphere of the LSA has important implications for the content of collective agreements. For example, in 2002 the British Columbia *Employment Standards Act* was amended to exclude workers covered by a collective agreement from the application of provisions concerning working time, statutory holidays, vacation, termination, and layoff, where the collective agreement addresses these issues.[7] In contrast, the Quebec LSA was modified in 1999 to include provisions making it illegal for employers to negotiate individual or collective agreements that treat workers performing the same work in the same establishment differently solely on the basis of their hiring date, with respect to wages, working time, public holidays, annual leave, family leave, and so on.[8] This amendment responded to the debate over controversial provisions known as "orphan" clauses, which allowed disparity of treatment in many collective agreements purely on the basis of a worker's hiring date. Another example is the more recent amendment to the LSA specifying that all collective agreements automatically contain protection against psychological harassment.[9]

Despite the government's stated intention in its 2001–3 Strategic Plan of addressing the issues surrounding non-standard forms of employment, specific proposals (besides introducing pro-rata compensation for legal holidays and reducing the number of years of service required for protection against unjust dismissal) were noticeably absent from the initial discussion document. This omission is not surprising because the government had mandated a committee to look into issues related to non-standard employment and its connection to precarious employment separately, outside the reform process, thereby fulfilling a promise made during the review of the Quebec *Labour Code*[10] in 2001. The Bernier Committee, composed of three independent labour law experts, examined the social protection needs of workers in non-standard employment, especially those in precarious situations. Less than two months after the 2002 reform became law, the committee came out with its comprehensive report on the "social protection needs of individuals in non-standard work situations" (Bernier, Vallée, and Jobin 2003).

The committee documented the evolution of employment forms and arrangements, surveyed non-standard workers, examined the application of labour and social security laws, and conducted a comparative analysis with the situation of workers in other Canadian provinces, the United States, and Europe. It made 53 recommendations on a wide variety of issues, including the need for legislative action to better protect workers in precarious employment – a broader group than those in non-standard forms of employment (Vosko, this volume), notably those in disguised employment relationships or false self-employment and temporary agency workers. These recommendations came too late to be considered within the reform process of the LSA, marking one more missed opportunity, given the improbability of another major review of the LSA in the near future. Meanwhile, the need to close the gap between the law and workers' experiences remains pressing.

REGULATORY CHALLENGES: MITIGATING PRECARIOUS EMPLOYMENT

The Scope of the Employment Relationship: Independent Contractor or Employee?

The existence of a subordinated employment relationship – the increasingly eroded "cornerstone of the edifice" of labour law, to use Kahn-Freund's expression – is a necessary precondition for the application of minimum employment standards legislation (Deakin 2002a; Supiot 2000). The basic question of determining who is covered by the legislation is crucial: Who is a genuine independent contractor and who is an employee? This preoccupation with the scope of the employment relationship crosses national and subnational borders and legal traditions and is not peculiar to Quebec (see Deakin 2002a; EIRO 2002; Fudge, Tucker, and Vosko 2002; Hunter 1992; ILO 2000b; Supiot 2000;). Indeed, the debate on the scope of the employment relationship is also ongoing at the international level. In 2003 the International Labour Conference studied the possibility of adopting an international recommendation (a non-binding legal instrument) to address the problem of "disguised employment relationships," or workers who are clearly employees, to ensure that workers have adequate protection and recourse at the national level (ILC 2003, 57). The debates over the definition of the boundaries of the employment relationship are symptomatic of the failings of the standard employment relationship as a model for legislative protection.

A range of different legislative initiatives has been adopted in Quebec in an attempt to limit uncertainties surrounding employee status. As early as 1979, a legislative amendment to the LSA introduced a new, broader definition of the term "employee," specifying that an employee is "a person who works for an employer and is entitled to a wage"; this definition includes workers who are party to a contract under which they perform work as directed by the employer, even if they have to provide the materials, equipment, or merchandise necessary to carry out the work and even if they deduct these expenses from their remuneration.[11] The definition is often held to include "dependent contractors," or workers who may otherwise be considered independent contractors but are economically dependent, essentially, on one provider of work (Dubé and Di Iorio 1992, 17; Hébert and Trudeau 1987, 39). Yet a certain amount of direction and control are required for workers to be covered by minimum employment standards provisions.[12] At the time of enactment, the purpose was to broaden the scope of the definition to include workers who, before 1979, were no doubt excluded from even the minimal protection of the law. This definition remains unchanged.

While determining employee status may at first glance appear relatively simple, this binary approach to coverage is fraught with ambiguity and, despite the identification of numerous criteria in Quebec case law, the factual reality of the relationship between worker and provider of work must be examined on a case-by-case basis.[13] Although the scope of the Quebec LSA is relatively broad, workers must still have recourse, often, to the courts to be recognized as employees. The actual situation in which workers find themselves, and not the contract's nomenclature, determines their status. The most important element is whether they follow the instructions of the provider of work and are under direct or even indirect supervision and control – that is, in a position of subordination with respect to an employer.[14] The provider of work needs only to be able to direct and control the work, rather than actually exercise control, for an employment relationship to exist. A lack of uniformity in the interpretation of the law on the part of tribunals and courts raises numerous questions, however, and fails to set out a clear path for workers in search of their employment status.

One of the issues often raised in determining employee status is the contractual freedom of the parties – the worker and the provider of work – to decide this status. Should the question whether particular workers prefer to be independent contractors, regardless of whether, in fact, they are employees, be relevant? Since the LSA is of public order, which means that no contractual derogations to the law are permitted unless otherwise specified in the legislation, it stands to reason that the parties should not be able to contract out of an employment relationship covered by the Act (Goyette 1998).[15] Case law on this question is nevertheless ambiguous[16] because tribunals and courts sometimes revert to the civil law precept of contractual freedom, ignoring the unequal bargaining power between worker and employer. This ambiguity is all the more surprising when we consider that tribunals and courts, including the Quebec Court of Appeal, agree almost unanimously that a worker's behaviour towards the tax authorities, for example, is irrelevant for determining employment status,[17] even though tax advantages appear to be one of the motivating factors behind voluntarily claiming to be an independent contractor (Bernier, Vallée, and Jobin 2003, 380).

A related question is whether it is possible to operate as a company and still be an employee under the law, since workers are often encouraged by employers to incorporate their "business," thereby transforming the relationship between an employee and an employer into a relationship between an incorporated business and a "client." Following a 1991 Quebec Court of Appeal decision, it has normally been held that if workers deal with the provider of work through a company, they cannot be an employee, unless the employer imposes creating a company as a condition for maintaining employment. In that case, the presence of a company can be ignored.[18] The Court of Appeal's reasoning was that a person should not be able to draw benefits from both tax and corporate laws and labour laws. This reasoning was revisited and revised in 2003, when a divided court determined that, even if incorporation is voluntary, the reality of the relationship between workers and the provider of work has to be examined, and workers do not necessarily forfeit their right to be protected by labour legislation.[19] Despite two schools of thought at the Quebec Court of Appeal, the 2003 judgment may dissuade some employers from suggesting that workers incorporate when they are, in fact, employees.

Although partially remedied with the 2002 reform, the inability of employees to contest their transformation into "independent contactors" under the

LSA is indicative of their limited bargaining power. Although recourse exists in the event of an employer trying to avoid the application of the law, including, in theory, disguising an employee as an independent contractor, the case law does not support this interpretation. Nor does it support the possibility of considering such a "transformation" of an employee's status to be equivalent to an illegal firing.[20] The possibility of contestation is even more remote if independent contractor status is a condition of employment at the time of hiring. While not on the initial legislative agenda in 2002, Bill 143 contained a provision aimed at curbing disguised employment relationships by specifying that workers have the right to maintain their status as employees when an administrative or operational reorganization of the firm has not, in fact, changed their status into that of independent contractors – or, to use the term in the bill, "contractor[s] without employee status."[21] Management rights remain essentially untouched by this proposal, which mirrors an almost identical amendment to the *Labour Code* in 2001 (Blouin 2003, 162).[22] However, this last amendment was adopted in another context, since its purpose is to force an employer to notify the union of transformations to independent contractor status which affect certification and the composition of bargaining units, and to provide the union with an opportunity to contest such changes. The proposed amendment in Bill 143 articulated the worker's right but did not offer any specific recourse to challenge the employer's actions. The final version of the law includes recourse in the event of an employer attempting to disguise an employment relationship.[23] The worker can file a complaint with the Labour Standards Commission, which will investigate the claim and bring it before the Labour Relations Commission (Quebec's specialized labour tribunal) if necessary. The Labour Relations Commission then rules on the "consequences" of the changes on the employment relationship. However, once it has determined that there is a disguised employment relationship, the tribunal's powers are unclear.[24]

This partial protection against disguised employment relationships will not remedy all the obstacles encountered by workers, but its educational value about the limits on disguised employment should not be underestimated, nor should the introduction of legal recourse for workers where none existed before. It remains to be seen whether this new right will dissuade employers who prefer to operate outside the bounds of the employment relationship and minimize their responsibilities under labour and social security legislation. At the same time, the amendment will not impede contracting out to ex-employees who are "real" independent contractors. Nor will it address the issue of "independent contractor" status as a condition of hiring, since the new provision, as written, applies only to persons who are already working for the employer. It could be contended that the new provision confirms the existing management practice of transforming employees into "real" independent contractors and fails to question the ensuing exclusion of many workers from protective legislation and the transfer of work-related risks (Morin and Brière, 2003, 1471).

The legacy of targeting minimum wage earners[25] in the LSA continues, despite the universal ambitions of the law. This outdated approach, moreover, has some pernicious effects. For example, management practices are sanctioned by another recent amendment which states that an employer cannot require an employee who is paid minimum wage to buy or pay for the maintenance or the use of material, equipment, raw materials, or merchandise needed to perform work for the employer.[26] This provision has the effect of explicitly confirming that an employer can ask employees for such payment as long as they receive at least the minimum wage once costs are deducted. This interpretation already dominated existing case law. The amendment is widely criticized because of its limitation to minimum wage earners (ABE and FDNS 2002; FFQ and CIAFT 2002; FTQ 2002). Even if the intention is to protect very low wage earners, the resulting amendment can be read to further legitimize the transfer of work-related costs to the vast majority of workers who earn more than minimum wage (for discussions of the notion of a poverty wage, see, this volume, Anderson; Cranford and Vosko). Employees should not be compelled to assume costs that are normally business expenses for the employer. Since the question of who assumes work-related costs is one of the criteria identified to determine employee status, the amendment could also reinforce the grey zone between employee and independent contractor status.

Although the contemporary tendency is to reinforce the universal coverage of the LSA, the temptation to revert to a sectoral approach to regulation for certain categories of workers is still in play, particularly by adopting specific legislation to exclude them from the purview of laws such as the LSA. Exclusions of this sort generally affect more vulnerable workers, shifting work-related risks from employers, and often the state, to workers (Fudge 2001, 5). Soon after coming into power in the spring of 2003, a new Liberal provincial government in Quebec introduced legislation to exclude certain workers from labour laws by deeming them to be independent contractors. The workers targeted by these two bills[27] are home child-care providers and intermediate resources in private dwellings in the social services sector, both recently determined by the courts to be salaried workers of state-controlled agencies.[28] These provisions, adopted in December 2003, exclude these workers from the LSA and other labour laws.

The use of this type of legislative technique is important for two reasons. First, it could signal a reversal in the trend towards the universal coverage of the LSA. The exclusion of specific categories of workers by deeming them to be independent contractors – in this case care workers, the vast majority of whom are women, for whom employee status could require more direct funding from the state – could become more widespread as employers (including the government) convince legislators that, in other specific cases, this exclusion constitutes a viable means to reduce costs and improve flexibility. Second, the use of such deeming provisions, to the detriment of workers, negates the dominant approach adopted by the courts. The courts have consistently held that the facts surrounding the actual relationship between workers and the providers of work have to be taken into account and that we must look beyond the parties' characterization of the workers' status. With these bills, workers in clearly subordinate employment relationships, under the direction and the control of the provider of work, and in many cases bearing the burden of work-related costs, will not be protected by labour legislation and will no longer have any means of contesting this situation. The legislator has decided to make use of deeming provisions regarding the employment relationship to exclude, rather than include, workers from labour legislation.

The Regulation of Temporary Help Agencies

The notion of "employer" is evolving: there is no longer necessarily a correlation between the employer and the firm for which an individual performs work. Whereas bilateral employment relationships were once the norm, the development of triangular employment relationships, with temporary employment agencies acting as an intermediary between workers and client firms, calls into question yet again the standard employment relationship as the norm. Such triangular relationships not only create confusion for the workers with respect to their rights but provide a means for employers to skirt round labour laws, including union avoidance, and to promote de facto deregulation of the labour market. Moreover, the temporary employment agency industry can be considered an important actor in the deregulation and the restructuring of the labour market (Peck and Theodore 2002; Vosko 2000).

The problems encountered by workers contracted through temporary help agencies are manifold and well documented (Bernier, Vallée, and Jobin 2003; Tapin 1993; Vosko 2000): difficulties in identifying the employer for the purpose of the application of labour and social security laws and in determining liability for legal obligations, disparities in working conditions and wages between agency workers and client firms' employees, abusive contractual provisions limiting the possibility of choosing work freely, and so on. Still, these issues remain unaddressed despite successive labour law reforms in Quebec. While the regulation of temporary employment agencies exists to a certain extent in several European countries (Clauwert 2000) and in some Canadian provinces (e.g., British Colombia),[29] their activities are entirely unregulated in Quebec, as are the working conditions and terms of employment specific to agency workers.

Legislation that once regulated agencies to some degree was repealed in 1982, a few years after the first major review of minimum employment standards. This law, the *Employment Bureaus Act* of 1964,[30] specified that employment agencies had to be public, with certain exceptions, and that their services were free. There were also provisions regarding the registration and the control of the agencies' operations. The *Employment Bureaus Act*, however, dated back to an era when recourse to temporary employment agencies was not as prevalent as it is now as a means of establishing and maintaining a flexible workforce, and when the often complex triangular employment relationships seen today were not even contemplated. The objective of the now repealed legislation was essentially to regulate employment bureaus – or private employment agencies – that simply brought together workers looking for employment and employers looking for qualified staff. The government of the day declared that the economic and social context had changed to such an extent that the legislation no longer had its *raison d'être* (Quebec 1982, 10883). Modern laws had replaced it, the government claimed, including the Quebec *Charter of Human Rights and Freedoms*,[31] which only specifically prohibits discrimination by employment agencies on the basis of a limited number of enumerated grounds, and the *Consumer Protection Act*,[32] which in theory protects "consumers" of the services offered by these agencies but contains no relevant provisions for workers in triangular employment relationships.

In 1993, a couple of years after yet another major reform of the LSA and another missed opportunity to address the issue of temporary help agencies, the government ordered a study on the subject, known as the Tapin Report (Tapin 1993). This report proposed several interesting avenues to remedy some of the problems raised by triangular employment relationships. In relation to the difficulties surrounding the identification of the "real" employer, it suggested that the agency and the client firm be held jointly liable for the employer's legislative obligations. It also proposed equal treatment in terms of wages for agency workers and client firms' employees, although it underlined the perils of such a proposal for an industry that depends on the profits from such salary gaps for its survival. In addition, it proposed giving "precarity pay" to compensate for benefits not available to agency workers (Vosko 2000, chap. 7). The report also recommended prohibiting clauses that restrict the right of temporary help workers to work directly, by way of a bilateral employment relationship, for client firms, and explored the possibility of limiting the use of temporary help workers to specific situations, where workers are needed on a short-term basis. Problems experienced by temporary help workers have in no way been remedied since the Tapin Report's publication, as the industry becomes increasingly transnational and institutionalized in the labour market. The Tapin Report was eventually shelved after a period of discussion at the government level (CNT 1995; CNT 1996). Some of the report's recommendations were resurrected 10 years later by the Bernier Committee (Bernier, Vallée, and Jobin 2003), but not until the reform process of 2002 had been completed.

Case law, the primary guide to the regulation of temporary help agencies in Quebec, is sorely lacking. A landmark Supreme Court decision in 1997, the *City of Pointe-Claire* case,[33] confirmed that the identity of the employer for the purpose of applying labour legislation to agency workers can vary from one law to the next. The client firm, then, could be determined to be the employer for collective bargaining purposes under the Quebec *Labour Code*, while the agency could be the employer under the LSA – an interpretation that might facilitate the application of standards dependent on continuous service with a single employer, such as protection against unjust dismissal. At the same time, this decision underlines the difficulties of applying legislation founded on bilateral employment relationships to situations where there are three parties to the employment relationship, as well as the need for legislative action to better reflect the realities of triangular relationships (Bich 2001; Grant and Laporte 1987). Although the position adopted by the majority of the Supreme Court may favour the agency worker in many respects (e.g., being able to benefit from the negotiated working conditions applying to the client firm's employees under the collective agreement), it does not necessarily facilitate the determination of who is responsible for ensuring that wages are paid and that decent working conditions are respected under minimum employment standards legislation.[34]

In the absence of regulation, no courts have stated that agencies cannot charge workers for their services or that penalty clauses negotiated by agencies and client firms, or imposed on employees, are illegal.[35] Only by the circuitous route of having a contractual clause declared by a court to be an abusive "adhesion" clause (i.e., imposed and non-negotiable)[36] have workers had some success in contesting such employer practices. In one case, *Agence de Placement Hélène Roy v. Rioux,*[37] an employee had signed such a contract with a temporary help agency specializing in providing personnel for financial institutions. Her contract stipulated that she could work for a financial institution only through the agency and that, if she did not respect the contract, she could be liable for a penalty of $1,200. The judge determined that the clause was abusive, and therefore null and void, because the agency had acted in bad faith by not fulfilling its promise of a fixed number of hours of work per week. In the judge's estimation, this restriction prevented her from gaining a livelihood. Presumably, if the agency had acted in good faith, the contract would have been declared legal.

The search continues for legislative solutions to ensure adequate working conditions and remuneration for temporary help workers and, ideally, equal treatment to curb recourse to the use of these workers. A European Directive on the question that would apply to all members of the European Union is under debate (Commission of the European Communities 2002).[38] The draft directive, whose protective scope is somewhat diluted by various exceptions, proposes a series of measures to counter some of the negative effects of triangular employment relationships. Although it does not call into question recourse to agencies, it provides for the equal treatment of agency workers and employees of client firms with respect to "basic working and employment conditions," such as working time, holidays, and remuneration. Access to permanent employment with client firms is not impeded, and agencies are not allowed to charge fees for their services. At the international level, after adopting the *Private Employment Agencies Convention* (no. 181) and the *Private Employment Agencies Recommendation* (no. 188) in 1997, further legitimizing the role of these agencies in the labour market (Vosko 1997), the International Labour Conference reached an impasse in 2003 concerning the further regulation of such triangular relationships and, more specifically, the problems related to the identification of the employer for the application of labour laws (International Labour Conference 2003, 57). Neither the convention nor the recommendation provides for the equality of treatment of agency workers. The convention does prohibit agencies from charging fees to workers and obliges member states to determine, at the national level, the respective legal obligations of agencies and client firms regarding working conditions and employment. In contrast to the draft European Directive, existing international standards on temporary employment agencies fail to embrace the principle of parity. (For a discussion of the potential of EU Directives, see Jackson, this volume.)

Parity between Workers in "standard" and "Non-standard" Work

There is growing concern over the disparity of treatment between workers in standard and non-standard forms of employment, putting this issue at the centre of the debate over the means available to mitigate precarious employment. Recourse to non-standard forms of employment stems largely from the advantages of this disparity for employers. More significant change has been achieved with respect to the regulation of part-time work than to regulating temporary help agencies. Parity between workers in standard and non-standard forms of employment has been promoted at both the European and the international levels, to varying degrees, with respect to part-time workers with the adoption of European *Directive 97/81/EC Concerning the Framework Agreement on Part-time Working* and the ILO *Part-time Work Convention*, 1994 (no. 175) and the *Part-time Work Recommendation*, 1994 (no. 182). The motivation behind the adoption of these instruments is, above all, a political agenda of promoting part-time work to create new employment opportunities. There is, however, a genuine fear that, by promoting part-time work, such instruments may actually serve to reinforce the segregation of part-time workers, the majority of whom are women and young people, in low-paying jobs (Murray 1999). Effective parity for part-time workers can only be achieved if the relevant instruments are drafted and interpreted in accordance with existing non-discrimination guarantees, including indirect discrimination (Murray 1999; Traversa 2003).

The idea of parity was introduced in Quebec in a 1990 amendment to the *LSA* on differences in treatment based on working hours.[39] These provisions specify that employees who work fewer hours than others and perform the same tasks in the same establishment cannot be paid less or be treated differently with respect to annual leave and vacation pay solely on the basis of the lesser number of hours worked. However, this provision applies only to employees who earn less than twice the minimum wage. Groups presenting at parliamentary hearings on the bill denounced this limitation, fearing that it will create new disparities in treatment between workers earning less than twice minimum wage and those earning slightly more. Opponents also contended that the limitation is incompatible with pay equity guarantees in the Quebec *Charter of Rights and Freedoms*[40] based on enumerated grounds (and later the *Pay Equity Act*),[41] since women and young people constitute the bulk of part-time workers (Quebec 1990b, CAS-3067ff). Yet surprisingly few decisions about the provision for equal treatment for part-time workers have been rendered under the Act.[42]

Another step towards parity occurred in 2002, though it imposed no conditions relating to rate of pay, continuous service, or prerequisites about the amount of time worked. Instead, the government introduced a new way of calculating compensation for legal holidays on a pro-rata basis, making it available to part-time and occasional workers and workers with non-standard work schedules who had previously been excluded from such compensation. This provision applies irrespective of continuous service accumulated for a single employer – in contrast to the previous legal holiday provisions, which required a minimum of 60 days. During the 2002 legislative review process, several groups recommended improving the parity provisions by extending the limited protection for some part-time workers to all casual workers, agency workers, home-workers, and workfare participants and by eliminating the requirement based on the minimum wage (ABE and FDNS 2002; FFQ and CIAFT 2002). They also recommended that these workers receive proportional monetary compensation to replace the benefits they cannot access because of their status. Although legislators did not heed these proposals, they were echoed by the Bernier Committee (Bernier, Vallée, and Jobin 2003, 253). Given the trend in Quebec, as well as at the international and European levels, the debate on the need for parity between standard and non-standard workers is far from over.

A NARROWING GAP BETWEEN EMPLOYMENT STANDARDS AND LABOUR MARKET REALITIES?

Over the years in Quebec, the trend towards universal coverage of minimum employment standards legislation has resulted in extending protection to many vulnerable workers previously excluded – specifically, caregivers in private homes and agricultural workers – while leaving regulators considerable discretion for exclusions from specific aspects of the LSA. This regulatory trend addresses precarious employment in part – specifically, dimensions of income and the extremely weak bargaining position of many workers due to a lack of union coverage – and it may also open space for labour market unionism (see Cranford, Das Gupta, Ladd, and Vosko, this volume). However, another facet of precarious employment, one that is not necessarily independent of income level and access to collective bargaining, is the spread of forms of employment deviating from the standard employment relationship (also described, in this volume, by Cranford and Vosko; Armstrong and Laxer; and Vosko and Zukewich). Without a doubt, there is increasing recognition that the traditional legislative model based on the standard employment relationship contributes, both in law and in practice, to the total or partial exclusion of large categories of workers from minimum employment standards legislation. This model also increases disparity of treatment between workers in the heterogeneous forms that make up the non-standard category. The 2002 reform of the LSA confirmed a continuing trend towards the regulation of non-standard forms of employment, albeit inadequately, with the adoption of provisions on disguised employment relationships and on equal access to compensation for public holidays. Faced with rising precariousness in the labour market and ever greater pressure from employers' organizations to regulate for flexibility and competitiveness, social actors concur on the need for the state to regulate in order to mitigate precarious employment (ABE and FDNS 2002; FFQ and CIAFT 2002; FTQ 2002; see also, this volume, Cranford, Das Gupta, Ladd, and Vosko; Schenk; and Vosko). Initiatives and discussions in Europe and at the ILO also demonstrate the inevitability of revisiting regulation based on the standard employment relationship. However, regulating is not without pitfalls.

The risk of legitimizing recourse to forms of non-standard employment exhibiting dimensions of precarious employment, such as solo self-employment, part-time work, and temporary wage work, grows when regulation is pursued in a piecemeal fashion. The new provisions in the LSA on disguised self-employment substantiate this claim. Limiting protection to certain categories of workers in non-standard forms of employment, on the basis of uneven and often unprincipled criteria, reinforces divisions between workers who may initially be only marginally less precarious along the continuum of precarious employment. Prohibiting employers from transferring work-related costs to minimum wage earners, to the detriment of slightly higher wage earners, reveals that basing entitlements on the minimum wage is outdated. These solutions inadequately address the fundamental issues of disparity of treatment between workers in general and which workers should assume work-related risks. At the same time, a total absence of legal regulation of temporary help agencies is institutionalizing their practices in the labour market.

Even with adequate legal regulation of non-standard forms of employment, difficulties related to compliance are exacerbated by the precarious situation of workers with limited bargaining power in many of these forms of employment. Even though they may work in the same place, many workers in such situations generally exhibit a lower level of solidarity, since they have little contact with one another (Cranford, Das Gupta, Ladd, and Vosko, this volume; Bernstein, Lippel, and Lamarche 2001). Such workers' precarious situation also contributes to a reluctance to file employment standards complaints, since their relationship with their employer, where one is identifiable, is always tenuous. Of course, compliance also depends on the priority given by government to enforcement and on resource allocation. Beginning in 2000, the Labour Standards Commission decided to put more emphasis on compliance through general inspections of workplaces following individual complaints (Lefebvre, Paradis, and Rivest 2003, 295). Nevertheless, of the 142,000 employers regulated only under the LSA (and not by collective agreements or decrees as well), only .02 per cent were subject to inspection in 2002–3. Of the 1,729,000 workers who are protected exclusively under the LSA, these inspections targeted only 25,052 employees (CNT 2003, 18). Adapting minimum employment standards legislation remains insufficient if compliance and the effectiveness of the legislation are not part of the equation (Collins 2000).

Using minimum employment standards legislation to mitigate precarious employment requires a delicate balancing of responding to new realities – and to "new" older realities such as temporary help work – and ensuring that the regulatory solutions will not inadvertently exacerbate the situation of already marginalized workers. To this end, it is necessary to look beyond the LSA and first analyse which workers are in a precarious employment and why that is the case. Systemic discrimination against women stemming from the male-breadwinner/female-caregiver model, for instance, exacerbates their experience of precarious employment (Fudge and Vosko 2001; Owens 1993). This model must be taken into account when designing new legislation. By limiting parity of treatment of part-time workers and failing to regulate temporary help agencies in the LSA, the legislator is neglecting this critical gender dimension.

In Quebec, the results obtained through legislative reform are mixed, yet the evolution of the LSA is best evaluated in historical perspective. From a more global standpoint, change-oriented legislative initiatives on many of the issues raised above date only to the early 1990s. Quebec has not kept pace with developments in Europe, but the principle of mitigating precarious employment is being introduced incrementally into the LSA, beginning with provisions targeting part-time workers and disguised employment relationships, as well as broadening the coverage of the Act. Universal coverage must be safeguarded, as the prime ambition of the LSA is to prevent further marginalization of specific categories of workers. The role of the *LSA* is to create a floor or threshold of entitlements for both unionized and non-unionized workers; hence, it is an appropriate vehicle for limiting precarious employment. The role of the *LSA* is particularly crucial in light of the inconsistencies of Quebec case law on questions relating to precarious employment. The 2002 reform represents a missed opportunity in many respects, but the gap between existing employment standards and the realities of the labour market is narrowing significantly in this jurisdiction, albeit mainly at the discursive level. Over time, it is hoped, this discursive shift will translate into legislative and policy reforms that mitigate precarious employment.

11

Precarious Employment and Occupational Health and Safety Regulation in Quebec

KATHERINE LIPPEL

This chapter provides an overview of the legislative framework governing occupational health and safety in Quebec as it applies to workers in precarious employment (Lippel 2004). Although in-depth studies of available literature clarify the health effects of various forms of precarious employment (Quinlan, Mayhew, and Bohle 2001a, b) and inform workers' compensation researchers of the importance of addressing both the forms and the dimensions of precarious employment (Quinlan and Mayhew 1999), little work has been done in developing the analytical tools necessary to evaluate regulatory failure from a purely legal perspective. A few studies examine certain types of regulatory failure with regard to specific groups of workers in precarious employment, including such groups as subcontractors (Johnstone, Mayhew, and Quinlan 2001; Thébaud-Mony 2000), the self-employed (Fudge, Tucker, and Vosko 2002), home-based workers (Bernstein, Lippel, and Lamarche 2001; Mayhew and Quinlan 1999; Vega-Ruiz, 1992), teleworkers (Blanpain 1997; Cox, Desmarais, and Lippel 2001; Montreuil and Lippel 2003; Ray 1996), and temporary or leased workers (Park and Butler 2001; Vosko 2000), though some neglect occupational health and safety legislation. Studies providing systematic analyses of occupational health and safety (OHS) legislation in a specific jurisdiction, and its effects on workers in precarious employment, are rare (notable exceptions include Bernier, Vallée, and Jobin 2003; Conseil du statut de la femme 2000; Quinlan 2002).

To explore the successes and failures of Quebec occupational health and safety legislation, the first section of this chapter identifies the relevant legislation and the forms of employment that are examined here. The second section outlines occupational health and safety issues of concern to workers engaged in precarious employment, with attention to such fundamentals as which workers are covered and who their employers are. The third section discusses the key difficulties confronted by workers in accessing compensation; in so doing, it identifies legal provisions demanding further scrutiny.

This chapter looks at legislation designed to prevent occupational injury and disease and also at workers' compensation legislation, which is designed to provide income support to workers disabled on the job. In Quebec there are two main laws in this area: the *Act Respecting Occupational Health and Safety (OHS)*, enacted in 1979, and the *Act Respecting Industrial Accidents and Occupational Diseases (AIAOD)*, adopted in 1985. Although their roots go back to the late 19th and early 20th centuries – occupational health and safety legislation was first enacted in 1885 in Quebec (Lippel 1981–82), and workers' compensation legislation was first adopted in 1909 (Lippel 1986) – both Acts were significantly redesigned in the last two decades of the 20th century. Since 1980, both compensation and prevention have been the responsibility of the Commission de la santé et de la sécurité du travail (CSST).

From a methodological perspective, evaluating the relevance of these statutes for the protection of workers in a changing labour market requires the design of the legal equivalent of a fine-tooth comb, a framework for analyzing legislation and case law which is designed to identify specific policy irritants. After defining the various forms of precarious employment potentially neglected under these laws, it becomes possible to scrutinize the case law of the specialized administrative tribunals with regard to specific legal problems that are predictable – for example, coverage and employer liability, but also problems in relation to specific employment statuses – in order to reveal actual situations involving workers in precarious employment whose attempts to access protection have led to litigation.[1] No single legal problem universally affects workers engaged in the dominant forms of precarious employment identified by Cranford and Vosko and by Vosko and Zukewich in this volume. With the notable exception of self-employment, moreover, no form of precarious employment is associated with complete regulatory failure, yet many problems arise for specific categories of employment. Interviews with injured workers and their advocates and with specialists from administrative agencies add texture to this fine-tooth-comb legal analysis.

Several forms of employment correlated with dimensions of precarious employment – low income, a lack of regulatory protection writ large, and a lack of control over the labour process – are explored in this chapter. These forms deviate from the standard employment relationship on the bases of duration or time, place of work, and contractual relationships. The forms comprising non-standard duration or time include part-time wage work, on-call work, short-term contracts, temporary work, and seasonal work. Non-standard place refers to home-based work, including telework, where new technology is used by employees working out of their homes. Non-standard contractual arrangements include self-employment (including independent and dependent contractors as well as workers in disguised employment relationships) and triangular relationships involving either subcontracting or work via employment agencies. Multiple job holders are also covered in this category, although they had not been initially targeted by our study. Legal difficulties apparent in the case law are particularly numerous for multiple job holders, many of whom are also part-time, on-call, and often even (partially) self-employed. The chapter does not address hours of work (long work days, shift work) or downsizing, although these realities of the new economy also have significant consequences for occupational health and safety (Quinlan, Mayhew, and Bohle 2001a and 2001b).

Regulatory failure is predictable in certain areas. Home-based work and telework is widely known to present challenges to labour inspection (Bernstein, Lippel, and Lamarche 2001; Cox, Desmarais, and Lippel 2001; Mayhew and Quinlan 1999), while small workplaces are associated with increased injury rates (Cedes 1993), poor injury prevention and OHS management strategies (Eakin 1992), and difficulties in terms of early return to work programs (Eakin, Clarke, and MacEachen 2002). Temporary work and work for employment agencies have both been associated with a plethora of problems, including higher accident rates (François and Lieven 1995), poor risk communication and training (Park and Butler 2001), ignorance of rights (Mayhew and Quinlan 2002), and subcontracting of risks (Thébaud-Mony, 2000). In the United States, where health-care access often depends on recognition of workers' compensation rights, some studies find that the contingent worker – a term defined more narrowly than precarious employment (see Cranford and Vosko, this volume; Vosko, Zukewich, and Cranford 2003) – is more, rather than less, likely to file a compensation claim (Park and Butler 2001), although the opposite is the case in other jurisdictions (Quinlan and Mayhew 1999; Mayhew and Quinlan 2002). In the Scandinavian countries, where there is a tradition of worker participation, vehicles to promote participation failed to effectively involve part-time workers and those who were in other forms of employment exhibiting dimensions of precarious employment (Aronsson 1999). Self-employment, involving both dependent and independent contractors, is well known to create regulatory confusion, prompting many people to fall through the cracks because they lacked information, they were deliberately misled, or their status was sufficiently ambiguous to undermine the system (Bich 2001; Fudge, Tucker, and Vosko 2002; Johnstone, Mayhew, and Quinlan 2001; Verge 2001). Compensation claims of temporary agency workers are more likely to be contested (Park and Butler 2001).

This summary of some of the issues dealt with in the literature helps to identify the legislative provisions that are of primary importance in evaluating Quebec OHS and workers' compensation legislation.

OCCUPATIONAL HEALTH AND SAFETY REGULATION

Section 46 of the Quebec *Charter of Human Rights and Freedoms* (*Charter*) specifically guarantees that "[e]very person who works has a right, in accordance with the law, to fair and reasonable conditions of employment which have proper regard for his health, safety and physical well-being." These rights become concrete if legislation governing these issues applies to "every person." The tangible outcome of this legislative provision is moot if OHS legislation fails to extend coverage to certain categories of "persons who work."

In Quebec, OHS legislation applies to all forms of precarious employment examined in this volume except the dominant form of self-employment, since self-employed people are not "workers" as defined in the Act. Section 1 provides that

"worker" means a person, including a student in the cases determined by regulation, who, under a contract of employment or a contract of apprenticeship, even without remuneration, carries out work for an employer, except

(1) a person employed as manager, superintendent, foreman or as the agent of the employer in his relations with his workers;

(2) a director or officer of a legal person, except where a person acts as such in relation to his employer after being designated by the workers or by a certified association.

Ironically, those self-employed who have incorporated their undertaking, whether or not they have employees, benefit from some protective provisions of the legislation; the unincorporated, in contrast, have certain obligations to protect others, but are under no obligation to comply with any provisions of the *OHS Act* if they are not in contact with "workers."

Although agents of the employer are excluded from the term "worker," section 11 reinstates the rights of the individuals described in paragraphs (1) and (2) to benefit from some of the rights granted to workers, including the right to "working conditions that have proper regard for his health, safety and physical well-being" (*OHS*, s. 9); the right to training, information, and counselling services in matters of OHS, including the right to appropriate supervision; the right to receive preventive and curative health services relating to the risks to which they may be exposed (*OHS*, s. 10); and the right to protective reassignment in cases where their health is compromised by exposure to a contaminant or where pregnant or breast-feeding workers are exposed to working conditions that could "endanger their health or that of their child

(Lippel 1998; *OHS*, ss. 32–48). Thus, the director of a corporation, with or without employees, has broader protection than the solo self-employed with no employees (see also Vosko and Zukewich, this volume).

The inconsistency arising from this distinction is well illustrated by the situation of hairdressers. Hairdressers work with products that justify protective reassignment in case of pregnancy, since the chemicals used in the products can be dangerous to the health of the unborn child. In an incorporated beauty salon, it is not uncommon to find the owner-operator, workers who are hairdressers or hairdressers' assistants, and self-employed hairdressers who rent a chair from the salon operator. If all three of these women are pregnant, the owner-operator and the assistant will be entitled to 90 per cent of their net salary if the only work available exposes them to the chemicals involved in hairdressing, while the self-employed hairdresser will either have to continue working with the products or withdraw from work without any financial compensation, given that the right to protective reassignment is not available to her.[2]

The declared purpose of the *OHS* Act is "the elimination, at the source, of dangers to the health, safety and physical well being of workers" (*OHS*, s. 2), and all its provisions are designed to promote that objective. Thus, the only provision specifically addressing the existence of the self-employed does so to ensure that they protect workers. Section 7 provides:

Every self-employed natural person who, for another person, and without the assistance of workers, carries out work in a workplace where there are workers is subject to the obligations imposed on a worker pursuant to this act and the regulations.

The person described in the first paragraph must, furthermore, comply with the obligations imposed on an employer in respect of products, processes, equipment, materials, contaminants and dangerous substances.

In practice, many self-employed people work alongside others, both waged workers and other self-employed people, so that the self-employed snow-remover, who works on a roof overlooking an area where workers may walk by, will be obliged to use protective equipment to keep himself from falling off the roof, as his fall could endanger a passing worker.[3] The self-employed working in isolation are not subject to any regulatory constraints and have no rights otherwise guaranteed under OHS legislation, which includes regulatory provisions adopted under the purview of the Act such as threshold limit values for exposure to toxic substances. Depending on the nature of the activity undertaken by the self-employed, other regulatory provisions may apply. Long-haul truckers are regulated in the interest of those who share the roads with them, and those performing work in construction are subject to regulations specific to that industry. However, most people working for themselves will fall below the radar screen of Quebec regulatory provisions designed to protect health and well-being.

From a health policy perspective, this situation is untenable, a conclusion shared by the authors of the Bernier Report (Bernier, Vallée, and Jobin 2003, 544–9). It was already an anomaly at the time the OHS Act was enacted in 1979, when 207,000 men and 57,000 women were self-employed (Matte, Baldino, and Courchesne 1998, 57), and by 2001 it had become an aberration, with close to double that number self-employed (Bernier, Vallée, and Jobin 2003, 56). Allowing individuals to undertake dangerous work in a totally unregulated fashion contravenes the spirit of the Quebec *Charter* and opens the door to abuse of vulnerable people who are ready to work under any conditions, regardless of danger. This situation not only undermines health protection for those who undertake such work but lowers the threshold of acceptable risk for all workers, since the totally unregulated self-employed are in a good position to underbid employers for contracts, putting pressure on employers to reduce costs by reducing protection to workers. Similar preoccupations with regard to unfair competition between the self-employed and employees have been voiced both by scholars (Engblom 2001, 227–8) and by unions in the European Union (CES). The Bernier Report also suggests that the self-employed have the right to refuse dangerous working conditions without fear of being held in breach of contract (Bernier, Vallée, and Jobin 2003, 548). Quebec's OHS legislation on this issue falls behind that of other provinces (Fudge, Tucker, and Vosko 2002), and the inclusion of the self-employed should be made a priority. The exclusion of many self-employed people from the purview of OHS legislation is its most central failure, in terms of this factor's potentially negative effect on the health and safety of all working people. Yet other forms of precarious employment contribute to difficulties in the application of specific provisions of the legislation. Home workers are covered under the OHS Act, and all provisions apply to them (Bernstein, Lippel, and Lamarche 2001),[4] in spite of an unnecessarily complex definition of the employer's establishment which leads some to contend that they are partially excluded (Bernier, Vallée, and Jobin 2003, 101). While employers can reasonably be expected to ensure that adequate working materials are provided to the home worker or the teleworker (Montreuil and Lippel 2003), inspection mechanisms are impracticable, because of privacy law issues (Bernstein, Lippel, and Lamarche 2001) and because the inspection of people's homes, where individual workers are employed, is simply not economically viable. British Columbia has addressed the privacy issue in a well-grounded provision specifically designed to accommodate privacy considerations and inspectorate imperatives (British Columbia, *Workers Compensation Act*, 1996), but even its forward-looking approach fails to guarantee effective inspection of thousands of small workplaces, let alone private homes.

Agency workers are undoubtedly workers under the OHS Act, but, again, the statute leaves open to debate the question of employer responsibility. Is the liable employer the placement agency or the employer responsible for the establishment in which the worker has been placed (Bernier, Vallée, and Jobin 2003, 160; Bich, Dion, Lemay, and Ratti 1997, 27)? Should the legislation be amended to provide for joint and several liability for both employers, at least in the context of OHS (Bich 2001, 295), or should Parliament opt for sole responsibility of the agency (Bernier, Vallée, and Jobin 2003, 503, 512)? In other jurisdictions, both parties have been held liable under penal statutes (Johnstone, Mayhew, and Quinlan 2001), and the wording of section 236 of Quebec's OHS legislation could permit the conviction of both, whether or not they were actually considered as employers, as "every person," and not just the employer, can be found guilty of contravening the Act. Given that fines in Quebec are currently set at a maximum of $500 (s. 236) for a first offence, and a maximum of $20,000 for the most serious of offences (s. 237), this problem will be of little practical interest until the penalties are increased.

Other issues are more difficult to measure through the case law but are well documented in the literature of other jurisdictions or were raised in the course of interviews. For instance, participatory mechanisms designed to promote prevention through worker participation often fail workers in precarious employment, particularly those who work part-time, on call, or through placement agencies (Aronsson 1999; Johnstone, Quinlan, and Walters, in press; Quinlan, Mayhew, and Bohle 2001a, b). Quebec OHS legislation (s. 112) provides that high-risk employment should be the subject of specific "Health Programmes," and workers should be closely monitored by public health officials, yet interviewees confirm that subcontractors and their employees are completely forgotten in the process.

Protective reassignment of pregnant workers is provided for in Quebec OHS legislation, but it fails the self-employed and many part-time multiple job holders. For example, public health doctors have determined that more than 20 hours of exposure to certain types of radiation justifies protective reassignment, yet the tribunal refused the appeal of a worker exposed for over 30 hours per week under two separate job contracts, since neither employer was responsible for more than 20 hours of exposure.[5] Similar difficulties arise when part-time workers refuse reassignment to a time slot for which they are unavailable because they are working elsewhere (Lippel 1998).

In Quebec, as elsewhere, workers in precarious employment are often the most at risk and the least well protected. When they are injured, they also encounter particular problems.

COMPENSATION FOR OCCUPATIONAL INJURY AND DISEASE

Workers' compensation legislation allows for economic compensation in the case of disability, either temporary or permanent, attributable to accidents arising out of or in the course of employment or to diseases contracted because of exposure to risk in the workplace. Quebec's compensation legislation was first enacted in 1909, but in 1931 the Act was completely revamped to ensure collective responsibility for the costs of disability attributable to work. All employers were obliged to contribute to the scheme, according to the level of risk engendered by their activities, and payments were pooled in a collective fund that was then redistributed according to the costs of claims.

Since the early 1980s the contributions for Quebec's workers' compensation scheme have become increasingly experience-rated or linked to the record of payouts to successful claimants over the previous years. The more the individual employer's experience is considered in the calculation of levies, the more costly a compensated injury in a given plant becomes for the individual employer, both because of the effect on future levies and because competitors within the same sector no longer pay the same amount, thus making it impossible to pass on the cost to the consumer. The larger the firm, the more individual experience is considered in the final calculation. In theory, the system is designed to provide incentives to prevent injury, though in many cases the effect is, rather, to prevent compensation for injury and even claims for compensation.

Strategies to reduce the cost of compensated injury include investment in claims management (Thomason and Pozzebon 2002) and subcontracting out the most costly and dangerous work (Johnstone, Mayhew, and Quinlan, 2001; Thébaud-Mony 2000). In many high-risk industries, such as trucking (Bernier, Marceau, and Towner 1999) and forestry (Bernier 1999, 157), restructuring involves transferring the risks to the worker or the small independent contractor. For instance, logging companies formerly employing truckers and lumberjacks increasingly do business with independent operators, often the very individuals who used to draw a salary from the company. These people have purchased expensive equipment from the company, assume the risks of an economic downturn, and are also obliged to assume the costs of disability insurance. Coverage under workers' compensation legislation is obligatory for all employees, though not for most of the self-employed,[6] so restructuring has led to a huge increase in the number of individuals without disability insurance of any kind. Although we have no figures for Quebec, in Canada only 38 per cent of the self-employed have some form of disability insurance (Akyeampong and Sussman 2003), and over 50 per cent of blue-collar independent operators have no insurance because coverage would be too costly (Delage 2002). In Quebec, when independent operators have at least one employee, including family members, they are obliged to pay premiums to the Commission de la santé et de la sécurité du travail for coverage of the employees, but their own coverage is not mandatory.

WHO ARE WORKERS? WHO ARE EMPLOYERS?

Coverage under the *AIAOD* is broader than under other Quebec labour legislation (Bernier, Vallée, and Jobin 2003) or under workers' compensation legislation in other Canadian jurisdictions (Fudge, Tucker, and Vosko 2002), except with regard to domestic workers and undocumented workers, who are covered in other Canadian provinces but not in Quebec (Bernstein, Lippel, and Lamarche 2001). All other workers are covered, regardless of the size of their firm or the nature of their activities. Contrary to other legislation, section 2 of the *AIAOD* includes a definition of independent operator – "a natural person who carries on work for his own account, alone or in partnership, and does not employ any worker" – and section 9 of the *AIAOD* guarantees coverage to those independent operators who comply with the stipulated conditions:

An independent operator who in the course of his business carries on activities for a person similar to or connected with those carried on in the establishment of that person is considered to be a worker in the employ of that person, unless

(1) he carries on the activities

(a) simultaneously for several persons;

(b) under a remunerated or unremunerated service exchange agreement with another independent operator carrying on similar activities;

(c) for several persons in turn, supplies the required equipment and the work done for each person is of short duration; or

(2) in the case of activities that are only intermittently required by the person who retains his services.

Criticized by some for being difficult to apply (Bich, Dion, Lemay, and Ratti 1997; Pratte 1995), section 9 is nevertheless of assistance to decision makers struggling to apply the definition of worker to truly independent operators and to other workers who could possibly be covered by a broad construction of the definition of worker but who clearly fall within the purview of section 9 (Lippel 2004). Workers and independent operators thus covered may receive compensation under the Act regardless of whether their "employer" or the deemed employer has paid the appropriate premiums, since section 26 of the Act guarantees that workers' rights do not depend on the fulfillment of the employer's obligations. No premiums are payable by workers or independent operators covered by section 9; the cost is borne solely by employers.

Even with coverage broader than that of other jurisdictions, many working people in Quebec assume they are not covered and never claim for their work-related injury. While this is true of many workers who clearly fall under the

Act, both in the United States (Biddle and Roberts 2003) and in Canada (Shannon and Lowe 2002), it is more troubling when workers or independent contractors have been wrongly led to believe they are not covered under the Act. In some cases, it is only when a worker has unsuccessfully sued his employer,[7] or when another government agency would otherwise have to pick up the cost of injury,[8] that a worker in a disguised employment relationship will file a claim. Even in these cases, because a claim must be filed within six months in Quebec, the worker who has been successfully duped by his employer may end up with no recourse. In one such case, it was held that section 9 is so complex that it is unfair to the employer for the courts to conclude it is the employer's responsibility to explain it to the worker, and that the worker is solely responsible for not having obtained competent legal advice with regard to his or her status and rights under the *AIAOD*.[9] In these circumstances, it is little wonder that employers find disguised employment relationships to be cost-effective.

Those independent operators not targeted by section 9, as well as domestic workers, employers, and company directors, are eligible for voluntary coverage, whereby they pay their own premiums in exchange for coverage for risks incurred during the period for which they have purchased coverage (s.18). This solution is not attractive to most of those who could opt for such coverage, since a grand total of only 27,292 individuals, including 19,978 directors of corporations, opted for coverage in 2003. The most vulnerable are the least likely to opt for voluntary coverage: only 13 domestic workers and 405 independent operators are included in the total figure.[10]

Once coverage has been determined, it is necessary to identify the employer. The identity of the employer is important, both to attribute the costs of injury to the employer obliged to pay levies and to determine who is responsible for the implementation of workers' rights and obligations. The employer must pay the first 14 days of benefits in Quebec (s. 60), an amount that will later be refunded by the Commission de la santé et de la sécurité du travail. The same employer has the right to temporarily reassign an injured employee to appropriate employment (s. 179) and must ensure that the immediate medical needs of the employee are met, including transport by ambulance from the scene of the accident to the hospital or the employee's home (s. 190). The right to rehabilitation implies that the employer will be invited to accommodate an injured worker, insofar as possible (s. 170); the worker maintains a right to return to work "to the establishment where he was working" or "in another establishment of his employer" (s. 236) for one or two years after the accident, depending on the size of the firm (s. 240).

The workers who have the most difficulty with regard to the identification of the employer are those involved in a triangular employment relationship, in particular employees placed in worksites by a temporary help agency. Case law, for the most part, has concluded that the agency, rather than the employer with whom the worker has been placed, is the employer,[11] but case law is not unanimous,[12] and the conclusion may vary according to the circumstances. The agency may reassign the worker to other work during the healing process, or after the injury is healed or stabilized, though some decision makers underline the importance of trying to relocate the worker at the client's workplace.[13]

Even if the case law were clear, it is often of little help; for example, a trucker interviewed, who was contracted out to a trucking firm by a placement agency, was injured several hundred kilometres from his home. Both potential employers, the owner of the truck and the placement agency, disputed liability for the cost of the ambulance that was needed to return the worker home. After spending hours in the waiting room of the community clinic, the worker eventually asked his wife to come and get him. Similar difficulties arose when it was necessary to know the size of the employer's workplace in order to determine the worker's right to return to work. As the agency had more than 20 employees and the client less than 20, the right to return to pre-injury employment expired in either one or two years. By the time the appeal was heard, both delays had expired and the worker was left without an effective remedy.[14]

A legislative provision, or a quasi-judicial interpretation of current legislation, that held both potential employers to be jointly responsible for the implementation of workers' rights would go a considerable distance in improving this situation. For OHS and workers' compensation issues, such a suggestion is viable, according to the Bernier Report (Bernier, Vallée, and Jobin 2003, 502, 504), and it would at least transfer the costs of ambiguity to the two potential employers, who are in a far better economic position to assume the costs of the necessary debate.

ACCESS TO COMPENSATION: KEY DIFFICULTIES

Proving Injury Is Work Related

Workers' compensation is payable to those who can prove they have suffered an employment injury, either because of a work accident or an occupational disease. Provisions governing work accidents apply without distinction, including section 28, which presumes "an injury that happens at the workplace while the worker is at work ... to be an employment injury." Thus, homeworkers and teleworkers have equal access to compensation for a work accident, even when it takes place in the worker's home.[15]

Recognition of occupational disease claims is far more problematic, particularly for multiple-job holders who have, either simultaneously or over a period of years, been exposed to risks while they are holding various forms of employment – some of which are covered and others, not. Aside from the difficulties temporary workers encounter when they have to prove exposure to a disease-causing substance they may have encountered at any number of job sites (Quinlan and Mayhew 1999), workers who have been exposed to disease-causing working conditions both during covered employment and while self-employed also encounter problems. Claims for industrial deafness,[16] psychological problems,[17] toxic exposure to isocyanates,[18] and musculoskeletal disorders[19] have all been refused in cases where the worker could not convince the tribunal that the most relevant exposure occurred while the claimant was an employee. If the tribunal is persuaded that the most significant exposure happened while the claimant was a worker, compensation should be payable as if the illness was solely attributable to that exposure, since the Commission de la santé et de la sécurité du travail is not permitted to provide partial compensation under the *AIAOD*.[20]

Calculation of Benefits

Once the occupational injury is accepted, it becomes necessary to determine benefits; it is in this process that the rights of individuals in precarious employment are the most in jeopardy. Quebec's compensation system is based on compensation for potential wage loss. A decision is first made as to the wage-earning capacity of the injured worker, and then the effect of injury on that capacity is measured. If the initial determination as to wage-earning potential underestimates the real earning potential of the injured worker, wage loss will be underestimated and economic compensation and the right to rehabilitation will be negatively affected. For instance, if it is assumed that a part-time worker at a fast-food outlet has an earning capacity equivalent to current earnings at the time of injury, minimum wage multiplied by the number of hours worked, the worker's right to compensation will depend on his or her inability to earn pre-injury wages, which will be less than minimum wage for full-time employment. Unless the injury causes permanent total disability, residual earning capacity will rapidly catch up with pre-injury earnings, so that access to a pension, or even to a retraining program, will not be provided, even though the injury has had severe economic consequences for the worker who was not employed at his or her maximum earning capacity at the time of injury.

The *AIAOD* actually provides for a partial solution to this problem, contrary to legislation and policy in other Canadian jurisdictions, such as in British Columbia and in Ontario, which have no minimum benefit level legislatively guaranteed. In Quebec, sections 6 and 65 of the *AIAOD* assume that pre-injury working capacity cannot be less than minimum wage for full-time employment (40 hours per week in 2005). In spite of the clear wording of the statute, McDonald's, in a series of appeals, several of which have been successful,[21] has maintained that the legislation should be construed as compensating only for the real wages lost, thus denying the recognition of a minimum earning capacity for all workers. Appeals involving other employers have refused to follow the restrictive interpretation proposed by McDonald's,[22] and the Commission de la santé et de la sécurité du travail still applies the law to guarantee benefits based on an earning capacity equivalent to full-time minimum wage, regardless of actual earnings at the time of injury.

Part-time minimum wage earners in Quebec are better protected than their counterparts in other provinces, yet the system is still unfair to part-time workers earning an hourly wage better than minimum wage. Although the same minimum benefit provision will be applied, the actual wage potential of a part-time nurse will be greater than minimum wage multiplied by 40 hours, yet most cases involving temporary or part-time workers will calculate benefits on the basis of minimum wage (Lippel 2004). Case law is constantly evolving on the issue of wage loss for short-term contracts, since previous practices allowing for the hourly wage to be annualized have been questioned by the Court of Appeal.[23]

Special provisions apply to seasonal and on-call workers (*AIAOD*, s. 68) and to multiple job holders (*AIAOD*, s. 71). Case law is currently divided with regard to compensation of multiple job holders, whose total real earnings are greater than those deemed to have been earned under section 71, which presumes a 40-hour work week. For example, a nurse's aid working 50 hours a week at two jobs will be compensated for only 40 hours under the more conservative reading of the legislation. If the worker worked 50 hours for the same employer, not only would she be compensated on the basis of the 50 hours worked but overtime rates would also be taken into consideration. The appeal tribunal has, on several occasions, pointed out the anachronistic nature of section 71, preferring to set aside the terms of the section so as to arrive at a more equitable result,[24] but the Court of Appeal has held that the unfairness of the results obtained under the application of section 71 will not justify intervention on judicial review,[25] so there are currently two conflicting streams of case law at the appeal tribunal level.

Other important issues (Lippel 2004) for injured workers include rehabilitation programs that retrain workers previously in standard employment relationships to access part-time jobs, home work, or self-employment. These practices seem particularly problematic, given that the self-employed are no longer eligible for benefits unless they choose to pay the premiums themselves. The right to return to work for many workers in precarious employment is often theoretical, either because the employer simply stops calling the on-call worker or the agency offers new employment at a work site at an unreasonable distance from the worker's home.

CONCLUSION

This chapter provides a glimpse of some of the problems arising when ill-adapted statutes are applied to workers in precarious employment. I characterize this discussion as a glimpse because many difficulties cannot be detected by a methodology based on an analysis of case law. The most vulnerable among workers and the self-employed are not likely to file claims, and even less likely to persevere to the appeal level.

In spite of this limitation, sufficient evidence is available to document the difficulties involved in making claims. In Quebec, OHS and workers' compensation issues confronting workers in precarious employment are, in many ways, similar to those in other jurisdictions. Precarious employment leads to the exclusion from coverage of people and activities that would have been covered previously. To this group, it is necessary to add the many potential claimants who wrongly assume they are not covered. As Quinlan and Mayhew (1999) make clear, the increase in precarious employment can wreak havoc on workers' compensation statistics, lulling policy makers and sometimes even researchers into the delusion that accident rates have shrunk, when in fact they are simply being less well documented because of reductions in claims, costs, and coverage.

This problem is not theoretical. It is evident at the level of claims data; and it is increasingly clear that working conditions are becoming more dangerous for wage workers because of pressure to increase productivity in order to compete with independent contractors, who are exempt from regulatory constraints. Lessons for prevention include the need to broaden the scope of OHS legislation to ensure that all people who work have both the right and the obligation to work in secure working conditions. No one should accept or be forced to accept work in conditions below that level. The situation in Quebec is lowering the threshold of acceptable risk for all workers.

Aside from the self-employed, many other workers are falling between the cracks, either because they are invisible to those responsible for OHS or because they are not sufficiently integrated into the system to allow participatory mechanisms designed to promote healthier workplaces to function as they should (Aronsson 1999). Information about risks in the workplace will not trickle down to those who work part-time or on call, or to those who change jobs on a regular basis.

This chapter has not looked at solutions in detail, but researchers in other jurisdictions are currently exploring new ways for regulatory mechanisms to be more inclusive of the needs of workers in precarious employment (Johnstone, Quinlan, and Walters, in press). These developments should be watched closely, as strategies in the European Union or in Australia may have relevance in the Canadian context.

Labour market restructuring, as well as the increased individualization of risks and costs because of experience rating, is also undermining the historical balance in workers' compensation schemes, which once allowed a sharing of the cost of risk. Collectively, all employers within a jurisdiction once subsidized each other in the event of work injury and, ultimately, the consumer picked up the cost of injury. Now this cost is no longer transferable to the consumer, as competitors are no longer sharing in the costs of employers who have higher accident rates. This change transfers the risks to the smallest and most expendable entity, whether the small subcontracting company, the recently independent contractor, or the under-compensated injured worker and his or her family. Costs appear to have been reduced because they are now invisible from an economic perspective. But from a social perspective, they are shared by the workers and what remains of the social security system, which, in Quebec, as in much of the rest of Canada, includes medicare and the welfare system (Hertzmann, McGrail, and Hirtle 1999).

Subcontractors, usually small employers, are less able to provide long-term positions to injured workers and more likely to use aggressive claims management strategies, given that they are also less likely to be unionized. Enforcement costs for government agencies mandated to apply OHS and workers' compensation legislation increase with the growth of small business, which, in other jurisdictions, has led to growing compliance concerns (Quinlan and Mayhew 1999). Several interviewees, both workers and policy makers, reported that subcontractors were more likely to contest claims, in some cases allegedly as a condition of obtaining contracts. Avoidance of OHS obligations and transferring costs of workers' compensation are encouraging the spread of precarious employment.

In terms of OHS and in the context of workers' compensation, the absence of compulsory coverage of the self-employed is of particular concern. Other jurisdictions, such as France (France 2001),[26] New Zealand (ACC), some Australian states (Quinlan and Mayhew 1999), and the Netherlands (Pennings 2002), have obligatory coverage for some or all of the self-employed and, in the case of the Netherlands, there are even mechanisms insuring that the more successful independent operators subsidize those, often in agriculture, who are the least able to ensure payment of adequate premiums. All these solutions need to be explored in order to guarantee all people who work the rights that are guaranteed in the Quebec *Charter*: the right to fair and reasonable conditions of employment that have proper regard for the person's health, safety, and physical well-being.

Will the Vicious Circle of Precariousness Be Unbroken? The Exclusion of Ontario Farm Workers from the *Occupational Health and Safety Act*

ERIC TUCKER

In the early evening of August 15, 2000, Henry Redekopp, a 23-year-old German-speaking Mexican Mennonite farm worker employed by Flinkert Dairy Farm, was operating a tractor pulling a manure spreader. He apparently noticed a leak, entered the tank to remove an object blocking the closing valve, and immediately was overcome by toxic gases from the liquid manure. Gary Ferrier and Erich Schulz arrived on the scene, and Gary Ferrier entered the tank to attempt a rescue. He, too, collapsed inside the tank. Erich Schulz ran to get a rope, ladder, and dust mask, entered the tank, and was also overcome. By the time the fire department arrived on the scene and removed the three men, they were dead from asphyxiation. There were no bars preventing human entry into the tank; a warning sign on the tank – written in English only notwithstanding the presence of workers who spoke and read German and Spanish – was covered by dried and hardened manure; and workers were not instructed in safety procedures (Ontario, Ministry of the Solicitor General 2001). Yet, at the time, none of these conditions violated any provincial statute[1] because workers employed on farm operations were not entitled to the protection of the Ontario *Occupational Health and Safety Act (OHSA),*[2] and no other legislation directly regulates the conditions of farm work.

This chapter explores the denial to agricultural workers of legal protections enjoyed by the overwhelming majority of workers, a situation made all the more anomalous by the norm of including agricultural workers in health and safety laws in Canadian, North American, and international law.[3] It does so through the lens of a modified resource mobilization theory that seeks to explain the likelihood of powerless groups mounting resistance to their oppression and of their being successful. The first section advances this theoretical framework and describes the vicious circle of precariousness that afflicts groups such as agricultural workers. The second section provides a brief historical overview of the conditions of Ontario farm workers and their exclusion from most labour and employment legislation. The third section paints a picture of agricultural employment in 2004, illustrating the dimensions of precarious employment that characterize it and undermining the normative myth of the family farm that provides the ideological justification for exclusionary legislation. The fourth section looks, more specifically, at the hazardous conditions that farm workers face, demonstrating that, by any measure, farm work is dangerous. This discussion is followed by an examination of the saga of the exclusion of farm workers from the Ontario OHSA and the inadequacy of the alternative regime that has been constructed. The conclusion discusses the recent decision to cover agricultural workers beginning in June 2006.

EXPLAINING THE VICIOUS CIRCLE OF PRECARIOUSNESS AND LEGAL EXCLUSION

Traditionally, workers have adopted two principal strategies to overcome employment insecurity: collective action to secure better contractual terms of employment, and political action to secure state-enforced minimum standards. Collective action was most available to skilled workers who enjoyed a partial monopoly of skill. Semi-skilled industrial workers lacked these advantages, but self-organization was aided by their concentration in oligopolistic mass-production industries. Their organizational resources and strategic ability to disrupt convinced politicians and many major employers to facilitate orderly industrial relations and to promote responsible unions through statutory collective bargaining schemes (Fudge and Tucker 2001; McInnis 2002; see also Cranford, Das Gupta, Ladd, and Vosko, this volume). The achievement of statutory minimum standards depended in part on organized workers engaging in political action but also on winning broader public support. Sometimes a successful reform coalition could be cobbled together through appeals to a common concern about the moral dangers posed by labour market conditions, as in the case of child and female labour (Backhouse 1991; Tucker 1990); in other cases there were shared beliefs that excess competition was driving down wages, pushing families onto relief, and having an adverse impact on aggregate demand, as in the case of male minimum wages (Cox 1987; Klee 2000; also see Bernstein, this volume).

Whether seeking greater security through collective self-organization or political action, workers need resources to be successful. Resource mobilization theorists take a number of different approaches to explain the emergence and success of social movements (Buechler 2000). Jenkins (1985) and Jenkins and Perrow (1977) have developed a particularly useful version of resource mobilization theory to analyze farm worker movements in the United States. They identified a number of interacting factors that shape both the likelihood that groups will challenge the status quo and their chances of success. First, the social structure conditions a group's indigenous mobilizing capacity. In general, the more economically secure the group, the more indigenous resources will be at its disposal. Second, the group's strategic position is central. Even the most powerless may be able to increase its leverage through strikes, riots, or other forms of mass defiance. However, the degree of power it can gain through such actions will vary widely depending, in part, on the potential impact of the disruptive activities. Third, strategic choices can affect mobilizations and their outcomes. The choice between relying on indigenous or professional organizers, targeting group members or third parties, or focusing on building solidarity networks or organizing for an immediate and specific objective are just some of the strategic issues whose resolution can influence the likelihood and success of mobilizations. Finally, the structure of political alignments and the ability of groups to promote and exploit divisions among and between political and economic elites may also be a key factor.

Resource mobilization theory, however, has been criticized on a number of accounts: its failure to engage more seriously with the role of the state; its lack of attention to the role of subjective and ideological factors, how issues are framed, and how these factors influence resistance struggles; and its failure to link resource opportunities to the larger political-economic context (Buechler 2000; Kuumba 2001; Mayer 1995). This study incorporates two additional factors into its analysis to partially remedy these lacunae. The first is the legal conditions under which mobilization occurs. A repressive regime with effective institutional and legal controls over potential opponents will make mobilization, even by well-resourced groups, difficult. Groups in liberal democracies that are deprived of rights that protect the exercise of freedom of association, or of other citizenship rights, such as the right to vote, are less likely to mobilize successfully and obtain effective redress than groups enjoying greater rights and freedoms that are more fully protected (Basok 2004). The second factor is ideology, which, in this context, refers to the ability of a relatively powerless group to frame its demands in a way that gives it legitimacy, both to its members and to the public. All these meso-level factors need to be situated within the macro-level political-economic context in which they operate.

Other things being equal, the fewer dimensions of precarious employment workers experience, the greater their chances of successfully mobilizing and

improving their situation through collective or political action; the more dimensions of precarious employment workers experience, the lower their
chances of mitigating precarious employment through these means. Agricultural workers[4] are a classic example of the latter group. For most of their history, they have faced structural conditions that adversely affect their indigenous
mobilizing capacity. They have been widely dispersed among small employers
and notoriously difficult to organize for the purposes of collective action. Despite the importance of agricultural products, the lack of indigenous organization makes it difficult for agricultural workers to exploit their strategic
potential to disrupt the food supply. Moreover, they have often faced high levels of coercion, both state sanctioned and vigilante, to curb disruptive activity
or even its possibility. Strategic choices have often been constrained because of
the lack of resources and the adverse conditions for organizing. Farm operators
and agribusiness have generally enjoyed high levels of political influence, leaving little scope to take advantage of cracks within the power structure. They
continue to operate under unfavourable legal conditions, having been denied
citizenship rights enjoyed by most other workers. Additionally, migrant agricultural workers, who constitute a significant component of the agricultural
workforce, lack the right to vote in Canada and face social exclusion in the
communities in which they reside, undermining their ability to obtain stronger
rights or to exercise the rights they enjoy (Basok 2004). Finally, their claims of
vulnerability have had to compete with those made by farm operators, who
emphasize their own economic uncertainty (Kelsey 1994). This vicious circle
leads Beatty (1987, 89) to describe agricultural workers as "among the most
economically exploited and politically neutralized individuals in our society,"
while Wall (1996, 517) notes that their "association with low status employment and the secondary labour market have helped reinforce the persistent dis-
regard farm labour has suffered in Canadian society."

Resource mobilization theory aims to do more than describe vicious cir-
cles; it also provides a way of thinking about how relatively powerless people
may break them. One dimension of that vicious circle was the exclusion of
agricultural workers from occupational health and safety laws in Ontario –
the central case study in this chapter. The theory also illuminates the struggle
that led to the decision of the Ontario government in June 2005 to promul-
gate Ontario Regulation 41415, bringing farm operators under the OHSA.

ENTRENCHING THE NORMS OF LABOUR MARKET PRECARIOUSNESS AND LEGAL EXCLUSION

Rural wage labour has been essential to agriculture production in Ontario
from the time of settlement onwards, although only a small portion of this
workforce ever conformed to the model of the standard employment
relationship. According to Parr (1985, 96), "agricultural workers have been

historically, as they are today, casual labourers dependent upon irregular spates of ill-paid waged work for several different employers in order to maintain material subsistence." During the early settlement days, many agricultural workers were themselves small holders or tenants seeking to earn enough to sustain themselves while they made their farms. However, by the latter part of the century, barriers to independent proprietorship rose. The children of established farmers increasingly opted to abandon the farm for the city, reducing the supply of unpaid family farm labour and making Ontario farmers increasingly dependent on wage labour. Between 1891 and 1941, both the absolute and the relative number of waged labourers increased in the agricultural workforce. A large proportion of workers were seasonal, many being village day labourers and the unemployed in nearby urban areas (Haythorne and Marsh 1941, chap. 9; Parr 1985, 101–2).

The pre-war agricultural world was a highly stratified one in which, according to John Kenneth Galbraith, "no hired man had full citizenship" (Galbraith 1964, 46, cited in Parr 1985, 100). As a result, farm workers were excluded from most early labour legislation. Occupational health and safety legislation developed in a piecemeal fashion from the last quarter of the nineteenth century. The *Thrashing Machines Act* (1874) was arguably the first occupational health and safety statute, and it required that certain protections be in place on steam-powered equipment, which was increasingly being used in agricultural production. Subsequently, legislation was passed to protect workers employed on railways (1881) and in factories (1884), shops (1888), mines (1890), and construction (1911),[5] but there has been no further legislation directly regulating hazardous working condition in agriculture.

Initially, injured agricultural workers were treated identically to other workers seeking compensation from their employers, as all workers were subject to a set of common law rules that made recovery extremely unlikely. These rules were modified by the *Workmen's Compensation for Injuries Act* (1886) to allow injured workers to succeed if they could establish that their injuries were caused by their employers' negligence or by the negligence of a supervisor or co-worker. The Act initially applied to agricultural workers, but in 1893 the Patrons of Industry, a farm organization, petitioned the government to be relieved of liability, and legislation to this effect was introduced. Organized labour protested, as did the leader of the opposition, William Meredith, who argued: "If the original act was based on a sound doctrine there was no sound reason why any class should be relieved from liability."[6] Supporters of the bill, however, justified the special treatment in terms that still resonate: the position of farmers is exceptional because they cannot exercise direct supervision over employees; the Act operated oppressively against farmers; and the law was aimed at corporations that mistreated employees, not farmers, who provided for workers who resided with them. Farm workers were also excluded from protection under no-fault workers' compensation legislation passed in 1914. Meredith, by then a judge, was the architect of the plan, and he had not changed his view that farm workers should be covered. He doubted, however, that "public opinion" would support their inclusion (Ontario 1913, xi). As a result, the entitlement of agricultural workers to compensation for work injuries continued to depend on the unreformed common law. Only in 1942, in a case brought by an Ontario farm worker against his employer, did the Supreme Court of Canada hold that an employer had a duty to provide a safe system of work, and that the duty was a personal one that could not be avoided by delegating responsibility to another employee or contractor.[7]

Farm workers were also excluded from other early twentieth-century Ontario minimum standards laws regulating wages and hours of work, including the *Minimum Wage Act* (1920), which established female minimum wages, and the *One Day Rest in Seven Act* (1922). An uneasy coalition government headed by the United Farmers of Ontario, a group established in 1914 to represent the interests of Ontario's farmers and supported by the Independent Labor Party, enacted both these statutes (Badgley 2000; Woods 1975). Depression and World War II-era employment legislation passed by a Liberal provincial government also excluded farm workers, including the *Industrial Standards Act* (1935), a male minimum wage act (1937), an hours of work vacation with pay act (1944), and collective bargaining legislation (1943). Federal unemployment insurance legislation passed in 1940 followed the same policy.[8]

The structure of farming in Ontario changed rapidly after World War II, particularly through the expansion of large farming operations. By 1971 there were half the number of farm operators in Ontario than in the interwar years, while the number of wage workers remained the same (Parr 1985, 79). Finding workers to fill these positions became increasingly difficult and the focus of annual federal-provincial agricultural conferences. Although agricultural wages increased rapidly between 1940 and 1950, farm work remained unattractive to Canadians, in part because of the absence of social security measures. Speaking to a 1949 federal-provincial conference on agriculture, the federal deputy minister of agriculture, Dr A. McNamara, advocated that farm workers be given unemployment insurance and workers' compensation coverage (Labour Gazette 1950, 9–10). In the early 1950s the federal Department of Labour (1954) published a brochure on farm safety and workers' compensation: "Farmers who take steps to ensure the safety of workers, and provide compensation in the event of an injury," it advised, "are in a better position to attract good workers than those who do not offer these benefits" (3). Despite these exhortations, few farm employers took advantage of the provisions made by most provinces for voluntary workers' compensation coverage for agricultural workers. A study in 1955 found that, of the 7,602 farm workers who had some coverage, 6,900 of them were in Ontario. This number represented less than 1 per cent of the total Canadian agricultural workforce (Labour Gazette 1957, 34–5).

Efforts to mobilize internal reserves of labour proved unsuccessful, while dependence on hired labour increased. A 1960 study of trends in the agricultural labour force found that farm wages remained lower than those paid to unskilled labour in other industries and that seasonal employment was growing (Canada, Department of Labour, Economics and Research Branch 1960; Labour Gazette 1960, 1001–2). Substandard social security conditions continued as well, even though unequal treatment of farm workers under law was becoming more difficult to justify (Neilson and Christie 1975). Instead, governments began turning to foreign workers to meet the demands of farmers for a reliable labour force, recruiting immigrants who were bound for two years to remain in agricultural employment, as well as free immigrants who came from agricultural backgrounds. But as these workers exited the agricultural workforce, in the mid-1960s the government turned to unfree migrant labour, recruited to come temporarily and restricted to agricultural employment. These workers continue to be brought into Canada under the Seasonal Agricultural Workers Program (SAWP), through which the Canadian government has entered into agreements with Caribbean and Mexican governments to regulate the flow and employment conditions of seasonal agricultural workers into Canada (Basok 2002; Satzewich 1991). The program primarily serves Ontario farmers.

Since the mid-1960s, agricultural workers have gained some legislative protection. In 1965 Ontario eliminated their exclusion from workers' compensation legislation and divided agriculture into two scheduled industries, for the first time making compensation coverage compulsory. Henry Rowntree, the provincial minister of agriculture, explained: "This is a major step forward. There is no question that accidents do happen, bearing in mind the nature and type of the machinery with which a modern farm, and indeed most farms in this province, are equipped. I think the time is ripe to take this step."[9] Yet when the provincial government enacted the *Employment Standards Act* (1968), it also promulgated regulations exempting agricultural workers. It was only in 1975 that fruit, vegetable, and tobacco harvesters were given some minimum standards protection. However, no change was made then to extend the protection of collective bargaining or occupational health and safety laws to agricultural workers. In 1971 the federal government extended unemployment insurance coverage to agricultural workers.[10]

THE PRESENT STRUCTURE OF PRECARIOUSNESS FOR AGRICULTURAL WORKERS

The labour market situation of agricultural workers at the beginning of the 21st century remains precarious, notwithstanding the continuing transformation of agricultural production in Ontario. One of the most striking features of that transformation has been the dramatic rate at which farming has become concentrated in a fewer number of large-scale, heavily capitalized operations.

From 1971 to 2001 the number of farms in Ontario decreased by 37 per cent, from 94,805 to 59,728 , while the average capitalization per farm has increased over elevenfold, from $72,819 to $845,998 . During that same period the number of total weeks of paid labour has increased by over 50 per cent, from 1,509,412 to 2,287,196. More heavily capitalized farms hire more labour. Two-thirds of Ontario farms had a capital value of over $500,000 in 2001, and they used 90 per cent of the paid weeks of labour. As well, the 1,144 Ontario farms that report annual sales of more than $1 million (1.9 per cent of all farms) pay 59.1 per cent of wages to non-family members. Clearly, it is a myth that the average farm labourer is a hired man on a small family farm.[11]

This growth of employment in capital-intensive farm operations improved the structural conditions that shape the indigenous mobilization capacity of farm workers. For some, especially those employed in large-scale, industrialized farming operations such as mushroom growing and hatcheries, that has been true. The reality, however, is that the great variation in the social organization of farming operations belies sweeping generalizations about the emergence of capitalist farming (Clement 1983, 225–43; Winson 1996). Despite important structural changes in farming, most farm workers remain in precarious employment.

Precarious employment is best understood as a multi-dimensional condition that takes account not only of the employment form but also of the level of regulatory protection, control, and income and the social location and social context of the worker(s) in question (Vosko, Zukewich, and Cranford 2003; see also Cranford and Vosko, this volume). Data on employment forms in agriculture are limited because the Census of Agriculture collects only the total weeks of paid labour and does not distinguish between family and non-family wage earners. Thus, it is impossible to assess how much farm work is full time or part time or whether there is a difference between family and non-family workers in regard to the seasonality of their work. With these limitations in mind, in 2001, nearly 40 per cent of paid farm labour in Ontario was seasonal. Although this proportion represents a decrease from 1990, when it was 43.5 per cent, seasonal labour remains significant. It is most prevalent on farms with high sales levels and on fruit and vegetable farms, while yearly labour is used most, relative to seasonal work, on mushroom, poultry, hog, and dairy farms.[12]

Given this historical lack of regulatory protection for farm workers, together with the saga of their exclusion from occupational health and safety laws, it is clear that agricultural workers are among the most poorly protected workers in Ontario. Because of the virtual absence of unionization due to their exclusion from collective bargaining legislation, agricultural workers enjoy little job security and have almost no control over the terms and conditions of their employment. The result is low income and long hours – two central dimensions of precarious employment. Even among those working full time full year, agricultural workers received lower earnings than any other occupational group, with the exception of babysitters, in 2000. Male general farm workers had average annual earnings of $25,306, 47 per cent of the provincial male average for all occupations of $53,923, while female general farm workers had average annual earnings of $19,164, 51 per cent of the provincial female average of $37,720[13] The average provincial hourly rate for all agricultural workers, including seasonal workers, was $10.74 in 2002, 58 per cent of the provincial average of $18.56.[14] The average usual weekly hours of agricultural workers in 2002 was 44.7, while the average weekly hours worked by all non-agricultural Ontario employees paid by the hour that year was 32.[15]

The social location of agricultural workers adds a further dimension to their experience of precarious employment. Given the poor working conditions, lack of union representation, and low levels of regulatory protection, few workers choose to remain in agricultural employment. A significant portion of that workforce is comprised of individuals who have limited mobility, either because of personal characteristics or because they are legally disabled from pursuing employment elsewhere. If we focus first on the non-migrant labour force, a distinctive characteristic of Ontario farm workers is that, as a group, their average level of educational attainment is lower than that of the general population. Three-quarters of farm workers have no post-secondary education, compared to 52 per cent of the general population. Almost one-fifth, 17.3 per cent, have less than a grade 9 education.[16] Data on the ethnicity of domestic farm workers is not available, but anecdotal reports indicate that a significant proportion of non-family paid workers are first-generation immigrants who experience difficulty integrating into the Canadian labour market (Bolaria 1992; Frenette and Morissette 2003; Shields 1992; Stultz 1987; Wall 1992).

The use of unfree foreign migrant workers introduces a group whose social location renders them particularly powerless. It is nearly impossible to calculate the percentage of the total weeks of paid seasonal labour performed by migrant workers, but it is generally recognized that they form the backbone of the tobacco, fruit, and vegetable harvesting workforce (Ernst and Young nd, 33). As a group, these workers tend to have low levels of education and are landless and poor in their home countries. While in Canada, they not only share the lack of access to regulatory protection that agricultural workers as a class face but also suffer additional deprivations of status and citizenship. Although they contribute to the Canada Pension Plan and to Employment Insurance, they are not eligible to receive benefits; they cannot gain permanent status through their participation in the program; they cannot enter the non-agricultural workforce; and they lack access to the political process in Canada, making it extremely difficult for them to challenge their various exclusions. Their lack of basic security in Canada and at home, their social exclusion in Canada, and their fear of being excluded from the program in the future reduce their willingness to assert whatever rights they do enjoy (Basok 2002, 2004; Bolaria 1992; Commission for Labor Cooperation 2002; Gibb 2002; Shimmin 2000).

UNSAFE AND UNHEALTHY WORK

Farm workers are exposed to a vast array of biological, chemical, ergonomic, mechanical, physical, and psychosocial hazards, as set out in table 12.1 (Bolaria 1994; Denis 1988; May 1990).

Exposure to these hazards materializes in numerous deaths, injuries, and diseases. Knowledge of the extent of these outcomes is partial because of serious reporting problems. Most worker injury data is derived from workers' compensation reports, but this source underestimates the incidence of work injuries because of reporting problems, recognition issues (particularly around disease claims), coverage issues, and administrative barriers (Ontario, Ministry of Agriculture and Food and Ministry of Labour 1985, 42–8). Because of the composition of the agricultural workforce and the precarious character of agricultural employment, reporting problems are even more severe in this sector than in others. Nevertheless, in 2001 every agricultural rate group except poultry and egg farming had a higher lost-time injury rate than the provincial average (see table 12.2).

Because of the frailties of workers' compensation statistics, researchers have developed an alternative method for collecting data on farm health and safety, one known as the Canadian Agricultural Injury Surveillance Program (CAISP). This program uses health record data sets to track farm injuries that result in fatalities and hospitalization as an in-patient. Based on this data, researchers found that, between 1991 and 1995, agriculture was the fourth most dangerous industry in Canada in terms of fatalities. They also found that the age-standardized death rate in Ontario agriculture was higher than the national average. Owner-operators were at the highest risk of death from work-related farm injuries, with tractors accounting for the largest share of fatal injuries. No separate death rate for hired agricultural workers was published (Pickett et al. 1999).

There may be disagreements over the precise dimensions of occupational health and safety (OHS) problems among agricultural workers, yet there is a consensus that farming is unsafe and unhealthy work. Notably, the exclusion of agricultural workers from OHS laws was never justified on the basis that their work was safe. Why, then, did the exclusion persist for so long?

THE VICIOUS CIRCLE OF PRECARIOUSNESS AT WORK IN HEALTH AND SAFETY

Historically, the voice of agricultural workers has been largely absent from discussions about their health and safety. This silence is a central feature of

Table 12.1
Farm Hazards

Type of Hazard	Examples
Biological	bacteria, parasites, viruses, grain dust, mould
Chemical	fertilizers, pesticides, fungicides, herbicides, farm gasses
Ergonomic	heavy lifting, stoop labour, reaching, repetitive motion
Mechanical	tractors, farm machinery
Physical	noise, vibration, compressed air, radiation, heat, sun
Psychosocial	stress, fatigue

the vicious circle of precariousness. Agricultural workers were unorganized and their indigenous mobilization capacity and strategic ability to disrupt was low. The trade union movement was not advocating on their behalf. Indeed, the Ontario Federation of Labour and the Canadian Labour Congress were putting more energy into developing relationships with small farm operators opposed to the increasing dominance of agribusiness than into addressing the concerns of agricultural labourers. In 1959, they began holding an annual farm-labour conference to address common concerns and to support the nascent Ontario Farmers Union (Farmer Labour Conference 1959; Ontario Farmers Union). But the issue of farm labour never reached the agenda in any annual farm labour conference. To the extent that public interest groups addressed health and safety issues, their major concern was the squalid living conditions of migrant farm workers, not the hazardous work they performed (Basok 2002).

The first legislative discussion of the denial to farm workers of the benefits of OHS laws occurred in 1977 after the introduction of Bill 70, the so-called omnibus OHS statute in Ontario. Unlike previous laws that were sector specific, this one set out a general scheme of OHS regulation, including both rights to protection and participation, that applied to all workers under provincial jurisdiction, except those specifically excluded. Agricultural workers were one of the excluded groups, although provision was made for them to gain coverage by regulation. This arrangement accorded with the wishes of farm operators, who had been consulted by the minister of labour, Bette Stephenson, when the bill was being drafted. At a meeting with the Ontario Fruit and Vegetable Growers Association, the minister noted that "resolving the apparent conflict between the employer's financial security and the employee's physical security is a difficult matter" (Ontario, Ministry of Labour 1977). In a joint brief presented to the minister of labour in August 1977, the Ontario Farm Safety Association, the Ontario

Table 12.2
Lost-Time Injury Rates:* Provincial Average and Agricultural
Rate Groups, Ontario, 2001

Rate Group	Lost Time Injury Rate
Provincial rate	2.23
Livestock farms	3.6
Poultry and egg farms	1.8
Field crop farms	2.4
Fruit and other vegetable farms	(2.5 in 2000)[†]
Tobacco farms	4.4
Mushroom farms	(4.6 in 2000)[†]
Fishing and miscellaneous farming	3.5

*Injuries per 100 full year employees.
[†] Data from 2001 not available.
Source: Workplace Safety and Insurance Board

Fruit and Vegetable Growers Association, and the Ontario Federation of Agriculture (OFA) indicated their support for OHS regulation in principle but insisted that special consideration had to be given to agriculture. For this reason, they contended that no part of the legislation should apply except by regulation and that an advisory committee, consisting of representatives of farm organizations and workers' compensation board officials, should be appointed to assist in the development of any such regulations. Their brief did not mention farm worker representation (OFA et al. 1977).

Bill 70 was introduced in October 1977. In the legislative debates that followed, only the New Democratic Party (NDP) demanded unconditional inclusion of agricultural workers. This party's new-found sensitivity to, and awareness of, the issue was likely influenced by the publicity that surrounded farm worker campaigns in the United States and efforts in Canada to organize boycotts in support of striking workers. Members of both the Liberal and the Progressive Conservative caucuses supported the approach of inclusion by regulation. Jack Riddell, a Liberal who claimed to speak for the agricultural industry, virtually read the agricultural lobby's brief as his speech in the Legislature. He emphasized that there was virtually no part of the omnibus Act that could be applied to agriculture without special provision being made. Coupled with a set of conditions for future implementation which ensured that agricultural interests would never be adversely affected, the strategy of acceptance in principle of the need for regulation, but delay in its implementation, was spelled out clearly: "Farm organizations support the application of health and safety regulations to agriculture, but only after careful study of the effect of such regulations on each segment of agriculture. Such regulations must be introduced over a period of time and under close consultation with the various farm organizations which I've already mentioned" (Ontario, *Legislative Debates* 1977, 2242–4).

Bill 70 was referred in February 1978 to committee, where a number of amendments were made, including one that would not allow any exemptions for agricultural workers after the end of 1978. The agricultural lobby immediately registered its dissatisfaction (OFA 1978) and, when the bill came back before the legislature in December, the new minister of labour, Robert Elgie, tabled an amendment restoring the exclusion. A bitter debate ensued, as both the Liberals and the Conservatives retreated to their earlier position, while NDP members, including Floyd Laughren, passionately decried the injustice of excluding "the group of workers who are least able to mount an offensive against your Act" (Ontario, *Legislative Debates* 1978, 6129). Both the Liberals and the Conservatives emphasized, however, that farming operations would be regulated. It was just a matter of time (Ontario, *Legislative Debates* 1978, 6132–3). The *Occupational Health and Safety Act*[17] passed, leaving the extension of protection to agricultural workers to be dealt with by regulation.

A notable feature of the debate over the agricultural worker exemption was that the voice of Ontario farm workers was silent. NDP member Ian Deans said it best when he accused the government of picking on "the most defenceless people to not extend good legislation to" (Ontario, *Legislative Debates* 1978, 6116). But even while the NDP spoke on behalf of inclusion, no organized group of farm workers mobilized to support its position. One reason why farm workers had such low mobilization potential was that they were excluded from the labour relations law that protected workers against retaliation for being union supporters or participating in union activities and that required employers to recognize and bargain with unions that enjoyed majority support. Unions had little incentive, then, to provide organizational resources, so long as they defined their goal as representing workers for the purposes of collective bargaining. The vicious circle was at work here: the legal exclusion of vulnerable agricultural workers from collective bargaining laws not only undermined their indigenous capacity to develop an organized voice but deterred organizations with resources from coming to their assistance. The result: agricultural workers lacked the resources and the capacity to fight against legal exclusions from OHS laws. That lack of capacity also undermined the ability of farm workers to loosen the political alignment of Conservatives and Liberals that placed the interests of farm operators and agribusiness above those of farm workers, both for electoral reasons and in furtherance of cheap-food policies (Shields 1992).

The absence of effective farm worker organizations continued into the 1980s, impeding the effort to hold the government to its promise to bring farm workers under the OHS law by regulation. Although the British Columbia–based Canadian Farm Workers' Union (CFWU) attempted to organize Ontario farm workers in the early 1980s, it gave up in 1983 because it lacked resources and was unable to overcome the unfavourable socioeconomic and legal organizing conditions (Stultz 1987; Tatroff 1994; Wall 1996). The NDP continued to press the government to develop appropriate OHS regulations for agriculture and, in November 1980, the Ministry of Labour (MOL) established an ad hoc steering committee that included representatives from the Ministry of Agriculture and Food (MAF) and farm organizations, but no hired farm workers. The committee never made any recommendations to extend protection to farm workers, but in 1983 it proposed that the MOL and the MAF establish a joint task force, comprised of a chair, two farmers accepted by the farm community, and two farm employee representatives. In October 1983 the Ontario Task Force on Health and Safety in Agriculture was appointed. Two farm employees were chosen, but the ministries decided to appoint four farm operators in addition to the chair, Dr N.R. Richards, the former dean of the Ontario College of Agriculture (Ontario, Ministry of Labour 1985, 5). The employee appointees did not seem to have any connection to a farm workers' or labour organization, and it is unclear how they were selected.

Between November 1984 and January 1985 the Task Force held hearings in 11 agricultural centres around the province. By this point, the farm lobby no longer accepted the need for regulation, even in principle. Rather, in the view of the OFA, the lead lobby group, "imposing the Occupational Health and Safety Act or similar legislation would not meet the needs of this industry. Rather we would propose that efforts to IMPROVE health and safety in the agricultural workplace must be directed to effective education programs and engineering improvements" (OFA 1984). The theme of "education, not regulation" was repeated in briefs from county federations of agriculture and farm safety associations, producers' associations, and Women's Institutes. Posed against this well-orchestrated campaign were a small number of briefs supporting regulation from an assortment of groups and individual farm workers. For example, the Ontario Farm Labour Information Committee, a group established in June 1983 to pursue research about farm workers, noted that a study it conducted found serious under-reporting of farm worker injuries to the workers' compensation board and widespread unsafe use of pesticides.[18] Its brief called for the inclusion of farm workers under OHSA and for the development of specific regulations addressing the hazards they faced (Ontario Farm Labour Information Committee 1984). The lack of a more coordinated effort to promote regulation reflected farm workers' lack of organizational resources. This problem was recognized in a briefing note prepared for the deputy minister of labour before the Task Force report was issued. "Because agricultural employees are not as strong and vocal as farm owners and because farm labour activist groups are not as well funded, it is possible that the Task Force recommendations may not fully address the concerns of paid farm workers"(Ontario, Ministry of Labour 1985, 8). This indeed proved to be the case.

The Task Force reported in December 1985, and its report tried to juggle two objectives. First, it clearly recognized that farm work was hazardous and that "there is an urgent need to develop greater occupational health and safety protection in farming" (Ontario 1985, 52). It did not, however, recommend that farm workers be covered by the OHSA, the most obvious and expeditious way of achieving that result. Rather, it gave greater weight to the second objective: cautious tailoring of OHS regulation to accommodate the "special" needs of agriculture. To meet this objective, the Task Force called for the creation of a new agency, under the joint auspices of the MOL and the MAF, with comprehensive responsibility for developing suitable protective measures, educational programs, and worker representation arrangements (141). By the time the Task Force issued its report, the longstanding Progressive Conservative government had been replaced by a minority Liberal government supported by the NDP. The Liberals, however, had strongly supported special treatment for agricultural in opposition and had appointed Jack Riddell, an outspoken opponent of farm safety regulation, as minister of agriculture and food. Neither ministry was enthusiastic about the joint agency recommendation. After another round of consultations, the MAF proposed the establishment of a joint implementation committee, a plan that met with some scepticism within the MOL because of concerns about delay, the failure to consider the threshold issue of coverage, and the marginalization of the MOL's involvement (Ontario, Ministry of Labour 1986, 1987). Nevertheless, after some negotiation, an agreement was reached and, in September 1987, the Agricultural Health and Safety Implementation Committee was appointed. It was co-chaired by assistant deputy ministers from the MOL and MAF, and three farm operators, two farm workers, and a representative from both the farm machinery and the agricultural chemical industries were appointed as members. Again, there is no indication of how the farm worker representatives were selected, but they had no apparent ties to any organization linked to farm workers or organized labour. The committee's report, publicly released in March 1989, completely rejected the Task Force's major recommendations. In its view, no agency was necessary and few, if any, mandatory standards were needed. Rather, it proposed that primary responsibility for agricultural health and safety be assigned to the Farm Safety Association, an industry body funded by the workers' compensation system, with a mandate to promote health and safety programs but no regulatory authority. Moreover, it completely marginalized MOL involvement (Ontario 1989).

The promise of the government in 1978 that the exclusion of farm workers was only temporary and that they would be brought under *OHSA* by regulation in a piecemeal fashion after consultation with the industry was proving to be empty. The absence of an organized group of farm workers, or of active support from the labour movement, left the farm lobby's influence unchecked. The issue, however, was not quite dead. It received a fresh boost in the context of Bill 208, the Liberal government's response to ongoing labour militancy in the 1980s over health and safety issues. As part of the consultation process, the bill was referred to the Advisory Council on Occupational Health and Occupational Safety (ACOHOS), a tripartite statutory body created, among other purposes, to provide expert advice to the government on OHS matters. ACOHOS was critical of the failure of the bill to adopt the principle of universality, and it specifically disagreed with the recommendation of the Implementation Committee. It stated that farm workers should be covered and that any sector-specific needs could be addressed by regulation (Ontario, ACOHOS 1989, 1990). In the legislative debates, the NDP was also critical of the exclusion of agricultural workers. Floyd Laughren argued that, in light of the dangerous conditions and the vulnerability of farm labourers, the government had a "moral obligation" and constitutional obligation to protect them under the law (Ontario, *Legislative Debates*, 1990, 1855). The Ontario Federation of Labour's brief on Bill 208 also called for the inclusion of farm workers. Not surprisingly, given its record on this issue, the Liberal government did not accept these recommendations, although it made some sections of the *OHSA* apply to self-employed persons.[19]

Notwithstanding these setbacks, some officials within the MOL were still concerned with the farm worker exclusion. In April 1990 terms of reference were drafted for a project to develop a regulation under the *OHSA* that would apply to farming operations (Ontario, MOL 1990b) and a report on the agricultural industry was prepared for that purpose. It noted the growth of "corporate agriculture" in the province and the increase in farm employment (Ontario, MOL 1990a). Later that year the NDP won the election and formed a majority government. For the first time, there was a party in government that had, at least in opposition, expressed strong support for the inclusion of farm workers in OHS laws. This victory represented a serious crack in the political alignment that had kept agricultural workers locked out of provincial collective bargaining and excluded from health and safety laws. Sensing that the time was ripe, ACOHOS revisited the farm worker exclusion. As part of its consultation process, it not only heard submissions from traditional Ontario farm organizations but also solicited the views of Jay Cowan, a former NDP minister of workplace health and safety in Manitoba, and of S. Boal, the president of the British Columbia branch of the Canadian Farmworkers' Union. In its report, ACOHOS noted three principal objections to applying the Act to agricultural operations: difficulties in implementing the legislation, given the diversity, management structures, and small scale of farm operations and the character of the workforce; conditions of work not under the control of the farm operator; and the instability of many farm operations. In response, it stated that the Act applied to small businesses that shared some of the features of agricultural operations and that distinctive conditions could be addressed through the development of regulations in consultation with the parties. The recommendation was forwarded to the minister of labour, Bob Mackenzie, who, as an MPP in 1977 and in 1990, had criticized the governments of the day for their failure to cover all workers (Ontario, *Legislative Debates* 1977, 2211; 1990, 1854–5). In his forwarding letter, the chair of ACOHOS, Julian Barling, noted that Mr Cowan had stated that his greatest regrets were not his mistakes but his failures to carry forward policies when opportunities opened up (Ontario, ACOHOS 1991). The Workplace Health and Safety Agency (WHSA), a bipartite body established by Bill 208 with oversight over health and safety training, also wrote to express its support for the inclusion of agricultural workers (WHSA 1991).

By this time the MOL was working with the MAF to prepare a set of policy options to be presented to Cabinet. As part of that process, it was consulting with agricultural interests that had formed a Labour Issues Coordinating Committee, which would also respond to MOL initiatives related to the inclusion of farm workers under collective bargaining and employment standards' laws. Sensing the changed political climate, the farm lobby retreated to the position it had adopted in 1977: acceptance of the need for health and safety regulation in principle but delay in implementation to allow ample consultation, so that any resulting regulation would be responsive to the industry's special needs (OFA 1991). Work proceeded on the development of options through 1991 and, in December, a discussion paper was completed. It presented a range of options for discussion, including the extension of the *OHSA* to some or all farm operations (e.g., "industrial" farming operations, or those with paid workers only) or the development of separate farm OHS legislation (Ontario, MOL and MAF 1991). The initiative, however, did not move forward. A briefing note, prepared in 1994, partially explains why: "This item did not, however, go forward to Policy and Priorities Board as planned and has since been on hold. At the time, the delay was linked to the government's plans to pass Bill 40, amending the Labour Relations Act. (Bill 40 maintained the exemption of agricultural workers from the LRA). Since Bill 40 the government has not shown an intent to revisit the issue of health and safety coverage for farms" (Ontario, Ministry of Labour 1994).

The other factor that likely influenced the government's decision was that it gave priority to the enactment of collective bargaining legislation for agricultural workers, an exercise that involved extensive consultations with major farm organizations and organized labour. The *Agricultural Labour Relations*

Act[20] (*ALRA*) was passed in 1994. The NDP government was routed in elections held the following year and replaced by an ideologically right-wing Conservative government, which promptly repealed the *ALRA* and eliminated any hope that farm operations would be included in the *OHSA*.

Despite these disappointments, the fight for inclusion continued, aided by a few key developments. First, the continuing concentration of agricultural production generated structural conditions in at least some of its branches which increased the mobilizing capacities of farm workers. In mushroom growing and hatcheries, in particular, a year-round workforce is employed in factory-like conditions. Indeed, the conditions of production so closely resembled industry that decision-makers were challenged unsuccessfully, in the late 1970s and 1980s, as to whether these types of operations fell under the farm operation exemption for both employment standards and collective bargaining purposes.[21] Second, the advent of the *Charter of Rights and Freedoms*, created a fresh avenue for challenging these exclusions despite the solidity of the political alignment supporting them. These two developments attracted some interest among trade unions in organizing farm workers. In the late 1980s the United Food and Commercial Workers (UFCW) undertook the organization of hatchery workers at Cuddy Chicks Ltd. The Labour Relations Board found that these workers were covered by the agricultural exclusion, but it also held that it had the power to determine whether this exclusion violated the *Charter*. The employer challenged the board's jurisdiction, which was eventually upheld by the Supreme Court of Canada,[22] but, by then, four years had passed and, in anticipation of the NDP's agricultural collective bargaining law, the employer agreed to recognize the union. The passage of the *ALRA* and the brief period in which it was in force temporarily disrupted the political alignment in support of exclusion and the UFCW successfully organized Highline Produce, a year-round mushroom factory employing 200 workers.[23] Two other UFCW certification applications were in process, one for a mushroom farm, the other for a hatchery, but the repeal of the *ALRA* resulted in the termination of acquired bargaining rights and the pending certification applications.[24]

Thus, when the Conservative government repealed the *ALRA*, the UFCW had a stake in defending its foothold in agriculture. It brought a *Charter* challenge on the grounds that the repeal deprived workers of freedom of association and equality rights. The Supreme Court of Canada's decision in *Dunmore*[25] held that freedom of association sometimes required the state to take positive action to protect its exercise, including protection against unfair labour practices and a requirement that employers listen to collective representations. But it did not require that powerless employees be given access to a statutory collective bargaining scheme that included compulsory recognition or a duty to bargain in good faith. The court did not address the equality

rights argument (Pothier 2002). The Ontario government responded with legislation that gives agricultural workers the thinnest set of rights that could
possibly pass constitutional muster.[26] Whether it has succeeded has become
the subject of another round of *Charter* litigation.[27]

At the same time that the Conservative government was denying agricultural workers access to a statutory collective bargaining scheme, it was also
refusing to extend the OHSA to farm operations. In its response to recommendations from the coroner's jury that investigated the deaths of the three
agricultural workers discussed at the beginning of this chapter, Deputy
Minister Tosine asserted that "the farming sector as a whole is characterized by unique working conditions and relationships and, as such, a legislative approach to occupational health and safety may not be appropriate in
this sector." The alternative she advanced on behalf of the MOL was to
leave farm safety with the Farm Safety Association, a body that is vested
with responsibility for promoting OHS through education but has no regulatory authority.[28] The other components of the current OHS regime for the
agricultural sector not mentioned by Tosine were experience rating, an economic incentive program operated by the Workplace Safety and Insurance
Board, and safety laws that indirectly protect agricultural workers, such as
the *Pesticides Act* and the *Farm Implements Act*.[29]

The UFCW adopted a two-pronged response to the continued OHSA exclusion. First, it opted for a long-term, community-based strategy (Cranford,
Das Gupta, and Vosko, this volume). Along with other labour organizations,
the UFCW is funding the Global Justice Care Van Project, which sends volunteers around Ontario to document the experiences of migrant farm workers
and to provide them with training. It also supports the Migrant Agricultural
Workers' Support Centre, which opened in 2002. Unhealthy and unsafe
working conditions have been a longstanding concern of both migrant and
local farm workers and have recently become a focus of community and
union activities. The Care Van Project made health and safety its key concern
in 2002, conducting training sessions and printing a Spanish-language manual (Health & Safety for Agricultural Workers 2002; Zwarenstein 2002).
Second, it launched a *Charter* challenge in summer 2003 on the ground that
the exclusion of agricultural workers violated their right to equality under
the law.

The campaign to extend the protection of the OHSA to agricultural workers got a decisive boost with the election of a majority Liberal government
in October 2003. Although in the past the Liberals had supported special
treatment for agriculture, they had never taken the position that agricultural
workers did not need legislative protection. Rather, they argued that the regulatory scheme had to be adapted to the special needs of agriculture and
that this should be done in consultation with the farming community. Previously, these consultation processes led nowhere, but this time there was

the threat that the courts would find the exclusion unconstitutional. As well, there may also have been a concern that the litigation challenging the exclusion of agricultural workers from an effective statutory bargaining scheme was going to be more difficult to defend because their exclusion from health and safety legislation provided clear and compelling evidence of their vulnerability.

Whatever their motivations, the MOL and MAF announced during Canadian Agricultural Safety Awareness Week in March 2004 that the government was developing new health and safety standards for farmers and farm workers. The announcement went on to state that the MOL and the MAF were working with the Labour Issues Coordinating Group (the farm industry group formed in 1990 to respond to NDP initiatives) and the Farm Safety Association to produce standards that would embrace the principles of the OHSA (MOL and MAF 2004).

This process culminated in the promulgation of Ontario Regulation 414/05 on June 29, 2005. It provides that the OHSA will apply to farm operations beginning on June 30, 2006. There are, however, a few modifications. OHSA will not cover farming operations conducted by self-employed persons without workers; joint health and safety committees will only be required on certain farm operations (mushroom, greenhouse, dairy, hog, cattle, and poultry farms) employing twenty or more workers; where committees are required, certified member requirements will apply only where there are fifty or more workers; and current regulations made under OHSA do not apply except for a few provisions specifically cited.

WILL THE VICIOUS CIRCLE BE UNBROKEN?

The vicious circle of precariousness and powerlessness, of which legislative exclusions is a part, operates to the detriment of agricultural workers in Ontario. The structural conditions that limited their indigenous mobilization potential undermined their ability to overcome their powerlessness through a credible threat to disrupt the economic or social order, notwithstanding chronic labour shortages. As well, because of their dispersion and their exclusion from collective bargaining laws, trade unions, until recently, did not evince much willingness to invest their resources in organizing campaigns that, realistically, could not produce dues-paying certified bargaining units. Finally, provincial political alignments have been hostile to the inclusion of agricultural workers in health and safety laws, notwithstanding the embarrassment that provincial governments have been made to feel, from time to time, about the denial of legal protection to such an obviously vulnerable group.

The vicious circle of exclusion can be broken, however. The changing structure of agriculture is producing industrial-type employment conditions in at least some areas of agriculture, increasing the mobilization potential of the affected workers and attracting attention and resources from organized labour. As well, the *Charter* can be invoked to disrupt the political alignment opposing inclusion and to shift the ideological climate that has, historically, been more sympathetic to the farm operator than to the agricultural labourer. Agricultural workers have also won victories elsewhere. In the United States, for example, the Farm Labor Organizing Committee, AFL-CIO, recently conducted a successful campaign in North Carolina that culminated in the signing of a union contract covering 1,000 farmers and 8,500 migrant workers from Mexico (Greenhouse 2004), while the California Occupational Safety and Health Administration approved an emergency regulation banning weeding by hand on most farms.[30]

The immediate lesson, then, is that breaking the vicious circle of precariousness requires an ongoing commitment to organizing (Cranford, Das Gupta, and Vosko, this volume; Shields 1992, 251; Tufts 1998). Overcoming legislative exclusion, however, is only the first step toward achieving effective regulatory protection (Bernstein, Lippel, Tucker, and Vosko, this volume). Unless appropriate regulations are developed, sufficient resources are devoted to enforcement, and farm workers are given access to a scheme of collective representation that is responsive to their conditions, it is unlikely that the vicious circle of their precariousness will have been truly broken by this act of inclusion.

13

Regulating Precarious Labour Markets: What Can We Learn from New European Models?

ANDREW JACKSON

Low wages and precarious jobs are not a necessary condition for high levels of employment. Improving job quality at the "bottom" of the labour market does not inevitably come at the price of unemployment. This conclusion is significant because the major objection by Canadian policy makers to labour market regulation aimed at protecting workers in precarious employment has been that such policies will hurt those whom they are intended to protect.

The experience of Scandinavian social democracy in the 1990s suggests that a virtuous combination of high employment, relatively equal wages, and real opportunities for workers in precarious employment is possible. It depends on regulating the labour market to create a wage floor and a compressed distribution of wages, achieved primarily via collective bargaining; keeping the non-wage costs of employment low by providing social and economic security primarily through public programs financed from general taxation; providing significant investment in active labour market policies to upgrade the skills of those at greatest risk of engaging in precarious employment; and building a distinct kind of "post-industrial" service economy based on a large non-market sector and high productivity private services. Relative success in securing high rates of employment in "good jobs" also depends on appropriate macroeconomic policies and good labour relations.

The social democratic labour market model is based on high levels of paid employment for both women and men, high levels of collective bargaining coverage, and a high level of "decommodification" of paid labour through universalistic social welfare programs and public services that reduce reliance on wages. In addition to the direct impact of collective bargaining on what would otherwise be precarious work, the model has limited the relative importance of precarious employment by shaping the nature of post-industrial employment, especially for women. The socialization of some caring responsibilities borne by households – such as child and elder care – has reduced the "double burden" of household and paid work on women, directly created many jobs of reasonably high quality for women in social services, and reduced the relative importance of private consumer services where precarious jobs are most likely to be found. However, women still perform a highly disproportionate share of "caring" work, and the unequal, gendered division of domestic labour has been only modestly attenuated. There is a highly gendered division of paid labour between women and men, with women excluded from higher-level jobs in the private sector, even in comparison with liberal countries like Canada. In short, the social democratic model is progressive from the standpoint of regulating precarious employment, and it holds lessons for Canadians. But it is still highly problematic from the standpoint of promoting labour market and wider equality between women and men.

In advancing this argument, the chapter is organized into five sections. The first section, The War of the Models: Liberal versus Regulated Labour Markets, summarizes the orthodox economic argument for deregulated labour markets as the key to job creation for workers deemed to be low-skilled. It demonstrates that levels of low pay and earnings inequality are high and are rising in countries embracing the liberal model of "flexible" wages and low unemployment benefits, yet these countries demonstrate no evidence of superior job creation performance compared to countries with high levels of collective bargaining coverage. The second section, Social Foundations of Job Creation: Labour Markets, Regulation, and Social Welfare Regimes, illustrates that high levels of collective bargaining coverage co-exist with other labour market policies that have different implications for the extent of precarious employment, notably employment protection legislation; the division of responsibility between the state and employers for financing social welfare; the extent of active labour market policies; and the extent of public services. The social democratic labour market model is the most "employment-friendly." The third section, The Economics of Labour Market Regulation: Positive Employment Effects of Labour Standards, argues that high labour standards can raise productivity in low-wage/low-productivity private services, countering the incidence of precarious employment. The fourth section, Denmark and the New European Labour Market Model, shows that Denmark, a key example of the new model, has been able to achieve very high rates of good-quality employment with very low levels of precarious work. The chapter concludes with an outline of the lessons to be drawn from this discussion for Canada.

THE WAR OF THE MODELS:
LIBERAL VERSUS REGULATED LABOUR MARKETS

In what has been termed the "War of the Models" (Freeman 1998), the "Great American Job Machine" was routinely contrasted to high-unemployment "Eurosclerosis." The highly influential OECD *Jobs Study* (1994) argued that the greater extent of labour market regulation in continental Europe, as compared to the United States and the United Kingdom, was a major (though not the only) factor behind higher unemployment. The orthodox view remains that labour market regulation militates against job creation for the relatively unskilled (OECD 2003). Its basic premise is that the level of employment and unemployment is determined by forces of both supply and demand and the extent to which wages are flexible. On the supply side, "overly generous" unemployment and related benefit systems are held to create barriers and disincentives to work by setting "reservation wages" that are higher than wages in available jobs. This benefit system creates disincentives to work, particularly for the relatively unskilled, who would qualify for only relatively low-wage jobs. On the demand side, wage floors, especially when combined with employment protection regulation and mandated employer payroll costs, reduce employers' demand for lower-skilled workers. High-wage floors set by minimum wages and/or collective bargaining mean that "low-skill" workers will be priced out of the low-productivity jobs that could otherwise have been created for the relatively unskilled.

At the economy-wide level, regulated labour markets are considered a cause of structural unemployment, the result of strong wage pressures from the employed even at high rates of unemployment and "inflexible" wages that slow adaptation to changing market conditions. In short, regulated labour markets deviate from the "ideal" labour market in which wages rapidly adjust to changing economic circumstances and closely reflect the relative productivity of different groups of workers. The dismal message to governments has been that there is a tradeoff between the quantity and the quality of jobs for lower-skilled and vulnerable workers, and that protective measures such as "generous" unemployment benefits and minimum wages come at a significant cost.

The orthodox view became a major influence on Canadian labour market policy in the 1990s. Employment insurance and welfare benefits have been substantially cut and entitlements restricted, with the explicit goal of increasing worker dependence on wage income to lower "dependency" and "structural" unemployment (Jackson 2000a). Minimum wages have fallen even further behind average wages (Battle 2003); employment standards have been eroded in terms of both coverage and substance; and labour laws have generally become much less facilitative in providing access to collective bargaining for precarious workers. As detailed elsewhere in this volume, precarious work is highly gendered, and much of the impact of neo-liberal labour market restructuring has fallen on women workers.

In fairness, orthodox economists recognize that factors largely unrelated to the structure of labour markets, such as innovation, industrial structure, and macroeconomic policy, also play a role in job creation. The deregulatory labour market policy message has also been balanced to some degree by support for measures to protect vulnerable and low-paid workers, such as earned income and child tax credits to "make work pay"; investment in the "human capital" of workers in precarious employment; and investment in "enabling" programs such as child care. However, labour market regulation to improve the income security and wages of workers in precarious employment directly has been virtually absent from the policy agenda in Canada.

The Canadian policy debate has largely ignored viable alternatives to deregulated labour markets. Evidence illustrates that profound differences remain between the labour markets of advanced capitalist countries; that regulated labour markets work far better for vulnerable workers in terms of distributional equity and access to opportunities; and that there is no clear-cut link between the extent of labour market regulation and employment performance (see table 13.1).

Canada has done reasonably well on the job front in raw quantitative terms since economic recovery began in the mid-1990s. Compared to other OECD countries, the employment rate for both women and men is high, and the long-term adult unemployment rate is very low (see table 13.2 below). However, as detailed elsewhere in this volume, gendered and racialized labour market segmentation has increased since at least the mid-1980s, and there has been a marked rise in the incidence of "precarious employment" (see, this volume, Armstrong and Laxer; Cranford and Vosko; and Vosko and Zukewich). About 1 in 4 Canadian workers – 1 in 5 men and 1 in 3 women, including 1 in 10 "core working-age" men and 1 in 5 "core working-age" women – are low paid, defined as earning less than two-thirds of the national median hourly wage (or less than about $10 per hour in today's dollars). The incidence of low pay has remained constant even in the economic recovery from the mid-1990s (Jackson 2003a). Most adult low-paid workers, particularly women and those with low levels of education, remain low paid and are excluded from opportunities to develop the skills and capacities that increase the ability of workers to access better jobs, to embark on lifetime career ladders, and to handle labour market risks such as permanent layoffs. There has been a significant widening of longer-term life prospects among Canadian workers from the mid-1980s (Beach, Finnie and Gray 2003). Many "working-poor" families cycle in and out of poverty as they find, or fail to find, enough weeks of work at decent wages in a year (Drolet and Morrissette 1998; Finnie 2000; for analyses of the implications of this trend, see also Lewchuk, de Wolff, King, and Polanyi, this volume).

Table 13.1
Incidence of Low-Paid Employment (mid-1990s)*

	All	Men	Women
US	25.0%	19.6%	32.5%
Canada	23.7%	16.1%	34.3%
Germany	13.3%	7.6%	25.4%
Sweden	5.2%	3.0%	8.4%

Wage Inequality[†]

	Men	Women
US	4.4	4.0
Canada	3.8	4.0
Germany	2.2	2.2
Sweden	2.2	1.8

Source: OECD Employment Outlook (1996)

*Per cent full-time workers earning less than two-thirds national median wage.

† Ratio of top of ninth decile to top of first decile i.e., minimum gap between top and bottom 10%.

As Cranford and Vosko (this volume) demonstrate, low pay is a key dimension of precarious employment. Canada stands out as a low-wage country among advanced industrial countries. In the mid-1990s, about 1 in 4 full-time workers in Canada (23.7%) were low paid – defined as earning less than two-thirds of the median national full-time wage – compared to 1 in 20 workers (5.2%) in Sweden and 1 in 8 in Germany (OECD 1996). One in 3 Canadian women workers are low paid, an even higher proportion than in the United States, compared to fewer than 1 in 10 women in Sweden. Further, the minimum distance between the wages of the top and the bottom decile of full-time workers is about 4 to 1, compared to a little more than 2 to 1 in Sweden and Germany. Canadian workers in hotels and restaurants and in retail trade – among the lowest-wage sectors – earn about 60 per cent as much as an average assembly worker in manufacturing, compared to 90 per cent in Sweden, where there is much greater compression of wages between the bottom and the middle of the wage distribution (for a discussion of the working conditions of hotel workers, see Schenk, this volume). Moreover, upward earnings mobility for low-paid workers is greatest in those countries with the lowest levels of earnings inequality, with Sweden and Denmark performing notably better than the United States (OECD 1996).

Recent data from Eurostat defines low pay as earning less than 60 per cent of the median wage and confirms the extraordinary level of wage equality in the Scandinavian countries. By the Eurostat definition, incidence varies from a low of 7 per cent in Denmark, to 13 per cent in France and 17 per cent in Germany, to a high of 21 per cent in the United Kingdom (EIRO 2002c). Low pay in Europe, as in Canada, is relatively concentrated among women working in consumer services, especially in small firms not covered by collective bargaining; among temporary workers; among mainly women workers working in caring services; and among men in unskilled blue-collar jobs.

Labour market institutions – wage floors set by collective bargaining and legislated minimum wages – play a major role in accounting for different levels of low pay and earnings inequality. Advanced industrial countries differ little in terms of the big structural forces shaping the demand for labour. All are exposed to increased international competition and technological change, widely believed to be tipping the scales against relatively low-skilled workers. The supply of skilled workers, driven by demographic factors and the quality of the education and training system, makes a difference to wage distributions. But there is a strong consensus that labour market institutions significantly shape the impact of supply and demand forces (Aidt and Tzannatos 2003; Clarke 2000; Dinardo 1997; Card, Lemieux, and Riddell 2003; Freeman and Katz 1995; OECD, 1996, 1997). As Anderson demonstrates in Part Four of this volume, collective bargaining raises the relative pay of workers who would otherwise be lower paid – women, minorities, younger workers, the relatively unskilled – and compresses wage differentials, particularly in countries with high rates of collective bargaining coverage. Further, owing to labour market deregulation and declining unionization, increases in wage inequality from the mid-1980s have been much greater in liberal labour markets than in the Scandinavian or continental European countries (Freeman and Katz 1995; OECD 1996).

The deregulated labour market model of Canada, the United States, and the United Kingdom differs profoundly from that in most continental European countries. It is common to distinguish "social welfare regimes" based on the level of income transfers, taxes, and public services, as well as the extent of labour market regulation (Esping-Anderson 1999; Pierson 2001; Scharpf and Schmidt 2000). The social democratic countries of Scandinavia and the "social market" countries such as Germany and the Netherlands differ in terms of the degree of development of public services and the extent of labour force participation by women. But they are both distinguished from liberal regimes by the relative generosity of income-support programs, such as unemployment insurance, and by the fact that the labour market and the workplace are still regulated by the "social partners." Collective bargaining coverage is very high and generally quite stable because of high union membership in combination with the de facto or sometimes legal extension of collective agreements to non-union workplaces on a sectoral or regional basis.

Wage floors set by bargaining protect the great majority of non-professional/managerial workers, including most part-time and even temporary workers. The more equal after-tax distribution of income and the lower poverty rates in these countries reflect the fact that the initial distribution of wage income by the labour market is much more equal than in liberal welfare states (Smeeding 2002).

Collective bargaining covers just 1 in 3 Canadian workers, and 1 in 5 private sector workers. While coverage is high compared to the United States, bargaining covers more than 80 per cent of workers in the Scandinavian and Benelux countries, and is about as high in Germany, France, and Italy, despite lower rates of union membership (EIRO 2002d; OECD 1997). Bargaining is the preferred instrument of labour market regulation in European Union (EU) countries other than the United Kingdom. In the Scandinavian countries, legislated employment standards in the Canadian sense are minimal, since the operative policy assumption has been that virtually all vulnerable workers are covered by wage floors and other standards set in collective agreements. In some countries, such as the Netherlands and France, agreements between unions and unionized employers are extended by legislation or custom to cover the wages of workers with non-union employers. Statutory minimum wages also play a major role in a few countries, notably France and Italy.

If the orthodox view of the way the labour market works were correct, relatively generous unemployment benefits, high-wage floors, and low-earnings inequality would come at the price of jobs. The social democratic and the social market regulated labour markets would lose the "War of the Models" hands down, particularly in terms of employment rates for the relatively unskilled. But major recent summaries of the empirical research by the World Bank and OECD find that there is no relationship at the economy-wide level between union density or collective bargaining coverage and economic or employment performance in the 1980s and 1990s (Aidt and Tzannatos 2003; OECD 1997). Union density is, overall, related neither to higher- nor lower-than-average rates of unemployment or economic growth. Moreover, evidence of a systematic linkage between other aspects of labour market regulation, such as EI generosity and national unemployment rates, is lacking even in the econometric work of the OECD (Baker, Glyn, Howell, and Schmitt 2002).

To be sure, the larger continental European economies such as France, Germany, and Italy performed poorly in terms of job growth and unemployment in the 1990s compared to the United States, and employment rates for women and youth in these countries lag well behind those in North America. But a number of smaller European countries with high levels of bargaining coverage and reasonably generous welfare states, notably Denmark and the Netherlands, performed well in employment terms in the 1990s (Auer 2000;

ILO 2003a; Jackson 2000b). The International Labour Organisation has recently highlighted the experience of some smaller European economies, particularly Denmark, in an explicit counterattack on the OECD prescription (Auer 2000; ILO 2003a; Sengenberger, 2002). The European Commission has also rejected the idea of a job quality/job quantity tradeoff for lower-skilled workers and highlighted the experiences of Denmark and the Netherlands as a desirable alternative to the US model (EIRO reports; European Commission 2001, 2002). The fundamental message has been that the liberal labour market gives rise to unacceptable levels of wage inequality and social exclusion, but that a *new* European labour market model can provide high levels of quality employment with low levels of insecurity.

SOCIAL FOUNDATIONS OF JOB CREATION: LABOUR MARKETS, REGULATION, AND SOCIAL WELFARE REGIMES

Labour market regulation combines with different key building blocks of social welfare regimes. As noted below, the social market and social democratic models have similarly high rates of collective bargaining coverage but differ profoundly in terms of the division of responsibility for social reproduction between the state and the family, and, relatedly, in the extent to which women participate in the workforce. Further, different countries combine labour market policies in different and distinctive ways, giving greater or lesser weight to training, to non-wage obligations imposed on employers, and to state regulation of the employment relationship.

Some countries, notably Germany, France, Italy, and Spain, impose serious restrictions on the ability of employers to lay off workers, either by the need for justification or by a requirement for long periods of notice or high severance pay. The impact of employment protection legislation on overall employment is relatively small, since lower inflows into unemployment balance off less new hiring. However, strict job protection legislation may have a negative impact on employment for women and may raise the incidence of long-term unemployment (OECD 1999a; OECD 2002). A high level of *job* security can perpetuate an insider/outsider labour market, since the incentive is for employers to hire the minimum numbers of permanent workers and to achieve "flexibility" through contracting out and the hiring, where possible, of temporary and contingent workers. The potential downside of "too much" job security has been recognized by the European Union and the ILO in their nuanced approach to labour market regulation. Tight *job* security has never been a major feature of the Scandinavian labour markets, which have stressed *employment* security through active labour market policies and high levels of worker training, as well as generous unemployment benefits as workers move between jobs in a changing labour market.

In the EU, the incidence of fixed-term temporary work has increased modestly, from 9.1 per cent in 1983 to 13.4 per cent in 2000 (EIRO 2002a). The increase in temporary work has been a major factor in strong job creation in some countries, notably the Netherlands, where it has increased from 5.8 per cent to 14.0 per cent of total employment over this period. Part-time job creation, mainly among women, also played a major role in strong job creation in the Dutch "employment miracle" of the 1990s. The European Commission has expressed strong concern over labour market segmentation associated with the growth of more precarious forms of work, especially among women, who disproportionately work in involuntary part-time and temporary jobs. One-quarter of EU jobs are judged to be of low quality, judged in terms of pay, access to career opportunities and training, job security, and conditions of work.

The regulatory solution has been seen as "flexicurity," rather than strong job security regulation or strictures on part-time and temporary work, as striking a better balance between the flexibility needs of employers and the security needs of workers. For example, part-time work is seen as not necessarily precarious, provided it conforms to certain minimum standards of non-discrimination compared to full-time work. Accordingly, the European Union has implemented binding directives mandating member countries to legislate non-discrimination against part-time workers (1997) and temporary workers (1999) with respect to pay and access to permanent jobs and training. The directive on fixed-term work, for example, requires states to set limits on the maximum duration of contracts or number of renewals. These directives set minimum standards that are quite low in relation to prevailing norms in EU countries, though not without application, for example, to the highly deregulated UK labour market. If Canada were covered by EU directives, significant wage and benefit gaps between otherwise comparable full- and part-time workers would likely be narrowed. European Union-wide minimum labour standards are thus a modest but innovative approach to labour market restructuring, which holds lessons for decentralized federations such as Canada. In summary, the EU approach is not so much to deregulate as to promote forms of regulation that reconcile job growth and job quality.

There are other major differences between the labour markets of OECD countries. The extent to which employers are expected to finance social security through payroll taxes or private pension, health, and other benefits varies greatly. Loading social welfare costs onto employers is common in the social market model, where social security has been primarily financed by employer and employee contributions rather than by general taxes. Non-wage costs can also be significant in liberal labour markets, where lack of public provision has been offset by bargained health care and pension benefits for "core" workers, increasing the divide between insiders and precarious workers. High non-wage costs are likely to lead to lower rates of job creation in labour-intensive sectors such as consumer services, where demand is highly sensitive to price, and in internationally exposed sectors where wage costs are a major competitive factor. In this respect, the social democratic model of services for all citizens financed from general taxes is the most "employment-friendly."

Further, countries differ greatly in terms of the extent to which they invest in public education and active labour market policies to promote labour adjustment and "lifelong learning" for vulnerable workers. Training for the unemployed and for workers in precarious employment helps equalize access to job opportunities and also creates a supply-side basis for higher-productivity and higher-quality jobs. Training can be a force for higher productivity and better jobs in low-wage private services (OECD 1999b; European Commission 2002). Active labour market policies directed to the relatively unskilled have long been a major feature of the social democratic model, but have been much less emphasized in the liberal and social market countries.

Finally, advanced industrial countries differ a great deal in terms of the structure of the service sector, which reflects the division of responsibilities for social reproduction between the family and the state, and the extent to which the "caring needs" of households, such as child and elder care, and a wide range of community services, such as health, have been assumed by the market or by the state (Esping-Anderson 1999; Pierson 2001; Scharpf and Schmidt 2000).Traditionally low rates of labour force participation by women in social market regimes went hand in hand with the assumption that the social reproduction needs of households would be met mainly by women in the home. Both social market and liberal welfare states have a relatively underdeveloped set of publicly financed and delivered social services compared to the Scandinavian countries. Here, state delivery of caring services has expanded the public sector, enabled women to work, and created new jobs that have mainly gone to women. State-delivered social services tend to have higher skill requirements than private consumer services, and wages and working conditions are usually covered by collective bargaining. Thus, the social decision to tax and spend on social services has had direct implications for the quality of services jobs. Moreover, higher taxes to pay for public services means that households have less disposable income for consuming private services, thereby limiting the growth of low-productivity and low-wage sectors. It should be noted that the system of individual rather than household-based entitlements to benefits has influenced the high rate of labour market participation by women in the Scandinavian countries compared to the rest of the European Union.

Esping-Anderson (1999) has highlighted distinctive "post-industrial employment trajectories" that have major implications for the extent of precarious work, particularly among women. In liberal social welfare states like Canada, employment rates for women are almost as high as in the Scandinavian countries, leading to a demand for caring services (child care, elder care, etc.) and services that substitute for household labour (cleaning services, fast food, etc.). These services are typically provided by the market, often supplemented, in the case of caring services, by not-for-profit delivery subsidized by governments. Demand for such services will be priced out of the reach of many households if wages are "too high." "Quasi-markets" organized by governments have also produced a low-wage social services sector.

In line with these forces, the structure of services employment differs profoundly between social democratic and liberal social welfare regimes. The ratio of private- to public-sector jobs ranges from 6 to 1 in the United States, to 4 to 1 in Canada, to 2.5 to 1 in Sweden and Denmark. Traditionally low-productivity and precarious personal services jobs are relatively much more important in North America than in Scandinavia. One in 6 of the total working-age population in Canada and the United States are employed in the retail trade, restaurants, and accommodation sectors combined, compared to about 1 in 10 in Sweden and Denmark (Scharpf and Schmidt 2000, vol. 1, Data Appendix; OECD 2000a). The structure of services employment, as divided between consumer services, public services, and not-for-profit services, has major implications for the extent of precarious work and the quality of employment for women.

It is important to recognize that, while the social democratic labour market model is progressive from the point of view of limiting the incidence of precarious employment among women, it is still problematic from a wider equality perspective. Denmark and Sweden have the lowest gaps in employment rates by gender among OECD countries, and a slightly smaller than average gender wage gap (OECD 2002). The presence of children in the household poses few barriers to the labour market participation of women. However, there is a very marked gendered division of labour in the Scandinavian countries, with a higher than average proportion of women employed in women-dominated occupations compared to Canada and the OECD average. The majority of women work in the public sector, concentrated in caring services, and women are relatively excluded from higher-level professional and managerial as well as blue-collar jobs in the private sector, even by comparison to liberal labour markets such as Canada.

Moreover, the socialization of caring responsibilities such as child and elder care, turning unpaid work by women in the home into paid work for women outside the home, has still left women with a significant and disproportionate burden of domestic labour, including primary responsibility for the care of children and the elderly. Domestic caring work has been socialized to a degree, reducing the domestic burden, but at the same time the relative absence of low-wage consumer services sectors means that other forms of domestic work, such as food preparation and cleaning, are performed as unpaid labour by women in the home, rather than as waged work. In short, the still unequal division of domestic labour between women and men as well as high levels of occupational segregation between women and men in the labour market remain unresolved gender equity issues. Glimpses of a more progressive model are to be found in Scandinavian initiatives to share caring and domestic work more equally by promoting longer parental leaves for men, and in the Netherlands model of reduced working time for both women and men to make possible a more equal division of both paid and domestic labour. The growth of part-time work in the Netherlands (which has a relative absence of formal child care) has seen the emergence of a new model among some younger families with children, in which both women and men work four-day weeks and men undertake a relatively high share of caring and domestic work.

Esping-Anderson argues that reliance on job creation in the public and the social services is the Achilles heel of the relative employment success of Scandinavian social democracy, since a high and rising tax burden ultimately becomes a barrier to further job growth. However, recent job growth in Denmark and Sweden has mainly been in the private sector, rather than in social services, and has generally been of quite high quality. There has been strong job growth in high-productivity producer services as well as in social services, and this growth helps explain why Scandinavian employment rates are as high as in the United States or Canada, even with a far smaller consumer services sector (OECD 2001).

THE ECONOMICS OF LABOUR MARKET REGULATION: POSITIVE EMPLOYMENT EFFECTS OF LABOUR STANDARDS

As noted, high rates of collective bargaining coverage do not necessarily lead to poor employment growth outcomes. Some high bargaining coverage countries such as Denmark, the Netherlands, and Sweden have done well, partly because bargaining has produced wage outcomes that have preserved cost competitiveness and maintained low inflation. Unions in Denmark and the Netherlands have consciously bargained, within a framework of loose national guidelines, to promote job growth. The ILO has underlined the importance of relative wage moderation in employment success, while noting that this factor has been consistent with real wage growth and reductions of working time in line with productivity. By bargaining for jobs rather than higher wages for "insiders," some labour movements have helped counter unemployment and precarious employment. Economists and post-industrial employment pessimists argue that wage floors destroy jobs by artificially truncating the wage structure at "too high" a level, pushing some low-productivity workers out of potential employment. To some degree, wage floors may indeed militate against employment in very low-wage or low-productivity firms and sectors. However, this barrier should be seen as a positive force. That was the case with the famous Swedish labour market model of the 1950s through the 1970s. "Solidarity wages" – the conscious pursuit through wage bargaining of very limited wage differentials by gender, skill, occupation, industry, or enterprise profitability – were explicitly intended by the Swedish unions to squeeze low-productivity firms and sectors, forcing them to raise productivity by investing in capital or skills or to go out of business. Accompanied by measures to retrain workers for jobs in expanding sectors where wages were relatively low in relation to profits, this policy resulted in a virtuous combination of high wage equality, rising productivity, and high employment. The model encountered serious intermittent difficulties from the mid-1980s, driven mainly by public/private sector tensions, difficulties in avoiding wage inflation, and setting a solidarity wage at the economy-wide level of productivity growth. But these difficulties have reflected tensions among workers rather than a breakdown in the economic logic of the model itself (Benner and Vad 2000).

Rather than just destroying jobs in private services, high labour standards may raise job quality and pay by raising productivity. Wage floors can lower worker turnover and increase experience and skills, reducing employer costs. The economic evidence, as comprehensively summarized by the OECD (1998), indicates that there are minimal negative effects from minimum wages at existing levels on the employment of adults. It is also important to distinguish between different wage-floor designs. Wage floors set by bargaining often vary by sector, occupation, and industry and are responsive to market conditions. Since bargaining has the effect of compressing the distribution of wages, higher wages at the bottom are paid for, in part, by lower wages for those at the middle and the top. Unskilled workers and women make more, so the more highly skilled and men make a bit less. Because bargaining redistributes wage income and equalizes gender wage gaps, it does not necessarily raise the total wage bill and thus reduce demand.

At the sectoral level, wage floors and generalized labour standards take wage costs out of the competitive equation, particularly in non-traded sectors such as consumer services. As recognized by work in this volume on employment standards, if all employers pay the same wage and benefit package, firms must compete with one another on the basis of non-labour cost issues, such as quality and customer service. The "high road" of firm competition on the basis of high productivity, training, and production of high-quality services is different from the "low road" of competing on the basis of low wages and poor working conditions. Unfortunately, the low road will prevail, especially in labour-intensive services, if higher wages and standards are not generalized. Unions in liberal labour markets have had great difficulty raising the wages and working conditions of workers in precarious employment precisely because they have not been strong enough at the sectoral and regional level to take wages out of competition.

There is good evidence that decent wages and high labour standards raise productivity at the firm level. The fact that employers come under pressure to pay good wages will lead them to invest more in capital equipment and training than would otherwise be the case. Further, labour standards can raise productivity by improving the social relations of production. In a major defence of labour rights and standards, Werner Sengenberger – a recently retired senior official with the ILO – argues that the neo-classical view of the labour market is profoundly misleading because it does not take account of the fundamental fact that "labour is not a commodity" or a "factor of production" (Sengenberger 2002). Rather, labour is a productive potential, linked to human beings with individual and social needs. Productivity – what a worker delivers in return for a wage – depends on what the ILO has termed "decent work." "A worker will be more or less productive, co-operative and innovative depending on how he or she is treated; whether the wage is seen as fair in relation to the demands of the job; whether the worker gets equal pay for work of equal value; whether training is provided; whether grievances can be voiced. In short, what the worker delivers is contingent on the terms of employment, working conditions, the work environment, collective representation and due process" (Sengenberger 2002, 48).

The work of Freeman and Medoff (1984) and more recent research summarized by the World Bank and the ILO (Aidt and Tannatos 2003; ILO 1995 and 1997) emphasize the importance of a collective voice that makes unionized workplaces more efficient precisely because they are more equitable. The participatory benefits of unions, combined with better wages and working conditions, reduce quits, giving an employer the benefit of more experienced workers and raising returns to investment in worker training. Job and/or employment security means that workers have an incentive to share their knowledge of production and to cooperate to raise productivity (see also Anderson, this volume). If workers know that changes in work organization will not cost them jobs, will not lead to poorer health and safety or working conditions, and know that the gains of higher productivity will be shared, then workers will cooperate in workplace change (see also Lewchuk, de Wolff, King, and Polanyi, this volume). The path to higher productivity, particularly in services, lies in the effective combination of new technologies, training, and changes in the organization of work to maximize the use of skills. Good labour relations can make a major contribution to the success of workplace restructuring (Black and Lynch 2000). In sum, there are good reasons to believe that high labour standards can raise the quality of private services jobs by raising productivity.

DENMARK AND THE NEW EUROPEAN
LABOUR MARKET MODEL

As noted, Denmark has been viewed by the ILO and the European Commission as a major success story in terms of both the quantity and the quality of employment. Although Denmark has many distinctive national features, it can be seen as a social democratic model that holds lessons for progressive Canadians as well as Europeans. This section summarizes some key features of the Danish labour market of the 1990s, especially in relation to the issue of precarious employment.

Table 13.2 provides comparative data for the United States, Canada, Denmark, and Sweden, to draw out contrasts between the liberal and the social democratic models as well as differences among the latter countries. As shown, employment rates are higher in Sweden and Denmark than in the United States or Canada, particularly for women. Notably, employment rates for unskilled adult workers with low levels of formal education are also significantly higher. If high levels of participation in paid work are seen as key to social inclusion, the development of individual capabilities, and gender equity, then the social democratic countries are the clear winners compared to Canada and the United States. High employment has also been twinned with very low unemployment rates, and, as in North America, by a low incidence of long-term unemployment.

Sweden and Denmark have very low levels of after-tax income inequality and child poverty compared to North America, reflecting much lower levels of earnings inequality and low pay, and also higher levels of social transfers as a share of GDP. Cash benefits (public pensions, unemployment, welfare, and disability benefits) are almost double the North American level. Taxpayer-funded public services as a share of GDP are, at 16 per cent, far higher than in the United States (6.7%) or Canada (9.8%). High levels of spending on public services mean that the share of national income spent on private consumption is correspondingly much lower.

In pure economic efficiency terms, the Scandinavian countries have also been very successful. The average annual growth of labour productivity in the business sector has been slightly higher in both countries than in the United States or Canada from 1995 to 2001. The average growth rate of real GDP per capita in the second half of the 1990s was comparable. (Denmark's performance looks better compared to the United States, and Canada's worse, for the 1990s as a whole.) If growth of GDP per capita were adjusted for time worked, Scandinavian relative performance would improve because of a lower incidence of long hours and longer periods of paid vacation. The average full-time Danish worker has a work week of 37 hours; long hours are very uncommon; and all workers now enjoy six weeks of paid vacation per year.

Table 13.2
North America v. Scandinavia: Key Economic and Social Indicators

		US	Canada	Sweden	Denmark
1	Average annual GDP growth per capita, 1995–2002	2.3%	2.5%	2.5%	2.0%
	Average annual growth of labour productivity in business sector, 1995–2002	1.6%	1.5%	1.7%	1.8%
2	Employment/population ratio, 2001				
	All	73.1%	70.9%	75.3%	75.9%
	Men	79.3%	75.9%	77.0%	80.2%
	Women	67.1%	66.0%	73.5%	71.4%
	Age 25–64 < upper secondary education	57.8%	55.0%	68.0%	62.5%
	Men	69.6%	66.1%	73.3%	70.9%
	Women	45.8%	43.3%	61.6%	55.1%
3	Unemployment rate, 2001				
	All	4.8%	7.3%	5.1%	4.2%
	Men	4.9%	7.6%	5.4%	3.7%
	Women	4.7%	6.8%	4.7%	4.8%
4	Long-term unemployment (> 6 months) as % of unemployed	4.8%	7.3%	5.1%	4.2%
5	Temporary employment as % total employment, 2001				
	All	4.0%	12.4%	14.7%	10.2%
	Men	3.9%	11.8%	12.3%	8.8%
	Women	4.2%	13.3%	16.9%	11.7%
6	Part-time employment as % total employment				
	All	13.0%	18.1%	17.8%	14.5%
	Men	8.1%	10.4%	7.1%	9.1%
	Women	18.2%	27.1%	29.3%	20.8%
7a	Net income replacement rate				
	(composite of four family types at two earnings levels, short- and long-duration unemployment)	41%	58%	80%	80%
7b	Unemployment compensation as % GDP	0.30%	0.72%	1.19%	1.35%

Table 13.2
North America v. Scandinavia: Key Economic and Social Indicators (*Continued*)

8 Child poverty rate	23.2%	14.2%	2.7%	3.4%
9 After-tax income gaps (minimum ratio to top to bo	5.57%	4.13%	2.61%	3.15%
10 Public social expenditure as % GDP				
a) Cash benefits	7.8%	8.1%	15.1%	14.0%
b) Public services	6.7%	9.8%	16.0%	16.1%
11 Public expenditure on labour market training as %	0.04%	0.17%	0.30%	0.85%
Unemployed/at risk participants as % workforce	0.99%	1.61%	2.32%	5.76%
Employed participants as % workforce	0%	0%	0.0%	10.15%

Except as Indicated, data are from OECD Social Indicators, 2002:

1 OECD Economic Outlook #73, 2003.

6 OECD Employment Outlook, 2002.

9 Smeeding, 2002.

Although in very broad-brush terms a variation of the Scandinavian social democratic model, Denmark differs from Sweden in many ways. It has an economy based much more on small firms in the services, food processing, and light industry, and less on large-scale industry. The social democratic party, while in government most of the time until 2002, has been less dominant, and the unions a somewhat weaker social force. As in Sweden and the Netherlands, recent employment success contrasts to experiences in the 1980s and early 1990s of high unemployment, fiscal crisis, and very strained labour-management relationships. And, as in the Netherlands, crisis led to a renewal of the social partnership model and to systemic reforms.

As noted above, the incidence of low-wage work in Denmark is very low because of the high-wage floor set by collective bargaining. More than 80 per cent of all workers are covered by collective agreements, though as many as 30 per cent of private sector workers may not be covered (EIRO 2002e). Coverage is almost universal in community and social services, and collective agreements cover the majority of workers in consumer services sectors such as retail trade (57%) and hotels and restaurants (50%). Bargaining coverage is stable or even increasing, despite erosion among some higher-paid professionals, and unions and employers have maintained that employee protection legislation is largely unnecessary because of continued high coverage of potentially vulnerable workers (EIRO 2002e).

Bargaining is conducted on a sectoral basis between employer associations and unions, within a loose framework of centrally agreed wage guidelines, with some enterprise flexibility to pay higher wages. The wage determination system has been characterized as "centralized decentralization." While wage moderation has been a feature of Danish success, it should also be noted that the major union federation, LO, recently conducted national strikes to win a sixth week of paid vacation and that real wages have increased more or less in line with those in Germany (Ploughman 2002). Wage inequality has not increased in the 1990s.

The incidence of precarious employment in Denmark is very low. Self-employment (which is disproportionately, though not universally, precarious) accounts for just 7 per cent of total employment, compared to about 20 per cent in Canada and an EU average of 15 per cent, and has been declining, from 9 per cent in 1990 (European Commission, 2002). Temporary or fixed-term contract employment accounts for 10.2 per cent of all jobs and is higher for women than for men, but fewer than 1 in 3 temporary workers report that this status is involuntary. The status of temporary workers generally compares well to other EU countries and to Canada (EIRO 2002f; OECD 2002). Temporary workers are covered by collective agreements; qualify for paid holidays, parental leave, and sick leave if they have worked for just 72 hours in the past eight weeks; and earn 78 per cent of the hourly wage of permanent employees (more when controlled for other differences in work status). However, they have much less access to training than permanent employees (OECD 2002). Similarly, the incidence of part-time work is low at 14.5 per cent, is falling (from 19.2% in 1990), and is generally voluntary (European Commission 2002).

The European Commission judges Denmark to have the highest overall quality of jobs in the European Union (European Commission, 2001, chap. 4). Measured by pay, working conditions, subjective job satisfaction, and opportunities for advancement, 60 per cent of Danes are in good jobs (the highest proportion in Europe), 20 per cent are in jobs of reasonable quality, and just 20 per cent are in jobs of poor quality (of which fewer than half qualify as really bad "dead-end" jobs). There are also very high rates of transition from lower-quality to higher-quality jobs, with 35 per cent of workers in low-quality jobs being in better jobs one year later, and 50 per cent in better jobs three years later (compared to 35% in the United Kingdom) (European Commission 2002, 93). Subjective job satisfaction is the highest in the European Union. Data from the European Survey on Work Conditions also suggest that jobs in the Danish services sector are, on average, much better than elsewhere in the European Union in terms of levels of work autonomy and the incidence of monotonous work (OECD 2001). It seems probable that the high level of social services jobs and high incidence of training have militated against "dead-end" (very low-skill/low-productivity) consumer services jobs.

The Danish labour market is remarkable in terms of its high level of labour mobility. Annual worker turnover is as high as 30 per cent. About one-half of annual job turnover is due to job destruction, but the level of voluntary quits to seek or take new jobs is also very high (Madsen 2003, 64; Ploughman and Madsen 2002, 21). Only about 2 in 3 workers have been in their current job for more than two years, the lowest proportion in the European Union, and one-quarter have been in their current job for less than one year, the highest proportion in the European Union (European Commission 2001, 72). There is a very low level of job protection by statute or collective agreement. On the OECD scale of strictness of employment protection, Denmark ranks low, just above Canada. Collective agreements typically specify periods of notice of layoff of two to three months for long-tenure workers. The union central, LO Denmark, has not called for stronger job protection, arguing that generous unemployment benefits and access to training serve workers better (LO Denmark website).

Despite quite high rates of entry into unemployment, perceived employment security is very high. A 2000 survey found only 9 per cent of Danish workers were afraid of losing their current job, the lowest in the European Union (Ploughman and Madsen 2002, 12). By contrast, one-quarter to one-third of Canadian workers have reported fear of job loss in recent years, according to the Canadian Council on Social Development Personal Security Index.

The annual incidence of unemployment is as high as 1 in 4 workers, but, for the majority, unemployment is very short term (less than 10 weeks). Per Madsen, who has written extensively on the Danish model for the ILO, talks of the "Golden Triangle" of the Danish labour market. As in liberal labour markets, there is a very low level of job security, which has encouraged job creation. However, in line with the principle of flexicurity and the traditional social democratic model, unemployment benefits are very generous, and there is a lot of emphasis on training and active labour market policy to promote employment security.

The great majority of unemployed workers belong to an Unemployment Insurance Fund administered by the unions and are eligible for benefits if employed for one year in the last three. The OECD calculated the relative generosity of benefits for unemployed workers for different family types and earning levels and found that the Danish and Swedish systems are by far the most generous. The income replacement rate for an average production worker is at least 70 per cent, rising to 90 per cent for relatively low-paid workers (Madsen 2003, 74). For an estimated one-third of unemployed men and one-half of unemployed women, benefits just about match prior earnings (Benner and Vad 2000). As shown in table 13.2, expenditure on so-called passive unemployment benefits was 1.3 per cent of Danish GDP in 2001, almost double the Canadian level despite similar unemployment rates.

Reforms to the system in the mid-1990s very modestly trimmed benefits and introduced individual employment plans. It is now mandatory for beneficiaries to participate in an active labour market program after one year, and after six months for younger workers. While this program has been equated with workfare in some critiques of "third-way" policies and is deliberately intended to counter "dependency," the carrots of good benefits and meaningful training opportunities are much more important than the stick of potential sanctions. Moreover, unemployed workers are clearly being trained for jobs at decent wages.

As set out in table 13.2, public expenditures on labour market training are, at 0.85 per cent of GDP, much higher in Denmark than in Sweden, and five times higher than in Canada. The main focus is on training for the unemployed, and about 2 in 3 unemployed workers, or 6 per cent of the total workforce, receive some public training each year. This training can be in private firms with a wage subsidy (which has been found in evaluations to be most effective), with a public sector employer, or in training or educational programs to fill future labour market vacancies. In addition, about 10 per cent of the workforce benefit each year from training programs directed to employed workers, compared to zero in Canada. There has been scepticism in Canada about the effectiveness of skills training for unemployed and vulnerable workers, but Danish government studies judge their programs to be effective in job placement and in raising skills (ILO 2003; Madsen 2003). Credit has been given to the decentralization since the mid-1990s of public training to the regional level, where it is run by the "social partners."

In addition, the Danish system features high levels of education and training for the currently employed. On top of a strong base of universal public education and high participation in post-secondary studies, the rhetoric of "lifelong learning in a skill-based economy" has been translated into reality through rights to individual educational leaves and opportunities to take education leaves funded by unemployment benefits. These leaves were quite popular when they were used to address high unemployment in the early to mid-1990s. Unions bargain access to training and help to run employer-sponsored training. Denmark has recently ranked high among OECD countries in terms of the extent of adult participation in training and equality of access for women (OECD 1999b). Average hours spent in training per worker are double the OECD average. Such training extends to workers in private consumer services, with participation rates of 70 per cent in hotels and restaurants, and 49 per cent in retail trade (European Commission 2002, table 9).

Both public and social services have been an important source of quality employment for women. These services account for about one-third of Danish employment, and fully one-half of employment for women. However, private services employment has grown faster since the mid-1980s, and two out of three new jobs created between 1993 and 2002 were in the private sector (Madsen 2003). Government policies have also avoided loading too many non-wage costs onto employers. In Denmark, tax reform in the mid-1990s trimmed already low payroll taxes and sharply reduced employer responsibility for funding active labour market programs. According to Madsen (2003, 60), "the direct costs of protecting the employee are borne to a large extent by the state and not by individual firms." Workplace pensions play a modest role compared to universal state pensions and the state-run work-based pension system. As a result, the proportion of social expenditures financed by employers is the lowest in the European Union – 8.7 per cent, compared to 46.5 per cent in France and 37.4 per cent in Germany (ILO 2003, 58) – and the percentage of non-wage costs in total labour costs is just 6.3 per cent, compared to 31.8 per cent in France and 20.7 per cent in the United States (ILO 2003, 61).

The Danish model is not without blemishes. In common with other socially homogeneous small states, the values of solidarity tend to be racially and culturally defined. Unemployment is relatively high among recent immigrants from developing countries, and the recently elected (conservative) government has limited immigrant access to full welfare benefits. As noted, occupational segregation of women and men is high.

LESSONS FOR CANADA

The central conclusion to be drawn from this chapter is that it is possible to have high levels of employment at decent wages and with decent working conditions. There is no ineluctable tradeoff between job quantity and job quality, even at the "low end" of the job market. Several European countries have achieved high employment rates even with "generous" welfare benefits and wage structures that are very compressed compared to the Canadian norm.

The Danish example is singular in some respects, but has wider lessons. First, a wage floor and the virtual elimination of low pay do not preclude job growth in private services. The theoretical link between good labour standards and higher productivity needs to be explored in detail, but it probably helps to explain Danish success. Further, a wage floor probably works best when combined with training policies, both public and private, which raise the skills of workers who might otherwise be precariously employed. The Danish example also suggests that high levels of public services, financed from general taxes, can make a positive contribution to high-quality "post-industrial" employment. Finally, the Danish example shows that generous social welfare benefits relative to wages in available jobs do not have to create serious disincentives to work, as is often argued in Canada. To the contrary, good child-care arrangements, a high wage floor, and active labour market policies are more effective than the stick of punitively low benefits.

Canada is a far more diverse and heterogeneous society than Denmark. This characteristic makes it more difficult, but not impossible, to link political projects to the values of equality and solidarity. Canada is also highly integrated with the deregulated US economy. Again, this integration poses policy constraints on Canada, particularly with respect to the level of taxes, but the experience of Denmark and Sweden strongly suggests that precarious work is not a precondition for high productivity, innovation, and competitiveness. Moving in a social democratic direction is not, then, impossible, and it could inspire change within North America as a whole. Finally, there are limits to the progressiveness of the social democratic model, which falls short of transformative change. But millions of precariously employed Canadian workers would be better off if Canada moved in this direction.

PART FOUR

Unions, Unionisms, and Precarious Employment

14

The Union Dimension: Mitigating Precarious Employment?

JOHN ANDERSON, JAMES BEATON,
AND KATE LAXER

Union status is intimately connected to precarious employment. An important indicator of control over the labour process, union membership is central to limiting precarious employment. Workers with standard employment relationships are often union members or covered by a union contract (Fudge 1997; Rodgers 1989; Schellenberg and Clark 1996; Vosko 1997; Vosko, Zukewich, and Cranford 2003). Many non-union, permanent, full-time jobs are also influenced by the kind of standards that unions establish in sectors such as steel or automobile assembly (Storey 1987).

Unionization in Canada is also situated within a broad matrix of economic factors and regulation, factors ranging from the magnitude and influence of the public sector to narrow industrial concentration. Regions of provinces relying on low-wage private sector jobs generally have lower rates of unionization, owing, perhaps, to their particular industrial profiles. The state of provincial employment standards, the ease with which unionization can occur, and the design of equity legislation also shape the union/non-union distinction. What Card and Freeman (1993) found when comparing Canada to the United States also holds true within Canada and among industries: "broader social safety nets, and labour regulations and institutions" can be more favourable to unionization than narrower policies.

At the level of the worksite, unions have often been a proxy for "good jobs." While the advantages of union coverage and the composition of union membership developed with the evolution of the Keynesian Welfare State, popular wisdom equating "good" and "better" jobs with unions seems generally to hold true. This chapter probes this truism by drawing on data from both the Statistics Canada Workplace and Employer Survey and the Survey of Labour and Income Dynamics to compare union and non-union jobs. It finds that the bifurcation between union and non-union jobs is important and that it highlights the superiority of union jobs to non-union ones.

Because the data considered here look only at the main jobs of individual workers and do not measure multiple job holding, and because they do not measure the periods of unemployment or reduced hours or the psychological toll on the precariously employed who never find secure employment, the chapter cannot capture the long-term advantages of unionized, permanent wage work compared to the long-term disadvantages of non-union precarious jobs. Many of the advantages of unionization cannot be measured in the short term or when the worker is young, since the full impact of relying on meagre government pensions may begin to be felt only as the worker approaches retirement. Women are more likely to hold precarious jobs and, therefore, less likely to accumulate good employer-sponsored pensions, yet, on the average, they also live longer than men. In these ways, they are doubly penalized. The absence of independent access to other benefits more common among women than men, such as drug and dental coverage, which may not be required to the same degree until the worker ages, also disproportionately affects women (Vosko and Zukewich, this volume). Another important finding of this chapter is that unionized jobs that are not full time and permanent, while superior to non-union jobs in the same category, are often vastly inferior in terms of wages and benefits to the better union jobs.

The discussion proceeds in three sections. The first section examines unions in Canada today. The second section maps union members and non-union members along indicators and dimensions of precariousness; by way of the methodology advanced in chapter 1, it considers the extent to which the mitigation of precariousness through unionization is a gendered and racialized process.[1] The third section considers what unions are doing to address issues related to precarious wage work both within and outside their membership.

UNIONS IN CANADA TODAY: WHAT IS THE OVERALL PICTURE?

The overall picture of Canadian unions today is characterized by seven features.

Canada is in the mid-range of countries in terms of union density   Canada falls in the mid-range of industrialized countries when it comes to union density. With a density of 31 per cent, it is between low-density countries in the 10–15 per cent range, such as France and the United States, and high-density

countries, such as Sweden, Norway, and Denmark, in the 70–80 per cent range
(ILO 1997). In its 1997 report, which surveyed 92 countries, the ILO listed
14 countries that had more than half their workforces unionized, and 48
countries with less than 20 per cent union density. Union density levels declined
between 1985 and 1995 in 72 of the countries surveyed (ILO 1997). Canada
sits in the middle group of 30 countries with between 20 per cent and 50 per
cent union density.

Canada is also in the mid-range when it comes to the pace of decline in
union density over the last 20 years. Canada's situation is distinguished
both from fast-paced decline countries such as the United States, where
union density dropped from a high of 30 per cent in the 1950s to 13 per
cent in 2002, and from low-decline counties such as Sweden, where union
density has remained fairly stable at 80 per cent in 1990 to 79 per cent in
2002. The decline of union density in Canada began in the late 1990s,
when union density dropped from a national record high of 36 per cent in
1994 to 31 per cent in 2002. This decline can be attributed to several factors, particularly to developments in the private sector. Jackson and
Schetagne (2003) note the dramatic decline of union density in the private
sector while the public sector remained stable. Yet, considering absolute figures, overall union membership in Canada is at its highest point, with
4.174 million members.

*Union density among men and women is now equal, although the numbers
alone don't mean equality* Levels of union density among men and women
equalized during the 1990s. This change took place rapidly in just under
15 years. In 1989, union density among women workers was 29 per cent, while
38 per cent of men were unionized. In 2002 union density for women and men
was nearly equal, at 30.2 per cent and 30.3 per cent, respectively (figure 14.1).
Comparing the gender breakdown between private and public sectors, men are
much more likely to be unionized in the private sector than are women, with
density at 24 per cent and 15 per cent, respectively. Unionization is lowest in the
kinds of private sector jobs that are precarious and that contain large numbers
of women workers; it is highest in the "good jobs," such as those in resource-
based industries, which employ the largest number of men. For example, in
2002 union density in the manufacturing sector was 36 per cent for men and
23 per cent for women. Meanwhile, in the public sector, women have a higher
level of unionization than men, at 77 per cent and 74 per cent, respectively
(Jackson and Schetagne 2003).

While equalization in union density has occurred, partly due to the increased
labour force participation of women in the public sector along with layoffs of a
primarily male workforce in the manufacturing sector, women's wages remain
far below men's. Though women are unionized in equal numbers to men,
women still, on the average, earn less and have access to fewer benefits.

Union members are an aging group   Another important indicator of unions' relevance to a major segment of workers in precarious employment is the age of union members. Union membership peaks for workers between the ages of 45 and 54 at 41 per cent, but membership among youth is relatively low at 14 per cent (figure 14.1). Precarious employment is much more common among younger workers who are concentrated in the private service sector, where union density is very low in general.

Workers of colour have lower union density   Studies such as Galabuzzi (2001) argue that unionization is one of the few mechanisms open to workers of colour seeking equality, yet workers of colour are less unionized than white workers. Both workers of colour and immigrant workers of colour have a lower degree of unionization, or an almost 33 per cent greater rate of not being in a union, than their white counterparts (figure 14.1). For example, union density is 26 per cent among workers of colour, and 35 per cent among white workers. Figures for immigrants of colour parallel those of all people of colour. While 33 per cent of workers of colour in Canada are Canadian-born, the discrimination they suffer is not simply the result of immigrant status. And while immigrant workers of colour are less unionized and more likely to be concentrated in precarious forms of employment, such as part-time and temporary wage work, they fare worse than both Canadian-born workers of colour and non-Canadian-born white workers. For example, immigrant workers of colour in part-time wage work have a unionization level of 16 per cent, compared to 26 per cent for white immigrant workers. These findings are consistent with the racialized gendering of jobs described by Cranford and Vosko (this volume).

Higher education means higher union rates   There is a relationship between education and levels of unionization. The union movement was born defending the interests of skilled and unskilled workers with generally low levels of formal education. Workers with post-secondary education were far from the core of the union movement until well into the post-World War II era. Since the 1960s, with the expansion of the public sector and the rise of post-secondary education in Canada, where Canada now leads all countries with its combined rate of university and community college education, many new jobs have been created in government, education, and health, jobs that require highly educated workers and have higher levels of unionization.

Along with the rise in qualifications needed for many jobs (e.g., nurses now often require a university degree), hiring policies in many industries often demand or favour higher qualifications than those needed for the job. At the same time, there has been a dramatic rise in public sector unionization rates, especially as groups such as university teachers (e.g., professors, contract faculty, and graduate students) face more difficult working conditions (Rajagopal 2002). In 2002, 35 per cent of workers with a university

Figure 14.1
Union membership density by sex, age, visible minority status,
and immigrant status, Canada

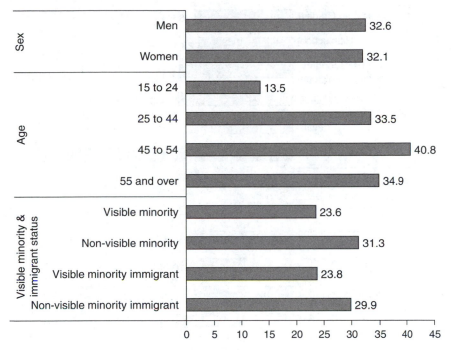

education were unionized, compared to 23 per cent with some high school
(figure 14.2). Precarious workers tend to have lower levels of education
and are more likely to lack union coverage.

*Union density is high in the public sector and in public administration, health,
and education*   In the public sector, unionization is almost at the level of
Sweden, with 76 per cent of all workers covered by a collective agreement. But,
in the private sector, union density approaches the national average in the
United States. Workers tend to be in precarious employment and to lack union
coverage in the private sector and in segments of the public sector experiencing
creeping privatization: there, overall levels of unionization fall below one in five
workers. Public administration, education, and the health-care industries have
much higher levels of unionization than do industries such as food and
accommodation, where there is also considerable precarious employment (this
volume, Armstrong and Laxer; Borowy; and de Wolff).

Location as a factor in union membership   Significant differences in levels of
unionization exist among provinces and cities. These differences are linked

Figure 14.2
Union membership density by education, sector, and industry, Canada

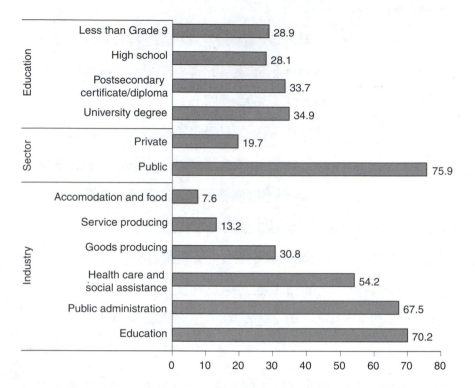

primarily to four factors: the economic and industrial make-up of a region or a province (e.g., in Windsor, high levels of unionization are, in part, linked to the high number of jobs in the auto sector); the importance of the public sector and the number of public sector jobs; the regulatory framework of the province (e.g., provinces with stronger labour codes have higher levels of unionization); and, finally, the history of unionization in a given industry and the strength of particular unions. In Canada, superior regulatory frameworks have been linked to the particular political parties that have been in power, but also, in Quebec, to the emergence of a "Quebec model" – which included high unionization rates – shared, at least until recently, by all parties. Higher levels of unionization prevail in Quebec, followed by Newfoundland, Manitoba, and Saskatchewan, compared to lower levels in provinces such as Alberta and Ontario. This same diversity also holds true for workers in precarious forms of employment. For example, the unionization rate for part-time permanent wage workers ranges from 15 per cent in New Brunswick to 34 per cent in Quebec. These stark differences are associated more with the form of employment than with provincial differences, though, together, they show the diversity in unionization across the country.

This diversity also occurs among different cities within provinces. At the margins are Windsor, the most highly unionized large city in Canada with a density of 40 per cent, and Calgary, with only 20 per cent of its workers unionized. Differences are also significant between Vancouver and Montreal compared to Toronto. Both Montreal and Vancouver have union density levels over 30 per cent, while Toronto trails at 23 per cent. These differences are related to unionization by form of employment, which varies dramatically by city. Among part-time permanent wage workers, for example, over 38 per cent are unionized in Montreal and just 16 per cent are unionized in Calgary.

Many factors can influence unionization rates. Some of these factors may include the dominant industries in particular geographic locales, labour militancy and resources available for organizing the unorganized, and government policy and legislation. Of course, the presence and influence of unions benefits not only unionized workers but also unorganized workers. Governments, often of social democratic persuasion, that remove obstacles to labour organizing may also develop policies benefiting unorganized workers as well, and thereby reduce the "gap" between those who belong to unions and those who do not. Certain policies, such as increasing the minimum wage and decreasing the number of allowable work hours in the week, can also benefit unorganized workers significantly.

What, then, are the differences in levels of precarious wage work among unionized workers by context and location, and between unionized and non-unionized workers?

UNIONS AND PRECARIOUS WAGE WORK: A RACIALIZED AND GENDERED ADVANTAGE?

Research shows that there are significant advantages to belonging in unions. Jackson (2003) finds that unionized workers tend to earn more in wages than non-unionized workers. Another advantage to having a unionized workforce is that union membership tends to place upward pressure on the wages and benefits of non-unionized workers. In addition to wages, unionized environments also provide a wide array of benefits such as job security, formalized processes around promotions, and restrictions on working time.

Workers covered by collective agreements are much less likely to earn under $10 per hour. Data from the Statistics Canada Survey of Workplaces and Employees indicate that among full-time workers earning less than $10 per hour in 1999, only 14 per cent had a collective agreement, whereas 86 per cent did not. Of those full-time workers earning more than $10 per hour, 30 per cent had collective agreements and 70 per cent did not.

Workers with low incomes are most likely to be covered by a collective agreement in manufacturing. Of this sector's workers, 20 per cent for those with an hourly wage of less than $10 per hour, and 34 per cent for those with an hourly wage above $10, are covered by a collective agreement. In education and health care, two sectors that are more heavily unionized, a similar level of coverage applies for low-wage workers. This finding is somewhat surprising and speaks to the issues dealt with by Armstrong and Laxer (this volume) – specifically, the rise of precarious employment in these sectors. The 60 per cent coverage rate for those earning over $10 per hour is not surprising. Those making less than $10 per hour are most likely to be covered in the 30–34 (13 per cent) and 35–39 (19 per cent) age ranges.

For those earning more than $10 per hour, the likelihood of being covered stands at a low of 22 per cent for workers under 25 and peaks at 38.5 per cent for those in the 45–49 age range. Of all occupations, clerical and unskilled labour positions are most likely to be covered by a collective agreement, regardless of what they earn. The coverage rate is 16 per cent for those with earnings of less than $10 per hour, and 40 per cent for those with earning above this figure. Two other interesting findings also emerged. Members of racialized groups earning over $10 per hour are less likely to have a collective agreement (23 per cent versus 32 per cent), while those earning less than $10 per hour are slightly more likely: 14 per cent to 11 per cent. One equity group, persons with disabilities, actually has a larger number of employees (39 per cent) with a collective agreement than the total of all employees with a collective agreement (31 per cent). Results from the Survey of Labour and Income Dynamics (SLID) confirm this finding, which could be linked to the hypothesis that unionized workplaces, because of sound equity policies, may be more likely than non-union workplaces to accommodate people with disabilities (see also Tompa, Scott, Trevithick, and Bhattacharyya, this volume).

Overall, unions provide greater income, security, and benefits to unionized and, in some cases, non-unionized workers. Since unionized workers have advantages not afforded to non-unionized workers, it is important to consider the distribution of these benefits and the extent to which they are gendered and racialized. How does unionization mitigate or fail to mitigate the effects of precarious employment, and how does this process relate to gender and "race"?[2] A series of measures is used to designate workers experiencing dimensions of precarious employment (see Cranford and Vosko, this volume). What is considered an indicator of precarious employment (i.e., union status) in the other chapters in this volume is the focus here, prompting a number of questions: Are unionized workers more or less precarious than non-unionized workers in the public and private sectors? Are unionized women and workers of colour more or less precarious than non-unionized workers? Finally, among unionized workers, how do women and workers of colour compare to men and white workers?

UNIONIZED WORKERS AND PRECARIOUS WAGE WORK IN THE PUBLIC AND PRIVATE SECTORS

In considering patterns of unionization by the public/private sector distinction, a definite hierarchy runs from unionized public sector workers to non-unionized private sector workers, where the latter experience multiple dimensions of precarious employment. Clearly, public sector environments are more unionized than private sector environments (see also Armstrong and Laxer, this volume). Yet it is important to consider the degree to which unionization mitigates precariousness in the public sector as well as how women compare to men within the private sector.

The emphasis on deficit and debt reduction over the last few decades of the 20th century, at the federal level and in many provinces, has translated into attempts by governments to reduce labour costs in the public sector by relying more heavily on private sector workers and non-unionized public sector workers. Figure 14.3 shows that those workers who are not unionized and in the private sector are most precarious on all the dimensions. Those who are least precarious on several different dimensions are unionized public sector workers. Non-unionized public sector workers are, in general, more precarious than unionized public sector workers but are less precarious than non-unionized private sector workers. This situation suggests that, for the non-unionized public sector workers, there are advantages to being in the public sector rather than the private sector, but there are even more advantages to being unionized in the public sector. The dimensions where the variation is the greatest are income and social wage. There is a large difference between unionized public sector workers and non-unionized private sector workers on the pension indicator, the poverty earnings indicator, and the industrial wage indicator. In negotiations with labour, governments often argue that pensions, benefits, and salaries are significant contributors to costs leading to deficits. The data illustrate that non-unionized public sector workers have less access to pensions, benefits, and higher wages than do their unionized counterparts. Interestingly, non-unionized public sector workers and unionized private sector workers have similar levels of precariousness on the industrial wage and poverty earnings indicators.

To understand precariousness among unionized and non-unionized men and women in both the public and the private sectors, figure 14.4 explores precarious employment by union status and sex. In comparing unionized and non-unionized workers by sex, a number of issues emerge. On the overall dimensions of income, social wage, and regulatory protection and control, non-unionized women are the most precarious, and unionized men are the least precarious. While unionized women are less precarious than non-unionized women, they remain, relative to unionized men, more precarious on the

Figure 14.3
Precarious wage work by public/private sector, Canada, 2000 (ages 25–54)

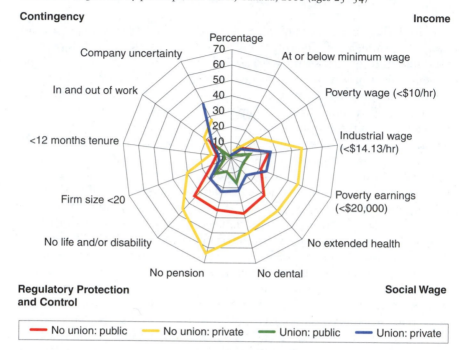

income, social wage, and regulatory protection and control dimensions. On the dimension of contingency, the differences narrow. There is a large difference in pension benefits between unionized and non-unionized men and women. More unionized women than unionized men earn less than the industrial wage. Unions make a difference for income between unionized and non-unionized men. The differences on the income dimension between unionized men and unionized women, where women are more precarious, suggest that unions need to focus greater attention on women's income.

Figures 14.1–14.4 have illustrated that non-unionized women are generally the most precarious group of workers and that the public sector is considerably less precarious than the private sector. It will be useful now to analyze the differentiation in precariousness among public sector workers.

Figure 14.5 examines precariousness among unionized and non-unionized men and women in the public sector. Within the public sector, non-unionized men and women tend to experience greater precariousness than unionized men and women. Non-unionized public sector women tend to experience the greatest level of precariousness on the different dimensions. As observed earlier with other indicators, non-unionized women are most precarious on the dimensions of social wage and income. There is a significant difference on the

Figure 14.4
Precarious wage work by union status and sex, Canada, 2000 (ages 25–54)

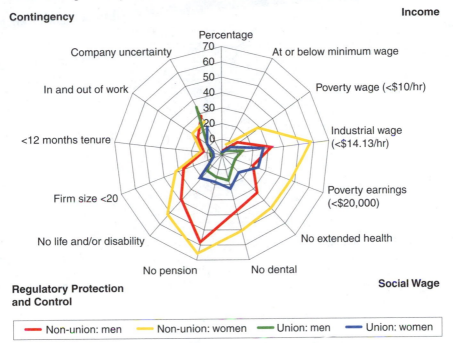

industrial wage, extended health, and dental and pension indicators. While non-unionized men are more precarious than unionized men and women, they seem to be significantly less precarious than non-unionized women.

These data highlight a gendered process whereby public sector environments are relying on non-unionized workers to reduce labour costs, leaving non-unionized women in the most precarious situation. Privatization is contributing to a tiered system of workers, where there are unionized employees who have advantages, such as higher income and social wage provisions including dental benefits, and a lower tier of non-unionized workers who generally have lower incomes and fewer social provisions. This difference highlights how important it is for unions to resist the privatization of public services and to transform non-unionized work into unionized work (Borowy, this volume).

UNIONS, PRECARIOUS WAGE WORK,
AND WORKERS OF COLOUR

As seen in the analysis above, women are generally more precarious than men. But to what extent does race influence precariousness in unionized and

Figure 14.5
Precarious wage work by union status and sex, public sector only, Canada, 2000 (ages 25–54)

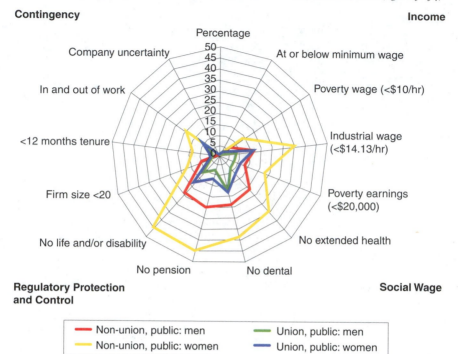

non-unionized workplaces? Figure 14.6 considers the relationship between dimensions of precariousness and union status among workers of colour and white workers. On the four dimensions, non-unionized workers of colour are most precarious, and unionized white workers are least precarious, although there are some indicators where this generalization is not the case. Non-unionized workers of colour experience precariousness in similar measure to non-unionized white workers. There is a significant reduction in precariousness for unionized workers along the social wage dimensions. Unionization benefits both workers of colour and white workers, albeit asymmetrically. Unionized workers of colour are more precarious on the income dimension than unionized white workers, suggesting that the processes and practices in place for winning wage gains for white workers do not benefit workers of colour to the same degree. Interestingly, the variation in precariousness among non-unionized workers of colour and non-unionized white workers is less than the variation among unionized workers of colour and unionized white workers. Although union membership seems to mitigate precariousness, workers of colour experience greater precariousness within unions than white workers do.

Figure 14.6
Precarious wage work, union status, and visible minority status, Canada, 2000 (ages 25–54)

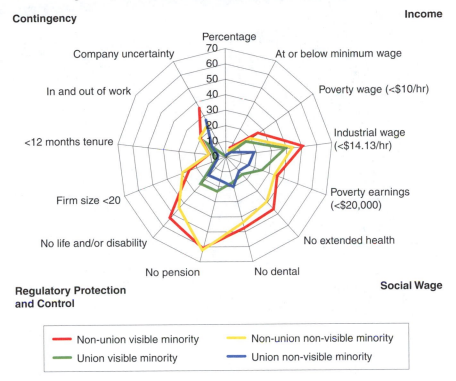

Figure 14.7 compares unionized men and women with attention to race. Women of colour are more precarious on the income dimension than men of colour. Predictably, the least precarious group is white men. Yet there is a large discrepancy between women of colour, with 47 per cent earning less than the industrial wage of $14.13 per hour, and men of colour, with 12 per cent earning less than the industrial wage. With respect to extended health and pensions, both men and women of colour are more precarious than white men and women.

Figure 14.8 examines unionized and non-unionized women, with attention to race. As with the other data, those who are non-unionized are most precarious on the different dimensions. Women of colour and white women who are non-unionized experience similar levels of precariousness. Yet unionized women of colour tend to be more precarious than unionized white women. On the income indicators, unionized women of colour are more precarious than the unionized white women. While non-unionized women are more precarious, the extent of variation among unionized workers on the basis of race is troubling.

Figure 14.7
Precarious wage work by visible minority status and sex, unions only, Canada 2000 (ages 25–54)

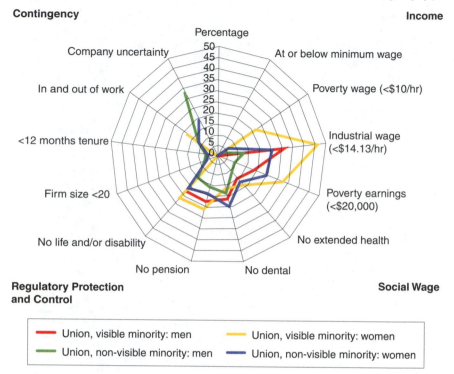

Although unionized workers are generally less precarious than non-unionized workers, the benefits of being unionized are not distributed equally, for they are both racialized and gendered. In terms of income and social wage, being a woman and a visible minority – even within a union – can mean greater precariousness. Consistent with Das Gupta's findings (this volume) about the persistence of racism inside and outside the trade union movement, this difference suggests that unions must make greater efforts to win and sustain gains in income and social wages for women and for people of colour. Additionally, while the public sector is generally thought to be a secure, protected environment, moves towards privatization have meant that public sector work is now stratified, with unionized workers who experience little precariousness alongside non-unionized workers who have lower incomes and fewer social benefits.

CONCLUSION

Unions mitigate precarious employment, and unionized workers are more secure, have higher incomes, and more of a social wage than non-unionized

Figure 14.8
Precarious wage work by union and visible minority status, women only,
Canada, 2000 (ages 25–54)

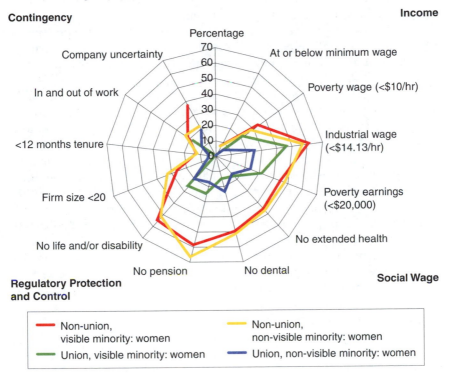

workers. Yet hierarchies exist among unionized workers: even among unionized workers, women and people of colour are more precarious, especially when it comes to income level and social wage benefits.

Additionally, while public sector workers are generally less precarious than private sector workers, (see, for example, Armstrong and Laxer, this volume), there is, with privatization and contracting out, a growing reliance on non-unionized workers in formerly public sector jobs. Privatization has particularly strong gendered implications, since non-unionized women are the most precarious workers in the public sector.

In Canada, no major governmental initiatives (federal, provincial, or municipal) are currently under way to regulate precarious employment or to increase unionization rates among low-income workers. Ontario increased the minimum wage in 2004, but, at $7.15, the rate is still well below the $10.00 per hour level set as a benchmark by many in the trade union movement and in community organizations. This limited progress in improving the situation of workers in precarious employment puts the onus of regulation squarely on the union movement. But resources available to unions in

Canada for overall organizing are limited. In *Innovation and Change in Labour Organizations in Canada*, Kumar and Murray (2003) note that, of the major unions surveyed, only 242 staff were working full-time on organizing and recruitment – and, of this group, only 27 per cent are women. Furthermore, only 45 per cent of the unions surveyed reported the presence of a person with overall responsibility for establishing policy and targets for organizing and recruitment, and only 42 per cent indicated that they have specific organizing or recruitment targets.

While 46 per cent of the unions indicated that organizing in the public service sector is a high or very high priority, private services, newly privatized or reorganized former public services, and goods production sectors were a much lower priority among unions with scarce resources. Organizing in existing areas of membership concentration (59 per cent) and in large units (42 per cent) was much higher than in new areas, where the union had fewer members (24 per cent), and in small units (28 per cent). Of the unions surveyed, 67 per cent agreed that organizing efforts focus primarily on traditional areas of membership strength. Still, as Yates (2001) observes, some unions are attempting to tackle the very sectors in which workers in precarious employment are concentrated, such as service and hospitality. Furthermore, various strategies, such as community unionism and sectoral and general unions, offer potential solutions to these problems (Cranford, Das Gupta, Ladd, and Vosko, this volume).

The fundamental challenge facing unions is to adapt their organizing strategies to deal with the realities of the growing number of workers in precarious employment. Yet it would be short sighted and unworkable, as a solution, to put all the onus for improving working conditions on the ability of unions to organize in these sectors. The examples from the European Union (Jackson, this volume), as well as the "laws flaws" in Canada (Bernstein, Lippel, Tucker, and Vosko, this volume), suggest that genuine progress also demands new regulatory frameworks in which governments, unions, and employers are directly involved. One important step in this direction would be to initiate public discussion on ways to improve regulatory effectiveness in the private sector. In the private sector, several countries in Europe, such as Sweden and Germany, have begun to regulate the temporary work sector with measures that have involved the participation of unions and major unionization initiatives in this sector. Another avenue for improving public policy would entail enlarging ongoing debates about what constitutes the public sector – debates in which unions representing public and quasi-public sector workers should be central.

Beyond these necessary changes at a regulatory level and greater roles for unions, the campaigns in place to improve laws both on the books and in practice at the municipal, provincial, industrial, and firm levels, such as those that are embodied in the current Living Wage movement in the

United States, could offer a powerful means to reach low-wage workers and people currently left outside union coverage and to improve the prospects of unionization. Living Wage campaigns aim to set living wage standards for wages of all employers contracting with a municipality or dealing with a university (Luce 2004). These campaigns, because they involve many different sectors of society, including unions, non-government organizations, municipal governments, and students, can have a positive effect on low-wage workers and on winning victories that, while neither province- nor country-wide, may still be significant for the workers involved (Niedt et al. 1999). As a complement to the notion of community unionism, living wage campaigns may also open the door to future unionization of previously non-organized sectors.

15

Racism/Anti-racism, Precarious Employment, and Unions

TANIA DAS GUPTA

Precarious employment is a highly gendered and racialized phenomenon (this volume, Cranford and Vosko; Vosko and Zukewich). Large numbers of women, immigrants, refugees, and people of colour labour under precarious conditions in Canada (Vosko 2000; Zeytinoglu and Muteshi 2000; Zwarenstein 2002). All workers who belong to unions have better working conditions, including wages, than those who are not unionized (Galabuzi 2001; Jackson 2002). Unfortunately, only 22 per cent of workers of colour[1] were covered by a collective agreement in 1999, while the rate for all other workers was 32 per cent (Jackson 2002,16). This finding is consistent with trends in the 1980s and early 1990s (Leah 1999).

According to Yates (2001, 2002), 63 per cent of all the workplaces in Ontario that unions tried to unionize in the years between 1996 and 1998 had no part-time workers, and 86 per cent had no casual or temporary workers (Ghosh 2003). Yates also found that workers of colour are more willing to join unions compared to the entire population of unorganized workers. Jackson (2002) reports a similar trend, quoting a study by the Canadian Policy Research Networks which concludes that 40 per cent of non-unionized workers of colour wish to join unions, compared with 25 per cent of other workers. Several questions flow from these findings: Why aren't more workers of colour, immigrant workers, and refugee workers unionized? Why aren't unions organizing with more workers in precarious employment? What factors contribute to the low rates of unionization among non-white and immigrant workers, many of whom engage in precarious employment? Jackson (2002) claims that racial segregation in the labour market is such that workers of colour are significantly represented in non-unionized sectors, some of which are low paid and others, high paid. In order for the unionization rate among workers of colour and white workers to converge, he argues, some sectors of unionized employment will have to hire more workers of colour (i.e., implement employment equity) and others will have to be unionized. Jackson predicts, further, that "the relatively low rate for workers of colour, particularly men, is probably more the result of hiring patterns than of conscious union discrimination" (2002, 17).

This chapter contests this assessment regarding racism, arguing that systemic racism in the labour movement is indeed one contributing factor, among many, to the lower unionization rate of workers of colour compared to white workers. It suggests, as Jackson does, that the racism may not be conscious – but racism is not always conscious. Systemic racism refers to standard and apparently neutral policies, procedures, and practices that disadvantage people of colour. Reproduced over time through written policies and laws, these practices become institutionalized. Other factors contributing to the low unionization rate of workers of colour include systemic racism practised by employers, which is demonstrated in racist hiring and promotional practices; fear and intimidation tactics of employers; and legal prohibitions or barriers against the unionization of certain groups of workers, along with anti-union sentiment in the community. The chapter argues further that the efforts of equity-seeking groups within the labour movement, including those of anti-racism activists, contribute to changes that could be more conducive to organizing workers in precarious employment.

In advancing this argument in the first section, the chapter considers the historical labour studies literature, particularly works written from an anti-racist, feminist perspective. In the second and third section it draws on 13 in-depth interviews with union organizers and activists, 10 of whom are people of colour and three of whom are white. These interviews were conducted either in person or over the phone during the summer and fall of 2003. Although each interviewee consented to being identified, some of them have been kept anonymous because of ethical considerations. Most of these interviews were a follow-up to another set of interviews, conducted in 1995 for another study (Das Gupta 1998). In those previous interviews, the names of interviewees were generated by a "snowball" method, where key informants recommended colleagues to interview. The rest were identified from conferences and workshops where union members deliberated on related issues.[2]

PRECARIOUS EMPLOYMENT, PRECARIOUSNESS AMONG WORKERS OF COLOUR

For most workers of colour, immigrant and refugee workers, precarious employment is not a new or an unusual phenomenon. In fact, before World War II, most people of colour in Canada held precarious jobs, since only a minority were entrepreneurs and professionals (Das Gupta 2000). This concentration reflected contemporary labour market requirements, which focused on land clearing, railway building, and farming.

Because of systemic discrimination and exclusion from professional sectors, people of colour were, historically, allocated to jobs that were the least desirable – jobs with low pay, insecurity, and gross exploitation. People of African heritage were brought over as slaves or entered Canada as refugees from slavery and war in the United States; they also held precarious jobs in the service and agricultural sectors. Workers of First Nations backgrounds were marginalized, disenfranchised, and relegated to precarious employment as well (Muszynski 1996).

For Aboriginal peoples, people of colour, and immigrant workers, the precarious labour market conditions in which they worked were an extension of their precarious condition in society at large, where they were socially constructed as dependents, as non-citizens and as non-workers, those deemed to be "others" in relation to employed white male citizens. Their otherness was marked by the colour of their skin, their "strange" customs and languages, their immigration status, and their lack of citizenship rights. While white women were also considered inferior under white patriarchy, they were valued as "mothers of the nation," as vehicles of reproduction of white Canada (Dua and Robertson 1999). Women of colour, in contrast, with their capacity to reproduce non-white citizens, were viewed as threats to the whiteness of the nation. They were, therefore, until the post-war period, either excluded or restricted from entering Canada (Das Gupta 2000), other than in small numbers in domestic work (Calliste 1991) – a highly precarious occupation characterized by a lack of citizenship status. Apart from domestic work, the few women of colour who entered the country worked under precarious conditions either as unpaid family workers in fishing, laundries, and restaurants or as waged workers in the fishing or garment industries. Before 1985, status Aboriginal women lost their status when they married anyone who did not have status – including non-status Aboriginal men. This policy was not only sexist but designed to assimilate Aboriginal members into white patriarchal values. Many Aboriginal women and men were forced to find jobs in non-Aboriginal enterprises because of the destruction of indigenous economies and ways of living, and they worked in deplorable conditions. The precariousness of immigrants, people of colour, and Aboriginal workers, including women, in the labour market was produced by their precarious citizenship status in Canada – and that lack of citizenship was due, in turn, to their racialization, their gender, their immigration status, to all the legal and social locations they occupied.

This precarious status was maintained by well-thought-out racist and sexist ideologies that characterized these groups as subhuman and unfit to be members of the nation. And these ideologies were institutionalized in both laws and policies. People of colour were said to be so inferior that they were biologically and culturally capable of working under subhuman working conditions, at super-exploitative wages (Creese 1992; Muszynski 1984; Ward 1978), thereby threatening the wages and working conditions of white male workers of the nation. They were viewed as threats to the nation by their otherness and as threats to the organized working class by their racialized capacity and supposed "willingness" to work at wages below those paid to white workers. Creese (1992) documents that white unionists considered Asians to be "unorganizable," leading unions to adopt a strategy of exclusionism (Das Gupta 1998; Leah 1999; White 1990). In so doing, they contributed actively to precarious employment among workers of colour as well as to their social precariousness. They spearheaded such groups as the Anti-Chinese Union, the Asiatic Exclusion League, and the White Canada Association. In addition to lobbying white politicians to restrict the entry of non-white workers to Canada, they also instigated popular hostility and violence against them (Das Gupta 1998).

By excluding workers of colour and, in some cases, reaching collective agreements that instituted labour standards differentiated by race, white unions took part in reproducing a racially segregated labour market. Creese (1992) writes that unions representing white tailors, garment workers, laundry workers, and restaurant workers were the most vociferous against Chinese and other Asian workers, who were paid much less because of employer racism and the lack of union protection. Instead of including Asian workers in existing unions in order to eliminate the wage competition, these unions took an exclusionary stance. The Hotel and Restaurant Employees Union, for instance, remained exclusionary until 1938, when a Chinese organizer was hired for one month.

Only a few radical, leftist unions were inclusive of workers of colour, including the One Big Union (OBU) and the Workers' Unity League, which actively recruited Chinese workers and opened leadership positions for them (Creese 1991). Unfortunately, these unions were short lived. Some research indicates that not all communist-inspired unions were egalitarian. For instance, Frager (1992) points to sexism in the Toronto cloak makers union in the interwar years, while Muszynski's (1996) research into fishing unions in British Columbia shows racist and sexist preferences in organizing practices and differential wage rates. She writes that, in 1968, an experienced female general fish worker received 9.3 per cent less than an inexperienced male fish worker, and 24.5 per cent less than an experienced male fish worker (8). Women fish workers were initially Aboriginal and later included Japanese and other non-English-speaking immigrant women.

Workers of colour did not acquiesce to this reality despite popular stereotypes of their passivity and lack of interest in organizing. They formed organizations of their own, including unions, relying on their ethnic, racial, and kin networks (Creese 1991; Ward 1978). Chinese workers struck for higher wages, shorter working hours, and licensing rights and against discrimination and the contracting system. The Amalgamated Association of Japanese Fishermen contested the government's proposal to reduce Japanese fishing licences, over time eliminating them altogether (Das Gupta 1998; Ward 1978). The Native Brotherhood of British Columbia negotiated the first agreement with canners on behalf of Aboriginal fish workers (Muszynski 1996). Many of these organizations exerted pressure on the labour movement, on government, and on other institutions to remove the racial bar against workers of colour. These groups were simultaneously fighting for labour rights as well as for social justice, specifically against racism and exclusion.

According to Ward (1978), racism in the labour movement began to be less overt around the 1920s. The movement began to dissociate itself from the rabid white supremacist organizations of previous decades. In its 1931 convention, the Trades and Labour Congress dropped its racially exclusionary position and called for extending voting rights to all Canadian-born people, including people of colour. The Cooperative Commonwealth Federation (CCF), also formed around this time, pushed for greater inclusion of Asian Canadians. The Jewish Labour Committee (JLC), founded in 1935, as well as the National Unity Association formed in 1943 by Black residents in Dresden, Ontario, and civil liberties associations, some unions, and women's and ethnic associations, were predominantly responsible for bringing pressure to bear on the labour movement as well as on the Ontario government of the time (Lukas and Persad 2004; Hill 1977).

In the 1930s, groups such as the Jewish Labour Committee pushed the Canadian Labour Congress to bring in human rights legislation. The National Committee on Human Rights was formed within the Canadian Labour Congress. Trade union committees for human rights were set up in Winnipeg, Toronto, Montreal, and Vancouver, and these committees worked against discrimination outside the scope of collective bargaining. They investigated and documented cases of discrimination in employment, housing, and services (Das Gupta 1998; Hill 1977) and conducted public educational programs. In addition, they organized for the enactment of human rights legislation provincially and federally. They supported those who suffered from discrimination in their jobs and in the community at large and negotiated anti-discrimination clauses in collective agreements.

Included, but Not Equal

Feminist labour studies scholars and labour activists have illustrated the continuing gender segregation and discrimination faced by women workers, even those who are unionized. In fact, they have demonstrated how union policies and practices perpetuated such divisions in some cases (Briskin and McDermott 1993; Forrest 1993; Frager 1992; Sugiman 1993). Parallels can be seen for workers of colour.

Although formal equality reigned in trade unions in the 1930s and 1940s, racism continued. Even in the years of supposed equality and access to unions, Muszynski (1984, 91) reports that one of the organizers of the Hotel and Restaurant Employees Union practised selective recruitment where white waiters and busboys were organized, to the neglect of waitresses and Chinese men working as kitchen help. The union signed agreements without any protection for Chinese and Japanese workers.

In 1940 the United Fishermen's Federal Union approached the BC government to force companies to hire white herring packers rather than Japanese packers. When the government refused, white women packers at one cannery walked off their jobs in protest. After fishers and cannery workers were unionized by the United Fishermen and Allied Workers' Union, Chinese workers were covered for the first time in 1947, when the union signed a supplement to the master agreement. In 1949 Chinese workers were included under the Male Cannery Workers' Supplement. Of the four groups in the supplement, Chinese workers were included in group IV (sundry workers) and were paid a maximum of $183 a month, while group I (machine workers) and II (boiler house) workers were paid to a maximum of $245 a month (Muszynski 1984, 99). Even so, by 1949, very few Chinese workers remained in fishing because many companies had stopped hiring them.

In the railways, Black males were segregated in portering (Calliste 1987). They were also paid lower wages compared to white porters. Black porters could not join porters' unions. Countering racist exclusion by the Canadian Brotherhood of Railway Employees (CBRE) until 1919, Black porters employed on the Canadian National Railways formed the Order of Sleeping Car Porters (Calliste 1987). As a result of pressure by the order on the CBRE for racial integration, the brotherhood incorporated the order as an auxiliary. Moreover, the CBRE created two separate units, where unit I was made up of higher-paid white conductors, inspectors, and stewards, while unit II was made up of lower-paid Black porters and cooks. Promotions could happen only within the same unit. This racial segregation lasted till 1964. Thus, the union reproduced practices of racial segregation adopted by employers.

Supported by the Toronto Labour Committee for Human Rights and the *Fair Employment Practices Act* of 1953, Black porters within various unions, such as the Brotherhood of Sleeping Car Porters and the Canadian Brotherhood of Railway Transport and General Workers, won promotional rights. Initially, however, they lost their seniority if they were promoted, though this practice was overturned after it was challenged by a local as racism. According to Calliste (1987), the Order of Railway Conductors resisted opening its organization to Black members, and the other related unions mentioned above never took responsibility for their own racism. Promotional and seniority rights of Black porters were won through legal challenges and supported by human rights committees and community organizations.

Industries with significant numbers of immigrant women and women of colour witnessed structural inequalities based on gender and/or race. Frager (1992), writing on the garment industry between 1900 and 1939, observes that Toronto's Jewish unions failed to include predominantly Jewish female workers and that the Canadian feminist movement failed to support them too. There were very few women in leadership positions, since the union did not provide any support for women who had childcare responsibilities. In 1933 the average woman cloak maker earned 44 per cent of what a man earned in the same trade (121). This practice was perpetuated largely because of women's confinement to jobs that were predominantly performed by women workers.

Winnie Ng (1995, 35), the first organizer of Chinese heritage hired by the International Ladies Garment Workers' Union (ILGWU) in 1977, commented on the continuing sexism and racism in the industry as well as in the union at that time:

In a union that represented a membership made up of over 85% immigrant women, the ILGWU, at that time, operated very much like an old boys' network. All the executive members were white men of European backgrounds within the Cutters and Pressers' Locals. In the union office, aside from the clerical staff, all the staff representatives and business agents were men. Servicing the membership was done in a patriarchal and patronizing manner such as "I'm going to take care of the girls" or "these poor girls, they don't speak the language ..." The union as a workplace was no different from a garment factory in upholding the pattern of occupational segregation on the basis of gender and race.

In 1979 Ng resigned from the union. She said it operated as a business union, making deals with the manufacturers and thwarting any challenges to their style of operation.

PRECARIOUS EMPLOYMENT
AMONG WORKERS OF COLOUR AFTER 1967

Although not all people of colour immigrating to Canada under the Points System introduced in the *Immigration Act* in 1967 engaged in precarious employment, a significant proportion of immigrants and non-whites, including women, were compelled to take up precarious jobs, even though many arrived with university degrees and professional qualifications. Their middle-class characteristics in terms of education level, languages spoken, and professional experiences should have resulted in secure employment. However, systemic discrimination in the forms of devaluation of previous education and professional experiences, demand for "Canadian experience," and lack of access to language and professional training streamed them into precarious employment. This trend continues in 2004 (this volume, Cranford, Das Gupta, Ladd, and Vosko; de Wolff).

A number of studies document racism in the Canadian labour market. Using 1999 data from the Survey of Labour and Income Dynamics, Jackson (2002) reports that people of colour[3] earned $19,895 in 1999, while all other workers earned $23,764, a difference of 16.3 per cent. On the basis of Census data from 1996, Galabuzi (2001) notes that individuals of colour had poverty rates of 35.6 per cent, compared to a general poverty rate of 17.6 per cent, and argues that economic apartheid exists in Canada.

Another study of the City of Toronto by Ornstein (2000), based on the 1996 Canadian Census, concludes that non-European groups suffered a family poverty rate of 34.3 per cent, one more than double that for Europeans and self-identified Canadians. Income disparities and high poverty levels reflect other factors such as higher unemployment rates and the segregation of workers of colour in low-end jobs in processing and manufacturing, sales and service, and industries such as clothing and textiles. Many of these sectors often have high concentrations of women of colour (Cranford and Vosko, this volume). High unemployment rates, overrepresentation in low-end jobs and industries, and underrepresentation in high-end jobs and industries occur through systemically racist hiring and promotional processes as well as through the devaluation of foreign education and professional experience. Henry and Ginzberg (1984) and Das Gupta (1996) demonstrate that racism in the form of exclusion or segregation in workplaces can result from such systemic practices as word-of-mouth hiring, differential treatment at the screening or pre-screening stages, biased interview processes, and the use of vague and subjective criteria in hiring, performance appraisals, and promotions. These policies, procedures, and practices amount to systemic racism as they disproportionately disadvantage people of colour. This issue is not restricted to immigrants (Pendakur and Pendakur 1995) but applies also to non-white, Canadian-born citizens.

Although racism is much more systemic and subtle in 2004 than it was in the past, it is very much present in the labour market. Precarious employment is still highly prevalent among non-whites, including non-white women. Many of these women are new immigrants or refugees, desperately trying to attain the "Canadian experience" that is demanded of them. Often their only recourse is to take up a job with a temporary agency, sell products and services door to door on commission, work as security guards, or drive a taxi – jobs that are synonymous with non-white workers and that often entail false self-employment or independent work (this volume, Bernstein; Vosko and

Zukewich). Many, lacking an adequate level of spoken English and denied the opportunity to learn the language, are left with no option but to work in factories, warehouses, farms, or in their own homes as homeworkers. Others, even more marginalized, enter Canada in semi-indentured conditions to work as live-in caregivers or as farm workers (Zwarenstein 2002). These sectors are usually non-unionized. Only the fortunate few are lucky enough to get a unionized job, with acceptable working conditions and benefits.

MOVING BEYOND INCLUSION

The days of the overt exclusion of workers of colour, Aboriginal workers, and immigrant workers by labour unions no longer exist, given the anti-racist efforts of these communities, a process documented by a number of authors including Calliste (1987), Das Gupta (1998), and Leah (1999). However, a focal question of anti-racist activism in the post-1980s relates to the nature of involvement of those workers of colour fortunate enough to be union members. Despite the move towards greater inclusion, the continued marginalization of many workers of colour within unions remains a pressing issue.

One key indicator of the marginalization of workers of colour is the predominantly white leadership in the movement, despite the number of dynamic non-white activists in local areas. This imbalance is reproduced systemically through old-boys' networks that are predominantly white. White women began organizing in the post-war period, particularly in the 1960s and 1970s (Briskin and McDermott 1993; Ng 1995; White 1990), against blatant sexism in the movement. However, Ng (1995, 38) writes that feminist activism within the labour movement did not incorporate the issues of immigrant women and of women of colour: "'women' meant white women only." Although white women were getting organized into committees within the labour movement and were able to push for staff positions dealing with women's issues, workers of colour remained marginalized. As Ng (1995, 38) states, racism remained a "taboo topic." This bifurcation in labour politics is reflected in labour studies scholarship. Leah (1999) writes that there are few integrated studies of the organizing experiences of women workers of colour. Studies of workers of colour generally exclude the experiences of women, while feminist studies on labour organizing neglect questions of race and racialization.

The role of women of colour within the labour movement has been, historically, to create the connections between anti-racism and anti-sexism as they embody this unity in their everyday lives. They experience both sexism and racism, in addition to exploitation as workers (Leah 1999). In making this connection, women of colour within the movement have had to confront racism from many white women. Some talk about not being supported in their

anti-racist activities because it is not seen as a priority, or of not being supported in their leadership aspirations (Das Gupta 1998; Leah 1999). Nevertheless, a number of statements, policies, and conferences organized by both
national and provincial trade union bodies attest to progress in developing
links between feminist and anti-racist efforts within the labour movement
(Leah 1993; Leah 1999). One of the most concrete indications was the collaborative work done by women and human rights committees within the
labour movement for employment equity in the 1990s in Ontario, a collaboration discussed below in relation to coalition building with communities
outside unions. Another convergence occurred in the Women's Work Project
(Canadian Labour Congress 1998), which generated a report, written by
Winnie Ng, on the effects of restructuring on women's work. The report outlined an approach and generated recommendations for organizing more
women, women of colour, and immigrants who were precarious workers.

Affirmative action and equitable representation within union structures
are major points of organizing among anti-racism activists. Anti-racism activists within the movement argue that equity policies can be better interpreted and applied if union staff and elected representatives at various
levels reflect the membership.

Representation for What?

Equitable representation in union leadership is not an end in itself. Still, it
indicates a recognition of racism and provides a means to challenge the historical marginalization of workers of colour and to change the basic structure and practices of unions. As Briskin and McDermott (1993, 95) note in
discussing "separate" organizing by feminist unionists, the aim is "unions
changing" rather than "individual women changing." They further argue
that separate organizing by women has changed organizing practices and
educational programs, brought in more social unionism, and enabled coalition building with groups outside the labour movement. At the level of
strategy, separate organizing by workers of colour has similar objectives.
Kike Roach (Rebick and Roach 1996, 113) says it most succinctly in characterizing anti-racist organizing within the National Action Committee on
the Status of Women (NAC): "We shouldn't think that becoming an anti-
racist organization just means having more women of colour members and
executive. It has to be about the anti-racist perspective, the analysis, the alliances created and the ongoing campaigns NAC develops and carries
forth ... Many are happy to 'include' but ignore, so our inclusion alone can
be superficial unless our presence makes a difference."

Anti-racism includes a reformulation of the hiring and servicing priorities
of unions. According to June Veecock, human rights and anti-racism coordinator of the Ontario Federation of Labour (OFL): "Those in leadership

need to understand that their unions need to reflect the membership ... Unions will do a better job if stewards were doing a better job. They [white stewards] don't understand how systemic racism works. They say there is no racism. They don't recognize racial segregation."[4] Veecock is contacted by workers of colour because they feel more comfortable with her than with their own shop stewards or staff members. More diverse representation would enable more effective service and support for members of colour and immigrant workers. More diverse staffing in unions would also influence organizing priorities. Bev Johnson of the Ontario Public Service Employees Union (OPSEU) observes that anti-racism and affirmative action have implications for union organizing: "Either pay attention or die ... How are you going to organize workers who are predominantly people of colour when you don't have any organizers who are people of colour? How are you going to service members effectively when they don't see themselves reflected in the union staff?"[5]

Hiring organizers of colour is crucial for organizing workers of colour in precarious employment, according to union organizers who have successfully reached them. Michael Cifuentes of the Hotel Employees and Restaurant Employees (HERE), whose members are largely immigrant women workers of colour, says: "The community workers are leaders. They are insiders. We explain to them the meaning of a union. What does a union stand for? The first meeting will be with them. These leaders are very important. These leaders have respect in the community."[6] Bryan Neath from the United Food and Commercial Workers Union (UFCWU), which has organized farm workers, had this to say about the representation of organizers: "For example, in the mushroom plant the main groups were Cambodian, Sudanese and Canadians ... If you want to be successful in organizing you need to find a leader in each community so they can communicate with the larger working community. If you don't find these leaders, you can forget it."[7] Some unions are starting to hire men and women of diverse racial and ethnic backgrounds to recruit members from those same communities. For instance, Neath notes: "We introduced something called SPUR (special project union representatives). This reflected the need to make the right contacts with [the] community. If we were organizing part-time workers, then we could get part-time workers who are unionized to go out and meet with them ... If the workers were workers of colour, we need workers of colour organizing ... If they are women, then we need women organizing."[8] The program trains selected workers as organizers. They are then involved in organizing drives in workplaces similar to theirs. They are paid their regular wages and they return back to their own workplaces once the organizing is over (CLC 1998).

Although SPUR is a highly successful program that has resulted in dramatic increases in membership in the UFCWU, including the precarious sectors, not all such programs function so effectively. Some concerns remain generally with contracting temporary organizers of colour. Some of them are contracted or "borrowed" for limited periods of time to sign up new members. Once that is done, their contracts are over. Although they may have been members of organizing committees, they were not treated like full-time organizers. When the organizers left, the new members, many of whom speak minimal or no English, had no one to connect with in the union. Community groups with workers who speak different languages get called by workers of colour unable to get through to their unions. Opportunistic methods of organizing often end up in failures, as workers have been known to decertify under such conditions or to end up with bad agreements. For example, after an intensive organizing drive of predominantly non-English-speaking contract workers of colour, a union signed a "bad deal," according to an organizer of colour, one in which she did not have any input. Similarly, a local of another union, composed predominantly of workers of colour, wanted to decertify because the union had no staff members who could represent them and it provided no translation services.[9] This point is captured by Hasan Yussuff of the CLC, who says that we need to consider "how we do organizing that is not just about bringing in a new membership dues base but integrates workers of colour fundamentally at every level" (CLC 1998, 28).

Anti-racism activists in the labour movement feel that more workers of colour in staff and elected positions will initiate changes in organized labour's priorities, practices, and policies. More emphasis will be given to the needs and issues of workers located in the most precarious forms of employment in society – immigrants, refugees, and workers of colour in unorganized sectors or in workplaces poorly serviced by unions. Greater effort will be put into working in coalitions with community groups, many of which are in touch with unorganized workers of colour in precarious employment, whether self-help organizations, ethnic networks, support groups in neighbourhoods, or worker centres. Trade unionists of colour self-organized within the labour movement, such as the Ontario Coalition of Black Trade Unionists in 1986, the Coalition of Black Trade Unionists (Ontario Chapter) in 1996, and the Asian Canadian Labour Alliance in 2000, have links with communities outside the labour movement. The Asian Canadian Labour Alliance, for instance, has a two-pronged strategy of bringing labour leaders and rank-and-file members of Asian heritage together, as well as bringing Asian activists together to create a union-friendly culture overall. The Coalition of Black Trade Unionists has been active on the campaign against racial profiling in the Black community. Bev Johnson, ex-president of the union, wants to reach out particularly to Black youth, to bring them into the labour movement as future leaders. She articulates a concern shared by a number of people interviewed about the younger generation of labour leaders being largely white.

Marie Clarke Walker, executive vice-president of the Canadian Labour Congress, says that she spent a year trying to connect her union with community issues when she was elected onto the Canadian Union of Public Employees (CUPE) executive committee in Ontario in 1999: "Members belong to communities before they belong to unions ... People don't just see you as a dues grabbing institution. They see you as genuinely concerned."[10]

A brief but important period of coalition-based organizing among various segments of the labour movement and community organizations occurred around the issue of employment equity in the early part of the 1990s in Ontario. The Ontario Federation of Labour and affiliated unions became integrally involved in drafting Bill 79, the precursor to the *Employment Equity Act*, which the New Democratic Party (NDP) would steer forward into law in 1994. The provincial labour movement and its equity activists were at the forefront of this development along with community organizations of women, people of colour, people with disabilities, and Aboriginal peoples. Union activists spent hundreds of hours on equity issues, and grassroots community activists facilitated workshops, prepared brochures, and informed people about the concept, fostering the environment for the successful adoption of legislation (Das Gupta 1998). The movement was pushed into taking this position by activists from outside and from within. Sadly, with the defeat of the Ontario NDP government in 1995, the *Employment Equity Act*, even the watered-down version that was passed, and all its infrastructure were scrapped overnight.

Another example of a community-labour coalition was the Coalition for Fair Wages and Working Conditions for Homeworkers, initiated by the International Ladies Garment Workers' Union (now Union of Needletrades, Industrial and Textile Employees, or UNITE) in 1991, which engaged in various public activities to voice the concerns of this very precarious group of workers (Borowy, Gordon, and Lebans 1993). Made up of labour, women's, immigrant, and church communities, the coalition focused on public education through press conferences and a large conference on homework. It put pressure on retail firms to improve the wages and working conditions of homeworkers, and it pressured the government for stronger legislative protection of homeworkers and for sectoral bargaining. In addition, the coalition spearheaded a campaign to raise the awareness of consumers about the exploitation of homeworkers for the production of garments and to develop a consumer campaign, called the "Clean Clothes Campaign," for fair wages and working conditions for homeworkers.

Changing Structures

The labour movement has made significant progress in addressing racism. In the words of the CLC's Yussuff: "The labour movement is dealing with equity.

It is in the mainstream. There is a recognition that it [racism] is a problem and that resources must be allocated to deal with it. Twenty years ago it may have been dismissed ... People of colour have tremendous opportunity to be confident in shaping the direction of the labour movement."[11]

While it is true that workers of colour are much better represented today (CLC 1997, 98; CLC 2002) than they were 20 years back, there are still lingering problems and resistance to equity in some quarters. Some of the interviewees, particularly women of colour activists, spoke about problems of co-optation, tokenism, harassment of women of colour, and their silencing.[12] Groups like the Coalition of Black Trade Unionists and the Asian Canadian Labour Alliance are still viewed by some as community groups because they are outside the labour structure and do not always agree with the labour movement. One member said that there is still a strong sense of control over caucuses through "report back" processes. There is still a fear among some people that community groups threaten the labour movement. These reactions all indicate resistance against anti-racism and change, as well as a lack of openness and democracy.

Anti-racism activists would like to see structural changes (CLC, 1997, 6) in the way in which the labour movement works, including how decisions are made and how meetings are conducted. The supposedly democratic structures are, in reality, often exclusionary. Marie Clarke Walker[13] told how a resolution to bring in two designated seats on the executive of CUPE, one for workers of colour and the other for Aboriginal workers, was defeated because it was brought in at the end of the day, when the audience had dwindled and no one was there to debate it. June Veecock of the Ontario Federation of Labour noted that leadership "education is good, but it does nothing to change the structure ... There are systemic barriers that need to be removed. They [people of colour] feel uncomfortable with those structures ... the onus is on people of colour to go back and make changes in structures."[14] Carol Wall, a former human rights director with the Communications, Energy and Paperworkers Union of Canada (CEP), observed that "structures don't help around equity and human rights issues. The democratic structures are used to silence."[15] A turning point in anti-racism within the Canadian Labour Congress occurred in Montreal during the 1990 convention. Dory Smith, a Black male member, ran against the white slate and received over a thousand votes. As one activist said, it "made the white boys sit up and take note." A resolution was passed to review the constitution and recommend changes to it. In the 1992 convention, a recommendation was brought forth to create a position on the executive committee for a member of colour. Many felt that this recommendation was tokenism. The Ontario Coalition of Black Trade Unionists and other anti-racist activists organized and achieved, instead, the designation of two seats. But structural change threatens many old-timers who want to maintain the status quo.

Exclusion – New Style

Just as union structures have sometimes resulted in the marginalization and silencing of unionists of colour, traditional methods of organizing exclude workers in precarious employment today. Most unions still function on the model of a traditional workplace and a standard worker who works 9 to 5 and is white, male, and English-speaking. Although these received practices and frameworks have been modified, to a certain extent, by the intervention of women and by non-whites, they need to be challenged even more. In order to organize workers in precarious employment, the assumptions that are taken for granted in the organizing process need to be examined and changed if necessary, and more creative strategies need to be incorporated. Ideas around organizing precarious workers have been greatly influenced by the writings of Kate Bronfenbrenner, director of Labour Education Research at Cornell University (CLC 1998). In 1995 she spoke at a conference on community unionism organized by the Ontario Federation of Labour. The following discussion is a reflection of some of her insights.

In order to include workers in precarious employment within the labour movement, organizing has to be seen as a longer-term project, not something that can be accomplished by speedy weekend campaigns or "blitzes" followed by worker sign-ups. The outreach process has to be more innovative, often requiring labour-intensive methods of contacting workers and then of building trust, a sense of community, and indigenous leadership through training and education programs. The current approaches do not allow that process in most unions. Longer, labour-intensive organizing campaigns require more resources – resources that are not always forthcoming. One success story is the organizing drive at Purdy's Chocolates (Ghosh 2003) in Vancouver, a campaign that included a minority of white, mainly full-time, workers and part-time workers who were originally from China, the Philippines, Vietnam, and Latin America. That campaign took six years to conclude under the Communications, Energy and Paperworkers Union of Canada (CEP). This long, costly campaign included two certification drives because the employer contested the first one. Cifuentes of the Hotel Employees and Restaurant Employees explains the process of organizing in one particular workplace:

There are four different ethnic groups. Now they are phoning and saying ... "Well, I signed the card, can I take the card back ... it is taking too long." We have to tell them that it sometimes happens like this, it takes some time. Each vote counts, so we have to make it clear, when the company hears of the organizing, they will work on the employee one by one, trying to convince him/her not to join. When there is someone who we identify that is not solid, then we make home visits. We need to resolve the confidence of the worker. Sometimes they think what they are doing is illegal. We have to explain everything ... the meaning of the union ... we have to explain everything ... [16]

All organizers interviewed about organizing workers in precarious employment spoke about the intensive and sometimes lengthy nature of the organizing process, particularly given the high level of employer intimidation tactics with immigrant workers and workers of colour and the stringent requirements for union certification under the former Progressive Conservative government in Ontario. These insights are substantiated by experiences in other successful organizing drives with precarious workers that have been documented by the CLC (1998). Those unions that are unable, for whatever reason, to allocate significant resources to organizing "stake out familiar territory," according to Galabuzi (Ghosh 2003), where it is easier to organize, mobilize, and develop leadership. Workers in this territory are also often better-paid standard workers and, consequently, their dues paying is more regular and reliable.

One informant[17] provided an even more critical perspective of this approach. Her union would take on organizing drives based on what, in effect, were ethnic and racial stereotypes. They assumed that workers of colour were more prone to unionizing if they came from a situation of collective struggle. In this mindset, Latin Americans, Filipinos, and Sri Lankans would unionize much faster than Chinese, for instance. The union would then prioritize its organizing strategy based on such assumptions. This approach is not only tantamount to racialized thinking but also opportunist. It promotes competition among organizers working within different communities, emanating from the "How many members have you signed up today?" mentality. It promotes organizing as piecework rather than a long-term process of building on a union base in a workplace or a community (this volume, Cranford, Das Gupta, and Vosko). This organizer, who challenged the mode of operation within her union by laying down different principles, was isolated and marginalized. By this logic, some workers of colour are still being excluded, although more systemically. It appears that certain groups are still being labelled by some unions as "unorganizable."

CONCLUSION

Systemic racism persists in the labour movement, although the movement has come a long way from the blatant exclusionism practised in the early 20th century. Racism today is characterized by authors as a "new" or "democratic" variety of racism (Henry et al. 2000) that employs non-racial discourses to "otherize" immigrants and people of colour. These discourses allow the co-existence of progressive policies and laws with racist practices and effects. Such discourses include "denial of racism," "blaming the victim," or "pathologizing the victim." While unions have been in the forefront of advocating for equity and combating racism, sexism, and various other discriminatory practices in the larger society, they have been slower in acknowledging racism within their own organizations. This trend is exemplified by the persistence of old structures, procedures, and practices that prevent unionists of colour from becoming central actors in the movement, despite the emergence of strong equity policies. At the same time, old union practices around organizing keep many workers in precarious employment out. Anti-racist union activists want a labour movement that moves issues confronting workers of colour to the centre of the agenda, including challenging racism and sexism in the workplace and in society at large, mitigating precarious working conditions, and facilitating greater access to the labour movement so more scope exists for their participation and leadership. The structural changes and union democracy desired by equity-seeking groups within the labour movement are the same changes that workers in precarious employment require to participate fully in the movement.

Union Renewal and Precarious Employment: A Case Study of Hotel Workers

CHRIS SCHENK

This chapter outlines the road to union renewal travelled by a group of hotel workers confronted with the threat of precarious employment and with challenges to their efforts to organize.[1] It is an ongoing story: an account of workers who, in the face of tremendous job-based difficulties, began first to organize themselves and then to unionize. As significant as these initial steps towards independent organizing were, they represented only the beginning of a series of efforts to bring about change. After the citywide local overcame its internal crisis and consolidated workers' most basic job-based rights, the hotel workers gained a new sense of purpose, greater solidarity, and the strength to confront the employer over outstanding grievances.

Following the introduction of a few core concepts in the first section, this chapter proceeds, in the second section, to outline key developments in the local union in both a historical and an international context. The third section then describes the situation of workers at the Journey Hotel, membership mobilization, and collective bargaining in Local 75 as a whole, as well as the five-month-long rank-and-file mobilization and strike in 2002. These activities resulted in a revitalized bargaining unit with a new collective agreement, in which virtually all attempts the workers had made to mitigate precarious employment – including increasing wage levels, introducing a benefit package, and reducing workload – were won.

Yet, just when the long struggle of these hotel workers had ended and the contractual improvements should have ushered in a period of improved labour relations and job security, new challenges surfaced. In addition to the usual cycle of economic recession and recovery that affects tourism, the Toronto hotel industry found itself faced with a new and little-known viral infection called SARS, the acronym for Severe Acute Respiratory Syndrome. The presence of the virus in this city resulted in a dramatic downturn in tourists and, therefore, hotel guests. Using this steep drop in the hotel occupancy rate as an example, the fourth section describes how even unionized, full-time employees, successful in securing contractual gains in wages, benefits, and working conditions, are vulnerable to precarious employment, partly because of their occupational context and income level, and especially in the face of unpredictable events.

CORE CONCEPTS: UNION RENEWAL AND PRECARIOUS EMPLOYMENT

Two distinct concepts frame this chapter: union renewal and the related notion of social unionism and precarious employment. The hotel workers in this case study participated in rallies and pickets for months in order to gain significant improvements in their terms and conditions of employment. Yet their high level of militancy was insufficient both to protect them from layoff in the ensuing crisis confronting the industry and to fight off an employer strategy focused on precarious employment.

The notion of union renewal relates to union revitalization on several dimensions: a growth in union members and the consequent rise in union density (Rose and Chaison 2001, 34); and, at the same time, changes in the internal life of unions in a way that makes them more participatory, inclusive, and democratic. This second aspect of union change is also characterized as "social unionism." Social unionism involves deliberate attempts to move beyond the "service model / organizing model" dichotomy, where the former focuses exclusively on bread-and-butter issues and uses top-down structures; while the latter goes beyond collective bargaining concerns to emphasize membership involvement, collective action, and organizing, yet is quite properly criticized for its failure to engage fully with internal issues of democratic renewal and alternative vision (Kumar and Murray 2003; Russo and Banks 1996; Schenk 2003).

Social unionism, according to Kim Moody (1997, 4), asserts the centrality of union democracy as "a source of power and broader social visions," and outreach as "a means of enhancing that power." Eisenscher (1999, 218) deepens Moody's claim by linking the issue of democracy to membership involvement, noting that activism and empowerment must be wed if unions are to be transformed and labour rejuvenated. The more that members have a say in their union, the more vital the union, the greater members' involvement in decision-making, and the higher the potential for a membership educated in the issues of the workplace and society at large.

This case study is concerned with issues of union renewal as they relate to increased internal democracy, rank-and-file activism, and membership participation in decision-making. New union structures that support or inhibit membership participation are therefore critical. But so, too, is a societal vision that extends beyond a particular worksite in promoting a worker-centred way of seeing the world.

Yet even where union renewal is strong, and struggles for workplace improvements result in substantive victories for both union members and society at large, there is no guarantee of employment stability. The nature of capitalist societies, with their recessions and recoveries, unexpected crises, the particularities of certain industries, and the existence of social and legal protections or the lack thereof, even in the presence of a collective agreement, make layoffs and slowdowns a fact of work life. Like many other workers in Canada, hotel workers have, since the early 1980s, increasingly confronted precarious employment.

In this volume, the notion of precarious employment is conceptualized by Vosko and developed statistically by Cranford and Vosko and by Vosko and Zukewich for, respectively, wage workers and the self-employed. The threat and experience of precarious employment among wage workers are the principal focus here. Yet several facets of this case study of hotel workers are unique. Anderson, Beaton, and Laxer provide evidence of the way union coverage mitigates key dimensions of precarious employment among wage workers. Yet, following Cranford and Vosko, they also observe that precarious employment is more common in certain industrial contexts than others, including in accommodation and food. The experiences of the hotel workers interviewed for this study bear out these complex findings – and they reveal, further, how even hotel workers securing full-time permanent work are vulnerable to certain dimensions of precarious employment, especially low wages and contingency.

BACKGROUND:
THE LOCAL UNION IN HISTORICAL
AND INTERNATIONAL CONTEXT

In the 1990s the citywide Local 75 of the Hotel Employees, Restaurant Employees Union (HERE), and its constituent bargaining units, developed a new vision, new layers of activists, and a new leadership. Yet the union itself is not a new organization. Its history dates to 1886, when bartenders, waiters, and catering trades people formed a local in Chicago (Tedesco 1977, 146). With the spread of more locals, a national union, known as the Waiters and Bartenders National Union, formed in 1891. As other workplaces unionized across the continent, they joined this early organization, which at first accepted "unskilled" workers only reluctantly. Space does not permit a lengthy history here, yet, over the decades, there were many struggles in this union involving thousands of workers all across Canada and the United States for workplace improvements. Issues of concern in the 20th century included wages, working conditions, and health and safety. The struggles for change often lasted decades before significant gains were won. Economic conditions, the wider political climate, the legislative framework, standards in the sector or occupation, as well as the perspectives and practices of individual employers and union locals all played a role in the outcome.

In addition to the conflicts between hotel owners and employees, particularly in relation to any new organizing, internal conflict inside the union was widespread. The union's image was tarnished in the 1930s and 1940s by some of its leaders' collusion with rampant corruption in the hotel industry. Other parts of the union were strongly influenced by socialists and communists. The allegations of corruption and actual charges lasted intermittently into the 1980s, when a court-appointed monitor in the United States was directed to oversee the union's activities following the removal of the corrupt leaders. The union itself now took the offensive and placed trusteeships on certain locals to rid them of racketeering. *Toronto Star* (June 18, 1989) writer Peter Edwards reported on a police investigation during the late 1980s which found a connection between the union and Frank Cotroni, Montreal's top mafia boss, a link that had lasted for more than 25 years.

Despite all the union's problems, thousands of well-intentioned, conscientious union members, together with many elected union officials and staff, struggled from the mid-century onwards to win improvements in wages and working conditions, including joining the fight for the eight-hour day. By the mid-1980s, media exposés, court proceedings, and membership agitation all came together to prompt a crisis that led to a very different union. The old-guard leadership was removed and new leaders were elected. In the 1990s HERE not only put these past problems behind it but, with new waves of immigrants entering the ranks of union membership, along with new issues and challenges, began to rebuild the union. The outcomes include more open and transparent decision-making processes in the union, more democratic practices and structures, and more rank-and-file participation. The final impetus preceding radical change in Local 75 surfaced in 1995, when the local was placed under a trusteeship and the old top-down leaders were removed. As Tufts (2002, 5) explains, that year HERE Local 75 "began a long process to reinvent itself as a strong and democratic force in the city's hospitality sector."

The international leadership of HERE also underwent dramatic change, with the union's organizing director, John Wilhelm, replacing International president Ed Hanley in 1999. On both the International and the Ontario level, then, change occurred at the century's end. These alterations enabled the union to chart a new course adopting the "organizing model," as opposed to the "service model," and embracing rank-and-file democratic participation on a scale not seen before (Schenk 2003). By 1995, Local 75 of HERE began the difficult process of changing its methods of operation, rethinking its structure, and elaborating a new perspective.

LOCAL 75 AND THE JOURNEY HOTEL

When the workers in a mid-sized hotel in downtown Toronto joined HERE Local 75, they were completely new to unionism. The hotel had never been unionized before, nor had many of its employees worked in unionized establishments previously. Nonetheless, the majority of employees signed union cards with surprising ease, as they viewed joining the union as a logical step in a process that had already begun. These hotel workers had already organized themselves on several occasions because of a number of problems in the workplace and the treatment they received from management. Employees at the "back of the house" – room cleaners and others – had formed friendship networks and even nascent committee structures, while those at the "front of the house" – those serving customers directly – were either young people receptive to unionization or in job classifications not numerically significant in the organizing drive.

At this point the Journey Hotel – the hotel in question – employed upwards of 50 full-time and part-time employees, most of whom were, and remain to this day, women who had immigrated from the Philippines.[2] Only a small minority were from countries in Eastern Europe or Latin America. About 12 members of the new bargaining unit were male – seven in the "back" positions and five in the "front." Room attendants were, and remain, the largest job classification, constituting approximately 50 per cent of the bargaining unit. Other classifications include housemen, laundresses, and maintenance staff. This hotel's bargaining unit includes front-desk employees, whereas in most hotels such employees are excluded from the union.

Hotels are known for their pyramid occupational structures, where workers at the front who interact with guests are ranked higher, paid more, and often excluded from the union. Workers in the back, in contrast, are ranked lower, paid less, and included in the union. This unequal ranking is intimately intertwined with workers' facility with English, gender, and race/ethnicity. White men dominate in the front positions. The back jobs tend to be occupied by immigrant women, many of whom have English as a second language (Wells 2000, 114). Yet, at this hotel, front-desk employees constitute approximately 25 per cent of the bargaining unit. The hotel is distinct for this reason as well as for not being a full-service hotel – it has no room service and it contains no restaurant or coffee shop.

In addition to the distinctness of the hotel, the citywide union local is also unique. In 1995, when the hotel bargaining unit was organized, the union local had been under trusteeship for a year, as stipulated by the International Union (HERE) and its Canadian office. As a result, and before the election of a new administration, the local engaged in serious reflection and internal change. The desired direction was towards social unionism.

The Principles of the Unity Team (see figure 16.1) and the Program of the Unity Team (see figure 16.2) outline the platform of the new slate of leaders, one that differentiated them from the previous regime of business or "service model" unionists. The new Unity Team stressed issues of democracy, with rank-and-file committees, membership training, and new avenues of communications and organizing. In so doing, it provided clear evidence of its desire to move in the direction of union renewal. In the interregnum between the old regime and the new, the internal union crisis enabled employers to move against the union by refusing to renegotiate a master agreement with major city hotels. Bargaining therefore returned to the status quo ante, with each hotel conducting separate negotiations with the union and concluding distinct collective agreements. This period also witnessed an attempt by major downtown hotel employers to withdraw from the joint (union/management) trusteed benefit package.

The hotel workforce unionizing at this time was capable but inexperienced in dealing with an international union and its crises. Nonetheless, it gained some basic rights with the first two collective agreements (1996 and 1999), such as due process with a grievance procedure, compensation and benefit increases, a functional shop steward system, and some dignity in the workplace. Given the time and effort involved in consolidating the improvements of these two collective agreements, the bargaining unit was viewed as being relatively "quiet" by the local union leadership. These first collective agreements, following earlier traditions, revealed the continued influence of the earlier union regime with its focus on improvements for male gratuity workers, such as doormen, compared with the larger and more poorly compensated female-dominated positions, such as room attendants.

Thereafter this "quietness" began to change. First, the union local level moved from trusteeship to a new and democratically elected leadership, which, together with new structures on the bargaining unit level, created more space for membership dialogue and participation. Second, the union successfully fought off raids from other unions, which were not part of the Canadian Labour Congress or the Ontario Federation of Labour, giving it more time to focus on workplace issues. Third, the local gradually recovered from the breakdown of its master agreement and successfully concluded individual collective agreements with the major downtown hotels.

In this more favourable context, the hotel bargaining unit moved from consolidating its unionized status and contractual improvements to considering unresolved issues, particularly those of the female-dominated, low-wage classifications at the back of the house. The issue of workload endured by

Figure 16.1
Principles of the Unity Team

Honesty and Integrity

Full disclosure of finances and regular reports to the Membership. Open and accessible leadership – forever aware of the value of our members' trust.

Democracy

The members are the ultimate authority. Active participation of the rank-and-file. Continue to encourage members' involvement in decision-making.

Strengh

Solidarity between workplaces. A presence and a voice in the community. Earn respect in our industry.

Hard Work

Dedicated to our Local 75 members. Committed to being there in times of need. Regular, dependable, and consistent effort on your behalf.

Source: HERE files

Figure 16.2
Program of the Unity Team

Committees

We have implemented and will continue to develop a committee structure to ensure rank-and-file input into decision-making and to bring forth leadership candidates.

Training

Courses and seminars for member-elected stewards
Health and Safety representatives
Members' union rights
Life-long learning fund

Communications

Membership meetings
Quarterly newsletter
Mailings to committees
Financial reports
Regular visits and workplace visibility

Organizing

Increase our members and our influence. Extend union rights to unorganized hotel and restaurant workers. Create justice, dignity, and equality in Toronto's hospitality industry.

Source: HERE files

room attendants gradually moved to centre stage on the union's bargaining agenda. Small changes in the hotel and in the industry as a whole, such as the introduction of products and equipment for hotel guests to make coffee and the supplying of bathrobes in each room, increased the workload of room attendants. But the major workload issue in the Journey Hotel was that room attendants (RAS) had to clean 18 rooms a day, when the norm in other hotels was 16 rooms.

Hotel RAS in a number of Toronto hotels discovered this discrepancy when some of them attended the International Union's convention in Los Angeles in 2001 and compared their workload and pay with RAS in California and elsewhere across North America. For the first time in decades, the various locals at HERE were also able to take time out from the convention proceedings and meet together informally to exchange experiences with other union members in the same occupations across the continent. No one from the Journey Hotel attended this conference, but word soon spread throughout the hotel industry regarding the differences and the commonalities among RAS relating to grievances over workload.

Following the convention in Los Angels, a conference on housekeeping was held by the Toronto local in October 2001. RAS in the hotels, and across the industry, now began to seriously question their workload and their lower level of compensation with comparable others. What were once individual complaints became collective concerns. Members recalled these experiences as "opening their eyes" and as "realizing they could do better." This perspective gained credence and gradually evolved into a broad, solidaristic consensus among RAS and members of other classifications in the bargaining unit. The union local and the hotel bargaining unit committed themselves through open dialogue and vote to making the workload of RAS a key issue in the coming round of negotiations.

Membership Mobilization and Bargaining

The bargaining round in 2002 was both long and difficult, but it was successful in terms of gains in membership activism, education, and collective bargaining. Hotel employers initially took the offensive in an attempt to build on their successful torpedoing of a multi-hotel master agreement in earlier negotiations. They were further embolden by the role of the Conservative government in Ontario, which had legislated numerous anti-labour amendments to the *Labour Relations Act,* creating an anti-worker political atmosphere in the province (Ontario Federation of Labour 1995; Martinello 2000).

The local negotiating team members proceeded to reformulate their strategy in favour of confronting the hotel industry as a whole through citywide bargaining, as opposed to accepting the employers' strategy and bargaining each hotel separately. The goal was not only to improve the compensation level of the members and to tackle the issue of workload but also to work towards the re-establishment of a master agreement with the major hotels across the city. To begin this endeavour, members from different hotels needed to come together to discuss and agree on a common strategy and specific bargaining demands. Bargaining issues were discussed at the house-keeping conference mentioned earlier, as well as at monthly contract committee meetings attended by workers from a number of hotels and in separate bargaining unit meetings in each hotel. The local leaders encouraged maximum attendance by members and their broadest possible participation in debate and decision-making.

A relatively new structure, known as an Action Committee, also encouraged participation at the workplace level. The current local leaders had introduced these committees in their fight with the former regime, with its top-down, autocratic way of functioning. The committees tended to represent the natural leadership of a particular bargaining unit or department, as opposed to the appointed supporters of the former local leadership. In these open rank-and-file structures, activists in each workplace met, discussed issues of concern, and planned the member participatory actions that eventually led to the union's success at the bargaining table and its revitalization along the path of union renewal.

Discussions of strategies and tactics concerning how best to achieve bargaining goals came next as the new leaders tried to get the widest consensus possible. As one member put it, "there was a lot at stake." "Either we won or we kept on cleaning 18 rooms instead of 16," said another. The strategy had to contain some flexibility, given the uncertainties of events, issues, and employer responses. The core of the strategy was to negotiate first with the "Big Three" downtown hotels – the Sheraton, the Hilton, and the Delta Chelsea – plus the Royal York Hotel. Once collective agreements with these hotels were successfully concluded, with equal wage increases, comparable benefit improvements, the same workload formula, and common contract expiry dates, the challenge would be to extend this pattern to the smaller hotels.

This strategy meant that bargaining units in the smaller hotels, such as the Journey, had to agree to wait for what was termed the "Big Three plus One" to settle before they could engage directly in bargaining – or at least before they could settle an agreement of their own. The union moved to hold city-wide events for all hotel workers. The goal was threefold: to activate as much of the membership as possible; to educate them about the goals of negotiations and the positions of the hotel owners; and to convince them that by sticking together – by solidarity – they could win. International president John Wilhelm came and spoke at a membership meeting and promised that the International Union would put pressure on hotels owned by the same employers in the United States. Presidents from other locals across Ontario came and offered moral and financial support. "It became clear to everyone," said one member, "that negotiations can't be limited to just one hotel. We must go global, just like the hotel owners." With both cross-border and regional support in motion, the local moved to hold a citywide rally. As with all such events, the action committees in each hotel were the key on-the-ground vehicles for motivating and activating members.

The union-sponsored rally held on June 10, 2002, featured Jesse Jackson, a well-known minister, politician, and social justice advocate. Jackson led a march for justice with hundreds of hotel workers in downtown Toronto (Local Newsletter, winter 2003). The union also felt that the threat of job action during the visit of the Pope to Toronto could prove to be an important bargaining tactic. Although that turned out not to be the case, it was evidence of a union membership and leadership thinking creatively and demonstrating a willingness to explore new and imaginative tactics – tactics that brought workers together from different workplaces, particularly low-wage immigrant women workers, and tactics that focused on issues common to the membership as a whole, that built solidarity, and did so in a manner that captured the public's attention.

Local members proceeded to assess themselves $5 per member each week over their regular dues to build a strike fund. Workers at the Journey Hotel were the first to sign on to the additional assessment, reflecting an awareness that gains might well come only with solidarity backed up by increased union resources.

As innovative as the overall union strategy was, each set of bargaining has its own dynamic. In this case, continued dialogue among bargaining unit and local union leaders soon saw the development of innovative tactics. In May 2002 hotel room attendants began "giving back" two of the 18 rooms assigned – that is, refusing to clean them. After several weeks of such action, the hotel management took the union to the Ontario Labour Relations Board (OLRB), charging an illegal strike.

The union denied that it "threatened, called, authorized, counselled, supported, encouraged or procured an illegal strike." It also noted that, in the collective agreement between the parties, "all bargaining unit employees, including room attendants, earn wages on an hourly basis." In short, "room attendants are not piece workers."[3]

Nonetheless, the board ruled that the employee actions constituted a strike. To avoid the penalties of an illegal strike, the union agreed to stop the "giving back" of rooms and asked members, temporarily, to continue to clean 18 rooms per shift, but encouraged them to file grievances over their workload. The bargaining team also assured all concerned that this issue of reducing the number of rooms to be cleaned per shift would be the key issue in the upcoming bargaining.

The result of these events was high membership participation in picketing on a daily basis. What began as picketing following the day shift (at 5 p.m.) was soon extended to morning "wake-up" pickets, complete with banging pots and pans. A star attraction was the huge balloon rat that accompanied the picketers. As the local's newsletter (winter 2003) noted: "Its presence was a gloomy reminder to customers to Boycott the Rat Hole." The picketing was to continue relentlessly for a full five months, making sleep difficult for guests and angering hotel management. Despite the union strategy of making a settlement with the Big Three hotels, plus the Royal York, a priority, bargaining unit members continued to picket. As the same newsletter explained: "Workers were so fed up with substandard conditions below that of other downtown hotels that, even though they were not in a strike position, they started picketing the hotel and kept it up for close to 100 days."

The hotel's location near apartment blocks, condos, and the University of Toronto attracted both supporters and some opposition from local residents. Individuals and anti-poverty community activists, as well as university students – known as the "Common Front" – joined the picket lines. Support also came from members of other unions. The Labour Council of Toronto and York Region's strike support committee brought out trade unionists to help on the picket line. Members of unions such as the United Steelworkers of America (USWA), the Canadian Union of Public Employees (CUPE), the Canadian Auto Workers (CAW), and the Ontario Public Service Employees (OPSEU) participated. As one activist stated in reference to the broad range of support, "without them moral would be low." Another stated, "Picketing is not easy; we needed all the support we could get."

As May and June passed into July, a contract was settled at the Royal York Hotel, but bargaining at the Big Three was still making little progress. Common Front supporters occupied the Journey Hotel lobby against the wishes of the local union and bargaining unit leadership, which was making some progress in employer-initiated negotiations. Between the daily picketing and the lobby occupation, the media heard about the dispute. Interviews with picketers on CBC Radio provided publicity to employees and their cause, while embarrassing hotel management.

In preparation for a strike, the bargaining unit members and Action Committee proceeded to set up the various committees, such as a food committee and a hardship committee. Training classes and programs were also established. The activation of the hotel workforce and the daily picketing in front of the hotel, accompanied by the 12-foot "rat," began to affect the number of hotel guests. The local's newsletter reported (winter 2003): "The customer boycott was in full swing as customers began to relocate to other [unionized] hotels." In particular, tour groups and an elder hostel that were regular customers were contacted. Hotel management felt the pressure.

Management now floated an informal offer of settlement, hoping to end the picketing and chaos and to reach an agreement before a pattern from the large hotels was foisted on them. But the offer was so poor that the union negotiator, with the support of the bargaining team, flatly rejected it. The union proceeded to conciliation as required under the *Ontario Labour Relations Act*. With the company failing to appear at conciliation, the union asked and received a "no board" report. Hotel employees were now in a legal strike position. Word of the rejection of the settlement offer spread throughout the industry and among many other hotel employees around the city. Picketing with the rat continued. Management in other hotels became increasingly worried that they, too, could be picketed and branded with the rat image if something wasn't done to solve the dispute.

International connections and support supplemented member mobilizations on picket lines at the major hotels. Paul Clifford, president of Local 75, flew to New York to meet with the Big Three hotel owners in the offices of HERE. An International vice-president of HERE attended, as did the Canadian director of the union. The meeting of August 24, 2002, finally achieved a tentative settlement with the Big Three hotels. It offered common contract expiry dates, wage increases, and increased job security, and the settlement was overwhelmingly accepted by a vote of the membership. At that point other hotels in the city began to negotiate with employees and to move towards the pattern settlement.

With the pattern set and a strike fund in place, the local moved from trying to hold off a strike at the Journey Hotel to favouring a strike, should hotel management offer anything less. Bargaining unit members at the Journey Hotel and workers in other hotels were inspired by the Big Three settlement. "We now knew that winning was possible," said one member. "The strategy actually worked," noted another with some relief. Picketing activity increased as workers from other hotels began to help out and join the picket lines. Many of these workers from around the city felt their "sisters and brothers" at the Journey were heroic, given their months of determined noisy picketing.

This support boosted the confidence of Journey Hotel workers and gave them a sense that they were "all in the same fight." When bargaining unit members were asked, "To what extent have your actions fostered a new awareness of the role of your employer? ... and of other employers?" the responses all claimed, "They increased our awareness." Others added that "these hotel owners are all the same." An Action Committee member explained that members felt that "hotel owners were more interested in making money, no matter how little we are paid." Some hotel workers viewed hotel owners as personally "greedy." Still others held that "even hotel guests are only a means to an end for the companies that own the hotels." Several indicated that "it isn't just hotel owners that put money before people, but all employers," indicating a view that distinct employer interests were involved.

As August passed into September, the union's press release "Toronto Hotel Workers Back on the Streets" described the conflict this way:

Film Festival goers visiting Toronto this week are being treated to stellar performances by the hotel workers of the [Journey] Hotel ... The workers, accompanied by a 12 foot rat, have been informing customers of the hotel and the many passers, how unfairly the [Journey] Hotel is treating them. The workers have been picketing outside the hotel since the beginning of May. This afternoon from 4–6 pm the Strike Support Committee of the Toronto and York Regional Labour Council will be holding a solidarity picket with music and the now famous ... Rat (September 12, 2002).

A strike date was set for October 4, but the preparations, determination, enthusiasm, and solidarity was such that, by the 3rd, everyone was on the picket line. At that point the hotel management gave way, withdrew its position, and offered virtually everything the bargaining team had asked for. The local newsletter (winter 2003) reported: "The commitment and dedication of the workers, and their committee leaders paid off. With a midnight strike deadline the company came in with a new position just hours before, that finally recognized that ... workers [at this hotel] deserved the same as other [hotel workers].

The next several days saw the workers at the Journey Hotel vote to accept the new contract. Over the life of the new collective agreement they achieved:

- full coverage under the jointly trusteed benefit plan (union/management) paid by the employer (drug plan and card, life insurance, sick leave, basic dental coverage and topped up paternity leave);
- wage increases: for example, housekeepers and room attendants, by far the largest classifications, saw staged-in increases from $10.95 per hour to $14.25 by January 2006;
- overtime to be paid at time-and-one-half following each 8-hour shift;
- workload reduction: rooms cleaned per day reduced to 17, and then to 16, over the life of the contract;
- job security from subcontracting (the employer could not lay off unionized staff as a result of contracting out any work during the life of the collective agreement);
- expiry of collective agreement: common expiry dates with other hotels organized by the same union – a major step towards regaining a master agreement with other hotels.

The long months of persistent activity, picketing, strike preparations, meetings, high morale, and solidarity had finally proved successful.

HOTEL WORKERS, UNION RENEWAL,
AND PRECARIOUS EMPLOYMENT

Since the early 1980s, workers in Canada have witnessed a growth in precarious jobs (Vosko, Zukewich, and Cranford 2003). Hotel employees are not immune from this trend but, rather, at the forefront of the receiving line. Yet the first two contracts of these hotel workers (1996 and 1999) achieved more full-time employment and less part-time employment and less temporary work. In these years, in contrast to other hotels, the hotels covered by these contracts did not use temporary help agencies. Yet crisis still ensued.

Tourism makes the difference between a full hotel and an empty one. The number of guests booking into a hotel rises and falls with the level of economic activity and the overall spending power of individual people. Employment trends, recessions and recoveries, even weather and political turmoil, including the September 11, 2001, attacks on New York, affect workers' job security more dramatically in the hotel sector than in many others.

By the time of the third contract at the Journey Hotel in 2002, there were up to 50 employees in the hotel bargaining unit, and all but four held full-time permanent jobs. The vast majority of these employees, therefore, fit the normative model of a standard employment relationship. These hotel workers enjoyed benefits and protections beyond the statutory minimum under their collective agreement. Yet the experience of this hotel, and others in the industry given pattern settlements, indicates how even full-time permanent workers, especially in vulnerable sectors, can be affected by the broader context of precarious employment.

The SARS crisis confronting Toronto in 2003 is a case in point. The infectiousness viral disease, by dissuading out-of-city Canadians and Americans from travelling to Toronto, caused more disruption and layoffs in the hotel industry in Toronto than did the attack on the World Trade Center in New York. The drop in tourism from the SARS outbreak was both dramatic and severe. Writing in the *Toronto Star*, Ann Perry noted that one hotel "gave its reservations department a new name: the cancellation department." Jack Boland of the *Toronto Sun* (May 10, 2003) quoted Zelda Davis, a room attendant and vice-president of Local 75, saying "she has worked only six times in the past six weeks and is fearful she may have to re-mortgage her home to make ends meet." Despite the successful struggle by unionized hotel workers to mitigate precarious employment at the Journey Hotel, SARS reduced the number of RAs by 80 per cent in the five months following its outbreak.

The lack of protections from layoff in the contract negotiated in 2003, given the instability faced by these hotel employees, is evidence that, even when certain dimensions of precarious employment (especially firm size and union coverage) work largely in employees' favour, other dimensions can tilt the balance towards precarious employment. In this volume, Cranford and Vosko take firm size to be one indicator of a degree of regulatory protection. Large firms are obliged to follow legislative and regulatory provisions, whereas small firms face less legislative enforcement (see also Fudge 1991; O'Grady 1991). While the Journey Hotel would be considered small to medium by industry standards, it is part of a larger chain of hotels with common ownership and employer policies and, therefore, subject to legislation and regulations similar to many other large chains. Both the hard-won prevalence of full-time permanent work in the hotel and the high level of regulatory protection afforded by labour law should provide a modicum of security to workers. However, exacerbated by the federal and provincial governments' failure to support hospitality workers affected by SARS, even the substantial size of this hotel chain failed to protect its employees.

Union status certainly extends workers a measure of control over the labour process (see Anderson, this volume). The presence or absence of a trade union influences employees' abilities to advance their collective agenda in collective bargaining and through other actions. Such actions also cultivate internal solidarity and, often, external alliances with other unions and community groups (Cranford, Das Gupta, Ladd, and Vosko, this volume; Levesque, 2003). The employees in this hotel were not only formally union members but actively involved in a long and ultimately successful struggle, substantially increasing their compensation level and benefit package and reducing their work load. Union status mattered in this case study, but it did not hold the line on layoffs.

A third and critical dimension of precarious employment is income level. A high income level may be an indicator of job security, and a low income level may be indicative of precarious employment. In the case of these hotel workers, despite unionization and wage increases gained through the five-month-long struggle for their latest collective agreement, the largest classification of RAS is located at the low end of the income scale. Wage level(s) moved up from $10.95 per hour (January 2001) to $11.95 per hour as of January 2003, and staged increases will occur through January 2006 to $14.25 per hour. Assuming a 40-hour work week, with the 2003 wage increase of $11.95, the annual gross income of an RA is still only $24,856. In addition, the reality for many hotel workers, particularly RAS, is that the hotel occupancy rate falls in the winter months, resulting in shorter work hours for many. Thus we find that workers in this hotel, as in many others, given the presence of pattern settlements, receive a low level of compensation, with consequent implications for job security. Indeed, interviews revealed that most full-time permanent hotel workers working as RAS either worked at a second job or were looking for a second job. Typical comments from hotel workers were, "We can't get by without some extra work" or "Everyone needs another job." Some members also noted the number of children they had: "I have to get extra work; I have three kids," or "My daughter is going to college this year," highlighting the necessity of multiple job holding. This point confirms the findings of Armstrong and Laxer and of Cranford and Vosko in this volume that context and location matter. Indeed, they make it necessary to conceive of precarious employment as a multi-dimensional continuum that is highly correlated with employment form (i.e., permanent full-time work) but also related to industry and occupation as well as to gender and race/ethnicity.

Many employees in the Journey Hotel were faced with layoffs because of the impact of SARS. But the impact was far from equal. Layoffs depended on a worker's job classification, which is intimately tied to social location. Front-desk employees retained their normal hours of work despite the shortfall in guests. In part, that was due to already low staff levels and to the tasks of their classification – someone had to be on the front desk at all times to register and assist, however few guests there were. Alternatively, the major classification at the back of the house, room attendants, faced the bulk of the layoffs. The SARS crisis reduced the number of RAS from over 20 to four, a reduction of about 80 per cent. While the reduction of hours and work occurred on the basis of seniority, a number of workers requested to be laid off completely for a number of weeks in order to qualify for Employment Insurance. Those in the mid-range of the seniority list were reduced to temporary part-time employment. Those near the bottom of the seniority list waited at home, hoping their employer would call them. If the hotel didn't call them by 11:00 a.m., they spent the rest of the day seeking extra work. Jack Boland of the *Toronto Sun* cites room attendant Zelda Davis saying, "You wait for the call-backs for work, but they never come. Friends of mine have stopped sending their children to school because they can't afford them bus tickets or money for lunches." The three or four original permanent part-time employees faced indefinite layoff.

The gains won by the hotel workers at Journey Hotel in their collective agreement were substantive, but they did not include provisions to protect them from layoffs in such circumstances. Despite efforts at the bargaining table, few collective agreements do. The major exceptions are those governing large auto and steel plants. Workers in these plants can opt in these circumstances for a shorter work week or for temporary layoff provisions in their collective agreements, in which they receive at least partial remuneration.

For hotel workers, the impact of SARS continued for months, improving only gradually with the onset of summer 2003. By the end of August 2003, the Journey Hotel, with a total of 209 rooms, reached only 60 per cent capacity. The number of RAS working full-time hours rose to between six and eight, depending on the number of guests that day. Thus, the job classification of RAS was still reduced by approximately 60 per cent. The remaining RAS continued to experience short hours. The threat of layoff or provisions allowing for shorter hours are an important industry-specific characteristic that shapes precarious employment among hotel workers, one that is akin to the importance of work arrangements among ancillary workers in the health-care sector.

CONCLUSION

The story of workers at the Journey Hotel is also a narrative of a union local in the process of revitalization – of becoming a social union with mass membership participation, increased rank-and-file involvement in decision-making, and new structures of democracy called action committees. These workers joined a union with a past riddled with corruption, but in transition to a new vision and new practices. The five-month campaign for a new collective agreement showed that the Principles and Program of the Unity Team were far more than mere electoral rhetoric. The union local and bargaining unit made every effort to involve the members in many meetings, rallies, and marches, such as the one led by Jesse Jackson. Participation in these activities was not for purposes of increased numbers of passive members; rather, members were encouraged to express their views, democratically arrive at decisions, and assist in carrying them out. The decision to picket every day at the end of the day shift, followed by the decision to extend such action with a morning "wake up" picket, involved virtually everyone in the bargaining unit.

The major organizational or structural change in the local was the development of action committees. These horizontal structures included key workplace members, sought direct rank-and-file participation, and collectively acted on committee decisions. Their role proved essential in mobilizing and educating members before and during the campaign for a new contract. The action committees focused on internal organizing, but they also embodied what Bronfenbrenner and Juravich (1998) termed "rank-and-file intensive strategy," in reference to external organizing.

There was also evidence of changed perspectives among these hotel workers. The recognition that they, as hotel workers, had interests in common at the Journey Hotel and at other hotels which were antithetical to hotel owners indicates the development of new perspectives on the part of those workers who were interviewed. The local union leadership and the Action Committee members, with their commitment to social unionism, were a further factor in encouraging a worker-centred view of the world and the permanency of such views. Still, even though the union local and the bargaining unit had demonstrated perseverance and solidarity in their struggle and had won substantive contractual improvements, the housekeepers who led the fight soon faced the brunt of layoffs and reduced work hours.

This change of fortunes is best understood through an extended notion of precarious employment, one sensitive both to context and to location. This concept moves beyond a simple dichotomous view of employment forms – a standard employment relationship versus non-standard forms of employment – to a continuum of employment forms of waged work moving from full-time permanent, to full-time temporary, to part-time permanent, and then part-time temporary. These forms of wage work are, in turn, linked to dimensions of employment – such as firm size, union status, and hourly wages – those dimensions considered in this book which enable readers to better assess the nature and extent of precarious jobs. In this case study, the relationship between "forms" of employment and the "dimensions" of precarious employment, in the context of conflictual labour relations, interacted in shaping the precarious employment among hotel workers, especially RAS. This experience also demonstrates that some employees are more precarious than others, that social contexts such as occupation and industry overlap with the social locations of gender, ethnicity, colour, and the overwhelming presence of immigrant labour at the back of the house.

Full-time unionized employees and permanent part-time employees in the hotel sector can also find themselves confronting precarious employment unless a strong collective agreement is in place. It is apparent that the threat of precarious employment is not limited to the fast-growing component of workers who are not in traditional full-time, permanent wage work. The evidence of this case study suggests that union status helps mitigate precarious work, but does not eliminate it. Countering precarious work needs ongoing resistance on a multi-workplace level, with the goal of social unionism leading to improved collective agreement language and to legislative change.

This conclusion provides further confirmation of the growing misfit between labour law and policy and the hotel workers in need of protection, as outlined in the introduction to this volume. Confronted with mass layoffs due to SARS, the union, with the passive support of the employer, sought financial assistance for affected employees. The initiatives of the Canadian Labour Congress to the federal government helped to get some training monies through Employment Insurance. Although a number of workers were assisted in this manner, the inadequacy of labour market policy to attend to the scope and nature of employment insecurity was obvious. More inclusive, timely, and permanent policies and programs need to be implemented for all employees confronting sudden layoff and unemployment. A cross-industry campaign by union members could well be the foundation for such a policy change.

Thinking through Community Unionism

CYNTHIA J. CRANFORD, TANIA DAS GUPTA,
DEENA LADD, AND LEAH F. VOSKO

The contemporary Canadian labour market is characterized by the growth of precarious employment. Job tenure is declining and more and more workers cycle in and out of employment. Workers in precarious employment often labour under atypical contracts and have high levels of job insecurity, high risks of ill health, and limited access to social benefits and statutory entitlements. A central consequence of rising precariousness is an increase in both the depth of poverty and the number of people living in poverty.

The rise of precarious employment exacerbates the already tenuous position of many women, immigrants, and people of colour in the labour market. Workers in precarious employment face considerable obstacles in securing a decent livelihood and in exercising their voice: laws regulating collective bargaining do not reflect their situation, and various elements of union strategy are out of sync with labour market trends.

This situation calls for innovative strategies aimed at enabling all workers to defend their rights. There is a pressing need for a plurality of representational forms that extend beyond the dominant model of a single worksite and a single employer (Fudge 1993; Vosko 2000; Wial 1993). A broader, more political social movement orientation is also needed to revitalize the labour movement and, in particular, to incorporate more women, immigrants, and people of colour (Leah 1999; Lévesque and Murray 2002; Robinson 2000; Tufts 1998; Wilton and Cranford 2002). No less than a coming together of broader-based "labour-market unionism" and "community unionism" is required (Fine 1998). Labour market unionism is collective bargaining beyond a single worksite, but the term "community unionism" is used in many different ways by different scholars. Most notions of community unionism do not focus sufficiently on the process of organizing, and many embrace a narrow notion of "community," yet attention to participatory processes and a broad notion of community are important components of any type of collective organizing, particularly among marginalized groups such as women and people of colour (Cranford 2001; Cranford and Ladd 2003; Das Gupta 1986; Leah 1999; Stall and Stoeker 1998). Union renewal efforts, such as that examined by Schenk in this volume, may be furthered by joining new representational forms with attention to the processes of community organizing.

This chapter thinks through community unionism with the aim of offering a new conceptualization. It also explores the potential of community unionism as a vehicle for precariously employed workers to improve their conditions of work. The analysis unfolds in four sections. Building on Part One of the volume, the first section explores the dynamics of precarious employment in Canada, with attention to the union dimension. With this backdrop, the second section describes labour market unionisms of "old" and "new" as well as complementary alternative legislative models of collective bargaining that could inform community unionism. The third section conceptualizes community unionism along two axes. The first axis is a continuum of *location* that includes constituency, site, and issue-based organizing. This continuum is defined by worksite-based organizing at one pole and "community" – constructed to fit a particular organizing agenda – at the other. The second axis is a continuum of *process*, defined by hierarchical organizations at one pole and participatory organizations at the other. Community unionism is located at the intersection of these two axes, and it is conceptualized here as a highly participatory process of organizing among workers around a variety of social locations, including a diversity of issues, sites, and constituencies, while maintaining a central interest on labour concerns. The fourth section demonstrates the utility of this conceptualization through a case study of Toronto Organizing for Fair Employment (TOFFE), a contemporary "community union" in Toronto. TOFFE organizes with workers across multiple and intersecting constituencies (immigrants, women, people of colour) and sites (occupation, sector, industry, and employment form), drawing on a participatory philosophy that is common in some community organizing yet focusing on labour issues. The chapter concludes by identifying the defining features of community unionism and assessing how these features might be harnessed to mitigate precarious employment among marginalized workers.

PRECARIOUS EMPLOYMENT IN CANADA AND THE UNION/NON-UNION DISTINCTION

Community unionism has (re)emerged in Canada because the worksite-based unionism that is dominant is unable to address the needs of a growing number of workers. In Canada, fewer than a third of the jobs are covered by a collective agreement. The need for a broader labour market unionism is evident in an examination of the union/non-union distinction as well as variations in union coverage among different forms of employment.

The union/non-union distinction is a key axis of gendered and racialized differentiation in the Canadian labour force (in this volume, see Anderson; Armstrong and Laxer; and Cranford and Vosko; see also Galabuzi 2004). Union coverage is an important indicator of precarious employment, reflecting both control over the labour process and regulatory protection, and it is highly correlated with other dimensions such as income and the social wage (Anderson, Beaton, and Laxer, this volume). An analysis of waged work illustrates that full-time permanent wage workers are most likely to be covered by a union contract, while part-time and full-time temporary workers are least likely to be covered. Women and people of colour are concentrated in these most precarious forms (Cranford and Vosko, this volume). Similarly, regardless of the conditions under which they labour and the degree to which they resemble wage workers, few self-employed workers are unionized, given the premises of collective bargaining legislation in Canada which exclude most self-employed workers from organizing in unions (Fudge, Tucker, and Vosko 2002). Women concentrated in part-time solo self-employment are the most precarious along multiple dimensions (Vosko and Zukewich, this volume).

Among liberal industrial democracies, Canada falls in the mid-range in terms of the levels of union density. It sits between low-density countries such as the United States and high-density countries such as Sweden, Norway, and Denmark (Jackson, this volume). The pace of decline in union density over the last two decades in Canada has also been slower than in the United States and faster than in Nordic countries (Jackson, this volume). Yet there is considerable evidence of low rates of union density among youth in Canada, and workers of colour are also underrepresented in unionized work (Das Gupta, this volume; Galabuzi 2004). Moreover, the convergence in women's and men's union coverage rates in the beginning of the twenty-first century is explained by white women's significant representation in the federal public sector (Fudge 2002). This gendered convergence minimizes the stagnation of private sector unionization, as well as the erosion of union gains in the face of privatization among part-time permanent wage-workers, many of whom are women and people of colour (Armstrong and Laxer, this volume).

An absence of union coverage is most pronounced among workers in precarious employment. Some of these workers engage in temporary work – they work on contract, on a casual or seasonal basis, or through a temporary agency. Temporary agency workers are highly precarious because they are party to a triangular employment relationship and often earn low wages, receive limited benefits, and require more hours of work to sustain themselves and their dependants (Vosko 2000). Other workers engage in "involuntary" solo self-employment, often resembling wage work but devoid of a full range of labour protections. The resort to subcontracting in industries such as clothing (ILGWU and INTERCEDE 2003) and construction (MacDonald 1998b), the persistence of exclusions from basic labour protections by occupation (in this volume, see Bernstein; Tucker), and privatization in health care and in the public sector more broadly reflect this trend (this volume, see Armstrong and Laxer; Borowy). Still others move between statuses such as temporary wage work and solo self-employment or juggle multiple statuses simultaneously, often in a single sector, occupation, or region, in order to piece together a living. Common to each of these groups of workers is the limited ability to express their voices collectively through dominant union structures (Cranford and Ladd 2003; O'Conner 1964a; Vosko 2000).

THE PROMISE OF LABOUR MARKET UNIONISMS "OLD" AND "NEW"

To secure adequate livelihoods for themselves, their households, and their communities, workers in these varied precarious employment situations require access to a combination of alternative unionisms and alternative legislative models of collective bargaining. Building a "labour market unionism" able to incorporate a plurality of "new" representational forms and supportive of a more political unionism is critical to meeting this need (Fine 1998; Levesque and Murray 2002). Labour market unionism grows out of the realization that in an economy which is largely non-unionized, such as the Canadian economy, organizing workers on a firm-by-firm basis is insufficient. Furthermore, with the spread of precarious employment, more and more workers cycle in and out of work; equally central, with privatization and the downloading of a range of social services onto households and communities, more and more workers also juggle multiple demands on their time, moving between paid and unpaid work (this volume, see Cranford and Vosko; de Wolff; and Vosko and Zukewich). The PC 1003 model, or the Canadian variant of Wagnerism, which grew to dominate in the post-war period, pivoted on the norm of the male industrial worker based in a single worksite. This model is outmoded. Unions must adopt strategies to organize geographically or by industry, occupation, and job-mobility path if they are to take wages out of competition in a city or region (Cobble and Vosko 2000; Fine 1998; Gordon 1999). They must also find ways to represent the interests of workers who move in and out of employment and the challenges they face across the labour market – in households and in the labour force.

Labour market unionism involves embracing bargaining beyond a single worksite, such as multi-employer and sector bargaining that allow workers to move up the labour supply chain (Cobble 1991; Fudge 1993; ILGWU and INTERCEDE 1993; Vosko 2000). The term also denotes the wide-ranging duties, and resulting needs, of workers in various forms of employment as well as those inside and outside the labour force. While the worksite-based model of organizing is often equated with industrial unionism, lessons may be drawn from the repertoire of broader-based models of old – those linked to both craft and industrial traditions – as well as campaigns launched under these models that address broad concerns across the labour market. Newer, alternative models of union representation also provide important seeds for renewal.

Craft and Industrial Trade Unionisms of Old

Until the mid-1990s, craft unionism was largely dismissed as a model for organizing workers in precarious employment because of the focus of the early craft unions on skilled workers – who were predominately white, male citizens – and the exclusionary, racist, and sexist unionism they practised (Milkman 1990; Moody 1988). However, the representational form of the craft union holds promise for a "post-industrial" workforce that is not employed in a single worksite by a single employer (Cobble 1991). As Cobble argues, craft unionism was also practised by waitresses, janitors, and other groups of workers in precarious employment, including women and immigrants. Cobble uses the term "occupational unionism," in the place of craft unionism, to emphasize this distinction between representational form and organizational culture.

The representational form of craft/occupational unionism, especially its organization of the labour supply and its adaptability to a mobile workforce, offers a range of lessons for organizing with workers in precarious employment. As practised by waitresses and garment workers (Cobble 1991), janitors (Gordon 1999) of old, truck drivers (Cobble and Vosko 2000), construction workers (MacDonald 1998a), and some artists today (Vosko 2005), it is neither worksite- nor firm-based. Nor are wages, benefits, and job security dependent on organizing workers employed by an individual firm. Rather, the ideal typical craft/occupational model organizes the labour supply around a given occupation or job mobility path (Wial 1993). For early craft unions like the International Brotherhood of Teamsters, "the issue was not fighting for tenure at an individual work site but increasing the overall supply of good, well-paying jobs and providing workers with the skills to perform those jobs" (Cobble and Vosko 2000). These aims were achieved through the development of hiring halls,[1] operated by the union, which performed management functions (including peer discipline), established performance standards, and sought to link workers with jobs. Some craft unions of old also embraced a "producerist consciousness," which enabled workers in a range of employment situations to band together. They rejected the narrow notion of worker, which precluded self-management and supervision, while at the same time limited the extent to which members could derive income from capital and employ others (Cobble and Vosko 2000). Under the craft/occupational unionism of the early International Brotherhood of Teamsters, as well as early waitresses unions, the chosen strategy was to use voluntarily negotiated agreements to bring workers in a range of situations into the union. Initially, there was little interference from the state; however, in the post-war era, especially in the United States but also in various jurisdictions in Canada, state interference limited the effectiveness of the voluntarism of these unions (Cranford, Fudge, Tucker, and Vosko 2005; Linder 1989, 558). However, a key question is whether workers with lower levels of socially recognized skills are able to use the craft model of organizing today.

Some of the earliest industrial unions also organized with mobile workers and workers without a single employer. Rather than organizing along the lines of a craft or occupation, the early industrial unions organized all occupations in an industry, sector, or strategic labour market. For example, the mining towns were sites where union organizing was a community affair, owing to the lack of distinction between workplace and the home (Avery 1979, 57–8). In addition, many of the early industrial unions were inclusive along race/ethnic lines. Established in 1905, the Industrial Workers of the World (the Wobblies) were one of the few labour organizations that incorporated Asian and European immigrant workers as well as domestic migrants and the unemployed. The Wobblies' representational form, characterized by low initiation fees and dues, transferable membership cards, and a mobile camp-delegate system, also fit the migratory work patterns of the most precariously employed workers (Avery 1979, 53). Born in Calgary in 1919, the One Big Union also organized precariously employed and mobile immigrant and migrant workers. As well, it sought to bring together skilled urban workers with the less-skilled migrants who came to the cities in search of work and relief. This union's inclusive unionism also influenced the formation of Women's Labour leagues and Women's Labour councils in western cities (Palmer 1992, 190, 201). Jumping forward to the late 1920 and early 1930s, Avery (1979, 117) argues that the Communist unions were the most successful in organizing immigrant workers, in part due to their alliance with the Ukrainian and Finnish organizations. This success was also related to their "superior organizational structure," which included organizing industrial unions in every sector through the Workers' Unity League and organizing the unemployed in the National Unemployed Workers Association (Avery 1979, 128, 132). These unions organized among Jewish workers in the locals of the Montreal and Toronto garment unions, which sought to establish industry-wide standards through mass demonstrations (Fudge and Tucker 2001, 147).

These inclusive and radical unions were repressed by the state, in no small part because of the red-baiting and deportation of immigrant activists; the state negotiated, instead, with the 'responsible' industrial unions, who took the divisions of the capitalist labour market as given (Fudge and Tucker 2001; Russell 1992, 125). In the current period, models exist of representational structures with the potential to foster, and expand on, the inclusiveness evident in some craft and industrial unions of old and in certain other of their practices.

New Alternative Legislative Models

Another highly complementary strategy of labour market unionism involves crafting legislation that facilitates collective bargaining among workers who are mobile across worksites and their multiple employers. Contemporary legislation in the construction industry, in provinces such as Ontario and British Columbia, and federal and Quebec legislation in the arts are two exemplars of this type of intervention.

In the case of artists, the federal *Status of the Artist Act* permits professional artists who are independent contractors to form associations and bargain collectively with federal producers. It introduces a collective bargaining regime centring on the production of artistic works rather than the performance of personal service and it does so by extending collective bargaining rights to independent professional artists and certifying organizations that are representative of artists in a given sector. On certification by a tribunal, artists' associations gain the right to bargain on behalf of all artists in the sector (Macpherson 1999). Yet, in contrast to most other collective bargaining regimes, artists' associations then negotiate scale agreements with producers. These agreements set minimum terms and conditions for various types of artistic work. They allow individual artists to negotiate contracts but prevent producers from paying any less than the amount provided in a given scale agreement to an artist working in a sector in which an artists' association has been certified, thereby attempting to minimize precarious work relationships in the arts (Vosko 2005).

In the case of the construction industry in Ontario, special legislation mandates single trade, multi-employer, province-wide bargaining in the industrial, commercial, and institutional sectors (ILGWU and INTERCEDE 1993, 50–2). Province-wide bargaining is facilitated by the designation of one employer bargaining agency and one employee bargaining agency, each of which holds rights in each trade. The agreement is binding to these bargaining agencies as well as to member employers and all member union locals, which are not permitted to negotiate outside the master agreement. Any newly unionized employer is automatically bound by the provincial agreement. Under this model, union locals control the labour supply by placing their members on various contracts through hiring halls – similar to the craft unions of old. Since the collective agreement prohibits non-union subcontracting, subcontractors are compelled to recognize the union in order to bid successfully for projects (MacDonald 1998a).

Linking Labour Market Unionism to Community Unionism

The review of older and newer forms of union organizing illustrates that different levels of inclusion have been practised in unions. For instance, the representational form of craft unionism has the potential to be inclusive of workers in different kinds of workplaces as long as they all practise the same craft. However, the fact that it excludes those who are unskilled in the craft has, in practice, led to the exclusion of many women, immigrants, and workers of colour. Similarly, industrial unions have the potential to include all workers in a given industry, regardless of skill or workplace location, yet many were still exclusionary well into the 20th century (Das Gupta, this volume).

The newer legislative models are seeds of a broader, more pluralistic labour market unionism. These models could be adapted for workers who move in and out of employment, since neither model described requires workers to be employed in order to belong to the union. They also suit those workers whose labour force trajectories reflect "job mobility paths" – a term coined by Wial (1993) to denote routes that low-wage workers travel in the labour force characterized by loose sector-based affiliations rather than the type of career progression associated with a given occupation. Yet fostering union structures that enable precariously employed women, immigrants, and workers of colour to organize requires more than advancing alternative legislative models. It requires linking new representational forms to praxes of community unionism. As Fine (1998, 133) argues: "Ultimately, labour market organizing is about re-imposing a set of community standards on wage and benefit levels in a community. It will never be possible to ... take wages out of competition. Thus, it is the community that must enforce standards." Community unionism entails efforts by groups to limit wage competition across a city, industry, occupation, or other grouping. It is a metaphor for labour-oriented community organizing inclusive of the employed and the unemployed, and it is based on the realization that mitigating precarious employment requires developing a mass base and engaging a range of actors. While much of the existing literature focuses on political alliances between recognized trade unions and community-based groups as essential for union renewal (Bickerton and Strearns 2002; Tufts 1998), greater attention must be paid to the process as well as the politics of organizing to ensure that new representational forms are inclusive of all workers.

CONCEPTUALIZING COMMUNITY UNIONISM:
LOCATION AND PROCESS

At the level of location and process, community unionism may be conceptualized by developing a typology with two axes. The first axis is a continuum of location that includes site, constituency, and issue-based organizing. The second axis is a continuum of process that moves from hierarchy to participation. Community unionism is located at the intersection of these two axes.

Location

The location continuum is defined by the ideal types of worksite-based organizing at one pole and "community" organizing at the other pole. Worksite-based organizing is located farthest to the left of community unionism. This location involves organizing that focuses on a single worksite, such as a factory, service provider, or public sector institution such as a university, where a single employer may be identified. Under this model, which represents a structural feature of collective bargaining arising from PC 1003, paid workers (normally employees) at one geographic site come together to collectivize their interests vis-à-vis their employer. They organize in bargaining units on the basis of a community of interest, normally defined by way of common work assignments and often by common employment relationships. Although it is dwindling, there is an age-old practice in Ontario of creating separate bargaining units for distinct occupational groups in a given worksite, such as clerical workers and assembly workers in a factory, and also for employees engaged in both part-time and full-time wage work (Fudge 1993; Forrest 1986). The assumption underpinning worksite-based unionism is that individual worksites, and subunits within them, are natural bargaining units.

This narrow view of the appropriate locus of organizing has a number of undesirable consequences for workers in precarious employment situations. It makes it extremely difficult for workers in precarious employment, such as temporary-help workers, to overcome the hard-bargaining tactics of employers in the long run because it isolates these workers in small units and often in small firms (MacDonald 1998a, 257; Vosko 2000, 265). Another problem is the principle of exclusivity – the practice of extending representation rights to a single union on the basis of majority role. These practices foster what Fudge (1993) labels a "symbiotic relationship" between bargaining unit structure and trade unionism, whereby union strategy is devised around the worksite norm. This worksite mode of organizing fails to take into account workers' needs to collectivize across a wide range of employment relationships (Annunziato 1990).

"Community," defined broadly, lies at the other end of the location continuum. This location is oriented to social location, and often a mixture of social location and social context, rather than a narrow worksite-based notion of location (for a discussion of the relationship between precarious employment, social location, and social context, see Cranford and Vosko, this volume). The notion of community employed here is highly fluid, constructed to fit a particular agenda. It may be a group of individuals linked by way of an issue-based campaign, such as Filipina hospitality workers denied access to Employment Insurance because of their short work weeks (Schenk, this volume). Alternatively, the notion of community may refer to a broad constituency, such as immigrant workers of colour who labour below legal standards. As a locus of organizing, community does not need to be tied to labour issues, although this chapter is concerned to identify forms of labour organizing oriented by a broad notion of community that extends beyond both the worksite and the labour force.

At the middle of this continuum, where community unionism takes expression, lie constituencies defined by hybrids of occupation and social location or by a common set of labour-related issues and concerns. At least two main types of community-oriented labour groups that are neither prototypical worksite-based unions nor community groups are evident: workers' associations and workers' centres. Workers' associations are organized around a specific labour market clustering. Examples include associations of domestic workers and homeworkers (Arat-Koc 1990; Bakan and Stasiulis 1997b; Borowy, Gordon, and Lebans 1993; Yalnizyan 1993). These associations are often seen as pre-union structures and are sometimes allied with trade unions. In contrast, workers' centres organize among workers from a range of occupations and industries around issues of fair labour standards and often include unemployed workers. The workers' centre is an institution/structure that challenges established modes of union organizing; this type of entity is neither a pre-union nor a typical community organization, although it focuses on workers' concerns and may provide limited legal and social services as well as training and education (Fine 1998). Examples of this organizational form include the Winnipeg Workers' Organizing and Resource Centre and the Immigrant Workers Centre / Travalleurs et Travalleuses Immigrant in Montreal. Although distinct in their focus, both organizational forms mix service provision and legal advice with labour organizing. Both groups are sponsored by charities, unions, or social service agencies that are relatively autonomous from the state or by a combination of such entities.

The two types of community-oriented labour groups are highly complementary: workers' associations organize on the basis of a specific labour force clustering, such as homeworkers or domestic workers, and have the potential to act as transitional union structures, while workers' centres are umbrella organizations that have the capacity to support these quasi-union structures but also to build a broader political base. Creating a political base of precariously employed women, immigrants, and people of colour also requires attention to the process of organizing.

Process

The "process" continuum is defined by the ideal types of hierarchical organizations at one pole and participatory organizations at the other. An extreme form of hierarchical working style can be visualized in an organization where one individual at the top makes the decisions. A more realistic scenario might involve the individual at the top making all the decisions in an executive committee, whose activities are also removed from rank-and-file members. Thus, such organizations reflect a particular leadership style, where one person and/or a small and exclusive group of individuals dominate. In such an archetype, local leaders, committees, and rank-and-file members have no opportunity to make any input or to affect ultimate decisions about the organization's activities. These organizations are undemocratic. Organizations of this type may be formalistic, rigid, and bound by traditions, constitutions, and rules. Alternatively, they may lack any formal structure at all and be run by informal rules of conduct defined by the person in leadership. Neither time nor resources are spent in reaching out to rank-and-file members. Instead, members are expected to contact the central office on their own volition. Typically, this process results in rank-and-file members making minimal or no contacts. It would also be difficult for workers at local levels to press for change within such a structure unless there was a mass movement from below to democratize the organization.

This hierarchical organizational form has been dominant in trade unions in various periods. The dominant form of unionism in the United States has, until the recent crisis period, been "business unionism." Business unionism emphasizes pragmatic bread-and-butter issues, rather than broad goals of social change, and focuses on servicing the members rather than empowering them or organizing new workers (Moody 1997; Robinson 2000). When new workers are organized, emphasis is placed on increasing membership dues rather than incorporating new members into the leadership of the union or the labour movement more broadly (Breecher and Costello 1996). The hierarchical structure discussed above is well suited to these goals. Although tendencies towards social unionism have been more common in Canada, particularly in the public sector, in the post-World War II boom, Canadian unions were also compelled by the state to make a compromise with employers – exchanging broad-based labour militancy for union recognition under the law. These developments influenced the increasingly worksite-based focus of trade unions as well as their increasingly hierarchical organizational forms (Fudge and Vosko 2001a).

A trade union adopting hierarchical organizational forms akin to a business is an undesirable organization for any rank-and-file worker, including prototypical standard workers. But it is particularly disadvantageous for precariously employed workers who require a variety of ways in which they can participate in a labour organization. Given their irregular work schedules and frequent fluctuation in location and forms of employment, a formal and hierarchical organization that offers activities and services at standard times and locations, discourages input from members, and functions in a paternalistic manner that would be counter to, or irrelevant to, their interests and needs. Moreover, many workers in precarious employment are women, immigrants, refugees, people of colour, and those for whom English or French is not their first language. A hierarchical structure would be inaccessible to them, not only because there are no entry points for them into the way the organization works but because such a centralized decision-making style is inappropriate for populations that have had minimal or no experience participating in labour organizations in Canada (Leah 1999).

At the other end of the process continuum lie participatory organizations. The small, grassroots organizations that follow a philosophy of community development is the ideal type (Das Gupta 1986; Stall and Stoeker 1998). These organizations view the involvement of members at every level as a principal objective. According to Stall and Stoeker (1998) and Das Gupta (1986), these organizations are particularly effective with poor, working-class immigrant women and women of colour. They place significant emphasis on conducting outreach, recruiting members, and providing information and training so they can take on leadership roles within the organization. In this organizational form, there are "many" leaders. In fact, every person is viewed as a potential leader. The concepts of self-help and self-organizing orient community development organizations. Outreach is aimed particularly at individuals and groups that are socially isolated, such as women with young children or those who are poor, elderly, live in remote areas, or experience language and other social barriers, including disabilities and systemic racism. Initially, outreach often takes the form of a "needs assessment" process or research into the needs of community members. Subsequently, individuals identified and contacted for the needs assessment become the basis for future activities. The research usually takes the form of an action research project, where members of the community become involved in defining the research methodology and in addressing the problems and needs identified through the research process itself (Das Gupta 1987).

To further facilitate members' involvement, specific accommodations are made, such as providing daycare or translation, or conducting meetings in more than one language led by indigenous leaders. Meetings may not be formally structured with a set agenda and Robert's Rules of Order. Rather, they may be relatively informal and participatory, where the chairperson is viewed as a facilitator and rotates periodically. Decisions are made not by moving motions but by reasoning, persuasion, checking with members outside the meeting structure, and reaching consensus. Such processes may not be conducive to short and quick decision-making, as discussions may continue until those affected by a decision have expressed their support of it and a consensus is reached.

Although such participatory processes are ideal for those who have been previously marginalized from formal organizations, including many groups that form the bulk of precariously employed workers, community organizations do not necessarily form around labour issues. Nor are they necessarily politicized (Aronowitz 1964; Williams 1964). The nature of a community development effort is unpredictable, as organizations following this philosophy emerge out of the process of sharing experiences of hardship and suffering by individuals at local levels. The agenda is never dictated from above. Moreover, the structure is loose, informal, and often temporary. An organization may form to address a particular problem in a local area, and it might fold up once the problem is addressed. Funding in these organizations is often very low or non-existent. Hence, continuity is not necessarily desirable or characteristic of this type of organization.

The reliance of some of these groups on state funding has created a certain dependence on government priorities, which may be antithetical to community development goals (Das Gupta 1999; Ng 1990). For example, in her study of a grassroots community employment centre for immigrant women and women of colour, Ng (1990) illustrates how state funding changed the centre's priorities from advocacy work for immigrant women to service provision for both employers and immigrant women. To sustain its funding base, the objective of the centre had to incorporate a measurable outcome, demonstrate "proper management," and spend more time on the production of documents – all of which compromised its community development goals and created tensions between staff and volunteer members (see also de Wolff, this volume).

At the middle of the "process" continuum, where community unionism lies, there is an effort to bring labour organizing together with the participatory nature of community development organizations. Specifically, the importance of educational and training programs for the empowerment of the most marginalized of workers is recognized (Ladd 1998; Leah 1999). Education becomes a vehicle to do outreach to unorganized workers, to inform them of their rights, to help them to develop the self-confidence to challenge their employers, and to become leaders or organizers in their own communities. The case of Toronto Organizing for Fair Employment (TOFFE) demonstrates the conception of community unionism offered here.

A CASE OF COMMUNITY UNIONISM: TORONTO ORGANIZING FOR FAIR EMPLOYMENT

Toronto Organizing for Fair Employment (TOFFE) is a worker-based community organization committed to improving the rights and working conditions of people in jobs that are unstable, low-paid, temporary, and contract.[2] TOFFE focuses most of its energy on the most precarious of these workers, such as temporary agency workers placed in factory and low-paid office work and those at the bottom of multiple subcontracting chains, rather than consultants who are better-paid and whose skills are recognized. Many of the workers that TOFFE connects with are precariously employed: they are in and out of work and constantly looking for a stable job. Thus, like the industrial unions of old, TOFFE also works with the unemployed. TOFFE consciously does outreach to recently arrived immigrant women and men of colour and sees its work as part of broader resistance to racialized and gendered class inequalities, as is the case in community development work. However, unlike much community organizing, TOFFE also targets employers. This set of circumstances has pushed TOFFE to practise community unionism. Community unionism takes expression in TOFFE's philosophy of organizing as well as its organizational form. TOFFE merged with the Workers' Information Centre in 2004 and, together, these two groups are developing an organization similar to many workers' centres.[3] The goal, and challenge, is to develop an organizational form that allows for a worker-centred philosophy of organizing (figure 17.1).

Philosophy of Organizing and Organizational Form

Like many community-based organizations, TOFFE must bridge the need for individual services with the imperative to organize collectively. In this climate of neo-liberal restructuring, community-based groups can become inundated with requests for services. This demand is not uncommon for grassroots groups focusing on labour issues. And the needs of recently arrived immigrant workers are great owing to the discrimination many experience on the basis of race, ethnicity, religion, legal status, accent, and gender (Das Gupta, this volume); the lack of recognition of credentials from the Global South; and the exclusion from, or marginalization within, other organizations, including some trade unions. TOFFE seeks to bridge the servicing/organizing divide through a worker-centred, self-organizing philosophy.

A self-organizing philosophy guides TOFFE's work. What is meant by self-organizing is the integration of leadership development, training, and education in all of TOFFE's work. The method of self-organizing is central to involving workers in strategizing about how to improve working conditions in their own lives and also in their given sector. Key components of the self-organizing approach are flexibility and openness to trying new organizing tactics that foster input from workers. This approach also involves frequent self-evaluation and critical reflection on strategy. As such, TOFFE's self-organizing model draws on a process-oriented philosophy of participatory democracy not unlike

Figure 17.1
Conceptualizing community unionism

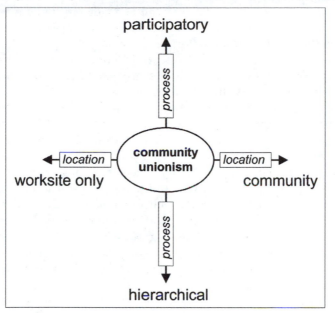

that of community development. It is focused on linking personal empowerment to community power through critical learning, self-reflection, and action.
In this way, TOFFE seeks to build a culture of organizing. However, it focuses
much more centrally on building a base of working-class resistance vis-à-vis
multiple employers than do groups engaged in community development.

TOFFE is developing an organizational form to fit this self-organizing philosophy. TOFFE and WIC are in the process of determining principles that
support self-organizing. Some of the principles that have emerged thus far
are maximum participation of those directly affected, leadership development, action for change, and shared learning. The flexibility of the self-
organizing model will allow for other principles to emerge if and when
appropriate. Key principles will serve as the questions members of the organization will ask themselves in order to evaluate the work. The working
idea envisions a process of worker involvement. First, workers engage with
TOFFE or WIC through a phone call asking for information about a particular problem at work or through one of the many workshops given by
TOFFE or WIC at employment resource centres. Second, workers are encouraged to stay in touch by inviting them to an educational workshop focusing on workers' rights. Others who are ready to get involved at a deeper
level move directly to the third stage, where workers are encouraged to
work on a concrete issue or campaign by joining a committee and/or getting

involved in membership meetings. In short, the idea is to merge information and education, both of which are traditionally driven by staff, with engagement and organizing so that decisions can be made largely by workers. Social change, at the level of both the law and employer practices, is envisioned through this process.

TOFFE's recent merger with the Workers' Information Centre has moved both groups towards a workers' centre focused on building a culture and capacity of organizing. Working together, the two groups are better able to bridge servicing and organizing. TOFFE and WIC have been working in partnership for three years. The specific mandate of WIC had been to provide phone-based and drop-in information and education to all workers encountering problems related to workers' rights and to address the full range of workplace rights (human rights, employment standards, workplace safety and insurance, labour relations provisions, occupational health and safety, and pay equity). TOFFE also provides information and education to temporary and contract workers who call the office, through workers' rights workshops and through its website.[4] Both groups seek to use these points of contact to involve people in organizing. TOFFE has always done outreach to a broad range of temporary and contract workers across occupation and, from its inception, it was committed to working with immigrants, people of colour, and women. For many workers, especially recent immigrants, people of colour, and women, permanent wage work mirrors many features of contract and temporary work. United, TOFFE and WIC plan to organize with contract and temporary workers as well as with workers with full-time permanent jobs where labour standards are regularly violated.

Drawing on the self-organizing model, TOFFE encourages workers to take leadership in defining strategy, organizing other workers in their sector, and building their organization. The goal is to institutionalize ongoing leadership development among workers, but also to recognize that the workers' precarious employment requires a varied and flexible structure. One way of reconciling these seemingly contradictory goals is to have important decisions about strategy and campaigns made not solely by the board of directors or the staff but in a multiplicity of worker-centred sites.

One site of building leadership is workers' committees. Over the course of its five years of organizing, TOFFE has mobilized several worker groups along various lines of solidarity and engaged in activities ranging from education to confrontation. The Tamil Temporary Agency Workers Committee, Scarborough, is made up of Sri Lankan Tamil women who are placed primarily in light manufacturing work. The work of the committee over the last year includes outreach to the Scarborough Tamil-speaking community by organizing drop-ins, through distributing flyers, and through a popular Tamil radio station. The group has made information about workers' rights accessible to this community by translating outreach materials into Tamil. Members of the committee have supported workers who have brought workplace problems forward and have helped to strategize how to improve working conditions.

One new initiative is a leadership-focused committee made up of a diverse group of women and men from the Tamil community, including temporary agency workers as well as community activists. It is focused on building organizing capacity to address employment issues in the Tamil community across Toronto. TOFFE also includes committees that work across ethnic and racial lines. The Downtown Temporary Agency Worker Committee is made up of workers from a range of industries, ethnic backgrounds, and geographical communities. This committee plans outreach, events, and work for temporary agency campaigns. The members created a temp-workers' booklet that they use to inform other temporary agency workers in various neighbourhoods. They hold monthly meetings and drop-ins to encourage others to get involved, to strategize about ways to address workplace problems, and to identify issues for education and lobbying. The value of flexibility, stemming from a philosophy of self-organizing, means creating space for the incorporation of other groups in the future as well as shorter-term committees. By the fall of 2004, six employer-specific committees had been formed focusing on employers who have violated the *Employment Standards Act*.

Many recently arrived immigrant workers and young workers have approached TOFFE for information regarding issues of unpaid wages or discrimination. Bringing them together to work collectively, TOFFE has provided training and support to speak publicly about their experiences, conduct media interviews, and speak out about the need to improve the ESA. Another multi-ethnic committee, one that also organizes across employment relationships, is the Action Committee. This group will bring together some of the concerns raised by specific unfair employer practices focusing more concretely on the problems with the ESA. To date, the group has helped to organize delegations to "bad bosses" and to formulate a campaign that addresses the problems with both the scope of coverage in and the enforcement of the ESA. This committee was formed at the first membership meeting, which is another place for worker leadership.

Membership meetings are envisioned as a key site for the building of worker leadership. Individuals who have connected with TOFFE on a particular issue, as well as longer-term members, are invited to these meetings. TOFFE had its first membership meeting in the fall of 2004, and it plans to have one each season. The meetings are envisioned as a place where newer workers can learn concretely about ongoing campaigns and be encouraged to participate as they meet other members and staff. The meetings are also seen as a place where workers can be involved in decision-making regarding future campaign and programming work. The way in which this vision may unfold in practice was evident at the first membership meeting: over 80 people attended this Friday evening meeting, attesting to a growing interest in organizing to challenge precarious employment. Followed by ample socializing over refreshments, the agenda included an update on the organizational development process by one of the worker representatives. Workers also shared stories that demonstrated the work of TOFFE as well as the possibilities for change. These stories illustrate the principle of shared learning. Shared learning is the process of sharing how one has learned to address a particular crisis, which in turn results in more collective reflection, strategic planning, and action. Shared learning also reflects the expansion of knowledge and experience beyond the staff to individual workers, and eventually to the broader membership. For example, at the fall membership meeting in 2004, a worker shared her experience participating in a delegation to a factory which owes over $35,000 in unpaid wages. Through this experience, others learned about the direct action tactics used by TOFFE. It is also important to share victory stories in order to show others what is possible. At this meeting, workers and staff performed a skit to illustrate how a dishwasher won $1,700 in unpaid wages by working with TOFFE. After demonstrating the success of delegations and other direct action tactics, the attendees were encouraged to join committees and get involved in organizing.

Through a multi-site and flexible organizational form, continuously crafted to fit a self-organizing philosophy, TOFFE and the Workers' Information Centre are engaged in innovative work to link individual services to collective organizing. The merits of this approach are clear from an examination of their organizing with temporary agency workers.

Organizing for Fair Employment in Toronto:
Temporary Agency Campaigns

The ways in which TOFFE is developing a broad base of worker organization is well illustrated through its campaign work. TOFFE has organized campaigns to address issues related to the lack of enforcement of employment standards, the lack of regulation in the temporary agency sector, and abusive subcontracting relationships. Following the self-organizing model, the goal of these campaigns is not just to achieve a specific demand, although individual and group victories are crucial. The ultimate objective is to build workers' power to enforce fair working conditions and to obtain secure employment. This objective can be broken down into a number of smaller goals: to support workers in fighting back against employers; to let employers know that workers, with the help of TOFFE, are seeking to enforce laws on the books; to encourage additional worker participation as they see that other workers, with TOFFE, have had success; and to create the political will to change the laws to suit temporary and contract workers.

One of TOFFE's significant campaigns focuses on temporary agency work. In this sector, the range of labour standards problems evident elsewhere in the labour market are multiplied by the triangular employment relationship between the client, the temporary agency, and the worker. Beginning with the experiences of workers in the Downtown and Tamil temporary agency committees and expanding to other workers, TOFFE documented several issues facing temporary agency workers: temporary agency workers often do the same work as permanent workers but do not receive equal pay; temporary agency workers are paid only when on assignment and are often not assigned sufficient hours, making it difficult to earn a living wage; employment agencies include anti-competition clauses in their contracts with clients, resulting in fees charged to clients who hire a temporary agency worker; because of the shifting of training and safety responsibility between the agency and the client company, there are high accident rates in temporary jobs; and temporary agency workers do not have the ability to form a trade union because of the single employer – single worksite collective bargaining model in Ontario. The final problems identified by TOFFE are related to the lack of fit between the *Employment Standards Act* and temporary agency work. Currently, temporary workers are entitled to the minimum paid vacation time stipulated in the ESA, but they have difficulty accessing it because of the stipulation of employment tenure of 12 months combined with low tenure among temporary workers. They are also entitled to unpaid sick days, but those who are able to afford to take unpaid days off, a small minority, face the likely possibility that the agency will not give them additional assignments. Lastly, temporary agency workers are often not paid for statutory holidays.

The inability of temporary workers to access paid statutory holidays developed into a full-blown campaign, one that highlights the link between violations of employment standards and the temporary employment relationship. Employment agencies have argued that temporary agency workers "elect to work." This legal notion means that a worker has the choice to elect to work or not when offered assignments *without penalty*. In Ontario, the ESA states that elect-to-work employees are exempt from public holiday pay entitlements. Temporary agency workers are routinely told when they sign an employment contract with a temporary agency that they elect to work. However, workers report that when they are not available or turn down an assignment, the agency does not call them again. In fact, when they register with an agency, workers are also often told that their attendance is expected.

The campaign for public holiday pay began with outreach activities to workers and public pressure on agencies. These activities represented a joint endeavour of the Tamil Temp Workers group and the Downtown Temp Workers group. They began when a member of the Downtown Temp Workers group shared her experience with her group of not receiving public holiday pay from the temporary agency. When TOFFE organizers reported this information to the members of the Tamil committee, the committee expressed an interest in participating in a campaign on this issue since its members had also experienced inconsistent payment for public holidays. Furthermore, through its contact with many more temporary agency workers in the community, the committee felt there was widespread abuse by temporary agencies of this provision of the Act. TOFFE further investigated and discovered that the Association of Canadian Search, Employment & Staffing Services (ACSESS), the temporary industry lobby group, informed its member agencies that temporary agency workers were not entitled to public holiday pay.

Temporary agency workers, with TOFFE staff, engaged in a number of actions to make visible the lack of public holiday pay for temporary workers. Much of the work was directed towards mobilizing workers. TOFFE conducted an education and training session on holiday pay with the temporary agency workers. Before each public holiday in May, July, and September, TOFFE members and other temporary agency workers informed other workers about their legal right to public holiday pay through leafleting, drop-offs of flyers at community centers, and posters in Employment Resource Centres and other places where people look for work. In December a volunteer dressed up as Santa Claus handed out flyers at busy street corners in neighbourhoods with a high number of temporary workers. Members also used community media to get the word out. The Tamil Temp Workers group organized a segment about holiday pay on the local Tamil radio station. Chinese and Filipino community newspapers also covered the campaign. TOFFE communicated this violation of the *Employment Standards Act* to frontline staff at community agencies working with newcomers, in order to involve them in tracking workers who had not been paid public holiday pay and in connecting these workers with TOFFE. Finally, TOFFE and its members directed their action towards employers. Just before the Christmas holidays, they faxed a bulletin to over 500 temporary agencies in the greater Toronto area arguing that, as employers, temporary agencies had the responsibility to pay statutory holiday pay. They also hand delivered a letter to the ACSESS Toronto Chapter board meeting to explain their concerns directly and demand a change in the board's position on workers' status as elect to work.

This worker outreach and employer pressure provided a successful policy dimension to the campaign and supported a broader review of the ESA by the Employment Standards Work Group in coalition with TOFFE and others. Within this broader umbrella, TOFFE and its members engaged in discussions with the Ministry of Labour over the issue of public holiday pay as an example of a grey area in the ESA as it applies to temporary agency workers. The Ministry's position is that the elect-to-work status can only be determined on a case-by-case basis. TOFFE met with the director of the Employment Standards Branch in October 2003 and requested that the ministry write to ACSESS to clarify the ESA provisions on holiday pay for temporary agency workers. As a result, the ministry did write to ACSESS regarding the incorrect recommendation to its member agencies that all temporary workers are in the elect-to-work category. TOFFE also supported two workers in filing claims with the Ontario Ministry of Labour through Toronto's Parkdale Communty Legal Clinic. In one case, the agency settled and paid the holiday pay. In the other, the employment standards officer sided with the agency. TOFFE and Parkdale appealed the decision, and it went to an arbitrator with the Ontario Labour Relations Board. The arbitrator made a decision in favour of the worker. That resulted not only in the agency having to pay holiday pay to the individual worker but also in a potentially important legal precedent on elect-to-work status. The arbitrator agreed that the worker did not have a choice to "elect to work" but, rather, that he would jeopardize further assignments if he did not take the assignment he was given. TOFFE continues to strategize as to how to use this decision in its ongoing organizing efforts. It is also working with its allies to recommend the removal of temporary agency workers from this elect-to-work classification as well as on other changes to the ESA.

This campaign won holiday pay for individual temporary agency workers and, most important, it also built worker leadership. The training, combined with TOFFE's organizational support, helped workers to demand holiday pay from temporary agencies. As in all its advocacy work, TOFFE trained individual temporary workers to negotiate with their employer as well as to apply pressure with knowledge of their rights. In many cases, temporary workers were successful in gaining their pay. In those instances where temp agencies refused to provide holiday pay, TOFFE phoned to give them information or wrote letters to request payment. As a result, a number of agencies called TOFFE, whose staff then informed them of their obligation to comply with the *Employment Standards Act*. Leadership development that supported this campaign included general training on organizing and mobilizing, including instruction on outreach, speaking to the media, and techniques for public speaking. It also involved specific attention to policy work, particularly employment standards as they relate to the temporary agency sector. These sessions have been critical in building confidence, focusing members' presentations on key messages, and motivating workers to speak out about their experiences. Through training and practice, the temporary workers became more confident and they told others in their community about their success. Thus, in addition to developing leadership, the number of temporary agency workers involved has grown. In turn, the posters and the radio show helped to inform a broader group of temporary agency workers, and TOFFE received more calls from temporary workers. TOFFE has worked with many temporary workers to assist them in seeking their employers' compliance with the Act and in obtaining outstanding holiday pay. More generally, this campaign built awareness among temporary workers about the issues they face collectively.

This process-oriented self-organizing model resulted in a growth in participation and in worker leadership in TOFFE. The public holiday campaign is only one example of how TOFFE is building worker leadership through an innovative organizational form. TOFFE engages in a range of outreach tactics, including frequent social events that provide workers with a space to build solidarities, have fun, and develop leadership. For instance, TOFFE held a barbecue in a local community park for workers and their families: the social and recreational aspects of such meetings are crucial in breaking the isolation and demoralization of precarious employment. TOFFE has begun a tradition of staging a public meeting during "temp week" in June to outreach to new workers and, at the end of the year, a winter party for members. Planning committees of workers help to organize these events, including extensive outreach to employment centres, community agencies, and other public places. The programs include music and food as well as discussions facilitated by TOFFE members and volunteers. These occasions provide a space for people to connect with each other, even as they are sites for learning and strategizing. For instance, a key objective of the June 2004 meeting was to gauge temp workers' demands for legislative changes in order to present them to the minister of labour in an upcoming meeting. The hundred workers in attendance organized into small group discussions, which were facilitated by committee members and other volunteers. At the end of the evening, each group wrote its message to the minister on pieces of materials that were then attached to a large 3 metre banner. This banner has become a visual document of the policy and the legislative demands of temporary agency and other precariously employed workers. Through these events TOFFE aims to develop a "culture of organizing, struggle and connection," to quote TOFFE coordinator Deena Ladd. With the new organizational structure, this culture of organizing will be increasingly harnessed to building a base of worker leadership.

CONCLUSION

Given its ability to bring together collective organizing outcomes targeting employers as well as participatory community organizing, community unionism has the potential to reach, organize, and enable precariously employed workers. As conceptualized here, community unionism fosters the organization of workers around labour concerns at the same time as it emphasizes the critical importance of processes and structures that enable the active participation of workers from various social locations.

Precarious employment is on the rise in Canada. One of its significant features is the lack of unionization, due partly to the type of unionization cultivated by the dominant model of collective bargaining: it assumes the norm of an adult white male citizen worker who holds a standard job in a single worksite. Reality departs from this image and, therefore, organizers and academics alike need to explore alternative models that cover workers who may be working from several worksites, at different times of the day or night, and for different lengths of time. These trends require a joining of labour market unionism and community unionism.

Labour market unionism is concerned with broader-based bargaining. In exploring new models of organizing suitable to the range of precariously employed workers today, a historical survey of labour market unionism is highly instructive. Some craft unions of old went beyond organizing in a single worksite and included all workers skilled in a trade. Indeed, in the early 20th century, workers in precarious situations, such as waitresses, janitors, and garment workers, used a variant of craft unionism in their efforts to limit wage competition. Industrial unions of old included both skilled and unskilled workers in the same industry, some of whom were women. A few of these industrial unions also went beyond narrow workplace preoccupations by organizing workers across industries and organizing the unemployed. In contemporary Canada, construction workers and artists have employed similar strategies and legislative innovations to bargain collectively for rights and standards over large geographic distances, cutting across worksites and employers. Community unionism is also essential to organizing precariously employed workers, especially women, immigrants, and workers of colour.

Community unionism lies at the intersection of two axes – *location* and *process*. Location refers to sites, constituencies, and issues. Process refers to levels of participation and styles of leadership. The extreme archetypes on this typology are business unions, with their preoccupation with single worksite-based bargaining and rigid, top-down decision-making style, and, as a contrast, community development organizations, whose boundary or focus of organization is highly fluid and where empowerment and participatory decision-making are paramount. Community unionism reflects the point at which there is, theoretically, a perfect balancing of locational diversity or hybridity and worker participation. The Toronto-based group TOFFE exemplifies a contemporary variant.

While placing importance on such ingredients as worker empowerment through support, education, and leadership development, TOFFE maintains a focus on organizing and advocating for fair employment for workers across various locations, including occupation, sector, industry, employment form, gender, and ethnic identity. The organization embodies several different forms and levels of politics that are inclusive. From its inception, TOFFE has deliberately chosen to ally itself with the most marginalized among workers, including recent immigrants of colour who work in such sectors as temporary agency work or subcontracted work. The organization also works with the unemployed and with people who cycle in and out of the labour force. While it nourishes solidarity among workers of the same ethnic group, in the same industry, or geographical setting – for example, Tamil temporary agency workers in Scarborough – it also organizes workers across ethnicity and race – for instance, temporary agency workers in downtown Toronto. In these multi-ethnic worker groups, solidarity is based on common forms and conditions of work. This solidarity is reminiscent of the early craft/occupational unionism, where workers asserted a common set of minimum standards that may or may not exist in law. This goal was evident in 2003, when temporary agency workers from different parts of Toronto, and placed in different industries, came together for a common campaign around holiday pay. Cross-sector and cross-ethnic solidarities are also built through social functions that bring workers together around the need to break their isolation and form a sense of community and common culture – TOFFE's work includes these activities as well. In its merger with WIC to form a workers' centre, TOFFE has moved from focusing solely on "contingent work" to addressing precarious employment along multiple dimensions.

Through attentiveness to multiple social locations and the wide-ranging issues around which organizing can take place, community unionism fosters the objective of building worker leadership and expanding worker consciousness from the level of the individual worker to membership in a larger community or collective. While TOFFE supports individual workers by providing information, advocacy, and translation, it also provides group support through socials, educational workshops about workers' rights, and training in advocacy, so that workers themselves are empowered to become organizers in larger campaigns. In this way, the principles of "empowerment" and "community" are integral elements of TOFFE. The commitment to a self-organizing philosophy is also evident in the various committees organized under the TOFFE-WIC umbrella as well as its emerging organizational form. The goal is to develop an organizational form that includes multiple sites for worker leadership to grow. This innovative idea has the potential to create strong and ensuring worker leadership, despite the workers' unstable employment situations.

It is impossible to generalize from any case study, for the value of ethnography is its ability to document processes in context. This study illustrates the utility of elevating process on a par with location in conceptualizing community unionism and in practical efforts at union renewal. This conceptualization of community unionism also leaves space for considering other elements that may be significant in organizing – for example, political ideology, neigh-bourhood, or other social locations such as legal status or disability. The broad notion adopted here may shed light on processes occurring in other groups. Given the need for a range of organizations and organizational forms, coalition politics is crucial in coordinating and sustaining larger-scale campaigns. However, these broader campaigns must also pay attention to processes of leadership in order to realize the potential power of community unionism. Alongside the structures of representation and alternative legisla-tive models examined elsewhere in this volume, a plurality of modes of orga-nizing is needed to encompass different issues, locations, and identities around which workers coalesce and to identify their varied concerns for so-cial change. Community unionism allows for this multiplicity.

What Is to Be Done?
Harnessing Knowledge to Mitigate
Precarious Employment

LEAH F. VOSKO

Precarious employment is growing in the Canadian labour market. Beginning in the mid-1970s and expanding through to the early 21st century, workers in Canada have endured the spread of forms of work often involving atypical employment contracts, limited social benefits and statutory entitlements, job insecurity, low wages, and high risks of ill-health. These trends are particularly acute for those workers in already marginalized social locations, such as women of colour and people with disabilities, and social contexts vulnerable to economic restructuring and privatization, such as ancillary workers in health care, meat inspectors, door-to-door sales people, and counsellors providing employment supports to recent immigrants. They are evident in statistical, sociological, legal, and policy analyses as well as in explorations of work organization and health concerned with the effects of employment uncertainty, regulatory failings, and challenges to institutions and practices critical to limiting labour market insecurity.

Collectively, these findings give rise to the fundamental question: What is to be done? What avenues are available for improving knowledge in the attempt to better workers' conditions of work and quality of health?

This chapter considers the conceptual and technical bases for making positive social change. Building on the conversation between theory, method, evidence, and practice orienting the volume, it advances four promising avenues for continued research oriented to mitigating precarious employment: the first avenue involves adopting a new statistical approach to conceptualizing and measuring precarious employment – one that reflects multi-dimensional rather than dichotomous understandings and is sensitive to social relations, occupation, industry, environment, and geography. The second avenue entails shifting away from job-level understandings of work organization and health to focus on employment relationships. The conventional notion of "job strain" – understood to result from the interaction between workload and control at work – does not reflect the experience of the precariously employed. This construct must give way to the notion of "employment strain," which captures the unique aspects of control in contexts where workers are constantly searching for work. The third new direction involves focusing analysis on regulatory effectiveness, moving away from studies of laws and policies on the books to broader analyses of their implications in practice. Given the misfit between law, legislation, and policy and the realities of the labour market, a growing number of workers are unprotected. They range from temporary agency and solo self-employed workers dispersed across varied contexts, whose employment status and/or form of employment shapes their limited access to regulatory protection, to workers excluded from coverage in key jurisdictions, unaware of their coverage, or ill-equipped to secure basic labour rights because of either a lack of knowledge or the paucity of enforcement measures. The fourth, and final, avenue involves joining praxis and theory in devising innovative strategies enabling workers in precarious employment to defend their rights. On the one hand, there is a need for a plurality of representational forms that extend beyond the dominant single worksite and single employer model. On the other hand, a politically oriented unionism, with a social movement emphasis, is necessary to address the representational needs of workers experiencing the full force of precarious employment.

CHARTING FUTURE RESEARCH

There is no simple formula for diagnosing a central ill of the Canadian labour market – precarious employment – but, rather, multiple approaches to knowing this phenomenon. It is nevertheless possible to arrive at a common understanding of precarious employment. As the chapters in this volume demonstrate, precarious employment may be distinguished from non-standard work. In contrast to this dominant and decidedly neutral moniker, it is best conceived of relationally, as shaped by employment status, form of employment, and dimensions such as limited control over the labour process, low income, a lack of permanency or a high level of uncertainty, and minimal regulatory protection. Contributors concur on a conception of precarious employment that is time, context, and location sensitive as well as process oriented. The main implication of this conception is that precarious employment takes expression in different ways over time, reflecting employment norms and the state of play of social relations, such as gender and "race" relations, both in households and in the labour force.

That precarious employment is relational is evident when we examine its diverse manifestations historically and geographically alongside the normative power and material strength of the standard employment relationship – an employment norm prevailing to date and identified with a full-time continuous employment relationship where the worker has one employer, works on the employer's premises under his or her direct supervision, normally in a unionized workplace, and has access to a social wage, and with a male breadwinner-female caregiver gender contract. Precarious employment is always shaped by struggles between workers and employers (often mediated by the state) and by the social and employment norms and household forms they reflect and engender. The dominant approaches to statistical conceptualization and measurement, to work organization and health, to the design of labour and social security law and policy, and to organizing strategies challenged in this volume are all products of this interplay.

Conceptualizing and Measuring Precarious Employment: From Dichotomous to Multi-dimensional Understandings

There is a pressing need to adopt approaches to conceptualizing and measuring precarious employment that reflect its relational nature. What is required is a movement away from the standard/non-standard dichotomy towards a methodological approach sensitive to the interaction between employment status and form of employment, dimensions of precariousness, and social context and location.

It is a mistake to equate precarious employment with non-standard work. Yet this slippage should not be surprising: the main commonality among the forms of employment and work arrangements comprising the non-standard work catchall is that they deviate from the standard employment relationship and are highly correlated with precarious employment, since this norm still organizes social and labour policy. Whether or not a worker earns wages from employment or income from self-employment, works full time or part time, or engages in shift work is critical to the experience of precarious employment. But employment status and form of employment, as well as work arrangements, are not definitive. For example, full-time permanent wage workers may be vulnerable to dimensions of precarious employment even though they hold jobs conforming closely to the standard employment relationship. As Schenk demonstrates in his case study of hotel workers, the gains of precariously employed workers, including securing full-time permanent wage work, are always tenuous, sensitive to economic restructuring and to human disasters. And, for certain groups, such as people of colour, even full-time permanent wage work may be poorly remunerated and devoid of a social wage. Furthermore, as Lewchuk, de Wolff, King, and Polanyi demonstrate by investigating the health implications of what they label the new "contract culture," and as I illustrate in my portrait of precarious employment in the Canadian labour force, the deterioration of forms of employment closely resembling the standard employment relationship is just as central to understanding precarious employment as the proliferation of so-called new forms of employment and work arrangements.

The need to break away from the standard/non-standard dichotomy is evident in the chapters in Part One, Mapping Precarious Employment in Canada: New Statistical Insights, and in chapter 14, "The Union Dimension," by Anderson, Beaton, and Laxer, which explore a central indicator of control over the labour process. Collectively, these chapters illustrate that statistical measures employing the notion of non-standard work to study labour market insecurity risk mystifying its nature and dynamics; this catchall provides only limited insight into dimensions of precarious employment.

The tendency to obscure forces driving continuity and change can be overcome through a new methodological approach. One logical step in responding to the overlap in the non-standard category is to adopt a mutually exclusive measure. However, chapters 2 and 3 illustrate empirically, for both wage workers and the self-employed, that considering the form of employment alone is insufficient to the task of understanding precarious employment. Legal and policy analyses focusing on the need to adapt minimum employment standards (Bernstein, this volume) and the failure of occupational health and safety regulation (this volume, Lippel; Tucker) substantiate these findings. Building on the early insights of European scholars, such as Rodgers (1989), and more recent work by Fudge (1997), Standing (1992), and Supiot (1999a), it is critical to consider dimensions of precarious employment such as control over the labour process, income level, and degree of regulatory protection in conceptualizing precarious employment statistically.

Casting attention to the dimensions of precarious employment adds depth to analyses of form of employment – in this way, the European scholarship of the late 1980s represented a major breakthrough (see, for example, Bettio and Villa 1989; Butchtemann and Quack 1990; Huws, Hurstfield, and Holtmaat 1989; Muckenberger 1989; Rodgers 1989; Rubery 1989). However, one contribution of this volume is that the dimensions of precarious employment enumerated originally are limited in several ways. The sheer size of self-employment in Canada (which stood at 15 per cent of total employment in 2003), and problems flowing from the tendency, at a policy level, to equate self-employment with entrepreneurship, illustrate that conceptualizing precarious employment demands a more expansive set of dimensions reflecting the changing nature of self-employment. While useful, most analyses of precarious employment assume the situation of a wage worker. To remedy this problem, chapter 3 advances several modified dimensions suitable to the self-employed – namely, regulatory protection and social benefits, job certainty, control over one's employment situation, and income adequacy – and applies suitable indicators to reveal a gendered continuum of forms of self-employment. Enlarging dimensions of precarious employment in this way is promising because it opens space for tailoring them to the employment status in question.

What other methodological challenges must be met to develop a relational conception of precarious employment at a statistical level? Are further steps necessary to secure the movement away from dichotomous to multi-dimensional understandings of this phenomenon? As the remaining chapters in Part One demonstrate, another methodological consideration relates to capturing how intersecting social locations, shaped by race, gender, (dis)ability, and age, as well as occupation and industry, shape precarious employment. This consideration is essential to achieving a location- and context-sensitive statistical approach. To this end, chapter 2 advances a new method using the metaphor of a map. In this case, the focus is wage workers, but Cranford and Vosko highlight how race and gender intersect with occupation in shaping precarious employment. In parallel, chapter 4 demonstrates how people with disabilities, especially women, dominate in forms of employment with low average annual earnings.

Applying this methodological approach in a specific context, chapter 5 takes the mapping method to a different level – Armstrong and Laxer develop occupation-appropriate indicators of the dimension of regulatory protection and control, such as poor schedule (e.g., night, rotating, on-call, split shifts), and apply them to ancillary workers in health care. Their analysis contributes richly to understanding the industrial and occupational dynamics of precarious employment by illustrating how, in the face of privatization, ancillary workers in health care increasingly resemble their counterparts in the private sector.

By way of this mapping approach, Anderson, Beaton, and Laxer, in contrast, elevate a dimension of precarious employment – control over the labour process – by centring the analysis in chapter 14 on the union/non-union distinction. The mapping approach advanced in this volume allows them to elevate a single dimension and consider it in relation to social location. Building on the notion of a "racialized gendering of jobs" advanced in chapter 3, and complementing Das Gupta's concern to discover how low rates of unionization affect people of colour, Anderson, Beaton, and Laxer illustrate that workers in some social locations lack control over the labour process more than others, and that union coverage brings greater benefits to some groups of workers than to others.

At both a conceptual and a technical level, the importance of breaking from dichotomous to more textured and multi-dimensional understandings of precarious employment should now be evident. Several chapters in this volume initiate this methodological departure. Yet more in-depth analyses of forms of employment and dimensions of precarious employment, as well as social location and context, are required to develop this approach and to test its merits and shortcomings. A sharper focus on place of work is especially important – both to expand analyses to other national and subnational cases and to take regional differences within Canada, especially rural and urban distinctions, into fuller account. Several chapters in this volume demonstrate that the location and choice (although often highly constrained) of the worksite shapes our understanding of precarious employment. Yet more empirical studies are needed to apprehend the often complex relationships between geography, industry, and social location.

The Health Effects of Precarious Employment: From Job Strain to Employment Strain

A second avenue for advancing knowledge on precarious employment involves replacing the narrow notion of job strain (Karasek 1979; Karasek and Theorell 1990) with the more expansive concept of employment strain in analyses concerned with work and health.

Evolving from exchanges across the Community University Research Alliance on Contingent Employment and elaborated in chapter 6 by Lewchuck, de Wolff, King, and Polanyi, the notion of employment strain reflects the lack of decision-making authority and unique forms of employment uncertainty facing workers in precarious employment. Job strain refers only to those dimensions of the control-demand-support trilogy captured in the labour process of a particular job, normally at a large, single, industrial, male-dominated worksite. It does not consider seriously the links between health and the employment relationship – specifically, how workers acquire and keep work and negotiate their working conditions. Employment strain, in contrast, adds dimensions of uncertainty over future job possibilities, earnings, work location, work schedule, and type of work to the well-known construct of job strain and elements of work-intensity or workload commonly experienced by workers in precarious employment, including the burden of job search, balancing multiple jobs, and pressures associated with constant evaluation by fellow workers and management.

Strains tied to the labour process at a particular job, as well as employment status and form of employment, affect the health of all workers. For the precariously employed, limited control and decision-making latitude on the job in terms of work schedule (Armstrong and Laxer, this volume), over the nature of the work contract (this volume, Borowy; Cranford and Vosko; De Wolff; Schenk), and across multiple employment situations (Lewchuck, de Wolff, King, and Polanyi, this volume), as well as over shifts from employment to unemployment (Tompa, Scott, Trevithick, and Bhattacharyya, this volume) contribute to high levels of uncertainty that can impact negatively on workers' health. The construct of employment strain and its four central components – employment relationship uncertainty (control), employment relationship workload, employment relationship support, and household insecurity – must move to the centre of discussions about the health implications of precarious employment.

The notion of employment strain is consistent with a central argument advanced across this volume – that limiting precarious employment requires analysts to think outside the labour force or the sphere of jobs and to re-examine commonplace understandings of "control," "uncertainty," and "constraint." Its components resonate in statistical analyses as well as in qualitative research demonstrating the many workers in precarious employment who cycle in and out of the labour force, hold multiple jobs simultaneously, and face considerable obstacles in exerting control over the labour process, often with significant consequences for their own health as well as the health of those they serve. Embracing the notion of employment strain, to supplement and move beyond conventional understandings of job strain, is critical to continued research aimed at limiting precarious employment, from efforts centred on changing laws and policies both on the books and in practice to those related to transforming institutions. Such efforts might well include more qualitative studies of workers' experience of employment strain over time as well as quantitative research linking survey research targeting specific groups to statistical instruments designed to capture broader trends in labour markets.

Achieving Regulatory Effectiveness:
From Laws and Policies on the Books to Legislative
and Policy Outcomes in Practice

Precarious employment is intimately intertwined with the legal regime governing work relations. Understanding it, therefore, requires consideration of the scope of coverage under a given law, regulation, or policy, yet it also calls for addressing labour market regulation more broadly – or the complex of formal and informal laws, institutions, policies, and cultural attitudes that organize and constrain the relationships and practices of paid work. As chapter 9 illustrates, at the level of the law the experience of precarious employment can relate to legal coverage, awareness of coverage, legal design, policies on application and enforcement (formal and informal), employer avoidance, and disparities of power and inequalities between groups of workers.

The most obvious, and indeed fundamental, example of exclusion due to a lack of legal coverage is the common requirement for the existence of a subordinated employment relationship for the application of a given law.

The distinction between a genuine independent contractor and an employee is of critical importance not only at a provincial level, as is the case in Quebec (Bernstein, this volume), but across national and subnational borders and legal traditions (Deakin 2002a; Fudge, Tucker, and Vosko 2002; ILO 2000b; Supiot 2001). The vicious cycle of precariousness experienced by migrant farm workers in Ontario also relates to a lack of coverage. Yet, in this instance, the justification for exclusion under the province's *Occupational Health and Safety Act* flows singularly from these workers' citizenship status (Tucker, this volume). The same is true for undocumented workers in Quebec, although not across all other provincial jurisdictions (Bernstein, Lippel, and Lamarche 2001).

Limited awareness of coverage among workers, especially if accompanied by employer avoidance, can also exacerbate characteristics of precarious employment, such as high risks of ill-health, and prolong recovery from injuries and return to work. Many temporary workers, for example, encounter difficulties with regard to the identification of their employer because they are involved in a triangular employment relationship; in this instance, a lack of clarity over who is the boss (e.g., the client or the agency) can lead to confusion on the part of the worker and the failure to comply with employment-related obligations on the part of the other parties to this relationship (Vosko 2000). Lippel illustrates this problem vividly in her analysis of the case law on occupational health and safety regulation in Quebec, where case law has found, for the most part, that the agency, rather than the client with whom the worker has been placed, is the employer. But she is careful to state that the case law is not unanimous. In reporting on disputes over who should bear the cost, Lippel relays the poignant story of a truck driver injured several hundred kilometres from home who ultimately had to telephone his spouse to bring him back from the hospital because of a lengthy dispute between the agency and the client over who was responsible for the cost of the ambulance ride deemed necessary by health-care officials.

In other cases, a lack of enforcement is the crux of the problem. As the ethnography of TOFFE illustrates, workers in precarious employment may be aware that they are covered under a given law or policy yet still lack the resources to seek enforcement; that was true of many of the temp workers seeking pubic holiday pay owed to them by their employers (i.e., the temp agencies that placed them with client firms) under Ontario's *Employment Standards Act*. These workers had to take enforcement into their own hands and educate the central temporary industry lobby group in Canada, as well as many of its members, that agencies' failure to pay temp workers for public holidays was illegal. Before they came together to respond collectively, due partly to their isolation and partly to their lack of access to formal union structures, fear of reprisal limited individual workers' capacity to seek justice as well as better terms and conditions of employment.

Laws on the books are of limited use in mitigating precarious employment where policies on application and enforcement are weak, employer avoidance is common, and disparities in power between employers and workers are sharp because of precarious citizenship status, high levels of job uncertainty, and other factors. A broad conception of regulatory effectiveness is necessary if future research is to address fully the growing array of labour market locations and their intersection with diverse social locations, and to cultivate innovative strategies enabling workers in precarious employment to defend their rights.

Towards "New" Unionisms

A decisive factor in shaping the response to precarious employment is the difficulty experienced by the mainstream labour movement in coping with employment statuses, forms of employment, and work arrangements deviating from the standard employment relationship. This difficulty relates to mounting legal obstacles to collective representation as well as a lack of understanding, on the part of some unions, of the needs of people of colour, women, people with disabilities, youth, and immigrants seeking to organize to improve their conditions of work.

Clearly, there is a need for reviving, developing, and sustaining representational forms that extend beyond the dominant model of the single worksite and the single employer. In response to this challenge, chapter 17 calls for reconsidering the age-old representational form of craft/occupational unionism. One of its main contentions is that this type of unionism could go considerable ways in enabling workers with complex job-mobility paths (Wial 1993) to gain collective representation, including temp workers and workers selling products and services door to door who are frequently misclassified as independent contractors, even though they work for a single subcontractor.[1] Consistent with other studies in this volume and elsewhere, however, the larger argument here is that a plurality of representational forms is necessary to meet the needs of workers in precarious employment (see, for example, Middleton 1996; Schenk 2003; Wial 1993). New legislative models departing from the prototypical craft union form, such as the federal *Status of the Artist Act* (and parallel legislation in Quebec), which allows professional artists who are independent contractors to form associations and to bargain collectively with federal producers, are also instructive in envisioning a collective bargaining regime centred on a sector that spans a large geography or where workers produce products or perform services for multiple clients (Farkas 1999; Macpherson 1999). Many workers in precarious employment lack access to basic employment standards – standards that could be enforced through scale agreements of minimum terms akin to those formerly existing in Ontario under the now defunct *Industrial Standards Act* and what remains of the decree system in Quebec (Grant 2004).

Alternative or innovative legislative models are no panacea, neither for enabling workers to secure their basic labour rights nor for building more inclusive forms of representation (Das Gupta, this volume). Rather, adapting organizing processes is a necessary ingredient in moving towards unionisms open to workers who occupy a diversity of social locations. Community unionism is particularly promising in revitalizing the labour movement to incorporate more fully not only women but people of colour and immigrants too (Das Gupta 1986; Fudge 1994; Leah 1999; Spink 2000; Wilton and Cranford 2002). As both TOFFE's association-building activities (chapter 17) and the pre-SARS hotel workers' struggle (chapter 16) attest, workers in precarious employment can make gains in control (broadly defined) and in income level and working conditions by joining in a highly participatory process of constituency, site, and issue-based organizing and maintaining a central interest in labour concerns. This strategic orientation encapsulates the practices of a key community partner in the Community University Research Alliance on Contingent Work, which traverses not only the workplace and the labour force but the labour market as well. Many of TOFFE's activities support workers both with jobs and without jobs, and its basis of unity lies beyond the worksite and challenges hierarchical models of representation. Moreover, this orientation is emblematic of a social movement that actors and analysts are both calling for in the union renewal efforts that are taking place elsewhere (Lévesque and Murray 2002; Robinson 1994).

Community unionism, in its dual concern with location and process, is an important resource in making the public costs of precarious employment known. The implications of precarious employment for individual workers, as well as groups of workers, their households, and their communities, should now be clear. However, it is equally important to emphasize its broader social costs. Contributions to this volume raise important questions about the links between precarious employment and public health scares (e.g., SARS, Walkerton, unclean hospitals), the failures of public sector regulation (e.g., meat inspection), and the increasing costs to the health-care system created by poor-quality unhealthy jobs – questions about systems of labour and social protection that affect the public at large. And community unionism, as an analytic and practical tool, is vital to making these linkages visible.

These avenues of future research oriented to action aim to harness knowledge in the struggle to mitigate precarious employment. They represent mere beginnings – the formulation of monumental social problems and the identification of potential challenges along the road to change – in what promises to be a long struggle to improve the work and health conditions of some of society's most vulnerable members. However, strategies for change become solutions only on the basis of the creativity and practices of the workers themselves.

Notes

1 "Gender" refers to the social processes through which cultural meanings become associated with sexual difference. Sexual differences are material to a large
degree (Armstrong and Armstrong 1983; Hennessy 2000; Jenson 1986), but
gender is socially constructed (Creese 1999; Lerner 1997; Scott 1986). It is the
social significance attached to sexual difference, which, in turn, "structures organizations, affects social and political relationships, and becomes intrinsic to
the construction of significant social categories and political identities" (Frader
and Rose 1996, 22). Contributors to this volume use the term both to refer
to historically and socially constituted relationships and as an analytic tool to
understand how social relationships and cultural categories are constituted
(Creese 1999; Frader and Rose 1996; Lerner 1997).

This definition of gender draws from Fudge and Vosko 2003 and from Vosko
2000.

2 "Race" is a social construct tied to racialization, a process of signification in
which human beings are categorized into "races" by reference to real or imag-
ined phenotypical or genetic differences (Miles 1987, 7; Satzewich 1991, 5).
Racial categories, including "visible minority," "Black," or "South Asian," and
"white," are constructed through processes of racialization embedded in daily
interactions, ideologies, policies, and practices.

Racialized identity categories are highly contested (Miles 1987). Yet the significance of identities for resistance and agency underscores the importance of retaining terms such as "Black" and "people of colour" (Das Gupta 2002;
Galabuzzi 2004; Mensah 2002; Mohanty 2003), terms that contributors use
across the volume.

3 Given the interdisciplinary orientation of the contributions to follow, a range of
subject- and discipline-specific terms are defined in greater depth in the glossary
of terms appended at the end of the volume.

4 See, for example, Arthurs 1967; Fudge and Cossman 2002; Glasbeek 1987; Fudge and Vosko 2001a, b; O'Grady 1992, 1991; Panitch and Swartz 1993; Russell 1990; Ursel 1992.

5 To bring them under the scheme, this modification based qualification on the amount of fish and type of fish caught and processed by a given fisherman and *his family* rather than on weeks of individual earnings (McCay 1988; Neis 1993).

6 The 1996 extension of employment insurance (as it is now known) to multiple job holders and the elimination of weekly minimum hours is a case in point.

7 These critics also raised questions about the extent to which such forms of employment and work arrangements were really "new"(see, especially, Gaudier 1987; Pollert 1989).

8 See also Broad 1991; Fernandez-Kelly 1983; Fernandez-Kelly and Garcia 1989; Jenson 1989; Rubery 1989; Walby 1989; Wood 1989.

9 Rather than surveying this literature, the ensuing discussion advances the conceptual framework orienting the contributions to this book, and subsequently its guiding methodological approach, based on a synthesis of the collective insights of the Community-University Research Alliance on Contingent Work and the large body of research on employment restructuring in Canada and internationally. (For detailed reviews of the literature by contributors to this book and to the Alliance more broadly, see Armstrong 1996; Fudge 1997; Cranford, Vosko, and Zukerwich 2003b; Vosko 2003. For reviews of the literature on precarious employment and related subjects outside Canada, see especially Huws, Hurstfield, and Holtmaat 1989; Portes, Castells, and Benton 1989; Rodgers 1989).

10 "Racialization" is analytically distinct from "racism," yet the two processes are historically intertwined. While racialization refers to a process of signification in which people are categorized into races, racism is an ideology that ascribes negatively evaluated characteristics in a deterministic manner to a group that is also identified as being in some way biologically distinct (Miles 1987, 7).

11 The term "standard of living" is often used in conjunction with social reproduction. It is defined as states of a historical process of social reproduction and understood to encompass historical, institutional, and moral elements separate from the price mechanism (Clarke 2000, 134).

Colloquially, standard of living is often used to denote a bundle of goods rather than a social process. For example, in calculating poverty, Statistics Canada uses a range of measures, such as "low-income cut-offs" and "low income measures" to assess the standard of living of low-income people, often following a "basic needs approach."

In this volume, contributors use standard of living in both senses (Picchio 1998, 197).

12 The "family" is a contested concept (Abbott and Wallace 1992; Hamilton and Barrett 1986; Luxton 1997; Luxton and Vosko 1998). At the level of public policy, it is used to denote a particular form of social organization bringing together

cohabitation and kinship centred on private household life and the notion a nuclear unit organized around a clear division of gender roles, with men as chief income earners and women focused on the domestic world of home and family. Notably, however, while this family form is dominant at a normative level, it is a minority lifestyle: only about 30 per cent of Canadian families with children maintain this household organization, and it accounts for only about 8 per cent of all households. Contributors in this volume use the term "family" critically, principally as a shorthand for describing a particular form of social organization dominant at a normative level and assumed by public policy, as well as to interrogate the racialized and gendered assumptions surrounding it.

13 This study criticizes dominant approaches to conceptualizing and measuring "non-standard work" and "contingent work" in Canada and the United States, respectively, and introduces an approach to breaking down total employment offering a framework for fostering more precise understandings of precarious employment.

14 Working time expressed in the full-time/part-time distinction also relates to income level – a fourth dimension of precarious employment. But this dimension is best explored through comparing hourly wages across form of employment by sex, race, and context – several chapters take up this challenge in the body of the volume.

15 The share of employed women aged 15–24 with a full-time permanent job fell from 53 per cent in 1989 to 36 per cent in 2003, while, for young men, the figure fell from 58 per cent to 45 per cent.

16 For many of these now solo self-employed workers, their former employer is a principal client (Lowe, Schellenberg, and Davidman 1999).

17 Men in couples with children performed, on average, 908 hours of unpaid work in 1961 and 1090 in 1992, while women performed 2,248 in 1961 and 2,024 in 1992 (Statistics Canada 1995).

18 For example, in 2000, 21.3 per cent of women and only 2.4 per cent of men reported that they engaged in part-time work in order to care for children or undertake other personal and family responsibilities (Vosko 2002, chart 6).

Time stress is also a factor in the "choices" women and men make: 38 per cent of women, aged 25–44 years, with children in two-parent households, versus 26 per cent of men, reported severe time stress in 1998.

19 The chapters in Part One focus on Canada as a whole, primarily for reasons of sample size. Adding texture to this portrait, the qualitative studies included in the volume focus more narrowly on developments in Ontario and Quebec, with particular attention to large urban centres. This emphasis arose from the nature of the Community University Research Alliance, with its focus on an Ontario-Quebec comparison. There is, however, a need for greater critical reflection on the relationship between place (i.e., geography and region) and manifestations of precarious employment in Canada (for a notable exception, see Winson and Leach 2001). Future work might usefully focus in this area, with more emphasis

to the rural-urban distinction, and with great attention to developments in both Atlantic Canada and western Canada.

CHAPTER TWO

Names are listed alphabetically to reflect equal contribution. The authors thank Valerie duPlessis, René Morrisette, Doug Norris, and Nancy Zukewich from Statistics Cananada, as well as John Anderson, Pat Armstrong, Stephanie Bernstein, Kate Laxer, Heather Scott, and Emile Tompa from the Community University Research Alliance on Contingent Work, for their valuable comments on earlier versions of the chapter; James Beaton for his inestimable work as a research assistant; and the Social Sciences and Humanities Research Council of Canada for its generous financial support of this project. Leah F. Vosko also thanks the Canada Research Chairs Programme.

1 In this chapter, the term "visible minority" is not taken as a conceptual or heuristic category. Rather, it refers to the specific variable defined by Statistics Canada composed of the racialized groups described in table 2.1.

 Following the *Employment Equity Act*, Statistics Canada defines "visible minority" as persons, other than Aboriginal peoples, who are non-Caucasian in race or non-white in colour (www.statcan.ca/english/census2001/dict/pop127.htm). However, racial and ethnic categories, including "visible minority" as well as "Black" or "South Asian" and "white," are socially constructed through processes of racialization embedded in daily interactions, ideologies, policy, and social relations in core institutions. This has led some scholars to call for the abandonment of the term "race" as well as racialized identity categories (Miles 1987). At the same time, people's continual experiences with racism as well as the importance of oppositional identities for resistance, in Canada and elsewhere, lead many scholars and activists to continue to use terms such as "Black," "people of colour," or "women of colour" (Das Gupta and Iacovetta 2000; Mensah 2002).

 Following these scholars, the term "people of colour" is used here to emphasize racialized social locations in the analytical sections of the chapter.

2 In this chapter, the term "wage work" refers to employees who earn salaries as well as hourly wages. Statisticians use the term "paid work" for what is labelled "wage work" here. However, the solo self-employed are also paid (by their clients), but they are not paid wages. Furthermore, in feminist scholarship, paid work is more commonly contrasted to unpaid work.

3 For a parallel exploration of self-employment, see Vosko and Zukewich, this volume.

4 See Cranford, Vosko, and Zukewich 2003a; and Vosko, Cranford, and Zukewich 2003.

5 In this chapter, the term "level of analysis" is used sociologically rather than to refer to units of analysis in data collection.

6 Work arrangements are also related to precarious employment. Workers who work on call, irregular shifts or split shifts, night shifts and rotating shifts are more likely to experience stress and ill-health (Lewchuck, de Wolff, King, and Polanyi, this volume). Owing to continuing unequal gender divisions of labour in households, unpredictable schedules make it difficult to plan for child-care, which exacerbates women's stress level (Armstrong and Armstrong 2001, 53), and women who work at night rarely get sufficient sleep during the day. However, the degree to which atypical work arrangements are precarious varies the most by form of employment and occupational context. This reflects the fact that work arrangements operate at a different level of analysis from the other dimensions (Vosko, Zukewich, and Cranford 2003).

   For these reasons, this chapter does not include work arrangements as a dimension of precarious employment. Rather, it leaves a more contextualized exploration of work arrangements to Armstrong and Laxer (this volume), whose chapter interprets the meaning of the indicator through a case study of the health-care sector.

7 Income would be more suitable to an analysis of all the jobs of a given individual or to an analysis of households.

8 Establishment size is a related indicator of regulatory protection that is often cited in the literature. However, according to Morrisette (1993), respondents report too often that they work in establishments with fewer than 20 employees, suggesting that the establishment size variable is not measured well by the SLID.

   In addition, employment in a small firm is a good indicator of precarious employment because larger firms are more likely to pay higher wages, have higher unionization rates, have higher pension plan coverage and other fringe benefits, and have lower risks of permanent layoffs (Cranford, Vosko, and Zukewich 2003a; Morrisette 1991).

9 We recognize, however, that geography is an important social context shaping, and shaped by, dimensions of precariousness among wage workers. For this reason, where possible, future research should address not only regional breakdowns but the urban/rural distinction.

10 So few part-time temporary employees in health occupations fall into the precarious categories of contingency, one indicator of regulatory protection (firm size less than 20) and two indicators of precarious income (below the minimum wage and poverty wage), that the sample size is not large enough for analysis; the same holds for occupations in social science, education, government service, and religion, except for the indicator "in and out of work."

11 In order to demonstrate this point empirically, the analysis focuses mainly on the intersecting social locations of gender and race and less on immigrant status, ethnicity, age, disability, or other important social locations.

12 Data available on request from the authors.

13 Data available on request from the authors.

14 In order to understand how precarious employment is racialized, we also need to examine diversity more fully within the category "visible minority," along the lines of place of birth and cohort of arrival, and to control for education.

CHAPTER THREE

The authors thank the Social Sciences and Humanities Research Council (Grant # 833-2000-1028) for funding the research on which this article is based, as well as Pat Armstrong, John Anderson, Cynthia Cranford, Valerie duPlessis, Judy Fudge, Karen Hughes, Gerald Kernerman, Kate Laxer, and Emile Tompa for their comments on earlier drafts of the chapter. Leah Vosko also thanks the Canada Research Chairs program for its support. This chapter reflects the views of the authors and not necessarily the opinions of Statistics Canada.

1 The slight decline in self-employment since 1999 appears to be a cyclical rather than a structural phenomenon (Delage 2002).

2 For parallel discussions of indicators of dimensions of precarious employment applicable to various groups of wage workers, see, in this volume, Armstrong and Laxer; Cranford and Vosko; and Scott, Tompa, and Trethivick.

3 Unpaid family workers are people, mainly women, who work without remuneration on a farm or in a business or professional practice owned by a family member living in the same household.

4 See, for example, Aronson (1991), Casson (1991, 1982), Holmes and Schmitz (1990), Kihlstrom and Laffont (1979), Rosen (1983).

5 For example, the Survey of Self-Employment does not ask people who say they became self-employed because of the lack of a suitable paid job to specify the main reason for self-employment from the other list of factors (flexible hours, independence, control, etc.).

6 The present analysis excludes unpaid family workers.

7 Indicators of each dimension are defined with respect to the data available in the Labour Force Survey and the Survey of Self-Employment.

8 See, for example, Armstrong 1996; Cranford, Vosko, and Zukewich 2003; Fudge and Vosko, 2001a and b; Spalter-Roth and Hartmann 1998; Vosko 2000; Walby 2000.

9 For example, the prevalence of severe time stress is higher for full-time employed women with children than for those without children, while the presence of children has no effect on severe time stress among employed men. Women are also more likely than men to work part time and to be absent from work for reasons of child-care or other family responsibilities (Women in Canada 2000).

10 It should be noted that part-time employers account for a marginal share of all self-employed workers (3 % in 2000). Consequently, sample sizes from the Survey of Self-Employment for this group were too small to yield statistically reliable estimates for most measures of precarious employment explored here, making it difficult to fully probe the employer/solo-worker aspect of polarization.

11 Full-time solo self-employed women and men have similar marital status and family profiles.

12 Part-time self-employed men are twice as likely to be aged 55 and over.

13 The exception here is source of dental benefits among the full-time solo self-employed, where the difference between men and women narrows slightly.

CHAPTER FOUR

1 In this chapter, the term "visible minority" is not taken as a conceptual or heuristic category. Rather, it refers to the specific variable defined by Statistics Canada composed of the racialized groups described in the introduction to the volume. Like Cranford and Vosko, the term "people of colour" is used in discussions pertinent to the social relations surrounding precarious employment, while the term "visible minority" is used in sections analyzing empirical data.

2 Average annual productivity growth rates were 2.8 per cent in the United States and 3.4 per cent in Canada in the 1960s, but were only 2 per cent in the 1970s and just above 1 per cent in the 1980s for both countries (Betcherman and Lowe 1997; Herzenberg, Alice, and Wial 1998).

3 The modest growth of GDP in the United States, combined with the continued decline in employment growth, may explain the lack of wage inflation in the late 1990s. Greenspan (in Collingwood 2003) attributes this to the widespread fear of layoffs that pervaded the labour force through much of this period.

4 Through the 1990s, the WHO continued to revise the International Classification of Disability and Handicap (currently called the International Classification of Disability and Functioning), modifying the terminology, definitions, relationships between concepts, and domains within the classification system (Final Draft, WHO 2001). The new terms for the four concepts are health condition, body function and structure, activities, and participation.

5 Beginning in 1986, the Federal Contractors program applied the same employment equity requirements to employers with over 100 employees bidding on federal contracts worth $200,000 or over.

6 The civil service was included through separate legislation from 1992 on, and by a policy of employment equity voluntarily adopted between 1987 and 1992.

7 The broader definition of pay equity relies on a range of job characteristics, such as skills and responsibility of the position, and allows comparisons across male- and female-dominated jobs, which would be impossible in "an equal pay for equal work" system.

8 The Rehabilitation Act requires that federally funded businesses not discriminate against disabled employees and that they provide "reasonable accommodation."

9 It represents a difference of 18 per cent. In 1994 the difference was only 9 per cent.

10 To make matters worse, the total monetary value of government transfers declined from $6,848 to $6,600 from 1993 to 1994.

11 Blanck et al. (2000) speculate that many of the self-employed with disabilities may have left paid employment because of experiences of discrimination at the hands of employers.

12 Both surveys exclude residents of the Yukon, Northwest Territories, Indian reserves, and people living in institutions.

13 Starting in 1989, the Labour Market Activity Survey included a question on disability status.

14 In 1999 a question regarding job permanence was added to the Survey of Labour and Income Dynamics. However, because the present study relies on a cross-sectional time-series analysis of labour market activity across multiple reference years, we were interested only in indicators that were available each year of the observation period 1989–2001.

15 In this analysis, therefore, the category of part-time employment includes part-time self-employment (both solo and employer) and part-time wage work (both permanent and temporary).

16 In the remainder of the chapter, the term "visible minority" is used to reflect the specific variable defined in the Survey of Labour and Income Dynamics and the Labour Market Activity Survey.

17 There appears to be some randomness in the data from the visible minority group due to its small sample. That makes the underlying trends less discernable.

18 Because Statistics Canada gave a note of caution for the Survey of Labour and Income Dynamics data for these questions for the 1999 survey year, the 1999 values were not considered in the trends analyses.

19 Unfortunately, there is no comparison group, since people who did not answer yes to one of the disability questions were not asked whether they were satisfied with the number of hours of work.

20 "Working poor" is defined as those economic families in which no member is aged 65 or over, total income is below Statistics Canada's Low-Income Cut-Off, and more than 50 per cent of total family income comes from wages, salaries, or self-employment

CHAPTER FIVE

Authorship is alphabetical to reflect equal contribution.

1 For the purposes of this analysis, we are using the Standard Industrial Classification (SIC) definition of "professional occupations." According to the SIC, this category includes physicians, dentists, and veterinarians; optometrists, chiropractors, and other health diagnosing and treating professionals; pharmacists, dietitians, and nutritionists; and therapy and assessment professionals.

2 The North American Industrial Classification System (NAICS) classifies employees according to who the employer is, not according to location of work. So, for example, a food services worker working in a hospital cafeteria that is

operated separately from the hospital will most likely be classified within the accommodation and food services industry.

CHAPTER SIX

The authors would like to thank Nicki Carlan, Simon Enoch, Cindy Gangaram, Brian Gibson, Erika Khandor, and Syed Naqvi for their contributions to the research on which this chapter is based. The research was funded by the SSHRC CURA program. Lewchuk received further assistance from a SSHRC INE grant. The researchers are members of the Alliance on Contingent Employment housed at York University.

1 The social health gradient developed by Marmot and his colleagues suggests that there is a pattern to health outcomes based on occupations. Health outcomes deteriorate as one moves from high-skilled to less-skilled occupations or as one moves from occupations with high control to occupations with low control.

2 For more details on the construction of employment strain, see Lewchuk et al. (2003).

3 The authors would like to thank David Robertson, Donald Cole, Ted Haines, Mickey Kerr, Dorothy Wigmore, and Joe Zsoldos, all of whom contributed to the design of a number of these questions. See Lewchuk and Robertson (1996 and 1997).

4 In order to gain access to part-time or contract university and homecare workers, the survey coordinator met with union representatives. Surveys were distributed to all members, either through the mail or during regular union meetings. In the latter situation, a member of the survey team was present at the meeting. Community workers were either current contract employees or graduates of a college community worker program who received the survey in the mail. In order to contact the diverse group, the coordinator primarily found workers as they searched for their next job. She attended community meetings, requested staff in a number of agencies to distribute the survey to clients, set up information tables, placed notices on public and electronic bulletin boards, and followed up on respondents' referrals to other workers.

5 A closer examination of this group has led us to think that as well as short-term contract, part-time, and self-employed categories of precarious employment, there is a fourth type in our sample – "full-time precarious." Over one-quarter of the homecare workers and close to one-tenth of the diverse group described themselves as permanent full-time employees. These workers have a full-time on-call relationship with an employer, and sometimes they work full-time hours. However, from week to week they had no guarantee of full-time work or pay. While marginally better off than their co-workers in the same sector, they were still a long way from the type of employment guarantee enjoyed by workers in standard employment relationships. Future work will explore the characteristics of this group of workers in more detail.

6 There are almost certainly interactions between the different components of the employment relationship, but the small sample size prevents a study of these possibilities at this point.

7 This is a rough estimate, as the logistic function is nonlinear and the actual difference in the probability of reporting a health outcome for an individual depends not only on the average difference in the employment relationship support measure but on whether the individual had a low or a high score on the index and on the value of the other characteristics in the model.

CHAPTER SEVEN

1 This chapter draws extensively on my MA thesis by the same title, completed in the Graduate Program in Political Science, York University, in May 2003. Special thanks go to OPSEU staff and members on the front lines, especially Paul Bilodeau, Pam Doig, Randy Robinson, Jojo Geronimo, and Frank Rooney. This project was completed thanks to the invaluable academic guidance and support of Leah Vosko, Ann Porter, Barbara Cameron, Meg Luxton, and Judy Fudge. Shelly Gordon and Patrick Rooney provided the support at home with love and tolerance.

2 *Crown Employees Collective Bargaining Act*, 1994, s. 32.

3 Hansard, David Tsubouchi, chair, Management Board Secretariat, Ontario Legislature, June 25, 2001.

4 Ontario Ministry of Finance, *Ontario Public Accounts*, Vol. 3, 1995–2002. These figures are based on the publicly recorded expenditures on temporary agencies for the Ministry of Health and Long-term Care. *Public Accounts* records the amount spent on temporary agencies and the name of the temporary employment agency. The expenditure on temporary agencies varies across all ministries, and it is difficult to obtain an accurate figure for each ministry. The total temporary agency figure is not necessarily public information. As we shall see later in the chapter, each individual manager has discretion to hire agency workers, and this independence may affect the aggregate recorded in *Public Accounts*.

CHAPTER EIGHT

I would like to thank Tariq Khan for conducting interviews, and the agency and program managers who were interviewed for their contributions to this study.

1 This message is central to most current employment advice. An Internet search in December 2003 for the phrase "there is no such thing as a permanent job" turned up quotes in employment advice websites (www.advancing.sw/ index.htm); in workers' survival strategies (www.helloap.com; www.cpsr.org; www.workingwounded.com/temping); on job-search websites (job-searchtech.about.com/library/weekly/aa031698.htm); and even in committee hearings of the Parliament of Ireland (www.irlgov.ie). Toronto's former mayor,

Mel Lastman, famously said in July 2002 that "no one has a job for life" during a strike that centred on job security issues for city workers (http://www.cbc.ca/stories/2002/07/04/tororntostrike020704).

2 The federal government renamed Human Resources Development Canada (HRDC) in early 2004. It has become Human Resources and Skills Development Canada (HRSDC). This chapter refers almost exclusively to HRDC because it was the name of the department during most of the changes that are relevant to this study.

3 For a discussion of how one community union works with this group, see Cranford, Das Gupta, Ladd, and Vosko, this volume.

CHAPTER NINE

Authorship is alphabetical to reflect equal contribution.

1 The use of the term "self-employed" is extremely problematic because it increasingly lacks a clear sociological, statistical, or legal referent (Fudge, Tucker, and Vosko 2002). Nevertheless, because it is still so widely used, we have opted to employ it to avoid confusing the reader.

2 *Occupational Health and Safety Act*, RSO 1990, Pt III.1.

3 The Quebec *Labour Standards Act* (RSQ, c. N-1.1) [LSA], for example, was modified in 1990 to permit the compensation of overtime by time off, at the employee's request or pursuant to a collective agreement or a decree extending a collective agreement to a certain sector, thereby recognizing the practices already prevalent in many workplaces (s. 55).

4 *Act Respecting the Professional Status and Conditions of Engagement of Performing, Recording and Film Artists*, RSQ, c. S-32; *Act Respecting the Professional Status of Artists in the Visual Arts, Arts and Crafts and Literature, and Their Contracts with Promoters*, RSQ, c. S-32; *Status of the Artist Act*, SC 1992, c. 33.

5 In Quebec, a special regime extending many of the provisions of certain collective agreements to non-unionized workers was created by the *Act Respecting Collective Agreement Decrees*, RSQ, c. D-2-A. See *Decree Respecting Building Service Employees in the Montréal Region*, RRQ 1981, c. D-2, r. 39; *Decree Respecting Security Guards*, RRQ 1981, c. D-2, r. 1.

6 In its 2003 report (Recommendation no. 45), the Bernier Committee recommended the creation of such a framework to enhance self-employed workers' bargaining capacity and to improve their social protection.

7 Legislation designed to correct historic disadvantage and discrimination, such as pay equity legislation, is an obvious exception to this rule.

8 "Among other things, intersectionality pushes for the legal recognition and delineation of specific status identities. The notion is that particular social groups (e.g., black people) are constituted by multiple status identities (e.g., black lesbians, black heterosexual women, and black heterosexual men). According to

intersectionality theory, the different status identity holders within any given social group are differently situated with respect to how much, and the form of,
discrimination they are likely to face. Intersectionality argues that, in ascertain-
ing whether a particular individual is the victim of discrimination, courts should
pay attention to the specific status identity that the person occupies." (Carbado
and Gulati 2001, 702).

9 *Dunmore* v. *Ontario (Attorney General)*, [2001] 3 SCR 1016.

10 *Labour Relations and Employment Statute Law Amendment Act*, 1995, SO
1995, c. 1, ss. 80, 81(1).

11 *Commission des droits de la personne et des droits de la jeunesse* v. *Sinatra*,
[2000] JL 45 (TDPQ), AZ-50067859, JE 99-2197.

12 *Les Restaurants McDonald du Canada Ltée.* v. *CLP et al.*, Superior Court 550-17-
000945–038, January 19, 2004, reversing *McDonald* v. *Nolet*, [2003] CLP 272.

13 *Employment Standards Act*, RSBC 1996, c. 113.

14 The Employment Standards Branch does not require that the "Self-Help Kit" be
used for a limited number of reasons, including complaints concerning a child or
where the company is insolvent, the employee is a victim of harassment in the
workplace, the complainant has problems understanding how to use the kit because of language or is unable to use the kit because of a disability, and the complainant is an agricultural worker, a textile or garment worker, or a domestic.
See the British Columbia Employment Standards Branch website at www.
labour.gov.bc.ca/esb/self-help/sh-start.htm (accessed on May 10, 2004).

15 *LSA*, RSQ, c. N-1.1.

CHAPTER TEN

1 *Labour Standards Act*, RSQ, C-N-1.1 (*LSA*).

2 *Act to Amend the Act Respecting Labour Standards and Other Legislative Provisions*, SQ 2002, c. 80. A series of provisions were targeted to come into force
in June 2004 or later.

3 *Minimum Wage Act*, SQ 1940, c. 39.

4 *LSA*, s. 124ff.

5 *LSA*, s. 3(2) and s.158.3. The law (s. 54(9)) does, however, exclude them from
the provisions on the normal workweek and overtime.

6 *LSA*, s. 81.18-81.20 and s.123.5-123.16.

7 *Employment Standards Act*, RSBC 1996, c. 113, s. 3(2).

8 *LSA*, s. 87.1ff.

9 *LSA*, s. 81.20.

10 *RSQ*, c. C-27.

11 *LSA*, s. 1(10).

12 See *Rivard* v. *9048–3082 Québec Inc.*, DTE 2000T-1023 (CQ); *Paquette & Asso-
ciés* v. *Côté-Desbiolles*, DTE 97T-1240 (CS); *Girardin* v. *Distribution Danièle
Normand Inc.*, DTE 2000T-228 (TT).

13 This observation is abundantly confirmed by Canadian and Quebec case law.

14 See, for example, *CNT* v. *2429–5040 Québec Inc. (Maison Dumontier)*, DTE 96T-602 (CQ); *CNT* v. *La Sanitation du Québec M.M. inc.*, DTE 97T-75 (CQ); *CNT* v. *Pouliot*, DTE 99T-1047 (CQ); *Simard* v. *Mutuelle du Canada (La) Compagnie d'assurance sur la vie*, DTE 2000T-33; *CNT* v. *Paquette* (2000), RJDT 169 (CQ); *Services Barbara-Rourke Adaptation Réadaptation* v. *Québec (Sous-ministre du Revenu)*, JE 2002–612 (CAQ) (interpretation under the Quebec *Pension Plan Act* (RSQ, C. R-9)).

15 *LSA*, ss. 93 and 94. See *CNT* v. *9039–5369 and Davlin Inc.*, DTE 2001T-1175 (CQ).

16 Compare *Godin* v. *Collège d'extension Cartier*, DTE 96T-1221 (CT), DTE 98T-390 (CS) (accepted), leave to appeal withdrawn; and *Charlotte Goudreault* v. *Axor, Experts Conseils Inc.*, DTE 98T-781 (CQ).

17 *North American Automobile Association Ltd.* v. *CNT*, DTE 93T-429 (CA); *Budai* v. *Pearl*, DTE 95T-1374 (TT); *Deere* v. *Marler & Associates*, [2000] RJDT 1084 (CT).

18 *Dazé* v. *Messageries Dynamiques* (1991), RDJ 195 (CAQ); *Technologies industrielles S.N.C. inc. (S.N.C. Defense Products Ltd.)* v. *Mayer*, DTE 99T-509 (CAQ); *Groupe Yoga Adhara inc.* v. *La Coopérative de travail le Collège de Saint-Césaire*, DTE 98T-943 (CS). For an example of a worker being determined to be an employee because incorporation was imposed as a condition of employment, see *Leduc* v. *Habitabec Inc.*, DTE 94T-1240 (CAQ).

19 *Services financiers F.B.N. inc.* v. *Chaumont*, [2003] RJQ 365 (CAQ), application for leave to appeal to the Supreme Court of Canada dismissed 11/09/2003 (SCC File no. 29683).

20 *LSA*, ss. 122(1) and 124. See *Provost* v. *Bureau d'éthique commerciale de Montréal inc.*, (1999) RJDT 233 (CT). In this case the plaintiff managed eventually to claim sums owed to her as an employee under the *LSA* in civil court even though the labour commissioner had determined that there was nothing she could do about the transformation of her status (*CNT* v. *Bureau d'éthique commerciale de Montréal inc.*, DTE 2000T-409 (CQ)). See also *Albert* v. *Pétrolière impériale*, DTE 2000T-281 (CT).

21 Bill 143, *Act to Amend the Act Respecting Labour Standards and Other Legislative Provisions*, art. 53, modified by the *Act to Amend the Act Respecting Labour Standards and Other Legislative Provisions*, LQ, 2002, c. 80.

22 *Labour Code*, s. 20.0.1.

23 *LSA*, s. 86.1.

24 As of October 2004, there was no case law for this provision.

25 In 2002, minimum wage earners represented 6.2 per cent of employees in Quebec, compared with 3.9 per cent in Ontario and 7.7 per cent in British Columbia. Institut de la statistique du Québec, 2004. "L'emploi au salaire minimum: différences et similitudes dans trois provinces du Canada," *Flash-Info Travail et Rémunération* 5 (1): 2.

26 *LSA*, s. 85.1.

27 Bill 8 (*Act to Amend the Act Respecting Childcare Centres and Childcare Services*) and Bill 7 (*Act to Amend the Act Respecting Health Services and Social Services*), now SQ 2003, c. 13, and SQ 2003, c. 12, respectively. The law defines an "intermediate resource" as a "resource attached to a public institution through which the institution provides a user registered for the institution's services with a living environment suited to the user's needs, together with the support or assistance services required by the user's condition, in order to maintain the user in or integrate the user into the community."

28 *Centre de la petite enfance La Rose des vents* v. *Alliance des intervenantes en milieu familial Laval, Laurentides, Lanaudière (C.S.Q.)*, DTE 2003T-763 (TT); *Centre du Florès* v. *St-Arnaud*, [2001] RJDT 1228 (TT), DTE 2002T-309 (CS), permission to appeal dismissed (CAQ, 2002–05-06, 500-09-012070–025). The previous government had also introduced a bill shortly before the end of its mandate providing for such a deeming provision in the case of intermediate resources, but it died on the order paper: Bill 151 (*Act to Amend the Act Respecting Health Services and Social Services*), introduced 13 December 2002.

29 *Employment Standards Act*, RSBC 1996, c. 113, s. 10 ff.

30 RSQ, c. B-10.

31 RSQ, c. C-12.

32 RSQ, c. P-40.1.

33 *Pointe-Claire (City)* v. *Quebec (Labour Court)*, (1997) 1 RCS 1015, par. 63.

34 An Appeal Court decision (*CNT* v. *Agence de personnel Parador Inc.*, [1986] AQ, no. 621) has, however, stated that regardless of who the "real" employer is determined to be, the agency can nevertheless be held responsible for the payment of wages.

35 In *CNT* v. *Agence de personnel Parador Inc.*, [1986] AQ, no. 621, the Court of Appeal stated that it would not decide if agencies could charge workers. The *Drakkar Ressources Humaines inc.* v. *Levy Transport Ltée*, DTE 2000T-1180 (CS), case, which does not specifically concern the legality of such clauses, appears to imply that they are legal. The agency in this case successfully sued a client firm for hiring drivers who had previously worked for the agency.

36 *Civil Code*, s. 1437.

37 *Agence de placement Hélène Roy* v. *Nancy Rioux*, (1997) RL 297.

38 This directive had not been adopted as of October 2004 because the Council of the European Union has yet to arrive at a common position. See 2512th Council meeting, Employment, Social Policy, Health and Consumer Affairs, Luxembourg, June 2003 (DN: PRES/03/152); and 2606th Council meeting, Employment, Social Policy, Health and Consumer Affairs, Luxembourg, October 2004 (Press: 264, Nr: 12400/04).

39 *LSA*, s. 41.1 and s. 74.1.

40 *Charter of Rights and Freedoms*, s. 19.

41 *Pay Equity Act*, RSQ, c. E-12.001.

42 This comment concerns published case law: there may be several unreported decisions. See *Maison Simons inc.* v. *Commission des normes du travail*, DTE 96T-18 (CAQ). Section 41.1 has also led to a handful of grievance arbitration decisions.

CHAPTER ELEVEN

1 In Quebec, the appeal tribunal (Commission des lésions professionnelles, or CLP) case law, and that of its predecessor, the Commission d'appel en matière de lésions professionnelles, or CALP, is available in searchable databanks that allow research methods that would be impossible if pre-selected cases were the only ones available to the public, as happens in many jurisdictions.

2 *Archambault et Salon de coiffure La Jonction*, CALP 29132-62-9105, 17 January 1992, M. Billard; *Bédard et Coifferie des Bouleaux*, CLP177952-31-0202, 16 April 2002, Jean-François Clément.

3 *François Bailleux déneigement*, CLP132588-32-0002, 1 March 2000, Guylaine Tardif.

4 *CSST et Lebel et Gérard Houle* (1997), CALP 1470; confirmed in review at CLP85524-04-9702, 30 October 1998, Michèle Carignan.

5 *Hôpital La Providence et Boily*, [1996] CALP 87, Louise Turcotte.

6 Except those included in s. 9, *AIAOD*.

7 *Barbeau et Récupération Emric Inc (Fermée)*, CLP159883-71-0104, 8 March 2002, Lucie Landriault.

8 *Constructions Deschenes ltée et Boucher et CSST*, CLP127095-07-9911, 18 October 2001, Bertrand Roy.

9 *Barbeau et Récupération Emric Inc (Fermée)*, CLP159883-71-0104, 8 March 2002, Lucie Landriault.

10 Interview with representatives of the CSST, 29 October 2003.

11 *Brassard et Gestion Yvon Marcotte Ltée*, CLP111807-71-9903, 7 July 1999, Neuville Lacroix; *Brisson et Recyclage Camco inc. et Thomson Tremblay inc.* CLP107008-62-9811, 28 March 2000, Hélène Marchand; *Bournival et Advantage Personnel Ltd*, CLP128588-04-9912, 6 December 2000, Sophie Sénéchal; *Zeller's Inc. et F.W. Woolworth Cie Ltée et Domtar Inc. et Les Agences de personnel Cavalier Inc. et CSST*, [1994] CALP 719; *2534 6115 Québec inc.*, [1998] CLP 352.

12 *Maisons Quebco Inc. et CSST*, [1995] CALP 1607; *Le Groupe Consel inc. et Groupe CRT inc. c. Cusson et CSST*, [2001] CLP 863 (SCQ).

13 *Jean-Louis et ProGroupe*, CLPE 2003 LP-38, Richard Hudon.

14 *Bournival et Advantage Personnel Ltd*, CLP128588-04-9912, 6 December 2000, Sophie Sénéchal.

15 *Duval c. CALP*, [1997] CALP 1840 (SCQ); *Vigneault et Ministère du revenu du Québec*, CLP120299-62B-9907, 7 January 2000, Nicole Blanchard.

16 *Giroux et Métallurgie Frontenac et Polybois inc.*, CLP125175-03B-9910, 12 June 2000, Robin Savard; *Amodei et Métaux industriels Adam ltée*, [2002] CLP 871.

17 *Violette et Pauline Violette Psychologue (fermée)*, CLP113034–64-9903, 17 September 2002, Claude-André Ducharme.

18 *Laflamme et Atelier Martin Robinson enr. et CSST*, CLP206898–01B-0304, 22 August 2003, J.-F. Clément.

19 *Bissonnette et F.X. Drolet inc.*, CLP114324–32-9904, 29 July 1999, Neuville Lacroix.

20 *Pelletier et Pelletier Maître Décapeur et al*, [1999] CLP 92.

21 *Les Restaurants McDonald du Canada Ltée et Demosthènes*, [1998] CLP 409, confirmed at [1998] CLP 1318; *Les Restaurants McDonald du Canada Ltée et Pelletier-Groleau*, CLP77174–60-9602, 19 June1998, Mildred Kolodny, confirmed on 16 March 1999, Santina Di Pasquale; *Restaurants McDonald et Reid*, CLPE 2002 LP-123, Michel Denis; Restaurants *McDonald et Barchichat*, CLP 173703–72-0111, 11 October 2002, Yolande Lemire. McDonald's appeal failed in *McDonald et Nolet*, [2003] CLP 272, but the Superior Court granted the employer's petition to quash the CLP decision: *Les Restaurants McDonald du Canada ltée v. CLP et al*, CS 550-17-000945–038, 19 January 2004, rectified 28 January 2004.

22 *Les Télécommuniations CNCP et Turpin*, CALP00782–60-8608, 3 May 1988, Guy Beaudoin; *The Gazette et Rosenblatt-Lazarus*, [1997] CALP 669; *The Gazette et Carrière*, CALP84865–60-9612, 18 December 1997, Simon Lemire; *Ville de Pointe-Claire et Fraser*, CLP141564–71-0006, 6 March 2001, Alain Suicco; *Boucher et Lalonde*, CLP149691–71-0011, 25 March 2002, Louise Turcotte; *Prelco Inc. et Lévesque*, CLP167287–01A-0108, 28 March 2002, Louise Desbois; *Butt et Ville de Pointe Claire et CSST*, CLP155727–71-0102, 23 May 2002, Lucie Landriault.

23 *Héroux v. Groupe Forage Major et CLP et Me Gilles Robichaud & CSST*, [2001] CLP 317 (CAQ), request for permission to appeal to the Supreme Court of Canada denied on 3 October 2002.

24 *Centre Hospitalier Ste-Jeanne-D'Arc et Goulet*, [1997] CALP 159; *Desgranges et Centre de réadaptation Gabrielle Major et Hôpital Maisonneuve-Rosemont*, [2001] CLP 56.

25 *Lehoux c. CLP*, [2002] CLP 975, (CAQ) request for permission to appeal to the Supreme Court of Canada denied on 11 September 2003.

26 Loi no. 2001–1128 du 30 novembre 2001 portant amélioration de la couverture des non-salariés agricoles contre les accidents du travail et les maladies professionnelles. *Journal officiel de la République française*, le 1er décembre 2001, 19106–11.

CHAPTER TWELVE

1 The actions of the employer may have violated the criminal law, but prosecutions for employer-created occupational hazards are few and far between

(Glasbeek 1988). A recent amendment to the *Criminal Code,* SC 2003, c. 21, may make it easier to prosecute health and safety crimes, but that remains to be seen.

2 *Occupational Health and Safety Act,* RSO 1990, c. O.1, s. 3(2).

3 Agricultural workers are included in basic OHS laws in British Columbia, Manitoba, New Brunswick, Newfoundland, Nova Scotia, Prince Edward Island, Quebec, Saskatchewan, and the federal jurisdiction. American and Mexican OHS laws also cover farm workers. The most recent ILO convention requires that agricultural workers be protected against hazardous conditions and be given participatory rights (*Safety and Health in Agriculture Convention, 2001* (ILO C184)).

4 This chapter's focus is restricted to paid agricultural workers. An argument could be made for including farm owner-operators and unpaid family members in the category of precarious workers who are exposed to hazardous working conditions and suffer high rates of occupational injuries and diseases, but salient socio-economic differences between the situation of these workers and hired labourers justifies separate treatment. For a discussion of the three-tiered structure of class relations in agriculture posing paid workers at the bottom, agribusiness on top, and owner-operators sandwiched in between, see Shields (1992).

5 *An Act to require the owners of Thrashing and other Machines to guard against accidents,* SO 1874. c. 12; *Railway Accidents Act,* SO 1881, c. 22; *Shops Regulation Act,* SO 1888, c. 33; *Mining Operations Act,* SO 1890, c. 53; *Building Trades Protection Act,* SO 1911, c. 71.

6 *Globe,* 18 May 1893, 1, 8.

7 *Workmen's Compensation for Injuries Act,* SO 1886, c. 28; *An Act to amend the The Workmen's Compensation for Injuries Act, 1892,* SO 1893, c. 26; *Workmen's Compensation Act,* SO 1914, c. 25; *Marshment v. Bergstrom,* [1942] SCR 374.

8 Farm workers were not excluded from the original *Industrial Standards Act,* SO 1935, c. 28, but this situation was reversed by SO 1937, c. 32, s. 13, *Minimum Wage Act,* SO 1937, c. 43 (s. 17 excluded farming operations); *Hours of Work and Vacations with Pay Act,* SO 1944, c. 26. (farm workers excluded by O. Reg. 8/44); *An Act to Provide for Collective Bargaining,* SO 1943, c. 4 (s. 24 excluded the farming industry); *Unemployment Insurance Act,* SC 1940, c. 44 (First Sch. Pt II, (a)).

9 Ontario, *Debates of the Legislative Assembly,* 2 March 1965, 884.

10 *Employment Standards Act,* 1968 c. 35 (O. Reg. 366/68, s. 3, excluded farm workers); *Fruit, Vegetable and Tobacco Harvesters,* O. Reg. 320/75; *Unemployment Insurance Act,* SC 1970–72, c. 48.

11 Census of Agriculture, various volumes; Statistics Canada Cat. 93-348, table 17; Census of Agriculture 2001, Special Run.

12 Census of Agriculture 2001, Special Run.

13 Statistics Canada, Earnings of Canadians, 2001; Census of Population 2001, 20 per cent sample.

14 Statistics Canada, Monthly Labour Survey, 2002.

15 Statistics Canada, Monthly Labour Survey, 2002; Statistics Canada, CANSIM, tables 281-0004 and 281-0008 and Catalogue no 72-0020XIB.

16 Statistics Canada 2001, Census of Population 20% Sample.

17 *Occupational Health and Safety Act*, SO 1978, c. 83.

18 The group was funded by the federal secretary of state. It later changed its name to the Tolpuddle Farm Labour Information Association, but dissolved by the mid-1980s (personal communication with Ellen Wall, 14 May 2004).

19 *An Act to Amend the Occupational Health and Safety Act and the Workers' Compensation Act*, SO 1990, c. 7 (Bill 208).

20 SO 1994, c. 6.

21 *Re. Ontario Mushroom Co. Ltd. et al. and Learie et al.* (1977), 15 OR (2d) 639; *Wellington Mushroom Farm*, [1980] OLRB Rep. 813; *Cuddy Chicks Ltd.*, [1988] OLRB Rep. 468.

22 *Cuddy Chicks Ltd. v. Ontario (Labour Relations Board)*, [1991] 2 SCR 5.

23 *Highline Produce Limited*, [1995] OLRB Rep. 803.

24 *Kingsville Mushroom Farms Inc.*, [1995] OLR.D No. 5221 (QL); *Fleming Chicks Limited*, [1995] OLRD No. 5223 (QL).

25 *Dunmore v. Ontario (Attorney General)*, [2001] 3 SCR 1016.

26 *Agricultural Employees Protection Act*, SO 2002, c. 16.

27 See *Kingsville Rol-Land Farms*, [2003] OLRD 2300 (QL).

28 Ontario. Ministry of the Solicitor General, Verdict of the Coroner's Jury into the deaths of Redekopp, Ferrier and Schulz (28 November 2001); Helen Tosine, Assistant Deputy Minister of Labour, to Dr. Anita Porter, Deputy Chief Coroner of Inquests for Ontario, 22 January 2003.

29 *Pesticides Act*, RSO 1990, c. P. 11; *Farm Implements Act*, RSO 1990, c. F4.

30 California Code of Regulations, Title 8, section 3456 (approved 23 September 2004).

CHAPTER FOURTEEN

1 In this chapter, the term "visible minority" is not taken as a conceptual or heuristic category. Rather, it refers to the specific variable defined by Statistics Canada composed of the racialized groups described in chapter 1. This term is used in depicting data from the Survey of Labour and Income Dynamics and the Workplace and Employer Survey.

In contrast, in the analytical sections of the chapter, the term "people of colour" is used to emphasize racialized social locations – that is, to acknowledge people's continual experiences with racism as well as the importance of oppositional identities for resistance, in Canada and elsewhere (see Vosko, this volume; see also Glossary of Terms). Consistent with the remainder of the volume, we also place "race" in quotation marks at first mention to reflect the socially constructed nature of this category.

2 The data for this section were generated from a special run of the Survey of Labour and Income Dynamics for Canada, 2000. We thank Valerie duPlessis of Statistics Canada for running this data.

CHAPTER FIFTEEN

1 Jackson notes that this category does not include Aboriginal workers and those workers who reported "didn't know" when asked about visible minority status.
2 CLC Women's Organizing Symposium, Toronto, October 20-22, 2002; Labour Council of Toronto and York Region, "Building Power: Aboriginal/Workers of Colour Conference," Toronto, June 14, 2003.
3 This category does not include Aboriginal workers or those who answered "didn't know" when asked about visible minority status.
4 Interview with June Veecock, Ontario Federation of Labour, June 17, 2003, Toronto.
5 Interview with Bev Johnson, Ontario Public Service Employees Union, June 17, 2003, Toronto.
6 Interview with Michael Cifuentes, HERE, September 25, 2003, Toronto.
7 Interview with Bryan Neath, UFCWU, September 4, 2003, Toronto.
8 Ibid.
9 Interview with anonymous organizer, September 8, 2003, Toronto.
10 Interview with Marie Clarke Walker, CLC, September 19, 2003, Toronto.
11 Interview with Hassan Yussuff, CLC, June 19, 2003, Ottawa.
12 Another article by this author describes in more detail these problems that exist in the labour movement. It is a chapter in *Union Responses to Equity in Canada*, edited by Gerald Hunt and David Rayside (Toronto: University of Toronto Press, forthcoming).
13 Interview with Marie Clarke Walker.
14 Interview with June Veecock, OFL, June 17, 2003, Toronto.
15 Interview with Carol Wall, Public Sector Alliance of Canada (PSAC), September 22, 2003, Ottawa.
16 Interview with Michael Cifuentes, HERE, September 25, 2003, Toronto.
17 Interview with anonymous organizer, September 24, 2003, Toronto.

CHAPTER SIXTEEN

1 I would like to thank all the hotel workers at the Journey Hotel who generously gave their time to answer my questions. My thanks are also extended to Paul Clifford, President of HERE Local 75, who helped me gain entrance into the local; to Michel Duncan, who willingly helped me access key information; and to Miguel Cifuentes, the bargaining unit staff representative.
2 The names of the hotel and the people interviewed have been changed or omitted to ensure confidentiality.

3 Response to Application Regarding Unlawful Strike or Lock-out (Form A-40). Before Ontario Labour Relations Board, W-Westmont Corp. and HERE Local 75. File No. 0235-02-U.

CHAPTER SEVENTEEN

Authorship is alphabetical to reflect equal contribution.

1 The hiring hall does have limitations, such as a top-down organizational structure and corruption (Fine 1998; Vosko 2000).

2 This description is from "Realities of Temp Work Today" by Toronto Organizing for Fair Employment (TOFFE), 10 June 2004. The analysis in this chapter includes events up to the end of 2004.

3 TOFFE and WIC were in the process of picking a name for the workers' centre at the time of publication. They merged to become the Workers' Action Centre in fall 2005.

4 In 2003–4 TOFFE had 825 new workers phone its telephone hotline with questions about rights in their workplaces. An additional 1,000 repeat calls were done to follow up with workers, intervene with employers, and ensure that violations were challenged and appropriate support was given. During this period, TOFFE has conducted workshops and drop-ins with over 760 workers. They have had 8,140 visits to their website, of which 4,925 were unique visitors. These figures do not include the information and educational work of WIC. See Toronto Organizing for Fair Employment, 2004, 5–6.

CONCLUSION

1 For case studies of self-employed workers dependant on their capacity to sell their labour power, temporary help workers, and agricultural workers who could benefit from the model of representation, see also Cranford, Fudge, Tucker, and Vosko 2005.

Bibliography of Secondary Sources

Abbot, Pamela, and Claire Wallace. 1992. *The Family and the New Right*. London and Boulder, Col.: Pluto Press.

ABE. See Au bas de l'échelle.

Acker, Joan. 1988. "Class, Gender and Relations of Distribution." *Signs: Journal of Women in Culture and Society* 12: 473–97.

– 1989. *Doing Comparable Work*. Philadelphia: Temple University Press.

ACOHOS (Advisory Council on Occupational Health and Occupational Safety). See Ontario, ACOHOS.

ACSESS. See Association of Canadian Search, Employment and Staffing Services.

Agocs, Carol. 2002. "Canada's Employment Equity Legislation and Policy, 1987–2000. The Gap between Policy and Practice." *International Journal of Manpower* 23 (3): 256–76.

Aidt, Toke, and Zafiris Tzannatos. 2003. *Unions and Collective Bargaining: Economic Effects in a Global Environment*. Washington: The World Bank.

Akyeampong, Ernest B. 2001. "Fact-sheet on Unionization." *Perspectives on Labour and Income* 3 (13): 46.

Akyeampong, Ernest B., and Deborah Sussman. 2003. "Health-Related Insurance for the Self-Employed." *Perspectives/Statistics Canada* 4 (5): 15–21.

Albo, Greg. 1994. "Competitive Austerity." In Leo Panitch, ed., *Socialist Register 1994*, 471–504. London: Merlin Press.

Anderson, K. 1991. *Vancouver's Chinatown: Racial Discourse in Canada*. Montreal: McGill-Queen's University Press.

Annunziato, F.R. 1990. "Commodity Unionism." *Rethinking Marxism* 3 (summer): 8–33.

Anon. 2000. *Women in Canada*. Ottawa: Statistics Canada.

Antecol, Heather, and Peter J. Kuhn. 1999. "Employment Equity Programs and the Job Search Outcomes of Unemployed Men and Women: Actual and Perceived Effects." *Canadian Public Policy* 25(1): S27–S45.

Arat-Koc, Sedef. 1990. "Importing Housewives: Non-Citizen Domestic Workers and the Crisis of the Domestic Sphere in Canada." In Meg Luxton, Harriet Rosenberg, and Sedef Arat-Koc, eds., *Through the Kitchen*. Toronto: Garamond Press, 81–103.

– 1997. "From 'Mothers of the Nation' to Migrant Workers." In Abigail B. Bakan and Daiva K. Stasiulis, eds., *Not One of the Family: Foreign Domestic Workers in Canada*. Toronto: University of Toronto Press, 53–80.

Armstrong, Pat. 1996. "The Feminization of the Labour Force: Harmonizing Down in a Global Economy." In Isabella Bakker, ed., *Rethinking Restructing: Gender and Change in Canada*, 29–54. Toronto: University of Toronto Press.

– 2004. "Thinking It Through: Women, Work and Caring in the New Millennium." In Pat Armstrong and Hugh Armstrong, eds., *Caring For and Caring About*, 4–44. Toronto: Garamond Press.

Armstrong, Pat, and Hugh Armstrong. 1983. "Beyond Sexless Class and Classless Sex: Towards Feminist Marxism." *Studies in Political Economy* 10: 7–43.

– 1994. *The Double Ghetto: Canadian Women and Their Segregated Work*. 3rd ed. Toronto: McClelland & Stewart.

– 2001. *Theorizing Women's Work*. Toronto: Women's Press.

Armstrong, Pat, Hugh Armstrong, and Pat Connelly. 1997. "Introduction: The Many Forms of Privatization." *Studies in Political Economy* 53 (summer): 3–10.

Armstrong, Pat, Mary Cornish, and Elizabeth Millar. 2003. "Pay Equity: Complexity and Contradiction in Legal Rights and Social Processes." In Wallace Clement and Leah F. Vosko, eds., *Changing Canada: Political Economy as Transformation*, 161–82. Montreal and Kingston: McGill-Queen's University Press.

Arnal, Elena, Wooseok Ok, and Raymond Torres. 2001. *Knowledge, Work Organization and Economic Growth*. Labour Market and Social Policy Occasional Paper No. 50. OECD.

Aronowitz, Stanley. 1964. "Poverty, Politics and Community Organization." *Studies on the Left* 4 (2): 102–5.

Aronson, R. 1991. *Self-Employment: A Labor Market Perspective*. Ithaca, NY: ILR Press.

Aronsson, Gunnar. 1999. "Contingent Workers and Health and Safety." *Work, Employment and Society* 13(3): 439–60.

Arthurs, Harry. 1967. "Developing Industrial Citizenship: A Challenge for Canada's Second Century." *Canadian Bar Review* 45: 787–806.

Arup, Christopher. 1995. "Labour Market Regulation as a Focus for a Labour Law Discipline." In Richard Mitchell, ed., *Redefining Labour Law: New Perspectives on the Future of Teaching and Research*, 29–44. Melbourne: Centre for Employment and Labour Relations Law.

Association of Canadian Search, Employment and Staffing Services (ACSESS). 2003. *Code of Ethics and Standards*. Accessed at www.acsess.org/english/aboutus.php?pageID=Code_of_Ethics

Atkinson, John. 1988a. "Recent Changes in the Internal Labour Market in the UK." In W. Buitelaar, ed., *Technology and Work: Labour Studies in England, Germany and the Netherlands*, 133–49. Aldershot, England: Avenbury.

– 1988b. Working Conditions and the Small and Medium-Sized Enterprises. European Foundation for the Improvement of Living and Working Conditions. Luxemburg: Office for Official Publication of the European Communities.

Au bas de l'échelle (ABE). 2000. *Une réforme en profondeur: c'est l'heure! Avis sur la Loi sur les normes du travail*. Montreal.

Au bas de l'échelle (ABE) and Front de défense des non-syndiqués (FDNS). 2002. *Mémoire d'Au bas de l'échelle et du Front de défense des non-syndiqués sur le document de consultation. "Revoir les normes du travail: un défi collectif."* Montreal.

Auer, Peter. 2000. *Employment Revival in Europe: Labour Market Success in Austria, Denmark, Ireland and the Netherlands*. Geneva: ILO.

Avery, Donald. 1979. *"Dangerous Foreigners": European Immigrant Workers and Labour Radicalism in Canada, 1896–1932*. Toronto: McClelland & Stewart.

– 1995. *Reluctant Host: Canada's Response to Immigrant Workers, 1896–1994*. Toronto: McClelland & Stewart.

Backhouse, Constance. 1991. *Petticoats & Prejudice: Women and Law in Nineteenth-Century Canada*. Toronto: Osgoode Society.

Badgley, Kerry. 2000. *Ringing in the Common Love of Good*. Montreal & Kingston: McGill-Queen's University Press.

Bakan, Abigail Bess, and Audrey Kobayashi. 2000. *Employment Equity Policy in Canada: An Inter-Provincial Comparison*. Ottawa: Status of Women Canada.

Bakan, Abigail Bess, and Daiva Kristina Stasiulis. 1997a. "Foreign Domestic Worker Policy in Canada and the Social Boundaries of Modern Citizenship." In Abigail Bess Bakan and Daiva Kristina Stasiulis, eds., *Not One of the Family: Foreign Domestic Workers in Canada*, 29–52. Toronto: University of Toronto Press.

– 1997b. "Making the Match: Domestic Placement Agencies and the Racialization of Women's Household Work." *Signs: Journal of Women in Culture and Society* 20 (2): 303–35.

– 1997c. *Not One of the Family*. Toronto: University of Toronto Press.

Baker, Dean, Andrew Glyn, David Howell, and John Schmitt. 2002. "Labor Market Institutions and Unemployment: A Critical Assessment of the Cross-Country Evidence." Centre for Economic Policy Analysis Working Paper 17. www.newschool.edu/cepa

Bakker, Isabella. 1996a. "Introduction: The Gendered Foundations of Restructuring in Canada." In Isabella Bakker, ed., *Rethinking Restructuring: Gender and Change in Canada*, 3–25. Toronto: University of Toronto Press.

– 1996b. *Rethinking Restructuring: Gender and Change in Canada*. Toronto: University of Toronto Press.

Baldwin, Majorie L., and William G. Johnson. 2000. "Labor Market Discrimination against Men with Disabilities in the Year of the ADA." *Southern Economic Journal* 66 (3): 548–66.

Baldwin, Robert, Colin Scott, and Christopher Hood. 1998. "Introduction." In Robert Baldwin, Colin Scott, and Christopher Hood, eds., *A Reader on Regulation*, 1–30. New York: Oxford University Press.

Barker, Kathleen, and Kathleen Christensen, eds. 1998. *Contingent Work: American Employment Relations in Transition*. Ithaca, NY: ILR Press.

Barndt, Deborah. 2002. *Tangled Routes: Women, Work and Globalization on the Tomato Trail*. Aurora: Garamond Press.

Barrett, Michelle. 1988. *Women's Oppression Today: The Marxist/Feminist Encounter*. London, England: Verson.

Bashevkin, Sylvia. 2002. *Welfare Hot Buttons: Women's Work and Social Policy Reform*. Toronto and Pittsburgh, Penn.: University of Toronto Press and University of Pittsburgh Press.

Basok, Tanya. 2002. *Tortillas and Tomatoes*. Montreal & Kingston: McGill-Queen's University Press.

− 2004. "Post-national Citizenship, Social Exclusion and Migrant Rights: Mexican Seasonal Workers in Canada." *Citizenship Studies* 8: 47−64.

Batavia, A., and K. Schriner. 2001. "The Americans with Disabilities Act as Engine of Social Change: Models of Disability and the Potential of a Civil Rights Approach." *Policy Studies Journal* 29 (4): 690−702.

Battle, Ken. 2003. *Minimum Wages in Canada: A Statistical Report with Policy Implications*. Kingston: Caledon Institute of Social Policy.

Beach, Charles, Ross Finnie, and David Gray. 2003 "Earnings Variability Stability of Women and Men in Canada: How Do the 1990's Compare to the 1980's?" *Canadian Public Policy* 29th Supplement (January).

Beatty, David. 1987. *Putting the Charter to Work: Designing a Constitutional Labour Code*. Kingston and Montreal: McGill-Queen's University Press.

Befort, Stephen F. 2003. "Revisiting the Black Hole of Workplace Regulation: A Historical and Comparative Perspective of Contingent Work." *Berkeley Journal of Employment and Labor Law* 1: 153−78.

Belkic, Karen, Dean Baker, Robert Karasek, Paul Landsbergis, Richard Peter, Peter Schnall, Johannes Siegrist, and Tores Theorell. 2000. "Psychological Factors: Review of the Empirical Data among Men." In Peter L. Schnall, Karen Belkic, Paul Landsbergis, and Dean Baker, eds., *The Workplace and Cardiovascular Disease. Occupational Medicine* 15 (1): 24−46.

Bellace, Janice R., and Max G. Rood, eds. 1997. *Labour Law at the Crossroads: Changing Employment Relationships. Studies in Honour of Benjamin Aaron*. The Hague-London-Boston: Kluwer.

Belzer, Mike. 2000. *Sweatshops on Wheels*. Ithaca, NY: Cornell University Press.

Benach, Joan, David Gimeno, and Fernando G. Benavides. 2002. *Types of Employment and Health in the European Union*. Dublin: European Foundation for the Improvement of Working and Living Conditions.

Benavides, Fernando G., and Joan Benach. 2000. *Precarious Employment and Health-Related Outcomes in the European Union*. Dublin: European Foundation for the Improvement of Living and Working Conditions.

Benjamin, Paul. 2002. "Who Needs Labour Law? Defining the Scope of Labour Protection." In Joanne Conaghan, Richard Michael Fischl, and Karl Klare, eds.,

Labour Law in an Era of Globalization: Transformative Practices and Possibilities, 57–92. Oxford: Oxford University Press.

Benner, Mats, and Torben Bundgaard Vad. 2000. "Sweden and Denmark: Defending the Welfare State." In Fritz Scharpf and Vivien Schmidt, eds., *Welfare and Work in the Open Economy*, vol 2: *Diverse Responses to Common Challenges*, 399–466. Oxford, NY: Oxford University Press.

Berg, Annika. 2000. *New Agreement Concluded from Temporary Work Agencies*. EIRO.

– 2003. *Social Partners Agree Guidelines for Implementation of European Telework Agreement*. EIRO.

Bernier, Jean. 1999. *Rapport du comité interministériel sur les rapports collectifs du travail en milieu forestier*. Quebec: Ministère du travail. http://www.travail.gouv.qc.ca/publications/rapports/forets_resume.html.

Bernier, Jean, Georges Marceau, and Michel Towner. 1999. *Rapport du Comité d'experts sur le statut des camionneurs-propriétaires*. Quebec: Ministère du travail.

Bernier, Jean, et al. 2001. *L'incessante évolution des formes d'emploi et la redoutable stagnation des lois du travail*. Ste-Foy: Presses de l'Université Laval.

Bernier, Jean, Guylaine Vallée, and Carol Jobin. 2003. *Les besoins de protection sociale des personnes en situation de travail non traditionnelle. Rapport final*. Quebec: Ministère du Travail. http://www.travail.gouv.qc.ca/publications/rapports/alphabet.html

Bernstein, Stephanie, Lippel, Katherine, and Lucie Lamarche. 2001. *Women and Homework: The Canadian Legislative Framework*. Ottawa: Status of Women in Canada. http://www.swc-cfc.gc.ca>publish/research/010419-0662854500-e.pdf

Betcherman, Gordon, and Graham S. Lowe. 1997. *The Future Work in Canada: A Synthesis Report*. Ottawa: Canadian Policy Research Networks Inc.

Bettio, Francesca, and Paola Villa. 1989. "Non-Wage Work and Disguised Wage Employment in Italy." In Gerry Rogers and Janine Rogers, eds., *Precarious Jobs in Labour Market Regulation: The Growth of Atypical Employment in Western Europe*, 149–78. Geneva: International Institute for Labour Studies.

Bich, Marie-France. 2001. "De quelques idées imparfaites et tortueuses sur l'intermédiation du travail." In Service de la formation permanente du Barreau, *Développements récents en droit du travail*, 257–319. Cowansville, Que.: Editons Yvon Blais.

Bich, Marie-France, Pierre Dion, Guy Lemay, and Normand Ratti. 1997. "La location de personnes, la problématique du travailleur autonome, la problématique de l'administrateur et du dirigeant." Rapport des travaux d'un comité formé par la Commission de la santé et la sécurité du travail, July 1997 (unpublished).

Bickenbach, J., S. Chatterji, E. Badley, and T. Ustun. 1999. "Models of Disablement, Universalism and the International Classification of Impairments, Disabilities and Handicaps." *Social Science and Medicine* 48: 1173–87.

Bickerton, Geoff, and Catherine Stearns. 2002. "The Struggle Continues in Winnipeg: The Workers Organizing and Resource Centre." *Just Labour: A Canadian Journal of Work and Society* 1: 50–7.

Biddle, Jeff, and Karen Roberts. 2003. "Claiming Behavior in Worker's Compensation." *Journal of Risk and Insurance* 70 (4): 759–80.

Black, Errol, and Lisa Shaw. 1998. *The Case for a Strong Minimum Wage Policy.* Ottawa: Canadian Centre for Policy Alternatives.

Black, Sandra, and Lisa Lynch. 2000. *What's Driving the New Economy: The Benefits of Workplace Innovation.* National Bureau of Economic Research Working Paper 7479.

Blais, Francois. 2002. *Ending Poverty: A Basic Income for All Canadians.* Toronto: James Lorimer.

Blakely, J., and E. Harvey. 1988. "Socioeconomic Change and Lack of Change: Employment Equity Policies in the Canadian Context." *Journal of Business* 3: 133–50.

Blanck, Peter D, Leonard A. Sandler, James L. Schmeling, and Helen A. Schartz. 2000. "The Emerging Workforce of Entrepreneurs with Disabilities: Preliminary Study of Entrepreneurship in Iowa." *Iowa Law Review* 85: 1583–1668.

Blanpain, Roger. 1997. *The Legal and Contractual Situation of Teleworkers in the European Union: The Law Aspects Including Self-Employed.* Consolidated Report, Working Paper No.: WP/97/28/EN European Foundation for the Improvement of Living and Working Conditions, Dublin.

Blouin, Rodrigue. 2003. "La CRT, le concept de salarié et les nouvelles réalités d'exécution du travail subordonné." In Service de la formation permanente du Barreau, *Développements récents en droit du travail*, 137–77. Cowansville, Que.: Yvon Blais.

Boland, Jack. "Hotel Staff Desperate: Fear of Virus Whacks Jobs in Tourism Trade." *Toronto Sun*, 10 May 2003.

Bolaria, B. Singh. 1992. "Farm Labour, Work Conditions, and Health Risks." In David A. Hay and Gurcharn S. Basran, eds., *Rural Sociology in Canada*, 228–45. Toronto: Oxford University Press.

– 1994. "Agricultural Production, Work and Health." In B. Singh Bolaria and Harley D. Dickerson, eds., *Health, Illness, and Health Care in Canada*, 2nd ed., 684–96. Toronto: Harcourt Brace Canada.

Borg, M.A., and A. Portelli .1999. "Hospital Laundry Workers: An At-Risk Group for Hepititis A." *Occupational Medicine* 49 (7): 448–50.

Borowy, Jan, Shelly Gordon, and Gayle Lebans. 1993. "Are These Clothes Clean? The Campaign for Fair Wages and Working Conditions for Homeworkers." In L. Carty, ed., *And Still We Rise: Feminist Political Mobilizing in Contemporary Canada*, 299–332. Toronto: Toronto Women's Press.

Borowy, Jan, and Teresa Johnson. 1995. "Unions Confront Work Reorganization and the Rise of Precarious Employment: Home-Based Work in the Garment Industry and the Federal Public Service." In Chris Schenk and J. Anderson, eds., *Re-Shaping Work: Union Responses to Technological Change*, 29–47. Don Mills: Ontario Federation of Labour.

Bourhis, Anne, and Thierry Wills. 2001. "L'éclatement de l'emploi traditionnel: Les défis posés par la diversité des emplois typiques et atypiques." *Relations industrielles/Industrial Relations* 56(1): 66–91.

Boyd, Monica. 1992. "Gender, Visible Minority and Immigrant Earnings Inequality: Reassessing an Employment Equity Premise." In Vic Satzewich, ed., *Deconstructing a Nation: Immigration Multiculturalism and Racism in the 1990s*, 297–321. Halifax: Fernwood Publishing.

Braverman, Harry. 1974. *Labor and Monopoly Capital: The Degradation of Work in the Twentieth Century*. New York: Monthly Review Press.

Breecher, Jeremy, and Tim Costello. 1996. "'A New Labor Movement': In the Shell of the Old?" *Labor Research Review* 24: 5–25.

Brenner, Johanna.1990. "Radical versus Liberal Approaches to the Feminization of Poverty and Comparable Worth." In K. Hansen, ed., *Women, Class and the Feminist Imagination: A Socialist-Feminist Reader*, 491–507. Philadelphia:Temple University Press.

– 2000. *Women and the Politics of Class*. New York: Monthly Review Press.

Briskin, Linda, and Patricia McDermott. 1993. *Women Challenging Unions: Feminism, Democracy and Militancy*. Toronto: University of Toronto Press.

Broad, David. 1991. "Global Economic Restructuring and the (Re) Casualization of Work in the Centre." *Review* 4 (Fall): 555–94.

– 2000. *Hollow Work, Hollow Society: Globalization and the Casual Labour Problem in Canada*. Halifax: Fernwood Publishing.

Bronfenbrenner, K., and T. Juravich. 1998. "It Takes More than Housecalls: Organizing to Win with a Comprehensive Union-Building Strategy." In K. Bronfenbrenner, S. Friedman, R. Hurd, R. Oswald, and R. Seeber, eds., *Organizing to Win: New Research on Union Strategies*, 19–36. Ithaca, NY: Cornell University Press.

Broughton, Andrea. 2002. Social Partners Sign Teleworking Accord. EIRO.

Buchanan, Ruth, and Sarah Koch-Shulte. 2000. *Gender on the Line: Technology, Restructuring and the Rise of the Re-organization of Work in the Call Centre Industry*. Ottawa: Status of Women Canada.

Buechler, Steven M. 2000. *Social Movements in Advanced Capitalism*. New York: Oxford University Press.

Bunch, Mary, and Cynthia Crawford. 1998. "Factors Affecting the Employment and Labour Force Transitions of People with Disabilities: A Review of the Literature." Unpublished.

Burke, Mike, Colin Mooers, and John Shields. 2000. *Restructuring and Resistance: Canadian Public Policy in an Age of Global Capitalism*. Halifax: Fernwood Publishing.

Burkerhauser, R., and M. Daly. 1996. "Employment and Economic Well-Being following the Onset of a Disability: The Role for Public Policy." *Disability, Work and Cash Benefits*, 59–101. Kalamazoo, Mich.: W.E. Upjohn Institute for Employment Research.

Burkerhauser, R., M. Daly, et al. 2001. "Economic Outcomes of Working-Age People over the Business Cycle: An Examination of the 1980's and 1990's." San Franciso: Federal Reserve Bank.

Butchtemann, C.F., and S. Quack. 1990. "How Precarious Is 'Non-Standard' Employment? Evidence for West Germany." *Cambridge Journal of Economics* 14: 315–29.

Calliste, Agnes. 1987. "Sleeping Car Porters in Canada: An Ethnically Submerged Split Labour Market." *Canadian Ethnic Studies* 19 (1): 1–20.

– 1991. "Canada's Immigration Policy and Domestics from the Caribbean: The Second Domestic Scheme." In Jesse Vorst et al., eds., *Race, Class, Gender: Bonds and Barriers*. Toronto: Society for Socialist Studies and Garamond Press.

– 1993. "Race, Gender and Canadian Immigration Policy: Blacks from the Caribbean, 1900–1932." *Journal of Canadian Studies* 28 (4): 131–46.

Cameron, Barbara. 1995. "From Segmentation to Solidarity: A New Framework for Labour Market Regulation." In Daniel Drache and Andrew Ranachan, eds., *Warm Heart, Cold Country: Fiscal and Social Policy Reform in Canada*, 193–212. Ottawa: Caledon Institute / Roberts Centre for Canadian Studies.

– 2001. *The Occupational Health and Safety Implications of Non-Standard Employment*. Toronto: Workplace Safety and Insurance Board.

Canada. 1960. *Trends in the Agricultural Labour Force in Canada from 1921 to 1959*. Ottawa: Queen's Printer.

Canada. Department of Labour, Economics and Research Branch. 1954. *Farm Safety and Workmen's Compensation*. Ottawa: Queen's Printer.

– 1960. *Trends in the Agricultural Labour Force in Canada from 1921 to 1959*. Ottawa: Queen's Printer.

Canadian Labour Congress. 1997. *Challenging Racism: Going Beyond Recommendations*. Report of the CLC National Anti-Racism Task Force.

– 1998. *No Easy Recipe: Building the Diversity and Strength of the Labour Movement: Feminist Organizing Models*. CLC Women's Symposium, November 1–3.

– 2003. Falling Unemployment Insurance Protection for Canada's Unemployed. March. Ottawa: CLC or www.unemployed.ca.

Cappelli, Peter, Laura Bassi, Harry Katz, David Knoke, Paul Osterman, and Michael Useem. 1997. *Change at Work*. New York: Oxford University Press.

Carbado, Devon W., and Mitu Gulati. 2001. "The Fifth Black Woman." *Journal of Contemporary Legal Issues* 11: 701–29.

Card, David, and Richard Freeman. 1993. *Small Differences That Matter*. National Bureau of Economic Growth. Chicago.

Card, David, and A. Krueger. 1995. *Myth and Measurement: The New Economics of the Minimum Wage*. Princeton, NJ: Princeton University Press.

Card, David, Thomas Lemieux, and W. Craig Riddell. 2003. *Unionization and Wage Inequality: A Comparative Study of the US, the UK and Canada*. National Bureau of Economic Research Working Paper W9473. February.

Carre, Francois, et al. 2000. *Non-standard Work Arrangements*. Wisconsin: Industrial Relations Research Association.

Carty, Linda, ed. 1993. *And Still We Rise*. Toronto: Women's Press.

Casey, Bernard, and Stephen Creigh. 1988. "Self-Employment in Great Britain: Its Definition in the Labour Force Survey, in Tax and Social Security Law, and in Labour Law." *Work, Employment and Society* 2 (3): 381–91.

Casson, M. 1991. *The Entrepreneur: An Economic Theory*. Worcester: Billing and Sons.

– 1982. *The Entrepreneur and Economic Theory*. Totowa, NJ: Barnes and Noble.

Cedes, Maurice. 1993. "Sur la prévention des accidents du travail et des maladies professionnelles dans les entreprises à faible effectif." *Droit Social* 5: 434–8.

CES. 2001. *Consultation des partenaires sociaux sur la protection de la santé et de la sécurité au travail des travailleurs indépendants: résponse de la CES, BTS,* April.

Cheal, David. 2003. "Finding a Niche: Age-Related Differentiations within the Working- Age Population." In Danielle Juteau, ed., *Patterns and Processes of Social Differentiation: The Construction of Gender, Age, 'Race/Ethnicity' and Locality*, 81–116. Toronto/ Montreal: University of Toronto Press/University of Montreal Press (French and English).

Chelius, James R., and John F. Burton. 1994. "Who Actually Pays for Workers' Compensation? The Empirical Evidence." In John F. Burton and Timothy P. Schmidle, eds., *1995 Workers' Compensation Year Book*, 1–153. Horsham, Penn.: LRP Publications.

Chen, Melody. 2003. "Outsourcing Played a Role in Outbreaks: CDC Head." Accessed at http://www.taipeitimes.com/chnews/2003/06/10/story/2003054672.

Chicha, Marie-Thérèse. 1999. "The Impact of Labour Market Transformations on the Effectiveness of Laws Promoting Workplace Gender Equality." In R. Chaykowski and L. Powell, eds., *Women and Work*, 283–304. Montreal and Kingston: McGill Queen's University Press.

Christofides, Louis, and Robert Swidnsky. 1994. "Wage Determination by Gender and Visible Minority Status: Evidence from the 1989 LMAS." *Canada Public Policy* 20(1): 34–51.

CIC. See Citizenship and Immigration Canada.

Ciscel, D.H. 2000. "The Living Wage Movement: Building a Political Link from Market Wages to Social Institutions." *Journal of Economic Issues* 34 (2): 527–36.

Citizenship and Immigration Canada. 2003. Contribution Accountability Framework (CAF) Newsletter (Issue 8, July). Accessed at http://integration-net.cic.gc.ca/inet/english/caf-cipc/documents/c/no1.htm, December 15, 2003.

Clarke, L. 2000. "Disparities in Wage Relations and Social Reproduction." In L. Clarke, Peter de Gijsel, and Jorn Janssen, eds., *The Dynamics of Wage Relations in the New Europe*, 134–9. London: Kluewer Academic Publishers.

Clauwert, Stefan. 2000. *Survey of Legislation on Temporary Agency Work*. Brussels: European Trade Union Institute.

CLC. See Canadian Labour Congress.

Clement, Wallace. 1983. *Class, Power and Property*. Toronto: Methuen.

– 1986. *The Struggle to Organize: Resistance in Canada's Fishery*. Toronto: McClelland & Stewart.

– 1988. *The Challenge of Class Analysis*. Ottawa: Carleton University Press.

CNT. See Commission des normes du travail.

Cobbaut, Robert. 2000. "'Corporate governance' et procéduralisation." In Philippe Coppens and Jacques Lenoble, eds., *Démocratie et procéduralisation du droit*, 351–63. Brussels: Bruylant.

Cobble, Dorothy Sue. 1991. "Organizing the Postindustrial Work Force: Lessons from the History of Waitress Unionism." *Industrial and Labor Relations Review* 44 (3): 419–36.

Cobble, Dorothy Sue, and Leah F. Vosko. 2000. "Historical Perspectives on Representing Workers in 'Non-Standard' Employment." *Industrial Relations Research Association, Year 2000*: 291–312.

Cohen, Marjorie. 1994. "The Implications of Economic Restructuring for Women: The Canadian Situation." In Isabella Bakker, ed., *The Strategic Silence: Gender and Economic Policy*, 103–16. London: Zed Books.

– 2001. *Do Comparisons between Hospital Support Workers and Hospitality Workers Make Sense?* Vancouver: Hospital Employees Union.

Collingwood, Harris. 2003. "The Sink-or-Swim Economy: The Recession Isn't So Deep, How Come You're Feeling So Bad? The Perils of Market Efficiency." *New York Times Magazine*, 42–5 (June 8).

Collins, Hugh. 2000. "Justifications and Techniques of Legal Regulation of Employment Relations." In Hugh Collins, Paul Davies, and Roger Rideout, eds., *Legal Regulation of the Employment Relation*, 3–27. Netherlands: Kluwer Law International.

– 2001. "Regulating the Employment Relation for Competitiveness." *Industrial Law Journal* 30: 17–48.

Collins, Patricia. 1990. *Black Feminist Thought: Knowledge, Consciousness, and the Politics of Empowerment*. London: Routledge.

Commission des normes du travail. 1995. *L'article 41.1 de la Loi sur les normes du travail et les agences de placement temporaire*. Quebec: CNT.

– 1996. *Document de travail présenté à des fins de discussion au Conseil d'administration de la Commission des normes du travail: Les agences de placement temporaire et la Loi sur les normes du travail*. Quebec: CNT.

– 2003. *Rapport annuel, 2002–2003*. Quebec: CNT.

– 2003. Wages. Accessed at www.cnt.gouv.qc.ca.

Commission for Labor Cooperation. 2002. *Protection of Agricultural Workers in Canada, Mexico and the United States*. Washington, DC: Secretariat of the Commission for Labor Cooperation.

Commission of the European Communities. 2002. "Amended Proposal for a Directive of the European Parliament and the Council on Working Conditions for Temporary Workers." Brussels, COM(2002) 701 final, 2002/0072 (COD).

Conaghan, Joanne. 2003. "Labour Law and 'New Economy' Discourse." *Australian Journal of Labour Law* 16: 9–31.

Congress of the United States, Joint Economic Committee. 1995. *50 Years if Research on the Minimum Wage*. Accessed at www.house.gov.

Connell, R.W. 1987. *Gender and Power*. Cambridge: Polity Press.

Conseil du statut de la femme. 2000. *Emploi atypique cherche normes équitables.* Quebec: CSF.

– 2000. *Travailler autrement: Pour le meilleur ou pour le pire? Les femmes et le travail atypique.* Quebec: CSF.

Contingent Workers' Project. 2002. "Breaking the Myth of Flexible Work: Contingent Work in Toronto." Toronto: unpublished report.

Cook, Judith A., and Jane Burke. 2002. "Public Policy and Employment of People with Disabilities: Exploring New Paradigms." *Behavioral Sciences and the Law* 20: 541–57.

Cooper, C.L. 2002. "The Changing Psychological Contract at Work." *Occupational Medicine* 59: 355.

Cossman, Brenda, and Judy Fudge. 2002. *Privatization, Law, and the Challenge to Feminism.* Toronto: University of Toronto Press.

Cox, Mark. 1987. "The Limits of Reform: Industrial Regulation and Management Rights in Ontario, 1930–7." *Canadian Historical Review* 68: 552–75.

Cox, Rachel, Jacques Desmarais, and Katherine Lippel. 2001. *Les enjeux juridiques du télétravail au Québec.* Quebec: CEFRIO, 145, or www.cefrio.qc.ca

Cranford, Cynthia. 1998. "Gender and Citizenship in the Restructuring of Janitorial Work in Los Angeles." *Gender Issues* 16(4): 25–51.

– 2001. "Labor, Gender and the Politics of Citizenship: Organizing 'Justice for Janitors' in Los Angeles." PhD dissertation, University of Southern California.

Cranford, Cynthia, and Deena Ladd. 2003. "Community Unionism: Organizing for Fair Employment in Canada." *Just Labour: A Canadian Journal of Work and Society* 3 (fall): 46–59.

Cranford, Cynthia, Leah F. Vosko, and Nancy Zukewich. 2003a. "The Gender of Precariousness in the Canadian Labour Force." *Relations Industrielles/Industrial Relations* 58 (3): 454–82.

– 2003b. "Precarious Employment in the Canadian Labour Market: A Statistical Portrait." *Just Labour: A Canadian Journal of Work and Society* 3 (fall): 6–22.

Cranford, Cynthia, Judy Fudge, Eric Tucker, and Leah F. Vosko. 2005. *Self-Employed Workers Organize: Law, Policy and Unions.* Montreal and Kingston: McGill-Queen's University Press.

Crawford, Cameron. 1998. "Disability-Status Transitions and Labour Force Activity Transitions of People with Disability: An Analysis Based on the Survey of Labour and Income Dynamics (1993 and 1994)." Unpublished.

Crawford, C. 2000. "Proposed Strategy for Researching Relevant Policy Issues on Disability: Phase I: Guide for Research Directions and Lines of Enquiry." Unpublished.

Creese, Gillian Laura. 1991. "Organizing against Racism in the Workplace: Chinese Workers in Vancouver before the Second World War." In Ormond McKague, ed., *Racism in Canada*, 33–44. Saskatoon: Fifth House Publishers.

– 1992. "Exclusion or Solidarity? Vancouver Workers Confront the 'Oriental Problem.'" In Laurel Sefton MacDowell and Ian Radforth, eds., *Canadian Working Class History: Selected Readings*, 311–32. Toronto: Canadian Scholars' Press.

– 1999. *Contracting Masculinity: Gender, Class, and Race in a White Collar Union, 1944–1994*. Don Mills: Oxford University Press.

Crenshaw, Kimberly. 1989. "Demarginalizing the Intersection of Race and Sex: A Black Feminist Critique of Antidiscrimination Doctrine, Feminist Theory and Antiracist Politics." *University of Chicago Legal Forum* 4: 139–67.

Critoph, Ursula. 2003. "Who Wins, Who Loses: The Real Story of the Transfer of Training to the Provinces and Its Impact on Women." In Marjorie Griffin Cohen, ed., *Training the Excluded for Work*, 14–33. Vancouver: UBC Press.

CSF. See Conseil du statut de la femme.

Das Gupta, Tania. 1986. *Learning from Our History: Community Development by Immigrant Women in Ontario, 1958–86*. Toronto: Cross Cultural Communication Centre.

– 1987. "Involving Immigrant Women: A Case of Participatory Research." *Canadian Women's Studies* 8(2): 14–16.

– 1996. *Racism and Unpaid Work*. Toronto: Garamond Press.

– 1998. "Anti-Racism and the Organized Labour Movement." In Vic Satzewich, ed., *Racism and Social Inequality in Canada*, 315–34. Toronto: Thompson Educational.

– 1999. "The Politics of Multiculturalism: 'Immigrant Women' and the Canadian State." In Enakshi Dua and Angela Robertson, eds., *Scratching the Surface: Canadian Anti-racist Feminist Thought*, 187–205. Toronto: Women's Press.

– 2000. "Families of Native Peoples, Immigrants and People of Colour." In Nancy Mandell and Ann Duffy, eds., *Canadian Families: Diversity, Conflict and Change*, 141–74. Canada: Harcourt Brace.

– 2002. "Racism in Nursing." Uunpublished report for Ontario Nurses' Association.

Das Gupta, Tania, and Franca Iocavetta. 2000. "Whose Canada Is It? Immigrant Women, Women of Colour and Feminist Critiques of 'Multiculturalism.'" *Atlantis* 24 (2): 1–4.

Daubas-Letourneux, V., and A. Thebaud-Mony. 2002. *Work Organization and Health at Work in the European Union*. Dublin: European Foundation for the Improvement of Working and Living Conditions.

Davidov, Guy. 2002. "The Three Axes of Employment Relationships: A Characterization of Workers in Need of Protection." SJD dissertation, University of Toronto.

de Jonge, J., and Jan de Jonge Marike. 1999. "The Incorporation of Different Demand Concepts in the Job-Demand-Control Model: Effects on Health Care Professionals." *Social Science and Medicine* 48 (9): 1149–60.

– 2000. "Linear and Nonlinear Relations between Psychosocial Job Characteristics, Subjective Outcomes, and Sickness Absence: Baseline Results from SMASH." *Journal of Occupational Health Psychology* 5: 256–68.

De Munck, Jean. 1999. "Rapport Supiot: Les trois crises du droit du travail." *Droit social* 5: 443–6.

– 2000. "Procéduralisation du droit et négociation collective." In Phillippe Coppens and Jacques Lenoble, eds., *Démocratie et procéduralisation du droit*, 261–311. Brussels: Bruylant.

de Wolf, Alice. 2000. *Breaking the Myth of Flexible Work: Contingent Work in Toronto*. Toronto: The Contingent Workers Project.

Deakin, Simon. 2002a. "The Evolution of the Employment Relationship." In Peter Auer and Bernard Gazier, eds., *The Future of Work, Employment and Social Protection: Dynamics of Change and the Protection of Workers*, 191–203. Geneva: International Institute for Labour Studies.

– 2002b. "The Many Futures of the Contract of Employment." In Joanne Conaghan, Michael Fishl, and Karl Klare, eds., *Labour Law in an Era of Globalization: Transformative Practices & Possibilities*, 177–96. Oxford: Oxford University Press.

Deber, Raisa, Sharmila Mhatre, and G. Ross Baker. 1994. "A Review of Provincial Initiatives." In Ake Blomqvist and David Brown, eds., *Limits to Care: Reforming Canada's Health Care System in an Age of Restraint*, 91–4. Ottawa: C.D. Howe.

Delage, Benoit. 2002. *Results from the Survey of Self-Employment in Canada*. Ottawa: Human Resources Development Canada.

DeLeire, T. 2000. "The Wage and Employment Effects of the Americans with Disabilities Act." *Journal of Human Resources* 35 (4): 693–715.

Denis, Wilfred B. 1988. "Causes of Health and Safety Hazards in Canadian Agriculture." *International Journal of Health Studies* 18: 419–36.

Di Pasquale, Verena. 2002. *New Law Passed on Temporary Agency Work*. EIRO.

Dinardo, John. 1997. "Diverging Male Wage Inequality in the United States and Canada, 1981–1988: Do Institutions Explain the Difference?" *Industrial and Labor Relations Review* 50 (4): 629–51.

Doeringer, Peter B., and Michael J. Piore. 1971. *Internal Labor Markets and Manpower Analysis*. Lexington, Mass.: Heath.

Drolet, Marie. 2001. "The Persistent Gap: New Evidence on the Canadian Gender Wage Gap." Ottawa: Statistics Canada, Business and Labour Market Analysis Division, No. 34.

Drolet, Marie, and René Morrissette. 1998. "The Upward Mobility of Low Paid Canadians, 1993–1995." Statistics Canada Cat. 75F002M.

Dua, Enakshi, and Angela Robertson, eds. 1999. *Scratching the Surface: Canadian Anti-racist Feminist Thought*. Toronto: Women's Press.

Dubé, Jean-Louis, and Nicola Di Iorio. 1992. *Les normes du travail*. 2nd ed. Sherbrooke: Editions Revue de Droit, Université de Sherbrooke.

Duffy, Ann, and Noren Pupo. 1994. *Part-time Paradox: Connecting Gender, Work and Family*. Toronto: McClelland & Stewart.

Duxbury, Linda, and Chris Higgins. 2001. "Work-Life Balance in the New Millennium: Where Are We? Where Do We Need to Go?" Ottawa: Canadian Policy Research Networks Inc.

Eakin, Joan. 1992. "Leaving It up to the Workers: Sociological Perspectives on the Management of Health and Safety in Small Workplaces." *International Journal of Health Services*. 22 (4): 698–704.

Eakin, Joan, Judy Clarke, and Ellen MacEachen. 2002. *Return to Work in Small Workplace: Sociological Perspectives on Workplace Experience with Ontario's "Early and Safe" Strategy.* Report on Research funded by the Research Advisory Council of the Ontario Workplace Safety & Insurance Board. Toronto: Institute for Work & Health. Online at http://www.iwh.on.ca/products/images/ESRTW.pdf.

Eardley, T., and A. Corden. 1996. *Low Income Self-employment.* Aldershot, England: Avebury.

Economic Council of Canada. 1990. *Good Jobs, Bad Jobs: Employment in the Service Economy.* Ottawa: ECC.

Edwards, Peter. "Metro's Powerful Hotel Union Boss Laughs at Link with Mafia Kingpin." *Toronto Star,* June 18, 1989.

Edwards, Richard C., Michael Reich, and David Gordon. 1975. *Labour Market Segmentation.* Lexington, Mass.: Heath.

Eichler, M. 1997. *Family Shifts: Families, Policies and Gender Equality.* Toronto: Oxford University Press.

EIRO. See European Industrial Relations Observatory.

Eisenscher, M. 1999. "Critical Juncture: Unionism at the Crossroads." In B.Nissen, ed., *Which Direction for Organized Labor?* 217–45. Detroit: Wayne State University Press.

Engblom, Samuel. 2001. "Equal Treatment of Employees and Self-employed Workers." *International Journal of Comparative Labour Law and Industrial Relations* 17(2): 211–31.

Equal Opportunities Commission of Northern Ireland. 1996. *Report on the Formal Investigation into Competitive Tendering in Health and Education Services in Northern Ireland.* Belfast: Equal Opportunities Commission of Northern Ireland.

Ernst and Young. Nd. *Horticulture Industry: Organizing for the Future.* Human Resources Issues and Opportunities, National Report Sponsored by Employment and Immigration Canada.

Esping-Anderson, Gösta. 1999. *Social Foundations of Post-industrial Economies.* Oxford: Oxford University Press.

Esping-Anderson, Gösta, Duncan Gaille, Anton Hemerilick, and John Myles. 2001. *A New Welfare Architecture for Europe?* Report submitted to the Belgian Presidency of the European Union.

Esping-Anderson, Gösta, and Joseph Mestres. 2003. *Unequal Opportunities and Social Inheritance.* Barcelona, Spain: University of Pompeu Fabra.

European Commission (Employment and Social Affairs). 2001. *Employment in Europe.*

– 2002. *Employment in Europe.*

European Industrial Relations Observatory. 2001. Annual Review for Denmark. www.eiro.eurofun.ie

– 2002a. Annual Review for Denmark. www.eiro.eurofun.ie

– 2002b. Collective Bargaining Coverage and Extension Procedures. www.eiro. eurofun.ie.

– 2002c. *Economically Dependent Workers, Employment Law and Industrial Relations: A Comparative Study.* Dublin: European Foundation for the Improvement of Living and Working Conditions.

– 2002d. Lifelong Learning and Collective Bargainig. www.eiro.eurofun.ie.

– 2002e. Low Wage Workers and The Working Poor. www.eiro.eurofun.ie.

– 2002f. Non-Permanent Employment, Quality of Work and Industrial Relations. www.eiro.eurofun.ie.

Evans, Robert G., Morris L. Barer, and Theodore R. Marmor, eds.1994. *Why Are Some People Healthy and Others Not? The Determinants of Health of Populations.* New York: Aldine De Gruyter.

Farkas, Lorraine. 1999. Untitled. *Workplace Gazette* 2 (2): 92–101.

Farmer-Labour Conference. 1959. *Can Farmer and Labour Cooperate?* Toronto: Farmer-Labour Coordinating Council and the Farmer-Labour Committee of the OFL with the cooperation of the Ontario Farmers' Union.

Fawcett, Gail. 1996. *Living with Disability in Canada: An Economic Portrait.* Ottawa: Human Resources and Development Canada, Office for Disability Issues.

FDNS. See Front de défence des non-syndiqués, under ABE.

Fédération des femmes du Québec and Conseil d'intervention pour l'accès des femmes au travail (CIAFT). 2002. *Mémoire sur le projet de loi 143 sur la Loi modifiant la Loi sur les normes du travail et d'autres dispositions législatives (présenté à la Commission de l'économie et du travail).* Montréal: FFQ.

Fédération des travailleurs et travailleuses du Québec. 2002. *Mémoire de la FTQ présenté à la Commission de l'économie et du travail sur les modifications apportées à la Loi sur les normes du travail et d'autres dispositions législatives.* Québec: FTQ.

Fernandez-Kelly, Maria Patricia. 1983. *"For we are sold, I and my people": Women and Industry in Mexico's Frontier.* Buffalo: SUNY Press.

Fernanadez-Kelly, Maria Patricia, and Anna Garcia. 1989. "Informalization in the Core: Hispanic Women, Homework, and the Advanced Capitalist State." In A. Portes, M. Castells, and Lauren A. Benton, eds., *The Informal Economy: Studies in Advanced and Less Developed Countries,* 247–78. Baltimore: Johns Hopkins University Press.

FFQ. See Fédération des femmes du Québec.

Fine, Janice. 1998. "Moving Innovation from the Margins to the Center." In Gregory Mantsios, ed., *A New Labor Movement for a New Century,* 119–46. New York: Monthly Review.

Finnie, Ross. 2000. *The Dynamics of Poverty in Canada.* Ottawa: C.D. Howe Institute.

Forrest, Anne. 1986. "Bargaining Units and Bargaining Power." *Relations Industrielles/Industrial Relations* 41 (4): 840–54

– 1993. "A View from Outside the Whale: The Treatment of Women and Unions in Industrial Relations." In Linda Briskin and Patricia McDermott, eds., *Women*

Challenging Unions: Feminism, Democracy, and Militancy, 325–42. Toronto: University of Toronto Press.

– 1995. "Securing the Male Breadwinner: A Feminist Interpretation of PC 1003." In Cy Gonick, Paul Phillips, and Jessie Vorst, eds., *Labour Gains, Labour Pains: Fifty Years of PC 1003.* Winnipeg and Halifax: Fernwood Publishing.

Frader, Laura L., and Sonya O. Rose. 1996. "Introduction: Gender and the Reconstruction of European Working-Class History." In Laura L Frader and Sonya O. Rose, eds., *Gender and Class in Modern Europe,* 1–33. Ithaca, NY: Cornell University Press.

Frager, Ruth A. 1992. *Sweatshop Strife: Class, Ethnicity and Gender in the Jewish Labour Movement of Toronto, 1900–1939.* Toronto: University of Toronto Press.

François, M., and D. Lievin. 1995. "Emplois précaires et accidentabilité: Enquête statistique dans 85 entreprises." Paris: INRS.

Fraser, Nancy. 1997a. "After the Family Wage: A Postindustrial Thought Experiment." In Nancy Fraser, ed., *Justice Interruputus: Critical Reflections on the "Postsocialist" Condition,* 41–68. New York: Routledge.

– 1997b. *Justice Interruptus: Critical Reflections on the "Postsocialist" Condition.* New York: Routledge.

Fraser, Nancy, and L. Gordon. 1994. "A Genealogy of Dependency: Tracing a Keyword for the U.S Welfare State." *Signs: Journal of Women in Culture and Society* 19 (2): 309–34.

Freedland, Mark. 1995. "The Role of the Contract of Employment in Modern Labour Law." In Lammy Betten, ed., *The Employment Contract in Transforming Labour Relations.* The Hague: Kluewer.

Freeman, Richard B. 1998. "War of the Models: Which Labour Market Institutions for the 21st Century?" *Labour Economics* 5 (1): 1–24.

Freeman, Richard B., and Lawrence F. Katz, eds. 1995. *Differences and Changes in Wage Structures.* Chicago: University of Chicago Press.

Freeman, Richard, and Morris M. Kleiner. 1999. "Do Unions Make Firms Insolvent?" *Industrial Labor Relations Review* 52: 4–40.

Freeman, Richard, and James Medoff. 1984. *What Do Unions Do?* New York: Basic Books.

Frenette, Marc, and Garnett Picot. 2003. "Life after Welfare: The Economic Well Being of Welfare Leavers in Canada during the 1990's." Analytic Studies Branch Research Paper Series 11 F0019, No. 192. Ottawa: Statistics Canada.

Frenette, Marc, and René Morissette. 2003. "Will They Ever Converge? Earnings of Immigrant and Canadian-Born Workers over the Last Two Decades." Analytic Studies Branch Research Paper Series 11 F0019M1E, No. 215. Ottawa: Statistics Canada.

Frick, Kaj, Per L. Jenson, Michael Quinlan, and Ton Wilthasen, eds. 2000. *Systematic Occupational Health and Safety Management.* Oxford: Pergamon.

FTQ. See Féderation des travailleurs et travailleuses du Québec.

Fudge, Judy. 1991. "Reconceiving Employment Standards Legislation: Labour Law's Little Sister and the Feminization of Labour." *Journal of Law and Social Policy* 7: 73–89.

– 1993. "The Gendered Dimension of Labour Law: Why Women Need Inclusive Unionism and Broader-Based Bargaining." In Linda Briskin and Patricia McDermott, eds., *Women Challenging Unions: Feminism, Militancy, and Democracy*, 139–62. Toronto: University of Toronto Press.

– 1997. "Precarious Work and Families." Working paper. Toronto: Centre for Policy Research on Work and Society, York University.

– 2001. "Flexibility and Feminization: The New Ontario Employment Standards Act." *Journal of Law and Social Policy* 16: 1–22.

– 2002. "From Segregation to Privatization: Equality, the Law and Women Public Servants, 1908–2001." In Brenda Cossman and Judy Fudge, eds., *Privatization, Law and the Challenge to Feminism*, 86–127. Toronto: University of Toronto.

Fudge, Judy, and Harry Glasbeek. 1995. "The Legacy of PC 1003." *Canadian Labour and Employment Law Journal* 3: 357–99.

Fudge, Judy, and Eric Tucker. 2001. *Labour before the Law*. Toronto: Oxford University Press.

Fudge, Judy, and Leah F. Vosko. 2001a. "By Whose Standards? Re-regulating the Canadian Labour Market." *Economic and Industrial Democracy* 22 (3): 327–56.

– 2001b. "Gender, Segmentation and the Standard Employment Relationship in Canadian Labour Law, Legislation and Policy." *Economic and Industrial Democracy* 22 (2): 271–310.

Fudge, Judy, and Brenda Cossman. 2002. "Introduction: Privatization, Law, and the Challenge to Feminism." In Judy Fudge and Brenda Cossman, eds., *Privatization, Law and the Challenge to Feminism*, 3–37. Toronto: University of Toronto Press.

Fudge, Judy, Eric Tucker, and Leah F. Vosko. 2002. *The Legal Concept of Employment: Marginalizing Workers*. Ottawa: Law Commission of Canada.

Fudge, Judy, Eric Tucker, and Leah F. Vosko. 2003a. "Changing Boundaries in Employment: Developing a New Platform for Labour Law." *Canada Labour Law and Employment Law Journal* 10 (3): 361–99.

– 2003b. "Employee or Independent Contractor? Charting the Legal Significance of the Distinction in Canada." *Canadian Labour and Employment Law Journal* 10 (2): 193–230.

Fudge, Judy, and Leah F. Vosko. 2003. "Gendered Paradoxes and the Rise of Contingent Work: Towards a Transformative Feminist Political Economy of the Labour Market." In Wallace Clement and Leah F. Vosko, eds., *Changing Canada: Political Economy as Transformation*, 183–213. Montreal and Kingston: McGill-Queen's University Press.

Gabriel, Christina. 1999. "Restructuring the Margins: Women of Colour and the Changing Economy." In Enakshi Dua and Angela Robertson, eds., *Scratching the Surface: Canadian Anti-racist Feminist Thought*, 127–64. Toronto: Women's Press.

Gaebler, T., and D. Osbourne. 1992. *Reinventing Government*. New York: Addison-Wesley.

Gahan, Peter, and Richard Mitchell. 1995. "The Limits of Labour Law and the Necessity of Interdisciplinary Analysis." In Richard Mitchell, ed., *Redefining Labour Law: New Perspectives on the Future of Teaching and Research*. Melbourne: Centre for Employment and Labour Relations Law.

Galabuzi, Grace-Edward. 2001. *Canada's Creeping Economic Apartheid*. Toronto: Center for Social Justice. Available from www.socialjustice.org.

– 2004. "Racializing the Division of Labour: Neo-Liberal Restructuring and the Economic Segregation of Canada's Racialized Groups." In Jim Stanford and Leah F. Vosko, eds., *Challenging the Market: The Struggle to Regulate Work and Income*, 175–204. Montreal and Kingston: McGill-Queen's University Press.

Gaudier, Maryse. 1987. *Labour Market Flexibility: A Magic Wand or the Foundation of a New Industrial Society?* Geneva: Institut international d'etudes socials.

Ghosh, Sabitri. 2003. "Immigrant Workers and Unions." *This Magazine* (January/February).

Gibb, Euan. 2002. "Agriculture Sweatshops in Canada." *Briarpatch* 31 (8): 3–10.

Girard, Magali. 2002. "La précarité de l'emploi chez les nouveaux immigrants: Une relation non linéaire entre stabilité et qualité." M.Sc. mémoire, Université de Montréal.

Glasbeek, Harry J. 1987. "Labour Relations Policy and Law as Mechanisms of Adjustment." *Osgoode Hall Law Journal* 25: 179–237.

– 1988. "A Role for Criminal Sanctions in Occupational Health and Safety." In *Meredith Memorial Lectures: New Developments in Employment Law*, 125–49. Cowansville, Que.: Editions Yvon Blais.

Glenn, Evelyn Nakano. 1992. "From Servitude to Service Work: Historical Continues in the Racial Division of Paid Reproductive Labor." *Signs: Journal of Women in Culture and Society* 18: 1–43.

Gordon, Colin. 1999. "The Lost City of Solidarity: Metropolitan Unionism in Historical Perspective." *Politics and Society* 27 (4): 561–80.

Goudswaard, A., and F. Andries. 2002. "Employment Status and Working Conditions." Dublin: European Foundation for the Improvement of Working and Living Conditions.

Government of Canada. 2002. *Technical Report Annexes: Advancing the Inclusion of People with Disabilities*. Ottawa: Government of Canada.

Government of Ontario. 2001. *Ontario Works Policy Directive 2.0: Principles for Delivery.*

Goyette, Renée M. 1998. "À la recherche du véritable statut: Salarié ou travailleur autonome." In Service de la formation permanente du Barreau, *Développements récents en droit du travail*, 19–53. Cowansville, Que.: Yvon Blais.

Grant, Michel. 2004. "Deregulating Industrial Relations in the Apparel Sector: The Decree System in Quebec." In Jim Stanford and Leah F. Vosko, eds., *Challenging the Market: The Struggle to Regulate Work and Income*, 135–50. Montreal: McGill-Queen's University Press.

Grant, Michel, and Pierre Laporte. 1987. "Salarié d'accord … mais de qui? (à la recherche du véritable employeur)." *Revue du Barreau* 47 (5): 1205–19.

Greenhouse, Steven. 2004. "Growers' Group Signs the First Union Contract for Guest Workers." *New York Times*, September 17.

Grievance Settlement Board. 2002. OPSEU and the Crown (Ministry of Health) Decision. Toronto: Grievance Settlement Board. February.

Grievance Settlement Board Decision. 2002. OPSEU and the Crown (Ministry of Transportation). October.

Griffin Cohen, Majorie, ed. 2003. *Training the Excluded for Work*. Vancouver. UBC Press.

Gunningham, Neil, and Richard Johnstone. 1999. *Regulating Workplace Safety: Systems and Sanctions*. Oxford: Oxford University Press.

Gurstein, Penny. 2001. *Wired to the World, Chained to the Home: Telework in Daily Life*. Vancouver: UBC Press.

Hamilton, Roberta, and Michele Barrett. 1986. *The Politics of Diversity: Feminism, Marxism and Nationalism*. Montreal: Book Centre.

Harris Survey of Americans with Disabilities. 1998. New York: Lou Harris and Associates.

Hay, Douglas. 2000. "Master and Servant in England: Using the Law in the Eighteenth and Nineteenth Centuries." In Willibald Steinmetz, ed., *Private Law and Social Inequality in the Industrial Age*, 227–64. Oxford: Oxford University Press.

Hay, Douglas, and Paul Craven, eds. 2004. *Masters, Servants, and Magistrates in Britain and the Empire, 1562–1955*. Chapel Hill: University of North Carolina Press.

Haythore, George V., and Leonard C. Marsh. 1941. *Land and Labour: A Social Survey of Agriculture and the Farm Labour Market in Central Canada*. Toronto: Oxford University Press.

Hébert, Gérard, and Gilles Trudeau. 1987. *Les normes minimales du travail au Canada et au Québec: Étude juridique et institutionnelle*. Cowansville, Que.: Yvon Blais.

Heery, Edmund, and John Salmon. 2002. *The Insecure Workforce*. New York: Routledge.

Hennessy, Rosemary. 2000. *Profit and Pleasure: Sexual Identities in Late Capitalism*. New York: Routledge.

Henry, Franes, and Effie Ginzberg. 1984. *Who Gets the Work? A Test of Racial Discrimination in Employment*. Toronto: Urban Alliance on Race Relations and Social Planning Council of Toronto.

Henry, Frances, and Carol Tator. 2000. *The Colour of Democracy: Racism in Canadian Society*. Toronto: Harcourt Brace.

Hepple, Bob. 2002. "Enforcement: The Law and Politics of Cooperation and Compliance." In Bob Hepple, ed., *Social and Labour Rights in a Global Context: International and Comparative Perspectives*, 238–58. Cambridge: Cambridge University Press.

Heron, Craig. 1989. *The Canadian Labour Movement: A Short History*. Toronto: James Lorimer. 2nd ed. 1996.

Hertzmann, C., K. McGrail, and B. Hirtle. 1999. "Overall Pattern of Health Care and Social Welfare Use by Injured Workers in the British Columbia Cohort." *International Journal of Law and Psychiatry* 22: 581–601.

Herzenberg, Stephen A., John Alice, and Howard Wial. 1998. *New Rules of a New Economy: Employment Opportunity in Post-Industrial America*. Ithaca, NY: Cornell University Press.

Hill, Dan. 1977. *Human Rights in Canada: A Focus on Racism*. Canadian Labour Congress.

Holmes, T.J., and J.A. Schmitz. 1990. "A Theory of Entrepreneurship and Its Application to the Study of Business Transfers." *Journal of Political Economy* 89: 265–94.

Horowitz, Sarah. 2000. "New Thinking on Worker Groups' Role in a Flexible Economy." In Francois Caree, Marianne A. Ferber, Lonnie Golden, and Stephen A. Herzenberg, eds., *Non-Standard Work: The Nature and Challenges of Changing Employment Arrangements*, 393–9. Chicago: IRRA.

Hucker, John. 1997. "Anti-Discrimination Laws in Canada: Human Rights Commissions and the Search for Equality." *Human Rights Quarterly* 19 (3): 547–71.

Hughes, Karen. 1999. "Gender and Self-Employment in Canada: Assessing Trends and Policy Implications." Canadian Policy Research Networks Study No. W/o4, Changing Employment Relationships Series. Ottawa: Canadian Policy Research Networks Inc.

Hughes, Karen. 2003a. *How Are Women Faring in the Entrepreneurial Economy?* Breakfast on the Hill Seminar Series. Ottawa: Canadian Federation for the Humanities and Social Sciences.

– 2003b. "Pushed or Pulled? Women's Entry into Self-Employment and Small Business Ownership." *Gender, Work and Organization* 10 (4): 433–54

Hughes, Karen, Graham S. Lowe, and Grant Schellenberg. 2003. *Men's and Women's Quality of Work in the New Canadian Economy*. Ottawa: Canadian Policy Research Networks Inc.

Hum, Derek, and Wayne Simpson. 1996. Canadians with Disabilities and the Labour Market. *Canadian Public Policy* 22 (3):285–99.

Hunter, Rosemary. 1992. "The Regulation of Independent Contractors: A Feminist Perspective." *Corporate and Business Law Journal* 6: 165–88.

Huws, Ursula, Jenny Hurstfield, and Riki Holtmaat. 1989. *What Price Flexibility? The Casualization of Women's Employment*. London: Low Pay Unit.

Hyde, Alan. 1998. "Employment Law after the Death of Employment." *University of Pennsylvania Journal of Labor and Employment Law* 1: 1–19.

Ichino, Pietro. 1998. "The Labour Market: A Lawyer's View of Economic Arguments." *International Labour Review* 137(3): 299-311.

ILC. See International Labour Conference.

ILGWU and INTERCEDE. 1993. *Meeting the Needs of Vulnerable Workers: Proposals for Improved Employment Legislation and Access to Collective Bargaining for Domestic Workers and Industrial Homeworkers*.

ILO. See International Labour Organization.

International Labour Conference. 2003. "Fifth Item on the Agenda: The Scope of the Employment Relationship (general discussion). Report of the Committee on the Employment Relationship." *Provisional Record No. 21*, Ninety-first Session. Geneva: ILO.

International Labour Organization. 1995. *World Labour Report, 1995–96*. Geneva: ILO.

– 1997. *World Labour Report, 1997–98*. Geneva: ILO.

– 1997. *World Labour Report, 2001–2002*. Geneva: ILO.

– 2000a. *Income Security and Social Protection in a Changing World: World Labour Report, 2000*. Geneva: ILO.

– 2000b. *Meeting of Experts on Workers in Situation Needing Protection (The Employment Relationship: Scope). Basic Technical Document*. Geneva: ILO.

– 2003. *Decent Work in Denmark: Employment, Social Efficiency and Economic Security*. Geneva: ILO.

– 2004. *More Women Are Entering the Global Labour Force than Ever Before, but Job Equality, Poverty Reduction Remain Elusive*. Geneva: ILO.

Jackson, Andrew. 2000a. *The Myth of the Equity-Efficiency Trade-Off*. Ottawa: Canadian Council on Social Development.

– 2000b. "The NAIRU and Macro-Economic Policy in Canada." *Canadian Business Economics*. July.

– 2002. "Is Work Working for Workers of Colour?" Canadian Labour Congress, Research Paper 18.

– 2003a. "Good Jobs in Good Workplaces: Reflections on Medium-Term Labour Market Challenges." Canadian Labour Congress, Research Paper 1, and Caledon Institute of Social Policy.

– 2003b. *In Solidarity: The Union Advantage*. Ottawa: Canadian Labour Congress.

Jackson, Andrew, and David Robinson. 2000. *Falling Behind: The State of Working Canada, 2000*. Ottawa: Canadian Centre for Policy Alternatives.

Jackson, Andrew, and S. Schetagne. 2003. *Solidarity Forever: An Analysis of Changes in Union Density*. Ottawa: Canadian Labour Congress.

James, A., D. Grant, and Cynthia J. Cranford. 2000. "Moving Up but How Far? African American Women and Economic Restructuring in Los Angeles." *Sociological Perspectives* 43 (3): 399–416.

Jamieson, Stuart Marshall. 1968. *Times of Trouble: Labour Unrest and Industrial Conflict in Canada, 1900–1966*. Ottawa: Task Force on Labour Relations.

Jenkins, J. Craig. 1985. *The Politics of Insurgency: The Farm Worker Movement of the 1960's*. New York: Columbia University Press.

Jenkins, J. Craig, and Charles Perrow. 1977. "Insurgency of the Powerless: Farm Worker Movements (1946–1972)." *American Sociological Review* 42: 249–68.

Jenson, Jane. 1986. "Gender and Reproduction: Or, Babies and the State." *Studies in Political Economy* 20: 9–46.

– 1989. "The Talents of Women, the Skills of Men." In Stephen Wood, ed., *The Transformation of Work? Skill, Flexibility and the Labour Process*, 141–55. London: Unwin Hyman.

– 1996. "Part-time Employment and Women: A Range of Strategies." In Isabella Bakker, ed., *Rethinking Restructuring: Gender and Change in Canada*, 92–108. Toronto: University of Toronto Press.

Johnson, J.V. 1991. "Collective Control: Strategies for Survival in the Workplace." In J. Johnson and G. Johnson, eds., *The Psychosocial Work Environment: Work Organization, Democratization and Health*, 121–32. Amityville, NY: Baywood Publishing.

Johnson, Laura. 2002. *The Co-Workplace: Teleworking in the Neighbourhood*. Vancouver: UBC Press.

Johnson, Laura C., and Robert E. Johnson. 1982. *The Seam Allowance*. Toronto: Alger Press.

Johnstone Richard, Claire Mayhew, and Michael Quinlan. 2001. "Outsourcing Risk? The Regulation of Occupational Health and Safety where Subcontracts Are Employed." *Comparative Labour Law & Policy Journal* 22 (2–3): 351–94.

Johnstone, Richard, Michael Quinlan, and David Walters. Forthcoming. "Statutory OHS Workplace Arrangements for the Modern Labour Market."

Jongbloed, Lyn. 1990. Difficulties in Shifting from Individualistic to Socio-political Policy regarding Disability in Canada. *Disability, Handicap & Society* 5 (1): 25–36.

Juteau, Danielle, ed. 2003. *Social Differentiation: Patterns and Processes*. Toronto: University of Toronto Press.

Karasek, Robert. 1979. "Job Demands, Job Decision Latitude and Mental Strain: Implications for Job Redesign." *Administrative Science Quarterly* 24 (2): 285–307.

Karasek, Robert, and T. Theorell. 1990. *Healthy Work: Stress, Productivity and the Reconstruction of Working Life*. New York: Basic Books.

Katz-Rosene, Ryan. 2003. *Union Organizing*. Ottawa: Canadian Labour Congress.

Kaufman, Bruce E., ed. 1997. *Government Regulation of the Employment Relationship*. Madison, Wisc.: Industrial Relations Research Association.

Kelsey, Timothy W. 1994. "The Agrarian Myth and Policy Responses to Farm and Safety." *American Journal of Public Health* 84: 1171-77.

Kessler-Harris, A. 1982. *Out to Work*. New York: Oxford University Press.

Kihlstrom, R.E., and J.J. Laffont. 1979. "A General Equilibrium Entrepreneurial Theory of Firm Formation Based on Risk Aversion." *Journal of Political Economy* 87: 719–48.

Kirton, John, and Michael J. Trebilcock, eds. *Hard Choices, Soft Law: Combining Trade, Environment, and Social Cohesion in a Global Governance*. New York: Ashgate.

Klassen, Thomas, and Steffen Schneider. 2002. "Similar Challenges, Different Solutions: Reforming Labour Market Policies in Germany and Canada during the 1990's." *Canadian Public Policy* 28 (1): 51–69.

Klee, Marcus. 2000. "Fighting the Sweatshop in Depression Ontario: Capital, Labour and the Industrial Standards Act." *Labour/Le Travail* 45: 13–51.

Krahn, Harvey. 1995. "Non-standard Work on the Rise." *Perspectives on Labour and Income,* winter: 35–42.

Kruse, Douglas. 1998. "People with Disabilities: Demographic, Income, and Health Care Characteristics, 1993." *Monthly Labor Review* 121 (9): 13–22.

Kruse, Douglas, and L. Schur. 2003. Employment of People with Disabilities following the ADA. *Industrial Relations* 42 (1): 31–64.

Kumar, Pradeep, and Gregor Murray. 2002. "Innovation and Change in Labour Organizations in Canada: Results if the National 2000–2001 HRDC Survey." Ottawa: HRDC.

– 2003. "Strategic Dilemma: The State of Union Renewal in Canada." In P. Fairbrother and C. Yates, eds., *Trade Union in Renewal: A Comparative Study,* 200–20. London and New York: Continuum.

Kuumba, M. Bahati. 2001. *Gender and Social Movements.* Walnut Creek, Cal.: Altamira Press.

Labour Gazette. 1950. "Social Security Benefits for Farm Workers Advocated," 9–10.

– 1957. "14th Annual Federal-Provincial Farm Labour Conference," 34–5.

– 1960. "Trends in the Agricultural Labour Force," 1001–2.

Ladd, Deena. 1998. *No Easy Recipe: Building the Diversity and Strength of the Labour Movement.* Feminist Organizing Models: Canadian Labour Congress Women's Symposium.

Laflamme, N., C. Brisson, J. Moisan, A. Milot, B. Masse, and M. Vezina. 1998. "Job Strain and Ambulatory Blood Pressure among Female White-Collar Workers." *Scandinavian Journal of Work, Environment and Health* 24 (5): 334–43.

Landsbergis, P.A., et al. 1994. "Association between Ambulatory Blood Pressure and Alternative Formulations of Job Strain." *Scandinavian Journal of Work, Environment and Health* 20 (5): 349–63.

Lane, Arja. 1983. "Wives Supporting the Strike." In Linda Briskin and Lynda Yanz, eds., *Union Sisters: Women in the Labour Movement,* 322–32. Toronto: Women's Press.

Langevin, Louise, and Marie-Claire Belleau. 2000. *Trafficking in Women in Canada: A Critical Analysis of the Legal Framework Governing Immigrant Live-In Caregivers and Mail-Order Brides.* Ottawa: Status of Women Canada.

Langille, Brian. 2002. "Labour Policy in Canada: New Platform, New Paradigm." *Canadian Public Policy* 28: 132–42.

Lavis, John N. 1998. *The Links between Labour Force Experiences and Health: Towards a Research Framework.* McMaster University Centre for Health Economics and Policy Analysis (CHEPA) Working Paper 98-4 (also available as Institute for Work & Health Working Paper 62).

Leah, Ronnie. 1993. "Black Women Speak Out: Racism and Unions." In Linda Briskin and Pat McDermott, eds., *Women Challenging Unions: Feminism, Democracy and Militancy,* 157–72. Toronto: University of Toronto Press.

– 1999. "Do You Call Me 'Sister'? Women of Colour and the Canadian La-
bour Movement." In Enakshi Dua and A. Robertson, eds., *Scratching the
Surface: Canadian Anti-racist Feminist Thought*, 97–126. Toronto: Women's
Press.

Leck, Joanne D., and David M. Saunders. 1992. "Hiring Women: the Effects of
Canada's Employment Equity Act." *Canadian Public Policy* 18 (2): 203–20.

Leck, Joanne D., and Isabelle Lalancete. 1995. "Wage Gap Changes among Organizations Subject to the Employment Equity Act." *Canadian Public Policy* 21 (4):
387–400.

Leeb, Gavin. 2002. "A Global Experience up Close and Personal: Ontario Government Workers Resist Privatization." *Canadian Labour and Employment Law
Journal* 9 (1): 1–35.

Lefebvre, Sylvain, Isabelle Paradis, and Robert L. Rivest. 2003. "La Commission
des normes du travail: ses pouvoirs et compétences en matière de processus d'enquête et d'intervention judiciaire." In Service de la formation permanente du Barreau, *Développements récents en droit du travail*, 287–364. Cowansville, Que.:
Yvon Blais.

Lemieux, Thomas. 1993. "Unions and Wage Inequality in Canada and the United
States." In David Card and Richard Freeman, eds., *Small Differences That Matter: Labor Market and Income Maintenance in Canada and the United States*,
69–107. Chicago: University of Chicago Press.

Lerner, Gerda. 1997. *History Matters: Life and Thought*. New York: Oxford.

Lévesque, Christian. 2003. "La mondialisation et le pouvoir des syndicats locaux."
Relations Industrielles/Industrial Relations 58 (1): 60–84.

Lévesque, Christian, and Gregor Murray. 2002. "Local versus Global: Activating Local Union Power in the Global Economy." *Labor Studies Journal* 27 (3): 39–65.

Levine, David. 1997. "They Should Solve Their Own Problems: Reinventing Workplace Regulation." In Bruce Kaufman, ed., *Government Regulation of the Employment Relation*, 475–97. Madison, Wisc.: Industrial Relations Research
Association Series.

Lewchuk, Wayne, and David Robertson. 1996. "Working Conditions under Lean
Production: A Worker-Based Benchmarking Study." *Asia Pacific Business Review*
2: 60–81.

– 1997. "Production without Empowerment: Work-Reorganization from the Perspective of Motor Vehicle Workers." *Capital and Class* 63: 37–64.

Lewchuk, Wayne, Alice de Woiff, and Andy King. 2003. "From Job Strain to
Employment Strain: Health Effects of Precarious Employment." *Just Labour* 3:
23–35.

Leys, Colin. 2001. *Market-Driven Politics: Neo-Liberal Democracy and the Public
Interest*. London: Verso.

Li, Peter S. 2003. "Visible Minorities in Canadian Society: Challenges of Racial
Dviersity." In Danielle Juteau, ed., *Social Differentiation: Patterns and Processes*,
117–54. Toronto: University of Toronto Press.

Lin, Z., J. Yates, and Garnet Picot. 1999. *Rising Self-Employment in the Midst of High Unemployment: An Empirical Analysis of Recent Developments in Canada.* Ottawa: Statistics Canada Research Paper Series.

Linder, M. 1989. "What Is an Employee? Why It Does, But Should Not, Matter." *Law and Inequality* 7 (2): 155–88.

Lior, Karen, and Susan Wismer. 2003. "Still Shopping for Training: Women, Training and Livelihoods." In Marjorie Griffin Cohen, ed., *Training the Excluded for Work,* 214–30. Vancouver: UBC Press.

Lippel, Katherine. 1981–2. "Droits des travailleurs québécois en matière de santé, 1885–1981." *Revue Juridique Thémis* 16: 329–82.

– 1986. *Droit des accidents du travail à une indemnisation: Analyse historique et critique.* Montréal: Éditions Thémis.

– 1998. "Preventive Reassignment of Pregnant or Breast-Feeding Workers: The Quebec Model." *New Solutions* 8 (2): 267–80.

– 2002. "Droit et statistiques: Réflexions méthodologiques sur la discrimination systémique dans la domaine de l'indemnisation pour les lésions professionnelles." *Canadian Journal of Women and the Law/Revue femmes et droit* 14 (2): 362–88.

– 2004. "Le travail atypique et la législation en matière de santé et sécurité du travail." *Développements récents en santé et sécurité du travail,* 307–83. Cowansville, Que.: Éditions Yvon Blais.

Lippel, Katherine, and Joseph Caron. 2004. "L'introduction de l'ergonomie dans la réglementation de la prévention des lésions professionnelles: balises et enjeux des législations nord-américaines." *Relations Industrielles/Industrial Relations* 59 (2): 235–72.

Lipsett, Brenda, and Mark Reesor. 1997. *Flexible Work Arrangements: Evidence from the 1991 and 1995 Survey of Work Arrangements.* Ottawa: Human Resources and Development Canada.

LO Denmark. 2000. *Labour Markets in the EU.*

Local News HERE 75. 2003. Toronto: Hotel Employees, Restaurant Employees Union.

Lochhead, Clarence, and Katherine Scott. 1997. "Are Women Catching Up in the Earnings Race?" Ottawa, Canadian Council on Social Development.

Longworth, Richard C. 1998. *Global Squeeze: The Coming Crisis for First-World Nations.* Chicago: Contemporary Books.

Lowe, Graham. 1999. Rethinking Employment Relationships. *CPRN Discussion Paper No. W/05, Changing Employment Relationship Series.* Ottawa: Canadian Policy Research Networks Inc.

– 2001. "New Employment Relationships as the Centerpiece of a New Labour Policy Paradigm." *CPRN Discussion Paper.* Ottawa: Canadian Policy Research Networks Inc. April.

Lowe, Graham, Grant Schellenberg, and Katie Davidman. 2001. *What's a Good Job? The Importance of Employment Relationships.* Changing Employment Relationships Series. Ottawa: Canadian Policy Research Networks Study No. W05.

Luce, Stephanie. 2002. "The Full Fruits of Our Labour": The Rebirth of the Living Wage Movement." *Labour History* 43 (4): 401–9.

– 2004. *Fighting for a Living Wage*. Ithica, NY: Cornell University Press.

Lukas, Salome, and Judy Persad. 2004. *Through the Eyes of Workers of Colour: Linking Struggles for Social Justice*. Toronto: Women Working with Immigrant Women and the Toronto and York Region Labour Council.

Luxton, Meg. 1980. *More than a Labour of Love: Three Generations of Women's Work in the Home*. Toronto: The Women's Educational Press.

– 1983. "From Ladies Auxiliaries to Wives Committees." In Linda Briskin and Lynda Yanz, eds., *Union Sisters: Women in the Labor Movement*, 333–47. Toronto: Women's Press.

– 1997. *Feminism and Families: Critical Policies and Changing Practices*. Halifax: Fernwood Publishing.

Luxton, Meg, and June Corman. 2001. *Getting By in Hand Times: Gendered Labour at Home and on the Job*. Toronto: University of Toronto Press.

Luxton, Meg, and Ester Reiter. 1997. "Double, Double Toil and Trouble: Women's Experience of Work in Family in Canada, 1980–1995." In P. Evans and G. Werkle, eds., *Women and the Canadian Welfare State*, 197–221. Toronto: University of Toronto Press.

Luxton, Meg, and Leah F. Vosko. 1998. "Where Women's Efforts Count: The 1996 Census Campaign and 'Family Politics' in Canada." *Studies in Political Economy* 56: 49–81.

MacDonald, Martha. 1991. "Post-Fordism and the Flexibility Debate." *Studies in Political Economy*, autumn: 177–201.

– 1997. *Gender and the Recent Social Security Reform in Canada*. Boston, Mass.: Radcliffe Public Policy Institute.

MacDonald, D. 1998a. "The New Deal Model of Collective Bargaining and the Secondary Labour Market." PhD dissertation, Northeastern University.

– 1998b. "Sectoral Certification: A Case Study of British Columbia." *Canadian Labour and Employment Law Journal*. 5: 243–66.

Macdonald, Roderick. 1985. "Understanding Regulation by Regulations." In Ivan Bernier and Andrée Lajoie, eds., *Regulations, Crown Corporations and Administrative Tribunals*, 81–154. Collected Research Studies of the Royal Commission on the Economic Union and Development Prospects of Canada (MacDonald Commission). Toronto: University of Toronto Press.

Macpherson, Elizabeth. 1999. "Collective Bargaining for Independent Contractors: Is the Status of the Artist Act a Model for Other Industrial Sectors?" *Canadian Journal of Labour and Employment Law* 7 (3): 335–89.

Madar, Daniel. 2000. *Heavy Traffic: Deregulation, Trade, and Transformation in North America Trucking*. Vancouver: UBC Press.

Madsen, Per Kongshøj. 2003. "'Flexicurity' through Labour Market Policies and Insititutions in Denmark." In Peter Auer and Sandrine Cazes, eds., *Employment Stability in an Age of Flexibility*, 59–106. Geneva: ILO.

Malles, Paul. 1976. *Canadian Labour Standards in Law, Agreement and Practice.* Toronto: Economic Council of Canada.

Marmot, M. 2000. "Social Class, Occupational Status, and CVD." In P.L. Schnall et al., eds., "The Workplace and Cardiovascular Disease," *Occupational Medicine: State of the Art Reviews* 15: 46–9.

Marshall, K. 2000. "Incomes of Younger Retired Women: The Past 30 Years." *Perspectives on Labour and Income* 12 (4): 9–17. Statistics Canada Catalogue 71-001-XPE.

– 2001. "Part-time by Choice." *Perspectives on Labour and Income* 13 (1): 20–7. Statistics Canada Catalogue 71-001-XPE.

Martin, Isaac. 2001. "Dawn of the Living Wage: The Diffusion of a Redistributive Municipal Policy." *Urban Affairs Review* 36 (4): 470–96.

Martinello, Felice. 2000. "Mr. Harris, Mr. Rae and Union Activity in Ontario." *Canadian Public Policy* 26 (1): 17–33.

Maxwell, Judith. 2002a. *Smart Social Policy: "Making Work Pay."* Ottawa: Canadian Policy Research Network Inc.

– 2002b. "Working for Low Pay." Canadian Policy Research Network Presentation to Alberta Human Resources and Employment, December 4.

May, John J. 1990. "Issues in Agricultural Health and Safety." *American Journal of Industrial Medicine* 18: 121–31.

Mayer, Margit. 1995. "Social Movement Research in the United States: A Perspective." In Stanford M. Lyman, ed., *Social Movements: Critiques, Concepts, Case Studies,* 168–95. New York: New York University Press.

Mayhew, Claire, and Michael Quinlan. 1999. "The Effects of Outsourcing on Occupational Health and Safety: A Comparative Study of Factory-Based Workers and Outworkers in the Australian Clothing Industry." *International Journal of Health Services* 29 (1): 83–107.

– 2002. "Fordism in the Fast Food Industry: Pervasive Management Control and Occupational Health and Safety Risks for Young Temporary Workers." *Sociology of Health and Illness* 24 (3): 261–84.

Matte, Denis, Domenico Baldino, and Réjean Courchesne. 1998. *Le marché du travail: L'évolution de l'emploi atypique au Québec.* Québec: Les publications du Québec.

McBride, Stephen. 1998. "The Political Economy of Training in Canada." Training Matters: Working Paper Series 98-07, Labour Education and Training Research Network. Toronto: Centre for Research on Work and Society, York University.

McCay, B.J. 1988. "Fish Guts, Hair Nets, and Unemployment Stamps: Women and Working Cooperative Fish Plants." In P.R. Sinclair, ed., *A Question of Survival: The Fisheries and Newfoundland Society,* 105–31. St John's: Institute of Social and Economic Research.

McDonough, P. 1997. "The Social Patterning of Work Disability among Women in Canada." *Journal of Disability Policy Studies* 8 (1–2): 75–95.

McDonough, P., and B.C. Amick. 2001. "The Social Context of Health Selection: A Longitudinal Study of Health and Employment." *Social Science and Medicine* 53: 135–45.

McElligott, G. 2001. *Beyond Service: State Workers, Public Policy and the Prospects for Democractic Administration*. Toronto: University of Toronto Press.

McInnis, Peter S. 2002. *Harnessing Labour Confrontation: Shaping the Postwar Settlement in Canada, 1943–1950*. Toronto: University of Toronto Press.

McKeen, Wendy. 2004. *Money in Their Own Name: The Feminist Voice in Poverty Debate in Canada, 1970–1995*. Toronto: University of Toronto Press.

McMullen, Kathryn, and Grant Schellenberg. 2003. *Job Quality in Non-Profit Organizations*. Ottawa: Canadian Policy Research Networks Inc.

Mensah, Joseph. 2002. *Black Canadians: History, Experiences, Social Conditions*. Halifax: Fernwood Publishing.

Middleton, Jennifer. 1996. "Contingent Workers in a Changing Economy: Endure, Adapt or Organize?" *New York University Review of Law and Social Change* 22: 557–620.

Miles, Robert. 1987. *Capitalism and Unfree Labour: Anomaly or Necessity?* New York and London: Tavistock Publications.

Milkman, Ruth. 1990. "Gender and Trade Unionism in Historical Perspective." In L.A. Till and P. Gurin, eds., *Women Politics and Change*, 87–107. New York: Russell Sage.

Mills, C. Wright. 1959. *The Sociological Imagination*. New York: Oxford University Press.

Mirchandani, K. 1999. "Feminist Insight on Gendered Work: New Directions in Research on Women and Entrepreneurship." *Gender, Work and Organization* 6 (4): 224–35.

Mishel, Larry, and Jared Bernstein. 2001. *Wage Inequality and the New Economy in the U.S.* Paper presented at the IRPP-CSLS Conference in Ottawa, Canada. Washington, DC: Economic Policy Institute.

Mockle, Daniel. 2002. "Gouverner sans le droit? Mutation des normes et nouveaux modes de régulation." *Cahiers de Droit* 43 (2): 143–211.

Mohanty, Chandra. 2003. "Sisterhood, Coalition and the Politics of Experience." *Feminism without Borders: Decolonizing Theory, Practicing Solidarity*, 106–24. Durham: Duke University Press.

Montreuil, Sylvie, and Katherine Lippel. 2003. "Telework and Occupational Health: Overview and Reflections Based on Empirical Research Conducted in Québec." *Safety Science* 41: 331–58.

Moody, Kim. 1988. *An Injury to All: The Decline of American Unionism*. London and New York: Verso.

– 1997. *Workers in a Lean World: Unions in the International Economy*. London and New York: Verso.

Morgan, Phillip, and Nigel Allington. 2000. "Employment Insecurity in the Public Service." In Edmond Heery and John Salmons, eds., *The Insecure Worker*, 78–112. New York: Routledge.

Morin, Fernand, and Jean-Yves Brière. 2003. *Le droit de l'emploi au Québec*. 2nd ed. Cowansville, Que.: Yvon Blais.

Morris, Jenny. 1993. *Independent Lives? Community Care and Disabled People.* London: Macmillan.

Morrissette, René. 1991. "Are Jobs in Large Firms Better Jobs?" *Perspectives on Labour and Income* 3 (3): 40–50.

– 1993. "Canadian Jobs and Firm Size: Do Smaller Firms Pay Less?" *Canadian Journal of Economics* 26 (1): 159–66.

Morse, Dean. 1998. "Historical Perspectives: The Peripheral Worker (1969)." In Kathleen Barker and Kathleen Christensen, eds., *Contingent Work: American Employment Relations in Transition*, 21–40. Ithaca, NY: ILR Press.

Muckenberger, Ulrich. 1989. "Non-standard Forms of Employment in the Federal Republic of Germany: The Role and Effectiveness of the State." In Gerry Roberts and Janine Rogers, eds., *Precarious Jobs in Labour Market Regulation: The Growth of Atypical Employment in Western Europe*, 167–86. Geneva: International Institute for Labour Studies.

Mudrick, Nancy R. 1997. "Employment Discrimination Laws for Disability: Utilization and Outcome." *Annals of the American Academy* 549: 53–70.

Murray, Jill. 1999. "Social Justice for Women? The ILO's Convention on Part-time Work." *International Journal of Comparative Labour Law and Industrial Relations* 15 (1): 3–19.

Muszynski, Alicja. 1984. "The Organization of Women and Ethnic Minorities in a Resource Industry: A Case Study of the Unionization of Shoreworkers in the B.C. Fishing Industry, 1937–1949." *Journal of Canadian Studies* 19 (1): 89–107.

– 1996. *Cheap Wage Labour: Race and Gender in the Fisheries of British Columbia.* Montreal: McGill-Queen's University Press.

Nagi, Saad Z. 1965. "Some Conceptual Issues in Disability and Rehabilitation." In M.B. Sussman, ed., *Sociology and Rehabilitation*, 100–13. Washington, DC: American Sociological Association.

– 1991. "Disability Concepts Revisited: Implications for Prevention." In A.M. Pope and A.R. Tarlov, eds., *Disability in America: Towards a National Agenda for Prevention*, 309–27. Washington, DC: National Academy Press.

National Institute for Occupational Safety and Health. 2002. *The Changing Organization of Work and the Safety and Health of Working People.* Cincinnati: NIOSH.

National Union of Public and General Employees (NUPGE). 1998. *In Defence of Employment Services.* Ottawa.

Neilson, Kathryn, and Innis Christie. 1975. "The Agricultural Labourer in Canada: A Legal Point of View." *Dalhousie Law Journal* 2: 330–68.

Neis, Barbara. 1993. "From 'Shipped Girls' to 'Brides of the State': The Transition from Familial to Social Patriarchy in the Newfoundland Fishing Industry." *Canadian Journal of Regional Science* 16 (2): 185–211.

Neumann, Rachel. 2001. "Living Wage 101." *Dissent*, fall: 59–63.

New Zealand. Accident Compensation Commission. 2002. Cover Plus Extra: Flexibility to Choose the Compensation You Need. December. Accessed at www.acc.co.nz.

Ng, Roxanna. 1990. "State Funding to a Community Employment Center: Implications for Working with Immigrant Women." In *Community Organization and the Canadian State*, 165–83. Toronto: Garamond Press.

Ng, Winnie Wun Wun. 1995. "In the Margins: Challenging Racism in the Labour Movement." MA thesis, University of Toronto.

NHS. See National Health Service.

NHSEstates. 2003. http://patientexperience.nhsestates.gov.uk/bhf/bhf_content/home/home.asp,28/02/2003a.

– http://patientexperience.nhsestates.gov.uk/ward_housekeeping/wh_content/home/hom...28/02/2003b.

Nichols, Theo, and Eric Tucker. 2000, "Occupational Health and Safety Management Systems in the United Kingdom and Ontario, Canada: A Political Economy Perspective." In Kaj Frick, Per Langaa Jensen, Michael Gary Quinlan, and Ton Wilthagen, eds., *Systematic Occupational Health and Safety Management*, 285–309. Amsterdam: Elsiver.

Niedt, Christopher, Greg Ruiters, Dana Wise, and Enca Shoenberger. 1999. *The Effects of the Living Wage in Baltimore*. Working Paper No. 119. Washington, DC: Economic Policy Institute.

NIOSH. See National Institute for Occupational Safety and Health.

NOD/Harris Survey of Americans with Disabilities. 1998. New York: Lou Harris and Associates.

O'Conner, James. 1964a. "Towards a Theory of Community Unions." *Studies on the Left* 4 (2): 143–8.

– 1964b. "Towards a Theory of Community Unions II." *Studies on the Left* 4 (3): 99–101.

O'Connor, Douglas. 2002. *Report of the Walkerton Inquiry: The Events of May 2000 and Related Issues*, Part I. Toronto: Ontario Ministry of Attorney General.

O'Grady, J. 1991. "Beyond the Wagner Act, What Then?" In D. Drache, ed., *Getting on Track*, 153–69. Montreal and Kingston: McGill-Queen's University Press.

OECD. See Organization for Economic Co-operation and Development.

OECD. 1994. *The OECD Job Study*. Paris.

– 1996. "Earnings Inequality, Low Paid Employment and Earnings Mobility." *OECD Employment Outlook, 1996*. Paris.

– 1997. "Economic Performance and the Structure of Collective Bargaining." *OECD Employment Outlook, 1997*. Paris.

– 1998. "Making the Most of the Minimum: Statutory Minimum Wages, Employment and Poverty." *OECD Employment Outlook, 1998*. Paris.

– 1999a. "Employment Protection and Labour Market Performance." *OECD Employment Outlook, 1999*. Paris.

– 1999b. "Training of Adult Workers in OECD Countries." *OECD Employment Outlook, 1999*. Paris.

– 2000a. "Employment in the Service Economy: A Reassessment." *OECD Employment Outlook, 2000*. Paris.

– 2000b. "Partial Renaissance of Self-Employment." OECD *Employment Outlook, 2000*. Paris.

– 2001. "The Characteristics and Quality of Service Sector Jobs." OECD *Employment Outlook, 2001*. Paris.

– 2002. "Taking the Measure of Temporary Employment." OECD *Employment Outlook, 2002*. Paris.

– 2003. "Structural Policies and Growth." OECD *Employment Outlook, 2003*. Paris.

OFA. See Ontario Federation of Agriculture.

OFL. See Ontario Federation of Labour.

Ogus, Anthony. 2000. "New Techniques for Social Regulation: Decentralization and Diversity." In Hugh Collins, Paul Davies, and Roger Rideout, eds., *Legal Regulation of the Employment Relation*, 83–98. Netherlands: Kluwer Law International.

OMAF. See Ontario Ministry of Agriculture and Food.

Ontario. 1913. *Final Report on Laws Relating to the Liability of Employers*. Toronto: L.K. Cameron.

Ontario. 1985. *Report of the Ontario Task Force on Health and Safety in Agriculture*. Toronto: Ministries of Agriculture and Food and Labour.

Ontario. 1989. *Report of the Agriculture Health and Safety Implementation Committee*.

Ontario. ACOHOS (Advisory Council on Occupational Health and Occupational Safety). 1989. *Eleventh Annual Report*. Toronto.

– 1990. *Twelfth Annual Report*. Toronto.

– 1991. *Thirteenth Annual Report*. Toronto.

Ontario. Government of. 2001. Ontario Works Policy Directive 2.0: Principles for Delivery.

Ontario. Ministry of Agriculture and Food. 1997–2002. Business Plans. Toronto.

Ontario. Ministry of the Attorney General (1997–2002). Business Plans. www.mag.gov.on.ca

Ontario. Ministry of Finance. 1994–2002. *Public Accounts*. Toronto.

Ontario. Ministry of Health. 1997–2002. Business Plans. Toronto.

Ontario. Ministry of Labour (MOL). 1977. "Notes for an Address by the Honorable Bette Stephenson, M.D. Minister of Labour, to the Ontario Fruit and Vegetable Growers Association, 18 January.

– 1985. Memo from Dr. Ann E. Robinson, Assistant Deputy Minister, Occupational Health and Safety Division, to Deputy Minister Tim Armstrong, 24 June.

– 1986. Memo from Dr. Ann E. Robinson, Assistant Deputy Minister, Occupational Health and Safety Division, to Deputy Minister Glenn R. Thompson. 10 December.

– 1987. Memo from Sandra Glasbeek, Manager, Strategic Policy Unit, to William Wrye, Minister. 4 February.

– 1990a. *Background Paper: Health and Safety in the Ontario Agricultural Industry*. Research and Analysis Section. Strategic Policy and Analysis Unit. July.

– 1990b. "Policy Project – Terms of Reference – Development of Regulations for Farming Operations." 12 April.

– 1994. "Briefing Note-Farming Operations – Exemptions from the Occupational *Health and Safety Act*." 17 February.

Ontario. Ministry of Labour and Ministry of Agriculture and Food (MAF). 1991. *Discussion Paper: Health and Safety Legislative Coverage for Farming Operations in Ontario*. December.

– 2004. "McGuinty Government Improves on Farm Safety." 17 March.

Ontario. Ministry of the Solicitor General. 2001. *Verdict of the Coroner's Jury into the Deaths of Heinrich Redekopp, Gary Ferrier, and Erich Schulz*. 28 November.

Ontario. Provincial Auditor General. 2002. *Annual Report 2002*. Toronto.

Ontario Conservative Party. 1995. *The Common Sense Revolution, 1995*. Toronto.

– 1999. *Blueprint for the 1999 Election*. Toronto.

Ontario Farm Council. 2003. *Ontario Farmer*. January: 3.

Ontario Farm Labour Information Committee. 1984. Submission to the Taskforce on Health and Safety in Agriculture. December.

Ontario Farmers Union. Nd. History. Accessed at http://www.nfu.ca/history.htm on December 17, 2003.

Ontario Federation of Agriculture. 1978. Letter to caucus members, 3 March.

– 1984. Brief to the Ontario Task Force on Health and Safety in Agriculture. December.

– 1991. "Brief to the Honorable Bob McKenzie, Minister, Ontario Ministry of Labour." Presented by Ontario Farm Organizations' Labour Issues Coordinating Committee, 9 September.

Ontario Federation of Agriculture et al. 1977. *Joint Brief to the Minister of Labour regarding Occupational Health and Safety* (reproduced as Appendix 4 in Ontario Task Force on Health and Safety in Agriculture, 1985).

Ontario Federation of Labour (OFL). 1995. *Submission to the Ministry of Labour on the Repeal of the Bill 40 Reforms and Other Proposed Changes to the Labour Relations Act*. Toronto.

Ontario Labour Relations Board Decision. 1998. OPSEU vs. the Crown and Private Temporary Agencies. G.T. Surdkykowski, Vice-Chair. Toronto. 5 November.

Ontario Management Board. 2000. *The Ontario Public Service in the 21st Century: Discussion Paper on the Public Service Act*. Prepared by the Secretariat of the Ontario Management Board. Toronto.

Ontario Public Sector Employees' Union (OPSEU). 1993. *The Lean Agenda in the Public Sector*. September.

– 1994–2002. Collective Agreements and the Crown.

– 1994–2002. OPS Populations Employee Lists for OPS Bargaining Unit.

– 1996. *Nothing Left to Cut*. Toronto.

– 2001–2. *Table Talk* and *Real Deal*: Bargaining Bulletins. Accessed at www.opseu.org.

– 2002a. *Frontlines*: Strike Bulletin. www.opseu.org.

– 2002b. *My Life in a Changing Workplace*. Toronto.

– 2003a. Interview 1, Staff 1 Communications Department, March; Interview 2, Local president, March; Interview 3, Court worker 1 (female), April; Interview 4, Court worker 2 (male), April; Interview 5, Court worker 3 (male), April; Interview 6, former temporary agency worker 1 (male), March.

– 2003b. *Survey of Contract Meat Inspectors*. Toronto.

OPSEU. See Ontario Public Sector Employees' Union.

Ornstein, Michael. 2000. *Ethno-racial Inequality in Toronto: Analysis of the 1996 Census*. Toronto: York University.

Orr, K.E., et al. 2002. Survival of Enterococci during Hospital Laundry Processing. *Journal of Hospital Infection* 50 (2): 133–9.

Owens, Rosemary J. 1993. "Women, 'Atypical' Work Relationships and the Law." *Melbourne University Law Review* 19: 419–30.

Palmer, Bryan D. 1992. *Working Class Experience: Rethinking the History of Canadian Labour, 1800–1991*. 2nd ed. Toronto: McClelland & Stewart.

Panitch, Leo, and Donald Swartz. 1993. *Assault on Trade Union Freedoms: From Wage Controls to Social Contract*. Toronto: Garamond.

Paquet, Esther. 2003. "Le statut d'emploi: Un élément constitutif de la condition sociale?" *Relations Industrielles* 60 (1): 64.

Park, Yong-Seung, and Richard Butler. 2001. "The Safety Costs of Contingent Work: Evidence from Minnesota." *Journal of Labor Research* 22 (4): 831–49.

Parker, S., et al. 2002. "Effects of temporary contracts on perceived work characteristics and job strain: A longitudinal study." *Personal Psychology* (55):689-708.

Parr, Joy. 1985. "Hired Men: Ontario Agricultural Wage Labour in Historical Perspective." *Labour/Le Travail* 15: 91–103.

Peck, Jamie. 1996. *Workplace: The Social Regulation of Labour Markets*. New York: Guilford Press.

Peck, Jamie A., and Nikolas Theodore. 2002. "Temped Out? Industry Rhetoric, Labor Regulation and Economic Restructuring in the Temporary Staffing Business." *Economic and Industrial Democracy* 23 (2): 143–75.

Pendakur, K., and R. Pendankur. 1995. *The Colour of Money: Earning Differentials among Ethnic Groups in Canada*. Ottawa: Department of Canadian Heritage.

Pennings, Frans. 2002. *Dutch Social Security Law in an International Context*. The Hague: Kluwer Law International.

Perry, Ann. 2003. "T.O. Hotels Struggle Post-SARS: 12,000 Staffers Out of Work in the City." *Toronto Star*, 10 May.

Picchio, Antonella. 1992. *Social Reproduction: The Political Economy of the Labour Market*. Cambridge: Cambridge University Press.

– 1998. "Wages as a Reflection of Socially Embedded Production and Reproduction Processes." In Linda Clarke, Peter de Gijsel, and Jan Janssen, eds., *The Dynamics of Wage Relations n the New Europe*, 195–214. London: Kluwer.

Pickett, William, et al. 1999. "Fatal Work-Related Farm Injuries in Canada, 1991–1995." *Canadian Medical Association Journal* 160: 1843–8.

Picot, Garnett, René Morissette, and John Myles. 2003. *Low-Income Intensity during the 1990's: The Role of Economic Growth, Employment Earnings and Social Transfers*. Ottawa: Statistics Canada, Business and Labour Market Analysis Division.

Pierson, Paul, ed. 2001. *The New Politics of the Welfare State*. Oxford: Oxford University Press.

Pierson, Ruth Roach. 1990. "Gender and Unemployment Insurance Debates in Canada, 1934–1940." *Labour/Le Travail* 25: 77–103.

Ploughman, Peter, and Per Madson. 2002. "Flexibility, Employment Development and Active Labour Market Policy in Denmark and Sweden in the 1990's." CEPA Working Paper 2002-04. New School University, Center for Economic Policy Analysis.

Polivka, Anne. 1996. "Contingent and Alternative Work Arrangements, Defined." *Monthly Labour Review* 119 (10): 3–9.

Polivka, Anne, and Thomas Nardone. 1989. "On the Definition of 'Contingent Work.'" *Monthly Labour Review* 112 (12): 9–16.

Pollert, Anna. 1988. "Dismantling Flexibility." *Capital and Class* 34 (spring): 42–75.

Pope, Andrew M., and Alvin R Tarlov, eds. 1991. *Disability in America: Towards a National Agenda for Prevention*. Washington, DC: National Academy Press.

Porter, Ann. 1993. "Women and Income Security in the Post-War Period: The Case of Unemployment Insurance, 1945–1962." *Labour/Le Travail* 31 (spring): 111–14.

Porter, Ann, ed. 2003. *Gendered States: Women, Unemployment Insurance, and the Political Economy of the Welfare State in Canada, 1945–1997*. Toronto: University of Toronto Press.

Porter, John. 1987. *The Measure of Canadian Society: Education, Equality and Opportunity*. Ottawa: Carleton University Press.

Portes, Alejandro, Manuel Castells, and Lauren A. Benton, eds. 1989. *The Informal Economy: Studies in Advanced and Less Developed Countries*. Baltimore: Johns Hopkins University Press.

Pothier, Diane. 2002. "Twenty Years of Labour Law and the Charter." *Osgoode Hall Law Journal* 40: 369–400.

Prasch, Robert, and Falguni Sheth. 1999. "The Economics and Ethics of Minimum Wage Legislation." *Review of Social Economy* 7 (4): 466–544.

Pratte, Pierre. 1995. "Le travailleur autonome et la Loi sur les accidents du travail: Le cas du sous-traitant." *Revue du Barreau* 55 (3), 553–83.

Prince, M. 2001. Canadian Federalism and Disability Policy Making. *Canadian Journal of Political Science* 34 (4):791–817.

Public Service Alliance of Canada. 1993. *Go Home...and Stay There? PSAC Response to Telework in the Federal Public Service*. Ottawa.

Pupo, Norene. 1997. "Always Working, Never Done: The Expansion of the Double Day." In A.D.G. Duffy and N. Pupo, eds., *Good Jobs, Bad Jobs, No Jobs: The Transformation of Work in the 21st Century*, 144–87. Toronto: Harcourt Brace.

Purcell, Kate. 2000. "Changing Boundaries in Employment and Organizations." In *Changing Boundaries in Employment*, 1–30. Bristol: Bristol University Press.

Quebec. 1982. "Étude du projet de loi n. 101: Loi modifiant diverses dispositions législatives (1)." National Assembly, Commission permanente de la justice in Journal des débats: Commissions parlementaires, 14 December.

Québec. 1990a. "Débats de l'Assemblée nationale. Projet de Loi 97: Adoption du principe." National Assembly, 21 November.

Quebec. 1990b. "Detailed study of Bill 97." National Assembly, Permanent Committee on Social Affairs, 28 November.

Québec. Ministère du Travail. 2001a. *Plan stratégique, 2001–2003*. Accessed at www.travail.gouv.qc.ca on 9 September 2003.

– 2001b. *Rapport du Comité interministériel sur le harcèlement psychologique du travail*. Direction de la planification stratégique, de la recherche et des politiques.

– 2002. *Revoir les normes du travail du Québec: Un défi collectif*.

Quinlan, Michael. 1999. "The Implications of Labour Market Restructuring in Industrialized Societies for Occupational Health and Safety." *Economic and Industrial Democracy* 20: 427–60.

– 2002. *Developing Strategies to Address OHS and Workers' Compensation Responsibilities Arising from Changing Employment Relationships*. Research project commissioned by Work Cover Australia. Report submitted in September.

Quinlan, Michael, and Clare Mayhew. 1999. "Precarious Employment and Workers' Compensation." *International Journal of Law and Psychiatry* 22 (5–6): 491–520.

– 2001a. "The Global Expansion of Precarious Employment, Work Disorganisation, and Consequences for Occupational Health: A Review of Recent Literature." *International Journal of Health Services* 31: 335–414.

– 2001b. "The Global Expansion of Precarious Employment, Work Disorganisation and Occupational Health: Placing the Debate in a Comparative Historical Context." *International Journal of Health Services* 31: 507–36.

Rajagopal, I. 2002. *Hidden Academics: Contract Faculty in Canadian Universities*. Toronto: University of Toronto Press.

Rapaport, David. 1999. *No Justice, No Peace: The 1996 OPSEU Strike against the Harris Government in Ontario*. Montreal and Kingston: McGill-Queen's University Press.

Raskin, C. 1994. "Employment Equity for the Disabled in Canada." *International Labour Review* 133:75–88.

Ray, Jean-Emmanuel. 1996. "Le droit du travail à l'épreuve du télétravail: une nécessaire adaptation." *Droit social* 4: 351–99.

Rebick, Judy, and Kike Roach. 1996. *Politically Speaking*. Vancouver: Douglas & McIntyre.

Reskin, Barbara F., and Patricia A. Roos. 1990. *Job Queues, Gender Queues: Explaining Women's Inroads to Male Occupations*. Philadelphia: Temple University Press.

Rifkin, J. 1995. *The End of Work: The Decline of the Global Labor Force and the Dawn of the Post-Market Era*. New York, NY: G.P. Putnam and Sons.

Roberts, Wayne. 1994. *Don't Call Me Servant*. Toronto: OPSEU.

Robinson, Ian. 1994. "NAFTA, Social Unionism, and Labour Movement Power in Canada and the United States." *Relations Industrielles/Industrial Relations* 49 (4): 657–95.

– 2000. "Neoliberal Restructuring and U.S. Unions: Toward Social Movement Unionism?" *Critical Sociology* 1 (1/2): 109–38.

Rodgers, Gerry. 1989. "Precarious Work in Western Europe: The State of the Debate." In G. Rodgers and J. Rodgers, eds., *Precarious Jobs in Labour Market Regulation: The Growth of Atypical Employment in Western Europe*, 1–16. Belgium: International Institute for Labour Studies.

Rose, J., and G. Chaison. 2001. "Unionism in Canada and the United States in the 21st Century: The Prospects for Revival." *Relations Industrielles/Industrial Relations* 56 (1): 34–62.

Rosen, S. 1983, "Economics and Entrepreneurs." In J. Ronen ed., *Entrepreneurship*. Lexington, Mass.: Lexington Books.

Rubery, Jill. 1989. "Precarious Forms of Work in the United Kingdom." In Gerry Rogers and Janine Rogers, eds., *Precarious Jobs in Labour Market Regulation: The Growth of Atypical Employment in Western Europe*, 49–74. Geneva: International Institute for Labour Studies.

– 1998. *Women in the Labour Market: A Gender Equality Perspective*. Paris: OECD.

– 1999. "Fragmenting the Internal Labour Market." In Peter Leisink, ed., *Globalization and Labour Relations*, 116–37. Cheltenham, England, and Northampton: Edward Elgar.

Russell, Bob. 1990. *Back to Work? Labour, State, and Industrial Relations in Canada*. Scarborough, Ont.: Nelson.

– 1992. "Reinventing a Labour Movement?" In William K. Carroll, ed., *Organizing Dissent: Contemporary Social Movements in Theory and Practice*, 117–33. Toronto: Garamond Press.

Russo, J., and A. Banks. 1996. "Teaching the Organizing Model of Unionism and Campaign-Based Education: National and International Trends." Paper presented at AFL-CIO/Cornell University Research Conference on Union Organizing. Washington, DC. April.

Sachdev, Sanjiv. 2001. "Contracting Culture: From CCT to PPP's." In *The Private Provison of Public Services and Its Impact on Employment Relations*. London: UNISON.

Santiago, A.M., and C.G. Muschkin. 1996. "Distangling the Effects of Disability Status and Gender on the Labour Supply of Anglo, Black, and Latino Older Workers." *The Gerontologist* 36 (3): 299–310.

Satzewich, Vic. 1991. *Racism and the Incorporation of Foreign Labour: Farm Labour Migration to Canada since 1945*. New York: Routledge.

Saunders, R. 2003. *Defining Vulnerability in the Labour Market*. Ottawa: Canadian Policy Research Network Inc. November.

Scharpf, Fritz, and Vivien Schmidt, eds. 2000. *Welfare and Work in the Open Economy*. Vol. 1: *From Vulnerability to Competitiveness*; Vol. 2: *Diverse Responses to Common Challenges*. Oxford: Oxford University Press.

Schellenberg, Grant, and C. Clark. 1996. *Temporary Employment in Canada: Profiles, Patterns and Policy Considerations*. Ottawa: Canadian Council on Social Development.

Schenk, Chris. 2001. *From Poverty Wages to a Living Wage*. Toronto: The CSJ Foundation for Research and Education and the Ontario Federation of Labour.

– 2003. "Social Movement Unionism: Beyond the Organizing Model." In Peter Fairbrother and Charlotte B. Yates, eds., *Trade Unions in Renewal: A Comparative Study*, 244–62. London and New York: Centenium.

Schiele, Alexandra. 2002. *Non-permanent Employment, Quality of Work and Industrial Relations*. EIRO.

Schnall, Peter L., P.A. Landsbergis, T.G. Pickering, J.E. Schwartz, and K. Warren. 1992. "Relation between Job Strain, Alcohol, and Ambulatory Blood Pressure." *Hypertension* 19 (5): 488–94.

– 1998. "A Longitudinal Study of Job Strain and Ambulatory Blood Pressure: Results from a Three-Year Follow-up." *Psychosomatic Medicine* 60: 697–706.

Schur, Lisa A. 2002. "Dead End Jobs or a Path to Economic Well Being? The Consequences of Non-standard Work among People with Disabilities." *Behavioural Sciences and the Law* 20: 601–20.

Scott, Allen J., and Michael Storper. 1986. *Production, Work, Territory: The Geographical Anatomy of Industrial Capitalism*, 301–11. In Allen J. Scott and Michael Storper, eds., Boston: Unwin Hyman.

Scott, H. 2004. "Reconceptualizing the Nature and Health Consequences of Work-Related Insecurity for the New Economy: The Decline of Workers' Power in the Flexibility Regime." *International Journal of Health Services* 34: 143–53.

Scott, Joan. 1986. "Gender: A Useful Category of Historical Analysis." *American Historical Review* 93: 1053-73.

Scott, Katherine. 2003. *Funding Matters: The Impact of Canada's New Funding Regime on Nonprofit and Voluntary Organizations*. Ottawa: Canadian Council for Social Development.

Sears, Alan. 1999. "The Lean State and Capitalist Restructuring: Towards a Theoretical Account." *Studies in Political Economy* 59 (summer): 91–114.

Seccombe, Wally. 1992a. *A Millennium of Family Change: Feudalism to Capitalism in Northwestern Europe*. London and New York: Verso.

– 1992b. "Labour-Power, Family Forms and the Mode-of-Production Concept." In W. Secombe, ed., *A Millennium of Family Change: Feudalism to Capitalism in Northwestern Europe*, 9–30. London and New York: Verso.

Sen, Amartya. 2000. "Work and Rights." *International Labour Review* 139 (2): 119–28.

Sengenberger, Werner. 2002. *Globalization and Social Progress: The Role and Impact of Labour Standards*. Germany: Friedrich Ebert Foundation.

Shannon, Harry, and Graham Lowe. 2002. "How Many Injured Workers Do Not File Claims for Worker's Compensation Benefits?" *American Journal of Industrial Medicine* 42: 467–73.

Shapiro, Evelyn. 1997. *The Cost of Privatization: A Case Study of Homecare in Manitoba*. Ottawa: Canadian Centre for Policy Alternatives.

Shepela, Sharon T., and Ann T. Viviano. 1984. "Some Psychological Factors Affecting Job Segregation and Wages." In Helen Remick, ed., *Comparable Worth and*

Wage Discrimination, Technical Possibilities and Political Realities, 47–58. Philadelphia: Temple University Press.

Shields, John. 1992. "The Capitalist State and Farm Labour Policy." In David A. Hay and Gurchan S. Basran, eds., *Rural Sociological in Canada*, 246–66. Toronto: Oxford University Press.

Shields, John, and Bryan Evans. 1999. *Shrinking the State: Globalization and Public Administration Reform*. Halifax: Fernwood Publishing.

Shimmin, Kevin. 2000. "The Tripartite Bargaining Model: The Struggle to Organize Migrant Farm Workers." MA thesis, McMaster University.

Smart, J.F., and D.W. Smart. 1997. The Racial/Ethnic Demography of Disability. *Journal of Rehabilitation* 63 (4): 9–15.

Smeeding, Timothy. 2002. *Globalization, Inequality and the Rich Countries of the G-20: Evidence from the Luxemburg Income Study*. Luxemburg Income Study Working Paper No. 320. July.

Smismans, Stign. 2003. "Towards a New Community Strategy on Health and Safety at Work? Caught in the Institutional Web of Soft Procedures." *International Journal of Comparative Labour Law and Industrial Relations* 19 (1): 55–83.

Smith, Vicki. 1997. "New Forms of Work Organization." *Annual Review of Sociology* 23: 315–39.

Spalter-Roth, R., and H. Hartmann. 1998. "Gauging the Consequences for Gender Relations, Pay Equity and the Public Purse." In K. Barker and K. Christensen, eds., *Contingent Work: Employment Relations in Transition*, 69–83. Ithaca, Cornell University Press.

Sparks, K., and C. Cooper. 1999. "Occupational Differences in the Work-Strain Relationship: Towards the Use of Situation-Specific Models." *Journal of Occupational Health Psychology* 72: 219–29.

Spink, Lynn. 2000. "Living on the Edge." *Our Times: Canada's Independent Labour Magazine*, July/August: 15–19.

Stall, Susan, and Randy Stoeker. 1998. "Community Organizing or Organizing Community? Gender and the Crafts of Empowerment." *Gender and Society* 12: 729–56.

Standing, Guy. 1992. "Alternative Routes to Labour Flexibility." In M. Storper and Allen J. Scott, eds., *Pathways to Industrialization and Regional Development*, 255–75. New York: Routledge.

– 1999. *Global Labour Flexibility: Seeking Distributive Justice*. London and New York: Macmillan Press/St Martin's Press.

Stanford, Jim. 1996. "Discipline, Insecurity and Productivity: The Economics behind Labour Market Flexibility." In J. Pulkingham and G. Termowetsky, eds., *Remaking Social Policy: Social Security in the Late 1900s*, 130–50. Vancouver: Fernwood Publishing.

Stanford, Jim, and Leah. F. Vosko. 2004. "Challenging the Market: The Struggle to Regulate Work and Income." In Jim Stanford and Leah F. Vosko, eds., *Challenging the Market: The Struggle to Regulate Work and Income*, 3–32. Montreal and Kingston: McGill-Queen's University Press.

Stasiulis, Daiva. 1999. "Feminist Intersectional Theorizing." In P. Li, ed., *Race and Ethnic Relations in Canada*, 2nd ed., 347–97. Don Mills: Oxford University Press.

Statham, Ann, Eleanor M. Miller, and Hans O'Mauksch, eds. 1988. *The Worth of Women's Work: A Qualitative Synthesis*. New York: State University of New York Press.

Statistics Canada. 1995. "Households' Unpaid Work: Measurement and Valuation." Catalogue No. 13-603E, No. 3: 44.

– 1997. *Labour Force Update: The Self-Employed*. Ottawa.

– 1998. General Social Survey.

– 2000. Catalogue No. 89F0133XIE.

– 2001a. *2001 Census Dictionary*. Statistics Canada Catalogue 92-378-XIE.

– 2001b. "Fact-Sheet on Unionization." *Perspectives on Labour and Income*. Catalogue #75-001-XWE 2 (8): 1-25.

– 2002. *Guide to the Labour Force Survey*. Statistics Canada Catalogue 71-543-GIE.

– 2003a. *Earnings of Canadians: Making a Living on the New Economy*. Catalogue 96F-0030-XIE-200113.

– 2003b. *Guide to the Labour Force Survey*. Statistics Canada Catalogue 71-543-GIE.

– 2003c. "Shaping Canada's Labour Force: Immigrants, Demand for skills and an Aging Workforce." *The Daily*, February 11.

Stephen, Jennifer. 2000. *Access Diminished*. Toronto: Advocates for Community-Based Training and Education for Women.

Stone, Katherine V.W. 2001. "The New Psychological Contract: Implications of the Changing Workplace for Labor and Employment Law." *UCLA Law Review* 48: 519–661.

Storey, Robert. 1987. "The Struggle to Organize Stelco and Dofasco." *Relations Industrielles/Industrial Relations* 42 (2): 366–85.

Strategic Policy and International Affairs – Labour Branch. 2001. *Labour Program – Database on Minimum Wages*. Ottawa: Human Resources Development Canada.

Stultz, Erma. 1987. "Organizing the Unorganized Farmwork in Ontario." In Robert Argue, Charlene Gannage, and D.W. Livingstone, eds., *Working People and Hard Times*, 293–6. Toronto: Garamond.

Sugiman, Pamela H. 1993. "Unionism and Feminism in the Canadian Auto Workers Union, 1961–1992." In Linda Briskin and Patrician McDermott, eds., *Women Challenging Unions: Feminism, Democracy and Militancy*, 172–88. Toronto: University of Toronto.

Summers, Clyde. 2000. "Employment at Will in the United States: The Divine Right of Employers." *University of Pennsylvania Journal of Labor and Employment Law* 3: 65–86.

Supiot, Alain. 1999a. *Au-delà de l'emploi: Transformations du travail et devenir du droit du travail en Europe. Rapport pour la Commission des Communautés européennes*. Paris: Flammarion.

– 1999b. "Wage Employment and Self-Employment." In Reports to the 6th European Congress for Labour and Social Security, Warsaw, 13–17 September: 129–64.

– 2000. "Les nouveaux visages de la subordination." Droit social 2: 131–45.

– 2001. Beyond Employment: Changes in Work and the Future of Labour Law in Europe. A Report Prepared for the European Commission. London: Oxford.

– 2002. "Towards an International Social Order? Preliminary Observations on the 'New Regulations' in Work, Employment and Social Protection." In Peter Auer and Christine Daniel, eds., The Future of Work, Employment and Social Protection: The Search for New Securities in a World of Growing Uncertainty, 115–56. Proceedings of the France/ILO Symposium 2001. Geneva: International Institute for Labour Studies.

Sverke, Magnus, Johnny Hellgren, and Katharina Nasvall. 2002. "No Security: A Meta-analysis and Review of Job Insecurity and Its Consequences." Journal of Occupational Health Psychology 7 (2): 242–64.

Swimmer, Gene, and J. Thompson. 1995. "Introduction." In Public Sector Collective Bargaining in Canada: The Beginning of the End or End of the Beginning. Kingston: IRC Press.

Tapin, Jean-Robert. 1993. Agences de placement temporaire. Québec: Ministère de la Main-d'oeuvre, de la Sécurité du Revenu et de la Formation professionnelle.

Tatroff, Daniel. 1994. "Fields of Fear." Our Times 13 (6): 22–7.

Tedesco, M. 1977. "Hotel and Restaurant Employees and Bartenders International Union." In G. Fink, ed., Labour Unions: The Greenwood Encyclopedia of American Institutions, 148–51. London: Greenwood Press.

Thébaud-Mony, Annie. 2000. L'industrie nucléaire: Sous-traitance et servitude. Paris: INSERM.

Thoemmes, Jens. 1999. "La construction du temps de travail: Normes sociales ou normes juridiques?" Droit et société 41: 15–32.

Thomason, Terry, and Silvana Pozzebon. 2002. "Determinants of Firm Workplace Health and Safety and Claims Management Practices." Industrial & Labour Relations Review 55 (2): 286–307.

Tilly, Charles. 1996. Half a Job: Bad and Good Part-time Jobs in a Changing Labor Market. Philadelphia: Temple University Press.

Torjman, S. 2000. "Employment Insurance: Small Bang for Big Bucks." Caledon Institute of Social Policy. Reprint from Global and Mail, 17 February.

Townson, Monica. 1997. "Non-standard Work: The Implications for Pension Policy and Retirement Readiness." Paper prepared for the Women's Bureau, Ottawa, Human Resources Development Canada.

Traversa, Enrico. 2003. "Protection of Part-time Workers in the Case Law of the Court of Justice of the European Communities." International Journal of Comparative Labour Law and Industrial Relations 19 (2): 219–41.

Treiman, Donald J., and Heidi J Hartmann. 1981. Women, Work and Wages, Equal Pay for Jobs of Equal Value. Washington: National Academy Press.

Tucker, Eric. 1990. *Administering Danger in the Workplace: The Law and Politics of Occupational Health and Toronto Safety Regulation in Ontario, 1850–1914.* Toronto: University of Toronto Press.

– 1992. "Worker Participation in Health and Safety Regulation: Lessons from Sweden." *Studies in Political Economy* 37: 95–127.

– 1995. "And Defeat Goes On: An Assessment of the Third Wave of Health and Safety Regulation." In Frank Pearce and Laureen Snider, eds., *Corporate Crime: Contemporary Debates*, 245–67. Toronto: University of Toronto Press.

Tufts, Steven. 1998. "Community Unionism in Canada and Labor's (Re)Organization of Space." *Antipode* 30: 227–50.

– 2002. "Getting in on the Ground Floor: Organizing the Unknown in 'Hole in the Ground' Hotels." Paper presented at the 2002 Congress of the Socialist Association, 29 May–1 June. Toronto.

UFCW Canada and CLC. 2002. "National Report: Status of Migrant Farm Workers in Canada." Brief presented to the Honourable Jane Stewart, Minister of Human Resources Development Canada.

Ursel, Jane E. 1992. *Private Lives, Public Policy: 100 Years of State Intervention in the Family.* Toronto: Women's Press.

Vega-Ruiz, Maria L. 1992. "Le travail à domicile: Vers une nouvelle réglementation?" *Revue internationale du travail* 131 (2): 209–27.

Verge, Pierre. 2001. "L'adaptation du droit du travail à la 'nouvelle enterprise.'" In Jean Bernier et al., eds., *L'incessante évolution des formes d'emploi et la redoutable stagnation des lois du travail*, 21–42. Sainte Foy, Que.: Presses de l'Université Laval.

Viswanathan, L. 2000. *Toronto Training Board, 2000–2001 Environmental Scan: Training for Toronto's New Economy.* Toronto: Toronto Training Board.

Vosko, Leah F. 1995. "Recreating Dependency: Women and UI Reform." In D. Drache and A. Ranikin, eds., *Warm Heart, Cold Country*, 213–31. Toronto: Caledon Press.

– 1996. "Irregular Workers, New Involuntary Social Exiles: Women and UI Reform." In J. Pulkingham and G. Ternowetsky, eds., *Remaking Canadian Social Policy: Social Security in the Late 1900's*, 265–72. Toronto: Fernwood Publishing.

– 1997. "Legitimizing the Triangular Employment Relationship: Emerging International Labour Standards from a Comparative Perspective." *Comparative Labor Law and Policy Journal* 19 (fall): 43–77.

– 2000. *Temporary Work: The Gendered Rise of a Precarious Employment Relationship.* Toronto: University of Toronto Press.

– 2002. "Rethinking Feminization: Gendered Precariousness in the Canadian Labour Market and the Crisis in Social Reproduction." Annual Robarts Lecture in Canadian Studies, York University, Toronto. Available at www.robarts.yorku.ca.

– 2003. "Gender Differentiation and the Standard/Non-standard Employment Distinction in Canada, 1945 to the Present." In Danielle Juteau, ed., *Patterns and Processes of Social Differentiation: The Construction of Gender, Age, 'Race/*

Ethnicity' and Locality, 25–80. Toronto and Montreal: University of Toronto Press/University of Montreal Press.

– 2004a. *Confronting the Norm: Gender and the International Regulation of Precarious Work*. Ottawa: Law Commission of Canada.

– 2004b. "Standard-Setting at the ILO: The Case of Precarious Employment." In John Kirton and Michael J. Trebilcock, eds., *Hard Choices, Soft Law: Combining Trade, Environment, and Social Cohesion in Global Governance*, 139–57. New York: Ashgate.

– 2005. "The Precarious Status of the Artist: Freelance Editors' Struggle to Organize and Bargain Collectively." In Cynthia Cranford, Judy Fudge, Eric Tucker, and Leah F. Vosko, *Self-Employed Workers Organize: Law, Policy and Unions*. Montreal and Kingston: McGill-Queen's University Press.

Vosko, Leah F. In press. "Ontario's Early Years Plan: One Province's Response to the Mounting Crisis in Social Reproduction." In Kate Bezanson and Meg Luxton, eds., *Rethinking Social Reproduction*. Montreal and Kingston: McGill-Queen's University Press.

Vosko, Leah, Nancy Zukewich, and Cranford, Cynthia. 2003. "Precarious Jobs: A New Typology of Employment." *Perspectives on Labour and Income*. Ottawa: Statistics Canada. October: 16–26.

Wa, Muraskin. 1995. "The Role of Organized-Labor in Combating the Hepatitis-B and AIDS Epidemics: The Fight for an OSHA Bloodborne Pathogens Standard." *International Journal of Health Services* 25 (1): 129–52.

Walby, Sylvia. 1989. "Flexibility and the Changing Sexual Division of Labour." In Stephen Wood, ed., *The Transformation of Work? Skills, Flexibility and Labour Proces*, 127–40. London: Unwin Hyman.

– 2000. "The Restructuring of the Gendered Political Economy: Transformations in Women's Employment." In Joanne Cook, Jennifer Roberts, and Georgina Waylen, eds., *Towards a Gendered Political Economy*, 166–85. New York: St Martin's Press.

Walkom, T. 1997. "The Harris Government: Restoration or Revolution." In G. White, ed., *The Government and Politics of Ontario*, 404–16. Toronto: University of Toronto Press.

Wall, Ellen. 1992. "Personal Labour Relations and Ethnicity in Ontario Agriculture." In Vic Satzewich, ed., *Deconstructing a Nation: Immigration, Multiculturalism and Racism in 90's Canada*, 261–75. Halifax: Fernwood Publishing.

– 1996. "Unions in the Field." *Canadian Journal of Agricultural Economics* 44: 515–26.

Wall, Toby D., Paul Jackson, S. Mullarkey, and Sharon Parker. 1995. "Further Evidence on Some New Measures of Job Control, Cognitive Demand and Production Responsibility." *Journal of Organizational Behaviour* 16: 431–55.

– 1996. "The Demands-Control Model of 'Job Strain': A More Specific Test." *Journal of Occupational Health Psychology* 69: 153–66.

Walsh, Kieron, and Howard Davis. 1993. *Competition and Service: The Impact of the Local Government Act, 1988*. London: HMSO.

Walters, David, dir. 2002. *Regulating Health and Safety Management in the European Union*. Brussels: Presses Interuniversitaires Européenes.

Wanner, Richard. 2003. "Entry Class and the Earnings Attainment of Immigrants to Canada, 1980–1995." *Canadian Public Policy* 29 (1): 53–71.

Ward, Peter. 1978. *White Canada Forever: Popular Attitudes and Public Policy Towards Orientals in British Columbia*. Montreal and Kingston: McGill-Queen's University Press.

Weber, Tina. 1997. *Commission Adopts Draft Directive on Part-time Work*. EIRO.

– 1999a. *Commission Adopts Draft Directive to Implement Fixed-Term Contract Agreement*. EIRO.

– 1999b. *Social Partners Reach Framework Agreement on Part-time Work*. EIRO.

Weil, David. 1991. "Enforcing OSHA: The Role of Labor Unions." *Industrial Relations* 30: 20–36.

– 1997. "Implementing Employment Regulation: Insights on the Determinants of Regulatory Performance." In Bruce E. Kaufman and E. Madison, eds., *Government Regulation of the Employment Relation*, 429–74. Madison, Wisc.: Industrial Relations Research Association Series.

Wells, M. 2000. "Immigration and Unionization in the San Francisco Hotel Industry." In R. Milkman, ed., *Organizing Immigrants: The Challenge for Unions in Contemporary California*, 109–29. Ithaca, NY: Cornell University Press.

White, Julie. 1990. *Mail and Female: Women and the Canadian Union of Postal Workers*. Toronto: Thompson Educational Publishing.

– 1993. *Sisters and Solidarity: Women and Unions in Canada*. Toronto: Thompson Educational Publishing.

Whitfield, D. 2001. *Public Services or Corporate Welfare*. London: Pluto Press.

WHO. See World Health Organization.

WHSA. See Workplace Health and Safety Agency.

Wial, Howard. 1993. "The Emerging Organizational Structure of Unionism in Low-Wage Services." *Rutgers Law Review* 45 (spring): 671–81.

Williams, James H. 1964. "On Community Unions." *Studies on the Left* 4 (2): 73–8.

Wilton, Robert, and Cynthia Cranford. 2002. "Toward an Understanding of the Spatiality of Social Movements: Labor Organizing at a Private University in Los Angeles." *Social Problems* 49 (3): 374–400.

Winson, Anthony. 1996. "In Search of Part-time Farmers: Labour Use and Farm Structure in Central Canada." *Canada Review of Sociology and Anthropology* 33: 89–110.

Winson, Anthony, and Belinda Leach. 2001. *Contingent Work, Disrupted Lives*. Toronto: University of Toronto Press.

Woods, Louis Aubrey. 1975. *A History of Farmers' Movements in Canada*. Toronto: University of Toronto Press.

Workplace Health and Safety Agency (WHSA). 1991. "Letter from Paul Forder, Labour Vice Chair, and Paul Parker, Management Vice Chair, to Minister of Labour Bob MacKenzie." 13 May.

World Health Organization (WHO). 1980. *International Classification of Impairments, Disabilities and Handicaps: A Manual of Classification Relating to the Consequences of Disease.* Geneva.

– 1989, 2001. *International Classification of Functioning, Disability and Health, Final Draft, Full Version.* Geneva.

Wotherspoon, Terry. 2003. "Aboriginal People, Public Policy and Social Differentiation in Canada." In Danielle Juteau, ed., *Patterns and Processes of Social Differentiation: The Construction of Gender, Age, "Race/Ethnicity" and Locality*, 155–204. Toronto and Montreal: University of Toronto Press/University of Montreal Press.

Yalnizyan, Armine. 1993. "From the DEW Line: The Experience of Canadian Garment Workers." In Linda Briskin and Patricia McDermott, eds., *Women Challenging Unions: Feminism, Militancy and Democracy*, 284–303. Toronto: University of Toronto Press.

Yates, Charlotte. 2001. *Making It: Your Economic Unions and Economic Justice.* Toronto: The CSJ Foundation for Research and Education and the Ontario Federation of Labour.

– 2002. "Expanding Labour's Horizons: Union Organizing and Strategic Change in Canada." *Just Labour* 1 (2): 31–40.

Yelin, E.H. 1997. "The Employment of People with and without Disabilities in an Age of Insecurity." *Annals of the American Academy* 549: 117–28.

Zavella, Patricia. 1997. "Reflections on Diversity among Chicanas." In Mary Hondagneu-Sotelo, and Peirrette and Vilma Ortiz, eds., *Challenging Fronteras: Structuring Latina and Latino Lives in the U.S. Romero*, 187–94. New York and London: Routledge.

Zeytinoglu, Isik Urla, and Jacinta Khasiala Muteshi. 1999. "Gender, Race and Class Dimensions of Nonstandard Work." *Relations Industrielles/Industrial Relations* 55 (1): 133–67.

Zukewich, Nancy. 2003. "Unpaid Informal Caregiving." *Canadian Social Trends.* Statistics Canada Catalogue 11-008-XPE, No. 70, autumn: 14–18.

Zwarenstein, Carolyn. 2002. "Smalltown Big Issues." *Our Times* 21 (3): 14–21.

LEGISLATION

Canada

Criminal Code, SC 2003, c. 21.
Status of the Artist Act, SC 1992, c. 33.
Unemployment Insurance Act, SC 1940, c. 44.
Unemployment Insurance Act, SC 1970–72, c. 48.

British Columbia

Employment Standards Act, RSBC 1996, c. 113.

Ontario

An Act to Amend the Occupational Health and Safety Act and the Workers' Compensation Act, SO 1990, c. 7.

An Act to amend the Workmen's Compensation for Injuries Act, 1892, SO 1893, c. 26.

An Act to Provide for Collective Bargaining, SO 1943, c. 4.

An Act to require the owners of Thrashing and other Machines to guard against accidents, SO 1874. c. 12.

Agricultural Employees Protection Act, SO 2002, c. 16.

Agricultural Labour Relations Act, SO 1994, c. 6.

Building Trades Protection Act, SO 1911, c. 71.

Farm Implements Act, RSO 1990, c. F.4.

Hours of Work and Vacations with Pay Act, SO 1944, c. 26.

Industrial Standards Act, SO 1935, c. 28.

Minimum Wage Act, SO 1937, c. 43.

Mining Operations Act, SO 1890, c. 53.

Occupational Health and Safety Act, RSO 1990, c. O.1.

Occupational Health and Safety Act, SO 1978, c. 83.

Pesticides Act, RSO 1990, c. P. 11.

Railway Accidents Act, SO 1881, c. 22.

Shops Regulation Act, SO 1888, c. 33.

Workmen's Compensation Act, SO 1914, c. 25.

Workmen's Compensation for Injuries Act, SO 1886, c. 28.

Quebec

Act Respecting Collective Agreement Decrees, RSQ c. D-2-A.

Act Respecting the Professional Status and Conditions of Engagement of Performing, Recording and Film Artists, RSQ, c. S-32.1.

Act Respecting the Professional Status of Artists in the Visual Arts, Arts and Crafts and Literature, and their Contracts with Promoters, RSQ, c. S-32.01.

Act to Amend the Act Respecting Childcare Centres and Childcare Services, SQ 2003, c. 13.

Act to Amend the Act Respecting Health Services and Social Services, SQ 2003, c. 12.

Charter of Human Rights and Freedoms, RSQ, c. C-12.

Consumer Protection Act, RSQ, c. P-40.1.

Employment Bureaus Act (1964), RSQ, c. B-10.

Labour Standards Act, RSQ, c. N-1.1.

Minimum Wage Act, SQ 1940, c. 39.

Pay Equity Act. RSQ, c. E-12.001.

Pension Plan Act, RSQ, c. R-9.

Glossary

*Refers to unique contribution of this book

accommodation   Any change or adjustment to a job or work environment that permits a person with a disability to participate in the job application process, to perform the essential functions of a job, or to enjoy benefits of employment equal to those enjoyed by employees without disabilities.

benefits   Benefits associated with employment that go beyond those required by law, such as extended holiday pay, sick pay, disability insurance, medical/dental coverage, and pensions that may come by means of collective agreements or individual contracts of employment, membership in a professional association, or by way of self-insurance.

broader-based bargaining   Models of negotiating where workers from different worksites (e.g., construction workers), bargaining units, or on a sector basis (e.g., taxi drivers and artists) negotiate for common terms of employment with providers of work (see Cranford, Das Gupta, Ladd, and Vosko).

*community unionism   A form of organizing that emphasizes worker participation at every level and may be focused on a social location (e.g., gender or ethnicity), a diversity of issues (e.g., fair employment or a living wage), sites beyond the workplace (e.g., a neighbourhood), and various constituencies (citizens as well as workers) while maintaining a central interest in labour concerns (see Cranford, Das Gupta, Ladd, and Vosko; Schenk; and Tucker).

contingent employment   A term used principally the United States denoting conditional, transitory, or temporary employment contracts.

contracting out   A term similar to outsourcing denoting a practice where an employer transfers work formerly done by his or her employees to another employer or self-employed person or intermediary.

craft / occupational unionism   A form of unionism that involves workers' organizing based on a common occupation or skill.

*dimensions of precarious employment   A way to conceptualize characteristics contributing to the phenomenon of precarious employment advanced in this book. Characteristics include uncertainty of continuing work; a lack of control over the labour process; low income; and limited social and regulatory protection.

employee   A person who is recognized in law as an employee. Typically, employee status connotes doing work for another for a wage under his or her control and direction.

employment status   The status of a person who participates in the labour force either as an employee or a self-employed person. Whether or not a person is an employee or self-employed is central to determining access to labour protection and social benefits.

*employment strain   Stress related to the employment relationship, particularly the interaction between high uncertainty over future employment and the expenditure of a lot of effort to obtain more work

family and household   *Family* is a particular form of social organization based on cohabitation and kinship and centred on the household. A *household*, in contrast, is a social institution central in the distribution of resources provided by the state and by employers, such as wages and the social wage.

feminization of employment norms / "gendering of jobs"   The *feminization of employment norms* is a broad concept that entails the erosion of the standard employment relationship and the spread of forms of employment exhibiting qualities of precarious employment associated with women. A central facet of this phenomenon, the *gendering of jobs*, refers to a process whereby jobs come to resemble the more precarious work associated with women and other marginalized groups assumed to have access to alternative sources of subsistence beyond the wage (see Cranford and Vosko).

*form of employment   Different categories of wage work or self-employment (e.g., part-time temporary wage work and full-time solo self-employment).

gender   Cultural meanings and structural relations associated with sexual differences that form the basis of inclusions/exclusions as well as inequalities in power, authority, rights, and privileges.

*indicators of precarious employment   Statistical measures used to signify the dimensions of precarious employment (e.g., union coverage as an indicator of control over the labour process).

industrial unionism   A multi-occupational form of unionism, distinct from craft unionism, organized around a single worksite or enterprise that takes the standard employment relationship as a norm. Labour law, legislation, and policy in Canada and Quebec commonly assume this form of unionism. Historically, this form of unionism has been organized around industries as opposed to occupations.

intersectionality   Understanding that people's identities are shaped by multiple social relations (e.g., class, gender, age, race, (dis)ability).

job strain   Stress related to the job, particularly the interaction between workload and control at work, leading to exhaustion, depression, job dissatisfaction, and stress-related illnesses such as cardiovascular disease.

labour force   People in jobs (wage work and self-employment) and the unemployed.

labour market regulation   The complex of laws, institutions, policies, and cultural attitudes that organize and constrain the relationships and practices of employment.

labour process   How labour is organized and employed in the production of goods and services.

lumping   Analysis based on what is common among people.

multiple job-holder   A person with two or more jobs that may include wage work and self-employment.

non-standard work   A catchall term covering forms of employment, such as part-time permanent wage work and full-time solo self-employment, as well as work arrangements differing from the standard employment relationship, such as on-call and shift work.

part-time employment Employment that is not full time and may be permanent or temporary. Part-time employment may entail wage work or self-employment.

permanent wage work Wage work that may be full time or part time and that has no predetermined end date and is expected to continue.

*precarious employment A complex concept that is the subject of this book and is used here in two different ways. One is to distinguish it from the often-called *standard employment relationship* (see standard employment relationship). The other is to assess the nature of the employment relationship along various dimensions. In this book, some analyses focus on how an employment relationship may be precarious or not, while others focus on how an employment relationship could be more or less precarious.

Precarious employment is shaped by employment status, form of employment, and dimensions such as income level and control over the labour process, as well as by social context and social location.

privatization The process of moving away from the public or the collective. Privatization take several forms, including the transfer of service delivery to for-profit firms through contracting out or the transfer of entire services; public-private partnerships for the delivery of services; the adoption of for-profit practices in the public sector; the transfer of payment responsibility to individuals or private organizations; and the transfer of work and responsibility to individuals or households.

race A social construct tied to racialization. Racial categories, including "visible minority," "Black," "South Asian," and "white," are constructed through processes of racialization embedded in daily interactions, ideologies, policies, and practices. Race is a concept that represents and symbolizes social conflicts and interests by referring to different types of human bodies (Omi and Winant 1994, 55). The significance of identities for resistance and agency underscores the importance of using terms such as "Black" and "people of colour" to challenge racism and other intersecting forms of discrimination (Mensah 2002; Mohanty 2003).

racism A system in which one group of people exercises power over another or others on the basis of socially constructed categories such as physical attributes like skin colour.

racialization A process of signification in which people are categorized into races.

regulatory effectiveness The degree to which regulatory protection is, in reality, provided to the labour force.

regulatory failure The phenomenon whereby existing mechanisms of regulatory protection fail to protect members of the labour force.

regulatory protection The protection of working conditions and standards of living by means of law and public policy.

self-employed employer A self-employed person with employees. Self-employed employers are normally excluded from coverage under labour and employment law.

self-employed person A person who participated in the labour force but who is not recognized in law as an employee. This diverse category ranges from true entrepreneurs to people who perform work under conditions similar to those of employees (see Bernstein; Lippel; and Vosko and Zukewich).

slicing Analysis based on the recognition of difference and the possibility of developing several angles into the same set of issues, circumstances, and evidence.

social context The contexts within which paid work takes place, including the occupation, industry, sector, or geographic location.

social location A term used to refer to groups of people affected differently by social relations of inequality such as gender, race, ethnicity, immigrant status, disability, class, and age, as well as their intersections. Examples include "women with disabilities," "men of colour," "women workers."

social reproduction The daily and intergenerational reproduction of people (Picchio 1992). Institutions connected to social reproduction include, but are not limited to, the state, education system, public sector, family, firms, and trade unions. Social reproduction occurs at various levels – including at the level of the household through unpaid work and at the level of the state through government transfers.

social wage The bundle of social benefits and statutory entitlements beyond earnings which shape the overall standard of living of workers and their households (see also benefits).

solo self-employed A form of self-employment, also known as own-account self-employment, where persons have no paid employees.

standard employment relationship A full-time continuous employment relationship where the worker has one employer, works on the employer's premises under his or her direct supervision, and has access to social benefits and entitlements that complete the social wage. The standard employment relationship is a normative model of employment or the basis around which most labour protections and social benefits are organized (see Vosko).

standard of living States of a historical process of social reproduction encompassing historical and institutional elements. The term is also used to denote a bundle of goods rather than a social process. For example, in calculating poverty, Statistics Canada uses a range of measures, such as low-income cut-offs and low-income measures, to assess the situation of people with low incomes.

subcontracting An arrangement whereby a contractor assigns some of the obligations of the job to another party, who might be a self-employed person, an employer, or an intermediary.

temporary employment Forms of work with a predetermined end date or with the expectation that the work will be of limited duration. Temporary employment may be full time or part time, seasonal or casual, or involve work through a temporary help agency.

triangular employment relationship An employment relationship involving a worker, an employment agency (or intermediary), and a client firm, characterized by an employment contract between the worker and the agency and a commercial contract between the client firm and the agency.

visible minority A contested term devised by the federal government referring to persons, other than Aboriginal people, who are non-Caucasian in "race."

work arrangements The conditions of employment, including place of work, scheduling, and supervision (e.g., on-call or shift work).

workers' associations Organizations of workers that may or may not represent pre-union structures built around workers' common identification, often with a sector, profession, or any other basis of identity that is appropriate, including "race," gender, ethnicity, and geography rather than a single employer (see Cranford, Das Gupta, Ladd, and Vosko).

Contributors

JOHN ANDERSON is the vice-president, Strategic Partnerships and Alliances, Canadian Council on Social Development, where he is responsible for the Community Social Data Strategy initiative as well as the Big Cities Social Development network project. He has worked on a number of research studies on such issues as *Poverty by Postal Code* with the United Way of Greater Toronto, expanding pay equity for the Pay Equity Task Force, as well as research on precarious employment and the living wage. A long-time social justice academic, he is the former director of research and senior economist for the Centre for Social Justice and the author of numerous research studies on social justice issues, including *The High Costs of Tax Cuts* (1999). He is also the co-editor (with Chris Schenk) of two books, *Re-shaping Work* (volumes 1 and 2), on technological change and the workforce, co-published by the Canadian Centre for Policy Alternatives and Garamond Press.

PAT ARMSTRONG is co-author or editor of such books on health care as *Caring for/Caring About, Exposing Privatization: Women and Health Reform in Canada*; *Unhealthy Times, Heal Thyself: Managing Health Care Reform*; *Wasting Away: The Undermining of Canadian Health Care*; *Universal Health Care: What the United States Can Learn from Canada*; *Medical Alert: New Work Organizations in Health Care*; *Vital Signs: Nursing in Transition*; and *Take Care: Warning Signals for Canada's Health System*. She has also published on a wide variety of issues related to women's work and to social policy. Over her career, she has served as chair of the Department of Sociology at York University and director of the School of Canadian Studies at Carleton University. Currently, she is a partner in the National Network on Environments and Women's Health, and she chairs a working group on health reform which crosses the Centres of Excellence for Women's Health. She holds a CHSRF/CIHR Chair in Health Services.

JAMES BEATON is working toward his doctoral degree in sociology at York University. His research focuses on corporate involvement in the university.

STEPHANIE BERNSTEIN is a law professor in the Faculty of Political Science and Law at the Université du Québec à Montréal (UQAM). The focus of her research and teaching activities is international and comparative labour, social security, and human rights law, the legal protection of workers in precarious employment, and the role of the state in labour market regulation.

SUDIPA BHATTACHARYYA holds a BSC. from the University of Toronto in biology and psychology. She is currently a research and administrative assistant at the Institute for Work and Health. Her research interests include stress and mental illness in the workplace, especially among disadvantaged groups (e.g., visible minorities, elderly individuals).

JAN BOROWY has promoted the rights of precariously employed workers for several years. Currently, she is a campaigns officer at the Ontario Public Service Employees Union. In former positions she was the workers' rights community legal worker at Parkdale Community Legal Clinic and the research coordinator at the International Ladies' Garment Workers Union in Ontario (now UNITE-HERE). She holds a Master's degree in political science from York University.

CYNTHIA J. CRANFORD is an assistant professor of sociology at the University of Toronto. Her research focuses on the intersection of economic restructuring, gender relations, and migrant labour. Her articles have been published in *Relations Industrielles/ Industrial Relations*, *Social Problems*, and the *American Sociological Review*. She is also co-author of *Self-Employed Workers Organize: Law, Policy and Unions* published by McGill-Queen's University Press.

TANIA DAS GUPTA is an associate professor in the School of Social Sciences, Atkinson Faculty, York University. She teaches, researches, and writes on race, gender, and class, with specific reference to paid workplaces, immigration and settlement, immigrant women, and related state policies. She has an interest in anti-racism activities, with an emphasis on community development concerns. Her publications in these areas include *Racism and Paid Work*, published by Garamond Press, and *Learning from Our History*, published by the Cross-Cultural Communication Centre.

ALICE DE WOLFF is a researcher and activist who has worked for many years with women's groups, unions, and community organizations. She has written about precarious employment, the transformation of administrative support work, training, and the tensions between paid work and social reproduction. She was the community director of the Community University Research Alliance on Contingent Work.

ANDREW JACKSON has been senior economist with the Canadian Labour Congress since 1989. He is also a research professor in the Institute of Political Economy at Carleton University and a research associate with the Canadian Centre for Policy Alternatives. During a leave of absence from the CLC in 2000–2, he was director of research with the Canadian Council on Social Development. His areas of interest include the labour market and the quality of jobs, income distribution and poverty, macro-economic policy, social policy, and the impact of globalization. He has written numerous articles for popular and academic publications and is the author of *Work and Labour in Canada: Critical Issues*, published by Canadian Scholars' Press in 2005.

ANDREW KING is the national health, safety, and environment coordinator and department leader for the United Steel Workers of America. He has worked extensively in the field of occupational health, both as a lawyer and as a labour representative. He is also a sessional instructor, teaching courses on occupational health and safety at McMaster University.

DEENA LADD is the coordinator of Toronto Organizing for Fair Employment. A long-time community organizer, she is also a researcher active in the Association Building Stream of the Alliance on Contingent Employment.

KATE LAXER is a doctoral candidate in sociology at York University. Her thesis research is on the restructuring of support services in health care in Canada.

WAYNE LEWCHUK is professor of labour studies and economics at McMaster University. He has written on the history of technology in the automobile industry and recent trends in work organization. His current work focuses on the relationship between work organization and health.

KATHERINE LIPPEL is a professor of law at the Faculty of Political Science and Law at the Université du Québec à Montréal (UQAM) and a member of the Quebec Bar. She specializes in legal issues relating to occupational health and safety and workers' compensation and is the author of several articles and books in the field. She currently directs three multidisciplinary research teams on the following themes: health effects of compensation

systems; policy, precarious employment, and occupational health; and interactions between law and medicine in the field of occupational health and
safety. She also co-directs, with Karen Messing, the research group Invisible
qui fait mal, a partnership with three Quebec unions oriented towards improvement of women's occupational health.

MICHAEL POLANYI works at KAIROS: Canadian Ecumenical Justice Initiatives in Toronto, where he coordinates research, education, and advocacy on Canadian poverty and social justice issues. He holds a PhD in
environmental studies from York University and has researched and written
about the impact of work on health, using participatory and qualitative
methodologies.

CHRIS SCHENK is the research director of the Ontario Federation of Labour. He has written numerous submissions to the Government of Ontario
as well as articles on labour relations and employment standards issues. His
most recent publication is "Social Movement Unionism: Beyond the Organizing Model," in P. Fairbrother and C. Yates, eds., *Trade Unions in Renewal: A Comparative Perspective*, published by Continuum Press in 2003.

HEATHER SCOTT is a doctoral candidate in medical sociology at the
University of Toronto. Her dissertation research examines the health consequences of work-related insecurity in new-economy firms. She also works
as a research associate at the Institute for Work and Health, investigating
the impact of precarious employment experiences on health.

EMILE TOMPA holds an MBA from the University of British Columbia,
an MA in economics from the University of Toronto, and a PhD in economics from McMaster University. A labour and health economist with a
background in aging and retirement issues, he is currently a scientist at the
Institute for Work and Health, an adjunct assistant professor in the Department of Economics at McMaster University, and an adjunct assistant
professor in the Department of Public Health Sciences at the University of
Toronto. His research focuses on three themes: the consequences of disability compensation system design features and other labour market policies and programs that bear on the health of individuals and populations;
the labour market experiences of people with disabilities and their health
and human development consequences, with a particular focus on precarious employment; and workplace interventions directed at improving the
health and well-being of workers, specifically the economic evaluation of
such interventions.

SCOTT TREVITHICK holds a BA from Huron University College, University of Western Ontario, and a Master's degree from the University of

Calgary. He is in the final stages of a PhD in history at the University of Toronto. He is also a research associate at the Institute for Work and Health. In the field of work and health, his interests lie in the labour market experiences of workers in precarious employment, in the potential health outcomes of these experiences, and in the social patterning of such experiences and their health consequences.

ERIC TUCKER is the author of *Administering Danger in the Workplace: The Law and Politics of Occupational Health and Safety Regulation in Ontario, 1850–1914* (University of Toronto Press 1990) and co-author of *Labour before the Law: The Legal Regulation of Workers' Collective Action, 1900–1948* (Oxford University Press 2001) (with Judy Fudge) and *Self-Employed Workers Organize: Law, Policy, and Unions* (McGill-Queen's University Press 2005)(with Cynthia Cranford, Judy Fudge, and Leah Vosko). He has also published numerous articles on contemporary occupational health and safety regulation. Professor Tucker provided an expert witness affidavit in support of the UFCW's *Charter* challenge to the exclusion of Ontario's agricultural workers from the *Occupational Health and Safety Act*.

LEAH F. VOSKO is associate professor and Canada Research Chair in Feminist Political Economy in the School of Social Sciences (Political Science), Atkinson Faculty, York University. She is author of *Temporary Work: The Gendered Rise of a Precarious Employment Relationship* (University of Toronto Press 2000), *Self-Employed Workers Organize: Law, Policy, and Unions* (McGill-Queen's University Press 2005) (with Cynthia Cranford, Judy Fudge, and Eric Tucker), and co-editor of *Changing Canada: Political Economy as Transformation* (McGill-Queen's University Press 2003) (with Wallace Clement) and *Challenging the Market: The Struggle to Regulate Work and Income* (McGill-Queen's University Press 2004) (with Jim Stanford). Her research has also appeared in a range of scholarly journals and edited collections. She was principal investigator of the Community University Research Alliance on Contingent Work.

NANCY ZUKEWICH is a senior analyst with the Housing, Family and Social Statistics Division of Statistics Canada. She holds a Master's degree in Canadian Studies, with a concentration in women's studies, and a Bachelor of Arts (Honours) in French and economics. Since joining Statistics Canada in 1991, her work has focused on gender statistics and the analysis of work and labour market issues. She has also worked as a policy analyst at Status of Women Canada and as a visiting analyst at the Social Sciences and Humanities Research Council. Her current research interests include the changing nature of employment relationships and the use of time-use data to measure and value unpaid caregiving work.

Index

Note: Page numbers followed by "f" denote a figure; page numbers followed by "t" denote a table; Page numbers followed by "n" denote a footnote.